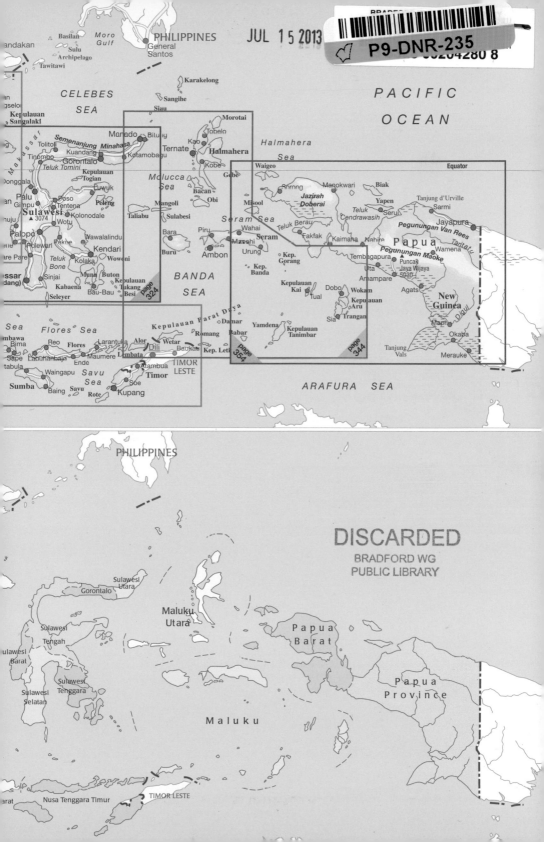

INSIGHT GUIDES
INDONESIA

APA PUBLICATIONS
Part of the Langenscheidt Publishing Group

INSIGHT GUIDE
INDONESIA

Editorial

Project Editor
Tom Le Bas
Series Manager
Rachel Lawrence
Design
Steve Lawrence
Map Production
Original Cartography Cosmographics,
updated by the Apa Cartography Dept
Production
Linton Donaldson, Rebeka Ellam and Tynan Dean

Distribution

UK
Dorling Kindersley Ltd
A Penguin Group company
80 Strand, London, WC2R 0RL
customerservice@dk.com

United States
Ingram Publisher Services
1 Ingram Boulevard, PO Box 3006,
La Vergne, TN 37086-1986
customer.service@ingrampublisher
services.com

Australia
Universal Publishers
PO Box 307
St Leonards NSW 1590
sales@universalpublishers.com.au

Worldwide
**Apa Publications GmbH & Co.
Verlag KG (Singapore branch)**
7030 Ang Mo Kio Avenue 5
08-65 Northstar @ AMK
Singapore 569880
apasin@singnet.com.sg

Printing

CTPS-China

© 2012 Apa Publications (UK) Ltd
All Rights Reserved

First Edition 1983
6th Edition 2012
Reprinted 2013

CONTACTING THE EDITORS
We would appreciate it if readers
would alert us to errors or out-
dated information by writing to:
**Insight Guides, PO Box 7910,
London SE1 1WE, England.**
insight@apaguide.co.uk

www.insightguides.com

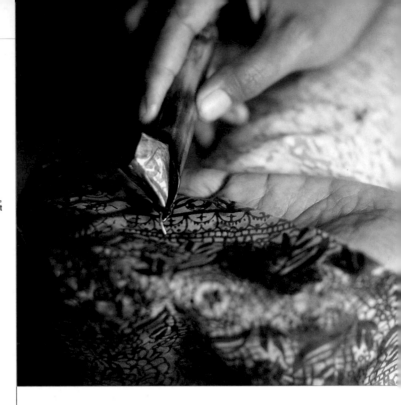

ABOUT THIS BOOK

The first Insight Guide pioneered the use of creative full-colour photography in travel guides in 1970. Since then, we have expanded our range to cater to our readers' need not only for reliable information about their chosen destination but also for a real understanding of the culture and workings of that destination. Now, when the internet can supply inexhaustible (but not always reliable) facts, our books marry text and pictures to provide those much more elusive qualities: knowledge and discernment.

How to use this book

Insight Guide: Indonesia is structured to convey an understanding of the sprawling archipelago and its culture, as well as to guide readers through its sights and activities:

◆ The **Features** section, indicated by a pink bar at the top of each page, covers the history and culture of the country in a series of essays.
◆ The main **Places** section, indicated by a blue bar, is a complete guide to all the sights and areas worth visiting in the country. Places of special interest are coordinated by number with the maps.
◆ The **Travel Tips** listings section, with a yellow bar, provides full information on transport, hotels, restaurants, activities from culture and shopping to sports, and an A–Z section of essential practical information. An easy-to-find contents list for Travel Tips is printed on the back flap, which also serves as a bookmark.

The contributors

The task of threading the 18,110 islands of the sprawling Indonesian archipelago into a palatable read was undertaken by **Tom Le Bas**,

LEFT: making traditional batik, Yogyakarta.

managing editor at Insight Guides' London office. He commissioned **Linda Hoffman**, a Yogyakarta-based journalist, to comprehensively update and rework the text for this new edition. Linda has contributed to several Insight Guides, including earlier editions of *Insight Guide: Indonesia*. She wrote all-new material for the Best Of Indonesia section, the Land of Many Lands, The People of Indonesia and Architecture chapters, new adventure destinations and features on Conservation and Torajan Culture, as well as overhauling many other parts of the book including an all-new Travel Tips section.

To assist her in the exhaustive task of updating the book, Linda assembled a team of experts from across Indonesia who ferreted out the latest facts about this rapidly changing country. Avid adventurer

Jacky Djokosetio of Jakarta was irreplaceable, contributing to the Jakarta, West Java, Sumatra and Papua chapters, as well as "Spice Islands Cuisine" and Travel Tips A–Z. **Joan Suyenaga** updated "Gamelan Music" and **Nia Fliam** reviewed the batik photo feature and **Textiles** chapter.

Also instrumental were **Andy Shorten** for the Maluku chapter, **Lucas Zwall** for Kalimantan, **Robert Arung** for Central and South Sulawesi, and seven other updaters in Java, Papua, Sulawesi and Nusa Tenggara.

This edition is indebted to the excellent foundations created by the writers and updaters of previous editions: **John Haseman**, **Joseph Yogerst**, **Julia Clerk**, **Genevieve Spicer**, **Dra. Asriati**, **Dave Heckman**, **Eric Oey**, **Satyawati Suleiman**, **Kathy MacKinnon**, **Peter Hutton**, **Made Wijaya**, **Kal Muller**, **Paramita Abdurachman**, **Michel Vatin**, **Bernard Suryabrata**, **Jacky Djokosetio**, **Dian N. Gafar**, **Lucas Zwaal**, **Sodersano** and **Rudolf V. Santana**.

The bulk of the photographs were the work of **Corrie Wingate**, who spent months travelling around Java, Bali, Lombok, Sumatra, Kalimantan and Sulawesi to capture the images that bring the pages to life.

The book was copy-edited by **Jane Hutchings**, proofread by **Neil Titman** and indexed by **Penny Phenix**.

Map Legend

▬ ▬ ▪ ▬	International Boundary
▬ ▬ ▬ ▬	Province Boundary
▪ ▬ ▪ ▬	National Park/Reserve
▬ ▬ ▬ ▬	Ferry Route
✈ ✈	Airport: International/Regional
🚌	Bus Station
❶	Tourist Information
✉	Post Office
⛪ † ✝	Church/Ruins
†	Monastery
✡	Synagogue
☾	Mosque
🏰 🏛	Castle/Ruins
∴	Archaeological Site
∩	Cave
🗿	Statue/Monument
★	Place of Interest

The main places of interest in the Places section are coordinated by number with a full-colour map (eg ❶), and a symbol at the top of every right-hand page tells you where to find the map.

Contents

Maps

Inside front cover:
Indonesia
Inside back cover:
Jakarta

THE BEST OF INDONESIA: TOP ATTRACTIONS

The astonishing array of Indonesian cultures and customs is equalled by the amazing landscapes and wildlife of this nation of islands

△ **Borobudur** Mesmerising Borobudur is the world's largest Buddhist monument. Dating from the 9th century, this gigantic stupa forms the shape of a mandala – a geometric aid to meditation. *See page 163.*

△ **Kuta, Sanur and Seminyak beaches** Visions of Bali almost always include its southern beaches, with Kuta in the limelight for surfers and young partygoers, followed by the trendier scenes at upscale Sanur and Seminyak. *See pages 224, 223 and 225.*

△**Yogyakarta (Jogja)** The Javanese art, dance and music cultivated by 18th-century royalty remain alive in Yogyakarta today, blending seamlessly with the modern-day life of students, farmers and handicraft makers. *See page 154.*

▽ **Orang-utans** The best places to see these magnificent creatures are the rainforests of Tanjung Puting National Park (Central Kalimantan) and Gunung Leuser National Park (North Sumatra). *See pages 311 and 193.*

△ **Gunung Bromo** Arrive before dawn to witness the sunrise illuminate one of the world's most remarkable volcanic landscapes. *See page 182.*

△ **Ubud** The cultural heartland of Bali, Ubud and its environs attract seekers of spirituality, wellness programs, health foods and tranquillity. Others are drawn by the wealth and handicrafts and artwork produced here. *See page 232.*

△ **Lake Toba** A water-filled ancient caldera, the largest and deepest in the world, Sumatra's beautiful Lake Toba is believed to have been formed by a series of super-eruptions nearly 900,000 years ago. *See page 195.*

▷ **Ikat-weaving villages** In remote Nusa Tenggara are many islands where ikat textiles are still woven on back-strap looms. Each village has its own motifs and colours, many of which are collected by aficionados. *See page 99.*

◁ **Tana Toraja** Tucked away in the green highlands of South Sulawesi, Tana Toraja is a land of breathtaking vistas, ancient funerary rituals and graves guarded by wooden effigies. *See page 327.*

▽ **Komodo National Park** In addition to its extraordinary reptiles, this remote corner of Indonesia offers some of the best diving and snorkelling in the Asia-Pacific region. *See page 279.*

THE BEST OF INDONESIA: EDITOR'S CHOICE

While Indonesia's best-known treasures are on most visitors' itineraries, others await those willing to go off the beaten track... Here at a glance are our recommendations for both familiar and lesser-known destinations

BEST SCENERY

Terraced rice fields Dazzling terraced rice fields stretch endlessly along the road from Antosari, passing through Belimbing, to Pupuan, West Bali. *See page 245.*

Volcano views Enjoy spectacular views of three of Java's mightiest volcanoes from the hilltop Gedung Songo temples north of Yogyakarta. *See page 167.*

Stormy seas View the stormy Indian Ocean crashing onto the shore from Bali's cliff-top Tanah Lot temple. *See page 226.*

Green valleys The lush, green valleys of South Sulawesi's Tana Toraja are dotted with stone graves, colourful traditional houses and picturesque farmland. *See page327.*

Crater lake Ascend through dense jungle to the ridge atop Lombok's Gunung Rinjani for fabulous vistas of the crater lake Segara Anak. One for experienced hikers. *See page 270.*

BEST DIVING SPOTS

Raja Ampat, Western Papua This remote spot has the world's greatest concentration of marine life for a region of its size, according to the World Wildlife Fund. *See page 360.*

Pulau Menjangan, West Bali Bali Barat National Park's crown jewel and the most accessible of Indonesia's many magnificent dive spots. *See page 247.*

Bunaken Marine National Park, North Sulawesi Several well-established, conservation-oriented dive centres abound in Manado, the gateway to the wonders of this national park. *See page 335.*

Wakatobi, Southeast Sulawesi Excellent dive sites plus local cultures and wildlife make Wakatobi Marine National Park ideal for groups that include non-divers. *See page 333.*

Maluku Currently centred around Ambon, the fabled Spice Islands' diving opportunities are rapidly extending north to Lembeh Strait. *See page 347.*

Alor In Nusa Tenggara, Alor's rich reefs attract sunfish *(mola-mola)*, whales, manta rays, whale sharks and migrating orcas; muck diving is also excellent. *See page 289.*

ABOVE: Balinese landscape. **LEFT:** Sulawesi scuba-diving.

ABOVE: Balinese kecak dance.
BELOW: Bali surf.

MOST UNIQUE CULTURES

Best variety The tiny, remote islands of the Solor and Alor archipelagos have Indonesia's highest concentration of unique cultures and handicrafts. See pages 288–9.

Asmat Known for their ritual woodcarvings, the Asmats of Papua still live in total isolation from the modern world. See page 357.

Dayak The Dayaks of Kalimantan's vast rainforests were once known as fierce head-hunters. See page 297.

Javanese The Javanese are Indonesia's largest ethnic group, and are known for their court cultures and refined manners. See page 59.

Balinese One of the regions's most sophisticated cultures. Many visitors have experienced the fabled spirituality and hospitality of the Balinese. See page 60.

BEST FESTIVALS

Pasola An exciting thanksgiving ritual, Sumba's Pasola is mock war on horseback held on a date determined by the migration of sea worms. See page 290.

Sanur Village Festival This four-day festival promises entertainment for all, with an international kite-flying competition, water sports, dance, music and food. See page 403.

Waisak Day The Buddhist Day of Enlightenment procession held at Borobudur, Central Java, attracts thousands of devotees from throughout Southeast Asia. See page 402.

Labuhan ritual Hundreds of Javanese in traditional attire form a procession to Parangkusumo beach, south of Yogyakarta, where sacrifices are made to the South Sea Goddess. See page 402.

Independence Day Every village and town is decorated two weeks before August 17, Indonesia's Independence Day, with games, food fairs and family fun punctuating the celebrations. See page 403.

BEST BEACHES

Kuta/Legian/Seminyak Kuta, Bali, leads the list as Indonesia's most famous hang-out beach and stretches north to Legian and Seminyak beaches and beyond. See pages 224–5.

Senggigi Lombok's west coast has the country's most beautiful beaches, centred on Senggigi, which blends north into Mangsit, and also includes the southwest peninsula. See page 269.

Sangalaki archipelago Currently being developed off the east coast of Kalimantan, the Sangalaki archipelago includes Derawan and Nabucco islands, dive resorts and white-sand beaches. See page 303.

Pantai Merah The fabulous Pantai Merah (Pink Beach) on Komodo island gets its name from the prolific red corals in surrounding crystal-clear waters. See page 281.

Togian islands In Sulawesi's azure Tomini Bay, the Togian islands' scenic limestone cliffs and secluded white-sand beaches are also excellent for snorkelling and diving. See page 332.

Maluku A premier dive destination, the Maluku islands' shores are lined with sparkling-white beaches, particularly at Ambon and in the Kai archipelago to the southeast. See page 346.

Traditional houses, Tana Toraja, South Sulawesi Traditional *Tongkonan* houses in Tana Toraja are decorated with carved wooden panels. The more buffalo horns displayed, the wealthier the owner. *See page 327.*

Restored Art Deco buildings, Bandung These Art Deco buildings are a remnant of the Dutch colonial era and are still in use today. *See page 150.*

Minangkabau architecture, West Sumatra The Tanah Datar area is the best place to see traditional Minangkabau architecture. The distinctive roofs resemble the horns of a water buffalo. *See page 10.*

Traditional houses, West Sumba The dwellings of this remote island feature steeply pitched roofs where the family's heirlooms are stored. Their four supporting posts are symbolically placed. *See page 290.*

BEST PERFORMING ARTS

Ramayana epic Performed seasonally on an open-air stage at Prambanan temple near Yogyakarta, the Hindu *Ramayana* epic epitomises Javanese culture. *See page 69.*

Hornbill dance In days of yore, Kalimantan's Dayak tribes welcomed returning warriors with a traditional hornbill dance, now seen at harvest festivals. *See page 85.*

Mock tribal wars Tribal battles – usually over land, wives or livestock – were, until recently, a way of life in Papua's Baliem Valley. Today, mock battles are staged for festivals and celebrations. *See page 361.*

Contemporary dance Performances by students at Indonesian Art Institution universities (ISI) in Bali and Yogyakarta often combine contemporary and traditional dance. *See page 89.*

Gamelan jegog Originating in West Bali, where competitions are held, *jegog* instruments are made of giant bamboo, their quality judged by resonance and tone. *See page 246.*

Dance and light shows At Bali Theatre in the Park in Gianyar, and seasonally at Borobudur, Central Java, dancers, animals and technology make for spectacular revues. *See page 90.*

TOP LEFT: legong dance. **ABOVE:** Torajan house.

BEST SHOPPING

Weaving villages Visit the far-flung villages of Nusa Tenggara –notably on Solor and Rote – for hand-woven ikat textiles. *See page 408.*

Pottery villages Banyumulek, Masbagik and Penujak villages, Lombok, for export quality hand-thrown pottery. *See page 405.*

Bali boutiques Numerous small shops along the main roads of Seminyak, for export quality fashions and home furnishings. *See page 225.*

Batik: Yogyakarta is the best place to look for traditional motifs in modern patterns and colours. *See page 405.*

Above: Javan rhino at Ujung Kulon National Park.

Best Wildlife and Trekking

Ujung Kulon National Park West Java's major wildlife reserve shelters the endangered Javan rhino and numerous other forest species. *See page 147.*

Way Kambas National Park In South Sumatra, Way Kambas is a sanctuary for Sumatran elephants and rhinos, assuring visitors the chance to spot them. *See page 210.*

Tanjung Puting National Park While orang-utans are the flagship species of Tanjung Puting, Central Kalimantan, also abundant are fun-to-watch proboscis monkeys. *See page 311.*

Bogani Nani Wartabone National Park In North Sulawesi, this area is home to rare, endemic Sulawesi animals including babirusas, anoas and Sulawesi warty pigs. *See page 334.*

Kerinci Seblat National Park Kerinci Seblat in West Sumatra shelters Sumatran elephants and tigers, clouded leopards, Malayan sun bears and tapirs, and over 375 species of birds. *See page 206.*

Travellers' Tips

Indonesia's sheer size and intricate customs can be overwhelming, particularly to first-time visitors. Below are a few insider tips to help smooth the way.

• When travelling away from the main tourist centres (Java and Bali), expect delays and be prepared to be patient. Using a reputable tour operator will reduce hassles.

• The Indonesian government discourages begging and giving gifts to children. Better to make a donation to an established social organisation or to a school headmaster.

• Be aware of customs and traditions, ie removing shoes before entering mosques and homes; wear a sarong and sash before entering Balinese temples; and dress properly – for ladies, cover midriffs, armpits and knees in Muslim areas; men and women should be fully clothed before leaving the beach anywhere in Indonesia.

• Outside fixed-price shops, bargaining is expected and should be done with a smile and a sense of humour. Away from the main tourist areas, English isn't readily spoken. Simplify sentences and speak slowly.

• Note that International airport departure taxes must be paid in rupiah.

ISLAND NATION

This land of untamed natural beauty offers a
plethora of unique opportunities for the
intrepid traveller

Few, if any, other countries on the planet offer
the mind-boggling array of holiday options that
Indonesia has within its borders. The bonus is that
a multitude of them are virtually untapped, giving those
who yearn for personal contact with exotic cultures, nature
or history such an abundance of choice that time is the
only constraint.

The world knows of Bali, Indonesia's primary tourist destination, and
to a lesser degree the court cultures and historic monuments of Central
Java and the beaches of Lombok. In recent years, travellers have begun
exploring further afield. Divers are flocking to remote Papua's Raja
Ampat, surfers are lured by the daring breaks along the
country's southern coastlines, and hardy climbers explore
the many volcanoes. But there is still so much more.
Granted, getting to many of these places takes an adventurous spirit, as infrastructure is weak off the beaten path, but
for those wishing for unique and authentic experiences,
with careful planning they are here for the taking.

For culture aficionados, art, theatre, dance, music,
rituals and handicrafts abound. In the remote forests of
Kalimantan live the former headhunting Dayaks, and amid
the hills and valleys of Central Sulawesi the Torajans still
hold elaborate funeral ceremonies. On the small islands
east of Lombok exist various ethnic groups whose isolated locations, far
from the country's commercial centres, have left their lifestyles and traditions almost untouched. Indonesia's easternmost outpost, Papua, is home
to extraordinary "lost world" cultures of great interest to anthropologists.

Wildlife-lovers may already know about the Komodo dragons, the rare
Javan rhino, Sumatran elephants and tigers, as well as both Sumatran and
Borneo orang-utans. But many aren't aware that most of these creatures
are found within Indonesia's national parks, which are untapped treasure
troves of rare species of mammals, birds and plants. In addition to diving,
surfing, trekking and climbing, opportunities for other outdoor sports
are prolific. And for those who prefer viewing nature in a more relaxed
way, scenic drives and sailing cruises afford spectacular scenery.

PRECEDING PAGES: Kuta Beach, Lombok; legong dance; orang-utans in the jungle.
ABOVE, FROM LEFT: *jajpongan* drummer; Banten mosque; shadow puppets.

A LAND OF MANY LANDS

The fourth-most populous nation in the world, Indonesia encompasses 6,000 inhabited islands and an extraordinarily diverse mix of cultures and landscapes

The far-flung islands of Indonesia span an impressively broad spectrum of world history and human civilisation – from ancient Hindu-Javanese temples to modern luxury resorts, Stone Age Papuan tribes to the immense metropolis of Jakarta. The country's motto, *Bhinneka Tunggal Ika*, or Unity in Diversity, is no mere slogan. The population of 238 million people is derived from more than 300 ethnic and perhaps several hundred sub-ethnic groups who speak 700 distinct languages. The common elements are a central government and a national language, Bahasa Indonesia, a derivative of Malay.

The fourth-most populous nation in the world, Indonesia straddles two geographically defined racial groups, the Asians to the west and the Melanesians in the east. The majority are Asians, particularly in the western part of the archipelago. Over the centuries, Indians, Arabs and Europeans have mingled with the indigenous people. The largest non-indigenous ethnic

group is the Chinese, who control a significant share of the nation's wealth while comprising only 3 percent of the population. Eighty-eight percent of Indonesians are Muslim, 8 percent are Christian and there are small Hindu, Buddhist and Confucian minorities. In most cases these beliefs are augmented by indigenous, centuries-old animistic traditions.

Indonesia's people are unevenly distributed across the archipelago and more than half inhabit Java and Bali alone, which cover only 7 percent of the total land area. With more than 120 million people living in Java – approximately 58 percent of the Indonesian population – the demands on its land and resources are considerable.

VOLCANIC FERTILITY

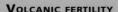

Active volcanoes dominate the landscape of many of the islands, their majestic smoking cones spewing forth millions of tonnes of ash and debris at irregular intervals. Eventually, much of this is washed down to form gently sloping alluvial plains. Where the soil is acidic, the land is infertile and practically useless. But where it is alkaline, as on Java and Bali and a few scattered locations on other islands, it has produced spectacularly fertile land. On both islands, abundant rainfall fills rivers that originate in the mountains and meander through farmlands. Java and Bali have always been Indonesia's primary rice-growing areas, and thus the centres of population and political power.

The archipelago is the world's largest. Its 17,508 islands are strewn across some 5,120km (3,200 miles) of tropical seas, straddling the equator. When superimposed on a map of North America, Indonesia stretches from Seattle to Bermuda. On a map of Europe, it extends east from Ireland to beyond the Caspian Sea.

Four-fifths of this vast area is occupied by ocean, and many of the islands are tiny – no more than rocky outcrops populated, perhaps, by a few seabirds. About 6,000 are large enough to be inhabited, and New Guinea and Borneo (Indonesia claims two-thirds of each) rank as the third- and fourth-largest islands in the world (after Australia and Greenland). Of the other major islands, Sumatra is slightly larger than Sweden, Sulawesi is around half the size of Germany, and Java is a little smaller than England. With a total land area of 1.9 million sq km (733,647 sq miles), Indonesia is the world's 15th-largest nation in terms of size.

Volcanoes, earthquakes and tsunamis

Befitting its reputation as the exotic Spice Islands of the East, Indonesia also constitutes one of the world's most diverse and biologically intriguing areas. Unique geological and climatic conditions have created spectacularly varied tropical habitats – from the exceptionally fertile rice lands of Java and Bali to the luxuriant rainforests of Sumatra, Kalimantan and Sulawesi, and from the savannah grasslands of Nusa Tenggara to the jungle-laced, snowcapped Gunung Puncak Jaya in Papua.

The geological history of the region is complex. The islands are relatively young; the earliest dates from only the end of the Miocene, 6 million years ago – just yesterday on the geological timescale. Since then, the archipelago has been the scene of violent tectonic activity, as islands were torn from jostling super-continents or pushed up by colliding tectonic plates, and then enlarged in earth-wrenching volcanic explosions. The process continues today – this is part of the Pacific 'ring of fire', with Australia drifting slowly northwards as the immense Pacific plate presses south and west to meet it and the Asian mainland. Indonesia lies along the lines of impact, a fact reflected in its geography and its seismic instability.

ABOVE, FROM LEFT: grey langur at a Bali temple; early-19th-century map of the East Indies.

Of Indonesia's major volcanoes, 18 are on Java, 12 dominate Sumatra and two are in eastern Bali. Kalimantan has no volcanoes.

Of the hundreds of volcanoes in Indonesia, over 167 are active, and hardly a year passes without at least one major eruption. On a densely populated island like Java, they inevitably bring death and destruction. When Krakatau, off Java's west coast, blew up in 1883 with a force equivalent to that of 10,000 Hiroshima atomic bombs, it created tidal waves

that killed more than 36,000 people on Java. The eruption was heard as far away as Sri Lanka and Sydney, and the great quantities of debris hurled into the atmosphere caused vivid sunsets all over the world for three years afterwards. But the Krakatau explosion was eclipsed by the truly cataclysmic 1815 eruption of Mount Tambora, on Sumbawa, the largest in recorded history. Around 90,000 people were killed and over 80 cubic km (20 cubic miles) of ejected material dimmed the sun for many months, producing a disastrous "year without summer" in distant Europe.

Already in the 21st century several devastating natural disasters have occurred here. The 2004 Indian Ocean tsunami, triggered by a 9.0-magnitude submarine earthquake, originated off the west coast of Sumatra; almost 170,000 people died and 500,000 were displaced in Indonesia alone. Thanks to international aid, early tsunami warning signals are now in place across 28 Indian Ocean countries, drills are regularly held and Indonesia's Disaster Risk Reduction programme has been introduced at international forums. A new, four-storey, multi-function evacuation centre has been built in Banda Aceh, one of the hardest-hit areas, topped by a helipad to facilitate rescue operations, and 140,000 houses have been built, most of them quake-resistant. There has been almost continual building work along Sumatra's west coast since 2004.

matters. In 2011 it sent a relief team to Japan following its 9.0-magnitude earthquake and ensuing tsunami. The Indonesian people were honoured to help, given that Japan had been one of the first to offer consultation and aid in Indonesia's time of need in the past.

Indonesians have also become more aware of environmental challenges. Farmers are experimenting with bio gas to fuel machinery. Returning to their forefathers' ways, they are using manure instead of chemicals as fertiliser. Local governments have planted billions of trees. Aid money has been used to buy solar-powered pumps, providing water to formerly parched areas.

At a few minutes before 6am one Saturday in May 2006, while many people were sleeping, a 5.9-magnitude earthquake originated deep in the sea along tectonic plate boundaries near Yogyakarta, Central Java. Ninety percent of the homes along the fault line collapsed, killing nearly 6,000 people. Refusing all foreign aid, the Indonesian government provided compensation to those who survived, but it was not enough to rebuild. Years later, it is estimated that the survivors owe a debt of US$5.86 million to state-owned banks.

The upside to these recent tragedies is that the country has greatly improved its preparedness and response to natural disasters, and is now a consultant to other nations on such

Scattered populations

As a result of its geographical peculiarities, Indonesia's hundreds of ethnic groups have been isolated from each other right through history, allowing them to evolve independently and resulting in a multitude of languages and traditions. It was not until road systems were put in place that many isolated villages became aware of the existence of other groups relatively close by. Yet while the implementation of a national language has been instrumental in uniting millions of dissimilar peoples into one nation, close scrutiny reveals how unique each group is even today.

In addition to their separation through geography, language and cultural traditions, Indonesia's people are divided by more commonplace factors such as wealth, social status, education and health care. Generally speaking, the further away from an urban area a village is, the more likely it is to adhere strictly to ancient traditions and rituals, the closer the family ties, the poorer the health care is, and the lower the education opportunities are likely to be.

At the same time, much of Indonesia has changed enormously in recent years. Modern highway systems connect hamlets to marketplaces and ports more efficiently than ever before. Improved transport includes not only public buses and ferries to help people get from one

channel at the minimum. In the past decade, sales of cellular phones have burgeoned, as the demand for landlines is so great that there will never be enough of them to go around. The internet has perhaps made the greatest impact of all, connecting citizens of even far-flung areas not only to other Indonesians but also to the situations and attitudes of the outside world.

All these factors have helped to minimise distinctions between people, for better or worse, but they have also created even larger gaps between those who have access to them and the millions who continue to live in poverty and relative isolation.

point to another, but there is now increased access to bank loans to finance the millions of motorbikes seen throughout the country. The growing number of budget airlines that reach hitherto inaccessible islands also makes flying more affordable to the growing middle-income group.

Communications, too, have vastly improved over the last decade. Until recently the biggest impact on Indonesians nationwide has been television – nearly every village no matter how small or remote has at least one TV and can receive the government-sponsored television

ABOVE, FROM LEFT: tropical forest on the lower slopes of Gunung Rinjani, Lombok; rescue workers search for survivors after Gunung Merapi erupts in 2010.

MERAPI ERUPTS

Following the 2006 earthquake, Central Java was plagued again in October and November 2010 when mighty Gunung Merapi, north of Yogyakarta, erupted. Area residents were evacuated to nearby refugee centres prior to the event, but 300 lives were lost, many through gas inhalation when returning to their villages to tend to their livestock. Blistering pyroclastic blasts and avalanches of house-sized rocks and debris continued for several days, replaced in the weeks following by flash floods. Among the half a million people who were displaced, 2,682 families returned to their villages on the slopes of the mountain, despite government offers to relocate them elsewhere.

DECISIVE DATES

Prehistoric era

1.81 million years ago
Solo Man (Homo erectus soloensis) inhabits Central Java.

1.66 million years ago
Java Man (Homo erectus) lives in Java.

40,000 years ago
Fossil records of modern humans found in Indonesia.

5,000 BC
Austronesian peoples begin moving into Indonesia from the Philippines.

500 BC–AD 500
Dong Son Bronze Age influences Indonesian arts.

Indianised kingdoms

AD 400
Hindu kingdoms emerge in West Java and East Kalimantan.

850
Sanjaya (early Mataram) seizes control of Central Java. Sailendran flee to Sriwijaya, southern Sumatra.

860–1000
The golden age of Sriwijaya.

910–1080
Political centre of Java moves to East Java; rise of Hindu kingdoms on Bali.

Singasari and Majapahit

1222–75
Singasari dynasty founded; controls maritime trade from Sriwijaya.

1292
Civil war ensues in Singasari; Mongol invasion joins forces against Singasari.

1294
Singasari falls to Majapahit kingdom, the most powerful in Indonesian history.

15th century
Majapahit and Kediri kingdoms are conquered by Islamic Demak, North Java. Hindu-Javanese aristocracy moves to Bali.

Mid-16th century
Islamic Banten and Cirebon sultanates established in Java.

Late 16th century
Second Mataram kingdom founded; Dutch arrive. Both fight to control Java.

Dutch colonial years

1602–3
United Dutch East India Company (VOC) establishes trading post in Banten.

1619
Dutch take over Jayakarta (now Jakarta) and rename it Batavia.

1613–1755
Mataram expands and attacks Batavia; Dutch prevail.

1740–55
A major conflict originates in Batavia. The Dutch acquire the right to collect tolls throughout Mataram. A new capital at Surakarta is established.

1755
Dutch partition Mataram into two courts, Surakarta and Yogyakarta.

1767–77
voc conquers eastern Java, abolishing Java's last Hinduised kingdom.

1799–1800
VOC is dissolved; Dutch assume control.

Resistance and repression

1811–16
English rule under Thomas Stamford Raffles.

1813
Raffles abolishes Banten and Cirebon sultanates.

1817
Raffles writes monumental History of Java.

1825–30
Yogyakarta sultanate's cataclysmic Java War against the Dutch. Sultan deposed.

1830–50
Dutch introduce the Cultivation System, a land tax payable by labour or land use. Famines occur; 250,000 die.

National awakening

1908
Dutch-educated Indonesians form regional student organisations; Indonesian nnational consciousness begins to take shape.

1910
Indonesian communist movement founded.

1910–30
Turbulent period of strikes, violence and organised rebellions.

1927
Sukarno tries to unite nationalists, Muslims and Marxists into a single mass movement. He is imprisoned by the Dutch and later exiled.

World War II and Independence

1942–4
Japanese invade Bali and Java, and promise independence for Indonesia.

1945
Japan surrenders. Nationalist leaders Sukarno and Hatta declare Indonesia's independence. Dutch return to resume control; war for independence breaks out.

1949
Dutch acknowledge Indonesia's independence under UN pressure.

PRECEDING PAGES & ABOVE LEFT: Prambanan Temple dates from the 9th century, the peak of Sriwijaya power. **ABOVE RIGHT:** Sukarno and his ministers, 1958. **RIGHT:** anti-government protest, as President Susilo Bambang Yudhoyono marked his 100th day in office in 2010.

Late 1950s
Separatist insurgencies prompt Sukarno to declare martial law and resurrect 1945 "revolutionary" constitution.

Sukarno and Suharto years

1959
Sukarno dissolves parlia-

ment; his sentiments become more militant.

1965
Bloodletting focused on Chinese ensues after failed communist coup.

1966
Sukarno persuaded to sign over powers to his protégé, Suharto, who takes over presidency. Until 1998, Suharto is re-elected six times in rigged elections.

1997
Asian economic crisis begins.

1998
Suharto refuses to reform economy and is forced to resign amid mass student uprising.

Contemporary Indonesia

1998–2001
Three presidents govern in quick succession.

2004
In historic first direct presidential election, Susilo Bambang Yudhoyono (SBY) comes into office.

2008
Suharto dies, ending a major chapter in Indonesian history.

2009
SBY is re-elected by overwhelming majority. Pledges at G20 summit to wean Indonesia off fuel subsidies to reduce greenhouse gas emissions. Poverty rate drops from 60 percent in 1990 to 14.1 percent.

2010
Amid global economic crisis, Indonesia emerges as the region's third-strongest economy after China and India.

2011
Indonesia chairs ASEAN and becomes key player in the Non-Aligned Movement. Establishes new corruption courts. Economic growth expected to continue.

BIRTH OF EMPIRES

Indonesians' prehistoric ancestors, Java Man
and Solo Man lived in a fertile region that later
saw the rise of great maritime empires

The late 19th-century discovery of hominid remains on Java island took the anthropological world by storm when they were identified as the first scientific evidence on the planet of *Homo erectus*. Early 20th-century findings of more fossils in nearby Sangiran (Sragen) proved to be even older, for a time establishing Java as the origin of the modern human race. Nearly a century later, when skeletons of nine small individuals were unearthed on Flores – who are now believed to have coexisted with dwarf *Stegodon* elephants – the scientific world rushed to Indonesia to prove whether or not they were a pygmy race, a controversy that remains unsettled.

These discoveries not only disparaged previous theories about the origin of man, but as some of them displayed definite Southeast Asian features, they threw new light on migration patterns. It is now generally believed that there were two great migratory waves into Indonesia. One was the Melanesian people who entered, perhaps via land bridges, from the north from mainland Asia. The other was the Austronesians, who were great seafarers and whose populations spread throughout Polynesia, Southeast Asia and to Madagascar.

It is an interesting turn of events that from these beginnings mighty empires arose that stretched as far afield as Cambodia, and that the fertile lands would produce spices sought after and fought over, extending Indonesia's influence from Europe to China.

Prehistory

Indonesian archaeological findings have contributed more than their share of controversy

LEFT: Brahma Amara Vihar Buddhist temple, North Bali.
RIGHT: *Homo floresiensis* skull.

in the past. In 1891, a Dutch military physician discovered a fossilised primate jawbone with human characteristics on the banks of the Bengawan Solo River in Central Java. The jawbone was at first discounted by anthroplogists who thought it was likely to belong to an extinct species of apes. But in the following year, two more humanoid fossils were uncovered. This caused a sensation: together the finds were believed to represent the world's first evidence of Darwin's "missing link". Darwin's evolutionary theories were still in dispute at the time and the discovery, dubbed Java Man, was only vindicated with the unearthing of similar fossils outside Beijing in 1921.

The most striking megaliths in Indonesia are the carved statues of riding men and wrestling animals found on the Pasemah plateau in South Sumatra. No definite date can be given for these.

It is now thought that the Java Man fossils are about 1.66 million years old. Originally named *Pithecanthropus erectus*, later reclassified *Homo erectus*, it justified migration theories between China and Indonesia. Until later discoveries were made in Kenya, anthropologists theorised

THE FLORES HOBBITS

Heated anthropologic debate began in 2004 with the discovery of the skeletons of nine people of diminutive size on Flores Island, nicknamed "Hobbits". The controversy centres around whether they were a race of pygmies, were malnourished or were victims of ill-formed brains. Currently classified *Homo floresiensis*, some fossils have been dated from 38,000 to 12,000 years ago, with one specimen about 74,000 years old.

Arguments, debates and extensive research of minuscule details continue and are likely to do so for many years to come, with the added intrigue of missing and damaged samples and blocked access to the discovery site in the early years of the exploration.

that the ancestors of modern humans were Asian in origin.

Then in 1936 German palaeo-anthropologist G.H.R. von Koenigswald discovered a larger collection of fossils in nearby Ngandong village, at Sangiran, 18km (11 miles) north of Solo. Dubbed "Mojokerto Child" (later called Solo Man), the finds were controversial from the outset due to the size of the cranium, debunking previous theories of the intellectual capacity of the now-extinct *Homo erectus*. After exhaustive studies and much debate, most scientists now concede that Solo Man (*Homo erectus soloensis*) was older than Java Man, about 1.81 million years, or about the same age as the Kenya fossils. As a result, it now appears that instead of a single origin of modern man, parallel evolutions occurred in two places at different rates. Interestingly, Solo Man seems to have survived until as recently as 20,000–50,000 years ago, perhaps living alongside *Homo sapiens*.

Beginning about 20,000 years ago, there is evidence of human burials and partial cremations in Indonesia. Several cave paintings (mainly hand stencils, but also human and animal figures) found in southwestern Sulawesi and New Guinea may be 10,000 or more years old.

The Neolithic centuries – which appear to have begun soon after the end of the last Ice Age, around 10,000 BC – are characterised here, as elsewhere, by the advent of village settlements, domesticated animals, polished stone tools, pottery and food cultivation. In Southwest Sulawesi and the East Timor plain, for instance, pottery vessels and open bowls dating from about 3,000 BC have been found, together with shell bracelets, discs, beads, adzes and the bones of pig and dogs.

The first agriculturalists in Indonesia probably grew yams before the introduction of rice. In fact, rice came to much of Indonesia only in recent centuries, and yams are still a staple crop on many eastern islands. Bark clothing was produced with stone-pounding tools, and pottery was shaped with the aid of a wooden paddle and a stone anvil tapper.

Neolithic Indonesians were undoubtedly experienced seafarers, like their Polynesian cousins who were spreading across the Pacific at this time. Today, the outrigger is commonly found throughout Indonesia and Oceania.

Dong Son bronze culture

It was once thought that Southeast Asia's Bronze Age began with the Chinese-influenced Dong Son bronze culture of northern Vietnam in the 1st millennium BC. However, the discovery of 5,000-year-old copper and bronze tools in northern Thailand raised the possibility of similar developments elsewhere. All early Indonesian bronzes known to date are clearly of the Dong Son type.

The finest Dong Son ceremonial bronze drums and axes are decorated with engraved geometric, animal and human motifs. This decorative style was highly influential in many fields of Indonesian art, and seems to have spread together with the bronze casting technique, as ancient stone moulds have been found in Indonesia. The sophisticated "lost wax" technique of bronze casting was employed, and such bronzes were found as far east as New Guinea.

Who were the Indonesian producers of Dong Son bronzes? It is difficult to say, but it seems small kingdoms based on wet-rice agriculture and foreign trade were flourishing in the archipelago during this period. Articles of Indian manufacture have been found at several prehistoric sites in Indonesia, and a panel from a bronze drum found on Sangeang island, near Sumbawa, depicts figures in ancient Chinese dress. Early Han texts mention the clove-producing islands of eastern Indonesia, and it is certain that by the 2nd century BC, trade was widespread in the archipelago.

Indianised kingdoms

Beginning in the 2nd century AD, a number of sophisticated civilisations emerged in Southeast Asia – civilisations whose cosmology, literature, architecture and political organisation were patterned on those of India. These kingdoms are known for the wonderful monuments they created: Borobudur, Prambanan, Angkor, Pagan and others. Yet their creators remain largely an enigma.

The most plausible theory is that Southeast Asian rulers Indianised their own kingdoms – either by employing Indian Brahmans or sending their own people to India to acquire knowledge. Sanskrit writing and texts, along with sophisticated Indian rituals and architectural techniques, afforded a ruler greater

organisational control, wealth and social status. They also enabled them to participate in an expanding Indian trading network.

The first specific references to Indonesian rulers and kingdoms are found in written Chinese sources. Using the South Indian *Pallava* script, the stone inscriptions were issued by Indonesian rulers in two different areas of the archipelago: Kutai on the eastern coast of Kalimantan, and Tarumanegara on the Citarum River, in West Java near Bogor. Both rulers were Hindus.

There is also the interesting figure Fa Hsien, a Chinese Buddhist monk who journeyed to

India in the early 5th century to obtain Buddhist scriptures and on his way home was shipwrecked and stranded on Java. Fa Hsien noted there were many Brahmans and heretics on Java and that the Buddhist Dharma there was not worth mentioning.

> Many Indian traders, unlike the Chinese, settled in Indonesia and intermarried with locals. In addition to introducing dance, music, literature, the Sanskrit language and religion, they brought military discipline and the division of labourers into castes.

At the end of the 7th century, a Buddhist kingdom at Palembang took over the vital

ABOVE, FROM LEFT: cave paintings at Maros, Sulawesi; a ceremonial Dong Son bronze drum.

Malacca and Sunda straits. This was Sriwijaya, which ruled throughout the next 600 years.

Sriwijaya's maritime trade

The Sriwijaya kingdom relied for existence not on agriculture, but on control of maritime trade. It has been speculated that Sriwijaya rose to prominence as a result of a substitution of Sumatran aromatics –*p'o-ssu* – for expensive Middle Eastern frankincense and myrrh. But Sriwijaya was also located in a strategic position – and is said to have had the largest ships in the world at the time – and apparently achieved regular

direct sailings to India and China by the late 8th century.

The nearest area suitable for wet-rice agriculture was in Central Java, where great Indianised kingdoms established themselves from the early 8th century onwards. They first supplied Sriwijaya with rice, and then later began to compete with that empire for a share of the trade.

Sanjaya and the Sailendra

The ever-present rivalry between Buddhist and Hindu ruling families in Central Java bore fruit with the supplanting of the Hindu rulers Sanjaya and his descendants by the Sailendra, a

KUBLAI KHAN SNUBBED

In the late 13th century, the Buddhist king Kertanagara's control of maritime trade was so complete that Kublai Khan, the great Mongol emperor from China, sent ambassadors to demand tribute from Java. Kertanagara not only refused but had the effrontery to disfigure the Mongol envoy, for which gesture the enraged Khan sent a powerful fleet in 1293 to Java.

The fleet landed only to discover that Kertanagara had been murdered by his vassal, Jayakatwang. The Chinese, with an ally in Kertanagara's son-in-law, Wijaya, stayed in Java for about a year and defeated Jayakatwang. Wijaya later turned on the Mongol generals and drove them off.

Buddhist line of kings from northern Java.

Both Buddhist, Sailendra and Sriwijaya maintained close relations and controlled Java for about a century. During this time, they constructed the magnificent Buddhist monuments Borobudur, Mendut, Kalasan, Sewu and numerous others in the shadow of Gunung Merapi.

Meanwhile, the Sanjaya line continued to rule over outlying areas as vassals of the Sailendra, building Hindu temples in remote areas of Java – at Dieng plateau and Gunung Ungaran. Around 850, the Sanjaya prince Rakai Pikatan married a Sailendra princess and seized control of Central Java. The Sailendra fled to Sriwijaya, blocking all Javanese shipping throughout the South China Sea for more than a century. Rakai

Pikatan commemorated his victory by erecting the splendid Prambanan temple, the Hindu equivalent of Buddhist Borobudur.

A succession of Hindu kings followed, but the capital suddenly moved to East Java around 930. A number of factors might account for this. The Sailendra kings, who were installed at Sriwijaya and had shut off the vital overseas trade from Java's north coast, may have threatened to return to Central Java. An eruption of Gunung Merapi may have covered Central Java in volcanic ash. There is also the possibility of an epidemic or of mass migration to the more fertile lands of East Java.

An eastern Javanese empire prospered in the 10th century and attacked and occupied Sriwijaya for two years. Sriwijaya retaliated later with a huge seaborne force that destroyed the Javanese capital, killed the ruler, King Dharmawangsa, and splintered the realm into petty fiefdoms. It took nearly 20 years for the next great king, Airlangga, to restore the empire.

Airlangga was the dead king's nephew, and he succeeded to the throne in 1019 after the Sriwijayan forces departed. He is best known as a patron of the arts and an ascetic who had Indian Sanskrit classics translated into Javanese. To appease his two ambitious sons, he divided the empire into equal halves, Kediri and Janggala (or Daha and Kahuripan). Kediri became the more powerful and is remembered today as the source of numerous works of old Javanese literature, mainly adaptations of the Indian epics in the poetic *kekawin* form.

Java prospered as never before under the rule of successive East Javan empires. At this time, the Javanese were the master shipbuilders and mariners of Southeast Asia. During the 14th century, at the height of the Majapahit Empire, they controlled the sea lanes in the Indonesian archipelago and to faraway India and China.

The Singasari dynasty was founded by Ken Arok in 1222. During his rule of Janggala, Ken Arok revolted against his sovereign, the ruler of Kediri, and set up his new capital at Singasari, near present-day Malang. The extraordinary Kertanagara, the last Singasari king, was a scholar and a statesman of the Tantric Bhairawa

ABOVE, FROM LEFT: Borobudur; Prambanan, an indicator of Sriwijaya's wealth.

sect of Buddhism. In 1275 and 1291, he sent successful naval expeditions against Sriwijaya and wrested control of the maritime trade.

Majapahit

Kertanagara's son-in-law Wijaya married four of Kertanagara's daughters and established a new capital in 1294 by the Brantas River (near present-day Trowulan) in an area known for its *pahit* (bitter) *maja* fruits. The new kingdom became known as Majapahit. Its extensive system of canals was probably used to transport rice and other goods downriver to the seaports.

Majapahit was the first empire to embrace

the entire Indonesian archipelago and reached its zenith in the mid-14th century under Wijaya's grandson, Hayam Wuruk, and his able prime minister Gajah Mada. Decline set in almost immediately after Hayam Wuruk's death in 1389. A smouldering struggle for supremacy erupted into civil war between 1403 and 1406, and although the country was reunited in 1429, Majapahit had lost control of the western Java Sea and the straits to a new Islamic power located at Malacca.

Towards the end of the 15th century, Majapahit and Kediri were conquered by the new Islamic state, Demak, on Java's north coast, and the entire Hindu-Javanese aristocracy then relocated to nearby Bali.

A TRADING POWER

Maritime trade was the conduit that brought foreigners, with their ideas, technology and religions, to Indonesia's shores

Ancient Chinese chronicles describe the islands of Indonesia as a wilderness of jungles, marshes, ferocious wild animals and naked natives who hunted and fished with poisoned arrows. Yet a few centuries later, when the Portuguese came to the archipelago, Indonesia's cities equalled the grandeur of those in Europe.

Early trade

The Chinese traded in Indonesia from at least 206 BC, and they were later followed by Persians, Indians, Arabs, Siamese and Burmese. This once-wild land became a transit point between the West and the East, where Indonesians exchanged precious stones, pearls, gold, silk, sandalwood and spices with foreign merchants in rudimentary trading activities. By the first century AD, Indonesians were sailing across the Indian Ocean to Madagascar in wooden outrigger boats. Establishing colonies there, they laboriously transported spices via the southern spice route to the Red Sea, to the Mediterranean and on to the Roman Empire. Financed by tiny kingdoms, these expeditions would have been small and the risks enormous, but the profits for such exotic cargo were extremely large.

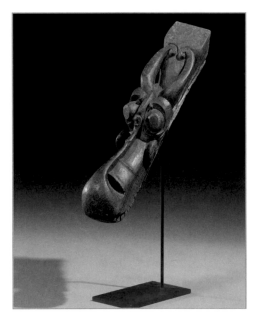

> The prices that nutmeg, mace, pepper and cloves attracted in Europe were as much as 2,500 percent over what traders paid for them in Indonesia.

With Chinese merchants came Buddhism, later followed by Hinduism from India. These religions began as court cultures, gradually extending their influence to city-dwellers but largely bypassing the rest of the population.

By the 7th century AD, the Buddhist Sriwijaya dynasty (based in today's Palembang, South Sumatra) was the greatest maritime empire in Southeast Asia. It controlled the Malacca Strait – the narrow channel between Sumatra and the Malay coast which functioned as a crucial conduit for all maritime trade between the Middle East, India and China – as well as the western part of Indonesia, most of the Malay Peninsula, and even claimed Sri Lanka. Sriwijaya became the centre of Buddhist learning for all of Asia and had a university where Chinese monks studied en route to India for continued learning. It was heavily involved in trade and owned ships that sailed to India and China. Sriwijaya's greatest glory occurred in 1200 when, together with Burma's Pagan kingdom and the Khmer kingdom in Cambodia, it was established as one of the three greatest empires in Southeast Asia.

Around the same time, the Javanese kings of the interior had adopted Hinduism from India as their faith. They surrounded themselves with the music, dance, art and language (Sanskrit) associated with that religion, while the ordinary Javanese retained their

not until Gujarat, an important Indian trading centre, fell into Muslim hands in the 13th century that Indonesian rulers began to convert to the new faith. The trading ports on the northeastern coast of Sumatra immediately saw the advantages of converting and became the first Islamic domains.

Islamic merchants, who controlled the overland Silk Road from China and India to Europe, via Persia and the Levant, had become increasingly powerful. With India's major textile-producing ports in their hands, they began to dominate the maritime trade routes through South and

original beliefs and traditions. In the 9th century, the reigning Hindu Sanjaya dynasty and rival Buddhist Sailendran dynasties merged through marriage, which was when Borobudur and its accompanying Buddhist temples were constructed.

Trade and Islam

Islam arrived in the Indonesian archipelago atop the crest of economic expansion along the trade routes of the East. Although Muslim traders had visited the region for centuries, it was

ABOVE, FROM LEFT: wooden dragon carving from a Dayak canoe; Islam became well established in the 13th century.

PROPAGATION BY THEATRE

The traditional account of the Islamisation of Java is interesting. According to Javanese chronicles, nine Islamic saints *(wali sanga)* propagated Islam through the Javanese shadow plays *(wayang kulit)* and gamelan music. They introduced the Islamic confession of faith and the reading of Koranic prayers, to performances of the Hindu Ramayana and Mahabharata epics. No better explanation could be given for the origins of Islamic syncretism in Java. Today, Islam is the professed religion of nearly 90 percent of all Indonesians and its traditions and rituals affect all aspects of their daily life.

East Asia. Conversion to Islam ensured that Sumatran rulers could participate in the growing international trade network and receive protection against the encroachments of two aggressive regional powers – the Siamese to the north and the Javanese to the east.

Islam received its greatest boost when, in 1436, a shrewd Malacca king converted to the faith upon returning from an extended

stay in China. Until then, Malacca had been a vassal of China ruled by descendants of the Buddhist Sriwijaya dynasty and peninsular

kings who had been attacked and evicted by the Javanese and Siamese during the 14th century. China had proved a valuable patron of Malacca since its founding in 1402, but by 1436, China's influence in the region was on the wane, and the Siamese were again demanding tribute. By 1500, Malacca was to become a major trading port in the region and the greatest emporium in the East, a city comparable in size to the largest European cities of the time.

Conquest

During the 15th century, all of the trading ports of the western archipelago were brought within Malacca's orbit, including the important ports along the north coast of Java. Traditionally, these ports owed their allegiance to the great inland Hindu-Javanese kingdoms, acting in effect as import-export and shipping agents, exchanging Javanese-grown rice for spices and other luxury items in a complex series of value-added transactions. After about 1400, however, the power of the inland Javanese rulers was rapidly declining, and the coastal rulers were seeking ways to assert their independence and retain the profits of the trade. Gradually, through intermarriage between leading Islamic traders and local aristocrats, relations were cemented with Malacca's Muslims.

A turning point was reached sometime in the late 15th century when the newly founded Islamic Demak kingdom on the north-central coast attacked and conquered the last great Hindu-Buddhist kingdom on Java, Majapahit.

GREEN CITIES

During the 16th century, Indonesia's cities were physically different from those in Europe, the Middle East, India and China. For the most part built without walls, they were located at river mouths or on wide plains, and relied upon surrounding villages for their defence. An official envoy from the Sultanate of Aceh to the Ottoman Empire explained that Acehnese defences consisted not of walls, but of "stout hearts in fighting the enemy, and a large number of elephants".

Indonesian cities tended also to be green. Coconut, banana and other fruit trees grew everywhere, and most of the widely spaced wooden or bamboo houses had vegetable gardens. The royal compound was the

centre for defence and might have walls and a moat. With perhaps no more than 5 million people in the entire archipelago, land had no intrinsic value except what people made of it. In 1613, when the English wanted some land to build a fortress in Makassar, they had to recompense the residents not for the space, but for the coconut palms.

With so few people and so much land, it is not surprising that the urban population of Indonesia in the 16th century at least equalled the agrarian population. Thus, the typical Indonesian of that period was not a peasant, but a town dweller engaged as an artisan, sailor, worker or trader.

They drove the Hindu rulers to the east and eventually on to Bali and annexed the agriculturally rich Javanese hinterlands. Demak then consolidated its control over the entire north coast, emerging as the master of Java by the 16th century.

During the 16th century, Islam continued to spread throughout the Indonesian archipelago, but the whole system of Islamic economic and political alliances was swiftly overturned in the dramatic conquest of Malacca by a small band of Portuguese in 1511.

The first Europeans arrive

By the time the Portuguese arrived, news of the hitherto closely guarded secret location of the fabled Spice Islands had leaked out, and greediness for the riches that possession of nutmeg, mace, cloves, pepper and sandalwood – then as valuable as gold – kicked in. In order to get to the Spice Islands, ships had to pass through the Malacca Strait. Thus, whoever had control over that protected stretch of sea held the keys to those treasures.

The first Portuguese ships that came were heavily armed men-of-war. Prior to their arrival, the exchange of goods was controlled by a feudal network of nobility and traders and had been peaceful except for pirates and political infighting among the kings. However, the Europeans – beginning with the Portuguese – brought a new, aggressive way of doing business backed by firepower, shocking the Indonesians, Arabs, Indians and Chinese who had been working together for centuries.

Portugal's first attack was on Malacca, which fell, but only after a bitter struggle that involved support from as far away as the Ottoman Empire. From Malacca, Portuguese ships proceeded to the rival kings at Ternate and Tidore in Maluku (the Moluccas), the world's only source of valuable cloves, while nearby, tiny Banda had the only nutmeg and mace. Tidore refused. About that time the Spanish arrived, under the leadership of an exiled Portuguese, Ferdinand Magellan.

ABOVE, FROM LEFT: Java grew wealthy on the proceeds of maritime trade, enabling the construction of great temples and mosques, such as the Grand Mosque at Demak; statue of first king of Majapahit (rule 1293-1309) at the Indonesian National Museum, Jakarta.

The Portuguese were successful at wooing the Ternate king in exchange for their protection against Tidore, and they built a fort in Ternate and one in Ambon. Fighting between the Spanish and Portuguese for control of the spice trade continued for 40 years until their governments in Europe agreed on a delineation of spheres of interest. Portugal kept the Maluku islands while the Philippines went to Spain.

By that time there was an uprising against the Portuguese. Ternate fort was continually besieged for six more years, while Ambon was eventually deserted. Portuguese Ternate fell in 1574, and Portugal's aura of invincibility was destroyed. Spain had already conquered Brunei and was standing by to take control of Maluku's spices, and certainly would have except for an astonishing event in Europe: King Philip II of Spain united Portugal to his throne in 1580.

Meanwhile on Java, Yogyakarta was now the centre of power, where the nobility continued to live according to ancient traditions. The major maritime power came from Makassar on the southwest coast of Sulawesi. While the Portuguese position in the Maluku islands slowly disintegrated and Spain's efforts were too weak to have any affect, the first English and Dutch ships arrived on the scene.

THE DUTCH COLONIAL YEARS

The hunt for highly prized spices drew the
Western powers to the East, where Indonesia's
resource-rich islands were a star attraction

The saga of the Dutch in Indonesia began in 1596, when four small Dutch vessels, led by the incompetent and arrogant Cornelis de Houtman, dropped anchor in Banten, then the largest pepper port in the archipelago. Repeatedly blown off course and racked by disease and dissension, the de Houtman expedition was a disaster. In Banten, the sea-weary Dutch crew went on a drinking binge and had to be chased back to their ships by order of an angry prince, who then refused to do business. Hopping from port to port along the north coast of Java, de Houtman wisely confined his sailors to the ships and managed to purchase spices. On arrival in Bali, the entire crew jumped ship, and it was months before de Houtman could muster a quorum for the return voyage.

Back in Holland two years later, with only three lightly laden ships and a third of the original crew, de Houtman's voyage was nonetheless hailed a success. So costly were spices in Europe that the sale of the meagre cargo sufficed to cover all expenses, even producing a modest profit. This touched off a veritable fever of speculation in Dutch commercial circles, and the following year five consortiums dispatched a total of 22 ships to the Indies.

The Dutch East India Company

Since the 15th century, ports of the two Dutch coastal provinces in northern Europe, Holland and Zeeland, had served as entrepôts for goods shipped to Germany and the Baltic states. Many Dutch merchants grew wealthy on this trade

and, following the outbreak of war with Spain in 1568, they began to expand their shipping fleets rapidly, so that by the 1590s, they were trading directly with the Levant and Brazil.

As a small country busy fighting its own battles back in Europe, many soldiers who fought in Indonesia on behalf of Holland were not Dutch. Among them were renegades, mercenaries, drunks and thieves; in short, the dregs of society.

Thus, when a Dutchman published his itinerary to the East Indies in 1596, it occasioned the immediate dispatch of de Houtman and later

LEFT: Jan Pieterszoon Coen led the Dutch campaign.
RIGHT: a Dutch East India Company shipyard.

expeditions. Indeed, so keen was the interest in direct trade with the Indies that all Dutch traders soon came to recognise the need for cooperation in order to minimise competition and maximise profits. In 1602, they formed the United Dutch East India Company (known by its Dutch initials, VOC), one of the world's first joint-stock corporations. It was empowered to negotiate treaties, raise armies, build fortresses and wage war in Asia on behalf of Holland.

In its early years, the VOC met with only limited success. Several trading posts were opened, and Ambon was taken from the Portuguese in 1605. But Spanish and English, not to mention the existing Dutch post, and proceeded to build a stone barricade mounted with cannons. The prince protested that fortifications were not part of their agreement; Coen responded by bombarding and destroying the palace. A siege of the fledgling Dutch fortress began in which the powerful Bantenese and a recently arrived English fleet joined the Jayakartans. Meanwhile, Coen escaped to Ambon, leaving a few men to defend the fort and its valuable contents.

Coen's cunning

Five months later, Coen returned to discover his men still in possession of their post. Although

Muslim, competition kept spice prices high in Indonesia and low in Europe. Then in 1614 a young accountant, Jan Pieterszoon Coen, convinced the directors that only a more forceful policy would make the company profitable. Coen was given command of VOC operations, and promptly embarked on a series of military adventures that were to set the pattern of Dutch behaviour in the region.

Coen's first step was to establish a permanent headquarters at Jayakarta (now Jakarta), on the northwestern coast of Java, close to the pepper-producing parts of Sumatra and the strategic Sunda Strait.

In 1618, he sought and received permission from Prince Wijayakrama of Jayakarta to expand outnumbered 30 to one, they had rather unwittingly played one foe against another by agreeing to any and all demands, but never actually surrendering their position due to the mutual suspicion and timidity of the three opposing parties. Coen set his adversaries to flight in a series of dramatic attacks, undertaken with a small force of 1,000 men that included several score of Japanese mercenaries. Jayakarta was razed to the ground and construction of a new Dutch town begun, including canals, drawbridges, docks, warehouses, barracks, a central square, a city hall and a church – all protected by a high stone wall and a moat. In short, another Amsterdam.

Coen subsequently learned that during the darkest days of the siege, many of the Dutch defenders had behaved in a most unseemly manner: drinking, singing and fornicating. Worst of all, they had broken open the company storehouse and divided the contents among themselves. Those involved were immediately executed and memories of the infamous siege soon faded – save one. The defenders had dubbed their fortress Batavia; the name stuck.

Coen's next step was to secure control of the five tiny nutmeg- and mace-producing Banda islands. He brought an expeditionary force there and, with the infamous Japanese samurai, rounded up and killed most of the 15,000 inhabitants within weeks. Three of the islands were transformed into spice plantations, managed by Dutch colonists and worked by slaves.

In the years that followed, the Dutch gradually tightened their grip on the spice trade. From Ambon they attempted to negotiate a monopoly on cloves with the rulers of Ternate and Tidore. But the smuggling of cloves and clove trees continued. Traders obtained these and other goods at the new Islamic port, Makassar, in southern Sulawesi. The Dutch repeatedly blockaded Makassar and imposed treaties barring the Makassarese from trading with other nations, but were unable for many years to enforce them. Finally, in 1669, following three years of bitter fighting, the Makassarese surrendered to the superior Dutch forces.

Dutch control

The Dutch achieved effective control of the eastern archipelago and its lucrative spice trade by the end of the 17th century. In the western half of the archipelago, however, they became increasingly embroiled in fruitless intrigues and wars, particularly in Java. This came about largely because the Dutch presence at Batavia disturbed a delicate balance of power in Java.

Batavia came under Javanese attack as early as 1628. Sultan Agung, the third and greatest ruler of the Mataram kingdom, was aggressively expanding his domain and had concluded a successful five-year siege on Surabaya. He now controlled all of Central and East Java, and intended to take West Java by pushing out the Dutch and conquering Banten.

ABOVE, FROM LEFT: Dutch warships off the coast of Java in the 18th century; a Javanese painting depicts a battle between Javan and Dutch forces at the Mataram capital, Kartasura (1684).

Agung nearly succeeded. A large Javanese expeditionary force momentarily breached Batavia's defences, but was then driven back outside the walls in a last-ditch effort by Coen. The Javanese were not prepared for such resistance and withdrew for lack of provisions. A year later, Sultan Agung sent an even larger force of 10,000 provided with huge stockpiles of rice for a protracted siege. Coen, however, learned of the stockpiles and destroyed them before the Javanese even arrived. Poorly led, starving and sick, the Javanese troops died by the thousands outside the walls of Batavia. Never again was Mataram a threat to the city.

Relations between the Dutch and the Javanese improved during the despotic reign of Amangkurat I (1646–77). They had common enemies – the pasisir trading kingdoms of the northern Java coast. Ironically, the Dutch conquest of Makassar later led to their ally's demise.

The Makassar wars of 1666–9 and their aftermath created a diaspora of Makassarese and Buginese refugees. Many of them fled to East Java, where they united under the leadership of a Madurese prince, Trunajaya. Aided and abetted by the Mataram crown prince, Trunajaya successfully stormed through Central Java and plundered the Mataram capital in 1677. Amangkurat I died while on the retreat, fleeing from the enemy forces.

Once in control of Java, Trunajaya renounced his alliance with the young Mataram prince and declared himself king. The crown prince pleaded for Dutch support, promising to reimburse all military expenses and to award the Dutch valuable trade concessions. The Dutch swallowed the bait and mounted a costly campaign to capture Trunajaya. This ended in 1680 with the crown prince, who styled himself Amangkurat II, being restored to the throne.

But the new king was in no position to fulfil his end of the bargain with the Dutch; his treasury had been looted and his kingdom was in ruins. All he had was territory, and although

EXPLOITATIVE CULTIVATION

The pernicious effects of the Cultivation System introduced by the Dutch in 1830 were apparent from the beginning. While in theory the system called for peasants to surrender only a portion of their land and labour, in practice certain lands were worked exclusively for the Dutch by forced labour. Java, one of the richest pieces of real estate on earth, was transformed into a huge Dutch plantation, imposing unimaginable hardships and injustices upon the Javanese. Private plantations largely replaced government ones after 1870, but some government coffee plantations continued to employ forced labour well into the 20th century.

Stamford Raffles was a brilliant scholar, naturalist, linguist, diplomat and strategist. He has been credited with rediscovering Borobudur, and he also wrote the monumental History of Java *(1817).*

much of West Java was ceded to the Dutch, the VOC still suffered a heavy loss.

In 1799, Dutch financiers received stunning news: the VOC was bankrupt. During the 18th century, the spice trade had become less profitable, while the military involvement in Java had grown costly. It was indeed a great war in Java (1740–55) that dealt the death blow to the already delicate Dutch finances. And once again, through a complex chain of events, it was the Dutch themselves who inadvertently precipitated the conflict. The details of the struggle are convoluted, but in a nutshell it began in 1740 with the massacre of the Chinese residents of Batavia, and ended 15 years later, after many bloody battles, broken alliances and shifts of fortune had exhausted almost everyone on the island.

Indeed, Java was never the same again. Mataram had been cleft in two, with rival rulers occupying neighbouring capitals in Yogyakarta and Surakarta. The VOC never recovered from this drain on its resources.

In the traumatic aftermath of the VOC bankruptcy, there was great indecision in Holland as to the next course. In 1800, the Dutch government assumed control of VOC's former possessions, now renamed Netherlands Indies, but for many years no one could make them profitable.

Raffles renaissance

A brief period of English rule under Thomas Stamford Raffles (1811–16) soon followed. In 1811, he planned and led a successful invasion of Java and was then placed in charge of its government at the age of 32.

Raffles's active mind and free-trade philosophy led him to make reforms almost daily, but the result was bureaucratic anarchy. Essentially, he wanted to replace the old mercantile system (from which the colonial government derived its income through a monopoly on trade) with one in which income was derived from taxes and trade was unrestrained. This enormous task had barely begun when the order came from London, following Napoleon's defeat at Waterloo, to restore the Indies to the Dutch.

Nevertheless, many of his land-tax ideas were eventually levied by the Dutch, and they made possible the horrible exploitation of Java later. This in turn led to the cataclysmic Java War of 1825–30.

Carnage to cultivation

So numerous were the abuses leading to the Java War, and so great were the atrocities committed by the Dutch, that the Javanese leader Pangeran Diponegoro (1785–1855) has been proclaimed a hero even by Dutch historians. He was indeed a charismatic figure: crown prince, Muslim mystic and man of the people.

His guerrilla rebellion against the Dutch and his own rulers might have succeeded but for a Dutch trick: luring him out of hiding with the promise of negotiation, Diponegoro was captured and exiled to Sulawesi. The cost of the conflict in human terms was staggering: 200,000 Javanese and 8,000 Europeans lost their lives, many from starvation and cholera rather than from death on the battlefield.

By then, the Dutch were in desperate economic straits. All efforts at reform ended in disaster, with the government debt reaching devastating amounts. New ideas were sought, and in 1829, Johannes van den Bosch submitted a proposal to the crown for what he called a Cultuurstelsel, or Cultivation System of fiscal administration in the colonies (see panel, opposite). His notion was to levy a tax of 20 percent (later raised to 33 percent) on all land in Java, and to demand payment not in rice but in labour or use of the land. This would permit the Dutch to grow crops that they could sell in Europe.

Van den Bosch soon assumed control of Netherlands Indies, and in the estimation of many from a Dutch perspective his system was an immediate, unqualified success. In the very first year, 1831, it produced a substantial profit. And within a decade, millions of guilders were flowing annually into Dutch coffers from the sale of coffee, tea, sugar, indigo, quinine, copra, palm oil and rubber.

With the windfall profits received from the sale of Indonesian products during the rest of the 19th century, the Dutch not only retired their debt, but built new waterways, dykes, roads and a national railway system.

Outside of Java, military campaigns throughout the 1800s extended Dutch control over areas still ruled by native kings. The most bitter battles were fought against the powerful Islamic Aceh kingdom in a 30-year war. Both sides sustained horrendous losses. In the earlier Padri War between the Dutch and the Minangkabau of West Sumatra (1821–38), the fighting was almost as bloody. In the east,

Flores and Sulawesi were repeatedly raided and finally occupied by the 1900s.

But the most shocking incidents occurred on Lombok and Bali, where on three occasions (1894, 1906 and 1908) Balinese rulers and their courtiers, armed with only ceremonial weapons, stormed headlong into Dutch gunfire after ritualistically purifying themselves for a puputan ("fight to the finish") rather than acquiesce to Dutch control.

In some ways, the tragic massacres symbolised the abrupt changes wrought by the Dutch: they had achieved the unification of the entire archipelago at the expense of indigenous kingdoms, sultans and tens of thousands of people.

ABOVE, FROM LEFT: Stamford Raffles led the English invasion of Java in 1811; the submission of Diepo Negoro in 1830, which ended the Java War.

MODERN INDONESIA

After the heady feeling of freedom that followed the departure of the colonial powers, people began to realise that things were far from perfect. In recent years, however, Indonesia's fortunes have been on a firmly upward trajectory

A t the beginning of the 20th century, signs of change were everywhere in the Indies. Dutch military expeditions and private enterprises were making inroads into the hinterlands of Sumatra and the eastern islands. Steam shipping and the Suez Canal (opened in 1869) had brought Europe closer, and the European presence in Java's cities was growing steadily. Gracious new shops, clubs, hotels and homes added an air of cosmopolitan elegance to the towns, while newspapers, factories, gas lighting, trains, buses, electricity and cars imparted a distinct feeling of modernity.

Indeed, thousands of newly arrived Dutch immigrants were moved to remark on the tolerable conditions in the colonies – that is to say, it was just like home, or even better.

In the Indies, nationalism was slow in developing but inevitable. A small but growing number of Indonesians living in cities were receiving Dutch education. The irony is that Dutch education provided much of the intellectual basis for Indonesian nationalism. As early as 1908, Indonesians attending Dutch schools began to form regional student organisations with political overtones. Small, aristocratic and idealistic, such organisations spawned an elite group of leaders and provided forums for a new national consciousness to take shape.

National awakening

In 1928, at the second all-Indies student conference, the concept of a single Indonesian nation (one land, one language, one nation) was proclaimed in the *Sumpah Pemuda* (Youth Pledge).

LEFT: Traffic at dusk, Jalan Medan Merdeka, Jakarta.
RIGHT: early oil exploration in Sumatra.

The nationalism and idealism of those students later spread through newspapers and the non-government Dutch- and Malay-language schools. But while the urban elite grew, the Dutch authorities were preoccupied with the nation's emerging pan-Islamic and communist movements.

The pan-Islamic movement's roots were in the steady and growing stream of pilgrims visiting Mecca and in the religious teachings of the *ulama* (Arabic scholars). What began in Java in 1909 as a small Islamic traders' association (*Sarekat Dagang Islam*) soon became a national confederation of Islamic labour unions (*Sarekat Islam*), with 2 million members in 1919. Mass rallies attracted tens of thousands, and many peasants came to see in the Islamic movement hope of relief from oppressive colonial conditions.

In 1910, the Indonesian communist movement was founded by small groups of Dutch and Indonesian radicals, with support from the working-class people. The movement soon embraced Islam, with many of its leaders gaining control of Islamic workers' unions and speaking at Islamic rallies. Following the Russian Revolution of 1917, they also maintained ties with the Comintern and increasingly espoused Marxist-Leninist doctrine.

The period 1910–30 was a turbulent one.

Shortly thereafter, Sukarno was arrested for making "treasonous statements". Although publicly tried and imprisoned, he was later released. A general crackdown ensued, and, after 1933, Sukarno and other student leaders were exiled to distant islands, where they remained for 10 years. The hope of independence seemed elusive.

Japanese occupation

In the 12th century, the Javanese King Jayabaya (sometimes spelled Joyoboyo) had prophesied that despotic white men would one day rule the Indonesian archipelago. But following

Strikes in cities frequently erupted into violence, and the colonial government arrested many Indonesian leaders. Moderate Muslim leaders soon disassociated themselves from political activities. The rank and file deserted their unions, and while the communists fought on for several years in Java and Sumatra to 1927, they too were crushed.

Leadership of the anti-colonial movement then reverted to the student elite. In 1927, a recently graduated engineer by the name of Sukarno, together with his Bandung Study Club, founded the first major political party with Indonesian independence as its goal. His *Partai Nasional Indonesia* (PNI) grew, and within three years had over 10,000 members.

the arrival of yellow men from the north, Java would be freed for ever from foreign oppressors and enter a millennial golden age. Therefore, when the Japanese invasion came, it was no surprise that many Indonesians interpreted this as a sign of impending liberation from the Dutch.

The immediate effect of Japan's 1942 invasion was to show that Dutch military might was a bluff. The Japanese encountered little resistance and, within weeks, had rounded up all the Europeans and placed them in concentration camps. Initially, there was jubilation. But it quickly became apparent that, like the Dutch, the Japanese had come to exploit the Indies, not to free them. Escalating

Japanese rice requisitions created famines and sparked peasant uprisings that were ruthlessly stomped out.

However, the Japanese found it necessary to rely on the Indonesians and to promote a sense of nationhood in order to extract their desired war materials. Indonesians were placed in many key positions held previously by Dutch nationals. The Dutch language was banned and replaced by Bahasa Indonesia. Nationalist leaders were freed and encouraged to cooperate with the Japanese. Most of them did.

When it became clear in late 1944 that Japan was losing the war, the Japanese promised independence to bolster faltering support. Indonesian leaders were brought in for discussions, and close to 200,000 young people were mobilised into paramilitary groups.

Independence declared

In 1945, on the same day that the second atomic bomb was dropped on Japan, three Indonesian leaders were flown to Saigon to meet with the Japanese military commander for Southeast Asia. The commander promised independence for all the former Dutch possessions in Asia and appointed Sukarno chairman of the preparatory committee and Muhammad Hatta the vice-chairman. They returned to Jakarta the day before Japan's unconditional surrender to the Allies. Following two days of debate, Sukarno and Hatta proclaimed *merdeka* (independence) on 17 August.

The following months were a chaotic struggle. News of the Japanese surrender spread like wildfire and millions of Indonesians echoed the call for *merdeka*. The Dutch tried to reclaim the islands, but Holland was in a shambles. Heroic sacrifices on the battlefield by tens of thousands of Indonesian youths placed them in an untenable position. Three Dutch "police actions" gave the returning colonial forces control of the cities, but each time the ragtag Indonesian army, under the inspired leadership of the youthful commander-in-chief, General Sudirman, valiantly fought back.

Finally, in 1949, the United States ceased the transfer of Marshall Plan funds to the Netherlands, and the UN Security Council

The democratic republic of Indonesia is run by a president and a parliament, the People's Consultative Assembly (MPR). In the past, the president was named by parliament, but since 2004 has been chosen by the people in direct elections.

ordered the Dutch to withdraw from Indonesia and negotiate a settlement. Dutch influence crumbled, and on 17 August 1950 – the fifth anniversary of the *merdeka* proclamation – the new government of the Republic of Indonesia took charge.

Euphoria swept through the cities and towns

of Indonesia following the withdrawal of Dutch forces. Mass rallies and processions were held; flag-waving crowds thronged the streets shouting "*Merdeka, Merdeka!*" Independence had come at last, and Indonesians were in control of their destiny.

The final chapters of early Indonesian nation-building were still to be written. The Dutch held on to the western half of New Guinea, called Papua, after granting independence to the rest of Indonesia. Pressure from the United Nations and the threat of all-out war by Sukarno eventually resulted in the transfer of the territory in 1962 and its integration as the country's 26th province, renamed Irian Jaya. In 1975, after Portugal abandoned its colony

---

ABOVE, FROM LEFT: image from the colonial era; a pro-independence march in progress.

of East Timor, Indonesia invaded and annexed that territory.

Headaches of a new nation

In Jakarta, the slow and arduous process of constructing a peacetime government began. While the unifying power of the revolution had done much to forge a national identity, the fact of Indonesia's complex ethnic, religious and ideological diversity remained. Moreover, massive economic and social problems faced the new nation – a legacy of colonialism and war. Factories and plantations were shut down, capital and skilled personnel

were scarce, rice production was insufficient to meet demand, people were overwhelmingly poor and illiterate, and the population was growing at a spiralling rate. A Western-style parliamentary system was adopted to deal with the problems.

From the beginning, however, the existence of more than 30 rival parties paralysed the system. A string of weak coalition cabinets rose and fell at the rate of almost one a year, and attempts at cooperation were increasingly stymied by growing ideological polarisation and by parochial loyalties. Sukarno, whose powers as president had been limited by the provisional constitution of 1950, and the army generals grew frustrated by the deadlock.

A series of separatist uprisings in Sumatra, North Sulawesi and West Java in the late 1950s gave Sukarno his cue. He declared martial law and gave the army a free hand to crush the rebels. In 1959, with the rebellions under control, Sukarno resurrected the "revolutionary" constitution of 1945 and declared a period of "Guided Democracy".

Under the new political system, power was focused in the hands of the president and the army generals. Militant nationalism became Sukarno's recipe for national integration, and the blame for most of the economic and political problems was placed at the feet of foreign imperialism and colonialism.

In the early 1960s, Sukarno became more militant. The long and successful campaign to wrest control of western New Guinea from the Dutch was followed by military confrontation with newly independent Malaysia in 1963. In 1965, he pulled Indonesia out of the UN, angry that Malaysia was made a member state. Domestically, however, it was Sukarno's nationalistic élan that helped create a nation out of disparate ethnic groups.

But Sukarno's reliance on charisma alone – he ignored day-to-day administration – created a vacuum in which the nation floundered. While he attempted to offset the growing influence of the military by courting the Partai Komunis Indonesia (PKI, Indonesian Communist Party), the economy crashed. Foreign investors fled, deficits left the government bankrupt, and inflation skyrocketed to 700 percent. Discontent was brewing, and by 1965, Indonesia was a political tinderbox.

Bloodbath

In the early hours of 1 October 1965, a group of radical army officers kidnapped and brutally executed six leading generals. However, the rebel officers soon lost the initiative to General Suharto, then commander of the Army Strategic Reserve. In a few hours, Suharto assumed command of the army, crushed the attempted coup and declared the PKI to be the culprit.

The nation was shocked by news of the execution and vengeance was demanded against the communists. A purge ensued, in which the military and moderate Muslims sought to settle old scores. Hundreds of thousands were killed as long-simmering frustration erupted into mob violence, first in North Sumatra, then later in Java, Bali and Lombok. The blood-letting continued for months, and the period from 1965 to 1966 is remembered today as the darkest in the republic's history.

> President Susilo Bambang Yudhoyono's final term of office ends in 2014, and contenders have begun tossing their hats into the ring. Among them are Megawati Sukarnoputri's and Gus Dur's daughters, as well as one of Suharto's sons.

Meanwhile in Jakarta, Suharto was slowly pushing Sukarno out of power. On 11 March 1966, Sukarno was persuaded to sign a document bestowing wide powers on General Suharto that charted Indonesia's course for the next 32 years.

Change came quickly. Martial law was declared and order was restored. Marxist-Leninist teachings were outlawed and thousands of alleged communists, including the prominent novelist Pramoedya Ananta Toer, were jailed. Existing political parties were weakened, and in 1967 the new government granted itself the right to appoint one-third of the representatives in the nation's highest legislative assembly. A major realignment in foreign policy restored long-fractured relations with the US and the West, and severed ties with China and the Soviet Union. Building political legitimacy on promises to revive the moribund Indonesian economy, Suharto placed a team of American-trained economists in charge of cooling inflation and restarting the economy.

These technocrats guided the rapid reintegration of Indonesia into the world economy, liberalised foreign investment laws and imposed monetary controls. Western aid was sought – and received – to replenish the nation's exhausted foreign exchange reserves. By the early 1970s, results began to show. Investors – Americans, Japanese and Indonesian Chinese – moved in to take advantage of Indonesia's vast copper, tin, timber and oil reserves and to set up factories.

Indonesia's mineral wealth made the job easier. In 1883, a Dutch planter sheltering from

a storm in a northern Sumatran shed noticed a torch burning brightly. On enquiring, he was led to a nearby spring where a viscous black substance lay thick across the water. The discovery led to the formation of Royal Dutch Shell and, eventually, to Indonesia's position as the world's fifth-largest and Asia's sole OPEC producer. Though the dominance of oil fell as the economy matured, it and other natural resources have remained Indonesia's primary source of foreign exchange.

During Suharto's reign, the country also made rapid gains in agricultural production and population control. An intensive family-

planning campaign was considered a model for the developing world, and Indonesia managed to reduce the birth rate to just over 1 percent annually. Still, Indonesia's main islands of Java and Bali were desperately overcrowded. In response, Suharto instigated a "transmigration" programme to ship the landless of Java and Bali to Papua, Kalimantan and other sparsely inhabited regions.

The New Order

Even as he liberalised the economy, Suharto undermined Indonesia's political institutions and cut off dissenting voices. Suharto and his supporters liked to call their regime the "New Order", to stress its departure from the past: less

ABOVE, FROM LEFT: Sukarno reads a statement to the press while his would-be successor Suharto looks on; Suharto in the mid-1990s.

populist, stridently anti-communist and more accommodating to international capital.

The new elite exerted total control through Golkar, the political vehicle of the new government. Newspapers were closed, dissidents were jailed and the military was given a free hand to deal brutally with opponents of the regime. For most of his reign, Suharto delivered on his promise of "Development yes, politics no!" He ensured political survival by stage-managing elections every five years and then ruled by fiat.

But politics had never gone away entirely. Many Muslims, despite being in the majority,

felt marginalised. By the mid-1990s, gratitude to Suharto for the progress made since 1965 was increasingly being replaced by anger at rampant corruption – particularly the vast business empires carved out by his children and a close circle of cronies. Rioting and religious tension became more intense. In 1996, a ham-fisted effort to discredit Megawati Sukarnoputri, the daughter of Sukarno who had risen to lead the strongest opposition party, backfired and led to rioting in Jakarta that frightened off investors and exposed the strains in Suharto's consensus-based polity. After 32 years of creeping change, Indonesia seemed poised to lurch backwards once more.

The eventual trigger echoed Sukarno's fall 33 years earlier. In July 1997, when Southeast Asia's financial crisis began, conventional wisdom had it that Indonesia, with its tradition of inflation control and restrained spending, would weather the storm better than its neighbours.

But as the rupiah fell alongside other regional currencies, it exposed massive fissures in the economy hidden by the glitter of the boom years. The foundations that the gleaming office towers, five-star hotels and state-of-the-art factories of the New Order rested on were riddled with debt. Corporations alone owed more than US$80 billion to foreign investors.

As banks collapsed and factories closed, prices for food and other basics soared. Millions lost their jobs, and even more saw their economic gains of the previous 30 years evaporate. By the end of October,

DEWI, SUKARNO'S FOIL

As Sukarno's grip on power began to loosen in the early 1960s and Indonesia's economy spun further out of control, his behaviour became ever more erratic and bizarre. He reputedly spent hours talking to spirits and ancestors and consulting seers. His usually flamboyant political speeches became filled with convoluted neo-colonialist plots. It was at this point that the ageing president found his perfect foil in the stunning young Japanese Naoko Nemoto.

Nemoto was under 20 when she married Sukarno in 1963, becoming Dewi Sukarno, the nation-builder's seventh and best-remembered wife. After his death, she made herself known as an international socialite

with a volatile reputation. In the early 1990s, she slashed a Filipino socialite at a Colorado cocktail reception with a broken champagne glass and served a month in jail. The 50-something Dewi went on to assault a Jakarta gossip columnist and released a book of mid-life nude photographs of herself that both titillated and shocked Indonesia.

She attended lectures by Indonesian politicians abroad and heckled them from the crowd. She also insisted Sukarno's ouster had been the direct result of a CIA plot. Nothing seemed to get her down. Upon emerging from the well-appointed Colorado prison, she said: "I will treasure [memories of the jail] for the rest of my life."

Suharto – who in 1992 had proudly echoed Sukarno's defiant "To hell with your aid" cry to the US – was forced into the arms of the International Monetary Fund. The fund arranged a US$40 billion support package, but at a price: the required economic reforms would strike at the monopolies and business groups of his friends and family.

While Suharto dragged his feet over the programme, the rupiah fell to one-seventh of its pre-crisis value, driving inflation and unemployment even higher. Students, the elite and disaffected officers began to move against him.

on. But one by one, his most trusted lieutenants abandoned him. On the morning of 21 May, he resigned. Joyful students frolicked in the fountain at parliament as Suharto's vice-president and close friend B.J. Habibie was sworn in as his successor.

During Habibie's short rule, he freed the press, allowed a referendum on East Timor (now called Timor Leste) and steered Indonesia to a democratic election that ended with his own October 1999 defeat – the first democratic political transition in Indonesian history.

Abdurrahman Wahid, the former head of

In March 1998, after Suharto was elected to a new term, opposition groups kicked into gear.

Reformasi!

Student protests took on a new, more urgent tone with *"Reformasi!"* (Reform) as their rallying cry. On 12 May 1998, six student protestors were shot and killed at Jakarta's Trisakti University, providing the spark for the capital's worst rioting in a generation. Foreigners fled and Jakarta's commercial districts became ghost towns. As flames swept the capital and army troops took charge, Suharto scrambled to hold

Above, From Left: Jakarta during the attempted coup d'etat in 1965; Student protests in 1998.

Nahdlatul Ulama (NU), a 35-million member Muslim social organisation, was Habibie's surprise successor. Though Wahid's National Awakening Party came in fourth in the general election, savvy politicking in the parliamentary assembly that selects the president won him his position over Megawati Sukarnoputri, whose Indonesian Democratic Party-Struggle (PDI-P) had run away with the general election.

Indonesia's fourth president was a study in contradiction. Gus Dur, as Wahid was popularly known, was devoted to a secular state. An avowed democrat, he was also a hereditary leader (NU leadership ran in the family). The partially blind Gus Dur was famous for his flip-flops, designed to confuse his opponents, some say. In the early 1990s, he had been a leader in the movement to oust Suharto, but as a crackdown loomed, he reconciled with the latter. This move cost Gus Dur many supporters – but kept him in the political fray, and ultimately helped him prevail.

Gus Dur's brief time in office was racked by continued fighting among various political factions, a worsening economy and violent ethnic conflicts, among many other problems. He was charged with incompetence and implicated in several corruption scandals. In July 2001, parliament impeached him, despite violent threats of retaliation.

Tarnished image

Vice-President Megawati replaced Gus Dur as head of state amid great rejoicing in the streets. With virtually no political experience other than being heir to a famous family name as daughter of Indonesia's first president Sukarno, the quiet housewife, who owned not much more than a florist shop and petrol station, selected a ministerial cabinet of capable advisers.

Megawati did not live up to expectations. As Indonesia's fifth president, she promised to eliminate corruption, rein in the military and reinvigorate the devastated economy. But rather than work on these pressing problems, parliament seemed more concerned with settling old political party rivalries and differences. Real reform remained stuck in the doldrums. In the meantime, ethnic and religious intolerance flared violently across the archipelago, while separatist movements in both Aceh and Papua were answered with harsh military responses – in spite of promises of greater autonomy. Thousands died in these struggles, but Megawati remained determined to keep Indonesia's immense territories intact as a legacy from her late father.

As a result, not much changed for Indonesia; the economy continued to spiral downwards and the ranks of the poor increased. Indeed, the image of the country suffered a severe beating among foreign investors nervous about stability in the country. Tourism, the nation's secondary income earner, took a beating. Threats posed by Muslim extremists and the unpredictability of natural disasters did not help matters.

21st-century democracy

In 2004, the current president, Susilo Bambang Yudhoyono (popularly known as SBY) – the country's first directly elected president – inherited a government burdened with decades of corrupt practices, enormous human rights violations, three provinces clamouring for independence, a weak economy and massive foreign debt.

Since Suharto fell in 1998, successive governments – some trying harder than others – have been chipping away to eliminate all vestiges of his autocratic New Order regime. Political exiles came home, East Timor became independent, and the military was stripped of its police powers and its vast holdings transferred to the state. Indonesia subsequently resigned from

TRANSITION TO DEMOCRACY

Sri Mulyani Indrawati, Indonesia's former finance minister (2005–10) and now a World Bank managing director, played a vital role in the country's evolution in its early years of transition. Her advice to emerging democracies is straightforward: widely publicised new laws must be established quickly, giving citizens freedom of expression and independent elections; corruption must be tackled; and new, independent judges and technical expertise must be found and put into place. Most importantly, she says, is that Indonesia learned during the process that there are no universal solutions; each country must address its challenges on its own terms.

OPEC and began diversifying its economy into other areas.

The transmigration programme, which proved to provoke strife between the newcomers and local villagers, took a back seat. Unfortunately, so did family planning, but it is now a priority once again. And although it may take many years to bring under control, SBY's administration has made a dent in the corruption problem, with daily headlines announcing yet another public official's arrest, and new corruption courts being set up across the country to ease the burden on the overwhelmed Jakarta judiciary system. Citizens and the press now have the right to speak openly, and all elections have been carried out peacefully. Today, Indonesia's economy is stronger than it has ever been, despite being one of the region's worst-affected economies during the 1997–8 financial crisis.

Analysts say that Indonesia's success so far as an emerging democracy is due to the fact that it has focused on the future instead of looking back. Unlike the Middle East and North Africa, which are seeking revenge on their former dictators, Indonesia's Suharto – and his children and cronies – disappeared from public life without reprisals. Deemed mentally unfit to stand trial, he was allowed to live out his remaining years peacefully at home, where – although he still had supporters – he died virtually in disgrace. None of the enormous fortunes his family and cohorts amassed and allegedly stashed in overseas accounts was recovered, much to the chagrin of millions.

An economic powerhouse

Indonesia's healthy economy today is due to good planning and leadership, but good luck comes into play too. Following the economic disaster that began in 2007 in the US and spread like the plague to Europe, investors' eyes turned to Asia, which has not only remained stable but whose economies continue to expand with impressive vigour. The spectacular success of China and, to a lesser extent India, are well known, but few in the West are aware that Indonesia is now firmly established as Asia's third-most successful

ABOVE, FROM LEFT: Acehnese people cheer the signing of a peace pact between the government and Aceh separatists in 2005; Susilo Bambang Yudhoyono, Indonesia's first directly elected president.

economy. Reliable markers of prosperity are here in abundance: the mid- to upper-income group is rapidly expanding, the banks are stable and the currency is strong. Furthermore, the sizeable population makes an attractive market for manufacturers of practically all products.

The president has further assumed responsibility by taking lead roles in G20 summits with strategies to reduce fuel subsidies, lower greenhouse emissions and protect long-abused forests, while simultaneously directing more cash to poor households and improving education and health care. As

president of the chairing nation in ASEAN, SBY is hosting meetings in various parts of the country, not only Jakarta and Bali, to expose more of Indonesia to the world in addition to sharing income-producing events with other regions.

In 2006, SBY was nominated for the Nobel Peace Prize for his role in the Helsinki Peace Accord, ending nearly three decades of fighting in Aceh. Re-elected by an overwhelming majority in 2009, his effectiveness is hampered by infighting in his coalition government as he nears the end of his final term of office in 2014. Only time will tell if his successor will continue leading the emerging democracy steadfastly forward into the future.

THE PEOPLE OF INDONESIA

Anyone travelling through the length of Indonesia will find the complexity and sheer diversity of peoples, languages and customs astounding

With over 300 ethnic – and perhaps several hundred sub-ethnic – groups, it is no easy task to identify all of Indonesia's peoples. Modern methods use language as the most important criterion in ethnic identity, and while there are known to be more than 700 distinct languages in Indonesia, many more are yet to be studied.

Java houses the largest proportion of Indonesia's total population, with 58 percent, followed by Sumatra with 20 percent and Sulawesi with 7 percent. Kalimantan has 6 percent, as do Bali and Nusa Tenggara combined. Maluku and Papua have a total of 3 percent. Each island is inhabited by several groups. The most heavily populated province is DKI (Special Province) Jakarta with 14,440 people per sq km, and the least crowded is West Papua with 8 people per sq km.

Ethnic groups

The Javanese are by far the largest ethnic group, with 42 percent of Indonesia's total population. Having an ancient court culture based in Central and East Java, with its long history of mighty empires and sheer numbers, it is no wonder that the Javanese tend to dominate the country's bureaucracy, military and politics. The majority of Javanese are Muslims, yet for many their religious and traditional rituals include pre-Islamic Hindu and animistic elements. With a definite segmentation within the culture, every Javanese knows which category

he or she falls within – the aristocrats, the merchants and traders, or the peasants – and that is indicated by which level of their hierarchical, three-pronged native language is spoken when addressing others.

West Java has Indonesia's second-largest ethnic group, the Sundanese, who form 15 percent of the population. They too have a long dynastic history, but they lack the elegance and the controlled manners that heavily influenced the Javanese. The form of Islam practised by the majority of Sundanese is not diluted, although lineage is equally important. In general, the Sundanese – who did not have the same rigid court structure as the Javanese – are more independent and individualistic.

PRECEDING PAGES: floating market, Kalimantan; young muslim boy. **LEFT:** Batuan mask makers, Ubud. **RIGHT:** traditional costumes are worn to welcome guests at a Torajan funeral ceremony.

Off the northeastern coast of Java on Madura island, the Madurese are renowned for their bravery and quick temper. Overpopulation and poor soils forced many Madurese into the maritime trade during ancient times. Their language is also divided into refined, medium and vulgar categories. The people are pious Muslims who accord high status to Islamic preachers.

Another of Indonesia's hot-headed groups is the clan-ruled, monogamous Batak, who inhabit the highlands around Lake Toba in North Sumatra. Primarily Christians, they are known for their outspokenness, their former reputation as cannibals, and their passion for singing raucous drinking songs and maudlin, melodic love tunes.

The Bugis and the Banjarese live in the southern part of Sulawesi. They are primarily Muslim seafaring people who are known as good sailors, skilled in shipbuilding, and shrewd businessmen. In the past, they often migrated elsewhere to earn a living and, at one time, almost controlled the trade of the region. The Bugis (pronounced boo-gees) were once the most feared pirates of the sea, and some say the Western expression "the Bogeyman" is named for this tribe.

Similar in numbers to the Bugis and the Banjarese are the Minangkabau of the breathtakingly beautiful hills of West Sumatra, whose matrilineal kinship system combined with a staunch belief in Islam and adherence to *adat* (traditional) laws is unique. Their coming-of-age ritual for men, *merantau* (seeking a fortune abroad), has scattered them throughout the archipelago, and they are quickly recognised by their *rumah makan* Minang or Padang food restaurants. Known as highly educated, keen entrepreneurs, Minangkabau include well-known writers and political leaders.

On the far northern tip of Sumatra is Aceh, the only province in Indonesia that has adopted Sharia (Islamic) law. With its strategic location at the entrance to the Malacca Strait, the gateway to Indonesia's spices and trade with China further east, Aceh was a crucial stopover for merchants from Arabia and India, and was the point of entry for Islam as early as the 13th century. The Achenese (1.9 percent of the population) are primarily known for their staunch adherence to Islam.

The Balinese

Although the Balinese are arguably the best-known Indonesians, they are a relatively small group in the grand scheme of things, comprising only about 1.5 percent of the total population. They have a unique culture and, except for small groups in Java and Lombok, are the last bastion of Hinduism in Indonesia. The islanders are not only gifted in the arts, but also live their lives by their religion, participating in the many rituals of life and agricultural cycles.

Balinese society is structured around a hereditary caste system that is far more relaxed than the Indian version. It does, however, carry certain rules of etiquette, as ordained in the Hindu scriptures. At the top is the Brahman caste; only

AUTONOMY

During the iron-fisted rule of Suharto, 100 percent of revenues earned by the provinces were under the control of the central government. Soon after Suharto fell in 1998, voices were raised, most notably in Aceh (Sumatra), Maluku and Papua, demanding autonomy. In 2000, the Wahid administration granted their wishes, and for the first time taxation, budgeting, infrastructure and trade became locally managed, with the lion's share of revenues remaining in the province. This was good news for some, such as resource-rich East Kalimantan; however, autonomy is not particularly beneficial for poorer areas, which must eke out their existence with loans, grants and other foreign aid.

Brahmans are allowed to be high priests. The Satriya form the second strata of society; they are the descendants of warriors and rulers. The merchants and administrative officials, or Wesia, occupy the third rank, and at the bottom are the Sudra, the common people, who account for 93 percent of Bali's population. The Sudras are not deemed inferior or denied access to specific professions; above all, an upper-caste background does not guarantee a high income or direct access to political power. In Bali, a university professor could be a Sudra or a waiter may turn out to be a Brahman.

"Unity in diversity"

It was Dutch colonialism that in its fervour to control the world's spice trade forced Indonesia's multiethnic and multi-religion society into what was to become one nation. Under Dutch rule, selected elites received Western educations, were governed by the same economic and administrative system and experienced similar, if not identical, problems. The Dutch provided a form of social cohesion that enabled the various ethnic groups to come together. The Japanese occupation, although lasting a brief 3½ years, was significant in that it provided Indonesians with military training and further stoked their zeal for independence. To their own ends, the Japanese also actively promoted nationalism, a movement which eventually gained Indonesia its independence and created a nation based on the boundaries of the former Dutch East Indies.

Another factor that helped to unite the ethnic groups was language. Although the language of a minority group, Malay was used widely as a medium of communication between different ethnic groups in trade relations and in the marketplaces. Campaigners used it to propagate the Indonesian nationalist movement throughout the diverse archipelago. When independence was achieved in 1945, a form of Malay was made into the national language, *Bahasa Indonesia*.

When Suharto ruled Indonesia, a transmigration policy was used not only to redistribute population density, but was also a guise to promote national unity. Java accounts for only 7 percent of the Indonesian territory, but 58 percent of the population live on the island. The policy put pressure on those who lived on Java and Bali, particularly the Javanese, to migrate to the Outer Islands, and the forced resettlement created much friction between locals and newcomers. Viewed as largely unsuccessful, the transmigration programme lost its zeal when the central government was regionalised in 2000 and the provinces and regencies were given full autonomy.

Java versus the Outer Islands

Throughout history, ethnic and religious conflicts have occurred between Java/Bali and the

Outer Islands, but more especially after independence. The people of the two regions are not only ethnically different but also dissimilar in their approach to agriculture. The principal farming method in Java and Bali is that of *sawah*, or wet rice-paddy cultivation, while the main method employed in the Outer Islands is lading, or slash-and-burn cultivation.

Until fairly recently, Java and Bali were collectively regarded as agricultural societies, in contrast to the Outer Islands, which were considered maritime. In an agricultural society, the need for close cooperation among villages is paramount, and people tend to be socialistic. In a maritime society, where the livelihood does not depend solely on agricultural products and

ABOVE, FROM LEFT: Dayak women with extended earlobes; becak driver in Yogyakarta.

trade is important for survival, people tend to be more individualistic. This split was emphasised by the aristocratic nature of Javanese society.

> *Traditional Javanese society requires one to be* sopan santun *(well mannered).* Rukun *(harmony) is the primary goal, achieved through knowing one's place in society and acting out one's assigned role.*

Defining "Indonesians"

It is difficult to define "Indonesians" and to generalise about how they think or feel about any given topic. Their particular ethnic upbringing plays its part, but there are vast differences – as there are in every country – between people who are educated and live or work in a metropolis where viewpoints are broader and those who are uneducated and remain isolated in country villages, which may be as much as 50 percent of the population.

In the cities, Blackberries, laptops and iPads are coveted either because they are essential to staying on top of the game or because having them is fashionable. Families and young people flock to shopping malls and cinemas in their spare time instead of waiting for harvest festivals to create entertainment. Indonesia has the second-largest number of Facebook users in the world and is third among Twitter-ers. These and other social networks not only link people to each other and enable them to voice opinions, they are also an educational link to foreign insights that are not accessible to the poor. More Indonesians than ever before are fluent English-speakers, as well as speaking other non-Asian languages, further widening the gap between those who are educated and those who are not.

University cities, such as Bandung and Yogyakarta, present another aspect of Indonesian identity. With an estimated 50 million university students in the country, when concentrated into smaller towns the ethnicity lines, while never forgotten, become blurred. Bright young students from across the archipelago are thrown together in these environments, many

Chinese-Indonesians today

Ill-feeling between indigenous Indonesians and Chinese immigrants dates back to the time when the Dutch tended to use Chinese traders and merchants as go-betweens in their dealings with the locals. Astute businessmen, the Chinese began to acquire wealth, while the vast majority of Indonesians remained farmers and labourers.

Obsessed by the threat of communism, when Suharto came to power he banned all things Chinese, including their media, schools, language and rituals. Thousands were banished, and those who remained were forced to change their names to Indonesian equivalents. He used the Chinese-communist connection as a scapegoat to divert the public's attention from his misdoings at every possible turn.

As a result of this enforced assimilation, millions of Chinese have grown up speaking Indonesian and have no ties to China. As the Indonesian economy has flourished, their wealth has been surpassed by that of non-Chinese.

Since Suharto's fall, the regulations discriminating against Chinese-Indonesians have been repealed. Chinese-language media is prevalent, dragon and lion dance troupes appear in nearly all celebrations, and Lunar New Year is a national holiday. In 2000, Indonesia added Confucianism as the sixth officially recognised religion.

of them away from their villages and families for the first time, and are exposed not only to new ideas through their studies but also to each other's customs and traditions. Nowadays, it is common among more sophisticated families for couples to be of different ethnicities, and even different religions, whereas mixed marriages are still taboo in rural villages. Even among the educated, however, tradition is still important, and one wedding ceremony often will be held in the bride's village according to her parents' customs and another in the husband's, followed by a party for the couple's friends in the city where they live.

of government from total control in Jakarta to the regions has helped, and now local administrations are responsible for providing health care to their citizens and for controlling spending.

Foreign funding also assists in training more doctors, nurses and midwives; constructing public clinics that hopefully one day will be accessible to all; and providing nutrition education, maternal and newborn care, as well as immunisations for children.

The Indonesian constitution states that all citizens have a right to free education, but currently the majority of regions only sponsor primary school grades 1–6. Even in the absence of a tui-

Education and health care

Although the number of people living in poverty, according to World Bank parameters, has dropped in the last decade from 60 percent to about 15 percent, many others (perhaps as many as 50 percent, around 120 million people) subsist close to this level. Thus, education and health care – both linked to poverty – are major issues to be dealt with.

Providing clean water and sanitation to all, especially those in remote locations, is a substantial challenge and is being addressed largely by international aid organisations. Decentralisation

tion charge, the cost of books and uniforms is beyond reach for many families. Nevertheless, primary school enrolment throughout the country is about 96 percent, although it drops to around 50 percent for junior secondary schools. The reasons for this low take-up include lack of access to schools or, particularly in rural areas, the need for boys to work in the fields and girls to look after younger siblings while the parents work.

The good news is that education spending has more than doubled since the fall of Suharto, with more spent on education than any other sector in recent years. But with over 50 million students and only 51 universities nationwide, there is still much work to be done. Gaps in access to lower education are filled by private and religious

ABOVE, FROM LEFT: urban youth, Jakarta; the school run, Ubud.

schools – which play a significant role – and in the higher-education realm by vocational secondary schools, colleges and academies. As with health care, foreign funding is significant.

A show of patriotism

Regardless of where its citizens live, what their ethnic background is and whether they are wealthy or not, the Indonesian nationalism that was fanned in the run-up to independence is still very much alive today in certain respects.

When it comes to defending their country's honour in sports arenas, against comments from outsiders that the people perceive to be slanderous or threatening, or when they feel one of their own has been mistreated, Indonesians tend quickly to adopt a patriotic stance. On the downside, many fall short in their ability to examine and analyse opposing points of view and are quick to accept, and repeat, popular opinion. This is the result of a weak education system that is in need of an overhaul. Although some are doing remarkable work, the vast majority of teachers, particularly at lower levels, have come up through the ranks of an archaic system that teaches by rote and punishment rather than encouraging young minds to think critically and form their

RADEN AYU KARTINI

Indonesian women have, in part, Raden Ayu Kartini to thank for their equal role in society. She was born into a noble family in 1897; traditions of the time demanded that Javanese girls of her ilk be sequestered and protected to prepare them for arranged marriages, often to polygamist husbands who had full authority over them. Not permitted to go to school after the age of 12, Kartini was largely self-educated, learning from Dutch books and magazines through which she developed feminist attitudes. Her letters to Dutch friends railing against Javanese restrictions that robbed women of freedom were published in Holland in 1911, influencing prominent figures. She began teaching women in 1903, and after her untimely death at the age of

25, other schools for girls were established in her name. Today she is seen as a leader of women's rights, and every year on her birthday, 12 April, her contributions are celebrated.

It might be surprising to know that in this country, with the world's largest Muslim population, there are several top-ranking female government officials. In addition to a former president, women in politics include the ministers of health, trade, national development planning and women's empowerment. The former finance minister, now managing director of the World Bank, is also female, demonstrating the moderate form of Islam practised by most Indonesians.

own opinions. Some progress has been made in training new teachers and reforming their teaching methods, but not nearly enough.

Indonesians have yet to appreciate how great their accomplishments have been in the last decade, and this is particularly true of the youth who did not grow up under the oppressive Suharto regime. Taking for granted the right to speak freely that was denied to their parents, when it is pointed out that Indonesia has the freest press in Asia, they are surprised. Quick to voice dissatisfaction that corruption has not yet been totally eradicated, they fail to note that the judicial system has been overhauled, independent judges

Indonesians abroad

An increasing number of Indonesians are attracting attention abroad in a variety of sectors, making them ambassadors for their homeland. Long known internationally are its Olympics-winning badminton teams and female weightlifters. Indonesia's Chris John has won the World Boxing Association's featherweight title 14 times since 2003. Singer-songwriter Anggun Sasmi from Java has had a successful career in France for over a decade, and the US became acquainted with Indonesian pop star Agnes Monica in 2011 when she recorded an album with Michael

have been hired, old judges are being weeded out and transparency is now the key word. They often forget, too, that Indonesia has made enormous strides at combating terrorism and that its unexpected success so far with democratisation is being used as a model for other developing countries. Many Indonesians also fail to realise how far human rights – including free elections – have come and that at last the regional and national governments are paying attention to the needs of the poor, education and health care, and how many millions of new jobs have been created.

ABOVE, FROM LEFT: Muslim girl on the way to the mosque; pioneering feminist Raden Ayu Kartini; festival preparations, Tabanan, Bali.

Bolton, whom she met while co-hosting the 2010 American Music Awards. Indonesian fashion designers are beginning to make a splash overseas, too. An exciting young couture designer, Tex Saverio, created the confection worn by Lady Gaga on the cover of a 2011 US *Harper's Bazaar* magazine.

Indonesia's people have just begun their journey to full-fledged democracy, and many challenges lie ahead. But in view of their enormous diversity, the hurdles they have overcome are nothing short of amazing. Virtually unknown outside Asia until the last decade, the Indonesian cultures certainly bear watching as the 21st century progresses and are an example to other evolving nations.

RELIGION

Muslim or Hindu, Buddhist, Confucian or
Christian, Indonesians are free to worship their
own faith

Although Indonesia has the world's largest Muslim population, it is not an Islamic state. Nearly 90 percent of its citizens are Muslim, with most of the remainder being Christian, Hindu, Buddhist and Confucian. Pockets of Christianity are found among the Batak people of North Sumatra, the Ambonese, Florinese and in Papua, and in a few areas of Kalimantan. Indonesian Christians are few in number but well represented within the educated military and political elite. Similarly, there is a small minority of Buddhist and Confucian Indonesians, mainly Chinese. As with Buddhism, Hinduism was at one time a significant power in the archipelago, but its presence is now limited to Bali, East Java and western Lombok.

Generally speaking, most Indonesians are staunch believers in their chosen faiths, but none of the religions is practised in the forms they are in other countries. Often enmeshed with animism, Hindu-Buddhist or customary practices, they are uniquely Indonesian. With so many ethnic and cultural groups, traditions, languages and religions, throughout Indonesia's history there has been a convergence of basic social, cultural and political needs. In many ways, the traditional tolerance that Islam teaches has permitted a give-and-take to this end. Although there are pockets of extremists, they are in the minority.

Animism

The native religion, animism – essentially the worship of spirits believed to preside in all living

or non-living things – is still practised on remote islands and is mixed freely with modern religions. Animism rests on the basis that both animate and inanimate objects are inhabited by living spirits.

Offerings of food are sometimes found beside a tree or a river, placed there in appeasement of the nearby deity in the hope of being granted a safe passage, a rich harvest or a good day's fishing. There is usually a spirit medium or *dukun* in each village who enjoys high status, since he plays the role of intermediary to the spirits.

Despite national statistics which claim high adherence to foreign religions, the spirit of animism continues to rule social behaviour. In everyday practical life, worship of mainstream faiths does not rule out ingrained fundamental

LEFT: a devout Muslim reading the Arabic script of the Koran, the Islamic holy book. **RIGHT:** Balinese temple courtyard.

beliefs in the power of spirits nor preclude the enactment of rituals of appeasement.

Islam

The most significant of the major religions in Indonesia is Islam, which became the fulcrum for the region's development. By the late 13th century, Islam had gained a foothold in Sumatra and, within a few centuries, had become embedded in Southeast Asia, anchored by a powerful Islamic commercial and political centre in Malacca during the 15th century.

Although Indonesia has an overwhelming majority of Muslims, religious tolerance and

freedom of religion is guaranteed by the constitution. Political parties based on moderate Islamic beliefs have had significant representation in parliament, but they do not dominate, whereas fundamentalist Islamist parties have had little impact in elections.

The faith is practised most traditionally in Aceh, North Sumatra, the only province that adheres to Sharia (Islamic) law. West Java, Madura (East Java), Southeast Kalimantan and western Lombok are other devoutly Muslim regions. Elsewhere, Islam may be the professed religion, but the strict rituals, of fasting and prayers for example, are less rigidly followed than in other Muslim-majority countries. On Java, perhaps one-third to a half of Muslims adhere to strict practices.

Islam's rituals are intertwined with the basic needs and acts of daily life and define the nature and quality of life itself and of the community. Islamic beliefs and practices are based upon two important touchstones: the *Koran (Qur'an)* and the *Sunnah*. The *Koran* is considered to be the word of God, as spoken to Muhammad (c. AD 570–632) during the last 22 years of his life, through the angel Gabriel. And as it is considered the word of God, the *Koran* in all its 114 chapters is irrefutable and faultless.

The *Sunnah*, less well known to outsiders, reflects the traditional norms regarding assorted concerns and issues, based upon what Muhammad himself did or said regarding those concerns. Although secondary to the *Koran*, it is a fundamental component for most Muslims.

Cousin to Christianity

Little known among non-Muslims is that Islam accepts most biblical miracles and prophets, in both the Old and New Testaments. Abraham, Moses and Jesus, for example, are important prophets. Adam was the first prophet, later forgiven by God for his sins. But they were early prophets. Muhammad came later as the last and final prophet, and thus revealed a more perfect word of God. The *Koran* itself is considered Muhammad's eclipsing miracle, as perfect as possible on earth. Islam regards all religions as essentially representations of the same divine truth, except that Islam is closest to that truth.

The Islamic Allah is omnipotent and singular, but there are permutations of this fundamental idea throughout Indonesia, where local and often polytheistic beliefs, and in some

---

ONE GOD

The Indonesian constitution guarantees freedom to worship as one pleases. Yet, only certain religions have been officially recognised (with Confucianism only added to the list in 2000). Pancasila, the state ideology created by Sukarno in 1945, demanded religions must recognise one god, Balinese Hinduism and others "appointed" a supreme being in order to qualify.

It is commonly believed that the one-god proviso was part of Sukarno's efforts to ensure that Indonesian identity was not defined as Islamic. Another theory is that by precluding primitive animistic worship, he could "civilise" Indonesia's varied peoples, or at least appear to the outside world to have done so.

places, from Hinduism and Buddhism, have been melded with Islam.

In common with Christianity, there is a heaven and a hell in Islam. The world's creation was an act of mercy by God; if God had not done so, there would be nothingness. Everything on earth has its function and form, defined towards making a harmonious world. Nature exists to be exploited by humanity, and the purpose of humans is simple: to serve God. But, unlike Christianity, which is more individualistic, Islam has it that humanity's responsibility includes the establishment of social systems that are pure and free from vice

and corruption. Allah also judges societies and nations, which are subject to the same transgressions and weaknesses as people.

The basis of an Islamic society is the sustenance of the community of the faithful, guided by Sharia, or Islamic law. This law defines a community's moral goals; in fact, in other majority-Muslim countries, Islam defines all the laws, both moral and legal.

According to the Koran, people are proud, if not egotistical, and susceptible to selfishness and greed. (Satan is a significant factor in earthly

ABOVE, FROM LEFT: almost 90 percent of Indonesians follow Islam; Christian wedding ceremony, Samosir Island, Sumatra.

affairs.) Belief in the *Koran* is said to assist people in rising above these inadequacies by establishing an inner ethical bearing called *taqwa*. Through this quality good and evil, and right and wrong, are recognisable. In the end, a person is judged by *taqwa*, not by earthly deeds or accomplishments. The role of the Islamic prophets has been to show individuals, as well as whole societies and even nations, the way to *taqwa*.

> Indonesia adapted Indian and all other religions to its needs. For example, the events and people recorded in Hindu epics such as the Ramayana and the Mahabharata have been shifted out of India to Java.

Balinese Hinduism

Most of Indonesia's Hindus live on Bali, where they form more than 90 percent of the Balinese population. Balinese Hinduism has developed local characteristics that distinguish it from Indian Hinduism.

Central to Balinese Hinduism – known as Agama Hindu Dharma – is the belief in the balance of two opposite forces, manifested as good and evil; light and dark; male and female; positive and negative; order and chaos, and so on. The two realms coexist and are equally important.

Good, as represented by benevolent gods such as Dewa and Bhatara, is to be emulated, cultivated and esteemed. Worship of these gods is marked by offerings of food, holy water and flowers, dancing and beautiful art pieces. Credit for a bountiful harvest, for example, is given to the popular goddess of rice and fertility, Dewi Sri.

The hierarchy of Balinese gods begins with Sanghyang Widi Wasa, the supreme invisible being who is manifested through the three gods: Brahma, Vishnu (also spelled Wisnu) and Shiva (also called Siva or Siwa). This main god qualifies Agama Hindu Dharma as a monotheistic religion under the terms of Pancasila.

The Balinese live for festive activities, which centre on the village temples, taking place once every 210 days or during a particular full moon in the lunar-solar year, when a communal birthday feast (*odalan*) is held on the anniversary of its consecration. In a typical celebration, delicately carved idols are brought out, wrapped in sacred woven cloths and then infused with the protective spirits of the villages before being borne in a colourful procession to the river or sea to be purified. On return to the temple, mediums tell if the celebrations have been satisfactory to the gods. If so, the villagers pray together and feast throughout the night.

Evil forces, in the form of earth demons, can cause ill fortune such as natural calamity, a breach of human relations or illness, and must be placated with purification offerings and rituals, such as ritual cleansings. Uncleanliness is a state that anyone can stumble into, for example, during menstruation, a long illness, a death in the family or a natural disaster such as a volcanic eruption. Central

the myriad array of gods. In its purest form, it offers a practical, moral way of life.

Buddhism's founder was an Indian prince named Siddhartha Gautama, who lived during the 6th century BC. He came to realise that pain and sadness were caused by desire, in itself an illusion. His solution was that by rising above desire and human attachments, human beings can live a life free from suffering. His spiritual recipe, called the Eightfold Path, set out steps to help an individual contain passion and emotion by focusing on wisdom, thought, speech, conduct, livelihood, effort, attentiveness and concentration. For Buddhists, the goal

to the cleansing ritual is the administration of holy water. To the Balinese, the mountains are holy because they are believed to be connected to Mount Meru in India and because they are the source of life-sustaining water. Due to this belief, all physical structures – houses, temples and schools – are aligned according to the direction of and proximity to sacred mountains and the sea.

Buddhism

Buddhism originated in India, penetrated China, and later entered Java and Sumatra with traders and wandering pilgrims. This gentle, contemplative offshoot of Hinduism has cast off the notions of caste differences as well as

is enlightenment and the bliss that comes with attaining non-attachment. The devotee is then freed from the endless cycles of rebirth and from human suffering.

Today, only small pockets of pure Buddhism remain in Indonesia, such as the monastery across from Mendut temple near Borobudur in Central Java. Most Buddhists in Indonesia are ethnic Chinese who mix Buddhism with ancestor worship, Taoism and Confucianism.

Catholicism and Protestantism

Roman Catholicism arrived with the Portuguese in the 16th century, beginning in Maluku, but more significantly in Flores, where a Catholic seminary remains today, eastern Timor (now called Timore Leste) and Papua. However, around the 17th century, the Dutch VOC banned the religion, and many Indonesian Catholics converted to Protestantism. After the VOC collapsed and Catholicism was legalised in the Netherlands, Dutch Catholic priests returned to Indonesia.

Dutch colonialists brought Protestantism to the country, avoiding Java and other predominantly Muslim areas. Followed by missionaries from other countries of various Christian religions, entire villages in some areas were converted. After the 1965 anti-communist coup, all Indonesian citizens were forced to register with the government and carry identification

outlining a code of conduct. It is believed that the first Confucian organisation was not formed until the early 20th century in Batavia (now Jakarta). Prior to Suharto's anti-Chinese regime, Confucianism was one of the original six religions which met the government's "one God" requirement *(see page 68)*, following the declaration of Confucius as a "god". It was then banned in 1978 following a decision by the presidential cabinet that it was not, in fact, a religion, and adherents were forced to register as Christians or Buddhists in order to maintain their citizenship. Following the fall of Suharto, fourth president Abdurraham Wahid declared Confucianism an official religion.

cards naming one of the then five officially recognised religions as their professed faith, and the smaller groups such as Lutherans and Presbyterians listed themselves as Protestant. Likewise, animists and others whose religions were not "acceptable" randomly chose a faith deemed to cause the least amount of conflict.

Confucianism

Perhaps one of the earliest religions to arrive in Indonesia, Confucianism was introduced by Chinese merchants and immigrants as early as the 3rd century AD. It is not a religion as such, but is a philosophy

ABOVE, FROM LEFT: villagers celebrating an *odalan* festival, Bali; Chinese temple at Glodok, Jakarta.

CHRISTIANITY AND CONFLICT

The Portuguese arrived in Flores during the 16th century and converted the local community to Catholicism, which then spread eastwards to parts of Nusa Tenggara and Timor. Dutch missionaries brought Protestantism to a few parts of the archipelago in the early 19th century, especially Minahasa in North Sulawesi, Maluku and parts of Kalimantan and Papua. German Christian missionaries also converted the Batak in North Sumatra. As with other religions, indigenous animist practices were integrated with Christianity in many places. Indonesia's minority Christian population has been targeted periodically by small, radical Muslim groups.

CUSTOMS AND RITUALS

The observance of *adat*, or local custom, lies at the heart of Indonesian morality and sense of community

All the religions practised in Indonesia are enmeshed with locally defined customs passed from one generation to another, called *adat*, and the manner in which this intermingling is manifested can be very confusing to outsiders. A classic example is of an average Javanese, a self-declared Muslim who firmly believes in the existence of Indian deities and in the indigenous folk heroes portrayed in the ever-popular *wayang kulit* shadow play, as well as in a host of deities, ghosts, spirits, demons and genies said to inhabit the worldly environment.

Typically, in addition to fulfilling the requirements of the Islamic faith, the Javanese hold frequent communal feasts *(selamatan)* to celebrate special occasions in thecommunity and to mitigate the disruptions of unsettling events. They will also seek the advice of a local *dukun* or mystic in times of distress, as well as trusting in the magical potency of an inherited *keris* dagger and a variety of other talismans.

Feasts

Central to the *adat* observances of most Indonesians is the ritual communal feast. In the Javanese *sesaji*, ceremonial foods are offered to the spirits in invitation, but are not eaten, whereas in Bali the food is an offering, publicly consumed to ensure well-being and to strengthen solidarity.

The most common example of such a feast is the Javanese *selamatan*, in which special foods are eaten (such as *tumpeng*, an inverted cone of yellow-coloured rice with various dishes), Islamic prayers are intoned and announcements or requests are made. A *selamatan* may

be given at any time and for almost any reason – to celebrate a birth, marriage, circumcision, death or anniversary, to initiate a new project or a new building, or to dispel bad luck or invite good fortune.

In Bali, festive activities centre on the village temple, where a communal birthday feast *(odalan)* is held on the anniversary of its

Visitors are welcome to attend odalan *festivals in Bali, provided they dress and behave respectfully. As every Balinese temple observes this ritual every 210 days, there are plenty to choose from. Most are one-day events.*

consecration. For several days beforehand, the entire village is engaged in the preparation of elaborate decorations and offerings. Most of these events last one day, but some extend over several days.

Everyone, from young children to great-grandparents, gets involved with the preparations, for it is a time for socialising as well. Women trim and pin together palm leaves into containers and ritual ornaments, mould coloured rice-dough into symbolic shapes and assemble countless offerings from a dazzling range of materials.

Meanwhile, the men of the village slaughter animals for meat offerings in addition to feeding those helping out in the *odalan*. They also construct temporary platforms and pavilions, repair shrines and climb trees to collect the necessary leaves, flowers and fruits that are used for the offerings.

When the offerings are presented, the deities and spirits consume the invisible essence of the offerings. The physical parts are considered to be "leftovers" and are eaten by the worshippers at the temple or brought home for a family feast. Clearly, the Balinese have the best of both worlds.

Jiwa

These and other types of communal feasts and rituals are frequently intended to enhance the fertility and prosperity of the participants by strengthening, purifying or augmenting something known to many Indonesian peoples as *jiwa* – the spirit or soul thought to inhabit and animate not only humans but plants, animals, sacred objects and also entire villages or nations. These spirits can be malevolent as well as benign, and it is believed that by boosting their own life-giving *jiwa*, people are able to achieve and maintain a fragile balance.

The *jiwa* of human beings is thought by some to be concentrated in the head and hair, and in the not-so-distant past, the Sulawesi Torajans, Kalimantan Dayaks and the Papua Danis sought to promote their own *jiwa* at the expense of an adversary through head-hunting raids. Skull trophies were once regarded as powerful talismans

that would enhance the prosperity of a community, and also ward off sickness, war, famine or ill fortune.

A ceremonial first haircut often serves to initiate an infant into human society. The exchange of snippets of hair is an integral part of some Indonesian marriage rites, while human hair curiously features in the costumes of many supernatural characters. Likewise, hair clippings are disposed of carefully (as are nail trimmings), lest they fall into the hands of an enemy sorcerer.

Blood, too, is thought to be infused with *jiwa*, which can be easily transmitted or conferred.

SOCIETY'S GLUE

Adat is often viewed as the glue that binds society and allows it to function with minimal conflict. With it, all community members have the same perspective of right and wrong. Some *adat* are of a superstitious nature, such as banishing twins of opposite sexes from villages because they are considered to bring bad luck. However, others are practical. In many forest communities, *adat* prohibits cutting certain trees or killing specific animals, thus promoting a balance between human needs and nature. Even in the 21st century, most Indonesians agree that *adat* is of vital importance to their daily lives.

ABOVE, FROM LEFT: a purification ceremony on a Bali beach; a colourful Torajan funeral.

On many islands, the pillars of a new house are anointed with the sacrificial blood of animals to render them strong and durable. And it used to be widely reported that, in many parts of the archipelago, victors in battle drank the blood of their slain enemies, or smeared it over themselves, to augment their own *jiwa* with that of the fallen.

Many Indonesians believe that this soul substance is also found in plants such as banyan trees. An interesting metaphor for human life is the powerful but sensitive *jiwa* associated with the rice plant, which is symbolic of important philosophical values.

humans can take on the characteristic of mature rice plants, their *jiwa* will become wiser, calm and humble, capable of accepting inner peace and achieving balance.

This philosophical merit is not reserved for older people but is also desirable in young people. Certain rituals are performed before babies are born, for infants and for teenagers to ensure they will be powerful, humble and wise in the future, while remembering their heritage. The ceremonies attempt to imbue these children with good *jiwa*.

All ancient and curious objects, as well as mountains and bodies of water are likewise

When still young, the rice grains are light because they are empty; thus the plant is straight, standing upright as if challenging the sky. This personifies the immature human soul, which is unstable, arrogant and lacking life experience. It also represents the rice plant's ingratitude to the life-giving nutrients and water of the earth.

When the plant grows older, the grains become full and heavy and it no longer stands upright but bends to the ground with the weight. This is symbolic of a mature human soul. The more educated one is, the more powerful and wiser. Therefore, like the rice, humans must humble themselves and give thanks to the origins that gave them life. If

thought to be imbued with a special *jiwa*. Bezoar stones, mineral deposits found in animals and in the nodes of certain bamboos, are traditionally used for magic and healing, while more generally, any object that is designated a *pusaka*, or sacred heirloom, is credited with harbouring a vital spiritual essence that requires special veneration and care. Antique *keris* daggers, lances, spear heads, cannons, jewellery, textiles, ceramics, manuscripts, gravestones and masks can all become *pusaka* and may be considered to contain a soul of their own or that of a previous owner. Such objects are often in the custody of a king, priest, chief or elder, a link between the living and the powerful ancestral spirits.

A place for souls

Much of a community's private and public ritual life often centres on the management of its human souls, both living and dead. In this, there are invariably certain individuals in the communities who possess specialised knowledge or skills in such matters. Special attention is always devoted to funerary rites, in which the dead are ritually venerated and can be transformed into protective clan or village deities.

It is commonly believed that the soul of a person may become detached during life, which can result in illness. Even under normal conditions, it is thought the soul assume the shape of a beautiful maiden, who waits at night beneath a banyan tree to seduce and emasculate passing men. Elaborate rituals must then be performed by a shaman to mollify the *hantu* and banish it from the area.

Good deaths must also, of course, be attended by a lengthy sequence of elaborate funerary rites. When a person dies, it is universally thought the soul is at first resentful and potentially harmful. Some rites are therefore designed to confuse the soul and dissuade it from returning. It is a widespread custom in Sumatra, Kalimantan, South Sulawesi and Halmahera, for instance, to send the corpse

wanders during sleep. Sorcery can entice unwitting souls away.

A distinction is made virtually everywhere between good and bad spirits, resulting respectively from good and bad deaths. A bad death, generally premature or violent, releases a vengeful ghost or *hantu* that may bring considerable misfortune on a household or community. The soul of a woman who dies at childbirth is pictured as a bird with long talons that jealously stabs and rents the stomachs of pregnant women. This *kuntilanak* can also

Cockfights are held at every Balinese temple festival. The blood spilled appeases the hungry forces of evil. Gambling is illegal under Indonesian law, but the police look the other way as cockfighting is considered to be a religious ritual.

out of the house through a gap in the wall or floor of the house, which is then sealed.

Observers of rituals should respect local customs concerning dress and silence. No one who has witnessed a Balinese funeral procession and cremation, a Torajan funeral sacrifice or a Dayak death ceremony will forget the dignity and colour of the events.

ABOVE, FROM LEFT: music plays a prominent role in many Indonesian rituals; Balinese priestess in a trance; a cremation ceremony, Bali.

SPICE ISLANDS CUISINE

Indonesian food is strong in flavours, with a delicious array of fish, unusual vegetables and fruits, and minimal meat. But only the brave should sample the chillies

Indonesia's cuisine is influenced by the culinary traditions of diverse nations such as China, India, the Middle East and the Netherlands. In fact, Indonesian cuisine is so varied that travellers can be assured of finding at least one dish that becomes a lifelong favourite.

Mealtime for most Indonesians is a quick, private and non-social activity. In most Indonesian homes the food is cooked in the morning to last the whole day. The prepared dishes are placed on the dining table at noon and again at dusk, and family members simply help themselves to a meal whenever they feel hungry. It is only on special occasions, such as on feast days or when having guests over, that the Indonesian family sits and eats together.

The Chinese influence is most evident in the use of stir-fried dishes cooked in a huge steaming wok, while Indonesia's popular curries can only have originated in India. Marinated meat on skewers, known locally as sate, owes its heritage to the Middle Eastern kebab, while the *rijstaeffel* (rice table) traces its roots to Dutch colonial times. In today's Indonesia, each of these various culinary traditions have blended and adapted to form distinctive regional cuisines across the archipelago.

Five pillars of the cuisine

Rice, coconut, banana, peanut and soya bean are the five pillars of Indonesian cuisine, and it is almost impossible to find a meal that does not include at least one of these items. Rice is the staple food on most of the islands, particularly the more fertile Sumatra, Java and Bali.

There are several kinds of rice in Indonesia: *beras putih* (white rice), *ketan putih* (sticky white rice), *ketan hitam* (sticky black rice) and *beras merah* (red rice). Nearly every menu offers dishes prefixed with the word *nasi*, which means they come with rice. Other starches like maize, tapioca, millet and sago are eaten in the drier islands east of Bali and in smaller archipelagos along the coast of Sumatra. In Roti and Savu islands, the staple food is sweet, nutritious juice tapped from the *lontar* palm.

Coconut and coconut products are central to Indonesian cooking. Every meal includes this versatile palm nut prepared in a variety of ways.

LEFT: wars were once fought in the islands of Maluku (Moluccas) for these ingredients. **RIGHT:** a welcome drink at a Balinese resort.

Coconut oil is the common cooking medium while *santan* (coconut milk) is used to thicken and add flavour to soups and curries and as a marinade for meats. Grated coconut is often added to various vegetable dishes to provide texture, flavour and an oil base. Fried shredded coconut is served as a condiment. Coconut is also a vital ingredient in Indonesian sweets.

There is an astonishing variety of bananas in Indonesia, ranging from the tiny *pisang mas* to the larger *pisang lembut* popular in Bali. Bananas can be eaten baked, fried or boiled, and are a popular snack. Even the banana flower is eaten as a vegetable and the leaves are

used as wrapping material for steamed meat, fish and vegetables.

Peanuts form an integral part of some meals in the form of a sweet and spicy sauce served with *sate*, *gado-gado* (steamed vegetables) and a host of other dishes. Much of the protein in Indonesian food comes from soya beans. They are eaten boiled or fermented to make *tempe* (soybean cake) and *tahu* (soybean curd). Peanuts are also fried and tossed together with *tempe*, either as a snack or served as a side dish to accompany a main meal.

Fermented soya bean sauces, *kecap asin* (salty) and *kecap manis* (sweet), are important flavouring agents used with gusto in almost every dish. Most Indonesian restaurants tend to use liberal amounts of MSG (monosodium glutamate) in their cooking, so let the waiter know beforehand if you prefer your food without this flavouring agent.

Kopi luwak *is the world's most expensive coffee. It is made from fermented coffee beans eaten and excreted by* luwak *(civets). In Lampung and Bali, civets are bred to cash in on the* kopi luwak *craze.*

Indonesians eat a large variety of vegetables. Most greens are picked wild and include tender tapioca, papaya and soya bean leaves, *kangkung* (water spinach) and *bayam* (Asian spinach). Other fruits and vegetables are grown in home gardens, including young jackfruits, papayas and bananas, all varieties of beans, squash and pumpkin, and carrots. Indonesians do not eat much meat for the most part, although it is common to find a few dried fish alongside a mound of white rice. Among other things, the choice of meat is determined by cultural and religious factors.

Main dishes are often accompanied by freshly made *sambal* (a thick chilli concoction), of which there are numerous varieties, ranging from a simple fried diced shallot, garlic and very hot chilli paste to a pungent fried version liberally laced with *terasi* (shrimp paste).

Regional cuisine

Typically, the food of Java tends to be relatively sweet compared with the spicier flavours of Sumatra and Bali. *Gudeg Jogja*, made

FESTIVAL FOODS

Almost every celebration in Java features *nasi tumpeng*, a cone-shaped steamed turmeric rice that symbolises a mountain, which is usually served with several side garnishes. *Babi guling* (suckling pig) is the main dish at ceremonies across Bali, North Sumatra and North Sulawesi. The Chinese minority celebrate Cap Go Meh 15 days after Imlek (Chinese New Year) with favourites including *lontong cap go meh* (special rice cakes) and *opor ayam* (chicken stewed in coconut milk). When Muslims celebrate Idul Fitri at the end of the fasting month, their festival foods almost always include *ketupat Lebaran* (Idul Fitri rice cake) with side dishes such as *semur daging* (beef stewed in soya bean sauce).

with young jackfruit, and *opor ayam*, chicken cooked in coconut milk, represent the sweet foods of Java. The Javanese eat a variety of meats (except pork), and favourite dishes are *soto ayam* (chicken soup), *sop buntut* (oxtail soup) and *ayam goreng* (fried chicken). The Sundanese of West Java prefer fish, grilled, fried or as *pepes* (wrapped in a banana leaf and roasted).

The Balinese favour duck and pork, with dishes including *babi guling* (roast suckling pig) and *bebek tutu* (spiced slow-cooked duck). The Sumatrans eat a lot of beef. One of the most popular dishes introduced by the West Sumatrans is *rendang* (beef chunks served in a rich and spicy sauce). The traditional Padang restaurant is Sumatra's great contribution to the national cuisine. It offers a bewildering array of tasty local dishes including *ayam* (chicken), *sapi* (beef), *kambing* (mutton), *sayur* (vegetables), *ikan goreng* (fried fish), various curries and maybe an assortment of entrails, plus a substantial serving of steamed rice.

Ayam taliwang, a Lombok dish featuring grilled chicken in hot chilli sauce served with steamed *kangkung*, is familiar throughout Indonesia. South Sulawesi is known for seafood dishes that run the gamut from shrimp, lobster and crab to carp, eel and sea slugs. *Iga sapi bakar* (grilled beef ribs) served with *konro* (rib soup) is on menus throughout the region. The coastal Papuans are said to offer the best *ikan bakar* (grilled fish) in the whole country. However, like Moluccans, their staple food is *pepeda*, sago porridge, eaten with a tuna soup flavoured with lime and turmeric.

Exotic fare

Some of the Dayak tribes of Kalimantan consider roast lizard a mouth-watering delicacy, while mice and bats are common fare in Minahasa kitchens in Sulawesi. Dog meat is commonly served during traditional celebrations on Flores, while rabbit and deer *sate* are common in West Java. Cobra meat added to soup and served as sate is believed to cure skin diseases and is offered in special restaurants in Java. In Bali, turtle meat is favoured but is now discouraged due to the endangered status of sea turtles. In Central Java, geckos are farmed and processed as crispy snacks, while grasshoppers

are captured to make crackers in Lampung or fried in hot chilli sauce in West Sumatra.

As a general rule, the more rural the area, the higher the chances of having meals prepared with meat and animal parts that may not agree with the palate. Once you go off the beaten track, it is a good idea to check what type of meat has been cooked if you're squeamish. Most Sundanese restaurants feature animal innards on their menus. Fried *ati ampla* (chicken livers and gizzards), *usus* (chicken or cow intestine) and *babat* (tripe) are among the dishes served. The term *jeroan* (meaning "inside") is widely understood in

Java to mean animal innards. *Gulai otak*, a curry dish made with cow brains, is easily found in Padang restaurants.

> In villages, the centrepiece of the traditional kitchen is a wood-fired stove and rice steamer. Other utensils include a pestle and mortar, wok and banana leaves for wrapping.

Vegetarian

Favourite vegetarian dishes include *gado-gado* (vegetable salad with peanut sauce) and *cap cai* (wok-fried vegetables), the latter being ubiquitous in Chinese restaurants. *Lotek* from West Java is similar to *gado-gado* with cooked vegetables, while *karedok* is raw vegetables, and is found on menus in Bogor. Both *lotek* and *karedok* are served with yummy peanut sauce. *Karedok* is more strongly flavoured than either *gado-gado* or *lotek* thanks to the pungent lesser galangal, a rhizome from the ginger family. *Pecel* from Madiun, East Java, is a popular vegetable salad. Minahasans eat sautéed *bunga papaya* (papaya flowers), while the Sundanese like plain raw vegetables, *lalaban*, a combination of cabbage, cucumbers, cassava and papaya leaves, basil and aubergine. *Sayur lodeh* (mixed vegetables in coconut milk) originated in Jakarta but is popular throughout Java.

Protein-rich *tahu* and *tempe* are also enjoyed by vegetarians, and both are served in a variety of ways throughout the archipelago, as they are popular with villagers who cannot afford to buy meat. In *arem-arem*, for example, *tempe* is combined with bean sprouts and chunks of compressed, glutinous rice covered with sweet soya sauce mixed with coconut water, and garnished with chopped peanuts and grated coconut.

SPICE UP YOUR DAY

It is no small wonder that spices are so readily used in the food of the Spice Islands, and make all the difference to Indonesian food. Spices can be either wet or dry. The wet type has fresh ingredients like shallots, onions, ginger, garlic and turmeric root ground into a paste, whereas the dry type includes powdered peppercorns, coriander seeds, cinnamon, cumin seeds, candlenut and *terasi* (shrimp paste). *Terasi* is an acquired taste and can be overpowering.

Fresh spices are first ground in a stone mortar and pestle, then fried to release their aroma before being added to meat, poultry or vegetables. Different spices are used with different kinds of meat. Pre-packaged spices are becoming common, available in local *warung* and supermarkets. However, in the villages, the woman of the house still prepares spices the old-fashioned way.

No spice mixture is complete without *cabai* (or lombok, chillies), as Indonesians love their food *pedas* (hot). The varieties include the long red *tabia Lombok* with its sweet flavour, the chunky red and yellow *tabia Bali* and the dynamite bird's-eye chillies. If you are unused to really spicy food, ask that it be prepared without chillies. In addition to being spicy, Indonesian food can be rather aromatic, as fresh bay leaves, lime leaves, basil and lemon grass are common ingredients. The best samplers are found in the Padang restaurants.

Foods found everywhere

One of the best ways to sample a wide variety of Indonesian food is to order *nasi rames* or *nasi campur*. These samplers are platefuls of steamed rice, chicken, fresh and preserved vegetables, fried egg, roasted peanuts, shredded coconut, fiery *sambal* sauce, and oversized crispy *krupuk* (fried prawn crackers).

The best-known rice dish is *nasi goreng*, fried rice with an assortment of vegetables and chicken, prawns or meat, or a combination of all three. If the word *istimewa* (special) appears, it means the dish comes with a fried egg on top. A cone-shaped mound of *nasi kuning* (yellow rice)

common throughout Indonesia, while *sate rusa* (deer) and *sate kelinci* (rabbit) are found in West Java. Soto comes in two varieties: one is clear soup flavoured with spices and the other has coconut milk added.

Fruits and sweets

The array of fresh tropical fruit available in Indonesia often astounds visitors. There are more than 40 varieties of bananas *(pisang)*, pomelos *(jeruk Bali)*, mangoes and pineapples *(nanas)*, plus an array of lesser-known delicacies. Durians might best be described as spiky green bowling balls that smell rather strange but taste like cara-

cooked with turmeric, coconut milk and spices is served on feast days on a banana leaf-lined platter. *Mi* (noodles) made from rice or wheat flour is another staple. In *mi goreng* (fried noodles), the noodles are fried in coconut oil with meat, vegetables and perhaps egg, with hot chilli shrimp paste and lime on the side. Both *mi goreng* and *nasi goreng* are popular breakfast dishes.

Lontong and *ketupat* are rice cakes that substitute for steamed rice and are usually eaten with *sate* and *soto* (soup). *Sate ayam* (chicken), *sate sapi* (beef) and *sate kambing* (mutton) are

mel peach. Rambutans are red or yellow, have a hairy exterior and a flavour very similar to lychee. And the skin of the *salak* (which has a crisp texture and sharp flavour) closely resembles that of a snake. Passion fruit *(markisa)* is a delicious refreshing fruit full of tiny, edible seeds. Other delicious local fruits include thirst-quenching watermelons *(semangka)*, mangosteens *(manggis)* and rose apples *(jambu air)*. The local tart green apples are surprisingly juicy and excellent to eat, as are several varieties of oranges.

Coconut milk, sticky rice, tapioca, mung beans, palm sugar and bananas are common dessert ingredients. Each island has its version of tiny cakes stuffed with sweetened mung beans, shaved coconut or banana, in a variety of colours

ABOVE, FROM LEFT: red-hot chillies at a market in Samarinda, Kalimantan; unusual meat, such as these bats, are often sold in village markets.

made with sticky rice cooked in coconut milk. Indonesians primarily use dark-brown palm sugar as a sweetener for desserts and other dishes.

Look *for kue lapis*, the Indonesian version of a light layered cake made of rice flour and fragrant coconut palm sugar, and *bubur ketan hitam* (black rice porridge cooked in coconut milk and sweetened with palm sugar). Delicious pancakes of all sorts, filled with fruit or palm sugar and shredded coconut, are available in nearly every big city. *Bubur kacang hijau* (green pea porridge) is also topped with coconut milk and palm sugar, as is *kolak* (steamed bananas, cassava and sweet potato stewed in coconut milk and brown sugar). *Kue pisang*, a coconut milk pudding laced with steamed bananas, is sold wrapped in banana leaves (or nowadays, in plastic) in almost all traditional markets.

Snacks

Indonesians eat three meals a day, which are interspersed with snack times. Snacking is a way of life here. Children cannot resist *krupuk* or a plate of *rujak* (spicy fruit salad). Fried *(goreng)* or steamed *(rebus)* foods are popular snacks, as the ingredients are readily available, and can include *pisang* (banana), *tahu* (soy bean curd), *ubi* (sweet potato) and *singkong* (cassava).

RIJSTAEFFEL

Much of the Dutch influence has long since faded away, but a remnant of it remains in the *rijstaeffel*, a more elaborate form of the Sumatran nasi Padang.

Rijstaeffel (literally, rice table) is a series of meat and vegetable courses, served with rice and spicy condiments, presented at the table with much ceremony by a string of sarong-clad waitresses.

Expect about five to six courses in a typical rijstaeffel, a far cry from Dutch colonial days when the serving might include as many as 350 separate dishes. Due to the elaborate nature of this meal, it is offered primarily at tourist restaurants and hotels.

Food vendors are ubiquitous, attracting customers by twanging a metal chime, beating a low wooden gong or a steam whistle. They serve *bakso* (meatballs), *bakpao* (steamed buns stuffed with meat) or simply a bowl of noodles.

People also get their meals and snacks at traditional Indonesian eating places known as *warung*, makeshift foodstalls set up on the pavements of busy streets and in marketplaces with rows of tables and rickety looking benches. Not the most romantic setting, but here, most of Indonesia's favourite dishes can be enjoyed at ridiculously cheap prices. Standards of hygiene are low, however, and refrigeration virtually non-existent, so cast-iron stomachs are a prerequisite for sampling street fare.

A popular dessert or snack is *es campur*, the Indonesian equivalent of the ice-cream sundae. There is no nationally accepted set of ingredients, but shaved ice is usually the base. A number of things can be poured over the ice, including syrup and coconut milk, bits of fruits, cubes of brightly coloured gelatin, jackfruit, fermented tapioca and various other sweet titbits.

Es cendol is another great refresher during hot weather, with green-coloured rice-flour jelly served in iced coconut milk and palm sugar. In Central Java it is called *es dawet*. *Es pisang ijo* and *es palu butung* come from Makassar, South Sulawesi, with bananas as the

usually available. Typically, most drinks come pre-mixed and tend to be very sweet, so do ask to have the sugar on the side. Sweetened tea, referred to as *teh botol* regardless of the brand, is widely sold in roadside coolers.

Fruit juices may be ordered fresh or pre-packaged. Among the popular choices of fresh juices are watermelon, papaya, pineapple and avocado. Fresh *es buah* is a mix of fresh fruits such as watermelon, papaya, pineapple and apple.

Local alcoholic beverages include Bintang beer (whose roots are traceable to the Dutch Heineken), *tuak* (palm wine), *brem* (rice wine), *badek* (rice liquor) and *arak*, the most potent of

main ingredient, topped with a rice-flour porridge, coconut milk and pandan leaf sauce.

Western food and other speciality cuisines are available at the more popular tourist destinations and in major cities. In recent years, Indonesians have developed a taste for western fast food and the popular chains are Kentucky Fried Chicken, McDonald's and Pizza Hut.

Drinks

Indonesians often drink sweetened hot tea with their meals, but iced tea *(es teh)*, local coffee *(kopi)*, fruit juices and bottled sodas are

ABOVE, FROM LEFT: Balinese sweets; fruit-juice vendor, Lombok; rijstaeffel, a reminder of Dutch rule..

rice spirits. Visitors are cautioned against buying locally made spirits, as they can be laced with added ingredients – even gasoline – to give them an extra kick and can cause illness or even death.

Kelapa muda, fresh young coconut, replaces body fluids quickly and is easily found in coastal areas. It can be served plain or with added sugar or vanilla syrup with ice.

In the highlands, where temperatures can be quite chilly, hot drinks are favoured. The Sundanese in West Java's highlands drink *bajigur*, a mixture of palm sugar with coconut milk. *Bandrek* is made with ginger and palm sugar and can be mixed with milk or coffee. In other parts of Java, ginger is also used in hot beverages, such as *wedang jahe* or ginger tea.

DANCE AND THEATRE

The most refined of Indonesian performing arts are found in Java and Bali, where court theatre has evolved as a highly stylised retelling of the classics. Other islands have their own distinct traditions

There is such a variety of dance and dramatic tradition throughout Indonesia that it is impossible to speak of a single, unified tradition. Each Indonesian ethnic and linguistic group possesses its own unique performing arts. Nevertheless, there are certain shared features among the groups, and most have several things in common.

Dance, storytelling and theatre are ubiquitous in Indonesia, elements of a cultural life that is all-encompassing and fulfils a wide variety of sacred and secular needs. Dancers, shamans, actors, puppeteers, storytellers, poets and musicians are members of the community, performing vital roles in informing, entertaining, counselling and instructing their fellows in the well-established ways of tradition.

Ritual dances

Most tribes have ritual dances performed to mark rites of passage – births, funerals, weddings, puberty – and agricultural events, as well as to exorcise sickness or evil spirits, and, in the past, to prepare for battle or celebrate victory. The primary purpose of these dances is to appease the spirits. The Batak *datuk* (magician) of North Sumatra, for example, holds a magic staff as he treads with tiny steps over a design he has drawn on the ground. At the climax of this dance, he hops and skips, thrusting his staff into an egg on the ground. The Hornbill dance performed by Kalimantan Dayak tribes for many generations celebrated warriors returning from battle. Nowadays used as part of harvest

festivals, the dancer, adorned with hornbill feathers, makes slow movements as though stalking and attacking the enemy.

Some dance schools teach boys to perform dance roles usually played by females. In the Javan town of Wonosobo, the lengger dance features men dressed as women, while the male Buginese bissu of South Sulawesi dances in a trance as a woman.

More refined ritual dances are performed by a select group, but in village dances, often all the males or females in the community join in. Female movements are generally slow and

LEFT: Legong dance performance, Ubud. **RIGHT:** the Barong dance dramatises the struggle between good and evil.

deliberate, with tiny steps and graceful hand movements; men lift their knees high and use their hands as "weapons", often in imitation of traditional martial-arts movements (*pencak silat*). Accompaniment is provided by chanting, pounding of rice mortar (*lesung*), and bamboo chimes or flutes.

Group dances often involve the entrancement and possession of participants, best known of which is the Balinese *Barong*. The Barong-Rangda dance-drama is a contest between the opposing forces of good and evil in the universe, represented by a good lion-like beast called Barong and the evil witch Rangda.

by musicians, masked clowns and perhaps also a masked lion, tiger or crocodile similar to the *Barong*. The riders begin in an orderly fashion, trotting in circles, until one of them becomes entranced and behaves like a horse, charging back and forth wildly, neighing and eating grass or straw. The others might follow his lead, and sometimes there is a confrontation between the masked animal and the horsemen. Eventually, the riders are brought out of the trance by their leader, and all ends well.

Another well-known trance dance from East Java is the *reog*, which tells the story of a prince who wants to marry a beautiful princess. He

The battle ends in a temporary quelling rather than complete victory.

In the Balinese *sanghyang* trance dances, the performers are possessed by gods and animal spirits. In the *sanghyang dedari*, or heavenly maidens dance, two young girls dressed in white enter a circle of 40 to 50 chanting men, the *kecak* chorus. The girls dance in unison with eyes shut, and when they are finally possessed by goddesses, they are clothed in glittering costumes and borne aloft on the shoulders of the men, touring the village to drive out evil.

In Central Java, one trance dance is variously known as *kuda kepang*, *kuda lumping* and *jatilan*, and consists of one or more riders on hobby horses made of plaited bamboo, accompanied

wears an enormous mask weighing 30–40kg (66–88lbs) adorned with a tiger or leopard head and peacock feathers, held in place by the performer's teeth. The dancer – the *singa barong* – goes into trance while demonstrating his strength and prowess in his efforts to impress the lady. On some occasions, children or young ladies ride on top of the mask to impress the audience. In other versions of the *reog*, young boys or girls riding hobby horses, similar to the *jatilan* horses used in Central Java, accompany the *singa barong*.

Court dances of Java

Before the turn of the 20th century, all traditional rulers of the coastal and inland kingdoms maintained palace dance and theatrical troupes. But following the Dutch conquests, most court traditions lapsed into obscurity. Only in Central Java are courtly performances and royal patronage of dancers, actors and musicians still found and appreciated.

Java has by far the oldest known dance and theatre traditions in Indonesia, as depicted in stone carvings dating from the 8th and 9th centuries. The walls of Borobudur, Prambanan and others are adorned with numerous reliefs depicting dancers and musical entertainers, from market minstrels and roadside revellers to sensuous court concubines and prancing princesses.

Most of the traditional dances in Central Java are attributed to rulers of one of several Islamic dynasties, particularly those of the 16th to 18th centuries, with rulers having dances choreographed for special occasions. One renowned Javanese court dance is the *bedoyo ketawang*, performed in the Surakarta palace on the anniversary of the Susuhunan's coronation. This is a sacred and private ritual dance said to have been instituted in the early 1600s celebrating a reunion between the descendant of the dynasty's founder and the powerful goddess of the South Seas, Ratu Kidul.

Nine female palace dancers perform the stately *bedoyo ketawang*, attired in royal wedding dress, and it is so sacred that they may rehearse only once on a given day. Until recently, no outsiders were permitted to witness the performance, as it is believed that Ratu Kidul herself attends and afterwards "weds" the king.

Another court dance from Solo, *serimpi*, was traditionally performed only by princesses or daughters of the ruling family. It portrays one or two duelling pairs of warriors, reflecting the balance of negative and positive cosmic forces. Following the rise of dance schools in the early 1900s, the *serimpi* became the standard dance taught to all young women.

Folk dances

Outside the courts, there have always been dances performed by the common people. Thought to be too crude to be performed for

ABOVE, FROM LEFT: kecak dance at Pura Luhur Uluwatu, Bali; in the Javanese *kuda kepang*, dancers often go into a trance.

royalty, these dances are relatively free of restrictions and change with the times.

Some folk dances, for example, are primarily for courtship. They are usually offshoots from fertility rites and women take the initiative, as in *gandrung* from Lombok. A female dancer selects male partners for short dance duets by tapping them on the shoulder with her fan. A similar dance, *jogged bumbung*, is performed in West Bali. In Kalimantan, young Dayak women perform graceful dances holding bunches of hornbill feathers as bachelors watch, hoping the ladies will approach them. In the past, in mainly Islamic Aceh (North Sumatra), women

were prohibited from dancing, as it was considered erotic. Now the *serampang dua belas* is performed by mixed pairs telling the 12 steps *(dua belas)* of introducing young people who are about to enter marriage.

From the 1950s, Indonesian performers began studying abroad, each bringing home new elements which they introduce into traditional dances or create new ones. The *jaipong* from Bandung, West Java, is considered by some to be vulgar, but its creator, Gumgum Gumbira, views it as humorous and spontaneous. Building on the past with *sarong*-clad female performers using some traditional body movements, the dance was intended to attract the attention of young people who were no longer interested in time-honoured dance.

Very popular, and now a Unesco cultural heritage treasure, is the *saman* dance from the Gayo highlands, near Aceh. Often called the "thousand hands" dance abroad, between eight and 20 male or female performers kneel on the floor in a line. There is no music; instead, the exuberant cadence is created by clapping hands, pounding the floor and slapping the chest, with one person reading a barely audible narrative in order to maintain the cadence. Energetic and dynamic, the performance

requires excellent coordination to keep the rhythm going.

Theatre

Some theatrical traditions incorporate dance to such an extent that they are typically referred to as "dance-dramas". In Java, all theatre seems to have its roots in the *wayang* (puppet) tradition, evident from the fact that all traditional Javanese theatre, whether performed by actors or by puppets, is referred to as *wayang*. Performed by actors on a stage, *wayang topeng* (mask drama) and *wayang orang* (dance-drama) are the most traditional,

BALINESE DANCE

There are clear indications that dance and drama closely tied to religion have played a central role in Indonesian life since time immemorial. Other dances, however, are ceremonial, teach life lessons, or are simply for entertainment.

In Balinese dance, the Indian influence is evident in the facial expressions. Balinese costumes, with their glittering headdresses and elaborate jewellery, are of Hindu-Javanese origin and, as in Java, Balinese dancers adopt the same basic stance. Javanese court dances, however, are performed with slow, controlled, continuous movements, with eyes downcast and limbs close to the body. In contrast, the Balinese dancer is charged

with energy, eyes wide and darting, feet lifted high, arms up, moving with quick, cat-like bursts that are startling.

Dances have evolved over long periods of time, and their original uses are now intertwined. In Bali, the *legong keraton* was originally a court dance developed for royal amusement, but it is now seen frequently at temple ceremonies. The *baris* warrior dance, often performed in groups and with weapons, appears to have developed out of a ritual battle dance. A solo *baris* performance is a true test of wits for the dancer and musicians, who must respond to each other's signals to produce the quivering bursts of synchronised energy that are the essence of the dance.

with many of the tales, choreography and characters' movements borrowed from the shadow play.

Wayang topeng may have been inspired by ancient masked dances, but it was not introduced in Yogyakarta courts until the early 20th century by the *pedalangan* (shadow puppetry) community. In Bali, mask plays are still popular, as they are in the courts of Central Java, and in some villages in the east and west of the island. Like puppet plays, masked performances are often used on television and in village performances to convey messages to the public, particularly satirical ones.

The highly stylised Javanese *wayang orang* or *wayang wong* (literally, human *wayang*) dance-dramas are said to have been created in the 18th century by one or another of Central Java's rulers. *Wayang orang* became a part of the state ritual in these kingdoms, performed in an open pavilion to commemorate the founding of the dynasty and the coronation of the king, as well as at lavish royal weddings. The great age of *wayang orang* was during the 1920s and 1930s, when

ABOVE, FROM LEFT: young Dayak women perform graceful dances holding bunches of hornbill feathers as bachelors look on, hoping the ladies will approach them; shadow puppet, Denpasar.

productions lasted days and would often employ 300 to 400 actors.

To keep up with the times, traditional dance and drama has in some cases blended with modern forms of entertainment to suit contemporary tastes. Javanese *kethoprak* (also spelled *ketoprak*) has connections to *wayang wong* because it uses classical costumes and gamelan music, but the dialogue is spoken rather than sung, the dancing is minimal and risqué humour is used to attract younger audiences. The topics are usually love stories, Javanese heroic romances or tales borrowed from Chinese folklore, and are frequently seen on television as well as at open-air venues. Evolving from this genre in order to relieve stress during times of political and economic change after Suharto's fall, *kethoprak* humour today remains slapstick and full of lowbrow puns and cross-dressing.

Modern trends

Although traditional dance and drama face competition from modern entertainment, many educated Indonesians are dedicated to keeping these arts alive. There are government and privately sponsored arts high schools and academies in Java and Bali and two fully accredited universities, one in Jogja and the other in Denpasar. With state-of-the-art visual, performing and recorded media arts, these schools are turning out not only traditional but contemporary performers, choreographers, musicologists and ethnomusicologists, as well as photographers, film-makers and interior designers.

While it might seem that the students at these schools would be primarily interested in contemporary arts, many Indonesians – and some foreigners – attend specifically to delve more deeply into traditions. Someone yearning to become a *dalang* (puppeteer), for example, has to study Bali's ancient Kawi language, Sanskrit or Java Kuno, and master vocal techniques to give personalities to each puppet character while simultaneously enrapturing the audience, sending the desired messages and ensuring their voices are strong enough to be heard. In addition, they need to learn hundreds of tales from the *Ramayana* and *Mahabharata* epics (see page 91), and many will learn to make their own puppets. Some students will study several genres until they find the right niche to pursue.

Excellent examples of performances mixing traditional and contemporary dance-drama can be seen on stage at Bali Safari & Marine Park in Gianyar and seasonally at Borobudur. Both use stunning costumes, animals and magnificent lighting effects.

In the performing arts realm, tourism helps by providing a commercial demand for the arts. A new generation of Indonesian choreographers, familiar with Western classical and modern dance, is now producing art-drama-dance (*sendratari*, literally translated as ballet),

which is essentially a traditional dance-drama, minus the dialogue, that incorporates some modern movements and costumes. One of the most popular is the *Ramayana* ballet spectacular performed on a large stage in front of the elegant 9th-century Prambanan temple complex near Jogja.

Also emerging from these schools and academies are theatre groups such as Teater Koma (Theatre Comma), which has been active since 1977. Its shows were often banned during the Suharto era for lampooning the government – both the system and leaders – but they persevered and today attract audiences that reach across the population, from university students to professionals to diehard theatre fans. In a lavish Chinese opera production staged in 2011, a series of 7th-century Chinese tales were woven together, incorporating elaborate costumes and make-up, and also brought in Javanese puppets and traditional martial arts. The dialogue in the 4-hour-long production included the satirical jabs that Teater Koma is known for.

The new generation of performers is also credited with finding overseas venues for local troupes and for inviting artists from abroad to combine talents with Indonesian actors, actresses and dancers, creating original contemporary work. One such collaboration between the Snuff Puppets Company of Melbourne, Australia, and Jogja artists has been ongoing for several years and has created a new genre using life-sized puppets, theatrical dances, popular music and cross-cultural dialogue about traditions and mythology in changing societies.

PUPPET THEATRE

Thought to be derived from ancestral worship, puppet theatre is limited to a few locations in Indonesia

The remarkable life-sized Batak *sigale-gale* puppet of North Sumatra is manipulated from below with cords and pulleys during funeral ceremonies. It is attributed to a local childless woman who, in somewhat macabre fashion, made an image of her dead husband and animated it to communicate with his soul. Some figures have water-filled sponges at the eyes to make them weep. Traditionally, at the end of the funeral, spears and arrows were shot at the figure to drive away evil spirits.

In Central Java, *wayang kulit* uses flat leather puppets that are perforated and fitted with movable arms for Ramayana and Mahabharata stories. In West Java, *wayang golek* (wooden rod puppets) perform tales from Indian epics and Islamic Amir Hamzah or Menak romances.

Balinese *wayang* refers to many types of shadow-puppet theatre with different repertoires. *Wayang Ramayana* stages stories from the epic of the same name, while *wayang parwa* performs episodes from the Mahabharata. An 11th-century Javanese exorcist legend of black magic is the focus for *wayang Calonarang*.

In Lombok, *wayang Sasak* works flat leather puppets to depict Islamic Menak romances, which were introduced from Java during the 17th century to spread the teachings of Islam.

Indian Morality Epics

Central to Javanese and Balinese drama are the two great Indian epics, the *Ramayana* and the *Mahabharata*, stories of love and goodness over evil

The *Ramayana* and the *Mahabharata* epics are the basis of the most important wayang stories in Java and Bali. These gripping tales, one about an everlasting love and the other about a great war, are products of India which entered Java with the propagation of Hinduism.

Filled with high drama, they are morality plays which over the ages have contributed largely to the establishment of traditional Indonesian values. Their fascination lies partly in the complex moral themes posed: life is never a case of absolutely black or white. Good heroes may have bad traits, and bad characters may have redeeming qualities. Although the forces of good do triumph over evil in the end, more often than not, the victory is incomplete; both sides suffer losses, and though a king may win a righteous war, he may lose all his sons as well.

The *Ramayana* is filled with examples on how to lead a good life. Written by the poet Valmiki about 2,000 years ago, it tells the story of Prince Rama, who had been predetermined by the gods to be a hero but would be put to the test many times. Rama is, in fact, an incarnation of the god Vishnu, and it is his destiny to kill the evil ogre king Ravana.

Owing to palace intrigues, Rama, his beautiful wife Sita (also spelled Shinta or Sinta) and his brother Laksamana are exiled to the forest. An ogre named Marica takes the form of a golden deer, luring Rama and Laksamana away. Ravana then carries off Sita to his island kingdom, Lanka. Rama's search for Sita is helped by the monkey god Hanuman and the monkey king Sugriva. Eventually, a full-scale assault is launched on the evil king and Sita is rescued. Sita, in turn, proves her chastity during captivity in a trial by fire before Rama accepts her.

The Mahabharata, which was written after the *Ramayana*, is a collection of stories centring on a

long-standing feud between two family clans, the Pandava and the Korava. The feud culminates in an epic battle during which the five Pandava brothers come face-to-face with their 100 cousins from the Korava clan. After 18 days of fighting, the Pandava emerge victorious and the eldest brother becomes king.

The great war portrayed in the *Mahabharata* is believed to have been fought in northern India in the 13th century BC. The war became a focus of legends, songs and poems, and at some point the vast collection accumulated over centuries was gathered into a narrative called *The Epic of the Bharata Nation* (India), or *Mahabharata*.

Important events that take place include the appearance of Krishna, an incarnation of Lord Vishnu, who becomes the adviser of the Pandava; the marriage of Prince Arjuna of the Pandava to the Princess Drupadi; the Korava's attempt to kill the Pandava; and the division of the kingdom into two in an attempt to end the rivalry between the groups.

In one scene during the great war, Arjuna becomes despondent at the thought of fighting his own flesh and blood. Krishna, his charioteer and adviser, then explains to him that the soul is indestructible and that whoever dies shall be reborn, thus there is no cause to be sad; it is the soldier's duty to fight, as the outcome of the battle is predetermined.

ABOVE, FROM LEFT: a Snuff Puppets Company production; acting out the *Mahabharata*.

GAMELAN MUSIC

The trance-like rhythms of the gamelan have earned it fame as a unique musical form. The contemplative Javanese strains contrast with Bali's sparkling sounds

Gamelan music is comparable to two things: moonlight and flowing water. It is pure and mysterious like the first and ever-changing like the second. Since 1893, when Claude Debussy first heard a Javanese ensemble perform at the Paris International Exhibition, the haunting and hypnotic tones of the gamelan have fascinated the West. This music has been studied by scholars – the earliest were Jaap Kunst and Colin McPhee – and is now recognised as one of the world's most sophisticated musical arts.

The term gamelan derives from *gamel*, an old Javanese word for handle or hammer, as most of the instruments in the orchestra are percussive. The interlocking rhythmic and melodic patterns found in gamelan music are said to originate in the rhythms of the *lesung* – the wooden mortars used for husking rice. Others ascribe the patterns to the chanting of frogs in the rice fields after dusk.

CONTEMPORARY SOUNDS

Aside from the classical beauty of gamelan music, Indonesia's popular music plays an important part in the social scene: ranging from *keroncong, dangdut, jaipongan, campursari* through pop, jazz, blues, and Javanese-language hip hop. Portuguese-influenced *keroncong*, which combines ukulele, cello (plucked), violin, mandolins, guitars and bamboo *suling*, was originally associated with the lower classes in Jakarta, but later gained respectability when it adopted nationalist themes during the war for independence. The romantic ballads remain popular today. The unmistakable driving beat of the enormously popular *dangdut*, originally influenced by Indian film songs, has swept the country and now gone international. There is no question that *dangdut* is

the choice of the masses. Jaipongan combines Sundanese instruments and Western rock music, while Campursari mixes Javanese gamelan instruments with keyboard, electric bass and drums for popular sing-along songs performed both in the traditional *wayang kulit* performances as well as at wedding receptions and parties.

With at least 400 Sundanese, Javanese and Balinese gamelan sets scattered throughout the world, gamelan music can now be considered truly international. The annual Yogyakarta Gamelan Festival, usually held in July, invites groups from around Indonesia, Southeast Asia, Japan, New Zealand, Europe and America to perform primarily their own contemporary compositions.

No one knows exactly when the first gamelan came into being. The manufacture of bronze gongs and drums is associated with the Dong Son bronze culture that is thought to have reached Indonesia from Indochina in the 3rd century BC. Since then, large bronze gongs have formed the heartbeat of this distinctive music, with a deep and penetrating sound that can be heard for miles on a quiet night.

Javanese gamelan

Gamelan ensembles are most commonly performed to accompany dance and theatre. *Karawitan* is the Indonesian term coined in the

played alone. Two instruments, the *rebab* (a two-stringed bowed lute, probably of Middle Eastern origin) and the *suling* (bamboo flute), are non-percussive and were probably later additions to the ensemble.

A basic principle underlying all gamelan music is that of stratification, in which the density of notes played on each instrument is determined by its register; higher instruments play more notes than lower ones.

Instruments are grouped according to their function. Gongs, for example, establish the basic foundation of the composition, while mid-register metallophones carry a basic

1950s by Ki Sindusawarno, the first director of the music conservatory in Surakarta, for the entire range of Javanese and Balinese performing arts incorporating gamelan music.

In Java, *karawitan* and related arts reached the height of refinement in the Islamic courts of the 18th and 19th centuries resulting in slow, stately and mystical music, designed to be heard in the large audience hall of the aristocratic home and to convey a sense of awesome power and emotional control.

Between five and 40 instruments make up a gamelan ensemble, and most of them are never

melody and other instruments provide more elaborate versions of that melody. The *kendhang* – wooden drums with skins stretched over both ends – control the tempo of the piece. Some musicians compare the structure of gamelan music to a tree. The roots, deep, sturdy and supportive, are the low registers; the trunk is the melody; and the branches, leaves and blossoms, the delicate complexity of the elaborating melodies.

In Central Java, the main *balungan* (skeletal melody) of a piece is played on the *saron* (small- to medium-size metallophones, with six or seven keys lying over a wooden trough resonator) and on the *slenthem* (metallophones with bamboo resonators). Faster variations on

ABOVE, FROM LEFT: gamelan instruments; a gamelan performance at Borobudur.

the *balungan* are played simultaneously on the elaborating instruments: the *bonang* (a set of small, horizontally suspended gongs), *gender* (similarly built to the *slenthem* but with two octaves), *gambang* (a wooden xylophone) and *celempung* (a zither with metal strings). Together with the *suling*, the *rebab* and the vocalists, they create the complex, rich sounds unique to gamelan music.

> The haunting melodies of the Sundanese kacapi suling *permeate restaurants and stores across the country. The ensemble comprises two zithers* (kacapi) *plus a bamboo* suling, *which play soothing, melancholic melodies.*

Vocals

Vocal parts in an ensemble were introduced in Java only in the 19th century and it is now common to have soloists as well as a chorus. Female *(pesinden)* singers are popular, but the sound of their voices is regarded merely as another element in the overall texture of the ensemble.

A common misconception of gamelan compositions is that they are improvised. This impression arises perhaps because written scores are rarely used. Most compositions *(gendhing)* have formal structures, but may be performed differently depending on the particular occasion. There are thousands of pieces, and every region of Java has its favourites. Each *gendhing* has its own name, often corresponding

to the character, dance or ritual for which the *gendhing* is played.

Gamelan musicians were traditionally taught by other musicians in their spare time, without any reference to written scores. In the Central Javanese palaces, a system of notation was developed. Some court musicians began to teach outsiders in the early 20th century. Since independence, government music academies have been founded and students now learn in a more formal setting.

At the village level, it is often difficult to distinguish amateurs from professionals.

THE FAHNESTOCK AND SMITHSONIAN RECORDINGS

The Fahnestock brothers, Bruce and Sheridan, sailed for Indonesia on the 42-metre (137ft) schooner Director II in 1940 with state-of-the-art recording equipment and 15 scientists. They had 3km (2 miles) of insulated microphone cable to enable them to record on shore while the equipment remained on board. Unbeknown to the public, the Fahnestocks were also spying for President Roosevelt, noting the sea defences of Java under cover of making the recordings.

The boat sank off Australia in 1941, but not before the discs were taken to New York. Bruce was killed in New Guinea during the war; Sheridan became a publisher. The original recordings were donated to the US Library of Congress, which accepted them as part of its Endangered Music Project. A selection of the recordings has been released by Rykodisc as Music for the Gods – The Fahnestock South Sea Expedition, Indonesia.

In the 1990s, with funding from the Ford Foundation, a joint team of American and Indonesian ethnomusicologists with the Indonesian Performing Arts Society (MSPI), in cooperation with the Center for Folklife Programs and Cultural Studies of the Smithsonian Institution, made recordings of lesser-known music traditions throughout the archipelago, including Sumatra, Riau, Flores, Papua, Kalimantan, Sulawesi and Maluku. This unprecedented project is available in a series of 20 audio CDs, complete with detailed background and field notes.

Many village artists are experts in the music of their region, but no special status is assigned to them, nor are they paid suitable fees for their services.

Some musicians are itinerant, making the rounds of traditional performances, be they theatrical or ceremonial, including the ever-popular *wayang kulit* circuit.

Court gamelan

Although gamelan instruments can be made of iron and brass, the best instruments are hammered out by hand from bronze. The highly decorative wooden frames and stands are made from teakwood, while the best wood for the drums is jackfruit. Good examples of Javanese court gamelan can be seen in the Keraton (Sultan's Palace) and the Museum Sono Budoyo in Yogyakarta (Jogja), and the Puro Mangkunegaran in Solo (Surakarta).

Once a year during the Sekaten festival, celebrating the Prophet Muhammad's birthday, the ancient court *gamelan sekaten* of Jogja and Solo that date to the 14th-century Majapahit kingdom perform in front of the Grand Mosque for one week, in clear defiance of fundamentalist Islamic beliefs regarding music, but in testimony to the enduring eclecticism of the Javanese culture.

Balinese gamelan

In Bali, the gamelan exhibits overwhelming variety. Dozens of completely different types of ensembles exist, some of which are found all over the island, others of which are restricted to isolated areas. Balinese musical performances are noted for their capriciousness, stridency and rhythmic vitality – particularly in contrast to the slow and measured gamelan performances of Java.

One of the most frequently encountered ensembles in Bali is the gamelan *gong kebyar*. *Kebyar* refers to a particularly flashy music style that originated in North Bali in 1915, but the ensembles that play it have since expanded their repertoire to include other styles. In the *gong kebyar*, four different gongs mark the musical phrase. They are, in order

of descending size: the gong, *kempur*, *kempli* and *kemong*.

The melodic theme is carried by two pairs of large metallophones: the *jegogan* and *calung*. Several *gangsa* (high-pitched metallophones) ornament the theme, and the reyong (Bali's version of the Javanese *bonang*) is played by four musicians producing a rippling stream of visceral, syncopated figurations. A pair of *kendhang* drums leads the group, interlocking with each other to produce spectacular rhythms. The drummer of the lower-pitched *kendhang* is generally the leader, teacher and composer for the ensem-

ble. A set of shimmering cymbals (*cengceng*) and several bamboo flutes (*suling*) complete the ensemble.

Balinese gamelan are normally owned and maintained cooperatively by village music clubs (*sekaha*). The Balinese religious calendar prescribes a hectic schedule of performances for temple festivals, and the provincial government has taken an active role in preserving lesser-known musical styles that may be in danger of extinction.

Island-wide, inter-village musical competitions have provided an impetus for Balinese composers and performers constantly to expand the expressive essence of the music.

ABOVE, FROM LEFT: gamelan instruments at the Keraton, Yogyakarta; *legong* dance performances are accompanied by gamelan music.

TEXTILES

Indonesia's great variety of peoples has produced an equally wide array of lovely and intricate textiles that express cultural identity and powerful symbolism

Indonesia is one of the world's greatest producers of fine traditional textiles. One of the oldest expressions of traditional art, handmade cloth is a vital component of Indonesian culture. Textiles are not only mere articles of clothing, but are also important to the cultural heritage of the country, as spiritually charged talismans, and symbols of wealth and status.

To understand the true value and meaning of Indonesian textiles, we have to examine their cultural context and the belief systems of the people who produce them. The materials, colours and motifs, along with rituals for their creation and use, all serve as powerful messages that convey wealth, social status, religious belief, the marriage contract and a connection to the spirit world.

Traditional textiles are works of art created by craftswomen who incorporate a medley of technical skills: weaving, dyeing and embroidery using any choice of natural fibres, including bark, cotton and silk. Some are embellished with shells, beads and gold or silver threads but use methods and techniques that have changed very little over centuries.

Symbol of birth

The process of manufacturing textiles is interwoven with taboos that define gender-role responsibilities to ensure the harmony of the community. Spinning, dyeing and the weaving of yarn are regarded as symbolic of the process of creation, and of human birth in particular. Weaving is generally an exclusively female activity. Men are permitted to participate only in the

LEFT: traditional batik, Brahama Tirta Sari Studio, Jogja. **RIGHT:** inside Jogja's Batik Museum.

dyeing of certain colours of the thread, analogous with their role in human conception. The dyeing process is carried out in the utmost privacy, behind partitions set up around the work area. Pregnant, menstruating or sick women are excluded from this work.

A traditional cloth produced with natural dyes once took many years to complete. The main natural dyes used in traditional textiles are indigo (*Indigofera tinctoria*), *mengkudu* (*Morinda citrifolia*), *soga* (a brown dye from root and bark) and mud dyes. Today, because of time and economic constraints, many textiles are coloured by chemical dyes.

In some areas, the mounting of threads on the loom is done on an auspicious day, otherwise the threads would break and bring bad luck. In several coastal villages, this means a full moon and a high tide. If a death occurs in the village, weaving stops at once to prevent the spirit of the departed from exacting vengeance by bringing sickness upon the weaver and causing the threads to lose their strength. Finished products are usually sanctified by metaphysical and psychological associations, and therefore regarded as powerful objects that can protect the weaver, cure illness, bring rain and are often necessary for life-cycle rituals.

Development

Cotton and silk have been used for making cloth for the past 3,000 to 5,000 years. As the spice trade developed over the last two millennia, Arab, Indian and Chinese traders discovered they could obtain valuable spices in exchange for Indian cotton and silk. Indonesians in turn found they could barter their easily gathered cloves, nutmeg, peppers and aromatic woods for fine textiles from the traders.

Many of the techniques and motifs in Indonesian textiles were adapted from foreign examples. As early as the 14th century, Indian fabrics were imported on a large scale, and the Indian textile revolution extended to fabrics that were considered rare and valuable, or even magical. The single most influential cloth is the Indian *patola*, a double-ikat silk fabric produced in Gujarat. Widely reproduced in Indonesia, it was incorporated into the ceremonial lives of many Indonesians and formed part of the costumes of kings on several islands, including Java. As fewer *patola* were imported after 1800,

weavers throughout Indonesia set about producing replicas. Today, the eight-pointed-flower or *chabadi bhatt* design is seen everywhere.

Indonesian textile decoration methods fall into three major categories: dye-resist, woven and embellished techniques. There are two dye-resist processes: the wax on cloth batik and the tie-and-dye process of warp, weft and double ikat. Warp and weft ikat are produced by the Batak (North Sumatra), in the Nusa Tenggara islands, East Java, Kalimantan and South Sulawesi. Weft ikat is produced in Bali, West Lombok, East Java, Palembang, Sumatra and in South Sulawesi, while double ikat is only

produced in Bali. Woven decoration includes supplementary warp and weft, tapestry, tablet-weaving, embroidery, appliqué, beadwork and shellwork. Embellished techniques include supplementary weft such as *songkets*, supplementary warp and warp-wrapping.

Batik

Batik is Indonesia's renowned textile art, especially Javanese batik, which is regarded as the world's finest. In the technique, dye-resist wax is applied to the cloth to prevent the dye from penetrating certain areas, thus resulting in a pattern in the negative. Finely detailed batik *tulis* ("written" design) is made possible with a tool called a *canting*. The *canting*, a

---

INDIGO DYE

Indigo dye from *Indigofera tinctoria* is the most widely used natural blue dye in the world. The recipe for the dye was once a guarded secret, but today it is known across the archipelago. The dye is prepared in a vat and goes through a fermentation and oxidation process. Indigo leaves are first soaked overnight in earthenware jars of water. The leaves are then removed and lime is added, causing chemical reduction. Cotton or silk threads dyed in this vat are then hung up to oxidise. This process is repeated until the desired colour intensity is achieved and the indigo threads deemed ready to be woven.

Geringsing is said to have protective powers. Kings once presented geringsing garments to warriors prior to battle.

small copper cup with a spout through which melted wax flows, is mounted on a handle and is wielded like a pen, allowing the artist to execute designs.

The first step is to draw a design on a piece of silk or cotton cloth. Areas not to be coloured in the first dyeing are covered with wax. This process alone can take hundreds of hours. The cloth is then immersed in dye and dried off.

In Central Java, certain motifs were once reserved for the royal court, such as the *parang rusak barong*, a broken sword design that consists of diagonal rows of interlocking scrolls. Today, out of respect for the descendants of the royal family, many locals will choose not to wear batik printed with motifs that were originally regarded as sacred to the royal court.

Batik *cap* is produced with the use of a metal printing block. The *cap* stamps are built out of thin strips of copper and wire soldered to an open frame. The *cap* is dipped into heated wax before it is pressed firmly onto the cloth. The

With natural dyes, repeated immersions and dryings are necessary, and a single dyeing can take months to complete.

For subsequent dyeings, either more wax is added to seal areas of the first dye before overdyeing with a second colour, or the cloth has to be de-waxed and waxed again. Wax is removed by boiling in water or by being scraped off. Dyeing and drying follow, and the process is repeated as many times as there are number of colours on the cloth.

Above, From Left: traditional methods of batik making, Brahama Tirta Sari Studio, Jogja; symbolic *hinggi* ikat from Sumba are used as dowry gifts and in funeral rituals.

advent of batik *cap* revitalised the industry in the 1890s, making mass-produced cloths that were affordable to all and creating an export trade from Java to the Outer Islands. For more on batik, *see page 102.*

Ikat

Warp ikat is a traditional method of weaving in which the warp threads (on the length) of a cloth are tie-dyed prior to weaving. The process of spinning cotton threads and preparing the dyes, binding the warp threads in a pattern that will resist the dye, and then repeatedly immersing, drying and re-binding them to achieve the desired colour requires tremendous skill and patience. In the hands

The sacred maa *cloths of the South Sulawesi Torajans are kept in special baskets and are essential for major rituals. Some* maa *are thought to be effective vessels for fertility spirits, and opening a powerful cloth is said to bring immediate rainfall.*

of a master weaver, the end result is intricate, detailed motifs executed in deep, rich colours. Weaving is done on a backstrap loom, with either discontinuous warp threads affixed to the loom's beams or a continuous warp bent around the beams so as to create a tube of cloth. While one beam is attached

to a grounded object (tree or house post), the other is secured to the weaver with the tension maintained by a strap placed around the weaver's back as she sits on the ground. String heddles are employed to create individual sheds, and sometimes a bamboo comb is introduced to maintain the spacing of a discontinuous warp.

The most famous warp ikats are the *hinggi* from East Sumba. These cloths are known for their rich colours, fine details and bold, horizontal fields of stylised human and animal figures. Normally produced in pairs, one to wrap around the body and one to drape over the shoulders, they have served as valuable trade goods for centuries and were exported extensively by the Dutch in the 19th century. *Hinggi* textiles are used in Sumba to seal a marriage contract and in funerals; it is not uncommon to wrap the body of a nobleman or woman in as many as 100 textile pieces.

The neighbouring island, Timor, is known for its brilliantly coloured warp ikat embellished by supplementary techniques such as *sotis*, a float weave using contrasting colours and usually woven into small panels. There is also the complex process of *buna*, which resembles heavy embroidery.

Another well-known warp ikat is the red, brown and white *ulos ragidup* (pattern of life) cloth of the Sumatran Bataks. This is presented by the father of the bride to the mother of the groom, who later presents the cloth to her daughter-in-law when she is seven months pregnant with her first child, as an *ulos ni tondi* or "soul cloth".

LURIK

References in old Javanese Hindu inscriptions (AD 851–82) mention striped and checked textiles that are today known as *lurik*. In Java, what remains of the *lurik*-weaving culture is centred in Jogja, Solo and Tuban, with the most obvious examples of *lurik* being the traditional coats worn by the palace guards at the Yogyakarta Keraton. However, the isolated Badui of West Java still weave *lurik* for their daily attire, and there are a handful of weavers in Banyumas, who call their cloth *kluwung*. Sadly, in Kudus in the northeastern part of Java, which once had a fairly wide range of motifs, only a few remain today. On Bali, these textiles are called keling and saudan, and remain ritually important.

Each motif on *lurik* cloths is defined by a specific palette and organisation of stripes and each has a symbolic meaning, is considered sacred, or thought to possess magical powers. Ancient rice paste-resist patterns on *lurik* textiles were probably the first Javanese batiks. *Lurik* is thought to pre-date tie-and-dye ikat textiles, though the origin of the latter is unclear.

Hand-woven *lurik* disappeared from favour with the advent of mechanised fabric factories producing a wider range of designs and colours at cheaper prices, but today it is experiencing a comeback thanks to a new generation of Indonesians who have great respect for old traditions.

Weft ikat (resist-patterning of the cross-wise threads) occurs primarily in Bali and the Islamic coastal trading areas of Gresik in East Java, Palembang and elsewhere in South Sumatra. Weft ikat is usually woven on a "fly shuttle" handloom.

The Palembang and Bangka weft ikat are extremely sophisticated, done on silk in rich tones of red, blue and yellow, often with supplementary gold threads in the weft. Indian, Javanese and Chinese motifs are all employed, sometimes simultaneously.

Today, weft ikat is a thriving cottage industry, with great amounts of cloth woven in bright colours and floral or geometric designs. A special weft ikat textile, *kain limar*, woven with gold threads, is worn by boys on the day of circumcision, a special rite among Muslim Palembang and Sumatran families.

Geringsing

The rare double ikat, known as *geringsing*, is made in Tenganan, a small village in East Bali, one of only three places in the world to produce this labour-intensive textile. The other two places are India and Japan. It can take several years just to complete a single *geringsing* piece. Both warp and weft threads are tied and dyed, then woven to produce an integrated motif on the finished fabric. Red being the predominant colour in most *geringsing*, the background is indigo overdyed with red to produce a midnight black.

Considered by the Balinese to be sacred, *geringsing* is used in many important ceremonies throughout the island, including tooth filings. In Tenganan, wearers of the cloth are thought to be protected from evil and illness, as *geringsing* means "without sickness".

Songket

Songket – cloth of gold or silver – is an ornately brocaded textile that has gold or silver threads worked into it. On a silk or cotton base, "floating" metallic weft threads are woven in to create a raised pattern that almost resembles embroidery. Areas with the best *songket* are Bali and Palembang, and those produced by the Minangkabau are sought after as well. Over

the years, the wearing of *songket* cloth became a sign of physical and spiritual blessings.

Palembang songket features gold threads woven onto bright red silk to form a fine geometrical pattern that often covers the entire cloth, while the Minangkabau's silver-threaded *songket* has a background of wine-red or black silk.

Once a favoured cloth by the royal class, *songket*, also known as *tanuk*, is worn today in a formal headdress by the Minangkabau women of West Sumatra. It serves as a display of wealth and the way it is folded also indicates which village the wearer is from.

Bark cloth

Bark cloths found among upland tribes in Kalimantan, Sulawesi and Papua display a high degree of artistry and techniques that date to the prehistoric era.

The Torajans boil and ferment the inner bark of *Pandanus*, mulberry or other trees before beating – with special wooden and stone mallets – the resultant pulp into extremely soft and pliable sheets. This cloth (*fuya*) is then dyed, painted or stamped using natural pigments.

Certain tribes in Kalimantan, Flores, Sulawesi and Timor produce warrior tunics from fibres by twining them, a simple process in which two weft fibres are alternately wrapped above and below a passive warp.

ABOVE, FROM LEFT: ikat from South Sulawesi; songket weaving at Sukarara weaving village, Lombok.

BATIK: ART ON FABRIC

Batik is the great leveller in Indonesian society. It is the formal attire of Jakarta urbanites and simple villagers working the paddy fields

Batik is one of the most prominent expressions of cultural identity in Indonesia. Nowhere in the world has the art of batik evolved into such high standards, fine-tuned over the centuries under the patronage of the Javanese royal courts. Today, the making and wearing of batik remains a source of national pride, a vital and unifying medium found in every conceivable form: sarong, dress, shirt, scarf, table-cover, wall hangings and more.

The Indonesian word *batik* (from *tik*, meaning dot) was originally a term used to describe the dye-resist technique; today, the term is used for both the process and the decorated fabric. The value of each piece is determined by the method of creation; the most highly prized and expensive is the labour-intensive *batik tulis* (literally "to write") using a canting tool. The best pieces are created by small cottage-industry workshops in Java. A cheaper alternative is the block-printed batik, produced using a metal printing stamp called *cap*. *Batik cetak* (printed batik) is mass-produced screen-printed fabric imitating traditional designs.

Each area of Java has its own unique style of batik which communicates ethnic identity and social status, while the folds of the *kain panjang* (waistcloth) convey one's gender. Special motifs with symbolic meaning, once reserved for the royal courts of Java, are today worn by all for ceremonies such as weddings, circumcisions, childbirth and burials.

ABOVE: the motifs created on the north coast of Java and Madura are known as *pesisir* batik. As exemplified by the Cirebon batik, pictured, foreign influence brought about by maritime trading introduced modifications in traditional Javanese motifs with bright colours and new designs.

BELOW: a wooden or copper block called *cap* is dipped into hot w and meticulously applied to the cloth, ensuring that wax left on the cloth by the edges of the block will not damage the motif.

LEFT: Javanese batiks are exported to other countries throughout the world, but are also found in every marketplace in Indonesia. A Torajan boy in Sulawesi shields himself from the weather with a *batik kain panjang* (sarong) from Java.

ABOVE: traditional methods of batik making *(canting)*, Brahama Tirta Sari Studio, Jogja.

CULTURAL TREASURES

When Unesco recognised Indonesian batik as a "Masterpiece of Oral and Intangible Heritage of Humanity" in 2009, the country swelled with pride and all citizens were requested to wear batik on Fridays to preserve this cultural icon. The result has been an enormous increase in the small and medium business local economy, as well as in exports, as designers began incorporating new fabrics, colours and motifs to meet the rising demand for the traditional cloth.

While traditional Javanese batiks range widely in colours and motifs from coast to coast, contemporary cloths can consist of classic designs in contemporary hues or entirely new creations influenced from abroad. Whether the preference is traditional or contemporary, however, collectors and fashion icons continue to acknowledge that the painstakingly hand-drawn *batik tulis* *(pictured above)* is textile art at its finest.

RIGHT: a traditional Javanese court motif is used on the batik sarongs of *wayang golek* puppets from West Java.

ABOVE: street stalls selling batik, Jogja. Mass-produced, printed fabrics, called *batik cetak*, are made into clothing, accessories and souvenirs.

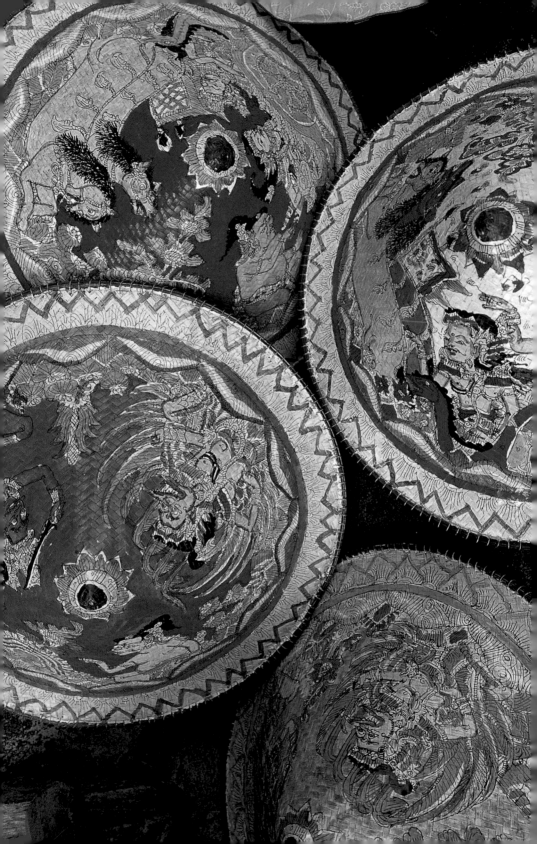

INDONESIA'S HANDICRAFTS AND ART

Many handicrafts produced by Indonesian artisans are exported worldwide, and art collectors flock to Jakarta auction houses to buy paintings produced by the new generation of Indonesian artists

As a crossroads for maritime trade, the Indonesian archipelago has for centuries been subject to foreign cultural influences, most notably Indian, Arab, Chinese and Dutch, as is evident in the art and culture of the Islamic coastal areas, the royal courts and in the architecture of ancient Hindu and Buddhist temples. In the remote interior and outer islands, many tribes lived in relative isolation until as recently as the 20th century, producing "primitive" art that was a medium of expression of their animistic beliefs.

Indonesian creative arts are primarily seen as a manifestation of the peoples' spiritual beliefs. As a result, traditional Indonesian art is surfeit with spiritually charged talismans. Creative arts serve to establish social and cultural identity, and fulfil social rites of passage such as birth, puberty, marriage and death.

In Central Java, the *loro blonyo*, painted wood statues that represent Dewi Sri, the goddess of fertility, and her consort Sedono, are placed in the home of newly married couples. Many objects of art are produced as the bride's dowry, such as the *mamuli* of Sumba, a decorative metal object given by the groom's family to the bride's family in exchange for textiles and other goods. A *mamuli* will also be placed in a grave for wealth in the afterlife.

Indonesia is a treasure trove of handcrafted items. Many artisans carry on the timeless tradition of fine craftsmanship, using traditional iconography passed on from one generation to the next. In many villages and tourist destinations, the main streets and local *pasar* (markets)

are full of artisans working at their trades in the open. Few other countries offer the opportunity of direct encounters with so many craftsmen practising skills that are centuries old.

The production process is usually divided between what is considered male and female. Male energy items use substances that are hard and strong or created with fire, as in the crafts of ironsmiths and woodcarvers. Female energy is expressed through what is soft and flexible, as in the weaving of textiles, basketwork and beadwork. There is no power struggle or competition between the sexes, but rather a desire to maintain the balance between the two in a unified symbol of an ordered universe.

LEFT: Javanese conical hats make good souvenirs.
RIGHT: demonic wooden faces from Bali.

In 1975 in a painting entitled Ken Dedes, named after a Majapahit Empire queen, Indonesian artist Jim Supangkat shocked Jakarta by depicting the revered lady bare-breasted and curvaceous, wearing unzipped jeans and high heels.

Puppets and masks

Indonesia is well known for its shadow puppets, or *wayang kulit*, flat puppets made of buffalo hide with finely chiselled, painted details, and rod puppets, or *wayang golek*, with carved and painted wooden faces. Puppets are typically

DAYAK BABY CARRIERS

Several ethnic groups, known collectively as Dayak, or jungle people, inhabit the Kalimantan interior and produce powerful and expressive art which maintains balance and harmony with the spirits of the supernatural world. Many Kenyah and Kayan Dayak baby-carriers are highly decorative works of traditional art. Carved out of wood with spiritually protective designs or made from rattan and embellished with ancient sacred beads and coins, they bear the claws and teeth of wild jungle animals and serve to protect the young child carried within. The amount of detail in the motif also indicates social stature.

used for performances of the *Ramayana* and *Mahabharata* Hindu epics, which impart complex yet subtle lessons in social behaviour. The oldest and best-known puppet makers are found in the environs of Yogyakarta (Jogja) and Surakarta (Solo), Central Java.

Ceremonial masks are found on many of the islands and believed to access the spiritual essence of the wearer's soul. Bali is famed for elaborately decorated and highly expressive *topeng*, carved softwood masks used in sacred temple ceremonial dramas. Cirebon masks from Java are used in theatrical pageants. Central and East Javanese masks celebrate the lives of past Javanese royalty. The Dayaks of Kalimantan make oversized wooden masks, *hudog*, with bulging eyes and large beaked noses, that are used in a ceremonial dance to keep maleficent spirits from taking over the "soul" of the rice. The Bataks of Lake Toba make carved masks and wooden hands that are symbols of their ethnic identity, copied from the *si gale-gale*, a life-sized puppet used in pre-Christian funeral ceremonies as artificial mourners for those who died childless.

Woodcarvings

Prized by museums and collectors throughout the world, many of Indonesia's woodcarvings are masterpieces of primitive art. Every island maintains a unique tradition, and today most produce countless "copies" of traditional sculptures, usually out of tropical hardwood. The woodcarvings of the Asmats of Papua are some of the most impressive of Indonesian primitive art. Decorative carved shields serve as vessels for ancestral spirits, and large spirit poles are the homes of the spirits of departed ancestors. In Sumatra, Batak ancestor statues called *si baso nabolon* are placed in the loft of a traditional house and serve as protectors against evil spirits. Kalimantan's Dayaks produce large carved wooden guardian poles, *hampatong*, with a stylised crouching ancestor figure, usually with an outstretched tongue; they are placed at the front of Dayak longhouses for protection against evil spirits.

The Javanese are known for their refined furniture-making skills, while the Balinese are known for their highly ornamental motifs found on doors, windows and posts.

From the 1600s, European and Chinese influences appeared in the form of enormous frame bcds used for wedding ceremonies, embellished with carved panels of flowers and birds and painted in the style of Chinese wedding beds. Today, furniture shops are filled with cabinets, beds, tables, chairs, chests and wall panels made of tropical woods.

Stone and metal

Religious stone statues of Hindu gods and Buddha have been carved for centuries in Java and Sumatra (excellent examples are found in Jakarta's National Museum). Newly made copies of these masterpieces are still produced in Central and East Java, as well as Bali. Batubulan

empu or master-smiths left today, and this dying art form is the preserve of a few ironsmiths in Central and West Java as well as in Kusamba, Bali, where a new *keris* can be commissioned.

Kalimantan and the Nusa Tenggara islands produce a functional cutlass, or *parang*, which usually has an ornate hilt of carved wood. The scabbard is sometimes decorated with old Dutch coins, rattan trim and the teeth of wild boar. At one time, *parang ilang* or *mandau* were used for head-hunting by Dayaks. Today, the finest *parang* are used ceremonially. Swordsmiths forge *parang* from scrap metal and employ bellows; the blade is repeatedly

village on Bali is dedicated to the creation of stone statues. Fashioned in *paras*, a soft ashy stone, Hindu gods are produced alongside fanciful garden statues. On other islands such as Nias, stone statues of ancestors are found.

Metalwork was introduced to Indonesia during the Dong Son Bronze Age around the 3rd century BC. To this day, metal items are produced either by forging or by wax-casting. One of the most revered examples of metal art is the ornamental dagger, *keris*, decorated with silver, gold or precious stones and thought to possess magical powers. Unfortunately, there are few

beaten, folded and hardened in cold river water.

Gold- and silversmithery have a long history in Indonesia. Early travellers were impressed by the riches and quality workmanship of the royal courts: parasol fittings, the bejewelled golden *keris* and exquisite ornate boxes fashioned of gold. Traditional jewellery is an important part of the bride price and each island produces its own distinctive style, ranging from the delicate filigree work of Bali and Java to the bold and expressive beaten gold of the Outer Islands. Indonesian gold- and silversmiths are masters of several decorative and labour-intensive techniques such as *repoussé* or embossing. For centuries, Balinese royal courts have expressed sacred and temporal power through art.

ABOVE, FROM LEFT: artisan crafting furniture from bamboo; stone-carving at Batubalan, Bali.

Kamasan village is still a centre for Balinese court arts, producing objects of silver and gold for ceremonial use. Statues of Hindu deities, offering bowls and containers for holy water, are embellished with intricate designs and mythological figures. A thriving business is modern silverwork for the tourist market. Celuk village in Bali is lined with rows of homes and shops producing silver jewellery and objects, while in Java, the silver centre is Kota Gede near Jogja. Most pieces are made with 90–95 percent pure silver, some set with semi-precious stones imported from Kalimantan.

Basketry and pottery

Indonesia has an inexhaustible supply of useful plant products derived from bamboo, coconut palms, rattan, *pandan* (screw pine), breadfruit trees, reeds and grasses. Basketry serves as a functional craft; fishing traps, baskets, backpacks, hats and all manner of useful containers are made. Men help to gather the materials, but it is traditionally the women who work the weaving or plaiting, usually with great speed and aesthetic and technical refinement.

In Lombok, bark and rattan boxes are used to transport wedding clothes, while large rectangular or round boxes made of palm leaf are decorated with split seashells and used for storing rice. The baskets of Sumatra are embellished with fine gold leaf and lacquer, while those made in Kalimantan display superb rattan palm-weaving skills.

Pottery has been made since Neolithic times. Earthenware vessels such as bowls and

kendi (water pitchers), decorative roof gables, animals and figures of Hindu deities serve both a functional and a decorative purpose. Terracotta pottery is usually only produced in villages that specialise in the craft and only by women who make the clay vessels. Lombok pottery, with entire villages now producing the high-quality earthenware, is exported worldwide.

Textiles

The making of high-quality handloom textiles *(see page 97)*, such as ikats, is the work of women and a skilled art, as is batik *tulis*. Today,

LOMBOK POTTERY

Lombok is well known for many of its traditional handicrafts, in particular earthenware pottery. With the assistance of the Indonesian and New Zealand governments, the Lombok Crafts Project was established two decades ago. Three villages initially received funds to build workplaces, warehouses and showrooms, and were supplied with technical and design advice as well as marketing and business ideas. The result was a thriving cottage industry producing high-quality decorative and functional pottery that continues today, with many women in Banyumulek and Masbagik villages *(see page 271)* owning lucrative businesses.

The grey-brown clay used for the pots is obtained by women from local riverbeds. They work it by hand, using a round stone and wooden paddle instead of a potter's wheel, a method that has changed little over the centuries. Geometric patterns are incised with a sharp bamboo stick.

The pots are left in the sun to set before being fired. Placed in a pit in the ground, they are covered with rice straw and husks that burn out quickly and leave a thick ash coating that retains the heat for the final stages of firing. A second firing using coconut husks, dung and wood turns the pottery jet black. After it cools, the finished product turns a rich red-brown.

Comic strips drawn by Indonesian artists appear in newspapers in Jakarta and Malaysia. Today's comic artists are adept at social commentary, particularly regarding the foibles of the government, which was forbidden until 1998.

mass-produced "copies" of traditional work are made for the tourist market using quick chemical dyes, and are found in most hotel shops and markets.

Beadwork is associated with agricultural fertility and femininity, and except for Sulawesi's Torajans, all beadwork is done by women. The Dayak regard beads as having magical power and use them in the necklaces worn by shamans and to embellish ritual objects such as baby-carriers. Antique beads came from as far away as Venice, introduced by the Portuguese and Dutch, while today most of the beads are from and Japan.

Indonesian art

In Java, one of the first modern painters of note was Raden Saleh (1816–80), who spent 20 years in European courts and later painted some memorable portraits of the royal families of Central Java.

In Bali, paintings were of religious objects commissioned as decorations for palaces and temples until the early 20th century. When European artists Walter Spies and Rudolph Bonnet promoted painting as an art form in Ubud, the Balinese began to depict naturalistic scenes of everyday life for the first time. Various local artist associations developed thereafter, including the Pita Maha Artists of Ubud (1936–42) and in the 1960s, the Young Artists group, which is known for its portrayal of Balinese life in vivid oils, inspired by Dutch artist Arie Smit.

Simultaneously, Yogyakarta and Bandung became the two crucibles of modern Indonesian art, and many accomplished artists appeared on the scene. Soedjojono (1913–86), Hendra Gunawan (1918–83) and Affandi (1907–88), for example, were strongly united in expressing their desire

for independence from colonial rule and in propagating a strong national awareness. After the Dutch left, Suharto's regime quashed all freedom of expression, and underground art colonies flourished. When his iron-fisted rule ended in 1998, artists were at last at liberty to express themselves openly, which they have taken great pleasure in doing ever since.

Today, there are there are two government-owned fully accredited art universities – one in Jogja and the other in Denpasar – as well as an arts high school in Solo. Together with the Fine Arts department of the Bandung

Institute of Technology, they are producing performing and visual artists who are creating cutting-edge themes with a freshness not often seen in the West.

In these cities, public spaces and galleries brim with expressions of unfettered enthusiasm on every possible topic. Jogja, in particular, gives artists – who see themselves as autonomous, removed from government or museum support – plenty of elbow room in which to discourse, debate, work and display. At the same time, a burgeoning art-auction market has evolved, with wealthy Indonesians joining foreigners as collectors. Agus Suwage and Entang Wiharso are both currently collectibles of international acclaim.

Above, From Left: an oversize water jar from Lombok; 'two women in a garden' at the Neka Art Museum, Ubud.

ARCHITECTURE

Architectural designs tracing Indonesia's
evolution from the 9th century until the present
reflect its rich history and cultural heritage

Indonesian architecture is a reflection of its various cultures, the influence of foreign arrivals and regional adaptions of universal styles. Its history can be traced through the remains of the ancient temples and bathing places of Hindu-Buddhist rulers, the mosques introduced by Islamic traders, the European influence brought by colonists, and the palaces of the last sultans. It is remarkable, however, that in many regions traditional houses (*rumah adat*) are still being constructed today in styles similar to those used centuries ago.

Traditional houses

Although all of Indonesia's varied ethnic groups have their own versions of *rumah adat*, many share similarities that are believed to have originated in Taiwan 6,000 years ago among the Austronesian group of related-language speakers that spread throughout Southeast Asia, the Pacific and Madagascar.

Built without nails from organic materials that grew nearby, the houses had four main hardwood posts, each with a symbolic meaning, and steep, thatched roofs suitable for shading residents from the tropical sun in the dry season and from torrential downpours when it rained. Most were also raised on stilts for ventilation and as protection from rival clans and marauding beasts in the thickly forested surrounds. *Rumah adat* had a separate cooking area, usually at the back of the house, which consisted of a stone base where meals were cooked in earthenware pottery over a wood

ABOVE, FROM LEFT: Tongkonan dwelling, Tana Toraja, Sulawesi; Batak architecture on Samosir Island, Sumatra.

fire. Strangers would never have been invited into the family quarters of the house, but would be greeted on a verandah or, if there was none, a small front room at the entrance, until sufficient meetings confirmed whether the visitor was friend or foe.

Because natural materials suitable for building were abundant in the forests, houses were more or less disposable. When the bamboo, thatching or timber began to rot, a new house was built and the old one left to disintegrate, or by that time perhaps area game had played out and hunter-gatherers simply moved on. The entire community played a role in building a new house, with each member having a particular speciality.

Borobudur's reliefs feature depictions of daily life, including dwellings, that provide a valuable record of Java's 9th-century architecture. This would otherwise have been lost, due to the perishable construction materials used.

Another recurring feature in *rumah adat* was communal living, with the house being the primary focus for extended families and communities for social contact as well as for protection from tangible and intangible forces, such as spirits. Examples of community houses can still be seen among the Dayaks in Kalimantan,

Hindu-Buddhist architecture

The examples of Hindu-Buddhist architecture (9th–15th century) that remain are temples – primarily in Central and East Java – and royal bathing pools in Bali. Many others had wooden frameworks that have long since collapsed. As the great empires of that era lapsed and structures were abandoned, many fell victim to looting, either by the local people for construction materials or by treasure hunters. A number of them were also lost to volcanic eruptions. In Java, it is still a common occurrence for a farmer ploughing his field to unearth a statue or part of a wall that belonged to one of these buildings.

the North Sumatran Bataks, the Torajans in Sulawesi and in the Mentawai islands.

There are other distinctive features among Indonesia's ethnic groups. The Minangkabaus and Torajans favour enormous roofs shaped like boats or saddles, and their buildings are also recognisable for their intricate exterior carvings. The elaborate, stilted *lumbung* (rice barns) of the Sasak on Lombok are known for their bonnet-shaped roofs. The *rumah adat* of Java and Bali are not built on stilts. However, the pyramid-shaped roofs of Java's *joglo* and *limasan* houses contain the same four, symbolic hardwood piles used in other traditional houses, while Balinese homes are a collection of buildings within a high-walled compound.

Although this form of architecture was ultimately inspired by Indian styles, local influences created a uniquely Indonesian form. The *candi* (temple, shrine or mausoleum), to take just one example, was usually a towering stone structure built on a base. At the top was a stepped-pyramid roof *(meru)*, as seen in Bali. These structures were symbolic representations of Gunung Meru, which in Hindu-Buddhist mythology is the abode of the gods. And each of these *candi* – as exemplified on the heights of Central Java's Dieng plateau and at Prambanan – had niches containing statues of the deities to whom the shrine was dedicated, representative of the caves where the gods were believed to reside on holy Gunung Meru.

It is interesting in Central and East Java, where the greatest number of temples remain, to be able to see how the architecture evolved. Java's oldest temples, dating from the early 8th century, are found on the cool heights of the Dieng plateau. It is believed that there were once as many as 400 *candi* here, but only eight are left standing. Dieng's temples are small and rather plain, and the *kala* heads – the toothy mythical demon seen over Balinese doors today – are not particularly ornate. Yet a century later, the magnificent Hindu Roro Jonggrang rose out of the Prambanan plains around AD 856. At about the same time, Buddhist Borobudur

structures that appear to have been dwellings are made of brick rather than organic materials and are very similar to the houses seen throughout Bali today. By 1450, the Hindu kingdoms had been pushed eastwards to Bali, replaced by Islamic empires.

Islamic influence

Beginning in the 12th century, Islam entered the archipelago with traders in coastal areas of Sumatra and Java. As with Hindu-Buddhist places of worship, the concept of mosques may have come from afar, but the architecture was strictly Indonesian, as existing architectural

was constructed (AD 750–850), and instead of being set on a stone base, a natural plateau was selected, the purpose of both types of base being to elevate the structures, making them appear even more magnificent than they already were.

Shortly after Borobudur was completed, temple architecture disappears in Central Java, shifts to Sumatra, and reappears in East Java in 1250. The structures almost continually being uncovered at Trowulan, even in the 21st century, are believed to be the 14th-century Majapahit Empire capital, a large city with public bathing places and water systems. For the first time,

styles were modified to meet Muslim requirements. New structures also had to be added, such as cemeteries, because cremation – the preferred method of disposing of the dead until that time – was forbidden by Islam.

By the 17th century the "new" religion had penetrated most of the archipelago, with trading ports and palaces the main architectural focus, leaving rural housing much the same as it had always been. Early mosques had four central posts like *rumah adat*, supporting a pyramidal roof, similar to the Javanese *joglo* and *limasan* houses, and the roofs were multi-tiered, as are contemporary Balinese temples. Domes did not appear atop mosques until the 19th century. The Grand Mosques at Aceh (1881)

ABOVE, FROM LEFT: Sasak rice barn, Lombok; Taman Tirtagangga water park, East Bali.

and Medan (1906) appear to be the beginning of the Moorish-style domed architecture, and since then Indonesian mosques have followed global Islamic design.

Cemeteries were placed behind mosques or on top of a hill, which can be traced to an ancient Austronesian tradition of reverence to ancestors. Surrounding mosques with walls provided a link to Java's Hindu-Buddhist past, with the walls being similar to those that surround modern Balinese temple complexes. The Grand Mosques in Demak (1474) and Kudus (1549) are two of Indonesia's oldest, and it is thought that the minaret at Kudus was the watchtower of an earlier Hindu temple. Kudus's minaret is not used for the vocal calls to prayer usually associated with mosques but houses the large drum traditionally used in Indonesia to summon the faithful. Similarly, drum towers exist throughout Bali, though not in mosques; the one at Pura Penataran Sasih at Pejeng contains a 2,000-year-old bronze drum from the Dong Son era.

Since royal palaces (*keraton* in Javanese, or *istana* in Indonesian) were at the centre of religions, they also adopted some Islamic features. The only *keratons* that remain are less than 200 years old, so it is not known how Islam affected early royal architecture. However, judging from existing examples in Java and Bali, it appears that Islam did little to influence them. None of the palaces were grand affairs, rather their power was expressed by symbolic alignment with water sources and mountains and with symmetry. The most imposing structure in the Yogyakarta *keraton* is the *pendopo*, a pavilion restricted to honoured guests where the ruler sat during ceremonial occasions, which has a traditional Javanese tiered roof supported by four posts, as in *joglo* houses. The residences surrounding the *keraton* within the inner walls of the city were occupied by the sultan's immediate family members and aristocracy. Beyond the walls were those who had regular dealings with the court, and outside that was the rural population, placing the sultan in the centre of the "universe".

While the *keratons* at Yogyakarta, Surakarta and Cirebon are generally Javanese, they have also borrowed elements of other styles. A gateway at the Cirebon *keraton* is repeated in both Yogyakarta and Surakarta, with arched entries from the Hindu-Buddhist era, a "cloud and rain" motif adopted from the Chinese, heavy emphasis on Javanese symbolism and

European gazebos. Balinese palaces resemble Javanese *keratons* somewhat, with a central pavilion (*bale*, in Balinese) placing the king at the centre and symbolic symmetry to emphasise power and sovereignty. At the Ubud palace, the central pavilion was replaced with a courtyard and a building where the king resided. At Karangasem, the pavilion "floated" (*bale kambang*) in a pond.

Colonial architecture

In the 16th century, new architectural features began to appear in Indonesian ports, introduced by European merchants and adventurers. In some cases new elements were integrated with local traditions; in others, they remained purely European. The best examples of Portuguese architecture are scattered throughout Timor. The Protestant church in Semarang (built 1778–1814) is mixed, with a Byzantine cupola and Baroque bell towers.

At the onset, the Dutch emulated cities from their homeland without factoring in the tropical climate. At Batavia (Jakarta), canals were constructed and city townhouses with few windows were built in rows, and all were enclosed in solid walls as protection from native revolts and attacks from other Europeans. The fortress housed the governor, officers, barracks, offices, a church and European merchants. Towns grew up beyond the fortress walls.

Many examples of Dutch architecture remain, particularly in Java: railway stations in neo-Gothic style still stand in Semarang and Jakarta, along with bank buildings, warehouses and trading centres in Jakarta, Semarang, Surabaya and a few in Medan, Makassar and Singaraja. Dutch tree-lined avenues are clearly visible in Bandung. As the cities grew, wealthy merchants began building country estates to escape the congestion. Better adapted to the climate, a new type of colonial architecture was born called the Indies Style. The four posts and the pyramid roof with overhanging eaves of the *joglo* were incorporated, and verandahs and porticoes appeared. European elements, such as neoclassical columns around the verandahs, were added, along with typical 18th-century Dutch-style windows for ventilation.

Modern architecture

By the 20th century, the Dutch had introduced many other architectural styles, such as Art Deco, best seen in Bandung. Modernist buildings, popular in Europe at the time, were the trend. Contemporary Indonesian architects were of two types: those who had been trained overseas and apprentices who had learned at home under the tutorship of foreigners. Thus, after Indonesia's independence architecture remained Modernist for several decades, with then-president Sukarno determined to erect modern cities equal to those in Europe and America. Factories, airports, office buildings and housing were constructed in rapid succession to keep up with the demands of a growing economy. The trend continued under Suharto's rule, and by the 1970s downtown Jakarta resembled every other major city in the world.

By the 1980s, following a boom in world oil prices which were directed towards development, a new generation of Indonesian architects was encouraged to create a national identity. There was a return to incorporating traditional styles, but it was limited to adding one or two local features to Modernist buildings, such as the multi-tiered roofs on the University of Indonesia. Taman Mini Indonesia Indah (Beautiful Indonesia in Miniature) theme park in Jakarta was constructed during this era, housing examples of indigenous architecture from each of its provinces to promote the country's rich cultural diversity. While this has at least preserved local designs, it did little to influence a new national identity, apart from resorts frequented by tourists with expectations of local environments.

As Indonesia continues to urbanise in the 21st century, its architects have kept up with global trends, and commercial skylines are filled with postmodern glass buildings, innova-

tive designs and atrocities, as in all major cities. Today's innovative Indonesian architects are taking environmentally-friendly designs to new levels, a trend that is hoped to continue.

CHINESE ARCHITECTURE

A few of the Chinese shophouses, of the type still seen in Singapore, survive in parts of Jakarta. They are well adapted for the tropics with high ceilings, ventilation grilles, airwells and extended eaves. Various old *klenteng* (Chinese temples) remain as places of worship in Jakarta, Yogyakarta, Semarang and Banten, as well as some outside Java, such as in Singaraja (Bali). Their symmetrically aligned courtyards and walled compounds follow *feng shui* principles which align buildings with natural landscape features. Roofs are swept up at the ends and are typically decorated with dragons. Their red colour – identified with fire and blood – symbolises prosperity, good fortune and virtue.

ABOVE, FROM LEFT: Medan's Mesjid Raya; the Keraton at Jogja features a range of architectural styles.

AMAZING BIODIVERSITY

Indonesia's volcanoes and forests, unique flora
and fauna and plethora of marine life make it
an ideal destination for outdoor activities and
adventures

The great tropical rainforests of Indonesia comprise some of the world's oldest and richest natural habitats, home to a fabulous variety of flora and fauna, including many species found nowhere else on earth. Indicative of this wealth of biodiversity is the fact that new species are continuously being discovered in the jungles of Papua, Sumatra and Sulawesi. There are also large areas of pristine mangrove forest and swamp, montane forests and savannahs, and thousands of miles of coastline harbouring colourful coral reefs.

The deep oceanic trench between Bali and Lombok that extends northwards to the east of Borneo marks a separation in the types of mammals and birds found in Indonesia. Named the Wallace Line in honour of the great 19th-century naturalist Sir Alfred Russel Wallace, to the west of the line the fauna is of Asian origin; that in Papua and some of Maluku's islands are Australian; and in the area in between (Sulawesi, Nusa Tenggara and parts of Maluku) are species of both origins. *(See photo feature page 320.)*

West of the Wallace Line

Kalimantan and Sumatra contain Indonesia's greatest expanses of jungle. Together with the forests of Sulawesi, Maluku and Papua, they are second in size only to the Amazon and house an astonishing variety of animals and birds. The Asian fauna west of the Wallace Line includes large mammals such

as elephants in Sumatra and rhinos in both Sumatra and Java, the Javan rhino being one of the world's rarest creatures. Big cats include leopards and small populations of tigers in Sumatra. Orang-utans are found in Sumatra and Kalimantan, along with gibbons, slow lorises and tarsiers in the mid-storey. Along the riverbanks in Kalimantan there are proboscis monkeys that chatter noisily and belly-flop from tree to tree.

Leopards also inhabit the Javan forests, and several smaller cats can be found in Sumatra. Kalimantan's jungles still shelter a few clouded leopards and reclusive sun bears, and Sumatra has Malayan tapirs, though they are rarely seen.

LEFT: young orang-utan at Camp Leakey in central Kalimantan. **RIGHT:** Gunung Bromo, with Gunung Semeru in the background.

On Java and Bali endemic birds include the Javan hawk eagle, Javan scops owl, Javan kingfisher and Javan barbet, but the rarest of all the avifauna is the Bali starling, with, until fairly recently, only 25 individuals left in the wild. Sumatra and Kalimantan host spectacular hornbills; the red jungle fowl lives in the forests of Sumatra, Java and Sulawesi; ornate Argus pheasants perform elaborate mating dances in Kalimantan; and the strutting green peacock is found only on Java.

These and other species can be seen in western Indonesia's national parks: 12 on Java and eight on Kalimantan. There is one national park on Bali and 11 on Sumatra.

The transition zone

Moving east from Lombok into Nusa Tenggara, the climate becomes more dry and lowland jungles are replaced by deciduous monsoon forests and open savannah. This transition zone between Asia and Australia, formed by explosive volcanic eruptions and with deep channels between the islands, has few large mammals, but birds of both origins are abundant. Lesser sulphur-crested cockatoos, sunbirds, drongos and bee-eaters

NATIONAL PARKS

A Forestry Department *surat jalan* (travel permit) is required before entering a national park. Most will have an on-site Forestry Department office, where permits can be issued on the spot. Some of the most popular parks are:

Ujung Kulon, West Java. Best accessed by chartered boat from Carita beach, a Unesco World Heritage Site and habitat of the Javan rhino. The park includes Anak Krakatau.

Bromo-Tengger-Semeru, East Java. Reached from the north by road from Pasuruan, home to active volcanoes Bromo and Semeru. Spectacular scenery.

Bali Barat, West Bali. Arrive via northern or southern trans-Bali highway. First-rate diving and snorkelling at Menjangan island; birdwatching; trekking.

Komodo, Nusa Tenggara. Take a chartered boat or public ferry from Labuanbajo, Flores or Sape, Sumbawa. A World Heritage and a World Network of Biosphere Reserves Site, it protects the Komodo dragon.

Gunung Leuser, North Sumatra. Transit through Medan. A World Heritage and World Network of Biosphere Reserves Site. Sumatran orang-utans, tapirs and other forest wildlife.

Tanjung Puting, Central Kalimantan. Fly to Pangkalanbun, then drive to Kumai and finally go upriver by chartered boat. A World Network of Biosphere Reserves Site with good populations of orang-utans and proboscis monkeys.

are representative, with the most unusual species being a mound-building megapode. The coral reefs in this region are particularly rich, with at least 1,000 fish species and more than 250 hard corals found in Komodo National Park alone.

The most remarkable creature in Nusa Tenggara is the world's largest monitor lizard, *Varanus komodoesnsis*, reaching up to 3 metres (10ft) in length and weighing up to 150kg (331lbs). The number of Komodo dragons has dwindled to fewer than 3,000 confined to a few islands in the park.

In addition to Komodo, there are four other national parks in Nusa Tenggara. Two of them surround volcanoes: the active Gunung Rinjani on Lombok and dormant Kelimutu on Flores. There are 15 major volcanoes in this region, the most prominent historically being Gunung Tambora on Sumbawa *(see panel page 277)*.

Endemic oddities

Many exceptions to Wallace's transition zone theory occur on Sulawesi, Indonesia's most biologically interesting island. Most of the island's mammals, including deer, monkeys, some civets and some tarsiers, are of obvious Asian origin; however, the two types of cuscus found here – the lesser and the bear cuscus – are marsupial and typically Australian. Additionally, some of Sulawesi's species are endemic and occur nowhere else in the world *(see page 320)*.

In Lore Lindu National Park are the world's smallest buffalo, anoa, and the curved-tusked babirusa – literally "pig-deer". Thought to be extinct until the late 1970s, the Sulawesi palm civet still exists, and there are at least five endemic species of macaques. Sulawesi's endemic avifauna includes two species of hornbills – the spectacular Sulawesi hornbill has a brilliantly colourful beak and casque. Among the 70 or so species originating from both the Asian and the Australian regions are kingfishers, drongos, babblers, cockatoos and sunbirds.

The wide variety of marine life at Bunaken National Marine Park *(see page 335)* ranges from bannerfish, orbicular batfish and bumphead

parrotfish to massive Napoleon wrasse, dogtooth tuna, pilot whales and giant green sea turtles. Seahorses, ghost pipe fish, mimic octopus and many varieties of nudibranch dot the shallows.

Sulawesi's mountainous interior is dotted with enormous lakes and forests. Situated on the island's extreme north arm are eight major volcanoes. Eight national parks protect Sulawesi's treasures: Bunaken and Wakatobi are marine preserves attracting serious divers, and Lore Lindu is a World Network of Biosphere Reserves site.

East of Sulawesi is Maluku, the fabled Spice

Islands that first drew Europeans to Indonesia. These days the area is best known for its incredible snorkelling and diving, with giant sea turtles and dugongs sharing the sea with colourful reef fish. Crocodiles, pythons and monitor lizards lurk topside, along with the endangered blue-tongued Ambon lizard related to the Australian sailfin variety.

Many of the islands are richly forested and house a plethora of birds: the salmoncrested cockatoo, red-breasted pygmy parrot, red-flanked lorikeet, red lorry and a rare bird of paradise, to name a few. Near the Banda Sea seabirds include masked, red-footed and brown boobies, frigate birds and red-tailed tropicbirds.

ABOVE, FROM LEFT: the forests of Kalimantan provide a habitat for sun bears; a green turtle.

There are several volcanoes and two national parks in Maluku, Aketajawe-Lolobata and Manusela, both established to protect marine life.

Eastern Indonesia's Australasian species

Remote Papua, the western half of New Guinea island, together with some of the eastern Maluku islands have a floral and faunal diversity equal to that of Kalimantan, with at least half of the known species endemic.

In the interior, Papua's terrain comprises thickly forested hills and montane jungles, with magnificent valleys stretching in between. Indonesia's highest mountain, Puncak Jaya (formerly called Carstenz Pyramid), is in the Lorentz National Park, towering 4,884 metres (16,024ft) and capped with permanent ice fields. In the south, in Wasur National Park, expansive savannahs, lowland forests and extensive swamplands dominate the landscape. All coastal areas are fringed by virtually untouched mangroves.

> Managed tourism can help conservation. Human presence deters illegal poachers and loggers, and tourist revenues can be used to maintain park security.

So large and dense is the Papuan forest that new species are still being discovered. In the Foja Mountains west of Jayapura, 8 million hectares (nearly 20 million acres) of undeveloped

rainforest make it a veritable Eden for species generation and as a carbon storehouse.

Also in Papuan forests are monotremes – egg-laying mammals such as echidnas – as well as marsupials: terrestrial and tree varieties of kangaroos, and wallabies, possums, large-eyed cuscus, and bandicoots, with many of the marsupials occupying the role monkeys hold in western Indonesia forests.

"Magnificent" barely begins to describe the avifauna, with lowland forests dominated by noisy cockatoos and hornbills. At slightly higher altitudes are flocks of 40 species of parrots and the large black palm cockatoo.

Waterbirds such as spoonbills, magpie geese, black-necked storks and cranes wade in the swamplands of Wasur National Park. Most spectacular of all are Papua's 42 species of birds of paradise, 36 of which are native to the island of New Guinea. The largest bird is the flightless cassowary, which frequents forests where ample fruit can be found.

Among divers, Papua's best-known national park is Cenderawasih Bay off the northwest tip of the Bird's Head peninsula where the Indian and Pacific oceans meet. The Nature Conservancy has recorded more than 1,000 fish species, 540 types of coral and 700 molluscs here, with new species being discovered on a regular basis.

INDONESIA'S RAINFORESTS

Two thousand years ago, tropical rainforests are thought to have covered as much as 12 percent of the Earth's land surface, but today the figure is below 5 percent, and falling. The largest unbroken stretch of rainforest is found in the Amazon basin of South America, with Brazil containing about one-third of the world's remaining tropical rainforests. The only other large tracts are found in central Africa and Indonesia, and the still-extensive jungles of Sumatra, Kalimantan and Papua New Guinea are the last refuge for many endangered species. Elsewhere in South East Asia, forest cover has been reduced into a patchwork of smaller forests, where species diversity is reduced.

Conservation in Action

Indonesians have enthusiastically embraced the need to protect their environmental riches and the results are beginning to show

From the time the phrase "climate change" was coined, Indonesia, due to its enormous expanse of forests and its long history of rampant illegal logging, has been top of the hit list for activists, and their efforts are beginning to pay off. In the last five years the government has implemented legislation and law enforcement and has improved forest management to ensure that all timber and its various products intended for export are produced from legal and sustainably harvested sources.

In addition, recent studies have shown that only 20 percent of deforestation is the result of the conversion of forest land to large-scale commercial agriculture – for example palm oil plantations. Their findings have tended, instead, to attribute environmental degradation to the millions of poor people who use the forests for food, fuel and shelter. The many NGOs working in Indonesia are now focusing on training villagers to do other jobs, thereby improving livelihoods and reducing greenhouse emissions caused by forest destruction and degradation.

In 2009, President Yudhoyono linked ocean environments to climate change at the World Ocean Conference in Manado, Sulawesi, and was successful in directing international attention on this issue. With some 55,000km (34,000 miles) of coastline and sharing maritime borders with 10 countries, Indonesia took the lead in setting up the Coral Triangle Initiative and quickly established a protected area of 3.5 million hectares (8.6 million acres) in the Savu Sea, a migration route for half the world's whale species and vast expanses of rare corals.

Marine conservation also includes protecting shorelines from erosion by planting extensive mangrove forests to reduce shoreline abrasion and seawater intrusion, which are exacerbated by climate change and can help lessen the effects of tsunamis.

Natural disasters greatly impact on Indonesia, which has more than its share of earthquakes, volcanic eruptions, landslides and tsunamis. Hardest hit are the poor – the vast majority of the population – who live in vulnerable areas on the coast, on mountain slopes prone to mudslides and on low-lying flood plains.

Growing awareness of environmental issues, particularly by young Indonesians, is beginning to make a difference. Green groups, bike-to-work programmes, school nature clubs and Scouts groups are gaining

popularity. There is an increasing number of backpacker organisations comprising young professionals, and Reduce, Reuse, Recycle campaigns instigated by corporate responsibility initiatives are influencing neighbourhoods to pitch in. Also, an increased demand for organic produce is encouraging farmers to return to traditional, pre-chemical practices.

There remains a great deal of work to be done, but Indonesians have proven themselves to be fast learners. More focus on reducing poverty and increasing education will impact on many problematic areas of this rapidly developing country, and protecting the environment is certainly one of these.

ABOVE, FROM LEFT: the crimson sunbird, an eastern Indonesian species; logging in Kalimantan.

WORLD HERITAGE SITES

Indonesia is unique in that it is the only country in Southeast Asia that has seven of its landmarks declared as Unesco World Heritage Sites

The United Nations has listed seven of Indonesia's natural and cultural wonders as United Nations Educational, Scientific and Cultural Organisation (Unesco) World Heritage sites, one of which, in Sumatra, is earmarked as a Natural Heritage in Danger.

The Buddhist **Borobudur** monument *(see page 163)* in Central Java, built from around AD 788, was "rediscovered" in 1814 buried in volcanic ash. Its restoration was completed by Unesco and Indonesia between 1973 and 1983.

Prambanan *(see page 168)*, also in Central Java, is the largest Hindu temple complex in Indonesia. Completed in AD 856, some 244 temple remains are still found in the outer compound.

Ujung Kulon National Park *(see page 147)*, West Java, has fewer than 50 endangered Javan (Lesser) one-horned rhinoceros and Java's largest lowland rainforests, housing hornbills, deer, wild boar, black panthers and green turtles. The offshore Krakatau island is part of the park.

Komodo National Park *(see page 279)* in Nusa Tenggara is primarily the home of the protected 2,740 carnivorous monitor lizards known as the Komodo dragons.

Lorentz National Park, Papua *(see page 359)*, the largest protected area in Southeast Asia, is one of the few areas in the world to have snow-capped mountains in a tropical environment. Its extraordinary biodiversity supports rare animals such as the spotted cuscus.

In 2011, three of Sumatra's national parks were named **Tropical Rainforest Heritage of Sumatra** for their great potential for long-term conservation of the distinctive and diverse biota. Sadly, it bears the label "World Heritage in Danger".

BELOW: the six lower terraces at Borobudur are carved with Buddhist bas relief scenes. Three upper tiers with 72 lattice-work miniature stupas each contain Buddha images that are unique in Buddhist art.

LEFT: at the Prambanan temple complex, niches within temples house statues, while exterior walls are decorated in reliefs from the Hindu Ramayana epic. Pictured here is Candi Plaosan.

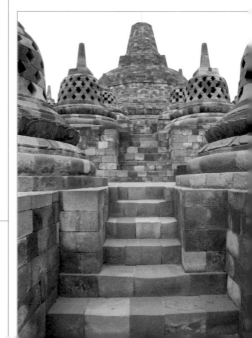

ABOVE: the Sangiran *Homo Erectus* site, Central Java.

SANGIRAN EARLY MAN SITE

In 1891, on the banks of the Bengawan Solo River near Surakarta (Solo), Central Java, Dutchman Eugene Dubois unearthed one of the world's first known specimens of *Homo Erectus* (upright man), the "missing link" that proved Darwin's evolution theory. The more complete remains (sometimes called Solo Man) found by G.H.R. von Koenigswald in 1936 are now thought to be as many as a million years older than Dubois's find, as old as those discovered in Kenya.

Many other fossils have been unearthed in the area, ranging from 1.2 million to 500,000 years old. Unesco proclaimed Sangiran a World Heritage Site in 1996, declaring this one of the most important places in the world for understanding human evolution.

BOVE: Lorentz National Park is home to numerous isolated tribes, cluding the Amungme, Western Dani, Nduga, Ngalik, Asmat empan, Komoro), Mimika and Somohai. It is one of the most ologically diverse national parks in the world.

ELOW: in 1883, Krakatau exploded and sunk, sank, re-emerging in 27 as Anak Krakatau, "Child of Krakatau". It remains active with equent eruptions, and is part of Ujung Kulon National Park.

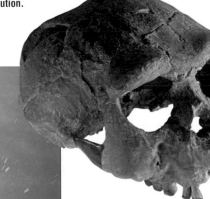

ABOVE: the skull of "Java Man" is displayed at Jakarta's National Museum.

PLACES

A detailed guide to Indonesia's principal sites, cross-referenced by number to the maps

Indonesia's choice of attractions and terrains is so vast that it has to be experienced to be believed. It is a country of more than 18,000 islands, large and small, which wraps itself around one-eighth of the world's circumference.

Java is home to nearly half of the nation's population, no mystery considering the land's lush volcanic landscape. Some of the country's most elegant aesthetic endeavours are here: music, dance and drama, textiles and antiquities. The capital city, Jakarta, a traffic-clogged metropolis, is not especially beautiful by day, but at night its electrified skyline can be elegant. To many Indonesians, it is the city of hope, the one place that best exemplifies a prosperous, forward-looking nation.

Sumatra is where spice traders first anchored after passage from India and China. The terrain is not especially good for farming, but there are verdant

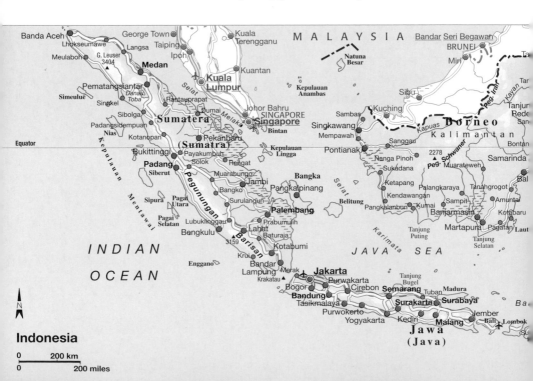

Indonesia

| 0 | 200 km |
| 0 | 200 miles |

jungles, still-plentiful wildlife, and perhaps Indonesia's most independent ethnic groups.

East of Java lies Bali, the epitome of an exotic tropical paradise. Beyond is Lombok, and then Nusa Tenggara, or what the colonials called the Lesser Sundas, a chain of volcanic islands with some tremendous scenery both terrestrial and marine.

Due north of Java is Kalimantan, Indonesia's portion of mystical Borneo. Kalimantan was once synonymous with remoteness, inaccessibility and headhunters; today it suggests timber wealth and oil frontiers, although vast tracts of forest remain, home to orang-utans and numerous other species.

This leaves Sulawesi and Maluku. Sulawesi is home to the remarkable Torajans, who bury their dead in the limestone cliffs, and exceptional wildlife. Maluku, formerly The Moluccas, are the original Spice Islands their lucrative crop of nutmeg, cloves and mace the subject of battles between European powers. Finally, the last outpost of this island nation is New Guinea, the western half of which belongs to Indonesia. Called Papua, it was a land of unknown peoples and mountain valleys until early in the 20th century. Even today it remains utterly remote and primitive.

PRECEDING PAGES: rice terraces near Candidasa, Bali; Borobudur on a misty morning; quiet beach on Nusa Lembongan, eastern Bali. **ABOVE LEFT:** sasak rice barn, Lombok. **ABOVE RIGHT:** Jalan Malioboro, Yogyakarta.

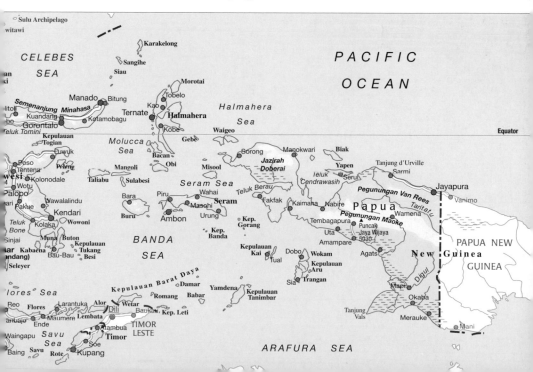

JAVA

Although it covers only 6 percent of the total area, Java is Indonesia's heartland, and its political and economic centre

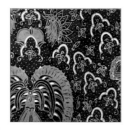

For 1,000 years, from the time of the great Hindu-Buddhist empires up to the early 1800s, Java's population of 3.5 million remained relatively stable. Wet-rice cultivation was the basis of civilisation, and as long as the population was small, farmers produced vast surpluses. Then in the 19th century a forced-labour cultivation system instigated by the Dutch to increase food supplies resulted in a spiralling birth rate. By 1900, the population had soared to 28 million and today stands at nearly quintuple that number, 136 million.

This is an island unlike any other in the archipelago. Its interior remains farmland, the soil made fertile by nutrient-rich ash deposits from 30 active volcanoes that rise magnificently amid the rice fields. Java is Indonesia's most densely populated island. More than half of its inhabitants live in traditional villages, eking out a subsistence lifestyle as farmers or fishermen. At the other end of the spectrum are its major cities: Jakarta, the nation's capital and the nucleus of Indonesian business, finance and politics, is here. A bustling metropolis, its people cohabitate with glittering skyscrapers, pricey shopping malls and bumper-to-bumper traffic. Surabaya, Indonesia's second-largest city, is a sprawling commercial centre and the primary trading port for the islands to the east. On the north coast is Semarang with its intriguing mix of descendants of traders from afar.

In the interior, the island's remaining forests are now limited to its 12 national parks protecting some of the Earth's rarest creatures. Trekking, climbing, birdwatching and wildlife-spotting at Gunung Bromo, Ujung Kulon and Gunung Merapi attract adventurers and naturalists. Two parks – Kepulauan Seribu and Karimunjawa – are marine preserves, luring water enthusiasts to their shores; Alas Purwo has some of the best pipeline surfing outside Hawaii.

At the heart of the Javanese culture is Yogyakarta, where painters, gamelan musicians, batik artists and dancers study and perform. Its rich court culture remains in the souls of every Javanese despite their contemporary facades. Outside its realm are Borobudur and Prambanan and countless smaller temples, remnants of past glorious kingdoms.

Left:: Gunung Bromo and Gunung Semeru at dawn. **Above Left:** traditional batik, Yogyakarta. **Above Right:** Java has a long seafaring tradition.

JAKARTA

The charms of this huge sprawling metropolis are well hidden, but Jakarta dwellers are proud of the cultural and intellectual life in their ever-changing, chaotic capital city

For the majority of its residents, Jakarta ❶ is a city of promise. The lure of jobs and a better life has caused the city's population to escalate at an alarming rate, to 9.5 million, with some 14,440 people crowded into each square kilometre. Visually unprepossessing, this is a city of monotonous skyscrapers, apartment buildings, shopping malls and traffic-choked highways, with few green spaces to break things up. More positively, the nation's largest metropolis has a rich cultural life, with an abundance of performing and visual arts and a laid-back, courteous persona.

Capital to the world's fourth-most populous nation, Jakarta is a city that verges on the chaotic. Just south of the harbour on Jakarta Bay and Ancol recreation park is Kota, the old Batavia area, where remnants of Dutch colonial rule reside. Heading south are *Pecinan* (Chinatown) and busy Glodok, the electronic, gadget and computer centre of the city. A major north–south artery, Jalan Hayam Wuruk, merges into Jalan Gajah Mada, lined with shops, restaurants, hotels and nightlife, ending at Monas (Freedom Square) in the heart of Central Jakarta.

The busy Jalan Thamrin-Sudirman corridor, south of Monas, is one of two major Central Business Districts (CBDs), a wall of glimmering glass and steel with some of the most interesting high-rise architecture in Southeast Asia. Creeping in bumper-to-bumper traffic, the thoroughfare in turn connects with Jalan Rasuna Said and Gatot Subroto, the second CBD and a golden triangle for national and international companies, banks, hotels, shopping malls and embassies.

Surrounding the city mayhem on all sides are residential areas, ranging

Main attractions

OLD BATAVIA HISTORICAL SITES
ANCOL DREAMLAND RECREATIONAL PARK
FREEDOM SQUARE
NATIONAL MUSEUM
TAMAN ISMAIL MARZUK
FIVE-STAR SHOPPING
RAGUNAN ZOO
BEAUTIFUL INDONESIA IN MINIATURE PARK
THOUSAND ISLANDS RESORTS

LEFT: gridlocked traffic along Jalan Sudirman. **RIGHT:** lighting incense in a Chinese temple, Glodok.

Jakarta

Waduk Pluit
(Pluit Reservoir)

Jl. Miara Baru

Jl. Pluit Timur Raya

Teluk Jakarta
(Jakarta Bay)

Kepulauan Seribu
(Thousand Islands)

Ancol
Marina

0   500 m
0   500 yds

N

Jl. Pluit Selatan Raya

Dunia Fantasi
(Fantasy Land)

Taman Impian
Jaya Ancol
(ANCOL DREAMLAND)

Sea World

A Pelabuhan Sunda Kelapa
(Sunda Kelapa Harbour)

Pasar Ikan
(Fish Market)

Pasar Seni
(Arts & Craft Market)

Jl. Pluit Raya

B Museum Bahari
(Maritime Museum)

Menara Syahbandar
(Dutch Lookout Tower)

C

Jl. Pluit Selatan Raya

Jl. Pakin

Jl. Tongkol

Jl. Lodan Raya

Kr. Bolong 5

P. Tritis Raya

Jl. Lodan Raya

Jl. Toll Pelabuhan

Harbour Tollroad

Jl. Bandengan Utara

Jl. Bandengan Selatan

Jl. Cengkeh

Museum Wayang
(Puppet Museum)

Taman
Fatahillah

F Museum Seni Rupa
(Fine Arts Museum)

Stasiun
Kampung
Bandan

Jl. R. E. Martadinata

Jl. Budi Mulia

Jl. R. E. Martadinata

Stasiun
Ancol

E Toko Merah (Red House)

D Museum Sejarah Jakarta
(Jakarta History Museum)

Stasiun
Kota

Jl. Jembatan Batu

International
Trade Centre

Jl. Mangga Dua

PADEMANGAN

HUTAN KOTA
KEMAYORAN
(KEMAYORAN URBAN
FOREST PARK)

Jl. Jembatan Dua

IKOTA

Gedong Panjang

Jl. Pintu
Besar Sel.

Pancoran

Perniagaan

Gereja Sion
(Portuguese
Church)

Stasiun
Jayakarta

Jl. Mangga Besar

Jl. Pangeran Jayakarta

Jl. Gunung Sahari Kanal

Jl. Hidup

Jl. Gunung Sahari

Jl. Baru

Jl. Landas Pacu Utara

Jl. Griya Utama

Stasiun
Angke

G Glodok
Plaza

GLODOK

Jl. Hayam Wuruk

Jl. Mangga Besar

Jl. Mangga Besar 13

Stasiun
Rajawali

Jl. Rajawali

Kelenteng Jin De Yuan/
Petak Sembilan
(Jin De Yuan/Petak
Sembilan Chinese Temple)

Stasiun
Mangga Besar

Jl. Karang Anyar Utara

Jl. Industri

Jl. Landas Pacu Barat/ Timur

TAMBORA

Jl. Kalianyar 9

Jl. K. H. Mohammad Mansyur

Jl. Tanah Sereal

Jl. Tambora

Pasar Karang Anyar
(Karang Anyar Market)

Jl. Kartini

SAWAH
BESAR

Jl. Gunung Sahari

Jl. Angkasa

Jl. Landasan Sel.

Stasiun
Duri

Gedung Arsip Nasional
(National Archives Building)

TAMAN
SARI

Jl. Gajah Mada

Jl. Wiryopranoto

Stasiun
Sawah
Besar

Jl. K. H. Samanhudi

Jl. Garuda

Stasiun
Kemayoran

KEMAYORAN

Jl. Duri Selatan

Jl. Tanah Sereal

Jl. Krukut

Jl. K. H. Zainul Arifin

Jl. Batu Jajar

Jl. Pecenongan

Jl. Pos

Pasar Kalibaru
(Kalibaru Market)

Jl. Tanah Tinggi Barat

GROGOL

Jl. Dr. Muwardi

Jl. Kyai Tapa

Jl. K. H. Hasyim Ashari

Jl. AM.

Jl. Sangaji

Jl. Ir. Juanda

Jl. Veteran

Gereja Kaledral
(Catholic
Cathedral)

I Kantor Pos Pusat
(Central Post Office)

Jl. Bungur Besar

Jl. Bungur Besar

Stasiun
Senen

Jl. Tanah Tinggi Barat/ Timur

Jl. Tomang Utara 1

Jl. Utara

Istana Negara
(Presidential Palace)
Istana Merdeka

Stasiun
Juanda

Mesjid Istiqlal
(Istiqlal Mosque)

J

Lapangan
Banteng

Patung Pembebasan
Irian Barat
(Freedom Memorial)

Jl. Senen Raya

Jl. Kramat Bunder

TOMANG

Jl. Tomang Raya

Jl. Kambola

Museum Taman Prasasti
(Ancient Inscription Museum)

Jl. Medan
Merdeka Utara

Jl. Kaledral

Jl. Prapatan

SENEN

Jl. Puto Gundul

Jl. Mandala

Jl. Cideng Timur

Jl. Cideng Barat

Jl. Tn. Abang 2

Jl. Muis

H Monas
(National
Monument)

Stasiun
Gambir

Gedung
Pancasila

TANAH

ABANG

Jl. Kyai Caringin

Banjir Kanal

Jl. Medan Merdeka Barat

I Museum Nasional
(National Museum)

Jl. Medan
Merdeka Selatan

GAMBIR

Gereja Immanuel
(Immanuel Church)

Jl. Medan

Jl. Kwitang

Jl. Kramat Raya

JOHOR

BARU

Jl. Letjen S. Parman

Jl. Jatibaru

Jl. Kebon Sirih

Jl. Kebon Sirih

Jl. K. H.
Wahid Hasyim

Stasiun
Gondangdia

Jl. Cikini 6

Jl. Cikini

Stasiun
Sentiong

Jl. Paseban

Stasiun
Tanah Abang

Jl. K. H. Wahid

Hasyim

Sarinah
(Sarinah
Department
Store)

Taman Ismail Marzuki
(Ismail Marzuki Arts Centre)

K

Merak, Cilegon

Museum Tekstil
(Textile Museum)

Jl. Kebon
Jati

Jl. Brigjen. Katamso Dharmokusomo

Jl. Slipi 3

c Said Na'um

Plaza
Indonesia

L

Jl. M. H. Thamrin

Patung
Selamat
Datang
(Welcome
Statue)

Jl. Cikini

Jl. Raden Saleh

Universitas Indonesia
(University of Indonesia)

Antique
Street

Stasiun
Cikini

Jl. Salemba Raya

Jl. Slipi 5

Jl. Alpka k. S. Tubun

Grand Indonesia
Shopping Complex

Jl. Sultan Syahrir

Jl. HOS Cokroaminoto

MENTENG

Museum Adam Malik
(Adam Malik Museum)

Jl. Diponegoro

Jl. Mataram

SENAYAN

Stasiun
Palmerah ← Taman Mini, Bogor

Jl. Gelora 1

Stasiun
Karet

Jl. K. H. Mas Mansyur

Jl. Jendral Sudirman

Stasiun
Sudirman

Jl. Karet Pasar Baru Barat

Jl. Karet Pasar
Baru Timur

Jl. Bendungan Hilir

↓ Blok M

Jl. Imam

Jl. Bonjol

Jl. Sultan Syahrir

Jl. Latuharhari

Stasiun
Mampang

Jl. Sultan Agung

Stasiun
Manggarai

Jl. Kawi

Cikampek

from upper- and middle-class streets to the most basic shanties. Scattered throughout are pockets that seem frozen in time, including diminutive residential districts with market gardens and makeshift *kampung* (village) dwellings that impart something of a village atmosphere to many back alleys.

Batavia

Starting out as a simple spice-trade harbour in the 14th century under the Hindu Pajajaran kingdom, Jakarta's waterfront grew into a major seaport as the lucrative maritime trade expanded with Indian, Chinese and Arab traders. In 1522, the Portuguese arrived in search of the legendary Spice Islands, followed later by the English and Dutch. The seaport was conquered in 1527 by the combined forces of the Javanese Banten and Demak Islamic kingdoms, renaming the area Jayakarta or "City of Victory".

But it was the Dutch who had bigger designs, taking Jayakarta by force in 1618, and claiming the land in the name of the VOC (East India Company). From here, the colonial Dutch ruled for the next 350 years.

In 1618, the architect of the Dutch empire in the Indies, Jan Pieterszoon Coen, moved his headquarters here from Banten and ordered construction of a new town at Jayakarta: Batavia. Under the VOC, Batavia's fortunes rose and fell. It had grown rich during the 17th century on an entrepôt trade in sugar, pepper, cloves, nutmeg, tea, textiles, porcelain, hardwoods and rice.

At the beginning of the 19th century most of Old Batavia was demolished to provide building materials for a new city to the south called Menteng, around what is now Medan Merdeka and Lapangan Banteng. The fashionable architectural styles of the period blended with newly laid out tree-lined boulevards and extensive gardens. By the turn of the century, Batavia's homes, hotels and clubs were in no way inferior to those of Europe.

During the brief Japanese Occupation of World War II, Batavia was renamed Jakarta. Following the nation's independence in 1945, hundreds of thousands of Indonesians flooded in from the countryside and outer islands, and Jakarta quickly outstripped all other Indonesian cities in size and importance, becoming what scholars term a primate city: the unrivalled political, cultural and economic centre of the new nation.

Around the waterfront

Hail a taxi and start your tour where the city's history began, the old spice trading seaport **Sunda Kelapa Harbour** . Early morning is the best time to walk along the 2km (1.25-mile) wharf among the ships' prows and gangways and witness one of the world's last remaining commercial sailing fleets. Filled with the romance of a bygone era, watch the unloading of cargo from the majestic wooden *pinisi* schooners built by the seafaring Bugis people of South Sulawesi.

The area around Sunda Kelapa is rich in history, and the best way to

The 19th-century Dutch Lookout Tower.

BELOW: drawbridge over a Kota canal.

Sunda Kelapa's graceful schooners are being fast supplanted by modern freighters.

BELOW: walking the plank at Sunda Kelapa Harbour.

survey the area is on foot. Near the river stands a 19th-century **Dutch lookout tower** (Uitkik), constructed on the site of the original customs house of Jayakarta. Behind the lookout stands a long two-storey structure dating from VOC times, now the **Museum Bahari** ❸ (Maritime Museum; Jalan Pasar Ikan No. 1; tel: 021-669 3406; Tue–Fri 9am–3pm, Sat–Sun 9am–2pm; charge). This warehouse, now a maritime museum, was built by the Dutch in 1646 and was used to store coffee, tea and Indian cloth. Inside are displays of traditional sailing craft from all corners of the Indonesian archipelago, as well as some old maps of Batavia. Down a narrow lane and around a corner behind the museum lies the **Pasar Ikan** (fish market), beyond which are numerous stalls selling nautical gear.

Further east along the waterfront is a giant seaside recreation area, **Taman Impian Jaya Ancol** ❸ (Ancol Dreamland). Once swampland, it now features beachfront hotels, a golf course, bowling alley and an arts and crafts market called Pasar Seni, where

a row of art kiosks and workshops mingle with cafés. There are also several theme parks, including **Sea World** (tel: 021-641 0080; daily 9am–6pm; charge), which has a tropical oceanarium, an underwater acrylic tunnel which allows you to view sharks, stingrays and a variety of fish native to local waters. In the same area is **Dunia Fantasi** (tel: 021-6471 2000; daily 9am–6pm; charge), an amusement park with a roller-coaster and Ferris wheel, very crowded at weekends and during school holidays. Close by is **Ancol Marina**, from where ferries depart to various islands (*see page 143*).

The Old City

Take a taxi to the area known as **Kota** in the old Batavia quarter that came to life in the 1620s as a tiny, walled town modelled on Amsterdam. Most of the original settlement – Old Batavia – was demolished at the beginning of the 19th century. Only the town square area survived and has been restored and renamed **Taman Fatahillah** (Fatahillah Square). Three of the surrounding colonial edifices

have been converted into museums, and the main square bustles at weekends with street entertainers, old-fashioned bicycle rentals, artists and food vendors.

Start at the **Museum Sejarah Jakarta ⑩** (Jakarta History Museum; tel: 021-692 9101; closed for renovations until 2014). It was formerly Batavia's city hall (*Stadhuis*), completed in 1710 and used by successive governments until the 1960s. It now houses memorabilia from the colonial period, notably 18th-century furnishings and portraits of the VOC governors, along with many prehistoric, classical and Portuguese-period artefacts. Dungeons visible from the back of the building were used as holding cells where prisoners were made to stand waist-deep in sewage for weeks awaiting their trials. Executions and torture were once commonplace in the main square as judges watched from the balcony above the main entrance.

The **Museum Wayang ⑤** (Puppet Museum; tel: 021-692 9560; Tue–Sun 9am–3pm; charge) is on the western side of the square. It has many puppets and masks, some of them rare buffalo-hide shadow puppets (*wayang kulit*), along with a collection of topeng masks, and tombstones of several early Dutch governors.

The **Museum Seni Rupa ⑥** (Fine Arts Museum; tel: 021-692 6090; Tue–Sun 9am–3pm; charge) occupies the former Court of Justice building, completed in 1879. Its collections include paintings and sculptures by modern Indonesian artists, and an important exhibition of rare porcelain, featuring many Sung celadon pieces from the Adam Malik collection, ancient Javanese water jugs (*kendhi*), and terracotta pieces dating from the 14th century.

Before leaving the area, walk over to the 16th-century Portuguese cannon mounted on the north side of Taman Fatahillah. Si Jagur, "The Robust One", as it is called, is regarded by many as a fertility symbol, perhaps because of the fist that is cast into the butt end of the cannon, with a thumb protruding between its index and middle fingers (regarded

The Museum Wayang on Fatahillah Square.

BELOW: Kampung Tugu.

Forgotten Portuguese

Nestled between busy Tanjung Priok harbour and the slums of the Cilincing warehouse district is one of Jakarta's oldest, but forgotten, villages. Kampung Tugu's residents are descendants of the Portuguese who took over Malacca in 1511. Enslaved by the Dutch after they conquered Malacca in 1641, in 1664 they were freed by their masters, given Dutch names and resettled east of Old Batavia. The village's 17th-century church, featuring a distinctive bell tower, Gereja Tugu, is still in operation. Alongside it are the graves of Portuguese settlers.

The community embraces its four-centuries-old Portuguese heritage, and some ancient rituals, such as a "bathing" ceremony, are still performed. Every January the ceremony begins with communal prayers and songs followed by applying powder to each other's faces as a sign of mutual forgiveness. The ritual ends with drinking beer and playing the *keroncong Tugu* music of their ancestors. The band is comprised of ukuleles, guitars, violins, flutes and cellos, and it is thought that the sound that the ukulele makes (*crong . . . crong*) was the origin of the name *keroncong*.

"Tugu" may have been derived from a stone inscription dating back to King Purnawarman of the Tarumanegara kingdom that was found in a nearby canal. Another explanation is that it comes from the middle syllable of the word *Por-tugu-ese*.

Jakarta History Museum.

BELOW: famous ex-resident.

as an obscene gesture in Indonesia). Occasionally, young couples are seen approaching it bearing offerings. Nearby is Café Batavia, once an old warehouse, now with eclectic furnishings and window tables that offer excellent views of the square.

Next, walk behind the Museum Wayang to view two Dutch houses dating from the 18th century. Across the canal and to the left stands a solid red-brick townhouse (Jl. Kali Besar Barat No. 11) that was built around 1730 by the then soon-to-be governor-general. The design and particularly the fine Chinese-style woodwork are typical of old Batavian residences. Three doors to the left is another house from the same period. Nearby is a historical drawbridge on the Kali Besar River called Jembatan Pasar Ayam (Chicken Market Bridge), as the area was once a market for chickens and vegetables.

Jakarta's **Chinatown** is immediately adjacent to the former European centre just to the south of the Old City in an area now known as **Glodok** , and is the centre for electronics, household goods and herbal medicines. There are two Buddhist temples deep within the convoluted back alleys. The public use of Chinese characters, banned decades ago during the failed but bloody communist insurgency, was lifted by then-president Abdurrahman Wahid in 1999.

Freedom Square

A circumnavigation of Central Jakarta begins at the top of the **Monas** (National Monument; tel: 021-384 0451/382 3041; Tue–Sun 9am–3pm; charge). A 137-metre (450ft) tall marble obelisk is set in the centre of **Medan Merdeka** (Freedom Square). There is an observation deck at the top surmounted by a 14-metre (45ft) bronze flame sheathed in 33kg (73lbs) of gold symbolising the spirit of freedom. It was commissioned by Sukarno and completed in 1961 – a combination Olympic Flame-Washington Monument with the phallic overtones of an ancient Hindu-Javanese *lingga*.

Barack Obama

US President Barack Obama lived in Menteng, Jakarta between the ages of six and ten. Going by his stepfather's name, he was registered in St Francis of Assisi and Besuki Menteng primary schools as Barry Soetoro. Before his first official visit to Indonesia in November 2010, a group of long-stay expats raised funds and erected a 2-metre (6½ft) statue of Obama as a child in Taman Menteng (Menteng Park).

Although most Indonesians have a deep affection for "Barry", as he is known here, he is not considered an Indonesian hero – largely because he was born elsewhere – and there was a degree of controversy when the monument was unveiled. The statue was eventually moved to a less visible location at Besuki Menteng School.

The National History Museum in the basement contains 12 dioramas depicting historical scenes from a nationalistic viewpoint. A high-speed elevator rises to the observation deck, where on a clear day there is a fabulous 360-degree view of Jakarta.

Double back to Medan Merdeka and pass behind the Presidential Palace, situated between Jalan Medan Merdeka Utara and Jalan Veteran. The palace building consists of two 19th-century neoclassical villas situated back to back. The older of the two, the Istana Negara, faces north and was built by a wealthy Dutch merchant around 1800. It was taken over some years later to serve as the town residence of the Dutch governor (whose official residence was then located in Bogor). The south-facing Istana Merdeka was added in 1879 as a reception area. President Sukarno resided in the palace and frequently gave lavish banquets in the central courtyard.

On the west side of Medan Merdeka lies one of Indonesia's great cultural treasures, the **National Museum** ❶, on Jalan Medan Merdeka Barat (tel: 021-381 1551/386 8172; Tue–Thur and Sun 8.30am– 2.30pm, Fri 8.30–11.30am, Sat 8.30am–1.30pm; charge). Known as Museum Gajah because of the bronze elephant statue in front, presented by King Chulalongkorn of Siam, it was opened in 1868 by the Batavian Society for Arts and Sciences – the first scholarly organisation in colonial Asia, founded in 1778. The museum houses valuable collections of antiquities, books and ethnographic artefacts acquired by the Dutch during the 19th and early 20th centuries. Objects of interest include Hindu-Javanese stone statuary, prehistoric bronzeware and Chinese porcelain. The star collection is housed in the Treasure Room – a stupendous hoard of royal Indonesian heirlooms. The Ceramics Room features the largest collection of Southeast Asian ceramics under one roof.

Central Jakarta sights

Head eastwards about 1km (0.5 mile) to the imposing white-marble **Mesjid Istiqlal** ❶ (Istiqlal Mosque) on Jalan Veteran. The largest mosque in all of Southeast Asia, it was built on the former site of the Dutch Benteng (Fort) Noordwijk. During the Islamic fasting month, Ramadan, the mosque is filled to capacity. Tours are available.

Lapangan Banteng (Wild Ox Field) lies just to the east, bounded on the north by the neo-Gothic **Catholic Cathedral** on Jalan Katedral, completed in 1901; note the rather interesting buildings on the east near the Supreme Court (1848) and the Department of Finance (1982), and on the south by the Borobudur Hotel with its lush gardens.

Returning to the eastern side of Medan Merdeka, are two more colonial structures: the 1830 Gedung Pancasila on Jalan Taman Pejambon, where Sukarno unveiled the five principles of the Indonesian state (Pancasila), and the small Immanuel Church on Jalan Medan Merdeka Timur, built in 1835 and resembling a Greek temple.

TIP

Members of the Indonesian Heritage Society conduct free guided tours of the National Museum in English, French and Japanese. Call ahead (tel: 021-381 1551/572 5870) for the schedule.

BELOW: the National Museum.

TIP

The best stop for souvenir-shopping is Pasaraya department store, packed with items from every corner of Indonesia, from Javanese batik to Dayak woodcarvings and Balinese art.

Southeast of the square, a short ride down Jalan Cikini, are two other noteworthy attractions. **Taman Ismail Marzuk ⓚ** (tel: 021-3193 7325; daily 8.30am–5pm) is a very impressive cultural centre that presents a programme of drama, dance and music from around Indonesia and the rest of the world. It also has a planetarium. Nearby, **Jalan Surabaya** is the city's so-called "antique street", with dozens of shops selling everything from wayang (puppets) to ship fittings, most of it brand new.

Shopping and dining

There is no shortage of places in Jakarta to shop in air-conditioned comfort and find something good to eat. Hail a taxi and cruise west across the upper-class residential area, **Menteng**, to the **Welcome Statue**, a busy roundabout with a statue of two waving youths and a fountain. Jalan Thamrin runs north and south here, turning into Jalan Sudirman a few more blocks south. The roundabout fountain is an urban anchor of Jakarta, built by Sukarno in the early 1960s. Harmless demonstrations are often staged here.

Surrounding the roundabout are the **Grand Indonesia Shopping Complex** and **Plaza Indonesia ⓛ**, two of the best shopping malls in Jakarta, offering designer and local-label goods and a huge array of eateries. Next door to Plaza Indonesia is EX Plaza entertainment centre, attracting a younger crowd. The Grand Hyatt is perched above Plaza Indonesia and is a wonderful place for afternoon tea – a ceiling-to-floor bay window allows you to look out on the heart of the city.

Further north from the Welcome Statue, Sarinah is historic as the first department store in Indonesia, built in 1962. Recently renovated, this five-storey building has fashion and jewellery, art and handicrafts, in addition to restaurants and shops as well as nightlife.

Further south on Jalan Sudirman, behind the Senayan sports field, home to national football games, is **Plaza Senayan**, another of the city's trendy shopping malls. The new **Senayan City** opposite Plaza Senayan is yet another shopping haven for branded goods and many food outlets.

BELOW: turtles at Kepulauan Seribu.

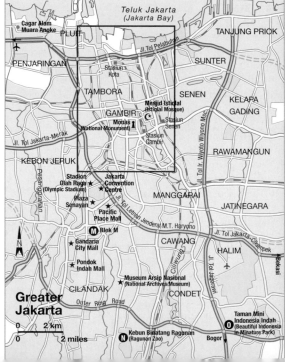

The final stop for downtown shopping is **Pacific Place Mall** in the Sudirman Central Business District: branded shops, local and international restaurants, fitness centres, cinemas and megastores in one location.

Away from the city's heart is the middle-class **Blok M** , bustling with street stalls and at least seven shopping malls, including Blok M Plaza and Blok M Mall, home of Pasaraya department store, which has a whole floor dedicated to Indonesian handicrafts and batik. In a wealthy southern suburb is **Pondak Indah Mall**. Two kilometres (1.25 miles) north is one of Jakarta's newest malls, **Gandaria City**.

South Jakarta entertainment

Still heading south, about 15km (9 miles) from the centre of the city, is **Ragunan Zoo** (tel: 021-780 6975/789 0615; daily 7am–6pm; charge). Set in a tropical garden park, with a pleasant relaxed atmosphere, it has more than 3,000 animals indigenous to Indonesia, along with species from other countries. This may be your only chance to see the infamous Komodo dragon, along with orangutans and Sumatran tigers.

Taman Mini Indonesia Indah (Beautiful Indonesia in Miniature Park; tel: 021-840 3400/840 9214; Tue–Sun 8am–5pm; charge) covers nearly 100 hectares (250 acres) of land near Kampung Rambutan. While not entirely successful in compressing the entire archipelago into a single attraction, the park nonetheless permits you a glimpse of the many thousands of Indonesian islands you will probably not visit. Taman Mini has 33 main pavilions – one for each of Indonesia's provinces – constructed in the traditional architectural style of each province and using only authentic materials. Six new provinces' pavilions were built in one integrated area. Housed inside each pavilion are interesting displays

of handicrafts, traditional costumes, musical instruments and other artefacts for which each region is known.

In addition, there are at least 30 other attractions here, including a tropical bird park, orchid garden, IMAX cinema, cable-car ride, transport museum, swimming pool, and the splendid **Museum Indonesia** (tel: 021-840 9246/840 9213; Tue–Sun 8am–5pm; charge) – a three-storey Balinese palace filled with traditional textiles, houses, boats, puppets, jewellery and wedding costumes.

Pasar Ikan, fish market

Also inside the park is **Museum Purna Bhakti Pertiwi** (Presidential Palace Museum; tel: 021-840 1687; Tue–Sun 8am–5pm; charge), established by the late First Lady Ibu Tien Suharto as a showcase for the family's private collection of antiques and art, along with the many diplomatic gifts Indonesia received while her husband was president.

Island getaways

One of the best ways to unwind and recapture a taste of the tropics after the bustle of Jakarta is to escape to clear blue waters and white-sand beaches at any one of the 600 small islands off the north coast of Jakarta, known as **Kepulauan Seribu** (Thousand Islands), one of Java's national parks.

Day trips can be taken to Bidadari, Kelor and Kahyangan islands near the coast. On Onrust island, explore the ruins of an old Dutch fort, which has remains of an 18th-century shipyard. Bokor and Rambut islands are home to bird sanctuaries; you need a permit from the national park office, PHKA, in Jakarta. Ferries depart every day from Ancol Marina *(see page 138)* to various islands at 7am and return at 2.30pm.

About 100km (60 miles) further out to sea lies a group of islands that have been developed into resorts: Pelangi, Putri, Matahari, Kotok, Ayer and Pantara. Each has fully equipped hotels with beachfront bungalows and restaurants. All bookings to island resorts have to be made in Jakarta through a travel agent. Activities include scuba-diving, snorkelling, swimming and fishing. Diving gear can be rented on most of the islands, but check with your travel agent to confirm.

WEST JAVA

This most populous region of Indonesia, home of the earthy Sundanese, offers majestic volcanoes, several national parks, a wild and rugged coast and refreshing highlands

West Java or Tanah Sunda (Sunda Land) can be roughly divided into two distinct regions: the volcanic highlands from Bogor east to Tasikmalaya and the northern, western and southern coastal plains. The highlands are dotted with volcanoes, rainforests and national parks, attracting trekkers and those wishing to escape from the lowland heat. There are a scattering of resorts along the coastline as well as some picturesque fishing villages, while the lowland Ujung Kulon National Park on Java's southwestern tip harbours the country's last viable population of Javan rhinos.

The inhabitants are mainly Sundanese, whose culture has remained alive despite the continual border incursions and sporadic warfare of the past. Unlike the refined Javanese, the earthy Sundanese value individualism, and possess a strong sense of humour. Although also Sundanese, the people west of Bogor prefer to call themselves *urang* Banten, or Bantenese. Casually dismissed as "mountain Javanese" by the people of the heartland, the Sundanese developed a strong culture of their own that pre-dates the great empires to the east. However, cultural performances – mainly *gamelan* and *angklung* music, popular *jaipongan* dances and lively *wayang golek* performances – are often confined to remote villages.

Banten Lama

Heading west from Jakarta on the Jakarta–Merak toll road for about 1½ hours is historical **Banten Lama** (Old Banten) **②**, the gateway to the once-grand Banten sultanate. During the 16th and 17th centuries, this was one of Asia's largest and most cosmopolitan trading emporiums. Once a grand

LEFT: wooden *wayang golek* puppets at Bogor.
RIGHT: pilgrims visiting the 16th-century Mesjid Agung mosque at Banten.

Fishing village at Banten Girang.

walled city, it was laid to ruin as trade was shifted to Jayakarta (Jakarta).

Today, it is a tiny fishing village with several interesting historical sites, such as the ruins of a large palace (Surosowan), which has been partially excavated. Looming over the village is the 16th-century Mesjid Agung (Grand Mosque) with a five-tiered roof typical of early Javanese Hindu-Islamic style. Climb the staircase to the top for a view. A small museum (charge) offers a glimpse into the seaport's great past. The Dutch fortress, Speelwijk, stands at the former river mouth.

Across the bridge is the Chinese Klenteng temple, one of the oldest in Java. The ruins of Banten Lama are 10km (6 miles) from Serang, also called Banten Girang (Upper Banten). It is best to go by hired car from Jakarta, or take the Jakarta–Serang bus, alight in Serang and then switch to a public minivan to the site.

West coast beaches

From Banten Lama, head south to Java's sandy and secluded west coast beaches (2½ hours, or 110km/70 miles west of Jakarta) to swim and relax in the cool ocean breezes. At Cilegon, the road branches off to the right and continues 13km (8 miles) to **Merak**, where ferries depart for Bakauheni on Sumatra.

Branching south towards the beaches, there are pretty bays and long stretches of deserted white sands lined with coconut palms. At **Anyer** ❸, several large resorts grace the coastline surrounding Dutch-built Anyer Lighthouse. Continuing 6km (4 miles) south is Karang Bolong, a huge rock forming a natural archway to the sea. Its pleasant beach is a popular weekend swimming spot for Jakartans.

Another 10km (6 miles) south is **Carita**, with sandy beaches situated in a lovely cove. Here there is beachside accommodation, a marina and sailing, jet-skiing, diving and snorkelling. In addition to sun, sea, sand and solitude, this palm-fringed coast has stunning sunset views of **Anak Krakatau** (Child of Krakatau).

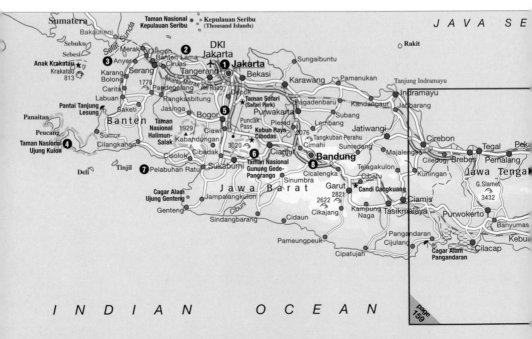

Although dormant for centuries, the original Krakatau volcano (known to the West as Krakatoa) achieved instant and lasting infamy in 1883, when it erupted with cataclysmic force, ripping out a huge chunk of the earth's crust to form a monstrous 40-sq km (16-sq mile) submarine caldera. The sea rushed in, and tidal waves up to 30 metres (100ft) high swept the coast, claiming more than 35,000 lives. Today, all that remains of the mighty volcano are Sertung, Panjang and Rakata at its crater rim.

In the decades that followed, under-sea eruptions continued and a new active crater emerged from the sea in 1927: Anak Krakatau. Boats can be chartered from Carita for day trips out to the volcano. It is 4 hours each way and another 3 hours to climb the peak. On clear days there are views of the Sunda Strait, Java coastline and Sumatra. Climbing Anak Krakatau is difficult, as the trails are steep and littered with slippery rock and gravel, and it can be extremely hot. Sunscreen and sufficient drinking water are highly recommended. Coastal areas arc forested and make an ideal resting place after trekking. At Legon Cabe bay at nearby Rakata island there is good snorkelling, and camping on the beach is allowed.

Many "guides" walk Carita beach promoting excursions, but it is best to make prior arrangements with your hotel or tour agent, and do check that the vessel is adequate before departure. Anak Krakatau is an active volcano and is regularly monitored by volcanologists at an observation post at Pasauran village, Carita. Warnings will be posted if it is unsafe.

Ujung Kulon National Park

A Unesco Natural Heritage Site, **Ujung Kulon National Park ❹** is located south of Carita on the southwest tip of Java. A 420-sq km (260-sq mile) reserve, it is the last refuge for the highly endangered and rarely sighted Javan rhino. The park also has other interesting animals, including leopards, macaques, leaf monkeys, mousedeer, crocodiles and indigenous wild oxen (*banteng*). Much of the area is dense lowland rainforest, open

TIP

There have been reports of tourists injuring themselves on the hike up Anak Krakatau or inhaling poisonous fumes, so exercise caution.

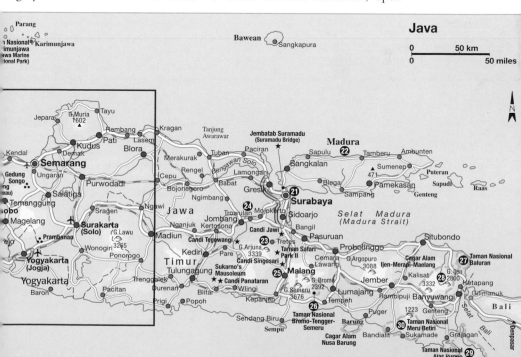

TIP

Pulau Dua can be reached by walking across mudflats at low tide from Banten Lama. During the mating season, the 8-hectare (20-acre) bird sanctuary attracts 40,000–50,000 migratory birds from as far away as China and India.

woodlands, and wetlands – excellent for birdwatching – with beaches in the north and south. Between April and August, migratory birds flock by the thousands to the nearby islands of Pulau Dua and Pamojan Besar in Banten Bay.

Peucang island, north of the mainland portion of the park, has basic bungalows and a restaurant, where deer, monkeys and monitor lizards are a common sight. About 10 minutes by boat from Peucang is Cidaon, the grazing ground for *banteng* and Javan peacocks. The highlight of the park experience is a canoe ride starting from **Handeuleum** island up the Cigenter River, where scientists monitor the Javan rhino activity. **Panaitan**, the largest of the offshore islands, is a good spot for diving and fishing. It's covered by hilly rainforest; there are several prehistoric Hindu statues at Gunung Raksa.

The best time of year to visit is during the dry season, from April to September. A permit is required from the PHKA (national park) office in Labuan (15 minutes south of Carita),

where accommodation, guide and transport can also be arranged. It is usually a 5-hour boat ride each way between Labuan and Peucang. Note that this can be a rough crossing in bad weather.

Bogor

The most scenic of West Java's major routes extends to the south of Jakarta, with the ascent to the dramatic Parahyangan highlands. First stop is **Bogor ❺** – only an hour's drive from central Jakarta via the Jagorawi Expressway. Situated about 500 metres (1,640ft) above sea level, the city is appreciably cooler (and wetter) than the coast. The main attraction here is the glorious **Kebun Raya** (Botanical Gardens; tel: 0251-831 8007; daily 9am–5pm; charge). Established by the British in 1817, it became world-renowned during the 19th century for its wide range of tropical botanical specimens and research into cash crops such as tea, cassava, tobacco and cinchona. The vast park with its rolling lawns, lily ponds and forest groves contains 15,000 species of trees and plants (including 400 types of palms) and orchid nurseries.

The elegant white **Istana Bogor** (Presidential Palace) stands at the northern end of the gardens. Constructed by the Dutch in 1856 as the official residence for the governors-general of the Dutch East Indies, it was a favourite hideaway of President Sukarno and contains paintings and sculpture from his vast collection. Sukarno lived here while he was under "house arrest" from 1967 until his death three years later. A permit is required to visit the palace, obtainable from the State Secretariat (ask your hotel to arrange).

Across the road from the Istana and down an alley is Pak Dase's **Sundanese *wayang golek*** (wooden puppet) **workshop** (Lebak Kantin RT 02/VI; tel: 0251-838 3758). Visitors can watch the puppets being made and see performances.

BELOW: the Istana Bogor within Bogor's magnificent Botanical Gardens.

Bapak H. Sukarna, a sixth-generation gamelan-maker, runs the last **gong and gamelan "factory"** in West Java (Jl. Pancasan 17, Bogor; tel: 0251-832 4132). Visitors can see how the instruments are forged from copper in tin by barefooted men over an open-pit fire.

Cool mountain air

East of Bogor is a favourite getaway for Jakartans, **Puncak Pass** (*puncak* means "summit"). Its cool, clean mountain air offers welcome relief from the oppressive lowland heat, but it can become very crowded over weekends and holidays because of its accessibility to the capital. The main road is lined with small hotels and restaurants, while further on are manicured landscapes of tea plantations. The 168-hectare (400-acre) **Taman Safari** (Safari Park; tel: 0251-825 0000; daily 9am–5pm; charge) is ideal for families. An open-air recreational park where lions, tigers, bears and giraffes forage in the open occupies one section; in the other there are rides for kids, educational animal shows and eateries.

Beyond Puncak Pass, a turn-off to the right leads to **Cibodas Botanical Gardens**, an extension of Bogor's Kebun Raya, and outstanding for its collection of montane and temperate flora from around the world. Next to the gardens' main gate is the entrance to **Gunung Gede-Pangrango National Park** ❻ (closed to trekkers and climbers Jan–Mar and Aug). The oldest park in Indonesia (founded in 1889) and a Unesco World Network of Biospheres Reserve, it is spread across the upper incline of two volcanoes. Its 15,000 hectares (37,000 acres) are home to rare Javan gibbons and leaf monkeys – both of which are often spotted – as well as a few leopards and a variety of bird species.

Cibeureum waterfall is a 90-minute walk from the park information centre at the main gate. Serious climbers can ascend Gunung Gede (2,958 metres/9,705ft) or Gunung Pangrango (3,020 metres/9,905ft), both requiring

overnight stays and appropriate clothing for cold nights. Although charges for day trips are paid on the spot, climbing requires a permit at least three business days in advance and is obtained at PHKA (national park) office in Cibodas.

Good accommodation and food are available in the nearby **Cipanas** mountain resort, a base for hiking through highland forests and tea estates, and other activities.

Halimun-Salak National Park

West of Gede-Pangrango National Park is another range of mountains. **Halimun-Salak National Park** (*halimun* means "misty mountain"), established in 1992, covers 113 hectares (280 acres) and is home to endemic Javan eagles, leopards and gibbons, as well as a multitude of insects and reptiles. The easiest access is from Kabandungan, about one hour south of Ciawi, where the head office and visitor information centre is located. Report for a permit, then continue another two hours west on an unpaved bumpy road to Cikaniki

TIP

In Puncak, stop by the historic Puncak Pass resort, built in 1928, where there are spectacular views of the valley below. Specialities at the restaurant include delicious pancakes and a refreshing drink, *wedang jahe* (hot ginger tea).

BELOW: picking tea near Puncak Pass.

research station for lodging. A guided canopy trail walk and rainforest trek to Citalahab tea plantation are offered.

South coast beaches

From Ciawi, the road continues south over the pass between Gunung Pangrango and Gunung Salak to the village of **Pelabuhan Ratu** ❼, where the ragged, wind-lashed Indian Ocean foams and crashes onto smooth black-sand beaches. When the boats moor in the morning the fish market does a roaring trade in freshly caught tuna, prawns, whitebait, sharks, stingrays and other delicacies. A number of good swimming beaches and hotels line the coast for several kilometres past the town, but be warned that the surf and undertow can be treacherous. Pelabuhan Ratu is part of the southern coastline that many locals believe is guarded by the legendary Nyi Loro Kidul, the Queen of the South Coast. Room 308 at the Samudra Beach Hotel remains empty and is reserved for the queen. There is a bat cave about 1km (0.6 miles) out of town; at sunset thousands take to the sky.

Bandung, City of Flowers

East of Ciawi, the road leads to **Bandung** ❽, another cool escape from Jakarta's oppressive heat. Located in a huge basin 700 metres (2,300ft) above sea level and surrounded on all sides by lofty volcanic peaks, it is a prosperous city with over 2 million inhabitants. Before World War II, it was a quaint Dutch administrative and university town of about 150,000 and was called the Paris of Java for its broad, shady boulevards, expensive shops and elegant homes. Although it is now a rapidly growing industrial city, Bandung is still green and attractive, and is often called Kota Kembang (City of Flowers).

Bandung's foremost industry is education, with more than 27 colleges and universities and thousands of students. But there is plenty for travellers, with an abundance of Dutch colonial Art Deco architecture, including the magnificent Gedung Sate, built in 1920 and home to the provincial government. Browsing in factory outlet shops along Jalan Cihampelas, a feast

BELOW: a Hindu ritual sacrifice off the coast at Pelabuhan Ratu.

for the eye as well as the pocket, is a popular pastime. Many of the shops have quirky façades fashioned from papier mâché, chrome or plywood. One even has King Kong peering down; another, a dinosaur crashing through a roof.

The **Museum Geologi** (Geological Museum, Jalan Diponegoro No. 57; tel: 022-720 3205/721 3822; Sat–Thur 9am–3pm; charge) is worth a visit for its extraordinary array of rocks, maps and fossils, including replicas of the famous Java Man or *Homo erectus* skulls found in Central Java. The campus of Bandung's Institute of Technology (ITB), Indonesia's oldest and finest university established by the Dutch, is also worth a visit. It has an interesting library built in the 1920s.

Spend some time, too, wandering around Jalan Braga, the old Dutch shopping district, and take a look into the remodelled Art Deco Savoy Homann Bidakara Hotel on Jalan Asia-Afrika. The town's large flower market is also nearby on Jalan Wastukencana. In the evenings, many theatres and clubs present Sundanese dance performances; check with your hotel or tour office for details.

An accessible volcano

Southeast of Bandung are the Parahyangan highlands (roughly, "Abode of the Gods") with vistas of manicured tea plantations, hot springs, waterfalls and the easiest-to-visit volcano in Java, **Gunung Tangkuban Perahu** (Overturned Boat Mountain), 30km (20 miles) north of the city. From Lembang, an old Dutch resort town surrounded by fruit, vegetable and flower farms, head east 9km (5.5 miles) to the park entrance and another 4km (2.5 miles) to the crater's rim. Morning clouds mix with sulphurous fumes rising from a perfect bowl-shaped centre to create a spectacular scene, surrounded by souvenir shops and restaurants. There are also several other smaller craters to hike around; exploration is best carried out during the dry season from April to September. Some 7km (4 miles) beyond Tangkuban Perahu is **Ciater**, where hot springs offer a soothing soak amid tea and clove estates.

Mist-shrouded Gunung Tangkuban Perahu, Java's most accessible volcano.

BELOW: Krakatau erupting.

From Bandung to Pangandaran

The 210km (130-mile) route southeast from Bandung to Pangandaran beach on the southern coast is both scenic and historic. A 2-hour drive from Bandung brings you to the mountainous Garut regency. Here, the only Hindu temple in West Java, Candi Cangkuang, is found in Leles village. **Cipanas** hot springs is popular with those who like to soak in the healing sulphurous waters flowing from Gunung Guntur. Five kilometres (3 miles) south in **Garut** town, Gunung Papandayan is visible. Day hikes set off from here to see its steam geysers, bubbling mud pools and fumaroles. Garut's distinctive batik is known throughout Java.

On the way from Garut to Tasikmalaya is **Kampung Naga**, where villagers still hold to their ancestors' rules and traditional way of life focused on simplicity in living and respect for the environment. **Tasikmalaya** is well known for its cottage industries: colourful paper umbrellas, batik, embroidery and *kelom geulis* (wooden clogs).

A further 4-hour drive southeast via Ciamis leads to **Pangandaran Nature Reserve**, home to *banteng*, deer, hornbills and grey langurs. At Pangandaran's white-sand beach there are many hotels and eateries offering seafood. Sunrises and sunsets are particularly spectacular here; local boat owners take visitors for a closer look at the marine park. Thirty kilometres (18 miles) west of the beach is **Green Canyon**, where caves and karst landscapes dominate.

CENTRAL JAVA

The glorious past of this region lives on today in the cultural capital of Yogyakarta and the spectacular World Heritage Sites of Borobudur and Prambanan. Majestic volcanoes lie to the north

Lapped by the Java Sea to the north and the Indian Ocean to the south, the landscape of Central Java is one of fertile agricultural fields dotted with forested volcanoes. The region's highlands, including mighty Gunung Merapi and less volatile Gunung Merbabu, give climbers, trekkers and birdwatchers ample reasons to come often and stay longer. Off the north coast, the Karimunjawa islands attract divers. To the south, the tempestuous Indian Ocean is flanked by beaches – some of black volcanic sand, some white-sand – offering freshly caught fish grilled to order. Part of the south coast is touched by a limestone karst mountain range riddled with caves, very few of which have been explored. Central Java's 35 million inhabitants live primarily in rural areas, where population densities are high. In the hinterland they are farmers and on the coasts they are fishermen, with a large number of handicraft-makers scattered throughout. North coast Semarang is the only industrial city.

The people of this region believe themselves to be "true Javanese", descended from Central Java's two great Mataram empires. The role of their royal courts as cultural centres is still deeply felt today. Often it is the cultural attractions that draw visitors here:

the sombre stillness of ancient Hindu and Buddhist temples, the sequestered courtyards of its 18th-century Islamic palaces and its traditional arts: gamelan, shadow puppetry and dance.

Much of interest is concentrated in and around the twin court cities, Yogyakarta (fondly called Jogja) and Surakarta (or Solo). It was here, on the well-irrigated banks of several adjacent rivers, that Central Java's two great Mataram empires – one ancient and one modern – flourished. The role of the Javanese courts as cultural centres

Main attractions
YOGYAKARTA: KERATON, PERFORMING ARTS, BATIK
KOTA GEDE SILVERSMITHS
BOROBUDUR
DIENG PLATEAU
PRAMBANAN
SOLO

LEFT: making traditional batik, Yogyakarta.
RIGHT: tobacco crop on the fertile soil of Central Java.

has long been recognised, but their vast catalogue of artistic wealth has only begun to be explored.

YOGYAKARTA AND ITS REGION

Sprawling **Yogyakarta** (**Jogja**) ❾ is situated at the very core of an ancient region known as Mataram, site of the first great Central Javanese empires. From the 8th to the early 10th century, this fertile plain was ruled by a succession of Indianised kings – the builders of Borobudur, Prambanan and dozens of other elaborate stone monuments. Around AD 900, these rulers suddenly and inexplicably shifted their capital to East Java, and

for more than six centuries, Mataram was deserted.

At the end of the 16th century, the area was revived by a new Islamic power based at Kota Gede, east of present-day Jogja. This second Mataram dynasty was founded around 1575 by King Panembahan Senopati.

The Yogyakarta and Surakarta (Solo) sultanates came into being in 1755 when the Dutch – fearful of Mataram's power – split the kingdom into two parts, further dividing each sultanate into two separate entities to dilute their influence. The present sultan of Yogyakarta is descended from one of two Yogyakarta royal families, hence

Bedoyo dancers at the Sultan's Palace in Yogyakarta, c.1860.

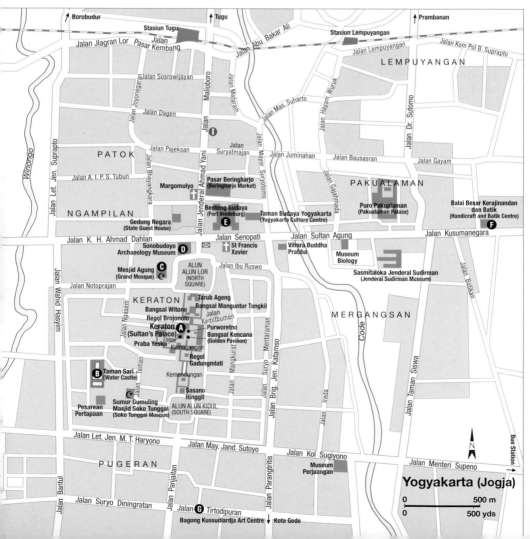

Yogyakarta (Jogja)

there are two palaces in Jogja. From the original Surakarta line, there are also two families and two palaces, Kasunanan and Mangkunegaran, both in Solo.

The Yogyakarta court was twice invaded by foreigners for failure to comply with colonial instructions – once by the Dutch in 1810 and again by the British in 1812. Later, it was swept into the Great Java War (1825–30), led by the charismatic crown prince of the ruling family, Pangeran Diponegoro.

In more recent times, Jogja served as the capital of the troubled Indonesian republic for four long years during the fight against the Dutch, from 1945 until 1949. This was a time of extraordinary social ferment. Six million refugees, more than a million young fighters and an enlightened young sultan (Hamengkubuwono IX) transformed the venerable court city into a hotbed of revolutionary idealism. Rewarded for its efforts by the new Indonesian government, Jogja was awarded Special Province status and enjoys the same privileges as the capital city, Jakarta.

The Sultan's Palace

Today, it is Jogja's cultural attractions that travellers come to see – ancient temples, palaces, batik, gamelan, dances and *wayang* puppet performances. Growing in popularity are nature-related activities. The city is a mere hour by plane from Jakarta or 9 hours by the Bima Express train; from Bali, it is 1½ hours by air or 12 hours by bus. Jogja is easy to get around: there are plenty of taxis, public buses and man-powered *becak* (pedicab). *Andong* (horse carts) are used both inside the urban areas and in the countryside.

The first stop is the **Keraton** Ⓐ (Sultan's Palace; Sat–Thur 8am–2pm; Fri 8–11am; charge), a two-centuries-old palace complex that stands at the heart of the city. According to traditional cosmological beliefs, the Yogyanese ruler is literally the "navel" or central "spike" of the universe, anchoring the temporal world and communicating with the mystical realm of powerful deities. In this scheme of things, the Keraton is both the capital of the kingdom and the

BELOW: coat of arms at Surakarta's Keraton Kasunanan.

TIP

Every morning at the Keraton, a classical Javanese court dance, gamelan music, leather or wooden puppet show or poetry recital is held. Check www.jogjapages.com for schedules.

hub of the cosmos, bringing the two together through the application of certain elaborate design principles.

The palace houses not only the sultan and his family, but also the dynastic regalia *(pusaka)*, private meditation and ceremonial chambers, a magnificent throne hall, several audience and performance pavilions, a mosque, an immense royal garden, stables, barracks, an armaments foundry and two expansive parade grounds planted with sacred banyan trees – all laid out in a carefully conceived complex of walled compounds, narrow lanes and massive gateways, and bounded by a fortified outer wall measuring 2km (1.5 miles) on every side.

Construction of the Keraton began in 1755 and continued for almost 40 years, throughout the long reign of Hamengkubuwono I. Structurally, very little has been added since his death in 1792. Today, only the innermost compound is considered the Keraton proper, while the maze of lanes and lesser compounds, the mosque and the two vast squares, have been integrated into the city. Long sections of the outermost wall *(benteng)* remain, and many of the residences inside are still owned and occupied by members of the royal family.

To step within the massive inner walls is to enter a patrician world of grace and elegance. In the first half of the 20th century, the interior was remodelled along European lines, incorporating Italian marble, cast-iron columns, crystal chandeliers and rococo furnishings into a classical Javanese setting. The "Golden Pavilion" or **Bangsal Kencana** (central throne hall) is its most striking feature – a *pendopo* or open pavilion consisting of an ornate sloping roof supported at the centre by four massive wooden columns.

There is much else to see within the Keraton, including the Keraton and Royal Carriage Museums, ancient gamelan sets, and two great *kala*-head gateways.

Puro Pakualam

About 2km (1.2 miles) east of the Keraton is Jogja's "second palace",

BELOW: a pavilion in the Keraton grounds.

Puro Pakualam. In an attempt to stabilise uprisings in Central Java and counterbalance the strength of Sultan Hamengkubuwono I, in 1812 then-Lieutenant Governor-General Thomas Stamford Raffles created a principality within the Yogyakarta sultanate and awarded it to one of the sultan's sons, Prince Notokusumo. After becoming Paku Alam I, the prince constructed this palace, which is now the official residence of Prince Paku Alam IX and a museum (Tue, Thur and Sun 9.30am–2.30pm; charge); performances are held here too.

Taman Sari

Behind the Keraton stand the ruins of the royal pleasure garden, **Taman Sari** Ⓑ (daily 9am–3pm; charge). It was constructed over many years, beginning in 1758 by Hamengkubuwono I and then abruptly abandoned after his death. Dutch representatives to the sultan's court marvelled at its large artificial lake, underground and underwater passageways, meditation retreats, a series of sunken bathing pools and an imposing mansion of European design.

The ruins of the mansion, named Water Castle by the Dutch, occupy high ground at the northern end of the huge Taman Sari complex, overlooking a colony of batik painters. The crumbling walls and a massive gate are all that remain of the building. A tunnel behind the castle leads to a complex of three restored bathing pools, **Umbul Bindangun**. The large central pool was designed for the use of queens, concubines and princesses, while the small southernmost pool was reserved for the sultan.

Further south, tucked amid a crowded *kampung* (village), lies **Pesarean Pertapaan**, an interesting royal retreat reached by passing through an ornate archway west of the bathing area, then following a winding path to the left. The main structure, a small Chinese-style temple with a forecourt and galleries, is said to be where the sultan and his sons meditated for seven days and nights at a time.

The most remarkable structure at Taman Sari is the **Sumur Gumuling** (circular well), a *mesjid* (mosque) with a well as its centrepiece. Folklore says the secret tunnels found there (now collapsed) led to the sea where the sultan could commune with Ratu Kidul, the powerful Goddess of the South Sea, to whom all Mataram rulers had been promised in marriage by the dynasty's founder and from whom they are said to derive their mystical powers. Access is by an underground passageway, whose entrance lies to the west of the Water Castle. The "well" is in fact a sunken atrium, with circular galleries facing onto a small, round pool.

Jalan Malioboro

Jogja's main thoroughfare, **Jalan Malioboro**, begins in front of the royal audience pavilion, at the front of the palace, and ends at a *tugu* (monument) dedicated to the guardian serpent spirit Kyai Jaga some 2km (1.2 miles) to the north. Jalan Malioboro derives its name from the

A keris dagger.

BELOW: the extraordinary Sumur Gumuling mosque.

TIP

The best way to explore Jogja is by *becak*, a three-wheeled man-powered pedicab, or *andong* (horse cart). Confirm the fare upfront, then enjoy the ride through scenic backstreets.

Sanskrit words *malya bhara*, meaning "garland bearing", as the royal processional route was always adorned with bouquets during ceremonial occasions.

Today, Jalan Malioboro is primarily a shopping district, though it is also an area of historical and cultural interest. Begin at the northern town square (*alun-alun*) and stroll up the street, stopping first at the **Mesjid Agung** 🅒 (Grand Mosque), built in 1773, and notice the two fenced-off banyan trees standing on either side of the road in the centre of the square. They symbolise the balance of opposing forces within the Javanese kingdom.

Nearby, on the northwestern side of the square, is **Sonobudoyo Archaeology Museum** 🅓 (Tue–Thur 9am–2pm, Fri 8–11am, Sat 8am–1pm; charge). Opened in 1935 by the Java Institute, a cultural foundation of wealthy Javanese and Dutch art patrons, today the museum houses important collections of prehistoric artefacts, Hindu-Buddhist bronzes, *wayang* puppets, dance costumes and traditional Javanese weapons.

Proceed northwards from the square through the gates and out across Jogja's main intersection. Immediately ahead on the right stands the old Dutch garrison, **Benteng Budaya** 🅔 (Fort Vredeburg; tel: 0274-586 934; Tue–Thur 8.30am–2pm, Fri 8.30–11am, Sat 8.30am–noon; charge), a museum and cultural centre complete with exhibition and performance halls. (Visit www.jogjapages.com for exhibitions, performances and times.) Opposite, on the left, stands the State Guest House. It was first the Dutch resident's mansion and, during the revolution, was also used as the presidential palace. Further along on the right, past the fort, is the huge central market, **Pasar Beringharjo** (9am–4pm), a rabbit warren of small stalls selling everything from fresh fruits and vegetables to batik, "antiques" and hardware. Bargain hard here.

Back out on Malioboro, both sides of the street are lined with handicraft shops selling a great range of batik, leather goods, baskets, tortoise shell, jewellery and endless knick-knacks. At dusk (4–10pm) the sidewalks explode

BELOW: *wayang kulit* shadow-puppet play at Sonobudoyo Archaeological Museum.

into an incredible street market of handicraft stalls and food and drink stands. Taste-test some of the traditional snacks such as *onde-onde* (rice flour balls filled with sweet mung bean paste), *lumpia* (spring rolls), *klepon* (green-coloured balls filled with palm sugar) or steamed coconut-coated *putu*.

Performing arts

Of the many art forms, *wayang kulit* or shadow-puppet play lies closest to the heart of the Central Javanese. All-night performances for *selamatan* ritual feasts, weddings or ceremonies occur regularly, often in village compounds. In addition to weekly *wayang kulit* plays at the Keraton, there is an 8-hour presentation on the second Saturday of every month at the **Sasano Hinggil** (daily 9am–5.30pm; charge), near the Keraton. **Sonobudoyo Archaeological Museum** (Jalan Trikora No. 6; tel: 0274-376 775) holds *wayang kulit* shows daily except Sunday (8–10pm, closed the night before public holidays; charge; camera fee). Dance and music performances, both traditional and contemporary, as well as changing visual art exhibitions, are held at **Taman Budaya Yogyakarta** (Jalan Sriwedari No.1; tel: 0274-523 512). Check programme on arrival to see what is currently on offer.

Court dances are also taught outside the Keraton at a number of private schools and government art academies in the city. The performances within the Keraton itself should not be missed, but also check out **Bagong Kussudiardja Art Centre** (Kembaran Rt. 04 Rw. 21 No. 148 Tamantirto, Kasihan, Bantul, in southern Jogja; tel: 0274-376 394; www.ybk.or.id), a large performing arts complex dedicated to creating new works within the framework of classical music, dance and theatre. Free monthly performances are open to the public.

Perhaps the ultimate in Javanese dance spectaculars is the Ramayana Sendratari Ballet. A modernised version (the lengthy dialogue in old Javanese has been cut) of the lavish *wayang orang* dance-drama, the entire epic (four episodes, one per night 7.30–9.30pm) is presented on

Tamin Sari water palace.

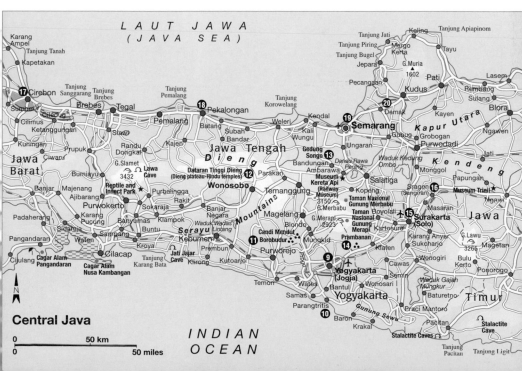

*Reprising the roles of
Rama and Sita in a
classical dance-drama.*

BELOW: getting
around by rickshaw.

four clear nights on and around the
full moon from May to October. The
elegant 9th-century Roro Jonggrang
temple at Prambanan *(see page 168)*
is the backdrop. (Check www.jogja-
pages.com for dates.) There is also an
indoor theatre at Prambanan where
performances are held during the
rainy season.

Batik town

Jogja's most famous handicraft is
still batik, now a Unesco Cultural
Heritage icon. Visit the **Balai
Besar Kerajinandan dan Batik** ❻
(Handicraft and Batik Centre) on
Jalan Kusumanegara. An individually
guided tour costs nothing, and is an
excellent introduction to the craft's
painstaking manufacturing process,
as well as to the staggering variety
of patterns and colours to be found
throughout Java. Batik courses are
taught here and at other centres.

Batik cloth is produced and sold all
over Jogja, but especially in the south
of the city on **Jalan Tirtodipuran**
❼, a street with more than 25 batik
workshops and showrooms, most

of which are happy to let visitors
observe production. Many of the
city's better-known artists, and a
number of aspiring ones, also produce batik paintings made with the
same resist-dye method, but specifically designed for framing and
hanging. For lower-quality souvenir
batik cloths and clothing go to Pasar
Beringharjo or Mirota Batik, both on
Jalan Malioboro.

Kota Gede

Long before Yogyakarta was established, **Kota Gede,** 4km (2.5 miles)
southeast of Jogja, was founded
in 1575 by Sultan Panembahan
Senopati as the first capital of the
Mataram Empire, where it remained
until his successor moved it to Kerta.
During its golden years, Kota Gede
attracted a myriad of wealthy traders, including Arab and Dutch, who
built mansions in exceptional architectural styles.

A pleasant way to arrive is by
andong (horse-drawn carriage),
about a 20-minute ride from Jalan
Malioboro. Now known for its

silversmiths, it is an interesting place to stroll around and imagine how it must have been in its heyday, while shopping for jewellery. Accommodation is available in some of the historic buildings, and there is a restaurant.

About 500 metres (yards) behind the *pasar* (traditional market) is the **Kota Gede Royal Cemetery** (Sun, Mon and Thur 10am–4pm, Friday 1–5pm; charge) dating back to Mataram times. Javanese attire is required to enter to see the graves of Senopati and other important figures, which can be "rented" at the desk where men guard the cemetery. Behind the cemetery is the oldest mosque in the Jogja area and across the street from the cemetery is a traditional Javanese house. While in the area, you may like to visit **Monggo Chocolate Factory** (Jalan Dalem KG III/978-RT 043 RW 10, Kelurahan Purbayan Kotagede; tel: 0274-710 2202; 9am–4pm Mon–Sat) to see "Belgian" chocolate being made, using Indonesia cacao of course.

Beaches, caving and climbing

The Indian Ocean is less than an hour's drive south of central Yogyakarta. **Parangtritis** ⑩ is a wonderful stretch of black sand backed by towering bluffs, both a popular recreation spot and a place of worship, where the legendary Ratu Kidul, Queen of the South Seas, is said to live. The rip tides are dangerous here, so swimming is forbidden. Nearby is the sacred **Parangkusumo beach**. Every year on 30 Rajab of the Javanese calendar (ask a local to check for you), a ceremony called Labuhan Alit is held to commemorate the coronation of the Yogyakarta Sultan and offerings are given to Ratu Kidul. The beaches can be done in a day trip from Jogja, but basic lodgings are available if you prefer to stay the night. There are great sunsets on Parangtritis hill, east of the beach.

Twenty kilometres (12 miles) southwest of Jogja via Bantul city are **Samas** and **Pandansimo beaches**. Both with the same stormy shores as Parangtritis, Samas is home to a village-run sea turtle conservation project, and Pandansimo is a Javanese

TIP

One of the best batik courses in Jogja is at Brahma Tirta Sari Studio and Gallery. Not only does it teach the process of batik, it also explains the philosophical meanings behind the traditional patterns (www. brahmatirtasari.org).

BELOW: Kota Gede gateway.

Durian stalls, Jogja.

BELOW: Parangtritis beach.

pilgrimage site. For swimming beaches, some with white sand, head 60km (40 miles) southeast of Jogja to Baron, Krakal, Kukup, Sepanjang, Drini, Sundak, Ngandong, Siung, Wedi Ombo, Sandang or Ngrenehan. While all are excellent choices for a day of relaxation away from the city's traffic, **Ngrenehan** is the best place to have a swim and enjoy some freshly caught fish cooked to order. At Ngobaran beach, 5 minutes from Ngrenehan by car, is Kejawen Hindu temple, built in 2005.

North of the beaches rises the **Gunung Sewu mountain range**, a length of karst limestone hills perforated by caves. Only a few have been explored, but with the cooperation of villagers who have developed homestays as part of a community project, two have been sufficiently explored by a local caving group to allow novices to participate in the adrenalin rush. The first, Jomblang, requires a vertical rappel down an inclined wall where there is a surprising subterranean forest, fed by the sun and rainfall entering through an enormous, gaping

hole at the entrance. Connected to Jomblang by a horizontal corridor is Grubug, a much riskier descent. A river flowing into Grubug is raftable in the rainy season. Nearby, on Siung beach, enormous limestone walls prove popular with cliff climbers. A paragliding jamboree is held in this area when the winds are favourable, March–April.

North of Jogja is volatile **Gunung Merapi**, popular with climbers until its violent eruption in late 2010. Trekkers and birdwatchers now head to safer environs, for example **Gunung Merbabu** further north. From Kopeng on its southern flank to Kenteng Songo, one of its two peaks, takes between 8 and 10 hours. The drive there via the Selo Pass affords fabulous volcano views.

Handicrafts around Jogja

The villages around Jogja specialise in handmade crafts, many of which are exported abroad and are the area's second-largest revenue earner after tourism. Shopping in the villages where the items are made means the craftsmen – not a middleman – reap the benefits with profits going back into the local area, and shoppers get a look at real life in the countryside. South of Jogja are Kasongan and Panjangrejo, which make earthenware pottery; Kota Gede is known for its delicate filigree silverwork; Manding produces leather bags, belts, shoes and jackets; wooden masks and other woodcarvings are found in Sendangsari-Krebet and Patuk; and *wayang* puppets and hand-forged ceremonial *keris* blades are specialities of Imogiri.

For authentic *keris* (ceremonial daggers; *see page 175*) – not the tourist variety sold at souvenir shops – Empu Sungkowo (*keris* maker) Harum Brodjo (Gatak, Sumberagung, Moyudan, Sleman; tel: 81-2273 1372) is a master craftsman. It takes two months to finish one dagger. You must make an appointment to visit him.

Borobudur and the Dieng Plateau

If your driver takes the scenic route through villages instead of the congested highway, a leisurely one-hour drive across riverbeds and rice fields leads to the steps of fabled **Borobudur** ⓫, 40km (25 miles) northwest of Jogja (daily, 6am–5.30pm; charge; licensed guides available), a Unesco World Heritage Site.

Allow yourself a minimum of two hours to tour the temple, though you could easily spend half a day here. This huge mandala, the world's largest Buddhist monument, was built sometime during the relatively short Sailendra dynasty between AD 778 and AD 856 – 300 years before Angkor Wat and 200 years before Notre-Dame.

Yet, within little more than a century of its completion, Borobudur and the other structures in Central Java were mysteriously abandoned. At about this time, too, neighbouring Gunung Merapi erupted violently, covering Borobudur in volcanic ash and debris, concealing it for centuries.

Borobudur's restoration

In 1900, the Dutch government responded to cries of outrage from within its own ranks and established a committee for the restoration of Borobudur. The huge task was accomplished between 1907 and 1911 by a Dutch military engineer with a keen interest in Javanese antiquities.

At this time, Borobudur was discovered to be a fragile mantle of stone blocks that had been built upon a natural mound of earth. Rainwater was seeping through the stone mantle and eroding the soft foundation from within, while mineral salts were collecting on the monument's surface, where they acted in conjunction with sun, wind, rain and fungus to destroy it. Grandiose plans for a permanent restoration were never realised, due to the intervention of two world wars and an economic depression.

During the 1950s and 1960s, it became increasingly evident that Borobudur was structurally endangered. Unesco was called to direct a rescue operation. Technical assistance

Highly volatile 2,923-metre (9,550ft) Gunung Merapi erupted in 2010, killing at least 300 people – primarily from pyroclastic blasts – and displacing half a million more. In 2004 the "danger zone" of the mountain was declared a national park, but government efforts to relocate the inhabitants failed because of their deep-seated spiritual beliefs about the mountain. Merapi's national park status is now being challenged in court.

BELOW: Borobudur and Gunung Merapi at sunrise.

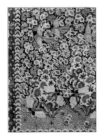

Pekalongan batik shows Japanese influences.

BELOW: individual dagobas, mini-stupas, at Borobudur.

and financing became available, and the project officially got under way in 1975. The scale of the project was spectacular. It took nine long years to dismantle, catalogue, photograph, clean, treat and reassemble a total of 1,300,232 stone blocks. Each stone had to be individually inspected, scrubbed and chemically treated before being replaced. In addition, a new infrastructure of reinforced concrete, tar, asphalt, epoxy and tin was constructed to support the entire monument, and a system of drainage pipes installed to prevent further seepage.

In the end, the work was completed at a cost of US$25 million, more than three times the original estimate. It is unlikely that the full import of Borobudur as a religious monument will ever be known. An estimated 30,000 stone-cutters and sculptors, 15,000 labourers and thousands more masons worked to build the original monument. At a time when the entire population of Central Java numbered less than 1 million, this represented perhaps 10 percent of the available workforce to a single effort.

Spiritual significance

Seen from the air, Borobudur forms a mandala, a geometric aid for meditation. Seen from a distance on the ground, Borobudur is a stupa, a model of the cosmos in three vertical parts: a square base supporting a hemispheric body and a crowning spire. The traditional pilgrimage route approaches from the east, and ascends the terraced monument, circumambulating each terrace clockwise in succession to see how every relief and carving contributes to the whole.

There were originally 10 levels at Borobudur, each falling within one of the three divisions of the Mahayana Buddhist universe: *khamadhatu*, the lower spheres of human life; *rupadhatu*, the middle sphere of "form"; and *arupadhatu*, the higher sphere of detachment from the world. The lowest gallery of reliefs, now covered, depicts the delights of this world and the damnations of the next.

The next five levels (the processional terrace and four concentric galleries) show in their reliefs (beginning at the eastern staircase and going

around each gallery clockwise) the life of Prince Siddhartha on his way to becoming the Buddha, scenes from the Jataka folk tales about his previous incarnations, and the life of the Bodhisattva Sudhana (from the Gandavyuha). These tales are illustrated in stone by a parade of commoners, princes, musicians, dancing girls and saints, with many interesting ethnographic details about daily life in ancient Java. Placed in niches above the galleries are 432 stone Buddhas, each displaying one of five mudra or hand positions, alternately calling upon the earth as witness and embodying charity, meditation, fearlessness and reason.

Above the square galleries, three circular terraces support 72 perforated *dagoba*s (miniature stupas), which are unique in Buddhist art. Most contain a statue of the meditating *Dhyani* Buddha. Two statues have been left uncovered to gaze over the nearby Menoreh Mountains, where a series of knobs and knolls is said to represent Gunadharma, the temple's divine architect. These three terraces are, in fact,

transitional steps leading to the 10th and highest level, the realm of formlessness and abstraction (*arupadhatu*), embodied in the huge crowning stupa.

Before leaving the park, have a look at two **museums** near the exit gate. One houses stones, Buddha images and other pieces from the original structure. The other houses an outrigger ship built to replicate vessels seen on the reliefs. The ship undertook an expedition to Madagascar in 2003–4, recreating the trade route that might have been used when Borobudur was constructed almost two millennia ago. The museum is well presented and the fully reconstructed ship is magnificent.

Every year, thousands of Buddhists arrive from all over Asia to walk in procession from nearby Mendut temple to Borobudur in celebration of Waisak (date changes annually), the holiest day of the year for Buddhists.

Pawon and Mendut

Two smaller, subsidiary *candi* lie along a straight line directly east of Borobudur. The closer of the two is tiny **Candi Pawon** (meaning "kitchen"

Reliefs show scenes from the Buddha's life.

BELOW: Borobudur lay hidden in the jungle for centuries.

The rediscovery of Borobudur

The story of Borobudur's "rediscovery" began in 1814, when the British governor of Java, Thomas Stamford Raffles (who later founded Singapore in 1819), visited Semarang and heard rumours of "a mountain of Buddhist sculptures in stone" near Magelang. Raffles dispatched his military engineer, H.C.C. Cornelius, to investigate. Cornelius found a hillock overgrown with trees, but curiously scattered with hundreds of andesite blocks.

For two months, Raffles directed a massive clearing operation, removing vegetation and layers of earth, until it became clear that an elaborate structure lay beneath. He dug no further, for fear of damaging the unknown monument. In the years that followed, Borobudur was laid bare and subsequently suffered almost a century of decay, plunder and abuse; thousands of stones were "borrowed" by villagers and priceless sculptures ended up as decorations in the homes of the rich and powerful.

In 1896, the Dutch gave away eight cartloads of Borobudur souvenirs to visiting King Chulalongkorn of Siam, including 30 relief panels, five Buddha statues, two lions and a guardian sculpture. Many of these and other irreplaceable works of Indo-Javanese art ended up in private collections, and now reside in museums around the world.

Javanese tourists, Borobudur temple,

BELOW: Buddha at Candi Mendut.

or "crematorium"; daily 6am–sunset; charge), situated in a shady clearing 1.7km (1 mile) from Borobudur's main entrance. It is often referred to as Borobudur's "porch temple" because of its proximity, and may well have been the last stop on a brick-paved pilgrimage route.

Just 1km (0.6 mile) further east, across the confluence of two holy rivers (the Progo and the Elo), lies beautiful **Candi Mendut** (daily 6am–sunset; charge). Unlike most other central Javanese monuments, which face east, Mendut opens to the northwest.

The base and both sides of the staircase are decorated with scenes from moralistic fables and folk tales, many of which concern animals. The main body contains superbly carved panels depicting *bodhisattva* and Buddhist goddesses. These are the largest reliefs found on any Indonesian temple.

The walls of the Candi Mendut antechamber are decorated with money trees and celestial beings, and contain two beautiful panels of a man and a woman amid swarms of playful children. It is thought that these two panels represent child-eating ogres who converted to Buddhism and became protectors instead of devourers.

Mendut contains three of the finest Buddhist statues in the world: a magnificent 3-metre (10ft) tall figure of the seated Sakyamuni Buddha, flanked on his left and right by Bodhisattva Vajrapani and Bodhisattva Avalokitesvara, each about 2.5 metres (8ft) high. The central or Sakyamuni statue symbolises the first sermon of the Buddha at the Deer Park near Benares, India, as shown by the position of his hands (*dharmacakra mudra*) and by the small relief of a wheel between two deer. The two *bodhisattva*, or buddhas-to-be, have elected to stay behind in the world to help Buddha's followers.

The Dieng plateau

Around 100km (60 miles) northeast of Borobudur are arguably the oldest temples in Central Java, dating back to the late 7th century. Travel to the **Dieng plateau** ⑫ via Kledung Pass, between Mounts Sindong and Sumbing, for breathtaking scenery and, in season, to see the tobacco plantations. Eight small temples stand on this 2,000-metre (6,500ft) high isolated plateau that is usually shrouded in mist. The temples are simple in detail, but it is the mysterious location and the close proximity to volcanic activity, brightly coloured sulphur springs and bubbling mud-holes that are of interest. There is an eerie quality to this site, which ancient Javanese felt to be a centre of supernatural powers. The remains of other temples (originally 400 structures stood here) and several wooden pavilions indicating perhaps a palace or monastery are spread among the sulphur lakes.

The main temples are named after the heroes of the *Mahabharata (see page 91)* and all are Hindu in design. To the east of Candi Bima is the **Telaga Warna** (Coloured Lake), with fluorescent hues caused by sulphur

vents. Close by are meditation caves. A visit to the plateau is a full day trip. Basic accommodation is available, as well as the lovely four-star Gallery Hotel Kresna in nearby Wonosobo. Visit Dieng plateau early before the afternoon clouds roll in.

East of Dieng plateau in the cool mountain air of the **Bandungan highlands** are the little-visited **Gedung Songo** ⑬ temples, the most spectacularly situated antiquities in Java. Successors to the *candi* at Dieng plateau, nine Sivaitic shrines were built by the Sanjaya dynasty in the 8th century and overlook the lofty peaks and verdant valleys of Central Java, but only seven remain. On a clear day three volcanoes and the Dieng massif can be seen from here. Arrive at sunrise and spend the day exploring the temples and inspiring landscape by foot or on horseback and soaking in the hot springs. Also in this area, near Ambarawa, is the wonderful **Museum Kereta Api** (Railway Museum, Jalan Stasiun No. 1, Ambarawa; tel: 0298-591 035), housing 21 German- and Dutch-built cogwheel locomotives and a restored train station. Rides through the scenic countryside are offered on weekends and holidays. Check timetables on arrival.

EAST TO PRAMBANAN AND SURAKARTA (SOLO)

Heading east from Jogja, past the airport, the main Jogja–Solo highway slices across a volcanic plain littered with ancient ruins. These *candi* are considered by the Javanese of Central Java to be royal mausoleums and the region is known as the Valley of the Kings.

In the centre of the plain, 17km (10 miles) from Jogja, lies **Prambanan** ⑭ (daily 6am–sunset; charge), a Hindu temple complex and a Unesco World Heritage Site. Completed sometime around AD 856 to commemorate a major battle victory, it was deserted within a few years of its completion and eventually collapsed. Preparations for the restoration of the central temple began in 1918, work started in 1937, and it was completed in 1953. Over time, other disasters have brought it

Candi Pawon.

BELOW: ancient temples on the cool heights of the Dieng plateau.

BELOW: intricate detail at Borobudur, the work of some 30,000 craftsmen.

harm. In 2006, a 5.9-magnitude earthquake hit Jogja, and 30–40 percent of the complex sustained major damage. Within a week after the earthquake, a rapid assessment mission was organised by the Indonesian government and Unesco to prepare the international emergency assistance to the compound. The majority of the restoration work has been completed, and most of Prambanan is open to the public, but the main temple – which sustained serious structural damage – is closed and may remain so for a few years.

Prambanan complex

The central courtyard of the main complex contains eight buildings. The three largest are arrayed north to south: the magnificent 47-metre (155ft) tall main **Candi Siva Mahadeva** is flanked on either side by the slightly smaller shrines **Candi Vishnu** (to the north) and **Candi Brahma** (to the south). Standing opposite these, to the east, are three smaller temples that once contained the "vehicles" of each god: Siva's bull (*nandi*), Brahma's gander (*hamsa*)

and Vishnu's sun-bird (*garuda*). Of these, only *nandi* remains. By the northern and southern gates of the central compound are two identical court temples, standing 16 metres (50ft) high.

Candi Siva Mahadeva, the largest of the temples and dedicated to Siva, is also known as **Roro Jonggrang** (often incorrectly spelled Loro), a folk name sometimes given to the temple complex as a whole. Local legend has it that Roro Jonggrang was a princess wooed by an unwanted suitor. She commanded the man to build a temple in one night, and then frustrated his nearly successful effort by pounding the rice mortar prematurely, announcing the dawn. Enraged, he turned the maiden to stone, and according to the tale, she remains here in the northern chamber of the temple as a statue of Siva's consort, Durga. In the other three chambers are statues of Agastya, the "Divine Teacher" (facing south); Ganesha, Siva's elephant-headed son (facing west); and a 3-metre (10ft) Siva (central chamber, facing east).

Java's ancient past

For the Central Javanese, the *candi* (ancient stone monuments) are tangible evidence of the great energy and artistry of their ancestors. For the foreign visitor, communion with one of these 1,000-year-old shrines provides an opportunity to ponder the achievements of a magnificent culture.

A great deal of effort has been expended since 1900 to excavate, reconstruct and restore their reliefs, study their iconography and decipher their inscriptions. Still, little more than the most basic symbolism of these structures is known, and even their chronology is in doubt. What is known is that they are among the most technically accomplished structures produced in ancient times, and that the awe inspired by their presence has formed a substantial part of their message.

One aspect of Roro Jonggrang's appeal is its symmetry and graceful proportions. Another is its wealth of sculptural detail. On the inner walls of the balustrade, beginning from the eastern gate and proceeding clockwise, the wonderfully vital and engrossing tale of the *Ramayana* is told in bas-relief (and is completed on the balustrade of the Brahma temple).

Prambanan's beauty and variety demand more than a single visit. One of the most romantic ways to view the temple is by moonlight, during an open-air performance of the *Ramayana*, staged on full-moon nights between May and October. During the rest of the year, abridged performances of the epic are held in the adjacent **Trimurti Theatre**.

Surakarta (Solo)

Located just 60km (40 miles) northeast of Jogja on the same highway as Prambanan is noble **Surakarta ⑮**, also known as **Solo**, only an hour away by car or train. Start early for a one-day visit or, if time permits, stay longer and enjoy a batik course, gamelan lesson or join one of the many meditation centres on nearby Gunung Lawu. Solo can also be reached by air from Jakarta and Bali. Although larger than Jogja, Solo is more sedate and has certain cultural characteristics that are different from Jogja's.

Solo's Keraton Kasunanan

On the banks of the mighty Bengawan Solo, Java's longest river, stands the **Keraton Kasunanan** (Sat–Thur 8.30am– 1pm; charge), constructed between 1743 and 1746. As with the Yogyakarta palace, Surakarta's Keraton defines the centre of the town and the kingdom as well as, metaphysically, the hub of the cosmos. Indeed, the similarities between the two courts, built within 10 years of each other, are striking. Both have a thick outer wall enclosing a network of narrow lanes and smaller compounds, two large squares, a mosque and a central or inner royal residential complex. Perhaps the major difference is that Surakarta has no north–south processional boulevard or pleasure palace.

The Keraton museum was established in 1963 and contains ancient

Temples at Prambanan.

BELOW: Prambanan, a Unesco World Heritage Site.

TIP

Rafting on the Progo River, which originates at Jumprit on Gunung Sindoro northwest of Borobudur, is an exhilarating sport in the rainy season. In February, the lower reaches are apt to flood and are extremely dangerous. However, in the dry season, the mighty tiger becomes a kitten and is gentle enough for beginners.

Hindu-Javanese bronzes, traditional Javanese weapons and three marvellous coaches. The oldest coach – a lumbering, deep-bodied carriage built around 1740 – was a gift from the Dutch East India Company to Pakubuwono II. The museum also displays some remarkable figureheads from the old royal barges, including Kyai Rajamala, a giant of surpassing ugliness, who once adorned the bow of the Susuhunan's private boat and is said even now to emit a fishy odour when daily offerings are not forthcoming.

Dance and music as high art

After visiting the Keraton, stroll through the narrow lanes outside, and be sure to pay a visit to nearby **Sasana Mulya**, the music and dance pavilion of the **Indonesian Arts High School** (STSI), located just to the west of the main (north) palace gate. This is an art school with an illustrious history: it was here that the first musical notation for gamelan was devised at the turn of the 20th century. Visitors are welcome to listen and observe as long as they do it unobtrusively.

Puro Mangkunegaran

About 1km (0.6 mile) to the west and north of the main Keraton Kasunanan is a smaller, more intimate palace of another branch of the royal family. Begun by Mangkunegara II at the end of the 18th century and completed in 1866, the **Puro Mangkunegaran** is open to the public (Sat–Thur 9am–2pm; Fri 9am–12.30pm; charge).

The Mangkunegaran's outer *pendopo* (audience pavilion) is said to be the largest in Java – built of solid teakwood, and jointed and fitted in the traditional manner without nails. Note the brightly painted ceiling with the eight mystical Javanese colours in the centre, highlighted by a flame motif and bordered by symbols of the Javanese zodiac. The gamelan set in the southwest corner of the *pendopo* is known as Kyai Kanyut Mesem ("Kyai Kanyut Smiles"). Try to visit the palace on Wednesday mornings at 10am, when it is used to accompany informal dance rehearsals.

BELOW: the tympanum of Puro Mangkunagaran palace, Surakarta.

The museum is in the ceremonial hall of the palace, directly behind the *pendopo*, and it mainly houses the private collections of Mangkunegara IV: dance ornaments, *topeng* (masks), jewellery (including two silver chastity belts), ancient Javanese and Chinese coins, bronze figures and a superb set of *keris*.

Solo's antiques and batik

Solo, with its sizeable "antique industry", where many dealers collect and restore old European, Javanese and Chinese furniture and bric-a-brac, is excellent for the unhurried shopper who likes to explore out-of-the-way places in the hope of finding hidden treasures. The starting point for any treasure hunt is **Pasar Triwindu**, just south of the Mangkunegaran palace. Solo is also the home of Indonesia's largest batik manufacturers, three of whom have showrooms in town with reasonable fixed prices for superb fabrics, shirts and dresses. Many smaller batik shops also line the main streets. To see why Solo calls itself the City of Batik, visit the huge **Klewer** textile market beside the Grand Mosque and near the Keraton. Just be sure to know what you are doing if making a purchase here – batik can sell for as little as US$1 or as much as US$100 a metre.

As with Jogja, Solo is renowned as a centre for traditional Javanese performing arts. It is one of the best places to see an evening *wayang orang* dance performance or *wayang kulit* shadow play, or listen to live gamelan music. Ornately carved leather puppets, contorted wooden masks and even monstrous bronze gongs sold here make highly distinctive gifts. Solo is also a major centre for meditation, and there are a few places which hold yoga courses for foreigners.

Gunung Lawu and beyond

High on the northwest slopes of **Gunung Lawu**, about 36km (22 miles) east of Solo, are two 15th-century temples. Little is known about these *candi* except that they were the last ones built before the Javanese kingdoms converted to Islam. The reasoning behind the Mayan pyramid-shaped **Candi Suku** (charge) remains a mystery, as do the stone altars, three of which are in the shape of giant tortoises. Higher up the slope past tea plantations is multi-terraced **Candi Ceto** (charge), which is unfortunately in very bad repair, with a large *lingga* pointing west.

Sangiran

Eighteen km (11 miles) north of Solo is **Sangiran (Sragen)** ⓰, where the remains of the 1.5 million-year-old Java Man were first unearthed in 1891 *(see page 123)*. A Unesco World Heritage Site, the small Museum Trinil (Mon–Sat 9am–6pm) in nearby Krikilan village unfortunately only holds replicas of Java Man's skull fragments and jawbone, but there are also mastodon tusks, artefacts from prehistoric settlements and fossils, some of them over a million years old. New discoveries in this area are frequent.

Java Man skull.

BELOW: batik at Jogja's Brahama Tirta Sari Studio.

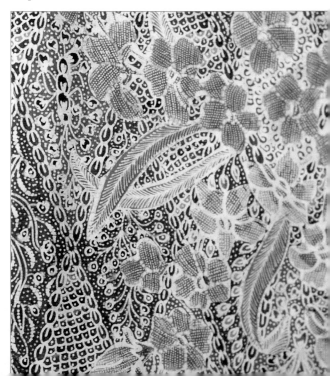

THE NORTH COAST

Java's northern coastal ports were once the busiest and richest towns on the island; they served as exporters of agricultural produce from the fertile Javanese hinterland, as builders and outfitters of large spice trading fleets, and as trading entrepôts frequented by merchants from all corners of the globe. Between the 15th and 17th centuries, when Islam was a new and growing force in the archipelago, these ports flourished as political and religious centres.

Beginning to the west, **Cirebon**  is an intriguing potpourri of Sundanese, Javanese, Chinese, Islamic and European influences. With a small harbour and a sizeable fishing industry, most sites are within walking distance, though a nice way to get around is by *becak* (pedicab).

Hindu deities in stone at Prambanan.

Cirebon's two major palaces were both built in 1678, giving each of two princes his own court. The **Keraton Kesepuhan** (belonging to the elder brother) sits on the site of the 15th-century Pakungwati Palace of Cirebon's earlier Hindu rulers.

BELOW: Cirebon's Keraton Kesepuhan.

Javanese in design with a Romanesque archway framed by mystical Chinese rocks, it is a spacious, pillared *pendopo* furnished with French period pieces. The walls of the Dalem Ageng (ceremonial chamber) behind are inlaid with blue-and-white tiles exhibiting biblical scenes. The adjoining museum has a coach in the shape of a winged and horned elephant grasping a trident in its trunk – a glorious fusion of Javanese, Hindu, Islamic, Persian, Greek and Chinese mythological elements.

Next to the Kesepuhan Palace stands the **Mesjid Agung** (Grand Mosque), constructed around AD 1500. Its two-tiered meru roof rests on elaborate wooden scaffolding, and the interior contains imported sandstone portals and a teakwood *kala*-head pulpit. Together with the Demak and Banten mosques, it is one of the oldest remaining landmarks of Islam on Java.

The **Keraton Kanoman** (palace of the younger brother) is nearby, reached via a busy marketplace. Large banyan trees shade the peaceful courtyard within, and as at Kesepuhan, the

furnishings are European and the walls are studded with tiles and porcelain from Holland and China. The museum has a collection of stakes still used to pierce the flesh of Muslim believers on Mohammed's birthday *(seni debus)*, as well as relics from Cirebon's past.

Taman Arum Sunyaragi, about 4km (2.5 miles) out of town on the southwestern bypass, was originally built as a fortress in 1702 and used as a base for resistance against the Dutch. It was cast in its present form in 1852 by a Chinese architect to serve as a pleasure palace for Cirebon's sultans. About 5km (3 miles) north of the city along the main north coast highway sits the hilltop **Tomb of Sunan Gunung Jati**, a 16th-century Cirebon ruler and one of the nine legendary *wali* who helped to propagate Islam on Java.

East to Semarang

About 220km (140 miles), a 4-hour drive, east of Cirebon is **Pekalongan** ⓲, which announces itself on roadside pillars as **Kota Batik** (Batik City). Quite apart from the many workshops and stores lining its streets, Pekalongan justifies this sobriquet by producing some of the finest and most highly prized batik on Java. The Pekalongan style, like Cirebon's, is distinctive – a blending of Islamic, Javanese, Chinese and European motifs.

Another 90km (55 miles) and 2 hours to the east, **Semarang** ⓳ rises out across a narrow coastal plain and up onto steep foothills. Known during Islamic times for its skilled shipwrights and abundant supplies of hardwood, it is today the commercial hub and provincial capital of Central Java. The Dutch Church, **Gereja Blenduk**, on Jalan Suprapto downtown, with its copper-clad dome and Greek cross-floor plan, was consecrated in 1753 and stands at the centre of the 18th-century European commercial district.

Semarang's most interesting district is its **Kampung Cina** (Chinatown) – a grid of narrow lanes tucked away in the city centre, reached by walking due south from the old church from

A gamelan musician plays a saron metallaphone.

BELOW: a market in Semarang.

Surakarta street scene.

Jalan Suari to Jalan Pekojan. Some old townhouses here retain the distinctive Nanyang style of elaborately carved doors and shutters and delicately wrought iron balustrades.

Half a dozen colourful Chinese temples and clan houses cluster in the space of a few blocks, the largest and oldest of which is on tiny Gang Lombok (turn right by the bridge from Jalan Pekojan). This is the **Thay Kak Sie temple**, built in 1772, which houses more than a dozen major deities. Those with time and an interest in things Chinese should visit **Gedung Batu**, Ming Admiral Cheng Ho's grotto on the western outskirts of town. Cheng Ho arrived in Java in 1405 and is credited with helping to spread Islam.

Demak and the teakwood towns

From Semarang, there are several towns to the east that may be visited as day trips. During the early 16th century, a Muslim kingdom centred on **Demak** ⓴ was the undisputed nonpareil among Java's coastal states; now, only the mosque remains. The city has become a place of pilgrimage – seven visits here is equal to a single pilgrimage to Mecca. The introduction of Islam to Java is credited to Sunan Kalijaga, a spiritual adviser to the Demak royal court, who used *wayang kulit* puppet shows to teach the illiterate masses about the new religion. His grave lies 2km (1.2 miles) southeast of the city. Another focal point is Demak's **Mesjid Besar** (Grand Mosque), considered the oldest and holiest mosque in Java. Built in 1466, its architecture combines Hindu and Arabic elements.

Neighbouring **Kudus** is renowned for beautiful hand-carved teakwood houses that grace the narrow lanes surrounding the Kauman area along its early 16th-century mosque and Muslim quarter. Kudus is also known as "Kota Kretek", or clove cigarette city, as several *kretek* companies are found here.

Jepara, 35km (20 miles) north of Kudus, has long been known for its teakwood carvings, catering to strong demand for finely detailed panels depicting scenes from the *Ramayana* and other Hindu-Javanese tales.

Symbolic Keris

The richly embellished dagger is not only a form of high art, but a symbol of male masculinity and an essential accessory for every Javanese man

Neatly tucked into the waistband of the traditional attire of the Indonesian man is the ceremonial dagger, or *keris*. No longer a weapon of defence, this ornate blade is rather an indication of social ranking and a source of cultural pride. An old Javanese proverb states: "Happy is the man who is the owner of a horse, wife, bird and keris." In many parts of Java, the *keris* is considered to be the most important item a man can own.

The traditional *keris* is a lightweight elongated dagger with a blade that is either straight or wavy, resembling a flame or serpent, coupled with a hilt and sheath. Originally worn for protection and used as a thrusting weapon, today it is an essential part of the groom's wedding and other ceremonial Javanese attire. So revered is the dagger that a man's *keris* can be a substitute in his absence at his own wedding.

Thought to possess a life of its own and endowed with magical powers, the *keris* is treated with great respect and reverence. There are many *keris* legends, including stories about wilful and bloodthirsty daggers that are capable of flying, turning into snakes, fathering children and taking human lives.

Stored in a place of honour, treated with perfumed oils and wrapped in silk and velvet, *keris* are passed down as sacred family heirlooms. Every year on the first day of the Javanese calendar, the Yogyakarta palace *pusaka* (heirlooms with spiritual powers), which include an assortment of sacred *keris*, are cleansed with scented water. Believing the objects to be magically endowed, crowds wait outside for the chance of receiving just a drop of the holy water used in the cleaning ritual, while the *keris* is carried from the palace in a coach.

The *keris* were (and still are) crafted by *empu* (master craftsmen), esteemed ironworkers imbued with divine status and who were so revered that they once came under the patronage of the court and were often considered members of the royal household.

Before beginning his work, the *empu* makes offerings, fasts, meditates and asks for divine inspiration. The blade is forged from several layers of nickel and meteoric iron, using a damascening technique which in turn produces the desired shades of light and dark patterns on the blade, the *pamor*. This pattern becomes visible after the blade has been polished and treated with citrus juice and arsenic. Each pattern has a name and meaning. *Wos wutah* (scattered rice grains), for example, represents prosperity.

Keris are distinguished by the number of curves (always uneven) they support. One wave represents god and king, while three, fire and passion. Each of these qualities is believed to have an effect on the life of the owner. If a man is not suitably matched to his *keris*, it can affect his life in a negative way. The hilt can be plain or carved with a mythical figure – believed to be capable of warding off evil spirits – in wood, bone or ivory and inlaid with precious metals and stones. The scabbard is usually wooden and encased in richly embossed brass, silver or gold.

RIGHT: a *keris* dagger.

EAST JAVA

Like Central Java, the eastern region is rich in archaeological interest and stunning volcanic scenery. Highlights are the traditions of ancient Surabaya and the splendour of Gunung Bromo

eographically and historically, East Java (Jawa Timur) may be divided into three regions: the north coast (including Madura island) with its old Islamic trading ports, the Brantas River Valley with its ancient monuments and colonial hill stations, and the eastern salient (known to history as Blambangan) with its spectacular volcanoes, secluded nature reserves and unparalleled scenic beauty nearly everywhere. The broad **Sungai Brantas** traces a circular path through the ancient and fertile rice lands of eastern Central Java, and around several adjacent peaks – Arjuna, Kawi and Kelud. For five centuries after AD 930, this valley was the undisputed locus of power and civilisation on the island. The great kingdoms of this period – Kediri, Singasari and Majapahit – bequeathed a rich heritage of art, literature and music.

With the arrival of Islam as a political force in the 16th century, and with the great fluorescence of the spice and textile trade, a struggle arose between the rice-growing kingdoms of the interior and the new Islamic trading powers of the coast. Muslim forces conquered the Brantas Valley around 1530, and many Hindus then fled eastwards to Blambangan and Bali.

Surabaya

East Java's provincial capital, **Surabaya ㉑**, has long been one of the largest and most important seaports in the archipelago. This is Indonesia's second-largest city, with 3.2 million people, known as a city of heroes because of the momentous first battle of the revolution in November 1945. Although the local rebels were driven out by the better-equipped British troops, they inflicted heavy casualties and proved that independence could be fought for.

Main attractions
DUTCH COLONIAL BUILDINGS IN SURABAYA
BULL RACES AT MADURA
TRETES MOUNTAIN RESORT
ANTIQUITIES AT TROWULAN
ANCIENT TEMPLES NEAR MALANG
GUNUNG BROMO AND GUNUNG SEMERU
BALURAN NATIONAL PARK
GUNUNG IJEN
ALAS PURWO NATIONAL PARK
MERU BETIRI NATIONAL PARK

LEFT: Gunung Semeru smoulders behind the caldera rim of Gunung Bromo. **RIGHT:** in Surabaya's Arab quarter.

TIP

From Java's easternmost point, Ketapang, near Banyuwangi, ferries make the crossing to and from Gilimanuk, Bali, four times a day, and six times a day during peak holiday seasons. Actual travel time is only 30 minutes, but factor in a lot of down time while waiting for ferries to arrive, unload passengers and cargo, reload, and get under way.

Dutch descriptions of the city in 1620 paint it as a formidable adversary surrounded by a canal, and with heavily fortified bastions measuring some 40km (25 miles) in circumference. Its army is said to have numbered 30,000 warriors. In the end, Surabaya succumbed to the powerful Mataram rulers of Central Java in 1625, but only after Sultan Agung's armies had devastated its rice lands and diverted its mighty river.

In the mid-18th century, Surabaya was ceded to the Dutch and developed into the greatest commercial city of the Indies – the chief sugar port and rail head on Java. Immortalised in many of Joseph Conrad's novels, this era was characterised by square-riggers in full sail, wealthy Chinese and Arab traders, eccentric German hoteliers, and lusty seamen brawling over the likes of Surabaya Sue (who really existed; *see panel, below*).

Arab and Chinese quarters

The most interesting areas of Surabaya are the old Arab and Chinese quarters at the northern end of the city, not far from the harbour. Spend some time wandering the narrow lanes east of Jalan K.H. Mas Mansyur, around the mosque and the **Tomb of Sunan Ampel**, one of the nine legendary *wali* saints who propagated Islam on the island. There is a bazaar that leads up to the mosque, with scores of stalls selling perfumes and handmade textiles from all over Java.

Hail a taxi and travel south to Jalan Dukuh II/2, to the **Hong Tik Hian temple**. And just across Jalan Kembang Jepun, on Jalan Selompretan, stands Surabaya's oldest Chinese shrine, the 18th-century **Hok An Kiong temple**, built entirely of wood by native Chinese craftsmen. The temple's central deity is the goddess Ma Co, the protector of waterlogged sailors. From the Chinese quarter, walk westwards along Jalan Kembang Jepun to the famous **Red Bridge** straddling Kali Mas canal. Nearby is **House of Sampoerna**, a restored Dutch building housing a museum, gift shop and café. Visitors can view the rolling, cutting, packing

BELOW: Arab quarter bazaar in Surabaya.

Surabaya Sue

Surabaya Sue was a Scottish national who was best known for her role as an Indonesian freedom fighter during the Japanese invasion. Born as Muriel Pearson in 1908, she travelled to Bali as a curious young girl in her 20s and fell in love with Indonesia. Known to the locals as K'tut Tantri, she seized the world's imagination as a brave spirit after she was captured, cast in solitary confinement and tortured for two years by the Japanese during their occupation of Surabaya.

She recounted her ordeal in the autobiographical and highly colourful (some would say "coloured") book, *Revolt in Paradise*. After she was set free, this foreigner joined the independence movement and fought alongside the Indonesians, smuggling arms and supplies between islands. She operated an underground radio station and broadcast news reports to gain the world's attention.

In this, she succeeded handsomely, and in the process earned the nickname "Surabaya Sue" given to her by the foreign media. After achieving Independence, the gratified Indonesian government put her up in a hotel in Jakarta.

Surabaya Sue lived a long and eventful life – she was closely associated with the raja of Bangli in Bali – before her death at age 89 in an old folks' home in Australia.

and wrapping of hand-rolled *kretek* (clove cigarettes).

Climb into a taxi and travel south from here, parallel to the river, past the **Heroes Monument**, to see how Surabaya has expanded in recent times. On Jalan Tunjungan is the old-world **Majapahit Hotel** (*see Travel Tips, page 379*), built in 1910 and wonderfully refurbished. From Jalan Tunjungan, the main shopping street with several shopping centres, turn left down Jalan Pemuda to the former **Dutch Governor's Mansion**. Constructed after the turn of the 20th century, this stood at what was then the new centre of colonial Surabaya, and which now is a major hotel district. **Joko Dolog**, a centuries-old statue of King Kertanegara, the last king of the Singasari dynasty (who died in 1292), is enshrined in a small, hidden park directly opposite.

A 20-minute drive south from the city centre is **Kebun Binatang** (daily 7am–5pm; charge), one of the largest and oldest zoos in Southeast Asia, housing Komodo dragons,

orang-utans and other fauna of Indonesia. In the same area is the **Centre Culturel Français** on Jalan Darmokali, periodically featuring exhibits and dance performances.

Madura

Madura ㉒ island is now accessible via Suramadu Bridge, the longest in Southeast Asia, in about 15 minutes. Madura is a popular destination during September–November – the time of the exciting annual bull races (*karapan sapi*). According to the Madurese, the races began long ago when plough team was pitted against plough team over the length of a rice field.

Today's racing bulls are never used for ploughing, but are specially bred; they represent a considerable source of local and regional pride. Only bulls of a high standard (condition, weight, colour) may be entered, and are judged on appearance as well as speed. District and regency heats are held all over Madura and East Java,

Service at the Majaphit Hotel

BELOW: bull races at Madura.

Artifacts in Trowulan museum.

BELOW: garuda close up at Candi Panataran.

building up to the finale in November in **Pamekasan**, the island's capital.

The main event is a thundering sprint down a 100-metre (328ft) long field lined with throngs of screaming spectators. These huge and normally slow-moving creatures attain speeds of over 50km per hour (30mph).

The Madurese have long enjoyed a reputation for toughness, and Madura's dry limestone terrain may account for this. The major industries here are fishing, tobacco-growing, salt-panning and batik. The southern coastal fishing villages exude a solid but slightly jaded Mediterranean air, and Madura has some good beaches. To the east is a modest but interesting palace at **Sumenep**, and a beautiful 18th-century mosque, **Mesjid Jamiq**. Close by is a small museum with examples of wonderfully carved wooden furniture, a skill that Madurese craftsmen are famous for, and an adjacent library with important manuscripts.

Mountain retreat

Tretes ㉓, just 55km (35 miles) south of Surabaya, is a delightful mountain resort offering fresh air, cool nights and superb scenery. Walk or ride on horseback in the morning to one of three valley waterfalls in the vicinity. Then spend the afternoon by a bracing spring-fed swimming pool, curl up with a good book and a huge pot of tea or coffee, visit one of the recreational facilities, take in a round of golf at one of three nearby courses or visit **Taman Safari Park II** (http://tamansafari2.com). Located on the highway between Surabaya and Malang near Tretes, the park includes animal shows accompanied by conservation messages and amusement park rides.

More active souls will perhaps want to hike up **Gunung Arjuna** (3,339 metres/10,950ft), located behind Tretes, through lush montane casuarina forests, or across the Lalijiwa plateau along a well-worn path to neighbouring **Gunung Welirang**, where sulphur is collected by villagers from hissing fumaroles. The area is also studded with ancient monuments, beginning with **Candi Jawi**, just by the main road 7km (4 miles) below Tretes. This slender Hindu-Buddhist shrine was completed around 1300, and is one of several funerary temples dedicated to King Kertanegara of the Singasari dynasty.

Candi Jawi overlooks **Gunung Penanggungan** to the north – a perfect cone surrounded on all sides by smaller peaks and regarded, because of its shape, as a replica of the holy mountain Mahameru. Penanggungan is littered with dozens of terraced sanctuaries, meditation grottoes and sacred pools – about 80 sites in all, most of which are on the mountain's northern and western faces. The most accessible and charming of these is **Belahan**, a bathing pool situated at Penanggungan's eastern foot. It is thought to be the burial site of King Airlangga, who

died in 1049. The pool is reached by a dirt road from the main Surabaya highway, only a few minutes' drive north of Pandaan.

Traces of the past

From Tretes or Surabaya, it is about an hour to **Trowulan village ㉔**, near Mojokerto, once the seat of Java's greatest empire, 14th-century Majapahit. Unfortunately, most of Majapahit's monuments were built of wood and soft red brick, so that only the foundations and a few gateways remain. The **Museum Trowulan** by the main road nevertheless has a fascinating collection of terracotta figures and fragments and a useful tabletop map of the area. From here, seek out nearby ruins: Candi Tikus (a royal bathing complex), Candi Bajang Ratu (a tall, brick entryway) and Wringin Lawang (a palace gate). Also visit the cemetery at **Tralaya**, 2 km (1.2 miles) south of Trowulan, site of the oldest Muslim graves on Java.

Malang and environs

Malang ㉕ is a pleasant highland town, with a cool climate and a colonial atmosphere, that is a 2-hour drive south of Surabaya. Through the centre of town runs the Sungai Brantas; the residential area lies to the north and the busy commercial hub to the south. A superb collection of Javanese and Chinese antiques and art is displayed in **Hotel Tugu Malang**. Even if not staying at this beguiling hotel, it's worth dropping by for a visit (*see Travel Tips, page 379*).

There are three interesting temples outside Malang. **Candi Singosari** is on the west side of the main highway from Surabaya, at Singosari. From Blimbing village, north of Malang, take the road to Tumpang, about 20km (12 miles) away. Just before the Tumpang market, a small road to the left leads to **Candi Jago**, begun in 1268 as a memorial to the Singasari king, Wisnuwardhana. All around the terraces are reliefs in the

distinctive *wayang* style of scenes from the *Mahabharata*, and a frightening procession of underworld demons.

East Java's only sizeable temple complex is **Candi Panataran**, located 80km (50 miles) west of Malang, just north of Blitar (best reached by taking the longer but more scenic route over the mountains via Kediri). This was apparently Majapahit's state temple, assembled over a period of some 250 years between 1197 and 1454. A series of shrines and pavilions arranged before a broad platform, it is assumed that the pavilions were originally roofed with wood and thatch, as was the body of the main temple.

Near Panataran (on the road to Blitar) stands **Sukarno's mausoleum**, the final resting place of the "father of Indonesian independence" who died in 1970. And on the way to or from Blitar via the scenic Malang–Kediri high road, make a detour north from Batu to Selekta mountain resort – interesting for its colonial bungalows, swimming pools and apple orchards.

BELOW: Majahapit ruins. Candi Bajang Ratu at Trowulan.

Sulphur mining is a profitable livelihood at Gunung Ijen.

BELOW: hire a pony to transport you to the Bromo crater.

Gunung Bromo and the Tengger highlands

The steep slopes of the active volcanoes Gunung Semeru and Gunung Bromo in **Bromo-Tengger-Semeru National Park** ㉖ have been the home of the Tenggerese people for several hundred years. One of the few remaining pockets of Hinduism on Java, they are believed to be descendants of the Hindu-Buddhist Majapahit kingdom that fell in the 16th century. As Islam swept through Java, Hindu priests and aristocrats fled to Bali, Blambangan (in South Java) and the Tengger highlands. Today, the Tenggerese maintain a special form of Hinduism mixed with animism and live as farmers working the fertile farmland on the slopes of Bromo. The region is a major vegetable-growing area, and the spectacular gardens and high-altitude pine trees are a lovely sight. But the main attraction of the area is a visit to the rim of Bromo's smouldering crater at sunrise.

Gunung Bromo (Mount Bromo) is an ancient caldera 10km (6 miles) across, with four smaller peaks rising in the centre, ranging between 300 and 400 metres (1,000–1,300ft). Surrounding these peaks on the crater floor is sand and lush vegetation; every few years cinder and ash pour forth in eruptions to carpet the countryside with nutrient-rich deposits.

There are two ways to take in the view: either from the crater's edge or a panorama of the entire caldera from afar (if time permits, watch the sunrise from both vistas). For the first, start from **Cemara Lawang** at 2–3am to catch an incredible sunrise at the peak. Make the trek across the sand-sea floor, either by pony or by foot, and once at the base of the crater, climb up an incline of 250 steps. At the top is a narrow lip from where you can look into the belly of the belching sulphurous centre of the crater and take in the 360-degree view of the entire caldera and the majestic **Gunung Semeru**, Java's highest peak at 3,676 metres (12,060ft). Temperatures can drop to freezing before dawn, so be sure to dress warmly and bring a torch.

For the panoramic view, hire a jeep to **Gunung Penanjakan**, 400 metres above Gunung Bromo and about 3km (2 miles) to the west; then it is a short hike along a paved road to the summit. Usually less crowded here, the view is just as amazing. All arrangements need to be made the night before. Both walks can be done in the pre-dawn period; if time is limited, enjoy sunrise at Gunung Penanjakan and after breakfast take a pony ride for the view of Bromo's navel. June–October, during the dry season, is the best time to visit.

Every year thousands of Hindu Tenggerese participate in a midnight procession to toss offerings into Gunung Bromo's caldera in a festival called Kasodo. Descendants

of those who fled to Bali when Islamic kingdoms overtook Central Java, their beliefs are more closely related to the Hindu-Buddhist religion of that time than to the Bali-Hinduism practised today in the neighbouring island. Their offerings to the spirits of Gunung Bromo are meant to assure blessings for the coming year.

There are several ways to reach the Tengger highlands, and transport can be arranged in Surabaya, Malang or even Bali. Public buses and the train go as far as Probolinggo; from here, there are tour companies with minivans to take you the rest of the way. There is modest accommodation in both Ngadisari and Cemara Lawang (closer to the rim), and the better rooms come with hot water. As Gunung Bromo is inside a nature park, a small charge is payable.

The far east

East of Bromo-Tengger-Semeru National Park are four other national parks that can be visited on the way to or from Bali (by the Ketapang–Gilimanuk ferry). The most accessible of these is the **Baluran National Park** ㉗ at Java's northeastern tip. The park is spread over 50,000 hectares (124,000 acres) inside an eroded volcano cone. This is a chance to observe dry-terrain wildlife not seen in other areas of Java, such as *banteng* oxen, *ajag*, a rare Javanese wild dog, and 150 bird species.

Southwest of Baluran is **Gunung Ijen** ㉘ and its haunting sulphuric crater lake. Miners carry 80kg (176lbs) or more of sulphur from the bottom of the crater in bamboo baskets on shoulder poles.

At Java's southeastern tip is **Alas Purwo National Park** ㉙. There is a watchtower for views of grazing *banteng*, wild boars, peacocks and some of the best surfing in Java.

Meru Betiri National Park ㉚ on the southern coast is a sea turtle conservation area surrounded by coffee and cacao plantations. Watch for splendid hornbills, Java warty pigs and giant owls as you trek to the beach to see the turtle nursery.

The tortured lavascape at Gunung Bromo.

BELOW: volcanic activity at Gunung Bromo has been on the increase in recent years.

SUMATRA

The extraordinary wealth of natural resources,
flora and fauna and unique tribes makes
Sumatra one of Indonesia's most rewarding
islands to visit

Exotic Sumatra (Sumatera) is one of the world's last
frontiers – an island of lush tropical rainforests,
extraordinary flora and fauna, and active volcanoes.
Home to Sumatran tigers, rhinos and elephants and a
host of dynamic ethnic groups, it is the third-largest
island in Indonesia and the fifth-largest in the world
(roughly the size of Sweden). It is vastly rich in natural
resources: over half of the country's exports come from the treasure
trove of Sumatra's bounty of oil, natural gas, hardwoods, rubber, palm
oil, coffee and sugar.

Situated at the western rim in the archipelago along the Strait of Malacca,
for centuries the region was the gateway for maritime trade
through Southeast Asia, receiving merchants from China,
India, the Middle East and Europe. The early coastal seaport
kingdoms were the entry points for the influx of foreign influence that left a lasting imprint on the very fibre of Indonesia's
culture. The first wave started in the 2nd century with the
Hindu-Buddhist Indian civilisation; later, in the 13th century,
Islam entered with traders.

Sumatra is a tapestry of ethnic groups mostly living in
rural communities: in the north are the independent and
devout Muslim people of Aceh; in the northern highlands,
the proud Christian Batak; and in the west, the business-savvy
Minangkabau. The Kubu and Rimbu in the south are forest tribes, while the
Orang Laut (sea people) live aboard boats and ply the seas among the hundreds of islands off the east coast.

Sumatra is a travel haven for nature-lovers, with surfing beaches and 11
national parks sheltering tigers, elephants and orang-utans. There is also
memorable Danau Toba, Asia's largest lake, along with impressive architecture, graceful mosques and Stone Age cultures. Allowing enough time is the
challenge. The thorns in the island's side are the west coast's susceptibility
to earthquakes and tsunamis, and forest destruction. The best time to visit is
the dry season in the months of June and July. For the intrepid traveller, the
rewards are worthwhile, while an added bonus is the warmth and friendliness
of the Sumatran people.

PRECEDING PAGES: verdant landscape in the mountains near Danau Toba.
LEFT: Minangkabau wedding. **ABOVE LEFT & RIGHT:** Batak architecture.

NORTH SUMATRA

This engrossing region is known for its great cultures in the Muslim Acehnese and the proud Batak, once fearsome cannibals, while its wildlife and rainforests attract adventurers

North Sumatra has historically been the Indonesian archipelago's first point of contact with external influences from as early as the 2nd century, when Hinduism and Buddhism were introduced by Indian traders. Later, Islam reached its shores through Arab and Indian Muslims in the 13th century.

Early north coast kingdoms took advantage of sea trade passing through the nearby straits. During the Golden Age under Sultan Iskandar Muda (1604–37), the Aceh kingdom expanded to include all the major ports of eastern Sumatra and several on the Malay peninsula. The Dutch declared war on Aceh in 1873, and it took more than 10,000 troops – the largest military force the Dutch ever mustered in the East Indies – before the eventual defeat of the sultanate in 1878. Guerrilla activities then spread inland to Gayo territories, where the rebel-controlled pepper trade financed the purchase and smuggling of arms from the British.

On 26 December 2004, tidal waves crashed into the coastal areas of North Sumatra, including part of the capital, Banda Aceh, causing devastation and loss of life on an unprecedented scale (*see below*). Today, travellers come to

North Sumatra for sojourns to scenic Lake Toba to relax and experience its flamboyant Batak culture, and a few venture as far north as staunchly Islamic Aceh because of its historical significance. Trekking in the ancient rainforests of Gunung Leuser National Park in search of orang-utans is another significant draw.

Banda Aceh

For nearly 30 years a separatist group, Free Aceh Movement (GAM), railed against the Indonesian government,

Main attractions

BANDA ACEH
GUNUNG LEUSER NATIONAL PARK
BOHOROK ORANG-UTAN CENTRE
DANAU TOBA
BERASTAGI MOUNTAIN RESORT
SAMOSIR ISLAND

LEFT: GAM freedom fighter in Banda Aceh addressing a crowd. **RIGHT:** Hotel Carolina on Samosir Island, Danau Toba.

Searching through debris, following the tsunami, Banda Aceh

Below: devastation from the 2004 tsunami

seeking independence from the republic. The resulting bloody conflict divided the Acehnese and drew international attention. Following the near-total destruction of Banda Aceh in the 2004 Indian Ocean tsunami, it became apparent that the provincial capital could only be rebuilt with the cooperation of all its citizens, and a radical transformation in the central government helped to create an environment that was favourable to peace talks. In August 2005, President Susilo Bambang Yudhoyono signed a landmark peace accord with GAM in Helsinki – for which he was awarded the Nobel Peace Prize – and GAM renounced its demand for full independence in exchange for political and economic autonomy for the province.

Banda Aceh ❶, capital of Nangroe Aceh Darussalam province, is located along the shores of two rivers, Sungai Krong Aceh and Sungai Krong Daroy. The original fortress and palace of the sultan of Aceh were destroyed along with the great mosque when the Dutch invaded in 1874, but vestiges of Aceh's glorious past can still be found around Jalan Teuku Umar. The **Gunongan** is a royal water pleasure garden built by Sultan Iskandar Muda in the 17th century for his Malay princess wife. Opposite this is the Pintu (door) Aceh, used only by the royal family, to enter the palace.

On Jalan Keraton are the tombs of 15th- and 16th-century Aceh sultans, while another series of royal tombs on Jalan Mansur Sjah includes that of Sultan Iskandar Muda, the heroic 12th sultan of Aceh. They in turn surround the **Museum Negeri Aceh** (Aceh State Museum; daily; charge). Inside, ceramics, weapons, clothes, jewellery and cooking equipment are on display, but the museum's pride is a large bell that was a gift from a Ming-dynasty emperor to the Aceh sultan in the 15th century.

Aceh's centrepiece is the beautiful **Mesjid Raya Baiturrahman**, located north of the museum. Designed by an Italian architect in the Moghul Indian style, it was built by the Dutch between 1879–81 to replace the destroyed Grand Mosque. At night, the huge white structure and its black domes are illuminated. The marble interior may be visited by non-Muslims, except during prayer times.

Heading southwest, there is a Christian cemetery on Jalan Iskandar Muda where many of the Dutchmen killed in the Aceh War, including generals and other senior officers, are buried. The entrance, through wrought-iron Art Nouveau gates, stands between two marble plates on which are engraved the names of all the soldiers.

In Lam Pisang, 6km (4 miles) north of Banda Aceh, is **Museum Tjut Nyak Dhein**, dedicated to the Acehnese heroine of the same name who assisted in the struggle for independence from the Dutch in 1875. Her original home was burned to the ground by the Dutch, and this replica is now a museum.

The nearby village, **Kampung Kuala Aceh**, is a place of pilgrimage.

Here lies the grave of Teungku Sheikh Shaj Kuala (1615–93), a holy man who translated the Koran into Malay. Aceh's university bears his name.

Banda Aceh itself is not Indonesia's Land's End. That distinction belongs to remote **Pulau Weh** (Weh island), reached by a one-hour ferry ride from Banda Aceh. The island's main town, **Sabang**, flourished throughout the 1970s as a duty-free port linked to Calcutta, Malacca, Penang and Singapore. The quiet islands offer beautiful white-sand beaches with aquamarine water, excellent for snorkelling and scuba-diving.

Gayo highlands

In the highlands south of Banda Aceh a scenic Japanese-built track constructed by slave labour during World War II connects Blangkejeren to **Takengon**, the Gayo capital that lies 1,100 metres (3,600ft) above sea level. Takengon is built on the banks of **Danau Laut Tawar** (Lake Tawar). The water is clean, cool and refreshing, but local people do not swim in it. Fearing they may be pulled into the underwater realm of a seductive fairy, they opt instead for the public baths and hot springs at **Kampong Balik**. A paved road follows the west side of the lake, affording spectacular views

Batak people are skilled musicians and famous for their emotive and powerful singing of Lutheran hymns. Apart from their gongs and drums, there is also a two-stringed mandolin and a wind instrument that sounds like a clarinet.

Sumatra

Medan skyline.

BELOW: Banda Aceh's
Moghul-inspired
Mesjid Raya
Baiturrahman.

of rice paddies and pine-clad mountain slopes. **Bireuen** is the chief marketplace for Gayo coffee, cinnamon, cloves and tobacco.

On the coast east of Banda Aceh is **Sigli**, known as Padri when it was the principal port from which Acehnese haji (pilgrims) departed to Mecca. The tragic Padri War started here in 1804; the Dutch took the town and completely destroyed it in the process. Remains of the *padri kraton* (fortress) can be seen on the outskirts of town, along the road to Banda Aceh. At nearby Kampong Kibet is the grave of Sultan Ali Mughayat Syah, the first Islamic sultan of Aceh, who died in 1511. Some 60km (40 miles) south along the coast and a short distance inland is **Lamno** village. Its inhabitants, said to be descended from Portuguese stranded here three centuries ago after a shipwreck, do indeed have green eyes and faces that are recognisably Iberian.

Medan

Most visitors enter North Sumatra via **Medan ❷**, a sprawling and crowded

city with one of the strongest economic growth rates and highest per capita incomes in Indonesia. Once the marshy suburb of a small court centre, Medan developed into a commercial city after the Dutch overran the Deli sultanate in 1872, and, 14 years later, became the regional capital.

Medan has retained architectural gems from its colonial days. The largest concentration of such examples is found along Jalan Jendral A. Yani and around Merdeka Square, including the General Post Office, the former White Societet (now Bank Negara), Hotel de Boer (now Hotel Inna Dharma Deli), and the estate offices of Harrison & Crossfield's (now P.T. London Sumatra Indonesia).

Chinese shops line Jalan A. Yani. Here also is the mansion of millionaire Tjong A. Fie who, despite enormous wealth acquired from modest beginnings as a horse trader, died of malnutrition in a concentration camp during the Japanese Occupation. His mausoleum stands in the Pulau Bryan cemetery.

The central market district is adjacent to the downtown area, and a

flow of buses, cars, motorcycles and pedicabs converges around the main, colourful markets Pasar Kampung Keling, Pasar Ramas, Pasar Hong Kong and the Central Market.

At the southern end of Medan's longest street, Jalan Sisingamangaraja, stands the magnificent **Istana Maimoon**, constructed by an Italian architect in rococo style in 1888. It is still the residence of the sultan's descendants and may be visited during the day. Cultural performances can be arranged, such as the colourful Malay and tribal dances of the many peoples of North Sumatra. One block east of the palace is the imposing **Mesjid Raya** (Grand Mosque). Built in 1906 to complement the palace's architectural style, it is the city's largest mosque.

Across the Sungai Deli, on the west side of Medan, lies the old European plantation town. Its wide avenues, flanked by huge colonial villas, are planted with flowering trees. The Art Deco **Immanuel Protestant Church**, erected in 1921, is on Jalan Diponegoro, while on Jalan Hang Tuah is **Vihara Gunung Timur**, one of Indonesia's largest Chinese temples. It is said to be such a powerful place that photographs taken within will remain unexposed. A Hindu temple, **Sri Mariaman**, off Jalan Arifin, is the spiritual centre for Medan's sizeable Indian community.

In south Medan, the **Taman Margasatwa** zoo (daily; charge) nurtures a varied collection of native Sumatran wildlife, including Sumatran tigers. The **Plaza Medan Fair** has permanent cultural and agricultural exhibits, as well as an amusement park. Rare Buddhist and Hindu statues, Islamic gravestones and Batak artefacts are on show at the **Museum Sumatera Utara** on Jalan Joni (Tue–Sun 8.30am–5pm; charge).

Deep forest: Gunung Leuser National Park

Northwest from Medan, some 3 hours by road, a narrow road winds up the Alas River Valley to **Gunung Leuser National Park** ❸, an 8,000-sq km

Aceh is Indonesia's only province ruled by Islamic Sharia law. Although only Aceh's citizens – not foreigners – are subject to its harsh punishments, visitors should dutifully respect Islamic mores, such as proper behaviour and attire. Alcoholic beverages, forbidden by Islam, are only served in selected hotels.

BELOW LEFT: young orang-utan. **BELOW:** jungle wildlife, Gunung Leuser National Park.

Marco Polo, the renowned 13th-century explorer, lingered in Sumatra for months waiting for the winds to change before sailing on. His writings acknowledge a fear of exploring the area because of the head-hunting Batak.

(5,000-sq mile) park covered in dense jungle that is home to elephants, rhinos, sun bears, tigers, 500 bird species and orang-utans. The park is both a Unesco World Heritage and a World Network of Biosphere Reserves Site. Surrounding sputtering **Gunung Leuser**, 3,404 metres (11,167ft) high and Sumatra's second-highest peak, the park reaches all the way to the west coast and is probably one of the most accessible in Indonesia.

On the eastern edge of the Gunung Leuser reserve is **Bukit Lawang**, where the **Bohorok Orang-utan Centre** is located. Although it no longer rehabilitates the red great apes, visitors are welcome. A 1-hour hike through the jungle brings you to the platforms used for early-morning and afternoon feeding of wild and semi-wild orang-utans. Permits are required from the PHKA office (take a photocopy of your passport with you). The well-run Bukit Lawang station provides comfortable lodging, decent food, and a superb visitor centre complete with slide shows and information concerning local wildlife. The

centre also arranges treks to Gunung Leuser, ranging from a couple of hours to several days. This type of trekking through jungle is not for the uninitiated: leeches, malaria and protection from dampness are major concerns.

The park's centre in **Kutacane**, situated in the heart of the Alas Valley, a 3–4-day hike north, is the jumping-off point for white-water rafting on the Sungai Alas and the base camp for other activities in the national park (Kutacane is a 6–8-hour journey from Medan). **Ketambe**, a 30-minute drive from Kutacane, is a research station for primates, elephants and Sumatran tigers. Friendship Guest House here offers trekking for 1–6 days around Gunung Leuser and to the top of neighbouring Gunung Kemiri.

Located in the Gunung Leuser National Park buffer zone, and encompassing Namo Sialand and Sei Seidang villages, is Tangkahan, a community-based ecotourism project. Among its activities are jungle trekking, elephant safaris and river cruises to observe the wildlife such as gibbons, orang-utans, sun bears and many bird species. For

Below: becak taxi, Medan.

adventurous travellers, Kalong cave is waiting to be explored.

Medan to Danau Toba

The main route from Medan to **Danau Toba** ❹ (Lake Toba) runs southeast along the coast through the market town of Tebingtinggi and inland to Pematangsiantar. Side roads along the first 50km (30 miles) offer access to fine beaches such as Cermin and Sialangbuah, renowned for its mudskippers that swim like fish and climb trees.

Pematangsiantar ❹, 130km (80 miles) south of Medan, is the second-largest city in North Sumatra. This cool highland rubber and palm-oil centre is notable for its **Museum Simalungun** (daily; charge) on Jalan Ahmand Yani, which contains an excellent display of Batak artefacts including *pustaha laklak*, bark-leafed books containing sacred formulas in Batak script used by ancient shamans. From here, continue west to Parapat and Lake Toba.

A longer, more westerly Medan–Parapat route runs through Berastagi, a hill resort and market town with Dutch-built villas and a cool climate, and the Karo Batak highlands. Located between two volcanoes – Gunungs Sibayak and Sinabung – Berastagi produces fresh vegetables such as carrots, cabbages and tomatoes and is known for its passion fruit, usually made into syrup. A 2-hour drive heading south leads to **Sidikalang**, popular for its coffee. Its **Taman Iman Park** represents Indonesia's five recognised religions in Indonesia living in harmony.

Only a short bus trip from **Kabanjahe**, north of Sidikalang, is a spectacular viewpoint near the northern tip of Danau Toba that overlooks the remote Tongging Valley and Sipisopiso Waterfall. In the surrounding area are **Barus Jahe**, a traditional Karo Batak village, and **Lingga**, with its massive, pyramid-roofed *rumah adat* (traditional clan houses), some over 250 years old. A lucky visitor

might stumble across a Karo Batak wedding or rice harvest festival. From here, the road skirts Toba's eastern shore, passes through the Monday-market village Haranggaol, and continues to Parapat.

The Bataks, one of the great highland peoples of Sumatra, inhabit a fertile volcanic plateau south of Medan that covers much of northern Central Sumatra. In the middle lies the lovely **Danau Toba**, a vast crater lake containing the lush Samosir island (nearly the size of Singapore). Danau Toba, the result of a great prehistoric eruption, is today one of the highest (900 metres/2,900ft) and deepest (450 metres/1,480ft) lakes on earth.

More than 3 million members of six distinct Batak tribes make their homes in the high country, which stretches 500km (300 miles) north–south and 150km (90 miles) east–west around Lake Toba. Each of these groups – the Toba, Karo, Pakpak, Simalungun, Angkola and Mandailing Batak – has its own dialect, customs and architectural style.

Canoe on Danau Toba.

BELOW: Ambarita village was once the scene of grisly beheadings.

A ferry crosses every hour from Parapat to Samosir Island

Samosir island

Around 170km (110 miles) from Medan, on the eastern shore of Danau Toba is **Parapat ⓑ**. A tourist resort since colonial times, today it offers de luxe hotels, golf courses, water sports and a refreshingly brisk climate. Parapat is nestled on the lake's eastern shore, and is a favourite weekend getaway for Medan residents. For most visitors, Batak sights are the main attractions.

The best place to experience Danau Toba's spell is **Samosir ⓒ**, a 1,000-sq km (380-sq mile) island in the lake. Samosir is regarded as the original home of the Bataks in Sumatra, and the Toba Batak, the "purest" Batak tribe. Boats depart from Parapat for Samosir daily. The main entry point is **Tomok**, a 30-minute ride across quiet water. The carved boat-like tomb of animistic King Sidabutar is here. In an enclosure opposite the tomb are ritual statues of a buffalo sacrifice. At the end of an avenue of souvenir booths leading from the jetty are dozens of stands selling *kain ulos* (hand-woven fabric), two-stringed

mandolins, ornate woodcarvings, Batak calendars and many other items of cultural interest. Other boats from Parapat will take visitors directly to the dozens of *losmen* scattered in Tomok, Ambarita and on the Tuk-Tuk peninsula. Most lakeside *losmen* have both electricity and hot water, and visitors do not lack for comfortable accommodation.

Tuk-Tuk ⓓ is a tourist village composed largely of small hotels. On the peninsula is a community hall for Batak dances and a few traditional houses, as well as inexpensive *losmen*. With the arrival of Christianity on Samosir in 1848, Toba Batak took enthusiastically to Lutheran hymnals. Sunday church services are fine entertainment, though there are many other opportunities to hear *ture ture* (tribal ballads) in village *warungs*.

Ambarita, an hour's walk from Tuk-Tuk, has three megalithic complexes. The first is just up from the jetty and is notable for its 300-year-old stone seats and the tomb of Laga Siallagan, the first *raja* of Ambarita. If an enemy was captured in Ambarita, neighbouring

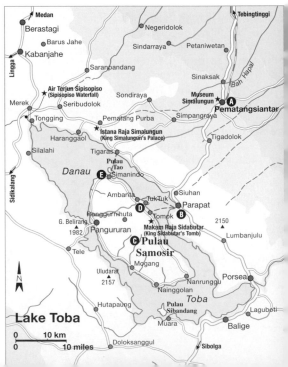

rajas were invited to this first hilltop complex for an initial conference before moving on to the second, a cluster of stone chairs where the fate of the prisoner was decided. The third complex is located south of Ambarita and includes a unique breakfast table. Here, the prisoner was beaten to death, decapitated and chopped up on a flat stone, cooked with buffalo meat, and eaten by the *raja*, who washed his meal down with blood.

Simanindo ⓔ, at Samosir's northern tip and a half-day walk from Tuk-Tuk, is 16km (10 miles) from Ambarita. Ferries run to Simanindo from Tigaras on the eastern shore north of Parapat. The village has a huge former king's house, which has been restored and is now a Batak **museum**. Look for the buffalo horns in front, one for each generation. A 10-minute boat ride off Simanindo is little **Tao island**, where a few tiny bungalows offer escape to those who find even Samosir hectic.

Although **Pangururan**, on Samosir's west coast, can be reached in half a day by the coastal path from Simanindo, a hike across the island's forested central plateau offers unforgettable views. From Tomok, the climb past the king's tomb to the plateau above takes about three hours. Pangururan is another 13km (8 miles) beyond and can be reached in less than 10 hours. Stay the night at one of the villages before pressing on to Ronggurnihuta and its swimming lake. It may frequently be necessary to ask directions from locals. In the wet season, this climb is extremely muddy and slippery. It is easier to take a ferry to Pangururan and then hike back to Tuk-Tuk.

Pangururan lies near the Sumatran mainland and is connected by a short stone bridge. Its main attraction is an hour's walk away – the *air panas*, or hot springs, halfway up the hill command a fine view of the lake. Every Sunday, a round-island cruise lasting most of the day departs from several villages, stopping at many of the islands and villages. Or take a stroll along the island's only road and listen to the glorious hymns at the many churches, an uplifting way to spend the morning.

Coffee beans grown in the rich volcanic soil of the Gayo highlands are considered to be the best in Indonesia – full-bodied and flavoursome.

BELOW: Batak dance performance.

The Batak

Wedged between two fervently Muslim peoples, the Minangkabau and the Acehnese, the Batak somehow remained isolated, animistic and cannibalistic until the middle of the 19th century, when German and Dutch missionaries converted many to a mystical sort of Christianity. But traditional *adat* and bygone customs are still practised. Cemeteries display stone sculptures of dead ancestors, shamans communicate with spirits, and priests consult astrological tables to make decisions for their clans.

When first discovered by the Dutch, the Batak were viewed as primitive cannibals isolated for centuries from the rest of the world. They seemed to be constantly warring with their neighbours; headhunting and cannibalism were common. But the Batak were anything but primitive. In fact, they were sophisticated and settled agriculturalists, possessing elaborate crafts, calendars and cosmological texts written in an Indic alphabet.

A Batak *marga* (clan) consists of several *huta* (communities) tracing descent from a single male ancestor. Kinship and clan loyalties are especially strong – in some cases fiercely defended – and weddings and funerals can draw kinsfolk in the thousands. Genealogies, some of which go back five centuries, are carefully kept as they determine status in personal relations and formal ceremonies.

WEST SUMATRA

The colourful Minangkabau culture is only one of the reasons that people come to mountainous West Sumatra; there are also three national parks, two Unesco World Heritage sites, fabulous surfing and dramatic scenery

est Sumatra's terrain, with its fertile valleys, lush rainforests and majestic peaks, offers some of the most memorable landscapes in all of Indonesia. Bukit Barisan Sclatan National Park, home of the few remaining two-horned Sumatran rhinoceros, the country's largest national park, Kerinci Seblat, and Bukit Tigapuluh National Park are all here. The region is also graced with two large crater lakes, the larger and more stunning of which is Maninjau just west of Bukittinggi, with smaller Singkarak to its southeast.

The highest peak in West Sumatra is Gunung Kerinci in the rugged, little-visited Kerinci Seblat National Park. Indonesia's second-highest volcano, it attracts climbers who like a challenge. Conservation groups there have trained local guides to take the adventurous on treks through the forest and climbing.

Just off the west coast lies a string of islands that lure visitors of entirely different sorts. The spectacular breaks at Nias have beckoned surfers for the last decade or two, some of whom have become volunteers in health care, community empowerment and disaster relief through SurfAid International, which has weathered the many upheavals of nature over recent years. The other islands, the Mentawais, draw extreme trekkers

who relish visiting the friendly Siberut people, who live in the forests and happily tell the stories that their tattoos represent.

While the attractions in this region are limitless, the number one destination remains the Minang highlands, home to the Minangkabau people who, despite their staunch Islamic devotion, make up the largest matrilineal society on earth *(see page 207)*. Property and wealth are inherited through the female line, and both men and women trace their lineage

Main attractions

BUKITTINGGI
MINANGKABAU CULTURE AND TRADITIONAL HOUSES
NIAS MEGALITHS AND SURFING
SIBERUT FOREST PEOPLE
BUKIT TIGAPULUH NATIONAL PARK
BUKIT BARISAN SELATAN NATIONAL PAR
KERINCI SEBLAT NATIONAL PARK

LEFT: surfing off the coast of Nias. **RIGHT:** Minangkabau matriarch.

Monkeys are a common sight in Padang.

BELOW: fishing boats at Padang.

through their mothers and retain loyalty to the clan houses of their grandmothers. Their distinctive traditional *rumah gadang* (clan houses) dot the countryside of the highlands, with elaborately carved exteriors and upturned rooflines that resemble the horns of a water buffalo.

Padang

The capital of and gateway to West Sumatra is **Padang** ❺, a thriving commercial centre. It is the island's third-largest city, and 90 percent of its population are ethnic Minangkabau. Home to the largest seaport on the western coast, **Teluk Bayur** is 6km (4 miles) south of the city centre. The harbour came into existence in the 18th century after the discovery of gold in the highlands and to accommodate the lucrative pepper trade. At one time, Sumatra supplied over half of the world's pepper needs. Today, the busy seaport loads ships with cargoes of coffee, tea, cinnamon, coal and wood.

Most travellers regard Padang as a stopover to the Minang Highlands or west coast islands. But the city does have some semblance of old-world charm, in the Dutch-built colonial homes and the shophouses lining the wide avenues in the area around **Kampung Cina** (Chinatown) and the **Pasar Raya** (Central Market) area. Best explored by walking or by horse-drawn cart, the route starts at Jalan Hiligoo and continues south along Jalan Pondak and onto Jalan Niaga to the old colonial waterfront. Here, both banks of the Sungai Muara are filled with hand-painted fishing boats and ferries. Cross over for a view of the Chinese cemetery before proceeding 4km (2.5 miles) south to **Air Manis** fishing village.

Padang offers few sights other than the **Museum Adityawarman** (daily; charge) which houses Minangkabau artefacts in a traditional *rumah gadang* (clan house). Regularly scheduled cultural dance performances take place nearby. (Check the programme with the tourist office or museum.) In the evening, head to the waterfront for a spicy Padang meal, cool ocean breezes and a view of the sunset over the Indian Ocean.

Bukittinggi

A 3-hour drive from Padang north through the lush tropical Anai Valley delivers you to picturesque hilltop **Bukittinggi** ❻, the heart of Minangkabau culture. Blessed with friendly people, a relaxed atmosphere and cool mountain air, Bukittinggi is the best base for visiting the surrounding Minang Highlands.

Bukittinggi, which means "Tall Hill", stands at 930 metres (3,050ft) and is surrounded by the Gunung Agam, Gunung Singgalang and Gunung Merapi volcanic peaks. It is a pleasant town to stroll through. The well-educated townsfolk, who have the highest literacy rate in the nation, are friendly and eager to practise their English. The cool mountain air also enhances touring on foot. In the centre of town,

a clock tower with a stylised roof stands as the city's landmark; nearby is the busy Pasar Raya (Central Market).

Taman Bundo Kanduang 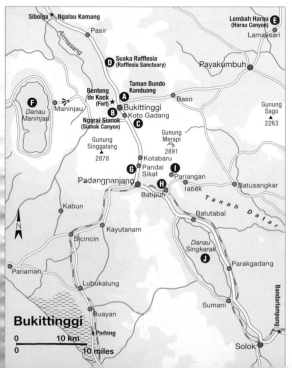 Ⓐ (Rumah Adat Baandjuang Museum; daily 7.30am–5pm; charge), a 140-year-old *rumah gadang*, marks the city's highest point. Exhibits include wedding and dance costumes, musical instruments, weaponry and other cultural artefacts.

Crossing a footbridge takes you to the remains of Benteng de Kock, built by the Dutch in 1825. The fortress itself does not hold much interest, but it provides a good vantage point to view farmland and the smouldering **Gunung Merapi** (2,891 metres/9,484ft) and **Ngarai Sianok Canyon** Ⓑ.

Better views of the spectacular canyon, sometimes referred to as the Grand Canyon of Indonesia, can be had at the lookout point in Panorama Park, a favourite leisure spot for locals. A pleasant hike through the 4km (2.5-mile) canyon is possible along a footpath that starts through rice fields. At the halfway point is a bridge; head up a flight of steps (slippery in the rainy season) to the silversmith village **Koto Gadang** Ⓒ. Here, delicate silver filigree jewellery and hand-embroidered shawls (based on Flemish laces) are made. From here, you can take public transport back to Bukittinggi.

North of Bukittinggi

An easy 12km (8-mile) drive north of Bukittinggi is the 3,100-hectare (750-acre) Rimba Panti Nature Reserve, which contains the **Rafflesia Sanctuary** Ⓓ, named after the world's largest flower, which can grow up to a metre (3ft) in diameter. The foul-smelling *Rafflesia arnoldii* only blooms between August and September. It may be necessary to hike over muddy paths in search of the bloom.

Continuing north another 15km (9 miles) is **Ngalau Kamang**, a limestone cave with stalactites and stalagmites. It also houses a small lake. Payakumbuh, 40km (25 miles) east, is the gateway to the cliffs and waterfalls at **Harau Canyon** Ⓔ, a lush reserve surrounded by 100-metre (330ft) high granite walls and home to various species of monkey and deer, as well as sun

TIP

West Sumatra is a good place to buy exquisite *songket* cloth – gold and silver brocade on silk or cotton. You will see many Minangkabau women dressed in traditional outfits made from *songket*.

BELOW: a Dutch colonial dwelling in the countryside outside Bukittinggi.

Sumatra once produced half of the world's pepper.

BELOW: rice paddies.

bears, leopards and even a few tigers. To get there from the main highway, head north past Payakumbuh for 10km (6 miles) to Lamaksari village. Turn left and proceed for another 3km (2 miles). Permits are sold at the entrance.

West and south of Bukittinggi

Heading west from Bukittinggi is the deep crater lake **Danau Maninjau** , renowned for its serenity and beauty. There is a wide range of accommodation and eateries there, along with canoes and motorboats for hire. For a day trip, the lake can be reached within 2 hours by bus from Bukittinggi. Even better, spend a few days relaxing and swimming in the cool, clear water. From the Embun Pagi lookout point, the road winds and zigzags an amazing 44 turns before arriving at the lake.

Just 12km (8 miles) south of Bukittinggi is the weavers' village **Pandai Sikat** ⓖ. Weaving has been a major business since the late 18th century, and women and girls here create by hand *kain songket* (cotton or silk base worked through with heavy gold or silver threads), which are popular with Jakarta women for formal events. Excellent-quality sarongs can be expensive and are sometimes just rented for the evening.

Continue southeast to the plains at **Tanah Datar**, where the ancient Minangkabau kingdom existed for half a millennium before succumbing in the Paderi wars of the early 1800s. The area has the finest examples of traditional Minangkabau architecture: *rumah gadang* with roofs turned up to resemble the horns of a water buffalo. The first stop in **Batipuh** ⓗ village is the traditional *surau*, or men's house, built entirely of wood in the Koto Piliang style.

A side road from here, heading east for 5km (3 miles) and skirting Gunung Merapi, goes to **Pariangan** ⓘ, believed to be the original Minangkabau village. Set in a beautiful valley, steps lead to the traditional clan houses and a royal tomb. Take a leisurely stroll here and see one of the last *surau* of its kind still in use. Back on

Batang Gadis

Lacking sufficient infrastructure to attract more than a few intrepid trekkers, the entry point to obscure **Batang Gadis National Park** is Panyabungan village, north of Padang. In addition to protecting strange and wonderful creatures such as Malayan tapirs and porcupines, Sumatran serows, tigers and elephants, and many varieties of rare cats, the park has 242 bird species and the huge, smelly Rafflesia flower. Also within park boundaries are natural and Japanese caves and Sorik Marapi volcano.

When Batang Gadis was established in 2004 it was unique in that it was Indonesia's first national park to be founded based on the requests of the local people, who were concerned about the illegal logging that was destroying their forests.

the main road, **Tabek** village has fine examples of traditional clan houses and the oldest building in West Sumatra.

Continuing east, the area between Bukittinggi and Batusangkar is arguably among the most scenic. Fertile lands grow many varieties of fruits and vegetables, as well as irrigated highland rice. Some 20km (12 miles) east of Padangpanjang, **Batusangkar** was once a residence of the Minangkabau kings. The main attraction, the royal palace Istana Pagaruyung, was destroyed by fire in 2007, and a new palace has been built.

South from Batipuh is the lovely **Danau Singkarak ❶**, larger than Danau Maninjau and easily accessible by rail or road, though not as developed. Beyond the lake is **Solok**, a mountain town known for its picturesque high-roofed houses and woodcarvings.

WEST COAST ISLANDS

Running parallel to Sumatra's west coast, about 100km (60 miles) offshore, is a string of ancient islands – peaks of an undersea non-volcanic ridge separated from mainland Sumatra by a deep trench. Simeulue, Nias, the Mentawai group and Enggano were first "discovered" in the 17th century by the Dutch. In the 19th century, missionaries arrived, and today 80 percent of the islanders are Christians, but they still retain strong animistic beliefs. The most visited island, Nias, is known for its stone-jumping rituals. Travelling overland from Medan or Padang will require an overnight stay in **Sibolga**. From here take a ferry to Gunung Sitoli on Nias, or go by one of the daily flights from Medan.

Nias island

The main points of interest on **Nias ❼** – the traditional villages and surfing beaches – are located in the south, a 4–7-hour journey on decent roads thanks to tsunami aid programmes.

The largest of the west coast islands, Nias is 100km (60 miles) long by 50km (30 miles) wide, and is home to one of Southeast Asia's most unusual ancient cultures, which

Maps pages 191 & 201

TIP

Before planning to climb Gunung Kerinci – or any Indonesian volcano – it is best to find out if it is active or not. The Indonesian Department of Volcanology website (http://portal.vsi.esdm.go.id) lists volcanoes that show activity. A blinking amber light means "danger"; a blinking red light means "stay away".

BELOW: Nias warrior in ceremonial garb.

revolves around stone: in architectural style, sculptures and rituals. In its most memorable traditional dance, *Fahombö*, Niasan tribesmen leap feet first over stone columns several metres high. *Tutötölö* is a warrior dance performed by young men leaping in combat.

Niasan villages are veritable fortresses, with great stone-paved central "runways". Stilt houses stand in parallel rows on hillsides, shielded by a thorny bamboo barricade from foreign attack. Northern Nias, raided by Acehnese slave traders for centuries, has few cultural remnants, although the capital, **Gunung Sitoli**, is found here. The remote centre of the island holds cultural interest, however. Amid jungle are the ruins of abandoned villages with huge *menhir*s, single standing stones.

Southern villages of Nias

All of the major tourist attractions are located in southern Nias. **Telukdalam** is the largest city and offers simple *losmen*. Most visitors head for the beautiful white-sand beaches and

aquamarine waves at **Lagundri**, proclaimed to be one of the best surf spots in the world. Simple *losmen* or stilted beach huts and a resort offering bungalow accommodation are available here.

Bawömataluwo, 15km (9 miles) from Telukdalam, is a village turned touristy because of its easy accessibility. Built more than 100 years ago on a summit for protection from Dutch attacks, it is reachable by a wide stone staircase of 480 steps along an alley between two rows of houses. The central "square" is the venue for stone-jumping performances and nearby is the ornate chief's house. There are stone statues and around 300 megaliths.

Hillisimaetano is a quiet village built in the past 70 years, where raising chickens and pigs – the main livelihood – goes on at a traditional pace. All 140 houses in the village face the chief's house located in the centre. **Gomo Lahusa,** 40km (24 miles) northeast of Telukdalam, and **Gomo** are both worth a visit to see fine old *menhir* stones.

Siberut island

South of Nias, **Siberut** ❽ is the largest and most visited of the Mentawai archipelago and is covered in dense tropical rainforest with isolated farming settlements. The indigenous inhabitants are forest people, living in close harmony with nature.

Siberut island measures about 110km by 50km (70 miles by 30 miles), and the port of entry is in the south at Muara Siberut, reached by ferry from Padang. There are no hotels or *losmen*, and travellers have to rely on the generosity of locals. The main attraction is the trek inland to visit remote villages where people live in traditional longhouses. **Rodok**, a 4–5-hour boat ride away, is a government village, and another 2 hours' journey leads to **Madobat**. Both are ideal locations from which to begin a trek inland.

The people of the interior live in small villages or in *uma* (longhouses). They are well known for the tattoos they incise over large sections of their bodies, and for their *puliajiat* rituals: these go on for several weeks to purify houses, in order to ensure harmony and reunite the souls of individuals with their bodies.

A Unesco Biosphere Reserve, **Siberut National Park** is home to a unique collection of flora and fauna due to its separation from any other landmass for over 500,000 years. Most notable are its endemic monkeys: primitive black gibbons (*Hylobates klossii*), Mentawai macaques, and two langurs, *Presbytis potenziani* and pig-tailed.

NATIONAL PARKS

Back on the mainland, east of Padang the **Bukit Tigapuluh National Park** is under tremendous threat from logging and palm-oil plantations, with two-thirds of the park already logged. With the park housing at least 10 critically endangered species, these operations have drawn the attention of wildlife conservation organisations worldwide. On the upside, orang-utan reintroduction has worked well here, and the World Wildlife Fund caught several rare Sumatran tigers on film using camera traps in mid-2011,

SurfAid International was established in 2000 by a doctor-surfer concerned by what he considered to be a lack of health care on Nias and Mentawai while on a surfing charter to the islands. When the December 2004 Indian Ocean tsunami hit, SurfAid was the first on the scene, and when Nias was devastated by an 8.7-magnitude earthquake, SurfAid was there.

BELOW: surfing off Nias island is top-class.

Gunung Kerinci, Indonesia's second-highest peak

BELOW: lone fisherman on Danau Maninjau.

intensifying the campaigns of several groups against further logging.

Along Sumatra's entire west coast, stretching from the northern to the southern tips, is the Barisan mountain range, and **Bukit Barisan Selatan National Park** encompasses 3,568 sq km (1,378 sq miles) of these heavily forested hills. This park joins Gunung Leuser and Kerinci Sebalat National Parks as a single Unesco World Heritage Site, and is home to three important Sumatran species – elephant, rhino and tiger – and has the only population of Sumatran striped rabbit ever recorded. The threat to this conservation area is not logging, but encroaching coffee plantations.

Two hours south of Padang is the northern border of Indonesia's largest reserve, **Kerinci Seblat National Park**, which covers an amazing 14,000-sq km (5,400-sq mile) stretch of jungle and mountains. Most visitors begin their explorations in the Kerinci district dominated by the active volcano **Gunung Kerinci**, which rises 3,800 metres (12,480ft), making it Indonesia's second-highest peak after Gunung Puncak Jaya in Papua.

Rare wildlife in this Unesco World Heritage Site park includes Sumatran tigers and elephants, clouded leopards, Malayan sun bears and tapirs, over 375 species of birds, and the world's largest and tallest flowers. There are no orang-utans, but occasionally sightings have been reported of the mysterious *orang pendek*, a bipedal ape similar to an orang-utan, and the mythical *cigau*, half-lion and half-tiger.

The national park office in Sungaipenuh (Mon–Fri) has a good visitor centre and some English-speaking staff. There are a number of simple hotels and a colourful market there. Homestays and trekking operators are available in Kersik Tuo, a tea plantation village at the foot of Gunung Kerinci, where treks start. From the south of Kerinci, trek on forest paths (2 days) to Renah Kenumu, a traditional village with many megaliths, hot springs and good wildlife-spotting.

The Matrilineal Minangkabau

They may be Muslims, but intriguingly in Minangkabau culture the women hold the key to social rights, identity and inheritance

The fertile highlands of West Sumatra are home to one of Indonesia's most interesting ethnic groups, the Minangkabau. With a reputation for being intellectuals, Minangkabau men feature prominently in the national government and are known for their keen business sense. Throughout Indonesia are restaurants run by Minangkabau men who serve up spicy Padang food.

What makes the Minangkabau so interesting is that while they are devout Muslims, they also belong to a matrilineal society, tracing social identity and inheritance through the female line. In fact, the Minangkabau are one of the few remaining matrilineal societies that still exist in the modern world.

Minangkabau can trace their descent to a *rumah gadang* (clan house), to which they pledge allegiance and maintain a social obligation throughout their lives. Each rumah gadang has descendants who can be traced back to a single grandmother.

All valuable property, land and house are owned in common by the clan, led by the grandmother and including all her female heirs and her eldest brother, and cannot be sold without group consent. The men are involved in the management of the communal property, but it is the women who maintain the rights of use, including landownership. Minangkabau women thus have a high economic status in society.

When a woman marries, she pays a groom price to her husband's female family members. After the wedding, the man goes to "visit" his wife in her home, but in the morning, he returns to his mother's house to work the crops and to raise his sisters' children. His nieces and nephews are his responsibility; his own children are in turn raised by his wife's brothers.

Men spend most of their time in the fields, and at night young boys go to the *surau*, the Islamic study hall. Young men are encouraged to travel in what is known as *merantau* ("to know about being without"), to seek their fortunes and experience the

world, When the seasoned wayfarer returns home with his wealth, he is deemed ready for marriage.

Households are the domain of the women, who are actively involved in daily affairs, while husbands and brothers live elsewhere. The men travel, but their hearts are always with the village, sending money home for ceremonies, the building of mosques and for the maintenance of the family's *rumah gadang*, a source of cultural pride.

The *rumah gadang* has a roof that resembles buffalo horns, and elaborately carved exterior panels are the pride of local woodcarvers. Other examples of the tribe's excellent craftsmanship are beautiful hand-woven *kain songket* textiles, fine silver filigree jewellery, lively music and a *silat* dance combining martial arts movements with dance.

Tradition has it that the Minangkabau derived their name – *minang* (victory) and *kabau* (buffalo) – from an ancient battle. In an effort to avoid bloodshed they proposed a contest between two water buffaloes. The Javanese brought to the arena a strong buffalo bull, while the Sumatrans entered a nursing calf that had been starved for days and had spikes affixed to its horns. The small calf quickly went in search of milk only to impale the underside of the bull, killing it. The Javanese returned home and left the Minangkabau in peace.

RIGHT: a Minangkabau in distinctive costume.

SOUTH AND EAST SUMATRA

Surf the waves at Krui beach on the southwest coast, trek through the jungles of Way Kambas National Park or relax in the beach resorts of Bintan island

outh and East Sumatra have never been hugely popular travel destinations due to lack of accessibility and infrastructure. Now, with scheduled flights to major cities and towns, it is becoming easier to get around.

In the east, broad alluvial lowlands no more than 30 metres (100ft) above sea level are drained by numerous meandering rivers, including the Sungai Batanghari, navigable for nearly 500km (300 miles) inland, and the Musi, Sumatra's longest river. In contrast, the west coast is mountainous, rising to volcanic peaks of more than 3,000 metres (10,000ft) before dropping sharply to the Indian Ocean at the former Dutch and British colonial outpost, Bengkulu. This area is home to five national parks, but only one of them, Way Kambas, has experienced any development to attract tourists. South of Bengkulu is Krui, one of Sumatra's popular surfing beaches.

Sitting off the eastern coast are Bintan and Batam and Bangka and Belitung islands, the former two part of a "golden triangle" project between Indonesia, Singapore and Malaysia. Bintan's northern beach is a sprawling complex of resorts and golf courses, while Batam is primarily industrial.

Bangka and Belitung are two of the world's largest tin producers, but as the 17th-century mines are playing out, watch for more resorts to pop up here.

Bengkulu

The seaport of **Bengkulu** ❾, formerly known as Bencoolen, was founded in 1685 by the British. Its fort, **Benteng Marlborough**, was constructed in 1713–19 and restored in the late 1970s. Old gravestones with English inscriptions can be seen in the gatehouse. Sir Thomas Stamford Raffles was

Main attractions
KRUI SURF BEACH
WAY KAMBAS NATIONAL PARK
BINTAN AND BATAM BEACH RESORTS

LEFT: an aerial view of the East Sumatran plains, characterised by slow, meandering rivers and large tracts of forest and swamp.
RIGHT: the elusive Sumatran rhino can be seen at Way Kambas National Park.

TIP

Both Batam and Bintan islands are easily accessible from Singapore. High-speed catamarans can whisk you to the resort islands in under an hour, and numerous travel agents in Singapore sell room-and-ferry packages.

lieutenant-governor of Bengkulu from 1818 to 1823. He introduced coffee and sugar cultivation, established schools and fought a royal decision to hand control of Sumatra over to the Dutch in 1824. His scientific zeal led to the naming of the giant Rafflesia flower in his honour. This can be found at the **Dendam Tak Sudah Botanical Gardens** near the lake of the same name 8km (5 miles) southeast of town.

East of Bengkulu is **Lahat**, gateway to the Pasemah highlands. Dotting this mountain plateau are carved megaliths, tombs, pillars and other stone ruins thought to date from about AD 100. They are considered the best examples of prehistoric stone sculptures in Indonesia. Oddly shaped rocks have been fashioned into figures of armed warriors riding elephants, wrestling buffaloes or fighting snakes. There are dolmens, sanctuaries, coloured cave paintings and other works of art around volcanic **Gunung Dempo**.

Heading south, near the southern tip of Sumatra, is **Krui beach**, known among surfers for its brilliant waves. There are several other good waves here and a choice of accommodation. From Bandar Lampung, it is a 6-hour drive to Krui town.

Bandar Lampung

Arriving from West Java, the Sumatran port of entry is Bakauhuni harbour near **Bandar Lampung** ⑩. The ferry passes within view of Anak Krakatau, which sits on the site of the former enormous Krakatau volcano that erupted in 1883 *(see page 146)*. The **Lampung Provincial Museum** on Jalan Teuku Umar (daily; charge) displays Chinese ceramics, Dongson bronze kettledrums, *kain tapis* (hand-woven ceremonial cloths) and archaeological finds from Labuan Meringgai.

There are hot sulphur springs at **Kalianda**, 38km (23 miles) north of the ferry terminal, where there are hotels and restaurants. Nearby are the remains of an old Dutch fort.

On Sumatra's southeast coast, **Way Kambas National Park** ⑪ comprises estuaries, marshes and open grassland and is the home of the **Sumatra Rhino Sanctuary**. Recommended is the 4-hour (one-way) boat trip through

BELOW: a poster for Laskar Pelangi. The film has helped to establish the fine local beaches on the tourist trail.

From tin to tourism

Bangka and Belitung islands are the biggest tin producers in Indonesia. Established in the 17th century, their mines are central to the local economy – although as both islands have a number of lovely beaches, the local governments have grand plans for developing tourism. Belitung's Tanjung Tinggi beach and its extraordinary granite formations along the coast are the most visited. The enormously successful Indonesian film *Laskar Pelangi* (Rainbow Troops) was shot here, and the movie's amazing beach scenes have already made it a popular holiday destination among locals. Tasty seafood and coffee shops are found everywhere. On Banka, new resorts are springing up on Remodong, Penyusuk, Parai Tenggiri and Tanjung Pesona beaches.

rainforests from Labuhan Meringgi, 12km (7 miles) south of the reserve, to the Way Kambas estuary, an excellent way to look for wild elephants, tigers and boars that come to the river's edge to drink. Birdwatching is also spectacular, with resident kingfishers, lesser adjutants, woolly-necked storks and pelicans. The park also houses an **Elephant Conservation Centre**, where the pachyderms are bred and trained to perform heavy work and to patrol park boundaries. Entertaining tourist shows featuring performing elephants are designed to educate villagers that elephants are not man's enemies and should be protected.

Palembang

Going north along the east coast, **Palembang** ⑫, a booming oil town, is Sumatra's second-largest city and sits on the banks of the mighty Sungai Musi. A major port for well over 1,200 years, Palembang was the capital of the Srivijaya kingdom in AD 600 and a spiritual centre where Mahayana Buddhist monks from as far away as China studied and translated texts.

Palembang was nurtured during the Dutch era as a riverine entrepôt, servicing the mines on **Bangka island**. Those who love fine beaches, refreshing sea breezes and azure waters can reach Bangka or neighbouring **Belitung** island by ferry or hydrofoil. Pantai Parai is the most visited beach on Bangka; Belitung's Pantai Tinggi has amazing rock formations.

Palembang's ornately carved lima-style houses and shops are raised on piles above the Musi, where river merchants ply their trade from boats. The region produces fine woven fabrics and has its own dances, including the *gending srivijaya*, dating from the 7th century. The **Museum Rumah Bari** (Tue–Sat 8am–4pm, Sun 8am–noon; charge), occupying several buildings, contains important megalithic statuary, Hindu and Buddhist sculptures, primitive ethnic crafts, weaponry and Chinese porcelain. An old Dutch fort is still used by the Indonesian army.

West of Bangka, on the east coast of the mainland, is **Sembilang National Park**, reached by motorboat from Palembang in about 4 hours. Its lack

TIP

On Jalan Sukarno-Hatta in Bengkulu is the house where Sukarno was held by the Dutch from 1938 to 1941. It is now a museum.

BELOW: Sumatran elephants.

TIP

Boats can be hired in
Canti village, near
Bandar Lampung, to
make the choppy 3-hour
crossing to Anak
Krakatau volcano.
Krakatau can also
be accessed from
West Java.

of easy access has prevented large-scale tourism development, which could be a good thing for the tigers, elephants, tapirs, giant tortoises, freshwater dolphins and otters that live there. This park is also excellent for birdwatching, as it is a habitat for migrating birds that come from as far away as Siberia.

At Sembilang's northern boundary, **Berbak National Park** is a Ramsar protected wetlands site. It owes its importance to is its large, undisturbed swamp forests, criss-crossed by muddy rivers.

Jambi

Further north, **Jambi** ⑬, the site of the ancient Melayu kingdom, is today a modern city, its growing economy based on palm oil, logging, rubber, coffee and tea exports. The surrounding forests are home to the Kubu people, the original inhabitants of the area who are hunter-gatherers. Clad in loincloths, they can sometimes be seen walking along the roadside en route to their forest homes.

Exploration of the city starts along the river, where a large number of people live on floating rafts or in houses built on stilts over the Sungai Batanghari. You can walk or ride on a *dokar* (horse-drawn cart), and visit the Pasar Raya (Central Market).

The Hindu temple complex **Candi Muaro**, 25km (15 miles) northeast of the city, is an hour by car or 30 minutes by speedboat. Accessible by four-wheel-drive along the Sungai Sengering are the 10 stalactite **Tiangko Caves**.

Relatively small **Bukit Duabelas National Park** is in Jambi province and consists of lowland tropical rainforest in the northern part, while in the south secondary forest is a result of logging. This park is the home of the Rimbu people, hunter-gatherers who live in small groups and are governed by traditional laws.

The Riau archipelago

Between the swampy shores of Sumatra and the Malay peninsula lies a chain of more than 3,000 small islands. These and the eastern mainland Sumatran lowlands comprise **Riau** province, one of the country's most rapidly developing areas.

BELOW: swanky pool at the Angsana Resort & Spa, Bintan island.

Pekanbaru ⑭, the provincial capital and the largest city in mainland Riau, is a thriving oil-production centre. This friendly Caltex oil town, with a large foreign population, is a good base for exploring nearby jungle abodes of the durian-loving Sumatran rhinoceros, as well as tigers, elephants and birds. Four hours downriver, at **Siak Sri Indrapura** village, stands a palace that was built in 1723.

Muara Takus, a temple near the hydroelectric plant, dates from the 9th century AD when the power of the South Sumatra-based Sriwijaya Empire was at its peak.

In this area at the **Tesso Nilo National Park**, the World Wildlife Fund and Indonesian forestry department operate a Sumatran tiger conservation unit. In a successful community empowerment programme, mahouts are selected from villages and trained to patrol the park on elephant-back. Called the Flying Squad, these groups herd wild elephants that threaten villages and crops back into the park.

Batam and Bintan islands

Change has come swiftly to Batam and Bintan islands. **Batam** ⑮ has been developed into a major industrial satellite of Singapore and is popular with weekend visitors from there, who come for its golf courses, beaches, duty-free shopping and seafood. Ferries and hydrofoils ply the waters to and from Singapore almost hourly, from sunrise to sundown.

Bintan ⑯ is the largest of all the Riau islands, and its northern shore is a string of high-end resorts catering to well-heeled Singaporeans and Indonesians. The energetic port of **Tanjungpinang**, situated on the island's southeastern coast, is just one hour by ferry from Singapore, and is also a jumping-off spot to nearby tiny islands and the Lingga archipelago. Attractions include the small but interesting **Museum Riau** situated on Jalan Brigjen Katamso in the eastern suburbs. You can catch a speedboat to **Senggarang**, a Chinese village

on the far side of the Sungai Riau. Its four shrines include the Banyan Tree temple, a 300-year-old clan house suspended in a giant banyan tree.

Just across from Tanjungpinang is **Penyengat**, home of the Riau sultans, their lavish court and royal city that encompassed nearly 10,000 citizens. A book entitled *Bustanul Katibin*, the first Malay grammar text, was published on Penyengat in 1857, laying the foundation for Bahasa Indonesia, the lingua franca of the entire country.

Spanning 14km (9 miles) along the north coast is **Pasir Panjang** beach, a sprawling complex of de luxe hotels, golf courses, spas and condos and the reason most tourists go to Bintan. A self-contained resort area, every water sport imaginable is available. From here, excursions can be arranged for trekking up Gunung Bintan; enjoying the cool breezes amid lush greenery at Lagoi Park and Reservoir; boating up the Sebung River for an eco-tour of the mangrove forests; interacting with bottlenose dolphins at Dolphin Lodge; and riding an elephant at Bintan Elephant Park.

Skewered meat is a street-food staple.

BELOW: measuring a Sumatran tiger being tracked at Sembilang National Park. The paw size is a good indicator of the animal's age and health.

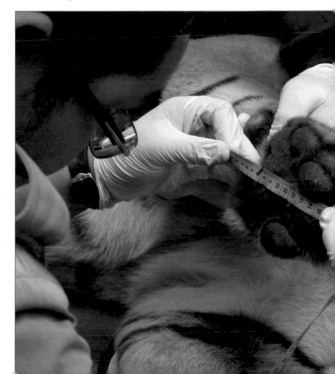

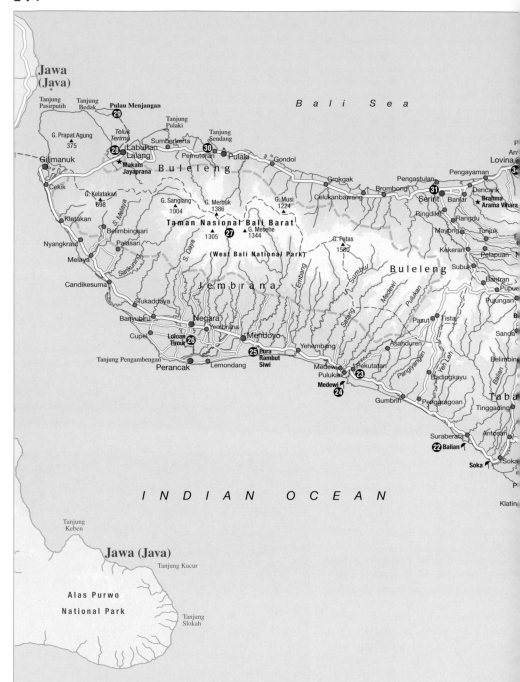

Jawa
(Java)

Tanjung
Pasirputih   Tanjung
Bedak   Pulau Menjangan
29

B a l i   S e a

G. Prapat Agung   *Teluk
Terima*   Tanjung
Pulaki
375   Sumberkerta   Tanjung
Sendang
Gilimanuk   28   Labuhan
Lalang   30   Pemuteran   Pulaki   Gondol
Cekik   ★ Makam
Jayaprana   B u l e l e n g   Grokgak   Brombong   Pengastulan   Pengayaman
G. Kelatakan   G. Sanglang   G. Merbuk   G. Musi   Celukanbawang   31   Dencarik
698   1004   1386   1224   Seririt   Banjar   ★ Brahma
Klatakan   Taman Nasional Bali Barat   Ringdikih   Arama Vihara
Belimbingsari   27   G. Mesehe   Rangdu
Nyangkraut   Palasari   1305   1344   Mayong   Tunjuk
Melaya   *(West Bali National Park)*   G. Patas
1580   Kekeran   Pelapuan
Candikesuma   J e m b r a n a   B u l e l e n g   Subuk
Tukaddaya   Bantran
Banyubiru   Negara   Pupu
Cupel   Yembrana   Mendoyo   Pasut   Tista   Pujungan
Loloan
Timur   26   25   Pura
Rambut
Siwi   Yehembang   Asahduren   Pangyangan   Sanda
Tanjung Pengambengan   Lemondang   Medewi   Pekutatan   Belimbin
Perancak   Pulukan   23   Badingkayu
Medewi   24   Taba
Gumbrih   Penggragoan   Tinggading

I N D I A N   O C E A N   Suraberata   Antosari
22 Balian   Soka

Tanjung
Keben   Klatin

Jawa (Java)
Tanjung Kucur

Alas Purwo

National Park   Tanjung
Slokah

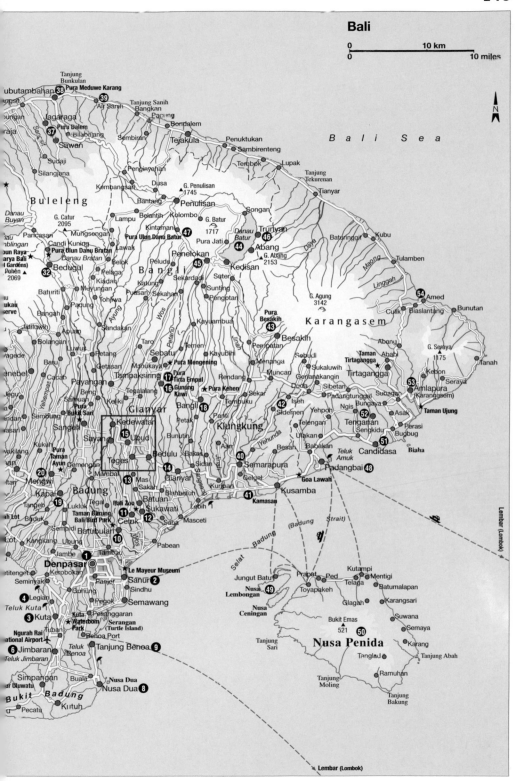

Bali

0 — 10 km
0 — 10 miles

Bali Sea

Buleleng

ubutambahan **38** Tanjung Bunkulan **Pura Meduwe Karang**
Pura Dalem **37** **39** Air Sanih
Jagaraga Tanjung Sanih Bangkan
Bilabalang Pacung
Sawan Bondalem
Sudaji Sembiran Tejakula Penuktukan
Silangjana Penginyahan Sambirenteng
Dusa Tembok Lupak
Danau Buyan Kembangsari G. Penulisan 1745 Tanjung Tekurenan
G. Catur 2095 Belantih Penulisan Tianyar
Lampu Kolombo Songan
Pancasan Mungsengan Kintamani G. Batur 1717 Trunyan **46**
Candi Kuning **Pura Ulun Danu Batur** **47** *Danau Batur*
32 **Pura Ulun Danu Bratan** Lawak Pura Jati **44** Abang
Bedugul *Danau Bratan* Penelokan G. Abang 2153
arya Bali (I Gardens) Belok **45** Kedisan Batoringgit Kubu
Pohen 2069 Peludu Suter Tulamben
Batuniti Meyungan Puasan Sekaban Sunting Linggah
Paqung Tohjiwa Sekahan Pengotan **54** Amed
Bangah Apuan Sandakan Kayuambua Abang Culik Biaslantang Bunutan
Jatiluwih Luwus Taro Temen G. Agung 3142 **Karangasem** G. Seraya 1175
Petang Manukaya Kayubihi Pemoatan Tanah
Catcal Getasan **Pura Mengening** Menanga **Pura Besakih** **43** Abong
Payangan Tampaksiring **17** **Pura Tirta Empul** Rendang Besakih Sebudi Ababi Tirtagangga
Beng Tegalalang **16** **Gunung Kawi** Muncan Sukaluwih **Taman Tirtagangga** Seraya
Samuan Keliki **★ Pura Kehen** Sekar Duda Geranakangin Tirtagangga Kebon
Pura **Gianyar** Bangli **18** Tembuku Iseh Sibetan Padangtunggal Subagan **53**
Bukit Sari Kedewatan Petak Panti **42** Sidemen Yehpoh Bungaya **Amlapura**
Sangeh **15** Ubud Bunutin Sidemen Ngis **52** Asak (Karangasem)
Pura Sayan Bedulu Bakas **Klungkung** Telengan Tenganan **Taman Ujung**
20 **Taman Ayun** Teges **14** Sidan Besah Babakan Sengkidu Perasi Bugbug
Mengwi Demenan Mambal **13** Mas Jungut Kuripan Ulakan *Teluk Amuk* **51**
Kapal Sakah **40** **Samarapura** **Candidasa** Biaha
19 Lukluk Tegal **Batuan** Blahbatuh Gelgel **Goa Lawah** **Padangbai** **48**
Baduk Sempidi **Bali Zoo** Sukawati **Gianyar** **41** Kusamba
Taman Burung **11** Celuk **12** Saba **Kamasan**
Bali Bird Park Batubulan Lebih Masceti (Badung Strait)
Kangkang Ubung **10** Pabean
Jambe Tambau *Selat Badung*
Denpasar Kutampi
Kerobokan Panjer **Le Mayeur Museum** Jungut Batu Prapat Ped Mentigi
4 Legian **Sanur** **2** Nusa Lembongan **49** Telaga Batumalapan
3 Kuta Pesanggaran Sindhu Semawang Toyapakeh Glagah Karangsari
Waterbom Park Serangan (Turtle Island) Nusa Ceningan Suwana
Ngurah Rai **6** Jimbaran Benoa Port Bukit Emas 521 **50** Semaya
National Airport *Teluk Jimbaran* *Teluk Benoa* **Tanjung Benoa** **9** **Nusa Penida** Karang
Simpangan Buala **Nusa Dua** Tanjung Sari Tanglad Tanjung Abah
Bukit **Badung** **Nusa Dua** **8** Tanjung Moling Ramuhan
Pecatu Kutuh Tanjung Bakung

Maong *Daya* *Jinah*

Lembar (Lombok)

N

BALI

Venture beyond the familiar southern resorts and the cultural attractions of Ubud to experience the "new Bali" – the rugged west, cool mountain highlands and east coast surf beaches

The name Bali evokes visions of mystical images and warm, naturally hospitable islanders, both of which have lured travellers for decades. Its culture is as captivating to visitors as are its stunning landscapes and beautiful beaches.

There are other facets to the "new Bali", however, that visitors are beginning to explore. Regional autonomy, giving each district control over its own destiny – and revenues – has stirred the creative juices of hitherto little-visited areas. The southern coastline of West Bali, for example, is filling up fast with new resorts. The difference here is that instead of luxury five-star international chain hotels, the accommodation is more of the boutique variety, with many places managed by Balinese who favour taking guests on scenic drives through the countryside to villages to soak in the local culture rather than staging in-house "shows". Trained, English-speaking trekking guides at West Bali National Park are chosen from local communities and are a part of village empowerment programmes. Resorts near the park help to patrol its boundaries and lead environmentally smart activities for local children. At nearby Pemuteran, resorts and dive shops teach and employ villagers to restore and protect reefs.

The north coast beaches are sprouting healing, well-being and yoga centres. Lovina has morphed from a sleepy alternative beach destination to a springboard for exploring the highlands to its south. Newly built family-run resorts now dot the highlands, along with more activities that cool mountain air-seekers can enjoy.

On the east coast, Amed is spawning bungalows and villas that are ideal for a combination sand-and-surf and inland exploration holiday. Offshore Nusa Lembongan no longer attracts only budget surfers, but also appeals to lovers of less crowded beaches as infrastructure continues to improve.

South Bali remains as busy – and enjoyable – as ever, but resorts are being developed further west to appeal to a more exclusive clientele, eventually flowing into expensive villa-mansions as far afield as Tanah Lot.

LEFT: legong dancer. **ABOVE LEFT:** an offering at a Balinese temple.
ABOVE RIGHT: ritual cleansing at Ubud..

SOUTH BALI

Many visitors do not venture beyond Bali's southern beaches, where hotels jostle with endless bars, shops and restaurants, and entertainment of every persuasion abounds

alinese cosmology considers south the most impure direction. Yet southern Bali attracts most travellers, where the infrastructure and commercialism are most developed. Moving south from Denpasar, office-block facades give way to signs advertising hotels, tours and shops.

Throughout the island's history, southern Bali has been the first to welcome or repel outsiders. Bali's first king, Sri Kesari Warmadewa, conquered invaders in AD 913. In later times, important Javanese priests trod these shores. Empu Kuturan came to Bali in the 10th century and introduced the *meru*, or multi-tiered roofed shrine. Bali's exposure to the West began when sailors from Dutch explorer Cornelis de Houtman's fleet were so entranced by the island that they jumped ship to stay for ever, beginning a trend that has continued to this day. The first hotel on Kuta beach was built by an American couple in 1936.

In addition to the sun, sand, sea and infrastructure (often lacking in other areas of Indonesia), visitors continue to flock to southern Bali beaches in part because of the local people's attitudes. Although they may not always approve of foreign shenanigans, the Hindu Balinese are more prone to look the other way than Indonesians elsewhere.

As South Bali continues on its developmental journey, the villages are taking an increasing role and are striving to create their own identities. While Kuta is happy to be backpacking, rabble-rousing nirvana, Tuban to its south has reinvented itself with five-star resorts. North of Kuta, Legian harbours those who want to be part of the Kuta scene, but prefer to sleep somewhere quieter. To the northwest, exclusivity comes in the form of beaches in Seminyak and Petitinget, or rural settings in Kerobokan and

Main attractions

MUSEUM NEGERI PROPINSI BALI, DENPASAR
TAMAN WERDI BUDAYA, DENPASAR
SANUR
KUTA
PURA TANAH LOT
BUKIT BADUNG
PURA LUHUR ULUWATU
NUSA DUA
TANJUNG BENOA

LEFT: shrine at Pura Jagatnata, Denpasar.
RIGHT: kecak dance.

Lillies, Pura Jagatnathn

BELOW: shadow puppets. **BELOW RIGHT:** Puputan Square statue commemorating the slaughter of Balinese by the Dutch in 1906 .

Canggu. On the opposite coast, Sanur remains its own special enclave of tourists and expats.

Further south, Jimbaran and the rugged cliffs of Bukit Badung create an entirely different atmosphere. Nusa Dua continues to draw those who seek total, luxurious escape, while Tanjung Benoa captivates a less staid crowd of sun- and sea sports-lovers.

In short, South Bali has something to suit every budget and taste, and it's very happy to share its glee with the rest of the world.

Denpasar

Denpasar ❶ is a traffic-clogged government and financial centre incorporating winding alleys, illogical one-way streets and pungent smells. If your mind has been unwinding on the beach, it may well be wound back up on an excursion into Denpasar. Once a parking spot is located, most of the city's main sights are within walking distance from each other.

Central to the city is **Taman Puputan** (Puputan Park), a large, grassy open space commemorating the battle between the *raja* of the Badung Empire and the Dutch militia in l906. Rather than being conquered by the Dutch, thousands of Balinese warriors, dressed in their finest regalia and armed only with *keris* daggers and spears, hurled themselves into battle in a heroic sacrifice, dying either by their own hands or by Dutch bullets in ritual suicide known as *puputan* (literally, "end"). Today, the slaughter of the estimated 600 to 2,000 is memorialised by a bronze statue. North of the square is the former Dutch governor's residence, where the *raja*'s palace once stood.

Catur Mukha, the great statue with four faces and eight arms at Denpasar's main intersection (at the northwestern corner of Taman Puputan), represents the Hindu god of the four directions.

Museum Negeri Propinsi Bali

East of the square is **Museum Negeri Propinsi Bali** (Mon–Thur 8am–3.30pm, Fri 8–11am; charge). Built in 1932 by the Dutch, it presents a comprehensive history of Bali's social and cultural

development from prehistoric times to the early 20th century. Items are well presented, although no specific dates of origin are given, but knowledgeable English-speaking guides are on hand. The museum is notable for its fine architecture, combining the two principal edifices of Balinese temples (*pura*) and palaces (*puri*): split gate with outer and inner courtyards, and the *kulkul* (wooden signal drum) tower.

The museum is representative of the entire island. The main building, with its wide-pillared verandah, resembles the Karangasem palaces of East Bali, with a porch used by officials in audience with the *raja*. The windowless building to its north reflects the Tabanan palace style of West Bali. The brick building, **Gedung Buleleng**, belongs to the northern palace style of Singaraja; inside are beautiful examples of wedding costumes and items used in religious rituals.

Next to the museum is the modern state temple, **Pura Jagatnata**, dedicated to Sanghyang Widi Wasa, the supreme god (manifested in

Bali's numerous local deities and ancestral spirits). Elaborate ceremonies are held here every full and new moon. The tall *padmasana* (lotus throne), made of white coral, symbolises universal order. The turtle Bedawangnala and two *naga* serpents represent the foundations of the world, while the throne signifies the cosmic mountain.

Denpasar means "north of the market". **Pasar Badung**, on Jalan Gajah Mada is a four-storey building housing Bali's largest traditional market. Locals shop for fruit and vegetables, meat and seafood, clothing, spices, baskets, ritual paraphernalia and everything else. Women wait outside offering market tours for a negotiable fee, with stops at shops where they earn a commission. Politely decline their assistance and stroll on your own. Across the Tukad Badung canal is **Pasar Kumbasari** (daily 8am–10pm), offering the same items as Pasar Badung plus handicrafts and art.

Nightlife in Denpasar revolves around the three huge colourful *pasar malam* (local night markets) that operate at Pasar Kumbasari, Pasar

Salak (snake fruit) at a Denpasar market.

BELOW: the Museum Negiri Propinsi Bali.

Kereneng, near the bus station off Jalan Kamboja, and the Pekambingan (Goat Penis) area just off Jalan Diponegoro. Here, an array of temporary stalls offer all kinds of cooked food, while hawkers push more unusual items like snake oil and charms as well as the ubiquitous T-shirts and sandals.

Pura Maospahit (daily during daylight hours; donation), on Jalan Sutomo, is the oldest temple in the city. It dates from the 14th century, when Majapahit Empire emissaries arrived from Java. Extensive earthquake damage in 1917 resulted in much of the temple being rebuilt; the section at the back is the only part that has remained unaltered for 600 years.

Denpasar's arts

A permanent exhibition of traditional and contemporary Balinese visual arts is at the **Taman Werdi Budaya** (popularly called the **Art Centre**; daily 8am–3.30pm; charge), 2km (1.2 miles) east of downtown, on Jalan Nusa Indah. Bali's numerous art disciplines are represented at this large complex, including painting, woodcarving,

shadow puppetry, silverwork, weaving, dance costumes and even ivory carving. Works by Bali's foreign artists are displayed in the museum.

The Art Centre was established in 1973 to showcase Balinese art and culture and includes teaching facilities, a restaurant, craft shop and an outdoor arena for traditional dances. The grounds are also home to the annual Bali Art Festival (mid-June–mid-July).

Next to the centre is **Sekolah Tinggi Seni Indonesia** (STSI; Mon–Fri 8am–2pm), the Indonesia Institute of the Arts, founded in 1967. Students study traditional dance, music and puppetry, and classical and contemporary choreography.

For serious study, the **Pusat Dokumentasi** (Documentation Centre) in Renon offers a collection of works in all languages on Balinese life and culture. Documents may not be removed, but can be photocopied on the premises. A lovely tree-lined "suburb" southeast of Denpasar, **Renon** is also the location of most foreign consulates and the respected Udayana University.

BELOW: beach volleyball at Sanur.
BELOW RIGHT: water sports at Nusa Dua.

Sanur

Local tradition maintained that ship-wrecks held bounty from Baruna, god of the sea, and thus anyone had rights to them. The Dutch had a different viewpoint. In 1904, a Chinese schooner was wrecked off the shores of **Sanur** ②. Pillaging by the local people breached a treaty between the Balinese and the Dutch, and this incident was just the excuse the Dutch needed to wage war against the Badung *raja*. The result was the *puputan* commemorated in Denpasar's Taman Puputan. Only one person, a child, survived the massacre.

Sanur became an enclave for artists around the world in the 1930s. By the 1950s, the first cluster of bungalows in Sanur was built, attracting international travellers. The Bali Beach Hotel opened in 1966, built with Japanese reparation money after World War II. When the 10-storey hotel first opened, it was a source of wonder to the Balinese with its running water, electricity and elevators. Bali's only high-rise structure at the time, and something of an eyesore, it was gutted

by a mysterious fire in 1992 but was rebuilt and reopened less than one year later as the Inna Grand Bali Beach Hotel.

Today, Sanur beach has all levels of accommodation, with access roads lined with shops and restaurants. Amid the development and tourism frenzy, Sanur has managed, remarkably, to retain much of its quaint heritage as a Brahman-dominated village, where trance performances are still staged during local temple festivals. Sanur's seas are calm and shallow, disappearing altogether at low tide, leaving little more than great swathes of sandy mud and coral stretching for hundreds of metres out along the reef. When the tides are high, however, Sanur offers windsurfing and sailing.

One of the few historical sites in Sanur is the home of Belgian painter Jean Le Mayeur de Mepres. He moved to Bali in 1932, where he lived until his death in 1958. **Museum Le Mayeur** (Sun–Thur 8am–3.30pm, Fri 8am–1pm; charge), just north of Inna Grand Bali Beach Hotel, has gardens full of statues, luxuriant gold-and-crimson

Museum Le Mayeur.

BELOW: exhibit at Denpasar's Art Centre.

Seminyak sushi bar..

carvings, and Le Mayeur's own paintings, mostly of his late wife, Ni Polok, a renowned *legong* dancer.

At the southern end of Sanur is the **Pura Belanjong** (daily during daylight hours; donation), notable for the island's oldest example of writing, the Prasasti Belanjong, an inscribed pillar dating from AD 913 and discovered in the early 1930s. The 177cm (70in) tall stone column is not much to look at, but close inspection reveals two forms of writing, ancient Balinese and Sanskrit.

Kuta, Tuban and Legian

In former times **Kuta** ❸ was a leper colony and slave station with poor soil; its original villagers were farmers, fishermen and metalsmiths. At the genesis of mass tourism, they looked askance at foreigners frolicking along the ocean, the Balinese idea of the underworld. But they soon saw there were profits to be made and invited travellers into their homes for clean, simple and cheap accommodation.

For many, Kuta is Bali, while others decry its plunge into rampant commercialism. As long as the pleasure

seekers are happy and villagers continue to leave *canang* – little offering trays – at the high-tide mark each day to pacify the spirits, Kuta beach seems to embrace both worlds. Both Balinese and foreigners are found along its golden sands surfing, sunbathing, strutting and selling. Kuta's surf break is among the best for learners, but the undertow is fierce, so be sure to swim in places marked by flags. The sunset here is usually glorious.

Inland from the beach, Kuta is packed with a dazzling array of pubs, bars, souvenir shops, tattoo parlours, travel offices, accommodation and handicrafts kiosks frequented by the young at heart. Nestled in between are temples, somehow retaining their dignity. Beach and street hawkers remain an annoyance, and this once-peaceful village is now punctuated by drugs, prostitution and muggings. Don't get too starry-eyed on the dark beach at night. South of Kuta, down Jalan Dewi Sartika, quieter **Tuban** village is an upmarket resort area. **Waterbom Park** (daily 9am–6pm; charge) has water slides, restaurants and spa

BELOW: lace shop at Seminyak; **BELOW RIGHT:** ridng the waves.

treatments. There are lifeguards on duty, but adults must accompany children under 12 years old. It can get crowded later in the day and especially at weekends with long queues, but is well worth the wait.

Just opposite Waterbom Park and next to Discovery Kartika Plaza Hotel is the modern Discovery Shopping Mall – right on the beach – with an array of shops and the Centro and Sogo department stores.

Legian ❹ is more sedate than Kuta and is preferred by Bali's young expatriate population. Their influence can be seen throughout the village in boutiques and a number of excellent restaurants, cafés and bars.

Seminyak, Kerobokan, Petitenget and Canggu

Further north, the decidedly hip **Seminyak** is home to exclusive hotels, designer boutiques, spas, trendy beachside restaurants and nightclubs, which are crammed into every available space. This is expat heaven, and expensive private and rental villas have replaced much of what once was the village.

Seminyak has the same wide sandy beach and thundering surf as Kuta, but without the heaving crowds. **Jalan Kayu Aya** at its northern boundary and **Jalan Abimanyu** at its southern end have also made a name for themselves: the former has a clutch of hip restaurants and the latter some equally trendy bars and clubs.

Northeast of Seminyak is **Kerobokan**, which is doing its best to get into the tourism game. Without a beach to lure travellers, it bills itself as a rural getaway, with rental villas the key draw. Along Jalan Raya Kerobokan are furniture shops and galleries catering to exporters.

Northwest of Seminyak is **Petitenget**. Formerly known to tourists only as a part of Seminyak (the dividing line is the north side of Jalan Kayu Aya), it is now establishing its own identity as upmarket, like its neighbour, but removed from the horrendous traffic further south. This condition may be short-lived, however, as new resorts, more villas, and expensive restaurants are popping up everywhere.

Offerings at Pura Tanah Lot.

BELOW: eating out at Seminyak.

Continuing northwest towards Tanah Lot, the coastline is an enormous construction zone. This is **Canggu**, once only known to surfers, but now being taken over by foreigners whose villas can more aptly be described as mansions. The village atmosphere they enjoy now will soon become another Seminyak.

Pura Tanah Lot

Continuing northwest from Canggu will bring you to one of Bali's most noted sites, **Pura Tanah Lot ❺** (daily daylight hours; charge). From the Kerobokan junction, turn west towards Canggu and follow the signs.

Set apart from the land on a stone pedestal carved by incoming tides, Tanah Lot's solitary black towers and tufts of foliage spilling over the cliffs recall the delicacy of a Chinese painting, although the gauntlet of souvenir stalls and hawkers on the temple approach may diminish this image. In caves surrounding the temple dwell striped sacred snakes, discreetly left undisturbed by Balinese. Only worshippers are allowed inside

the temple, but visitors get a dramatic view from the adjacent hill, especially at sunset.

Tanah Lot is attributed to the 16th-century priest Danghyang Nirartha. During his travels, Nirartha saw a bright light emanating from a point on the west coast and came to this spot to meditate. The disciple of a local spiritual leader became fascinated by Nirartha and began to study with him. This angered the local priest who, filled with jealousy, challenged Nirartha. The unflappable Nirartha simply moved his meditation spot into the ocean, and this point became known as Tanah Lot, or "Land in the Sea".

Jimbaran and Bukit Badung

An exclusive resort area is found along the coast south of **Jimbaran ❻**, housing hotel bigwigs such as Four Seasons and InterContinental. All of them face the sea within easy reach of Jimbaran village and its justly celebrated beachside seafood restaurants.

Connected to the mainland by a low, narrow isthmus, the limestone tableland at **Bukit Badung**, a

BELOW: Pura Tanah Lot.

peninsula rising to 200 metres (660ft) above sea level, is a striking contrast to the lush Bali mainland. Vantage spots along the road that crosses the hill afford breathtaking northern vistas rising to the peaks of distant volcanoes; an ideal place to catch beautiful sunsets. The ultra luxurious Bvlgari Resort – from the Italian jeweller of that name – is nestled between the cliff and the ocean near Uluwatu.

Pura Luhur Uluwatu

At the western tip of Bukit Badung, where rocky precipices drop almost 100 metres (330ft) to the ocean, is **Pura Luhur Uluwatu** ❼ (daily daylight hours; charge), 70 metres (230ft) up on a dramatic promontory. Originally dating from around the 16th century, it is one of the Sad Kahyangan, or Six Temples of the World, revered by all Balinese. The holy Javanese priest Danghyang Nirartha established this temple, and it is said he achieved enlightenment here. The innermost sanctuary, *jeroan*, is off-limits to non-worshippers but can be viewed from the side. South of the temple and car park, a panoramic short path leads along the cliff top.

The area just north of the temple is well known among surfers. Only experienced riders should attempt the dangerous reefs, strong currents and tricky waves from April to September. Viewers can watch the action from the shore, but the sea here is not ideal for swimming.

Nusa Dua and Tanjung Benoa

Nusa Dua ❽, on the east coast of Bukit Badung, is a slightly sterile paradise in a ribbon-wrapped package. A purpose-built, luxury hotel enclave, sprawling in the middle of a coconut grove and alongside a white-sand beach, Nusa Dua caters decidedly to the upmarket traveller. In many ways, Nusa Dua is thin on local ambience, having been built on unused land in a concerted government effort

to prevent tourism from affecting the island's cultural sanctity. Luxury hotels wrap around the beach, among which are several international chains. Water sports available here include spectacular parasailing, and jet-skiing. The well-regarded **Bali Golf & Country Club** has a championship golf course, with nine holes heading towards the sea and nine holes inland. At least seven temples are within Nusa Dua's bounds.

For many years, **Tanjung Benoa** ❾, a fishing village north of Nusa Dua on a long peninsula, was overlooked by hotel developers blinded by the obvious potential of Sanur, Kuta and Nusa Dua. The peninsula is now lined with four- and five-star hotels, as well as lower-end accommodation and restaurants. Benoa offers an attractive stretch of white-sand beach which, like Sanur, is susceptible to the tides. A walk north up the peninsula reveals a bustling morning market and a multicultural community, evolved from decades as a trading centre, reflected in Chinese and Muslim cemeteries, and Chinese, Muslim and Hindu temples.

Artist at work in Legian.

The cremation ceremony

Balinese Hindus believe a soul borrows a physical human body, so upon death this body is returned to the five elements – wind, earth, fire, water and ether – to release the soul and enable it to reincarnate on earth or unite with the divine Supreme Being. No weeping or grief is openly displayed, as this makes the soul unwilling to leave.

Cremation ceremonies are so costly that a family often waits years to share expenses in a joint ceremony. In the meantime, the body is purified and buried in the village cemetery. Once a cremation date is set, ritual specialists, priests, friends and neighbours help mobilise the communal spirit. If a body has been buried, the bones are exhumed or the body is placed in a sarcophagus inside a colourful cremation tower.

A noisy procession leads the way as dozens of men carry the tower on their shoulders to a field where the cremation will take place, spinning it at crossroads to confuse the soul so that it cannot find its way home to disturb the living.

After the corpse is reduced to ashes, the family gathers and pulverises the charred bone fragments, and puts them in a yellow coconut that they cast into the sea. Purification ceremonies for the community who participated in the cremation are held three days later.

CENTRAL BALI

Beyond the tourist centres lie a series of craft villages, a timeless affirmation of the spirit of Bali – where art, as material culture, is an authentic part of everyday life

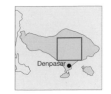

Central Bali is best known for Ubud, the island's artistic centre, and many visitors perch there and are content to wander its narrow streets on extensive shopping expeditions or relax in its healing centres, perhaps taking in a dance performance in the evenings. Situated in the hills north of Denpasar and only accessible by narrow, winding, often traffic-laden roads, Ubud is the epitome of Bali for many travellers.

Beyond the now overcrowded town, much of the rich history of Balinese culture lies peacefully hidden from the tourism masses and can be enjoyed on day trips of scenic drives taking in memorable vistas of rice fields and deep river gorges. Antiquities dating from the 11th century abound in the outlying areas west, north and east of Ubud, with one rare artefact dating back to Indonesia's Bronze Age. And along with these treasures are glimpses into the deep-rooted traditions that remain very strong within the Balinese people today.

The road to Ubud

The first "village" outside Denpasar is **Batubulan** ⑩, stretching for about 2km (1.2 miles) and distinguished by stone-carving shops lining the roadside. Soft *paras* stone, found in nearby ravines, is used to create deities and

demons for temples, households and, now, tourists. Males carve in groups at roadside "factories", reproducing designs formed by their ancestors and, increasingly, those which appeal to visitors.

Batubulan holds daily performances of the Barong dance on a stage near Pura Puseh temple. The drama depicts the age-old struggle between good and righteousness – the path of *dharma*, or right-doing – and the negative forces which seek to destroy them.

Main attractions
BATUBULAN STONE-CARVERS
CELUK SILVER- AND GOLDSMITHS
SUKAWATI WAYANG KULIT MAKERS
MAS MASK MAKERS
GIANYAR ANTIQUITIES
UBUD ART GALLERIES
GOA GAJAH, BEDULU
MOON OF PEJENG, PEJENG
TAMPAKSIRING TEMPLES

LEFT: legong dance performance.
RIGHT: Batabulan stone carving village.

Craftsman at work, Batubalan.

Taman Burung Bali Bird Park (daily 9am–5.30pm; charge), just to the north of Batubalan, houses over 1,000 specimens of 250 exotic bird species in a well-designed aviary and is dedicated to the conservation of rare and endangered birds from Indonesia and elsewhere. Paved paths lead through 2 hectares (5 acres) of gardens representing deserts, rainforests and marshlands. The park has an attractive open-air restaurant and gift shop.

Continuing along the road to Ubud, numerous wood- and stone-carving shops are interspersed among the houses of **Singapadu**, but the village is more famous for producing some of Bali's talented musicians and dancers. Take time to visit the workshop-home of **I Wayan Tangguh** (tel: 0361-298 685), one of Bali's best mask makers. Look for the sign with his name on it on the main road. Here you will see a chunk of wood evolve into a beautiful work of art in

BELOW: gamelan music is essential for ceremonies.

addition to viewing his collection of exquisite masks.

Celuk to Gianyar

At the main junction before the bird park, the route turns eastwards to Gianyar. **Celuk ⑪**, some 4km (2.5 miles) from Batubalan, beckons visitors. Here local smiths create sterling silver and gold brooches, gem-studded bracelets and earrings of all descriptions using simple hand tools. Don't miss the shops on the road north and perpendicular to the main road, as many fine jewellers dwell off the beaten track.

Across the Wos River, **Sukawati ⑫** anchored an extremely powerful kingdom in the 18th century. The town now sports an art market and is home to some of the best *dalang* (puppeteers) on Bali. *Wayang kulit* – shadow puppetry – is a difficult art. Aside from manipulating different puppet characters, memorising hundreds of stories, singing, cueing the musicians, and creating a variety of voices, a *dalang* must be clean in mind, body and soul. He is akin to a

priest in many respects and can even make the holy water so necessary for Balinese rituals (an honour usually reserved for Brahman priests). *Wayang kulit* stories are imbued with innuendo and impart the values of daily life to the audience.

Many *dalangs* make their own puppets, delicately carved out of buffalo hide and then painted. A number of *dalangs* live in the *banjar* behind the Sukawati market, where visitors can watch them work. In Puaya village, north of Sukawati, cowhide also is made into dance accoutrements, such as traditional costumes with ornamented filigree leather headdresses, colourful gilded clothes and beaded epaulets.

Sukawati's **Pasar Seni** (Art Market; daily 9am–5pm) is a two-storey building filled with woodcarvings, clothing and knick-knacks, ceremonial umbrellas, statues, bamboo flutes and basketry. If passing Sukawati early in the morning, look through the *pasar pagi* or morning market, about a block behind the Pasar Seni. In this steaming, packed, warehouse-like barn is every trinket that is on sale in Kuta, but for half the price. The market closes mid-morning.

The family-friendly **Bali Zoo** (tel: 0361-294 357; daily 9am–6pm; charge) in Sukawati is a 4.6-hectare (12-acre) landscaped zoo that houses many species of exotic birds and other rare creatures such as lesser ape *siamangs*, crocodiles and Komodo dragons.

The **Pura Desa** (village temple; daily during daylight hours; donation) in **Batuan** dates from the 11th century, with fine examples of temple carvings. Head west at the bend in the road. The temple is located directly across from an open-air pavilion.

Mas ⑬ (north of the "Fat Baby Statue" T-junction to Sakah) is best known for its intricate woodcarvings and masks. Along the main road is Ida Bagus Anom's studio, an artist renowned for new designs in masks. On the west side of the main road is Njana Tilem Gallery.

Many of the inhabitants of Mas are *brahmana* who trace their roots to the great Brahman sage Danghyang Nirartha, the founder of **Pura Taman Pule** (daily during daylight hours;

On the full moon of the fourth Balinese month (Sept–Oct), villagers bring a sacred stone for ritual cleansing at Pura Tirta Empul. Dated AD 962, the inscription on the stone – deciphered in the early 1900s and which describes the bathing of the stone – was something the villagers had unwittingly been carrying out for over 1,000 years.

BELOW LEFT: shadow puppets for sale, Sukawati village.
BELOW: making shadow puppets.

donation), which is just behind the football field.

At the gamelan factory in Banjar Babakan, **Blahbatuh**, barefoot men pump bellows to stir up the heat for forging. They squat with large hammers, bending bronze alloys into the desired shape for the metallophones and knobbed kettles used in gamelan. After they are cooled, the master adjusts the instruments' tuning with a bamboo tuning fork. Gamelan casings are assembled and painted here, and instruments for entire ensembles (worth well over US$10,000) may be purchased.

On the back road, 1km (0.6 mile) east from Blahbatuh, is **Belega** village, where bamboo furniture of all sorts is produced. Another 1.5km (1 mile) northeast is **Bona**, which specialises in products woven from dried fan palm leaves. Bona is also the place where the dramatic *kecak* dance was born.

Gianyar

The richly cultural Gianyar region is part of the old kingdom of the same name, and extends from Central Bali to the southern coast. With bountiful fields and harvests, the people here have had ample time to cultivate artistic talents, resulting in an ideology where aesthetic excellence takes place in everything – carving, painting, weaving, music and dance.

Kota Gianyar ⓮ is now a sleepy and overgrown, but contemporary, village. During Dutch confrontations, the Gianyar regency was sympathetic to the colonists and thus suffered considerably less violence than other southern kingdoms. The last *raja* maintained his figurehead position until his death in 1999. The former palace, Puri Agung Gianyar, opposite Gianyar field, is not open to visitors.

The speciality of the area is woven *kain endek* (weft ikat cloth) used in traditional wear. Numerous factories conduct informal tours, where visitors can watch the dyeing and weaving process.

UBUD

Northwest of Gianyar is **Ubud** ⓯. Named after *ubad*, or medicine, it refers to the healing properties of plants growing on the Campuhan

BELOW: Ubud market.

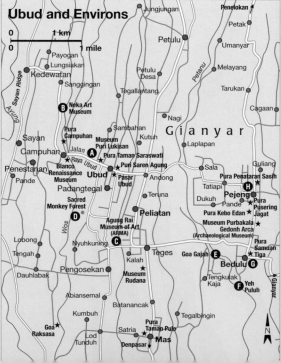

Ubud and Environs

River at the western end of town. Ubud was also the seat of a 19th-century aristocratic family, whose descendants continue to command great respect among the locals.

The first few foreigners to settle here, from Europe in the 1920s, were artists seeking inspiration within their surroundings. The masses that followed in subsequent decades brought commercialisation, which in turn benefited growth of the arts.

Ubud's tourism foundation, **Yayasan Bina Wisata** (west of the main market, daily 8am 8pm; www.ubudvillage.com) unifies the needs of both travellers and citizens. Visitors are asked to respect local ceremonies, wear traditional clothing when appropriate and learn about the area's people. The foundation's staff helps to answer questions and plot journeys, and a message board carries details of area festivals, ceremonies and cremations.

The arts quarter

West of the Ubud market on Jalan Raya Ubud is **Museum Puri Lukisan** Ⓐ (daily 9am–5pm; charge). Founded in 1953, the excellent collection showcases the richness of traditional and modern Balinese art. The main building exhibits older works, a second displays paintings by the spirited Young Artists of the 1960s, and a third houses temporary exhibits. Further west is the **Blanco Renaissance Museum** (daily 9am– 6pm; charge), which sits at the top of a steep driveway, just past Campuhan Bridge. The ornately decorated museum displays the works of the late self-professed Spanish-Filipino "maestro" – mainly erotic paintings of his favourite models: his Balinese wife and their daughter.

To understand Balinese art better, a visit to **Neka Art Museum** Ⓑ (Mon–Sat 9am–5pm, Sun noon–5pm; charge) beyond Campuhan is essential. This wonderful display of paintings was assembled by former schoolteacher Suteja Neka, one of Bali's foremost art connoisseurs. Nearly 400 artworks are chronologically displayed and well documented with descriptive labels in English and Japanese, providing an excellent background to the development of

Preparing for a festival, Pura Saman Tiga.

BELOW: Batuan mask makers.

In the 1930s, fearful of tourism's effect on the quality of art, Ubud artists established the Pita Maha association. Painters, sculptors and others joined, seeking to make all artists aware of the need to maintain aesthetic quality and to exhibit work outside Bali.

BELOW: *Waiting to Dance by Abdul Aziz, Nekka Art Gallery.*
BELOW RIGHT: *Pasar Bali by Anak Agung Gde Sorbrat, Museum Puri Lukisan, Ubud.*

Balinese painting. The multilingual staff are both friendly and knowledgeable. The museum also has an extensive research library, well-stocked bookstore and souvenir shop, and a café with spectacular panoramic views. For works for sale, visit **Neka Art Gallery** (tel: 0316-975 034; daily 9am–5pm) on Jalan Raya Ubud.

Further east along the same street is **Seniwati Gallery of Art by Women** (Tue–Sun 9am–5pm; free), established in 1991 by British expatriate Mary Northmore. The gallery represents female artists from Bali and other parts of Indonesia, as well as foreigners.

South of Ubud, in the direction of Pengosekan village, lies **Agung Rai Museum of Art (ARMA) ❸** (daily 9am–6pm; charge), showing an extensive collection of works by Balinese, Indonesian and foreign artists. A side room features a small painting attributed to German artist Walter Spies. Works are titled in English, Indonesian and Japanese. ARMA also promotes Balinese performing arts and has a bookshop and library.

Continue south on the main road towards Denpasar to **Museum**

Rudana (daily 9am–5pm; charge). Its massive building shows works in the Kamasan, Ubud and Batuan styles, paintings by well-known contemporary Indonesian artists, and exquisite wooden sculptures.

Central Ubud

Pasar Ubud (daily 9am–2pm), at the junction of Jalan Raya Ubud and Monkey Forest Road, tempts shoppers with clothing, handicrafts, souvenirs and fresh produce. Across the road from the market, on the northeast corner of the intersection, is **Puri Saren Agung**, from where Ubud was ruled from the late 1800s until World War II. The buildings were erected following a devastating earthquake in 1917. Evenings here see traditional dance performances.

Take a stroll down shop- and hotel-lined Monkey Forest Road to Ubud's **Sacred Monkey Forest ❹** (8am–6pm; charge), for a walk through beautiful and dense tropical jungle. Like all "monkey forests" in Bali, the experience is punctuated by roving gangs of mischievous,

annoying and fearless macaques, which ostensibly protect the temple. They are amusing up to a point, usually breached when one of them pinches keys, sunglasses or any other shiny object, and runs off with it. This walk is best done in the cooler early morning or late afternoon. A temple in the forest, **Pura Dalem Agung Padangtegal**, is dedicated to Durga, the goddess of death, who often takes the form of Rangda, the queen of the underworld.

Around Ubud

West from downtown beyond Campuhan, the road turns north to **Kedewatan**, a village blessed with outstanding views. South from Kedewatan is **Sayan**, a small Ubud "suburb" that teeters on the edge of the beautiful Sayan ridge, with the Sungai Ayung tumbling down below. The entire ridge from Sayan to Kedewatan and north to **Payangan** is now an enclave of villas owned by foreigners and super-de luxe resorts. The Ayung is a popular spot for white-water rafting trips. The two-hour journey floats through 25 Class II rapids, giving an adrenalin rush without too much danger.

Penestanan, between Sayan and Ubud, grew from obscurity when Dutch-born Arie Smit, who lived and worked here as a respected artist, established a small art group during the early 1960s. With Smit's encouragement and enormous freedom of subject matter and style of expression, young painters produced imaginative, Naïve-style scenes of village life and rituals which became known as the Young Artists style.

East of Ubud, **Peliatan** gained fame in the 1950s for its *legong* dancers, who took New York and Paris by storm while on tour. Today, their descendants continue the tradition. One of the few all-female gamelan troupes (gamelan *wanita*) in Bali rehearses in Peliatan.

Beyond Ubud

Northwest of Ubud is another noted monkey forest. Sangeh's legendary history can be traced to the Hindu *Ramayana* epic, in which the monkey-general Hanuman went to search for magical healing herbs that grew on a

There are elements of both Hinduism and Buddhism found at Goa Gajah. The cave may be an early precursor to the Hindu-Buddhist character which to a large degree defines Bali today.

BELOW: schoolgirls, Ubud.

Offerings and incense

Consecrated offerings of food, flowers and palm-leaf figures are essential to the religious rituals of Bali. The island's Hindu-Dharma religion is a fusion of Hinduism, animism and ancestor worship. Ancestors and deities of fertility and nature are worshipped along with the Hindu Trinity – Brahma, Vishnu and Shiva – and the Buddha.

The prime god is Sanghyang Widi Wasa, and all gods are considered mere manifestations of him. Hindu-Dharma is founded on the Balinese system of cosmology that strives to maintain the harmony between the cosmos, its divine principles and human existence. Gods and demons are worshipped equally, and daily rituals are performed to maintain this balance. Religious life revolves around sacrifices, offerings and purification ceremonies.

The common daily offering, *canang*, is a small palm-leaf tray of flowers and cooked rice, sprinkled with holy water and anointed with incense. Offerings presented to the gods are made from gifts of nature and left to decay naturally or, if containing food, are later taken home to be eaten by the family who made them. Offerings made to demons or evil spirits are left on the ground, while those to gods are put on high altars, with incense used to carry the essence of it upwards to heaven.

Door detail, Neka Art Museum.

BELOW: Pura Taman Pule Hindu temple on Koningan Day, a major Balinese festival during which the ancestors' souls are revered.

mountain. Unable to find the plants, he broke off the peak, but part of the mountain fell to the earth in **Sangeh**, along with a group of monkeys from his army, whose descendants remain there to this day to pester travellers. A moss-covered 17th-century temple, **Pura Bukit Sari**, lies in the heart of the woods.

An "elephant cave" lies off the Ubud–Gianyar road, east of Peliatan in Bedulu. **Goa Gajah** Ⓔ (daily 9am–5pm; charge) is mentioned in the 1365 *lontar* (palm-leaf) manuscript of a Javanese court poem as a Balinese place called Lwa Gajah (Elephant River), a Buddhist priest's dwelling, which may refer to the Petanu River, near the cave. Goa Gajah, dating from at least the 11th century, was excavated in 1923.

The entrance is actually a carved head of a monster with a gaping mouth and hands which look as if they are trying to pull apart an opening for people to enter. All around the entrance are fantastically carved leaves, animals, waves and humans. Inside is a 13-metre (43ft) long passage stopping at a T-junction 15 metres (50ft) wide. At one end of the passage is a

four-armed statue of elephant-headed Hindu deity Ganesha. At the opposite end is a set of three *lingga* (phalluses). Sleeping niches and Buddhist ruins outside the cave suggest religious syncretism. To the side of the entrance is a 1,000-year-old statue of Hariti, a Buddhist demoness-cum-goddess. Large male and female figures spout water from their stomachs in a bathing place in front of the cave.

Continue down the road and turn south at a statue to see rarely visited 14th-century reliefs at **Yeh Puluh** Ⓕ (daily during daylight hours; charge). This 25-metre (80ft) long, 2-metre (7ft) high rock wall is carved in high relief. Aside from Ganesha, there are no religious themes, only scenes from daily life. The sequence begins with a *kakayonan*, the cosmic tree of life used in *wayang kulit* performances.

Bedulu and northwards

Bedulu Ⓖ village was once the site of the early Mahayana Buddhist Warmadewa dynasty dating from the 5th century. By the late 10th century, Balinese religion lacked cohesion due

to conflicts between the different sects. Several holy men gathered with the king at **Pura Samuan Tiga** (Temple of the Tripartite Meeting; daily during daylight hours; charge). Out of this exceptional meeting emerged the fusion of Balinese religion as practised today, with the three elements of animism-ancestor worship, Buddhism and Shivaism.

North of Bedulu is the archaeology museum, **Museum Purbakala** (Mon–Thur 8am–3pm; Fri 8am–noon; charge), with four buildings displaying megalithic and Bronze Age artefacts from throughout Bali.

The **Pejeng** ⓗ area has a cluster of important old shrines and sacred springs. Across the road in the rice fields is **Pelinggih Arjuna Metapa** (Shrine of the Meditating Arjuna). Loincloth-clad statues of Arjuna, warrior-hero from the Hindu *Mahabharata* epic, along with two servants are displayed in a small pavilion with a few other relics.

Just up the road on the same side is **Pura Kebo Edan** (Crazy Water Buffalo Temple; daily during daylight hours; donation). The site is remarkable for its more than 3-metre (11ft) tall statue called the Pejeng Giant, showing a masked male figure dancing upon a wide-eyed figure, perhaps a corpse. His huge penis, its tip adorned with balls, swings to the left and indicates the more sinister aspects of Balinese worship.

Still further north is **Pura Pusering Jagat** (Navel of the World Temple; daily during daylight hours; donation). It has a shrine with large and unusually realistic stone figures of a *lingga* and *yoni*. Childless couples bring offerings, pray and touch the shrine to ask for offspring. The temple also houses the Pejeng Vessel, Naragiri (Mountain of Men), a cylindrical vessel carved with a scene of the gods and demons churning the ocean of milk to produce the elixir of immortality.

One of the most impressive antiquities in this area – in all of Indonesia, for that matter – is the **Moon of Pejeng** at **Pura Penataran Sasih** (daily during daylight hours; charge), on the main road to the north of Bedulu. This temple was probably the religious centre of the old Pejeng-Bedulu kingdom.

BELOW: the Moon of Pejeng, the largest single-cast bronze kettle drum in the world.

Feeding the wildlife at Ubud's Monkey Forest.

A large 190cm (75in) bronze kettledrum, the Moon of Pejeng, dates back to Indonesia's Bronze Age, which began in 300 BC. It is said to be the largest metal drum in the world cast as a single piece. Shaped like an hourglass, the rare drum is decorated with eight stylised faces displaying wide-open eyes and earlobes distended by big rings. Other ornamentation suggests that it probably originated in northern Vietnam during the Dong Son era.

Legend says that the drum was a moon that fell from the heavens one night and landed in a tree. The brilliant light disturbed a nocturnal thief, so he climbed up the tree and urinated on it. The moon exploded and killed him, cracking and losing its shine as a result (thus explaining its present condition). Today, no one dares touch the drum, not even the temple priests.

Tampaksiring temples

BELOW: Gunung Kawi, Ubud.

Continuing north to **Gunung Kawi** ⑯ (daily during daylight hours; charge), a complex of rock-hewn temples and monks' meditation niches overlooks the Pakerisan River in a valley near **Tampaksiring**. There are 10 temple facades here. Legend says that Kebo Iwa, powerful prime minister of Bedulu, used magic to carve the monuments, using his fingernails, in just one night. This 11th-century "Mountain of Poets Temple" complex is remarkably preserved. Mistakenly called tombs, research indicates that the temple facades are monuments commemorating the Warmadewa dynasty. Royal funeral cults in which kings, queens and consorts were deified after death began in Bali around this time.

Up the road is **Pura Mengening** (Clear Water Temple; daily during daylight hours; donation). In a reconstructed temple on a hillside is a free-standing structure similar in form to those hewn from rock at Gunung Kawi. This temple has a spring of pure water, as indicated by its name, and feeds into the Pakerisan River. It might be the commemorative temple of the Warmadewa king Udayana.

Just to the east, the Balinese believe the sacred **Pura Tirta Empul** ⑰ (Bubbling Water Temple; daily during daylight

Lifestyle centre

Amid the designer fashion and jewellery boutiques, five-star resorts, and some of the best dining on the island, Ubud is more or less returning to its ethnic roots as a healthy lifestyle centre. Healing centres such as Como Shambhala (www.como-shambahala.como.bz) and Fivelements Puri Ahimsa (www.fivelements.com) specialise in short- and long-term wellness programmes, and The Yoga Barn (www.theyogabarn.com) and Intuitive Flow Sanctuary for Yoga and Healing (www.intuitiveflow.com) include yoga and meditation. Others, such as Bali Botanica Day Spa (www.balibotanica.com), focus on massage. The Ubud Organic Farmer's Market (www.indonesiaorganic.com) supports local farmers by selling their produce at the ARMA Museum on Wednesday mornings.

hours; charge) spring at Tampaksiring was created by the god Indra when he pierced the earth to create the elixir of immortality to revive his fallen warriors. The bathing place was built in the 10th century and its waters are said to have curative powers. Balinese from all over the island come to purify themselves here. After presenting a small offering to the spring's deity, men and women go to different sides to bathe. The waters have a common source, but each spout has a different ritual function.

Pura Kehan

As you climb the slopes of the volcano, the weather turns cooler. Bamboo forests line the roads, and plots abound with sweet potatoes, peanuts, corn and spices on the way to **Bangli** ⑱, capital of an 18th-century kingdom of rulers descended from the Klungkung royal house. The largest and most sacred temple of the district is **Pura Kehen** (daily during daylight hours; donation), an ancient terraced mountain sanctuary and state temple of Bangli.

Below the foot of the stairway is an old temple that houses a collection of bronze plate inscriptions. Statues of mythological figures line the first terrace to Pura Kehen, from which steps lead to a magnificent gate that the locals call "the great exit". Above the gate is the frightening face and splayed hands of Bhoma, the demonic son of the earth who prevents harmful spirits from entering the temple. On both sides of the opening are figures of villagers gesturing in welcome.

An enormous banyan with a *kulkul* (warning drum) nestled in its branches shades the first courtyard, where the upper walls are inlaid with Chinese porcelain plates. An 11-tiered *meru* (pagoda) dedicated to the god Shiva dominates the inner sanctuary. In the northeast corner of the courtyard is a high throne with three compartments for the Hindu Trinity of Brahma, Vishnu and Shiva.

Just 3km (2 miles) west of Bangli is a road to **Bukit Demulih**. It is well worth climbing this "Hill of No Return" for superb views of Central Bali on a clear day. To reach the volcanoes Batur and Agung, continue north from either Bangli or Tampaksiring.

Making an offering at Pura Kehen.

BELOW: Pura Kehen.

BALINESE CEREMONIES AND FESTIVALS

The frequency of Balinese ceremonies and festivals means that most visitors will be able to attend at least one celebration during their stay

The Balinese believe in the eternal cycle of reincarnation and view their life on earth as just one stage in their continued existence. As part of these beliefs, a person's life is marked by rites of passage that are celebrated by the whole community.

The first ritual is performed at birth, when the baby's placenta is buried in a coconut shell near the entrance to the family house. Babies are regarded as being the reincarnation of ancestors. They are therefore thought of as being holy and are treated with reverence. At puberty the tooth-filing ceremony takes place, although to save money this expensive custom is often delayed until marriage.

The final and most important rite in the cycle of life is cremation. Cremation rituals are seen by the Balinese as joyous occasions, as they release the soul from the body of the departed.

Temple Festivals

An *odalan* community festival takes place every 210 days or once a year during a particular full moon to mark the "birthday" or dedication of a temple. It can be a brief one-day affair or an elaborate event that goes on for weeks and involves months of preparation.

The most important of Balinese festivals is Galungan. During this time, the deified ancestors descend from heaven and take up residence in their family temples, where they are worshipped by their descendants for five days. As part of the festivities, all over the island streets are lined with penjor, tall bamboo poles decorated with palm-leaf ornaments, fruits and biscuits.

ABOVE: in the days before the end of the lunar-solar year, which varies according to the Balinese calendar, villagers take their temple artifacts to the sea for ritual cleansing. The new year begins with Nyepi, the "Day of Silence" when no one is allowed outside. Fires and lights are extinguished, and noise is forbidden so that evil forces leave in the belief that the island is deserted.

BELOW: a wedding takes place after the groom's family sends a delegation to the bride's home to officially ask for her hand. The couple dress in their finest garments for the ceremony.

LEFT: women carrying offerings to temples are a comon sight. In addition to their own village temple's *odalan*, many families also participate in ceremonies at the temples of their ancestors and at temples dedicated to their professions.

Days of Honour

Tumpek are days set aside to honour physical things that make life possible. During Tumpek Landep, *keris* daggers are ritually cleansed and presented with offerings to fortify their protective powers. Other metal objects, such as cars and motorcycles, are also treated with respect.

Small packets of rice cake are tied around trees on Tumpek Wariga, or Uduh, to thank them for their fruits, flowers and wood. Songbirds and gamelan instruments are honoured on Tumpek Krulut because of the beautiful sounds that they make. Domesticated animals such as cattle, water buffaloes and pigs are fed better food on the special days set aside for them, called Tumpek Uye or Kandang.

Sacred masks and dance costumes along with *wayang kulit* (leather puppets) used for ceremonies are presented with offerings on Tumpek Wayang. A special day honours Betari Dewi Saraswati, goddess of learning and knowledge. Offerings are given to *lontar* (palm-leaf manuscripts) and books. No reading and writing are allowed, and students pray to Saraswati to ask for her blessings.

Above: most Hindu Balinese make ritual pilgrimages to Besakih Temple to obtain holy water during an *odalan* or at full moon.
Top Right: villages celebrating their *odalan* temple festival, Seseh, Tabanan.

Right: *canan sari* petal tray offering, Air Panas Banjar.
Far Right: worship at Pura Ulun Danu Batur, Gunung Batur.

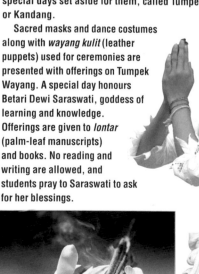

WEST AND NORTH BALI

For a slower pace and more intimate encounter with this magical island, head to the shores and mountains of the west or establish a base in the north to explore the cool highlands

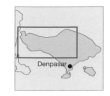

Denpasar

An increasing number of visitors are escaping the congestion of South Bali and Ubud in favour of other areas of the island that are ideal for quieter getaways with fewer crowds. In the west the landscape is much drier, and off the coastal highway that leads from Pura Tanah Lot to Gilimanuk, the beaches are experiencing development that promises to continue for several years. Once only remote surfing areas, their newly built resorts and villas are good bases for taking in the refreshing sea air and for scenic mountain drives to the north. Menjangan island in West Bali National Park is Bali's premier dive destination, with the north coast's Pemuteran a close second.

The north coast highway grips the shore, passing through Lovina, an excellent starting point for exploring the scenic Bedugal highlands to the south. Also along this road are even more developments: villas and resorts catering to well-being, yoga, meditation and healing that continue east of bustling Singaraja.

WEST BALI

North of Pura Tanah Lot, Tabanan regency is one of Bali's most prolific rice-growing areas. It has

also long been home to some of the island's most admired gamelan orchestras and dancers. New tourist resorts are springing up throughout the region, particularly on the coast, which is popular with surfers. At the end of every side road from the main highway leading to the shore are long, often black-sand beaches with surf that sometimes breaks over 3 metres (10ft) high. Be aware that the undertow and currents are treacherous.

Main attractions
BALIAN BEACH
MEDEWI BEACH
NEGARA BUFFALO RACES
WEST BALI NATIONAL PARK
MENJANGAN ISLAND AND DIVING
PEMUTERAN DIVING
BEDUGUL HIGHLANDS
LOVINA
SINGARAJA

LEFT: Pura Beji detail. **RIGHT:** colourful flowers at Tabanan.

TIP

Dolphin-watching, a popular activity in Lovina, is increasingly controversial. Convoys of early-morning boats carrying dolphin-seeking tourists go on a chase which very likely disturbs the dolphins' morning reveries.

Mengwi and Tabanan

Northwest of Denpasar, at the start of the highway that goes on to hug the southern coastline, **Kapal** ⑲ shelters the most important temple in the area, Pura Sada (daily during daylight hours; donation), an ancestral sanctuary honouring the deified spirit of Ratu Sakti Jayaningrat, whose identity remains uncertain. The temple's original foundations may be as old as the 12th century, but the temple itself was rebuilt during the 17th century. The oldest of the Mengwi state shrines, Pura Sada was destroyed in the great earthquake of 1917 and restored in 1949.

Mengwi ⑳ principality, 6km (4 miles) north of Kapal, was, until 1891, the centre of a powerful kingdom dating from the Gelgel dynasty. Pura Taman Ayun (daily during daylight hours; charge), built in the 18th century, has a surrounding moat, giving the impression of a garden sanctuary, explaining the name *taman*, or garden. The temple is a *penyawangan*, or a place to worship the gods of other sacred sites. The shrines here are a place to worship Bali's holy mountain peaks Agung, Batukau and Batur, as well as the gods of other sacred sites, for example Pura Sada.

Dipping down off the main road to a southern bypass, in **Kerambitan** ㉑ the Tabanan royal family has two palaces – **Puri Anyar** and **Puri Agung** – where they showcase their *tektekan* gamelan ensemble of bamboo drums and wooden cow bells. For a fee, anyone can book a "royal" evening, including either a *joget* (flirtation dance accompanied by a bamboo gamelan) or a *Calonarang* (trance performance), complete with a dinner. If it is just the surroundings you are interested in, there is a guesthouse in Puri Anyar.

Balian beach stopover

Continuing west along the southern Trans-Bali highway, the environment begins to change and the landscape becomes increasingly dry. About 10km (6 miles) west of Antosari, a side road through Lalang Linggha village leads to the crashing surf at **Balian beach** ㉒. With the exception of a couple of locally owned *losmen* catering to

BELOW: Medewi beach.

Belimbingsari and Palasari

From Cekik on the far western coast, travel 15km (9 miles) south to Melaya and turn inland to Belimbingsari village. Home to Bali's largest Protestant community, its impressive church has distinctly Balinese design elements and a *kulkul* (warning drum) instead of a bell to signal the start of Sunday services, which begin at 9am.

A short drive to the south is the 1,500-strong Catholic community in Palasari. Like Belimbingsari, the early converts settled in remote West Bali by choice after being shunned by the Hindu Balinese. The cathedral, built in 1958, is adorned with Balinese touches, and is a stunning piece of architecture in the middle of nowhere. Friday mass at 5.30pm and Sunday mass at 6.30am are good times to visit.

budget travellers, all the other lodgings and villas are new, and most of them are owned by foreigners. There is a homestay here serving very tasty Western food and a medium-sized, rather upmarket resort catering to surfers right on the beach that makes a wonderful stopover for a bite to eat while taking in the enormity of the sea.

Medewi to Gilimanuk

At **Pekutatan** ㉓, a side road heads north over the mountain and descends to the northern coast at Pengastulan. This narrow, paved road is among Bali's most beautiful routes, its 10km (6 miles) passing through exquisite rainforest and coffee, cocoa and clove plantations. The destination is a giant old *bunut* tree which is so large that its aerial roots descend on both sides of the road, which passes through the tree. A holy site for Balinese-Hindus, there is a shrine on one side of the tree, and many motorists stop there to ask the spirits for permission to continue their journeys by making a small offering.

For several decades, extreme surfers have kept the eastern reaches of Medewi beach ㉔ to themselves, staying in basic lodgings and picking their way across the rocky shore to reach the good waves, carefully avoiding the dangerous undertow. Now, upmarket resorts are going up and others are being renovated along this stretch of coast, where black-sand beaches far removed from their crowded counterparts in South Bali are luring an increasing number of travellers. Almost all the resorts still cater mainly to surfers, but instead of the nomadic hardcore dudes who dominated Medewi in the past, there is a new generation of novices who are eager to learn the sport in safer environments and with the benefit of babysitting services, spas, restaurants and cultural tours for those times when the sun gets too hot.

Near Medewi stands the tranquil **Pura Rambut Siwi** ㉕ (Lock of Hair Temple; daily during daylight hours; donation), founded by High Priest Danghyang Nirartha in the 16th century. Perched on a cliff overlooking the sea, the pavilions west of the temple offer panoramic views over

TIP

West of Lovina, turn left at Dencarik and continue for about 3km (2 miles) to **Brahma Arama Vihara** (daily 8am–6pm) in Banjar. The striking Thai-style Theravada Buddhist temple, with its bright orange roof and colourful statues of Buddha and other figures, was founded in 1958 by a Balinese monk and rebuilt in this location in 1971. The views down the coast are stunning, and visitors are welcome as long as they dress modestly, lower their voices and walk quietly barefooted.

BELOW: Belimbing rice terraces, Tabanan.

The reef at Pemuteran is one of the most colourful on the Bali coast.

BELOW: fisherman at Labuhan Lalang.

rice fields and the ocean. It is said that Nirartha's stopover here relieved the village of a devastating epidemic, and before moving on, he presented the people with a lock of his hair, explaining the temple's name. His hair and some of his personal belongings are enshrined in the inner courtyard of the main temple.

West of Pura Rambut Siwi is **Negara**, the provincial capital. There is little to see here, except that every year between July and October the town's prized buffalo take part in annual racing competitions, which are fun to watch. Wearing colourful banners, their horns decorated and with wooden bells tied around their necks, they race along the 4km (2.5-mile) track at speeds of up to 50kph (30mph). The daredevil charioteers twist the bulls' tails to give them extra motivation. Rehearsals are held every second Sunday and the competitions are staged in August, around Independence Day, and in October.

One kilometre (0.6 mile) south of Negara is **Loloan Timur** 26. Its residents are Muslim Buginese who

originated from Sulawesi, and they continue to build their homes in the Buginese style on stilts. The bamboo musical instruments they play, gamelan *jegog*, which accompany traditional dances, sound like thunder. Today there are nearly 50 ensembles, mostly located in the Sangkar Agung area.

Further south, along the coastline near Perancak, villages run a sea turtle conservation programme. Small donations to tour the area and an adopt-a-nest scheme help to fund the hatchery. While in Perancak, look for the fishing boats painted in bright colours that line the shore.

The north and southwest coast roads meet at **Cekik**, where a short spur road continues a few kilometres north to **Gilimanuk**, the access point for a 30-minute ferry journey (but much longer wait), operating 24 hours a day across the Bali–Java Strait. Accommodation in Gilimanuk is limited to homestays. The Bali–Java Strait is just 3km (2 miles) wide, but its waters are treacherous.

West Bali National Park

In order to visit **West Bali National Park** 27 (Taman Nasional Bali Barat; park headquarters Mon–Thur 7.30am–3.30pm, Fri 7.30am–1pm), first obtain a hiking permit and ticket from the visitor centre in **Labuhan Lalang** 28 (daily 8am–4pm; tel: 0361-61060) on Teluk Terima (Reception Bay). You can also book tours and treks at the centre.

Official guides, who usually speak English, are a requirement for trekking within the park, and are part of a community empowerment programme. The 760-sq km (300-sq mile) conservation area, much of which is off-limits, is home to deer, civets, monkeys, rare wild Javan buffalo and the nearly extinct Bali starling or Rothschild's mynah (*Leucopsar rothschildi*), a small white-crested bird with brilliant blue streaks around its eyes and black-tipped wings. Many wild birds live on the gentle slopes of **Gunung Prapat Agung**, which anchors Bali's western tip. There

are several trails from which to choose, designed to suit different interests and capabilities. Short and medium treks (1–3 hours) focus on mangrove and mountain forests and savannahs for birdwatchers. Longer treks (6–7 hours) can be customised. All guided tours must be booked in advance.

The park is known for its spectacular diving and snorkelling off **Pulau Menjangan** ❷❾ (Deer Island), about 10km (6 miles) offshore. Now considered Bali's best dive site, it is surrounded by deep waters, coral reefs, sandy slopes and walls housing a wide variety of large and small marine life. There are eight dive sites, and at Pos 2 a shallow reef attracts snorkellers. Walking around the perimeter of the uninhabited island takes about 45 minutes, and there are some stunning panoramic views of volcanoes and mountains on Java from here.

Boats to the island can be hired at Labuan Lalang and at a second pier at Banyumandi, near Mimpi resort. On Menjangan there is an ancient temple, Puri Gili, and Balinese-Hindus often depart from Banyumandi to make offerings here. There is a modest canteen, and showers and changing rooms are available for a small charge. Wait until other divers appear and share the cost of the boat. Overnighting on the island is forbidden.

There are four upmarket resorts in the area; for cheaper accommodation most people stay at nearby Pemuteran, where transport to and from Menjangan can be arranged.

Near Labuan Lalang and still within the park is **Makam Jayaprana**, a local hero's tomb and temple, which is worth the hike for the view.

NORTH BALI

A rather sleepy fishing village, **Pemuteran** ❸❾ is the nearest place to the West Bali National Park and has a wide range of low- to medium-priced bungalows and hotels, and some exquisite luxury villas, all catering to divers, snorkellers and nature-lovers. For many years, Pemuteran was only a place to sleep and eat, but it has earned a good reputation for diving and snorkelling in its own right thanks to the Reef Seen Aquatics Dive

The Reef Seen Dive Centre runs trips out to the reef at Pemuteran..

BELOW: Negara bull races.

Grapes bound for the market at Lovina.

Center and Taman Sari Bali Resort, which pioneered reef restoration here over a decade ago. Now joined by other dive shops and local businesses, an effort that began simply has blossomed considerably.

A community project called Reef Gardeners teaches local people the importance of environmentally sound fishing practices and that keeping the reefs healthy is an economic plus. Village divers who have been trained by the co-op patrol reefs regularly looking for signs of lawbreakers and plagues that may devastate the corals. They also operate a sea turtle egg rescue centre, hatchery and release programme, Proyek Penyu, which can be visited. Donations for tours are welcome and keep the programme running.

Using local divers and products, the project has also created an astonishing submarine wonderland by sinking several traditional boats, some at great depths and one only 5 metres (16ft) from the surface at low tide. The main attraction is the Taman Pura (Temple Garden), a re-creation of a Balinese Hindu temple complex under the sea comprising 25 carved sandstone statues.

Inland detour

A road leads south at **Pengastulan-Seririt** ㉛, climbing over the mountains and through rice fields and clove plantations before eventually descending to the coast in South Bali. Several scenic routes are possible, among which is a beautiful but meandering drive that goes through Ringdikit and Rangdu villages. Just south of Rangdu, a turn eastwards at Mayong continues to Lakes Tamblingan and Buyun, nestled in hillside coffee plantations, and Bratan in the **Bedugul highlands**.

Bedugul ㉜, 1,300 metres (4,300ft) above sea level, is a mountain-lake resort area favoured by Indonesians for weekend retreats. In the not-so-distant past, tourists limited their visit there to a day trip from Ubud or Lovina to see **Danau Bratan**, a lake filling the long-extinct, often mist-veiled Gunung Catur crater, and its temple, **Pura Ulun Danu Bratan** (daily during daylight hours; charge), sitting on a small promontory and arguably the most

photographed site on the island. The lake is an essential water source for surrounding farmlands, and Bedugul people honour Dewi Danu, the lake goddess, here. Nowadays, improved accommodation and an increasing choice of activities are luring travellers to stay longer and soak up the clean, cool climate. The spectacular Bali Handara Kosaido Country Club golf course is here.

North of Bedugul proper is Bukit Munggu market, popularly called **Candi Kuning**, where wild orchids and colourful flowers are sold alongside vegetables. Nearby is **Kebun Raya Eka Karya Bali** (Bali Botanical Gardens; daily 8am–6pm; charge). This refreshing 1.5-sq km (370-acre) park is sliced by hiking trails through towering forests, and the sprawling grounds are home to more than 2,000 plant species, focusing on orchids, medicinal and ceremonial plants, roses and cacti. There is a library and café, and guides are available for a nominal additional cost.

Southwest of the Bedugal highlands, along the winding artery skirting the mountains, is one of Bali's most venerated temples, **Pura Luhur Batukau** ㉝ (daily during daylight hours; charge), situated near Batukau on the slopes of Gunung Batukau (2,276 metres/7,467ft high). The western Batukau highlands are famed for magnificent landscapes, and the view from **Jatiluwih** village takes in the whole landscape of southern Bali. Nearby, **Yeh Panas** surges hot water from the riverbank, graced by a small temple for prayers and offerings. The springs are part of a modest resort and are open to visitors for a fee.

Pengastulan-Seririt to Singajara

Back to the north coast highway, from Pengastulan-Seririt heading east there are pockets of resorts away from the main highway on the north shore dedicated to healing, meditation and yoga. Set almost alongside these is an astonishing number of private villas, many of them for rent. The road is lined with vineyards that feed Bali's blossoming wine industry.

BELOW: Singajara.

Dolphin-watching at Lovina.

Further east is a 12km (8-mile) long stretch of black-sand beach encompassing Pemaron, Tukad Mungga, Anturan, Kalibukbuk, Kalisasem and Temukus villages, collectively called **Lovina** ❸. In the 1970s and 1980s, Lovina was the escape of choice for crowd-weary former Kuta enthusiasts, but as development continued it was transformed from quiet fishing village to a Kuta clone, minus the bars. After a slump, when it became threadbare and musty, it has taken on new life; modern resorts and renovations abound, but it is no longer the quiet haven it once was. The diving has never been spectacular here – the biggest attraction is early-morning dolphin-watching boat trips – and today's travellers use it primarily as a base for exploring North Bali and the highlands with sand and surf on the side rather than the other way around.

The next stop is Singaraja, formerly Bali's capital city. In contrast to the south, citrus fruit orchards, tomatoes, vanilla, coffee, cacao, grapes and cloves replace the familiar rice paddies. About 10km (6 miles) south of Singaraja, the **Air Terjun Gitgit** (daily during daylight hours; charge) waterfalls flow vigorously during the rainy season. The soft pink sandstone that gives North Bali's temples their distinctive character was quarried near here.

Singaraja ❸ has a cosmopolitan flavour, derived from centuries as an important trading port until 1953 when shipping was moved to the more convenient Benoa Harbour in the south. Bali's second-largest city after Denpasar, its population comprises Buddhists, Javanese, Arabs and Chinese. The **Gedong Kirtya** historical library (Mon–Thur 8am–4pm, Fri–Sat 8am–noon; charge) on Jalan Veteran is a repository of old books and Balinese manuscripts established by the Dutch in 1928. It has a fine collection of *lontar* manuscripts – books inscribed on palm-leaf strips and preserved between two pieces of wood or bamboo. The ancient volumes cover subjects such as literature, mythology, history and religion.

There are some Dutch-era buildings hidden behind clutter on Jalan Ahmad Yani, and across a small bridge, a gift from the queen of Holland, is the old harbour. Just over the bridge is **Ling Gwan Kion** Chinese temple, an interesting structure dating back to 1873, with beautifully manicured gardens. Someone will be happy to show you around and tell you about the historic accoutrements that remain here. Some of the old waterfront buildings are being restored and the restaurants on stilts make an excellent lunch stop, serving grilled fish amid cool ocean breezes. From Singaraja, a major north–south highway goes to Denpasar.

Singaraja to Air Sanih

East from Singaraja, the land becomes increasingly dry as the road winds around the east coast, eventually passing an area devastated by the 1963 Gunung Agung eruption north of Tulamben. Deep, black gashes in the earth caused by lava flows replace all forms of agricultural life here.

In **Sangsit** ㊱ an unusual 15th-century *subak* (irrigation cooperative) temple, **Pura Beji** (daily during daylight hours; donation), dedicated to rice goddess Dewi Sri, is garnished with many *naga* – serpents that symbolise water and fertility. The road from nearby Kubutambahan going south leads to Danau Batur and Kintamani.

About 15km (10 miles) southeast of Singaraja at **Jagaraga** is **Pura Dalem** ㊲ (Temple of the Dead; daily during daylight hours; donation). Interesting reliefs portray life before and after the arrival of the Dutch, including scenes such as two Europeans in a Model T Ford attacked by armed bandits and a Dutch steamer under siege by a sea monster. Southwards is **Sawan**, a village with gamelan makers and a talented gamelan *angklung* orchestra.

Further east on the coast road, **Pura Meduwe Karang** ㊳ (daily during daylight hours; donation), is a dry-land agriculture temple. Just as *subak* temples ensure irrigated crop harvests, this 1890 temple gives "blessings" for plants grown on non-irrigated land. It has many fertility themes, including numerous portrayals of erotic acts. Carvings in this "Temple of the Landowner" show ghouls, domestics, lovers, noblemen and even a bicycle-riding Westerner, believed to be Dutchman W.O.J. Nieuwenkamp, who travelled all over Bali by bicycle at the beginning of the 20th century.

Further east, 17km (11 miles) from Singaraja, at **Air Sanih** ㊴ (Yeh Sanih; daily during daylight hours; donation) travellers, for a small fee, can dip in a cool, spring fed swimming pool. Facilities include luxury villas and spas as well as budget lodgings and restaurants. Continuing east, the road and villages become simpler, the land grows more arid and the number of tourists dwindles.

Air Panas Banjar.

BELOW: Air Panas Banjar.

EAST BALI

The inland east is for those seeking relaxation and reflection. Slow and steady does it, in a realm where timeless rice terraces, palaces and temples dot the countryside fringed by black-sand beaches

Denpasar

East is the most auspicious of compass points in the Balinese worldview, and an excursion among the temples, palace ruins, crater lakes and black-sand beaches of this area reveals why. Less developed and simpler than the island's south, eastern Bali has a different ambience defined by lava-strewn landscapes, ancient kingdoms and good diving and snorkelling, making it a tourist destination in its own right. Partly hidden by the eastern coastal ranges is the colossal **Gunung Agung**, Bali's tallest peak at 3,142 metres (10,308ft), which on clear days can be seen soaring above the countryside.

Whereas formerly the majority of travellers explored East Bali on day trips from an Ubud base, an increasing number are settling in at less crowded Amed or Candidasa instead. In addition to snorkelling and diving at both locations, excursions inland can be easily arranged at most hotels. From Candidasa, explore the dazzling agricultural panoramas from Sideman to Besakih, or from Amed visit Tirtagangga, Amlapura and Lake Batur in the Kintamani highlands.

Semarapura (Klungkung)

As the seat of the Dewa Agung (the title of the reigning king), **Semarapura** ⑩ (formerly called Klungkung) holds a special place in the island's history and culture. The palaces of Klungkung's *raja* and noblemen have supported and developed the styles of music, drama and the arts that flourish today in Bali.

The kingdom's capital was moved to Semarapura from nearby Gelgel in 1710 and a new palace was built here. The great gate is all that remains of

LEFT: scenes from the Mahabharata adorn a ceiling at Taman Gili's Kerta Gosa pavilion *(bale)*, Semarapura. **RIGHT:** statues outside the building.

Pura Besakih is the most revered of all Balinese temples

BELOW: weaving double ikat fabric.

the Puri Semarapura palace, razed in a *puputan* battle with the Dutch in 1908. It stands within the grounds of **Taman Gili** (8am–2pm Mon–Thur, 8am–1pm Fri; charge), a compound housing the remains of Bali's most powerful kingdom, at the town's main intersection.

One of the two focal points of the park is **Kerta Gosa** (Pavilion of Peace and Prosperity), an open *bale* (pavilion) beautifully decorated with exquisite examples of Kamasan paintings and Klungkung architecture. Eighteenth-century ceiling murals depict scenes from the *Mahabharata*, including punishments and rewards of deeds, either in the present lifetime or the next.

Kerta Gosa was the "courtroom" where disputes were adjudicated, but only if they could not be settled among families or individual villages. The Klungkung *raja* ruled all of Bali, with the other kings serving as his consultants, and Kerta Gosa was the island's highest court, and by far the strictest.

Next to Kerta Gosa is **Bale Kambang** (Floating Pavilion), surrounded by a moat, which is similarly decorated and

was used by the royal family as a place to rest and be entertained. Also in the compound are a small museum and a tourist information office, and across the street is Puri Agung, the home of the current *raja*, who was elected by the local people in 2010. The son of the last Klungkung king, who gave up his rank when Indonesia became a republic in 1945, he has no official powers, but the family remains highly regarded throughout Bali.

Kamasan ㊶ lies 2km (1.2 miles) south and is a pleasant place to stroll around and see the artists at work. Using natural pigments, they illustrate episodes from Javanese classic literature, and the figures look like *wayang kulit* shadow puppets. Although Kamasan-style paintings are sold all over Bali, cheaper and better-quality works are found here. Stop by I Nyoman Mandra's painting school (ask for directions), where young artists imitate the master's strokes.

Mountain villages

From Klungkung, turn north, passing through Bukit Jambul's astonishing

A new era of kings

When Indonesia declared independence in 1945, all the *rajas* and sultans throughout the archipelago relinquished their powers and pledged allegiance to the new republic, ending a centuries-long era of often-warring fiefdoms and empires.

This stance started to change in 1989 with the crowning of the king of Pemecutan, one of Denpasar's three royal houses, and again in 2005 when Tabanan reinstated the title. In 2010, Semarapura followed suit, naming the son of the last colonial-era Klungking *raja* their new king amid great pomp and ceremony, incorporating elaborate Bali-Hindu rituals and sacred dances.

While the new kings have no official authority, some analysts see this symbolic gesture as a return to traditional values and cultural wisdom.

landscapes. In **Sidemen** 🄸, every household is engaged in some aspect of textile-weaving. This is one of the centres of *endek* (weft-ikat cloth) weaving, and the clack-clack-clack of the looms can be heard from the road. *Songket* cloth – cotton or silk with an overweft of silver or gold threads – is also produced here. The agricultural fields here are astonishingly beautiful, and there are *losmen*, frequently filled with expatriates from South Bali who come here for weekends to soak up the solitude.

Pura Besakih and Gunung Agung

Folklore has it that when the deities made mountains for their thrones, they set the highest peak in East Bali. In every temple a shrine is dedicated to the spirit of **Gunung Agung**. The tapering form of cremation towers, *meru* (pagodas) and even temple offerings bear the shape of a mountain, mirroring reverence for this holy volcano.

On the slopes of Agung lies **Pura Besakih** 🄳, the Mother Temple (daily during daylight hours; charge; camera fee). Easily accessed from Besakih village, the temple houses ancestral shrines for all Hindu Balinese, who regard the complex as the pinnacle of sanctity. Besakih originated in the 8th century as a terraced sanctuary honouring Gunung Agung's gods. Over a period of more than 1,000 years it was enlarged, and today it comprises 30 public temples with hundreds of shrines. Nonworshippers are not allowed into the inner temple unless they wish to pray, but the layout can quite easily be seen from the open gates. Do not enter the grounds unless invited, and be sure to be dressed in *sarong* and a temple sash.

Pura Penataran Agung is the paramount sanctuary in the Besakih complex. Steps ascend in a long perspective to split gates. Inside the main courtyard is a triple-throned shrine for three aspects of god: Siwa, as creator;

Pramasiwa, god without form; and Sadasiwa, god as half male and half female. Others interpret this trinity to be Vishnu, Brahma and Shiva. Only worshippers may enter, but visitors can circle the outer walls for a view of the courtyard.

During festivals, the shrines are wrapped in coloured cloths in three sacred colours: red, symbolising the earth as lava and associated with Brahma; white, as light, associated with Shiva; and black, as both water and heaven, and associated with Vishnu. Yellow cloth – a colour symbolising compassion – is also used to cover the shrines during festivals.

Gunung Batur

The road north from Besakih leads to the crater lake **Danau Batur** 🄴. Bali's largest lake, Danau Batur is cradled within the **Gunung Batur** caldera, an active volcano. At 1,717 metres (5,635ft) above sea level, it is considered to be the female counterpart to Gunung Agung's male. The crater itself is 11km (7 miles) in diameter and 200 metres (660ft) deep. Try to

Carvings at Pura Besakih.

BELOW: a temple festival at Besakih.

TIP

If you've forgotten to bring a sarong and temple sash, they can be "hired" outside Bali's many temples or purchased from the numerous area vendors as a souvenir.

arrive in the early morning, before the mist descends.

Penelokan , at 1,450 metres (4,800ft) above sea level, is a spectacular point to take in views of Gunung Batur and the lake. The cliff is lined with tourist restaurants with large glass windows, and can be a nice coffee stop to enjoy the panorama protected from the cold and mist. A steep, winding road descends to lakeside **Kedisan**. On the volcano's flank at **Toya Bungkah**, hot springs are reputed to have medicinal qualities. Travellers who climb Batur use Toya Bungkah as a staging point.

Trunyan ⑯, a Bali Aga village across the lake, is inhabited by the aboriginal Balinese who rejected changes brought by Muslim Majapahit invaders in the 14th century. The villagers practise unusual burial customs with the dead left under a sacred tree in the open air for nature to eliminate, covered only by a cloth. The name Trunyan comes from the *taru menyan* (fragrant tree) that grows in the cemetery. Isolated for centuries from mainstream Bali,

Trunyanese keep under wraps – in a *meru* – Bali's largest traditional statue, a 4-metre (13ft) high patron guardian they believe is the "God of the World's Centre". Be aware that visiting the village is not altogether pleasant, as the local people have a habit of scamming tourists and are highly aggressive at begging.

Gunung Batur intermittently spews lava, ash and steam, but nothing drastic has occurred since 1926. Treks across the barren landscape resulting from the eruption – where there is an active reforestation programme – can be arranged through the trekking guides' association office at Toya Bungka. It is not advisable to bring guides from outside the area for tours here.

"Head of the Lake" temple

Back on the main road from Penelokan heading towards Kintamani is Bali's second-most important temple after Besakih, **Pura Ulun Danu Batur** ⑰ (daily during daylight hours; charge). As it is a major *subak* (irrigation) temple, rituals here are linked with the veneration of the Goddess of the Lake, Dewi Danu.

Inscriptions from the 10th century indicate that nearby **Kintamani** – a mountainous area taking its name from the windy town at 1,500 metres (4,920ft) up – was one of Bali's earliest kingdoms. A paved road at Sukawana leads to Pinggan on the crater's north side, with a flight of 300 steps rising to the mountain sanctuary, **Pura Tegeh Koripan** (daily during daylight hours; charge), the highest temple in Bali at 1,745 metres (5,725ft). From Kintamani the road leads north to Kubutambahan, east of north coast Singaraja.

East coast explorations

Back to the east coast road, **Gelgel** is the former capital of the Klungkung dynasty. In the 1400s and 1500s, Gelgel's Dewa Agung held immense power, but the dynasty's influence declined in the 17th century as it lost battles and allegiances. This misfortune was attributed to a curse which

BELOW: Puri Agung Karangasem, Amlapura.

had fallen on the palace. Consequently, the palace was moved to Klungkung, but there was no improvement in fortune. Small conflicts and jealousies broke out among the kings, and the result was the creation of numerous minor kingdoms.

Exquisite hand-woven *songket* and *endek* are made in many homes in Gelgel. To the east is **Pura Dasar** (daily during daylight hours; donation). During the full moon in October, dozens of villagers come here to take part in a very colourful temple ceremony.

Eastwards, a perfectly shaped bay is cradled by the hills at **Padangbai** ⓲. The entire length of beach is crowded with *losmen*, cafés and dive shops, but the beach itself is ideal for a quiet escape. Up on the hill at the end of the bay is an upmarket private villa complex overlooking the sea where some are for rent. A steep climb down (and back up again) brings you to secluded Blue Lagoon, excellent for snorkelling at high tide. The dive shops can arrange boat trips to diving spots offshore.

The reason most people come to sleepy little Padangbai is to catch boats to neighbouring Lombok and Nusas Lembongan and Penida. Tickets can be bought at the ferry terminal beside a huge, ugly car park at the harbour where trucks laden with goods and cars wait for boats to arrive. Another option is to join a scheduled small-boat crossing, buying tickets at the kiosks on the beach or bargaining directly with private boats waiting in the bay.

Nusa Lembongan and Nusa Penida

Nusa Lembongan ⓴ is a popular water-sports area, currently in the throes of development. Accommodation ranging from primarily foreign-owned budget to luxury lines the beaches on the western side of the island, with some at the southern tip. The best surfing is off the south and west coasts, and good diving can be found off the west and east coasts. Be careful of dangerous undertows. Many boating companies in South Bali offer day trips here; some include lunch at a

Prayer, Pura Ulun Danu Batur.

BELOW: Pura Ulun Danu Batur.

TIP

Don't be surprised to find that the Kintamani people are significantly more abrupt and aggressive than the more laid-back South Balinese.

resort and jet-skiing and other water activities.

East of Lembongan is the much larger **Nusa Penida** ⓾, a dry, sparsely cultivated island, which can also be accessed by boat from either Padangbai or South Bali. Far less developed for tourism, here the highlight is the largest free-flying population of Bali starlings in the world, thanks to the breeding efforts of Friends of the National Park and Begawan Giri Foundation. There are basic lodgings at their field station where, for a small fee, someone will guide you on a birdwatching trek and to see their reforestation and community environmental education programmes. In 2011, 20,057 hectares (49,560 acres) of sea surrounding Nusa Penida were named a marine protected area.

Candidasa and environs

Back on the east coast road, the next destination is **Candidasa** ⓾, first passing through Manggis, where there are two luxury resorts overlooking the sea on Balina beach. Unfortunately

BELOW: Crystal Bay on Nusa Penida.

Candidasa's shores are blighted by jetties protruding into the water, intended to stop the erosion, making it impossible to walk more than 50 metres (160ft) on the beach, which is only visible at low tide. Nevertheless, Candidasa has a good range of hotels and restaurants, so is a convenient base to explore East Bali.

Tenganan

West of Candidasa is a turn-off northwards to **Tenganan** ⓾ (daily during daylight hours; charge), a Bali Aga village. Within its bastions, all houses are arranged in identical rows on either side of wide, stone-paved lanes running the length of the village. There is evidence the Tengananese originated from Bedulu, but some accounts say they came from East Java.

Tenganan communally owns large tracts of well-cultivated land and is one of the richest villages in the area. Traditionally, the men do not work in the fields. The aristocratic Tenganan people instead rent out their land to neighbouring villagers and spend their time inscribing dried palm leaves to make illustrated *lontar* manuscripts or crafting an especially fine quality of basketry.

The women still weave the incredible *kain geringsing*, a cloth believed to have the power to immunise the wearer against evil and sickness. Only the finest *geringsing* pieces are worn as ceremonial dress by the Tenganan people; imperfect ones are sold, and even these fetch high prices on the market.

Amlapura (Karangasem)

Amlapura ⓾, further east, is the capital of Karangasem regency. The former kingdom, founded while the Gelgel dynasty waned in the late 1600s, turned into the most powerful state in Bali during the late 18th and early 19th centuries.

Puri Agung Karangasem (daily 9am–5pm; charge) long served as the residence of these kings, who extended their domain across the eastern strait.

to Lombok. During the Dutch conflict at the turn of the 20th century, the raja of Karangasem cooperated with the conquering army and was allowed to retain his title and powers. The palace where the last *raja* was born is a 20th-century amalgam of European and Asian architecture. The main building, **Bale Maskerdam**, contains furniture gifted by the Dutch royal family. Opposite is the ornate **Bale Pemandesan**, used for tooth-filing ceremonies and embellished with Chinese features.

The kings of Karangasem created delightful water gardens to escape the heat of East Bali. Some 8km (5 miles) south, near the beach, lies **Taman Ujung** (daily 8am–5pm; charge), a vast complex of pools and pavilions built in 1921. Destroyed by an earthquake in 1979, it was renovated and reopened in 2004, and is indeed a heavenly garden worthy of a visit once again.

Taman Tirtagangga (Water of the Ganges Park; daily 8am–5pm; charge), 6km (4 miles) north on the road to Culik, is another royal water park with beautiful gardens. Locals flock here just before sunset to bathe in pools fed by natural springs gushing out from animal fountains and statues, believing the waters to have healing properties. There is an upmarket resort and excellent restaurant overlooking the bathing pools owned by descendants of the royal family.

East coast beaches

At Culik, continue east to **Amed** ㊴, where bungalows and a few villas line a stunning shoreline. Actually a compilation of seven villages and beaches all collectively called Amed, this is an ideal choice for dropping out for a little while. The snorkelling is good at high tide, with coral reefs just off the beach, and there are dive spots further afield. From here, dives at **Tulamben**, where the well-known World War II *Liberty* cargo shipwreck lies, can be easily done in a day trip, as can visits to Tirtagangga, when you've had enough sun and surf.

From Amed, the road north runs close to the coast all the way to Singaraja *(see page 250)*. Village life in this area is simple and rustic, and there are occasional views of the ocean.

Nusa Lembongan, with Mt Agung visible in the distance.

BELOW: Nusa Lembongan.

NUSA TENGGARA

Lombok aside, the islands of Nusa Tenggara are remote and little-known, and make up one of the poorest parts of Indonesia

This sparsely inhabited archipelago extending eastwards from Lombok to Timor is formed by the protruding peaks of a giant submarine mountain range that stretches to Sumatra. Sandalwood rather than spices was the treasure that foreign merchants sought in this southern corner of the East Indies, always something of a backwater in Indonesian history. Nusa Tenggara translates as "Southeastern Islands" in Javanese.

The first Portuguese ships reached the area in 1512, and by the end of the century they had hijacked the Timorese sandalwood trade and established fortresses on Flores and Solor. The Dutch wrested much of the spice trade away from their rivals in the 17th century, but what remained of the area's sandalwood was largely depleted by then.

One of Indonesia's poorest and least fertile regions, most of its 9.2 million inhabitants are subsistence farmers or fishermen, and many of them still worship nature and ancestral spirits under a thin veneer of Islam or Christianity. Imagine, then, how the discovery of Indonesia's second-largest gold reserves on Sumbawa has changed the lives of the people on the island.

While many visitors have discovered Lombok, the few who undergo the rigours of travelling further east largely seek the mystifying array of cultures from one region to the next, the myriad fine hand-woven ikat textiles that they create, excellent water sports, or the splendid nature of the national parks and reserves, including the Komodo dragon. Surfers have frequented the south coast villages for decades, and the superb marine life attracts divers to Alor. But as elsewhere in Indonesia, it is the people of Nusa Tenggara, with all their differences in physical features, personality traits and traditions, who are the most stunning.

In some ways it's a pity that the infrastructure in Nusa Tenggara isn't better developed, allowing more visitors to wander from one island to another to marvel at the differences between the cultures and landscapes. Since the region continues to receive relatively few foreign visitors, modest dress and politeness out of respect for ancient cultures and religions are imperative.

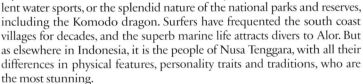

PRECEDING PAGES: an idyllic stretch of beach near Senggigi on Lombok's well-developed west coast. **LEFT:** spice market, Mataram. **ABOVE LEFT:** Gili Trawangan. **ABOVE RIGHT:** songket-weaving.

LOMBOK

Bali's eastern neighbour is favoured by some for its quieter and more laid-back island experience. Lombok offers lovely beaches fringed by beautiful coral reefs, some fabulous surfing and a spectacular volcano

Most often thought of only as an alternative to Bali, Lombok could be a major destination in its own right if it were properly promoted. Rather than touting itself as home to some of Indonesia's greatest beaches – as it certainly is – it is content to wait patiently for travellers to discover the island themselves.

The people of this medium-sized island are something of an enigma. The Sasak, the majority ethnic group, comprise about 95 percent of its population, with Balinese, Bugis, Chinese, Javanese and Arabs making up the remainder. The Sasaks are divided into two distinct groups: the Wetu Telu – who primarily subscribe to an unorthodox form of Islam but whose rituals are basically animistic with some Muslim and even Balinese-Hindu influences – and the Wetu Lima, who inhabit the lowlands and the coasts, and are orthodox Sunni Muslims. At Pura Lingsar, the Wetu Telu pray alongside Buddhists and Hindus.

Most of western Lombok is green and lush, but to the east and south the island becomes increasingly arid. Along the west coast are some of the snowiest-white beaches imaginable, and while Senggigi beach has been its main calling card in the past, its five-star resorts are beginning to take a back seat to Mangsit and other

LEFT: the beach at Gili Air. **RIGHT:** Sasak villagers at Sade.

beaches further north, which offer hip boutique hotels.

The three small "Gilis" – Trawangan, Meno and Air – once only popular with budget divers and snorkellers now attract more mature travellers as well, with more upmarket hotels and villas being built to accommodate them. Other dive resorts have sprung up on Lombok's southwestern peninsula, and with an influx of foreign investment, the southern beach, Kuta (also spelled Kute), is set to blossom. Mataram, the island's main city, is the

Main attractions
SOUTHWEST PENINSULA BEACHES
PURA LINGSAR
SENGGIGI BEACH
MANGSIT BEACH
THE GILIS: GILI TRAWANGAN, GILI MENO, GILI AIR
GUNUNG RINJANI
POTTERY-MAKING VILLAGES
KUTA AND MAWUN BEACHES

Sunset from Gili Trawangan.

BELOW: the crater lake at Gunung Rinjani.

provincial seat of West Nusa Tenggara, which includes its eastern neighbour, Sumbawa. Inland, the mighty volcano of Gunung Rinjani – at 3,726 metres (12,224ft) the third-highest peak in Indonesia – presents challenges to even the most experienced climbers.

While Lombok does not have the overwhelming commercialism of Bali, and its cultural experience is more restrained, the flipside is that it possesses a greater sense of adventure.

Western Lombok

Three main towns in western Lombok – Ampenan, Mataram and Cakranegara – meld together to create what is, for Lombok, an urban sprawl. **Mataram ❶** is the administrative centre of political and cultural life, with provincial government offices, banks, mosques, bookstores, the General Post Office and Mataram University.

In Mataram, the **Museum Nusa Tenggara Barat** (Jalan Panji Tilar Negara No. 6; tel: 0370-632 519; Tue–Thur and Sat–Sun 8am–2pm, Fri 8–11am; charge) houses artefacts from Lombok and Sumbawa, and

occasionally hosts special exhibitions. Displays include exhibits on geology, history and culture. The **Taman Budaya** cultural centre on Jalan Majapahit presents traditional music and dance nightly. The provincial tourist office is on Jalan Langko.

The **Gunung Pengsong Temple** (daily 8am–5pm; donation), 9km (5 miles) south of Mataram, sits atop a peak with vistas of rice fields, Gunung Rinjani and the sea. Populated with monkeys, this is the hill the Balinese had aimed for in the mythical account of their initial arrival in western Lombok. Today, it is an area populated by a significant community of Balinese Hindus. In March or April, a buffalo is sacrificed here to ensure a rich harvest. At that time of the year, houses are repainted and the entire village spruced up to honour the rice goddess Dewi Sri.

Merging into Mataram on its west side is **Ampenan**. With its numerous shops, cheap hotels, dusty roads, plentiful horse-drawn carts called *cidomo*, Islamic bookstores and an Arab quarter, it is easily the island's

most colourful town. Early Arab traders were drawn to Ampenan when it was the only harbour for incoming and outgoing ships. Nowadays, it is used only for fishing and shipping cattle. On special holidays, the beach is a venue for performances of the *gandrung* social dance or for the *wayang Sasak* shadow play.

Market town

Cakranegara ❷, abutting Mataram at its eastern boundary, is Lombok's main market centre. It is also home to many Chinese and Balinese, who make up more than 50 percent of the town's population. Many weaving and basketry industries are located in Cakranegara – items of which are sold in Bali at many times the Lombok price.

Several important Balinese temples occupy Cakranegara and the surrounding area. **Pura Meru** (daily 8am–5pm; donation), built in 1720 by Balinese prince Anak Agung Made Karang, is the island's largest temple. Its giant *meru* (pagoda) for the Hindu Trinity – Siwa (Shiva), Wisnu (Vishnu) and Brahma – is the "centre

of the universe" for the Balinese here, and its annual festival, held over five days during the September or October full moon, is the largest Balinese Hindu event on Lombok. The outer courtyard hall has drums that call the devout to ceremonies and festivals. Two buildings with raised offering platforms are in the centre courtyard, while the interior enclosure holds 33 shrines and three multi-tiered *meru*.

Across the street stands the Mayura Water Place and its **Pura Mayura** (daily 8am–5pm; donation), built in 1744 as the court temple of the last Balinese kingdom in Lombok. A large artificial lake holds a *bale kambang* (floating pavilion) that was once used as a platform where justice was dispensed and meetings held. Today the gardens are a playground for children and a pasture for grazing cattle. The temple sits behind sedate water gardens.

The structures and pool at **Taman Narmada** (daily 8am–5pm; donation), 10km (6 miles) east of Cakranegara, were reportedly built in 1805 as a replica of Gunung Rinjani and Segara Anak, the lake within Rinjani's caldera.

International dance sport judge Marcel de Rijk has a studio in Lombok. The Dutch grandson of an Indonesian freedom fighter, de Rijk has lured several International Dance Sport Championships to Mataram, spawning a craze for the sport in Indonesia.

BELOW: market at Cakranegara.

Alfred Russel Wallace

Although 19th-century biologist Alfred Russel Wallace developed the theory of evolution at the same time as Charles Darwin, he is best known for his studies of bio-geography, concerning the spread of species through the Indonesian archipelago. He theorised that the deep oceanic trench that runs between Bali and Lombok, distinctly separated the flora and fauna of mainland Asia from that of the islands to the east. This divide is now known as the Wallace Line.

Apprenticed as a surveyor, Wallace spent eight years travelling through the "Malay archipelago" – now part of Indonesia – collecting over 125,000 insect, bird and mammal specimens. During that time he noticed a marked difference between the mammals, banyan trees and hornbills of the western islands and the marsupials, eucalyptus and birds of paradise in the east.

Over the years Wallace's theory has been refined. It is now clear that many Asian species were able to migrate into the eastern islands and many Australian species are found towards the west, depending on their abilities to float, swim or fly.

The islands from Lombok to Timor are known as Wallacea in his honour, and this area is recognised as a transitional zone between the flora and fauna of the two land masses.

The coral reefs off the Gili Islands offer superb snorkelling.

When the elderly king Anak Ngurah Gede Karangasem of Mataram could no longer make the trek to Segara Anak, he built Taman Narmada. The annual pilgrimage and offering at Rinjani's crater lake continue today, and the festival at **Pura Kalasa** coincides with them during the full moon of either October or November. The Narmada gardens are splendid, with traditional dances performed on special occasions. Some of the pools are open to swimmers and are popular with local children.

The southwest peninsula

Most of the goods shipped to Lombok today arrive at **Gerung ❸**, near **Labuan Lembar**, to be distributed. Gerung is the village of the *cepung*, a men's social dance in which they read and sing from the *lontar monyet* (monkey manuscript), drink *tuak* (palm wine), dance and imitate *gamelan* instruments vocally. The road southwards continues to the westernmost point of the island – a sheer cliff standing above Bangko Bangko beach. Turning on the road to **Sekotong** south of Lembar, you will eventually skirt the

coastline and witness beautiful scenery of turquoise sea and blindingly white beaches. There are cottages and fine snorkelling at **Gili Nanggu**, accessible by boat from either Lembar or Tawun. The snorkelling is good at Palangan beach, and this is the place to catch boats to Gili Gede, Gili Ashan and others. The route ends at **Bangko Bangko ❹**, with a stunning forest and a white-sand beach surrounding Lombok's best surfing area, Desert Point.

Exploring central Lombok

East of Cakranegara in **Lingsar ❺** is **Pura Lingsar** temple complex (daily 8am–5pm; donation). Originally built in 1714, this is the main temple of Lombok, not only for Hindus but also for the Wetu Telu, an unorthodox Islamic sect. Buddhists, Christians and occasionally traditional Muslims (Wetu Lima) pray here for prosperity, rain, fertility, health and general success.

Located a few kilometres northeast of Narmada in **Suranadi** is the oldest and holiest of the Balinese temples in Lombok, **Pura Suranadi ❻** (daily 8am–5pm; donation), a complex of

BELOW: Pura Lingsar.

three temples founded by a Javanese priest, Danghyang Nirartha. Chilly spring water bubbles up into restored baths, which are open to swimmers. Beyond Suranadi is **Hutan Wisata Suranadi** (daily 8am–5pm; admission charge). Stroll through the botanical garden, where specimens are labelled, to see birds, monkeys and butterflies.

The northwest coast and northern Lombok

Heading north from Ampenan is **Pura Segara**, where, following cremations, the Balinese who live on Lombok come to scatter the ashes of their loved ones into the sea. En route to Senggigi, the road passes **Batu Layar**, an important *makam* (ancestral grave) where nominal Muslims come to picnic and to pray for health and success. Nearby is **Pura Batu Bolong** (daily 8am–5pm; donation), an interesting Hindu temple on a cliff facing Bali. It sits beside a large rock with a hole, from which the temple takes its name. This is a great sunset point with fantastic vistas of Bali.

About 10km (6 miles) north of Ampenan is beautiful **Senggigi** ❼, with glorious beaches, picturesque views of Bali's Gunung Agung to the west, good coral for snorkelling and diving, and millions of dollars invested for tourism. Senggigi is an attractive place to stay, with several de luxe hotels as well as budget accommodation.

While Senggigi has always had the lion's share of visitors to itself, there is now competition from sheltered **Mangsit** ❽ beach to its north. Taking the place of international chain hotels here are villas and stylish boutique hotels offering a friendly, personalised service. Expect more development along this stretch of beach.

North of Mangsit along the scenic and hilly coastal road, there is a variety of terrain and villages. First is **Pemenang**, followed westwards by **Bangsal** ❾, which has an attractive

beach. Boats depart from here for the three islands fondly called "The Gilis": Gili Air, Gili Meno and Gili Trawangan. For decades they have attracted visitors from around the world for their pristine waters, great diving and snorkelling and their laid-back charm.

Gili Trawangan ❿, the largest and most distant of the three islands, has two types of visitors: partygoers, who flock to the southwest side of the island to enjoy gorgeous white-sand beaches, cheap (and not so cheap) accommodation, and of course, parties. North coast visitors spend their days in quiet relaxation, sunbathing and diving. **Gili Meno** ⓫ is the least developed of the three islands. Its attractions are uncrowded beaches, Meno Wall off the west coast, popular with divers, and quiet walks under the stars. **Gili Air** ⓬, closest to the mainland, has the largest local population and a range of dive shops that service all the needs of divers. It has basic as well as moderately priced accommodation.

There is no fresh water on the Gili islands, which means saltwater

While Bayan is considered to be the centre of Lombok's Wetu Telu (unorthodox) Muslims, to the west are Buddhists. Local Hindus hold their ngulam pekelem ceremony at Segara Anak Lake on Gunung Rinjani.

BELOW: Pura Meru.

The women of all Penujak and neigbouring villages have been making pottery since the early 16th century.

BELOW: monkeys are a common sight at Lombok temples.

showers and the absence of lush gardens. Most water is shipped from the mainland, so there is a need to conserve it. Drink only bottled water, eat only cooked food, and choose accommodation with mosquito nets.

Back on the mainland, the south-facing beach at **Sira**, along the peninsula north of Bangsal, is a good launch spot for snorkelling on the offshore coral reef. This is also the site for the **Kosaido Country Club**, an 18-hole course with magnificent sea views. Around the point, in Medana Bay, is the luxury Oberoi resort.

Northeast of **Gondang**, along the coast, is **Tiu Pupas** waterfall, a 20-minute walk beyond the end of a poorly marked, rocky road. While the spring-fed falls may be disappointing during the dry season, they flow into a deep pool suitable for swimming. Trekking through a traditional Sasak village, **Kerurak**, makes the effort worthwhile. Dusty **Segenter** village, 20km (16 miles) from Gondang and inland at Sukadana, provides a glimpse into the harsh reality of life on the island's dry side. The 300 villagers in

this northern interior village eke out a living growing corn and beans, yet they welcome visitors with smiles.

Bayan ⓭ maintains old dance and poetic traditions, as well as *kemidi rudat*, a theatre form based on the *Thousand and One Nights* fables. One of the most important Wetu Telu mosques in Lombok is in Bayan. In nearby **Sedang Gile**, the waterfalls are among the island's most spectacular and are worth the effort of descending 200 vertical steps to view them.

Start planning the ascent to **Gunung Rinjani** ⓮ with a visit to Rinjani Trek Centre (daily 7am–5pm; tel: 868-1710 4132; Mataram office, Hotel Lombok Raya, Jalan Usaha No. 11; tel: 641 124) or the Rinjani Trekking Club (www.rinjanitrekking.com) in **Senaru**. Funded by the New Zealand government, both offer a series of programmes for climbing the volcano and for trekking in the Rinjani National Park, all of which involve the local communities. Inside the Gunung Rinjani caldera is a crater lake, **Danau Segara Anak** (Child of the Sea), with a second steaming volcano growing at the edge. It is a difficult climb; go with an authorised local guide and wear warm clothing.

Eastern and central Lombok

South of the north coast road are **Sembalun Bumbung** and neighbouring **Sembalun Lawang**, located in a valley on the slopes of Gunung Rinjani. Both villages are alternative points for climbing Gunung Rinjani, and there are a number of tourist agencies which organise treks in the region, as well as several homestays. Be warned that climbing Rinjani is not for amateurs. What starts out easily enough becomes a steep winding path to the ridge. The final ascent to the summit is over loose gravel, rising steeply, and there's also the cold, wind and low oxygen levels to contend with. Gunung Rinjani National Park is closed to climbers and trekkers in

the rainy season, which is roughly December to March.

Southeast of Gunang Rinjani, Lenek is well known as a source of traditional Sasak music and dance, including *tari pakon*, a medicinal trance dance. A local cultural patron of the arts has established an organisation to reinvigorate the performing arts, and visitors are welcomed for a rustic stay here. To the west is **Pringgasela**, a village steeped in tradition and a major centre for *ikat*-weaving. Visit the small houses and shops here to purchase hand-woven fabrics.

Tetebatu ⓯, at the southern foot of Gunung Rinjani, is a cool mountain retreat with views of beautiful rice terraces. The area is wet and misty during the rainy season. About an hour's trek north of Tetebatu through a monkey-filled forest is **Jeruk Manis waterfall**. (Be advised to stay well away from the mischievous monkeys, who are known to nip tourists, and steal food, bags and jewellery.) **Bonjeruk**, in central Lombok, is a village of *dalang*, or puppeteers, for the *wayang Sasak* shadow play; many of the puppets are

made here. Near **Lendang Nangka** is Jojang spring, with great vistas and a forest inhabited by black monkeys. In August, Sasak boxing takes place in the village.

To the south

Praya ⓰ is a crossroads and the hub of the south. Home of the Saturday market, it is central to many of the area's handicrafts villages. Southwest of Praya is **Penujak** ⓱ one of three traditional pottery-making villages sponsored by the New Zealand government. The other two are **Banyumulek**, south of Mataram, and **Masbagik** Timur, in East Lombok.

The women of all three villages have been making pottery since the early 16th century, with skills being passed from one generation to the other. Visitors can watch as a greyish-brown clay that comes from local riverbeds is manipulated into shape by hand, sometimes using a wooden paddle. Instead of a potter's wheel, the women walk around the jar, building up and scraping the walls as they go. After drying in the sun, the earthenware is

Rambitan villagers.

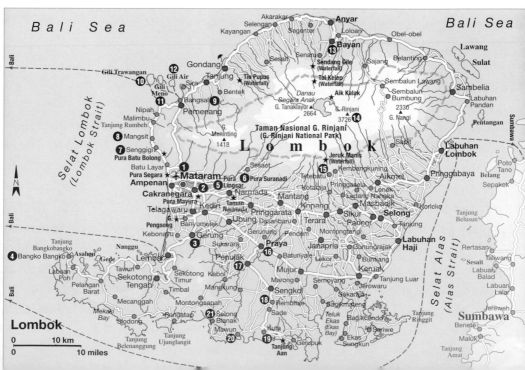

BELOW: Penujak pottery village.
BELOW RIGHT: Nyale sea worms.

baked in pits where the clay turns a rich reddish-brown in the process.

Magnificent giant water pots, incense boxes, cooking pots, tableware, lamp bases and garden lanterns have joined the line of *kendi* (drinking vessels), also produced in Java.

On the road leading south from Praya to the coast are two traditional Sasak villages sandwiched between the main road and rice fields. On the west side of the road is **Rembitan** ⑱, an authentic hilltop village with the oldest mosque in Lombok, **Mesjid Kuno**. Only Muslims may enter this thatched-roof house of worship. An interesting walk through the village is encouraged by residents, who act as guides for a small fee. On the east side of the road is **Sade**, a village with clusters of thatched *lumbung* or rice barns, that is open to tourists.

Kuta ⑲, 45km (28 miles) southeast of Cakranegara, is fronted by an expansive and beautiful white-sand beach. The architecturally interesting Novotel Lombok Mandalika hotel on Mandalika beach is moderately priced, and the homestays in the area

are cheap. Kuta's market (early on Wednesday and Sunday mornings) is a lively cacophony of chickens and local chatter and is brightened by colourful fruits and woven baskets. The 15-year-long logjam to develop this beach has been broken by the investment of a Middle East company. This influx of revenue is good news for the southern Lombok people, but not so great for those who liked Kuta exactly as it was.

Mandalika beach is also the site of the annual Bau Nyale festival commemorating the legend of the beautiful Putri (Princess) Mandalika, who long ago was sought as the bride of every Lombok *raja*. When she could not choose between the suitors, she threw herself into the sea from a headland, saying, "*Kuta*", or "Wait for me here". When she jumped, hundreds of *nyale* sea worms floated to the surface. Thus, every year on the anniversary of her fateful demise, the *nyale* worms return to the site. Thousands of residents – including young people who flirt and strut while watching the sea worms spawn – gather for the festival. Associated

with fertility, the *nyale* are ground up, and the resulting mixture is either placed in irrigation channels to ensure farmers will have a good harvest, or fried and eaten in the manner of a love potion.

Astonishing landscape

West of Kuta village, the beach at **Mawun** ⓴ runs the length of a perfect half-moon bay, flanked by massive headlands. This deserted spot off the beaten track is barren of trees, which accentuates the spectacular scenery and the sound of the sea. Apart from the occasional fisherman or young girls selling sarongs, it is possible to have this fine beach all to yourself. It can also be reached by bicycle from Kuta, although the road is a bit steep.

A picturesque little fishing village lies on the fringe of the wide, sweeping **Selong Blanak** ㉑ beach, west of Mawun. Colourful, small fishing *prahu* (boats) rock in gentle waves at the eastern end of the bay. What sets this site apart from other beaches is the scale of the surrounding landscape, which is of continental, not island, proportions. The sand, sea and distant hills are painted in an astonishing palate of colours, making this an ideal place to bask in nature's beauty.

East of Kuta lies a series of beautiful, untouched beaches. **Tanjung Aan** has spectacular scenery off the peninsula, just a few vendor shacks and a virtually undisturbed beach. Another 3km (2 miles) east is **Gerupuk**, well known as a surf location and ideal for windsurfing or body-surfing. Local fishermen harvest seaweed in the nearby bay.

Further east, beyond **Batu Nampar**, is the infrequently visited **Batu Rintang**. With its traditional thatched-rice barns and huts, this village offers a realistic look at local life. Outside Batu Nampar are salt works and floating seaweed frames, farmed by migrants from South Sulawesi and Madura. South and east, respectively, are found the coastal settlements of **Ekas** and **Tanjung Luar**, inhabited by Bugis fishermen from Sulawesi, who arrived here during the early 1600s.

TIP

A festival held at Pura Lingsar temple (*see page 268*) during the November or December full moon presents sacred Balinese Hindu and Islamic Sasak performing arts. This is the only event on the island that unites the two groups.

BELOW: Kuta beach.

SUMBAWA

Some of the best surf in the world off the coast of little-known Sumbawa. Non-surfers can trek through forests, snorkel off the south coast of Pulau Moyo or view ancient stone sarcophagi

Larger than Bali and Lombok combined, Sumbawa's contorted form is the result of violent volcanic explosions. It was Gunung Tambora that isolated the people of the west from the Bimanese for centuries. So separate are they that the native language of the Sumbawanese is more akin to those of the Balinese and the Lombok Sasaks, while the Bima language is more like those of Flores and Sumba. When islanders say "Sumbawa", they mean the western part of the island. The east is simply called "Bima". Javanese Hinduism never made it this far east, and most Sumbawans are devout Muslims: visitors should wear respectful attire away from the beaches, particularly in the east.

Until fairly recently, there were only two reasons to visit this little-known island: to hire a boat from Sape in the east heading for Komodo National Park, or to catch a big wave on its west or southeast coasts. Improved air service to Labuhanbajo, Flores, from where the sail to Komodo is much easier and prettier, has negated the first reason, leaving surfing as the island's biggest attraction. The breaks at Hu'u attract championship surfers, and sunsets from the beaches are absolutely stunning.

There are a few other relatively unnoticed things to do and see in Sumbawa. The rich and famous use part of Pulau Moyo, off the north coast, as a luxury remote getaway. Moyo is also a nature reserve protecting forest and wildlife, and there are trekking opportunities. The mighty Gunung Tambora is waiting to be climbed, and there are megaliths believed to be related to those in Sumba.

West Sumbawa

Ferries from Lombok arrive at Poto Tano in West Sumbawa, where buses await passengers bound for the surfing beaches or Sumbawa Besar.

Main attractions
WEST COAST AND HU'U SURFING
BATU TERING MEGALITHS
MOYO ISLAND SNORKELLING AND
  TREKKING
GUNUNG TAMBORA CLIMBING
BIMA

LEFT: tribesman on horseback. **RIGHT:** a bicolour blenny on the coral reef south of Pulau Moyo.

TIP

Sumbawa is known throughout Indonesia for its wild honey, reputed to have special powers that enhance the sexual prowess of men. Ask for *madu Sumbawa* at any local market.

On the west coast from Taliwang south to Sekongkang beach (familiarly called Yo-Yo's), the scenic coastline has superb white-sand beaches. There is prime surfing at Scar Reef near **Jereweh**, at Supersucks near Maluk, and at Yo-Yo's on the south coast. **Maluk ❶** and neighbouring **Benete** are bustling centres of goods and services to satisfy the needs of the copper- and gold-mine employees who work near Maluk. Budget hotels, bars and restaurants cater for surfers.

On the north coast at **Sumbawa Besar ❷** is the **Dalam Loka**, the former sultan's palace. Made entirely of wood, it is raised on 99 stilts to remind followers of the 99 names given to their god. It is now a museum used for cultural activities. The late sultan's heirlooms are kept in nearby Balai Kuning (Yellow House) where his daughter lives, and can only been seen by appointment.

The hills east of Sumbawa Besar contain large stone sarcophagi, carved in low relief with human forms and crocodiles. **Batu Tering ❸**, about 29km (18 miles) south of Sumbawa

Besar, has megaliths said to be the royal tombs of ancient chiefs, a Neolithic culture that thrived about 2,000 years ago. About 2km (1.2 miles) beyond is Liang Petang (Dark Cave), with stalactites and stalagmites resembling humans and weaving looms.

Travelling west from Sumbawa Besar brings you to **Pulau Moyo ❹**. Two-thirds of the island is a game reserve to protect the island's deer, *banteng* wild ox, 21 bat species and wild boars. The flora here ranges from savannah to dense jungle containing teak, tamarind and banyan trees. There are two waterfalls; the one near Labuan Aji village is an easier trek. South of the island the water is crystal clear and the reefs undisturbed, ideal for snorkellers and divers, with a white-sand beach opposite the island at Tanjung Manis.

Moyo is accessible in about 45 minutes by speedboat from Sumbawa Besar. Alternatively, fishing boats can be hired from Ai Bari. Simple accommodation is available at Tanjung Pasir on the mainland. The luxurious Amanwana resort, with modified villas

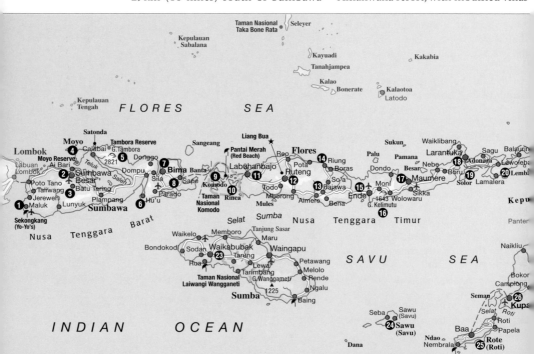

using canvas tent toppings, is also on Moyo. It's totally isolated, and bookings have to be made in advance.

East Sumbawa

Heading east from Sumbawa Besar, the land narrows connecting West with East Sumbawa. From here, fertile river valleys with shimmering velvet-green rice fields are replaced by the monotony of rolling scorched brown hills. Picturesque bays and harbours shelter *bagan*, fishing platforms. Along the coasts, families line the shores damming up sea water to make salt.

Serious climbers may want to ascend **Gunung Tambora ⑤**. In 1815, some 100 cubic km (25 cubic miles) of debris were ejected into the atmosphere with a force equivalent to that of several hydrogen bombs, creating "the year without summer" in 1816. Located on the northern peninsula of Sumbawa, the gaping, 2,821-metre (9,250ft) high caldera offers spectacular views on a clear day. The ascent begins at **Calabai**, a small logging town on the coast. It is a very difficult three-day climb and a guide is imperative.

Due south of Dompu is **Hu'u ⑥**, where long tube rides break off outlying reefs at Periscope, Nangas, Lakey Peak, Pipeline and Cobblestones, attracting international championship surfers. Lakey beach has beautiful white sand, and at low tide there is good reef-walking. Swimming and snorkelling are possible in small inlets.

At **Bima ⑦**, if there is a festival going on, you may catch *pencak silat* (martial arts) and other dance performances at the sultan's palace. At the *pasar* (local market), you'll see women wearing colourful Islamic headscarves that are unique to this region; unmarried women must cover everything except their eyes.

There are several traditional villages in the hills east of Bima, where the people fled to escape Islamisation in the 17th century. **Donggo** is the oldest. Women here still weave indigo cloth, from which they make their traditional clothing. The Donggo people adhere to a traditional animistic religion.

Look out for picturesque rice storage barns along the hilly road that connects Bima and **Sape ⑧**, from where boats depart for Komodo.

Sumbawa is famous for its surf

BELOW: a highland village in eastern Sumbawa.

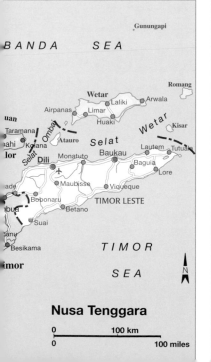

B A N D A   S E A

Gunungapi

Romang

Wetar
Laliki
Airpanas · Limar · Arwala
uan · Huaki · Wetar · Kisar
Taramana
pahi · Kolana · Atauro · Selat · Lautem · Tutuala
lor · Dili · Monatuto · Baukau · Baguia
· · Lore
ade · Maubisse · Viqueque
bua · Bobonaru · TIMOR LESTE
· Betano
anu · Suai
Besikama

T I M O R

imor

S E A

N

Nusa Tenggara

0 — 100 km
0 — 100 miles

KOMODO AND RINCA

The main attraction of these inhospitable islands is the remarkable Komodo dragon, the largest lizard in the world

A Unesco World Heritage Site, **Komodo National Park** lies in the strait between Sumbawa and Flores and is the habitat of the world's largest reptile, *Varanus komodoensis*, the Komodo dragon. This giant monitor lizard is one of the world's oldest species, a close relative of the dinosaurs that roamed the earth 100 million years ago. Although there are dragons on two other nearby islands, in order to protect wild populations visitors are only allowed on Komodo and Rinca (pronounced *ren-cha*).

Most visitors couple Komodo dragon-spotting with snorkelling and diving while in the park. During low tide at Pantai Merah (Red Beach), near Komodo, reefs teeming with colourful fish are very near the shoreline. Divers will appreciate the slopes, boulders and small rocky outcroppings nearby. The strong currents here provide plenty of plankton for small fish to feed on, in turn attracting larger ones, and provide migratory paths for whales and dolphins. Sea turtles are frequently seen here, too. Divers who venture further from the coast should be be aware that extreme undertows have claimed lives.

Komodo island is home to several human settlements, including its largest village, Kampung Komodo (population about 1,300), located only a few kilometres west of Loh Liang ranger station. Villagers make a living primarily from

fishing. They speak their own language and although predominately Muslim, also adhere to strong traditional beliefs. Modestly dressed visitors are welcome, particularly if they are interested in buying one of the locally carved Komodo dragon statues, seed pearls or souvenirs from elsewhere in West Nusa Tenggara.

Visiting Komodo National Park

The highlight of a visit to the national park is seeing the dragons in their natural habitat. On **Komodo** ❾,

Main attractions
KOMODO DRAGON-SPOTTING
TREKKING
DIVING AND SNORKELLING
PANTAI MERAH (RED BEACH)

LEFT: Komodo island. **RIGHT:** a throwback to the age of the dinosaurs.

TIP

When visiting Komodo, whether arriving by government ferry or by a private boat chartered on Sumbawa or Flores, be aware that the currents around Komodo are very strong and the seas usually rough. When swimming, keep an eye out for sea snakes, which are plentiful in these waters, and always be mindful of currents and rip-tides.

the most popular trek is a 2km (1.2-mile) walk to **Banunggulung**. With prior arrangement, those who wish to see more of the elusive reptiles away from the tourist crowds can continue past Banunggulung to **Poreng**, in the northeastern part of the island, or as far as **Sebita** on the coast. Shorter walks are also possible from the ranger station at **Loh Liang** (where basic tourist accommodation is sited) to Kampung Komodo to the southwest.

Trekkers on both islands must be accompanied by a park ranger, whose expertise at knowing where to look for and spotting wildlife is invaluable. In addition to being responsible for your safety, the rangers will also point out other interesting flora and fauna en route. Although it is tempting to focus on photographing the beasts encountered, be constantly aware of everything else around you, including poisonous snakes. Keep your distance from all wild animals, and remember that the dragons can move very quickly if disturbed, that they are dangerous creatures and that medical attention is far away.

There are several other trails to choose from, and park regulations require that all visitors be accompanied by a ranger (whose fee is nominal). The most frequented long-haul trek is to **Gunung Ara** (730 metres/2,390ft), one of a chain of mountains that extends along the northern part of Komodo. It is a one- or two-day excursion, and from the summit you can take in great panoramas of the islands, their craggy peaks, sandy bays and the sparkling turquoise sea. Similar views can be enjoyed from **Gunung Satalibo**, at 740 metres (2,420ft) high, the island's tallest peak. The trails are those used by foraging animals, bordered by tall grasses concealing large stones, so sturdy walking shoes and trousers are recommended.

Scuba-diving and snorkelling in the park waters are reputed to be some of the best in the Asia Pacific region. The 260 species of reef-building corals, sheer-drop walls and around 1,000 species of fish and marine mammals, including manta rays, sharks, sea turtles, dolphins and whales, are paradise to snorkellers and divers. With the

BELOW: the visitor centre at Komodo National Park.

KOMODO NATIONAL PARK
Indonesia

THE WORLD HERITAGE SITE

marine area constituting 67 percent of the park, diving brings a significant number of tourists. The waters to the south of the park are cooler than those to the north, creating an ideal habitat for corals and reef fish, while to the north, rich plankton and nutrients attract a wide variety of temperate marine life. For snorkellers, **Pantai Merah** (Red Beach) offers butterfly, parrot and trigger fish, giant clams and colourful corals at close range. The gorgeous beach is pink due to an abundance of red coral in the region.

As Komodo National Park is in the transition zone described by 19th-century naturalist Sir Alfred Russel Wallace *(see page 267)*, birdwatchers will find a mixture of Asian and Australian species. Squawking cockatoos and noisy friarbirds flock in tropical kapok and gnarled tamarind trees, disturbing green Imperial pigeons, black-naped orioles, sunbirds and flowerpeckers. On the forest floor there are jungle fowl, the forebears of domesticated chickens, quails scratching for insects and mound-building megapodes.

Rinca

Not having received the same publicity as Komodo, **Rinca** ⑩ island is not as crowded as its more famous neighbour in the high season (July and August), and provides a far more natural experience.

On Rinca, there are two moderately easy treks (2–3 hours each) from the ranger station at **Loh Buaya**, which also has limited basic accommodation. One, to the east of the compound, is up and across a ridge where there is a breathtaking view of the Komodo group of islands, with Flores rising from the sea at one point. Watch for herds of wild horses, which are absent from Komodo. The other trail goes in the opposite direction through monsoon forest, where wild buffaloes wallow in streams.

There is a shortage of park rangers on both islands in July and August, the busiest tourist season. Those wishing for longer treks requiring a ranger may be happier visiting during the off-season. It is best to leave on expeditions in the early mornings so you can see the animals at their most active, and you can avoid the extreme midday heat.

Warm blue waters, perfect for swimming and snorkelling.

BELOW: the saliva produced by Komodo dragons is highly septic.

The dragons of Komodo and Rinca

The dragons of Flores and Rinca display genetic similarities, whereas on Komodo and Gili Montang there is a clear pattern of genetic divergence. According to a 2011 census there are 2,740 Komodo dragons on Komodo, Rinca, Gili Montang and Nusa Kode. The greatest threat to the monitors is from deer poachers, who kill off the animals on which they feed.

Male dragons can reach 3 metres (10ft) or more in length and weigh an average of 70kg (154lbs). Females usually attain only two-thirds of this size and lay up to 30 eggs at a time.

The reptiles are carnivores, favouring rotting meat, which they track by flicking their forked tongues into the air to identify odours. However, they can hunt when there is no carrion available; by lifting their massive bodies up on muscular legs they can sprint briefly at 20kph (12mph). Stealth predators, they lie in wait to ambush using claws and tails to knock victims senseless. If the lizard has managed to sink its serrated teeth into the victim's flesh, the creature will usually die from septicaemia due to the toxic bacteria in the dragon's saliva.

During the mating season (July to August) Komodo dragons prefer to attend to the business at hand in seclusion, making them more difficult to spot.

FLORES

Named for its untamed verdant beauty, Flores is crowned by Gunung Kelimutu, with three crater lakes that constantly change colour. High-quality ikats are woven in numerous villages around the island

lores extends a long arm east from Komodo towards the Solor archipelago, its highland landscape punctuated by volcanic cones, its coastal waters fringed with nature reserves and a marine park. Diverse cultures with ancient traditions have survived in the isolated villages of the interior.

A 750km (470-mile) highway runs the length of Flores in a series of curves and switchbacks from Labuhanbajo in the west to Larantuka in the east and is plagued by landslides in the rainy season. For the hardy, a trip across the Trans-Flores highway offers a look at many facets of one of Indonesia's most interesting islands. In the west are the primarily Muslim Manggarais and in the east the majority Roman Catholic Sikkas of Portuguese descent.

By breaking the journey up into overnight stops, on one day travellers can be awed by the patterned rice fields near Ruteng, revel in the cool mountain air at Bajawa and snorkel at the marine national park in Riung. The next day could include Flores's largest city, Ende, and sunrise at Kelimutu's three crater lakes at Moni, passing cocoa, vanilla, coffee and pineapple plantations along the way. The third leg of the journey leaves the volcanoes behind and dips down to a gorgeous azure sea and enters former

Portuguese strongholds at Maumere and Larantuka.

Named Cabo das Flores (Cape of Flowers) by the Portuguese in the 16th century, Flores was already established as a vital link in inter-island trade with the 15th-century Hindu-Javanese Majapahit Empire and later with South Sulawesi's Gowa kingdom, which began converting coastal communities to Islam. The Portuguese built a fort on Solor island, further to the east, to protect their trading interests in malaria- and cholera-ridden

Main attractions

RUTENG AND KAMPUNG RUTENG
BAJAWA
BENA AND NEARBY TRADITIONAL VILLAGES
GUNUNG KELIMUTU
MAUMERE

LEFT: an elderly woman from eastern Flores.
RIGHT: Catholic missionary in Flores, c.1920.

TIP

While in Manggarai, travellers may see a spectacular *caci* whip duel, held as part of weddings or other important ceremonies. Combatants are fitted with buffalo-hide shields, and attack each other with long rattan whips tipped with rawhide tassels, steeped in ancient symbolism. The aim is to overcome the physical and spiritual defence of one's opponent. Welts and scars are admired, and blood drawn is offered to the land.

Timor and established a Catholic mission at Larantuka.

The Dutch acquired the Portuguese settlements on Flores in 1859 in exchange for Portuguese holdings in eastern Timor with a proviso that Catholicism be encouraged. They also bombarded Muslim Ende twice and exercised increasing authority here, but fully controlled the island only after subduing a bloody rebellion in 1907–8. Thereafter, Catholic missionaries flooded Flores, sparking a new wave of conversions.

Western Flores: Manggarai

The western third of Flores is called **Manggarai**. Primarily Muslim, Manggarai is self-sufficient in rice, and exports fine coffee and livestock. **Labuhanbajo** ⓫ sits on a beautiful harbour filled with the outriggers of local fishermen, and its primary importance from a tourist's perspective is its proximity to the Komodo National Park. Boat charters, snorkelling and diving trips and tours to Komodo can be arranged through local travel agencies, and the sail to the national park is far more scenic and the waters calmer than the crossing from Sape (Sumbawa) to Komodo.

Batu Cermin (Mirror Rock) is a series of caves and canyons about 5km (3 miles) from Labuanbajo by car, and from there on foot. A large grotto contains stalactites and stalagmites, and while some of the caves are narrow and dark, others receive sunlight from above.

A three-hour drive southeast of Labuhanbajo (83km/52 miles) brings you to the volcanic Lake Sano Nggoang region and the 15,000-hectare (37,064-acre) **Mbeliling Forest Nature Reserve**. It is in the throes of being developed as a community-based ecotourism site with the assistance of BirdLife Indonesia; villagers have been trained in first aid, food preparation and search-and-rescue techniques and serve as guides, porters, cooks and administrative staff. A two-day trek includes birdwatching for prevalent swamp species, hiking to Savanna Peak for panoramic views, and visits to healing sulphuric hot springs and an old wooden church and parish houses.

Continuing east from Labuhanbajo, the road winds up to **Ruteng** ⓬, a pleasantly cool town situated up in the western hills. Watch for the traditional *lingko*, spider's web-shaped rice fields near **Cancar**, before reaching Ruteng.

Ruteng is primarily a government centre and a good stopping-off place to break up the overland trip. The top of **Golo Curu** (Welcome Mountain) has great sunset views and an old Dutch church (5 minutes by *bemo* or a 45-minute walk). Rainforest-covered **Gunung Ranaka** (2,400 metres/7,874ft) looms over Ruteng – it is a four-hour walk to the summit – and is a good venue for birdwatching.

Kampung Ruteng, just outside Ruteng, features a stone ancestral altar. **Todo** village, 21km (13 miles) from Ruteng, is known for its megalithic stones and a drum whose head is reputedly covered by a woman's skin.

BELOW: cacao plantation near Labuhanbajo.

From Todo, drive to Denge village via Dintor and make a four-hour mountain trek up to **Waerebo**, 1,000 metres (3,280ft) above sea level. This is the only remaining village in Manggarai where traditional houses still exist. Built on five levels, with high-pitched straw roofs, the living areas are at the bottom and the top four levels are used for storage. With the assistance of BirdLife Indonesia, the 35-member Waerebo Tourism Body was formed to improve the local economy through environmental conservation and low-impact tourism. A local travel agency can arrange an overnight stay in one of the houses, which is inhabited by eight families.

About 12km (7½ miles) north of Ruteng is **Liang Bua**, where the fossils of *Homo floresiensis* were found by a joint Indonesia-Australia team. The tiny skeletons, nicknamed "Hobbits", are believed to be a new human species that existed alongside modern humans as recently as 12,000 years ago, yet may have descended from *Homo erectus*, which arose some 2 million years ago *(see Birth of Empires, page 30)*.

Central Flores: Ngada

The next stop is **Bajawa** ⑬, whose attractions are its cool mountain air, exquisite yellow-on-black supplementary warp *sarongs* and traditional villages. More than any other area of Flores, the Ngada region has retained its traditions and rituals despite the veil of Catholicism. Bena, Luba, Langa, Gurusina and Nage villages offer examples of Ngada's ancient culture. All have *ngadhu* shrines, with carved tree-trunk bases, and *bhaga* – miniature houses in the village centre. The *ngadhu* and *bhaga* symbolise male and female tribal ancestors who are said to live in the shrines. Interesting megalithic stones are easiest to find at **Bena** and at nearby **Wogo Tua** (Old Wogo). The week-long Reba festival begins in Bena in late December, then moves to other villages according to dates

selected by their *adat* (local customs) leaders. Wearing traditional ikats, the people dance around the village and sing to reconcile humans and nature.

A deer hunt in **So'a** is a fertility ritual associated with puberty rites: circumcision for the boys and tooth filing for the girls. Strong taboos against sex are enforced throughout the hunt, including a prohibition against the consummation of recent marriages. After the hunt, young women dip their hands into the blood of slain deer to enhance their fertility.

Langa and Bena lie in the shadows of a perfectly coned volcano, **Gunung Inerie** (2,227 metres/7,306ft). It can be climbed in 3–5 hours, depending on your level of physical fitness. **Gunung Ebulobo**, one of Flores's most magnificent volcanoes, can be climbed from Mulakoli village, off the main road to Ende.

From Bajawa, it is a three-hour drive to the northern coastal village of **Riung** ⑭, an excellent side trip for those with time to spare and who are interested in snorkelling in the **Seventeen Islands Nature Reserve**. Riung is also one of the few sites

This Ngadhu shrine in Langa features a human figure on its rooftop.

BELOW: traditional thatched dwellings in Bajawa.

The fossilised remains of a marabou stork that lived 20,000 to 50,000 years ago and stood 180cm (71ins) tall, weighing 16kg (35lbs), have been discovered on Flores.

inhabited by Komodo dragons outside Komodo National Park.

Eastern Flores: Ende to the east coast

On the main road east from Bajawa, it is 125km (80 miles) and about four hours to **Ende** ⑮, one of Flores's two major towns. In contrast to the other, Maumere, Ende has a distinctly Islamic flavour; it was an important Islamic trading port from the late 17th century to the 19th century. During the Japanese Occupation, the city was the regional capital for the eastern archipelago. Sukarno was exiled here in 1933, and Ende was later bombed by the Allies. Today, commerce is largely in Chinese hands.

A couple of hours' drive northeast of Ende are three adjacent volcanic crater lakes on **Gunung Kelimutu** ⑯, the island's main tourist attraction. The lakes, at an altitude of 1,640 metres (5,380ft), are separated only by low ridges and, curiously, are of different colours. Like chameleons, their colours have been constantly changing since Gunung Iye

in Ende erupted in 1969. Theories for the changes in colours range from imbalances in bacterial and micro-organisms to dissolving minerals as the water eats through the rock. Village elders say the colours remain constant, but optical illusions make them appear to be different. The best time for viewing is at sunrise. The trip up to the lakes can be arranged at your lodgings in Ende or in **Moni** where, in addition to a new Australian-standard eco-lodge, there are several *losmen*.

Around Ende is the beginning of the ikat-weaving area, producing exquisitely woven cloths in which intricate designs are tie-dyed on to the threads before weaving begins. In Ende ikats the designs are of a solid colour, usually reddish brown. Some 12km (7.5 miles) east of Kelimutu, at Wolowaru, turn south to **Nggela** coastal village to see superb textiles being woven. From Ende to Maumere, the road cuts diagonally across the island towards the north coast. The distance is 150km (90 miles), but the winding, scenic drive can take seven hours.

BELOW: misty descent from Gunung Kelimutu.

Catholicism and animism

Catholicism claims about 95 percent of Flores's 2 million inhabitants. The Church has put heavy emphasis on improving living conditions through its schools, health services and agricultural programmes. And although the clergy in Flores are well aware of the continued existence of many traditional beliefs and customs, they make no systematic efforts to eliminate them.

The ancient traditions that have survived are many and varied. Some islanders still worship their ancestral spirits. They also believe in Dewa, a god who lives in the sky, and Nitu, a goddess who lives beneath the earth, in the water, in large trees and in the ocean. Pythons were once worshipped in Flores, lending the island another former name, Snake Island.

Maumere **17** is the entrance into Flores for many visitors, as flights are more reliable than into Labuhanbajo. The Catholic Church, with its large coconut holdings, is behind much of the development here. Although the town and nearby Catholic seminary were severely damaged in a 1992 earthquake and tidal wave that killed 2,400 people along the north coast of Flores, little evidence remains of the tragedy. Visit Maumere's market to see local women with swept-up hairdos dressed in traditional weavings, bright green or yellow blouses and heirloom ivory bracelets. While made in the same manner as Ende's, the ikat cloths of Maumere have a greater variety of colours. Watch weavers at work in nearby villages Watublapi, Sikka or Nita. Snorkelling and diving off Maumere's fine beaches have suffered from dynamite fishing.

Ledalero Museum on the outskirts of Maumere has an interesting collection of regional ethnological objects. The little museum is run by Ledalero Catholic Seminary, where many of Indonesia's priests study and are ordained. It is attached to the church, and visitors are welcome – ask at the church for the museum to be opened.

A slice of Iberia

A 140km (87-mile) road journey takes you to **Larantuka 18** on the eastern tip of Flores. For about 300 years it was a Portuguese colony, and the Catholic rituals reflect that Iberian influence. Men dressed in white hoods carry the coffin of Jesus through the streets during Good Friday processions, stopping along the way for prayers and hymns in a version of the *Via Dolorosa*. But local beliefs creep in. A statue of the Virgin Mary is bathed in holy water. The statue is said to have been found on the beach by a local man, who reported to the king that he met a beautiful lady. But when the king reached the beach, the lady was not there. Instead, they found a statue and a message in the sand that said: *Renha Rosari* (Queen of the Rosary). Larantuka is a departure point for excursions to the small islands to the east.

BELOW: the coloured lakes of Kelimutu.

ELSEWHERE IN NUSA TENGGARA

Kupang

This remote region is way off the tourist trail, but there is a great deal of interest in the traditional cultures of Alor and Sumba and Rote's world-class surfing

Main attractions
SOLOR
SHOPPING FOR IKAT FABRIC
ALOR DIVING
TRADITIONAL VILLAGES, SUMBA
SURFING OFF ROTE

BELOW: weaving ikat cloth on Sumba.

F ew tourists make it to the far-flung islands that are scattered south and east of Flores. Yet for anyone with an interest in traditional culture, these outposts are richly rewarding to visit. The inhabitants' ancient animistic-based rituals, their megalithic tombs and symbolic architecture have long attracted researchers, while collectors worldwide are drawn by the hand-woven ikat cloth in an astonishingly wide variety of colours and motifs for such a small area.

Eastern Nusa Tenggara's biggest draw these days is its waters. Surfers have long sought out the great breaks at Rote. But the ocean, now acknowledged to be one of the world's most varied marine biodiversity areas, also attracts divers from near and far. Part of the Coral Triangle, which reaches north to the Philippines, a large sweep of the Savu Sea is a Marine Protected Area.

At the far eastern end of the archipelago is Timor. The provincial capital, Kupang, was transformed from a sleepy village to a booming transit point a decade or so ago, serving as a link between Indonesia and Timor Leste and Australia.

Solor archipelago

East of Flores lies the Solor archipelago, which includes Solor, Adonara and Lembata. Larantuka is the gateway, and boats frequently ply the waters between these islands.

Solor ⑲ is guarded by a Portuguese fort, constructed in 1566 and still in good shape. The entrance is covered by an impressive arch and, in one corner, rusting cannons have survived and stand to attention over approaches from the sea. But it is the traditional weaving that visitors come here to see. Unique among all other *ikat* cloths of the region, Solor's fabrics have a brilliant red background instead of the dark indigo used elsewhere.

To the east, the women of **Lembata** ⑳ are known for producing ceremonial ikat cloths. A good "bride's

wealth" weaving sells for hundreds of dollars due to its importance as part of the wedding arrangements. Top-quality cloths are given to the groom's family, who in turn give the bride's family a gift of equal value – heirloom ivory tusks, first brought to the area in the 14th century. The island is also noted for its primitive whaling industry centred in **Lamalera**. When a whale is sighted, a harpooner balances precariously on a narrow plank extending from the bow of a wooden boat and thrusts his harpoon into the whale's back.

Towering over Lembata is **Gunung Ile Ape** (also called Lewotolo), revered by Lembata people who retain animistic beliefs. Ile Api can be climbed from its northern slope in four hours of fairly easy walking, but take a guide and go early, before the clouds cover the sulphurous crater.

Alor archipelago

East of the Solor islands lies the Alor archipelago: Pantar and Alor. To reach the islands, either hop on a ferry or catch one of the two daily flights in Kupang. At **Pantar** ㉑, Gunung Sirung awaits climbing for views of the yellow crater and the aroma of sulphurous fumes.

Alor ㉒ has always been known for its bronze kettledrums, *moko*, replicas of those from the 2,000-year-old Dong Son era of northern Vietnam. Hundreds and perhaps thousands of the drums are kept as heirlooms and are an essential part of the bride price here. Although the *moko* found on Alor were cast in either Java or China, how they ended up on this island, which was not part of traditional trade routes, remains unknown.

Today, however, it is the spectacular diving that attracts visitors. Renowned worldwide as one of Indonesia's top three dive destinations, Alor's rich reefs and diverse marine life are equalled by excellent visibility. Sunfish (*mola mola*), whales, mantas, whale sharks and migrating orcas are just some of the highlights, as well as muck diving.

A short drive from the major town, **Kalabahi**, is Takpala, perched atop a mountainside giving spectacular views

BELOW: an Alor tribal elder takes aim.

BELOW: a bronze moko drum on Alor.

of Maimol Bay on the northern coastline. Traditional dances can be pre-arranged here.

Sumba

South of Flores, **Sumba** is barren throughout the long dry season, but it teems with remnants of an ancient pagan culture. In past centuries it was a source of sandalwood, slaves, horses and cannibal tribes, but today Sumba's attraction is its sculptured megalithic tombs, war game ritual *(Pasola)* and intricate *hinggi* ikat textiles.

West Sumba is lush and green during the rainy season, and its people live in distinctive houses with high-peaked roofs. Ancestral and land worship are still strong here. Traditional villages with elaborate megalithic tombs are scattered throughout the district: near **Waikabubak** ㉓ there are a number of ancient mausoleums, and in nearby **Tarung** there are tombs and houses decorated with water buffalo horns and other souvenirs of sacrificial feasts. **Sodan**, 25km (16 miles) southwest of Waikabubak, is perhaps the most

interesting of the traditional villages. The area is steeped in magic and taboos.

In West Sumba's exciting *Pasola* ritual, scores of colourfully arrayed horsemen on bareback charge one another in a dramatic mock war. Held in several villages *(see Activities, page 402)*, the event begins after the full moon during an annual migration of *nyale* sea worms.

East Sumba is dry, rocky and inhospitable. Most of its people live near or on the coast, and an extensive handloom industry has flourished here for several centuries, producing distinctive *hinggi* ikats known for their bold, animistic designs. To see the process, set out for **Prailiu**, just outside of **Waingapu**. Some 70km (40 miles) southeast of Waingapu is **Rende**, which is known for good ikats as well as for megalithic tombs with unusual carvings. In the vicinity of **Ngalu** and **Baing**, 125km (80 miles) south of Waingapu, whole villages produce the fabulous *kombu* woven cloths – bargaining is expected.

Rote and Savu

Rote and Savu are two seldom-visited islands off the west coast of Timor. With little rainfall to encourage rice-growing, both learned centuries ago to rely on a sturdy drought-resistant palm, the *lontar (Borassus sundaicus)*, for sustenance when there was no other food available. The liquid taken from the inflorescence from two or three trees is enough to support a family during times of drought by reducing it to treacle and storing it in clay pots. Often farmed plantation-style, parts of the palm are also used for building materials and household tools.

Savu ㉔ (also spelled Sawu and Sabu) has a reputation for some of the most beautiful women in Indonesia. Ask any seaman about Savunese women and wait for the swoon. Equally beautiful are the island's ikat weavings, which are far more elegant than others nearby. Historians will more likely remember Savu as one of

the islands visited by Captain Cook in 1770 on his expeditions aboard the *Endeavour*.

Savu is also known for its small "sandalwood" horses, similar to those found on Sumba. Much stronger than they look, the little horses are used for transport and are ridden bareback in mock battles.

Rote ㉕ (also spelt Roti), a land of dazzling white-sand beaches and rolling plains, shelters 18 different ethnic groups, each of which was formerly ruled by its own *raja*. Rotenese men are known for their debating skills, and many attorneys and administrators throughout Indonesia are Rotenese. The island's south coast is a paradise for surfers.

Ikat cloths produced by the Rotenese are far more colourful than those of their neighbours, containing a good deal of red, white and black. Unique to the island is the *sasando*, a mandolin-like instrument made of *lontar* leaves which produces soft lyrical sounds. Also sought after here is silver jewellery from neighbouring **Ndao** island.

Timor

For many centuries, **Timor** island was known as a source of fragrant sandalwood, a draw for foreign traders. The Portuguese and the Dutch later fought to control the trade and subsequently divided the island into Dutch West Timor and Portuguese East Timor. Indonesia claimed Dutch West Timor in 1975 and Portuguese East Timor in 1976, but in 1999 East Timor gained independence and is now called Timor Leste.

The capital of East Nusa Tenggara province, **Kupang** ㉖ has regular air and ferry services to and from the rest of Indonesia. Kupang's attractions include the town market and the **Museum Negeri Kupang** (Museum of East Nusa Tenggara; Mon–Thur 8am–2pm, Fri 8–11am, Sat 8am–12.30pm, Sun 10am–2pm; donation). Ask about cultural performances here.

Timor also offers good cave diving and snorkelling and a great variety of fine textiles. On the main road between Kupang and Dili (Timor Leste), **So'e** is a bustling little town with a cool, pleasant climate. Don't miss its colourful daily market.

Chickens at a Sumba market.

BELOW: Rote island beachcombers.

KALIMANTAN

This vast, wild territory used to be known for its head-hunters. Today orang-utans head the list of attractions

Kalimantan is Indonesia's name for its two-thirds share of Borneo, the world's fourth-largest island (after Australia, Greenland and New Guinea). Borneo's north coast comprises Malaysia's Sarawak and Sabah and the tiny independent oil-rich Brunei sultanate. Kalimantan, with an area of 540,000 sq km (200,000 sq miles), represents nearly 30 percent of Indonesia's land area, but is occupied by barely 6 percent of the population.

Although the name Kalimantan may be unfamiliar, many of us have notions about Borneo: impenetrable jungles concealing Dayaks – the former head-hunting tribes with long earlobes – and dangerous wild animals may leap to the minds of romantics; the plight of endangered orang-utans evokes passionate conversation among animal-lovers; and forest degradation catches the attention of global warming-watchers.

From Kalimantan's hinterland of low-altitude mountain ranges great rivers cascade, serving as crucial "highways" for hundreds of kilometres as well as channels of communication between the people of the interior and those on the coast. Particularly in the east, where infrastructure is better developed, the rivers attract tourists who want to travel deep into jungle regions to visit the Dayak tribes.

Few tourists visit South Kalimantan, but its capital, Banjarmasin, is one of the island's most colourful towns. West Kalimantan is the most unexplored of all of Indonesia's Bornean territories, with poor infrastructure the major cause. Trips upriver to Dayak longhouse settlements are long and rigorous and are definitely not for casual visitors. However, if transportation should improve, these two provinces with six national parks full of wildlife are waiting to be discovered, and will be a treasure trove for adventurers.

Tanjung Puting National Park's orang-utans are Kalimantan's biggest tourist draw. They were perhaps first brought to the world's attention by Birute Kaldikas, who started studying them at Camp Leakey in the 1970s; this is the most accessible area for wildlife-viewing, and as the nature-loving world continues efforts to protect some of the planet's oldest forests, interest in the furry red apes is not likely to wane.

PRECEDING PAGES: orang-utans at Tanjung Puting National Park. **LEFT:** on the river at Tanjung Puting. **ABOVE LEFT:** red-hot chillies at a Pontianak market. **ABOVE RIGHT:** Dayak architecture.

EAST AND SOUTH KALIMANTAN

Journey upriver into the forested interior to see Dayak tribes and extraordinary wildlife. The passage of time and global concerns have little meaning here

Kalimantan Timur (East Kalimantan), or Kaltim for short, is the destination of choice for many "soft" adventurers happy to travel by air-conditioned houseboat up Sungai Mahakam (Mahakam River) to see Dayak settlements, while doing a bit of wildlife spotting en route. For extreme trekkers, however, the possibilities are endless, with the only limitations being time, money and stamina.

Covering an area about the size of England and Scotland combined, the Sungai Mahakam and its tributaries criss-cross Kaltim, serving as "roads" for a scant 2 million inhabitants. Many Dayak tribes – with their extended earlobes, communal dwellings and exquisitely beaded artwork – live inland, while on the coast remnants exist of two rival kingdoms that ruled from the 13th century until the last surviving sultan relinquished his authority to the Indonesian government in 1960.

Much smaller and far more densely populated, Kalimantan Selatan (South Kalimantan), or Kalsel, is separated from its two neighbouring regencies by the densely forested Meratus Mountain Range, with the Barito and Martapura rivers servicing the hinterland. Dayak tribes live upriver; on the coast, fringed by vast mangrove forests, are the primarily Muslim Banjar

people, whose ancestors include Malays, Javanese, Arabs, Chinese, Buginese and Dayaks, as befits the people of an important trading port.

While Dayak tribes are not as plentiful here as they are in Kaltim, an adventure on the Sungai Amandit (Amandit River) makes Kalsel worth exploring, and Banjarmasin itself is a charming town.

EAST KALIMANTAN

The usual port of entry to East Kalimantan is **Balikpapan ❶**, a busy oil and timber town with a population

Map on page 301

Main attractions
MAHAKAM RIVER
KERSIK LUWAI NATURE RESERVE
APOKAYAN REGION
KAYAN MENTARANG NATIONAL PARK
KUTAI NATIONAL PARK
SANGKALAKI ARCHIPELAGO / PULAU DERAWAN
BANJARMASIN FLOATING MARKET
SUNGAI AMANDIT RAFTING
SAMBOJA LESTARI ORANG-UTAN REHABILITATION CENTRE

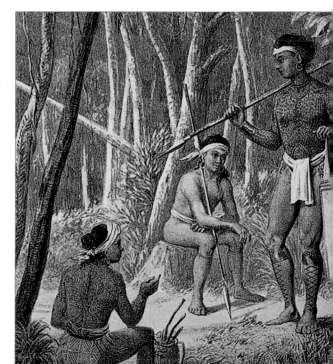

LEFT: Dayak boy in festival finery.
RIGHT: a 17th-century Dutch lithograph of indigenous Borneo tribals.

A totem on a Dayak Longhouse.

BELOW: the Islamic Centre at Samarinda.

of 600,000. It's not a place that holds great interest for travellers, who generally head straight to Samarinda by air or via the 115km (70-mile) paved road to begin their journeys up the great Sungai Mahakam.

Samarinda ❷, a similar-sized city, is the jumping-off point for visits to Dayak country and is the capital of Kaltim province. There is not much to see here aside from waterfront activity: freighters loading or discharging, coal barges being shoved around, rafts of logs under tow to nearby lumber mills. Half a day is enough in Samarinda, giving you time to check out timetables for planes or boats heading inland.

Sungai Mahakam trips

Sungai Mahakam is the main "highway" into the hinterlands. Its source is in the Muller Mountain Range and from there it rushes, meanders, twists and turns downstream. Along the river are Dayak settlements, which are the major attraction for visitors. Also in the area are four lakes harbouring strange and wonderful animals, such as freshwater dolphins and Siamese crocodiles (*Crocodylus siamensis*).

Tour packages, arranged in Samarinda, are the best way to traverse the Mahakam, with some offering overnight stays either on houseboats or in longhouses set up for visitors. For all riverboats, the first major stop out of Samarinda is **Tenggarong ❸**, the former sultan's capital, about 2–2½ hours away. En route, watch for sawmills and barges laden with coal – evidence of two of Kaltim's major industries – and daily activities in riverside villages. There is a **museum** housing Ming-dynasty ceramics and Dayak handicrafts that is worth a visit.

Alternatively, a new toll road links Samarinda to Tenggarong. The drive takes about 30 minutes, and the tour allows travellers to visit Tenggarong's museum and then join a cruise boat for short trips on the Mahakam or longer trips upriver. Tenggarong is also home to the Erau festival, held every 22–28 September, celebrating the town's founding and honouring former royalty. Dayaks come from

miles away to perform traditional dances and recreate pagan rituals such as funeral ceremonies, contrasting greatly with the more sedate dances of the Kutai Muslims, who don their best ceremonial costumes for the occasion.

The next major stop, **Kota Bangun ❹**, lies 6 hours upstream from Tenggarong and is the last chance for accommodation with modern conveniences. From here, travellers can hire a motorised canoe into the upstream hinterland.

Riverside **Muara Muntai**, 2–3 hours from Kota Bangun, is home to both Kutai Dayak and transmigrants. It is also the departure point for exploring the mid-Mahakam lakes region, the beginning of Dayak country. Small motorised canoes can be rented here for the 2-hour run to **Tanjung Isuy ❺**, a Dayak village on **Danau Jempang** (Jempang Lake), sometimes called Green Lake due to massive amounts of a rampant water weed. Welcome rituals and dances are often performed for tourists here, the most popular destination in the Kaltim area. At **Mancong** village, a rebuilt *lamin*

(longhouse) with 24 doors – the only two-storey longhouse in Kalimantan – gives an idea of past splendours. There has been a communal house on this site for more than 300 years.

Danau Semayang, one of the two other lakes in the region, harbours freshwater dolphins and several bird species, such as lesser adjutants and egrets. Connected to Semayang is Danau Melintang, whose forested shores include leaf and unusual proboscis monkeys and at least 298 bird species. Siamese crocodiles are also found in this area.

Dayak country

Melak ❻, the district capital, is a busy little town, and is home to the Tanjung Dayaks. There are lodgings and a modest restaurant, and local handicrafts are for sale. Downriver from Melak is the **RASI Freshwater Dolphin Information Centre**, located at the Bolongan River Delta at Muara Pahu. The centre supplies information about spotting freshwater dolphins.

There is a local road system out of Melak with transport (jeeps or

The Mahakam River, a transport artery for eastern Kalimantan.

BELOW: Dayak child and longhouse.

Cruising the Mahakam River

The most popular way to reach Dayak country is by houseboat up the Mahakam River. Many tour operators offer packages, and they are more or less the same with a few basic differences. The first is the size of the boats: large ones for groups and smaller ones for individuals. Most are fully air-conditioned with Western toilets and hot-water showers, and they have two decks. Downstairs is a kitchen, where cruise meals are prepared, and a salon for dining and relaxing. Upstairs on the smaller boats is a sleeping room and a terrace, the larger boats have 10 cabins.

The main destinations of nearly all Mahakam cruises are Tenggarong, Muara Muntai, Danau Jempang, Tanjung Isuy, Mancong and the Melak area (Eheng and Kersik National Park). Nowadays houseboats cannot travel further upriver than Tering in mid-Mahakam.

One Samarinda tour operator, De'gigant Tours, includes Muara Pahu in its cruises due to the excellent wildlife-spotting on the Bolongan River, with freshwater dolphins as the highlight. *(See Travel Tips page ###.)* Stops at Dayak villages and watching life along the river are also attractions, as well as the changes of the river from vast and wide to narrow channels, while small hinterland villages are replaced by towns, and rather solitary travel becomes crowded with ships of all sizes getting ready to haul cargo through the Makassar Strait.

A bead panel from a Kayan baby carrier.

motorcycles) for visiting the **Kersik Luwai Nature Reserve**, 10km (6¼ miles) to the south. The 5,000-hectare (12,355-acre) reserve is ideal for trekking, sheltering 100-plus species of orchids, including the famous "black" variety, *Coelogyne pandurata*, which blooms April through December. Nearby Dayak villages Pepas Eheng and Ombau Asa have lived-in longhouses. Pepas Eheng can be reached in 1 hour by car from Melak. There's a beautiful waterfall, Jentur Gemuruh, at Ombau Asa. Ask around if you wish to witness a funeral ceremony in progress; the rituals feature the sacrifice of a water buffalo performed with spears.

Upriver from Melak is **Barong Tongkok**, where the nearest authentic longhouses are located. Beneath the T-shirts and shorts worn by most villagers in the area beat the hearts of followers of the traditional religion, Kaharingan (meaning "life"). Influenced by Hinduism, Kaharingan focuses on the supernatural world, and involves ritual practices such as shamanic curing. A nice place to overnight, Barong Tongkok has lodgings, shops and motorcycles to take visitors to other Dayak villages. Between Barong Tongkok and Tering is an ancient megalithic site reachable by trekking 40km (25 miles).

Six hours upstream from Melak, year-round river navigation stops at **Long Iram**, more than 400km (250 miles) from the coast. Some of the larger passenger boats make the Samarinda–Long Iram run in about 36 hours, have bunks and mattresses for a small surcharge, and kitchens serving simple meals. Several larger riverside towns offer basic accommodation, and their restaurants serve rice-based meals. Beyond Long Iram, there is only the hospitality of the Dayaks or government officials. Many of the Dayaks in this area, and also further upstream, belong to the Roman Catholic Church, which tolerates and even encourages some traditional rituals.

If the river level is not too low boats can reach **Long Bagun** in 4–6 hours from Long Iram. Several Dayak groups are settled along this stretch of the Mahakam, including

the Kenyah, who are known for their huge sculptures and paintings in communal buildings.

Beyond Long Bagun, logistics are a problem because a series of rapids choke off most river travel, with only an occasional powerful twin-outboard longboat roaring through. Chartering a boat may entail a long wait. It is a great experience, but unless you have plenty of time, the best way to reach the uppermost areas of the Mahakam is to fly from Samarinda to **Data Dawai**, a landing strip near Long Lunuk village. From Data Dawai, charter a boat to go upriver to Long Apari, the last village on the Mahakam.

The Apokayan region

Near the border with Sarawak, the forested highlands of the **Apokayan region ❼** are relatively untouched by time. The isolated Kenyah residents are some of the most traditional Dayaks in Kalimantan. Travel to this area is not for the casual tourist, but for adventurers it offers a glimpse of one of Indonesia's most remote regions.

Currently air travel is the only means of access, other than weeks of trekking. Be warned that flights are often delayed or cancelled, and it is advisable to avoid this scenario if time schedules are tight. On the bright side, roads to Apokayan are now under construction, and in time the area will be more accessible.

Located on the uppermost reaches of the Sungai Kayan, a dozen villages are strung out on either side of the landing strip at **Long Ampung**. Due to its isolation and difficulty in obtaining essentials, most Apokayan inhabitants have migrated to more accessible locations. Those who remain usually live in longhouses, and the prolific artwork of the Kenyah is still in evidence. There are good trails for trekking, and distances between villages can be covered in a few hours or by boat on small rivers.

Among the highlights is **Long Uro**, a 2-hour walk from Long Ampung, where there are Dayak carvings in front of the village and a cemetery. An easy hour's walk away is **Long Lindung Payau**, with ancient stone relics.

TIP

Travel in Kalimantan is expensive because, due to poor infrastructure, several forms of transport must be chartered to get from one place to another. Take plenty of time, money and patience, and prepare for the adventure of a lifetime.

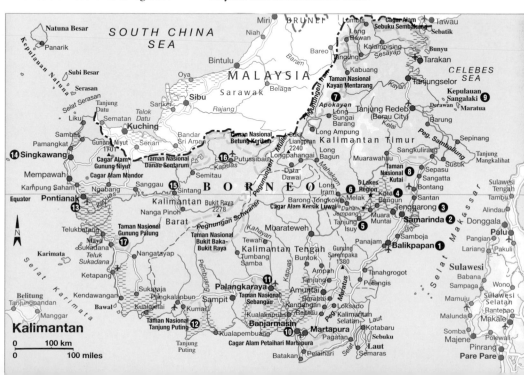

TIP

Changing foreign currency into Indonesian rupiah can be difficult in Kalimantan. Therefore, it's best to handle these financial matters before arriving.

The last human settlement on the Sungai Kenyah, **Long Sungai Barang**, is a demanding 4-hour walk over hills and through jungle. On a lake surrounded by mountains, Long Sungai Barang is an excellent place to rest for a few days and gather strength for the trip back to "civilisation".

Kayan Mentarang National Park

In the heart of the Apokayan region is **Kayan Mentarang National Park**, 13,605 sq km (5,253 sq miles) of untouched rainforest, the largest block of its kind on Borneo. The park protects a wealth of flora and fauna, many species of which are endemic. Much of the park is lowland and hill forest populated by *Dipterocarp* trees, while the remainder is cloud forest.

Wildlife, including pangolins, proboscis monkeys, slow lorises and tarsiers, three hornbill species and Bulwer's pheasants, may be difficult to spot due to hunting by the several thousand Dayak people who live here. The WWF has five regional field offices and a research station at Long Alango that can help with information.

Inside the park are the **Krayan Mountains**, near Long Bawan. Krayan forms a plateau 1,700 metres (5,570ft) above sea level where ancient, impenetrable cloud forest with dense undergrowth and sandstone valleys dominates. Further east, **Sebuku Sembakung** is a protected area where rarely seen pygmy elephants reside.

Access to the area is difficult due to its remote location, and trips are expensive. It is essential to make arrangements with a local tour operator. Small aircraft do fly into the area, but they require booking one month prior to departure.

Kutai National Park

On Kaltim's east coast, the principal attraction at **Kutai National Park** ❽ is orang-utans. There are another 60 mammal species and 300 species of birds here, including proboscis monkeys, clouded leopards, tarsiers and hornbills, as well as monitor lizards, crocodiles and pythons.

BELOW: clouded leopard.

To reach the park, travel from Balikpapan either by road (about 300km/106 miles, 6–7 hours), by bus to Sangatta village (1–1½ days), or fly from Balikpapan to **Bontang**, the site of a natural gas plant on the coast. At Bontang, report to the park office for a permit before beginning your journey. From Bontang, take a motorised canoe to riverside Sangatta for the best wildlife viewing. Park facilities are limited to two basic rooms. Nearby is excellent birdwatching, the only place in Kalimantan where eight hornbill species can be spotted.

Sangalaki archipelago

North of Bontang, **Tanjung Redeb** (Berau) is the entry point to the **Sangalaki archipelago** ❾, which is growing in popularity as a dive destination. The town itself is nothing to brag about, but there is a replica of the Gunung Tabur palace across the river, now a museum, which was damaged by Japanese bombs during World War II.

The archipelago consists of several islands, and the sea gardens here are spectacular, with several hundred species of reef fishes and corals, dugongs, lobsters and endangered sea turtles. Several varieties of dolphins are also prolific here, and humpback and other whales frequent deeper waters.

At **Derawan** there is a WWF-sponsored sea turtle sanctuary. To reach it, fly from Balikpapan into Tanjung Redep and go overland to Tanjung Batu (about 2 hours). From here it is 30 minutes by speedboat to Derawan, where there is a dive resort.

Palm-fringed **Nabucco** island, with white-sand beaches, also has a dive resort. A 30-minute boat ride takes you to Big Fish Country, inhabited by barracuda, sharks, rays, groupers and bumphead parrotfish. Water-skiing and wake-boarding are also available here. A resort on **Maratua** island offers water-skiing and diving.

Sangalaki island's main diving draw is manta rays, which feed on plankton north of the islands. The reefs here are 4–40 metres (13–130ft) deep and there is a shipwreck, attracting scorpionfish, jawfish, frogfish and ribbon eels. A local foundation that

The Derawan islands off the east coast are rich coral reefs, turtles and fish.

BELOW LEFT: proboscis monkey.
BELOW: orang-utan at Kutai.

TIP

Travelling solo in Kalimantan requires fluency in Bahasa Indonesia, the national language, because so few people here speak English. It is highly recommended to arrange expeditions through a licensed tour operator who can provide an English-speaking guide.

protects green turtles allows visits to the hatchery and to the beach to see turtles laying eggs at night.

Nearby is **Wehea**, a Dayak community that set up a small ecotourism business with money received in settlement from a logging company dispute. There is a lodge and campsite, and canoes are available for wildlife spotting and village visits. At least 600 orang-utans inhabit the forest here.

SOUTH KALIMANTAN

Kalimantan Selatan (Kalsel), often called the "Land of a Thousand Rivers", is a small, swampy province on the southeast coast. There are frequent flights to the capital city, **Banjarmasin** ⑩, interesting for its colourful floating markets and bustling canals. The majority of Kalsel's people are Banjarese. Largely Muslim, with a sprinkling of Protestants and Catholics, the Banjarese are strict adherents to their religion, with thousands making the pilgrimage to Mecca each year. Modest dress is required while travelling in the region.

Criss-crossed by rivers and tributaries, Banjarmasin teeters at the brink of sea level, dipping below that when the tide is in. Perched on the banks of the intersection of the Martapura and Barito rivers, floating houses line the waterways, water taxis ply the riverine "highways", and *jukung* (dugout canoes) replace streetside shops.

There are a couple of places (under the Yani Bridge and at Kuin Pertamina) to rent a *klotok* (motorised canoe) to tour the Sungai Barito. Start early to visit one of the charming floating markets. **Pasar Terapung**, 30 minutes from town, is the most famous and has been bobbing along the Sungai Kuin for 400 years. It gets under way before dawn and the activity peters out a couple of hours after sunrise. Female vendors glide through the canals in canoes selling fruit, vegetables and fish or light refreshments to housewives whose front (or back) doors open onto the water.

Closer to town, the Martapura or the Barito are good places to experience riverside life at its bustling

BELOW: a green turtle.

best. Take a *klotok* or a *bis air* (water bus) up a branch of the Sungai Martapura just beyond the Trisakti docks – which are for large ships – to see a modern lumber mill, where cranes lift enormous felled trees out of the river. A short way up the Martapura, open-fronted stores sell brightly coloured plastic items to water-borne shoppers. Housewives gossip and exchange pleasantries as they handle laundry chores, while naked children bathe.

A bit further on, graceful Bugis-style schooners *(pinisis)* are constructed from sturdy ironwood along the riverbank. Just beyond, there is an all-night fish market and a red-light district. Sunsets on the rivers can be bewitching.

The ultra-modern **Mesjid Raya Sabilal Muhtadin** (Grand Mosque) rests on land formerly occupied by a Dutch fortress and is one of Asia's largest places of worship. Its metallic flying saucer-shaped dome is clearly visible from the river. Inside, beautifully finished stone panels with copper inlaid inscriptions from the

Koran line an open space for praying. Doors and windows are decorated with reliefs taken from traditional Banjarese designs. As when visiting any mosque, dress modestly (women should have their knees, midriffs and arms covered), and remove footwear before entering.

Gemstones and gold panning

At **Cempaka**, about 45km (28 miles) from Banjarmasin, workers dig shafts 10–15 metres (33–49ft) deep, shored up with bamboo scaffolding and fitted with steps, where men wait downhole to pass baskets of soil, clay and gravel to the surface. The search is for gems, and they hope to duplicate the 1965 find of the 100-plus-carat Trisakti Diamond. Attentive women puddle the dirt, sift it through a screen, then pan it, watching with experienced eyes for even the smallest diamonds, sapphires, amethysts, garnets and gold. In nearby **Martapura**, the gems are cut and polished. Some stones purchased in this area have been appraised in the West at a higher value than that which was

Boats are the main form of transport in Kalimantan.

BELOW LEFT: rough and ready stilt houses on the canals of Banjarmasin. **BELOW:** a floating market near Banjamarsin.

paid. Shopping with reputable dealers is advised, paying particular attention to quality.

For another look at mining, 65km (40 miles) southeast of Banjarmasin in **Pelaihari** is a gold-mining region started by Chinese settlers at the request of the Banjar sultan six centuries ago.

Sungai Amandit

Itineraries on the Sungai Amandit range from half- to 2-day trips poling downriver by bamboo raft from Loksado through white-water rapids past scenic mountains. The river originates in Gunung Meratus, flows through Loksado and meets the Barito further downstream. Treks at Meratus can also be arranged.

The Amandit can be navigated in two segments: from Loksado to **Muara Hatip**, near Kandagan (Class 1–2.5 rapids), including a night's stay at a simple lodge at Muara Hatip. Stage two is from Muara Hatip to **Batu Laki**, where the rapids increase to Class 3 at the mouth of the Sungai Muara Harang.

Getting to **Loksado**, 40km (25 miles) east of Kandangan, and Dayak country, is not for the faint-hearted. Twenty-four kilometres (15 miles) east of Kandangan is Lumpangi, which can be reached by car in about 2 hours. From here, Loksado (Muara Hatib) can only be reached by trekking about 4 hours over mountains, through forests, and across hanging bamboo bridges.

There are about 20 longhouses around Loksado, but they do not have the long verandas seen in other parts of Kalimantan although the concept is the same. They can house 10 families or as many as 120 people. Aruh Ganal, a tribal ceremony, is held during the harvest season. The reward for the arduous journey is seeing nature at its best, with 500 bird species, 150 snake species, and many other reptiles, amphibians and several hundred varieties of freshwater fish.

Sungai Amandit can also be reached by car via Kandangan, continuing by local public transport in approximately 6 hours or by chartered car in about 4 hours.

Orang-utans: The Fight for Survival

At orang-utan rehabilitation centres across Kalimantan the race is on to protect the apes' habitat from deforestation and to educate the community

O rang-utans have grabbed world headlines not only for their endangered status but also because their numbers have dropped dramatically over the last few decades. With only two subspecies, one in Sumatra and the other in Borneo, scientists and activists have latched on to the cause with great vigour, drawing attention to Indonesia's poor forest-management practices in the process. In the past, poaching was the greatest threat due to the high prices their cute young faces and intelligence commanded from private individuals, zoos and theme parks. Today, the larger culprit, as for most protected species, is dwindling habitat caused by fires, logging and forest-clearing for commercial plantations.

In the wild, an infant orang-utan stays with its mother for the first seven to eight years of its life. During this time, it learns to distribute its weight while moving through the trees, to build a fresh sleeping nest each night, and to identify edible forest foods.

Indonesia's first rehabilitation centre was established in Sumatra in 1971, and since then several others have been created as surrounding release sites reached capacity. The best known of these centres is Camp Leakey in Tanjung Puting National Park, Central Kalimantan. The centres' jobs are to teach the orang-utans basic skills so they can survive in their jungle habitats, and to release them back into the wild.

Above: seeing orang-utans in the wild is a highlight of any trip to Indonesia.

Whether or not orang-utan rehabilitation programmes are successful is debatable, but through their work they attract global attention to the problem, thereby forcing state and local officials to take action. Nowadays, most centres focus, too, on protecting remaining forests and replanting which, in turn, helps to secure the futures of other species. Efforts also include community development: providing jobs and environmental education.

One especially noteworthy project is at Samboja Lestari, 40 minutes from Balikpapan, East Kalimantan, an area damaged by drilling, logging and forest fires. Operated by award-winning Borneo Orang-utan Survival Foundation (BOS), in addition to reforestation, rehabilitation and community involvement, they operate a Sun Bear Sanctuary.

BOS also manages several other forest and wildlife reserves in Kalimantan, a primate conservation education programme in Jakarta and a satellite monitoring centre that keeps track of deforestation, commercial plantations and illegal logging. Visitors are welcome at its Samboja Lodge – all revenues go to BOS conservation projects – which also offers trekking excursions into virgin rainforest in search of wild orang-utans, to orang-utan "islands" and into nearby Dayak tribal villages. There are also volunteer opportunities aplenty for those who want to be more deeply involved. For further information, visit www.sambojalodge.com.

CENTRAL AND WEST KALIMANTAN

Less visited than the eastern half, the west and
centre of Kalimantan is home to vast swathes
of jungle protected in several national parks, as
well as Dayak culture

Central and West Kalimantan are both huge provinces that are rarely visited by tourists due to poor infrastructure and lack of promotional effort by the tourist industry. Although Pontianak, the capital of West Kalimantan, is a busy trading centre, its equivalent in Central Kalimantan, Palangkaraya, isn't much more than a small government administrative town. For both provinces the major industries involve deforestation – logging, palm oil and mining – placing them under the watchful eye of a carbon emissions-oriented world.

For adventurous souls, the still-extensive rainforests that survive in both areas hold many attractions. Six national parks protect remaining habitats, with orang-utans bringing the most international attention. But there are many more endangered species to search for, such as sun bears, Malayan tapirs, clouded leopards, a wide variety of gibbons, proboscis monkeys, tarsiers and slow lorises. Crocodiles and false gharials swim the rivers that criss-cross both regions, while pythons sun themselves in trees and hornbills soar above forest canopies.

Dayak tribes, who have their own deep-seated cultural heritage, also attract tourists. The Ngaju of Central Kalimantan, for example, held so fiercely to their religion, *Kaharingan*, that they fought the Indonesian government and won the right to have it acknowledged as one of the country's officially recognised faiths. So strong is the Dayak influence in Central Kalimantan that the province also recognises their traditional laws. In West Kalimantan, many Dayak tribes live in the upper reaches of the Kapuas River and deep within the isolated national parks.

Main attractions

TANJUNG PUTING NATIONAL PARK
PONTIANAK
DAYAK TRIBES
REMOTE NATIONAL PARKS

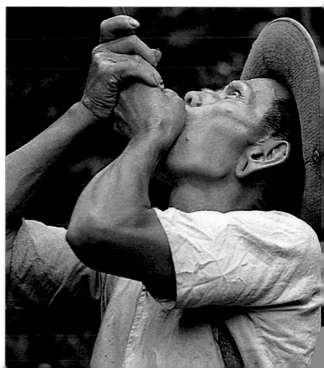

LEFT: Dayak child tucked into a carrier adorned with animal teeth. **RIGHT:** hunting by blowpipe.

Young orang-utan at Camp Leakey.

BELOW: forest at Tumbang Samba.

CENTRAL KALIMANTAN

Kalimantan Tengah (Central Kalimantan), or Kalteng, is the Dayak province par excellence. For centuries dominated by the Muslim Banjarmasin, the local Dayak fought a short guerrilla conflict to obtain separate provincial status, which was granted to them by former president Sukarno in 1957. The Ngaju Dayak predominate among the province's several groups. Many were converted to the Protestant faith and became aware of their cultural identity thanks to German missionaries in the late 19th century.

Palangkaraya

The capital of Kalteng, **Palangkaraya** ⑪, has a population of around 100,000. Most of the commercial and business activities are concentrated in the Pahandut district, where a village once existed on the Sungai Kahayan before the place was selected as the provincial capital.

There are two docks on the river: Rambang, the lower one, serves boats heading downriver. Flamboyant is for upstream passengers. While in Palangkaraya, see Dayak artefacts at **Museum Negeri Probinsi Kalimantan Tengeh Balanga** (Museum Balanga; Tue–Thur 8am–1pm, Fri 8–10am, Sat–Sun 8am–noon; free). It is located near the Pasar Kahayan market at the 2.5km mark, just off the paved road running parallel to the river.

Dayak country is found up the Sungai Kahayan. There are daily passenger boats heading upriver as far as **Tewah**. Speedboats that allow stops along the way can also be chartered. From Tewah, where regular river traffic usually stops, hire a motorised canoe to **Tumbang Mire** and beyond, to the traditional Ot Danum Dayak land with longhouses and funerary structures. Travel here depends essentially on water levels. Try to reach Tumbang Korik, on a tributary, or **Tumbang Maharoi**, the last village on the river.

Alternatively, let a tour operator do all the logistical work, something which is difficult without a basic knowledge of the Indonesian language. Otherwise, from Palangkaraya you can arrange boats on the Katigan (Rangkan) River for two full days, camping or staying

overnight in village homes in **Tumbang Samba** and **Penda Tangaring**. It is a 3-hour hike from Penda Tangaring to a Dayak longhouse built in 1870 by a member of the Kahayan Dayak tribe. In front of the longhouse is a mausoleum where the bones of ancestors were placed following the customary *tiwah* funerary ceremony. *Sepundu* poles, carved to represent humans, were used in days gone by to tie up sacrificial animals (and slaves) awaiting their fate.

The Borneo Orang-utan Survival Foundation has a rehabilitation centre at Nyaru Menteng, 28km (17½ miles) north of Palangkaraya, which can only be visited with a permit acquired in advance. Visitors are not allowed to come in close contact with the orangutans, but the information centre is open to the public on Sundays, and many local people enjoy strolling through the forest.

South of Palangkaraya, **Sebanggau National Park** is centred on a river by the same name, which is black from decaying plant material. The park is an important research area for its large population of orang-utans and agile gibbons, but it is difficult to reach with virtually no infrastructure to facilitate tourism.

Tanjung Puting National Park

Orang-utan-watching in **Tanjung Puting National Park ⑫** is the province's major attraction. The starting point is **Pangkalanbun**, which is accessible by air. Scheduled arrivals and departures ply routes to and from Pontianak, Ketapang, Banjarmasin, Jakarta, Semarang and Surabaya.

Once in Pangkalanbun, it is necessary to obtain an entry permit at the park office. From there hire a taxi for the 20-minute drive to **Kumai**, a riverside village that is the entry point to the park, a Unesco Biosphere Reserve. At the harbour, either hire a *klotok* (local motorised boat) or a speedboat to go upriver. While speedboats are faster, the noise they generate may nullify whatever chances there are for birdwatching or quiet enjoyment of the *nipah* and mangrove ecosystems along the muddy jungle river.

There is one lodge and a homestay on the river, both with basic amenities

There is a longhouse at Tumbang Anoi that was the site of a conference of all Kalimantan's Dayak tribes called by the Dutch over 125 years ago. During this meeting a treaty was signed which ended the head-hunting commonly practised in those days. The longhouse has an interesting collection of sandung funerary posts.

BELOW: visitor notice at Camp Leakey.

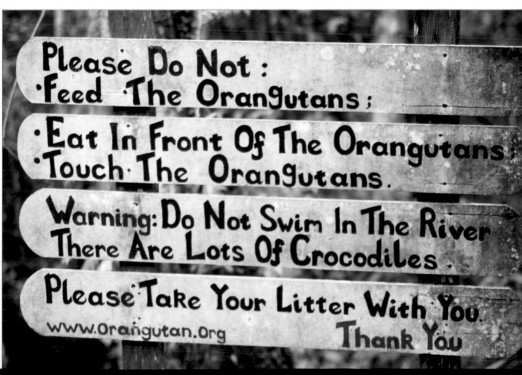

Klotok boat (floating hotel) along the river at Tanjung Puting National Park

BELOW: kids in Pontianak.

and food service, or serious adventurers can elect to sleep aboard the *klotok*. If choosing the latter, buy supplies in Kumai (include enough for a two-man boat crew), and one of the crew will prepare simple meals.

Friends of the National Parks Foundation (FNPF) runs a small guest house at the Tanjung Harapan post and can also arrange upriver expeditions. All money received helps support FNPF's conservation and village projects.

The highlight of the Tanjung Puting National Park experience is the orangutan feeding sessions (check times upon arrival) at one of the three park outposts. The first, **Tanjung Harapan** – directly opposite the Sekonyer River Ecolodge – cares for orphaned infants and new arrivals and has a visitor information centre. By far the most famous of the three, **Camp Leakey** can be somewhat of a circus during high season (June–August), with visitors who are less conservation-oriented clamouring to walk down jungle paths to see the red apes in action. Older orangutans, sometimes with their offspring, can be found at **Pondok Tanggui**.

During the feeding sessions at Camp Leakey and Pondok Tanggui, orangutans that hover near the stations are offered bananas and milk to supplement seasonal lack of food in the forest. Allowing tourists the experience achieves an additional benefit: raising awareness of the plight of orang-utans and the shrinking forests. It is a joy to sit quietly and watch as semi-habituated orang-utans, lumbering hand over heavy hand through the trees, arrive at the feeding platforms. Their gregarious antics can be amusing.

Best wildlife viewing

The best wildlife viewing is possible from the river. At sunrise, proboscis monkeys begin their day's foraging. Occasionally, one will belly-flop into the river, his lightly webbed toes enabling him to swim against the currents. During these times, the birds are particularly active. Azure-hued kingfishers, greater coucals and three species of hornbills are among the 220 species recorded in the park. Along the riverbanks, watch for mudskippers and archerfish, pythons sunning themselves

on branches, and estuarine crocodiles. In the late afternoon, the groups of proboscis monkeys, one male and his female harem per tree, settle in for the night and are easy to spot, with their long straight tails hanging down from their branch roosts. For a sublime jungle river experience, ask the boatman to stop the engine for a while to allow the boat to drift quietly. Sunsets can be spectacular.

WEST KALIMANTAN

Kalimantan Barat (West Kalimantan), or Kalbar, covers another huge area, enveloping essentially the Sungai Kapuas Basin. In the 1600s, diamond fields attracted the attention of the Dutch, and these were quickly depleted. In the 1700s, the sultan of Sambas imported Chinese coolies to work alluvial gold deposits, which continued until the beginning of the 19th century. The 18th century also saw Pontianak established as the resistance headquarters for Dutch efforts to stave off advances from Englishman James Brooke, the "White Raja", who ruled the neighbouring territory now known as Sarawak.

Dominated by the Kapuas, Indonesia's longest river, Kalbar's transport, communications and economy revolve around its waterways.

The provincial capital, **Pontianak** ⑬, lies near the sea at the junction of branches of the Kapuas and Landak rivers, their bridges giving views of riverborne markets, floating houses and a working port. Pontianak is an unusual name. Taken from the Malay "*Perempuan Mati Beranak*", it means a female vampire who died during childbirth. Believed to haunt the town, precautions are taken to prevent her and her kind from rising and becoming ghosts.

While the city's **Museum Negeri** (State Museum; Tue–Sun 8am–noon; charge), housing prehistoric and historic artefacts as well as ceramics, is worth a visit if there is time, the old wooden **Keraton Kadriah** or Istana Qadriah (Sultan's Palace) on the far side of the Kapuas from downtown, is excellent and a must-see. The main entrance to the palace is in the shape of a Portuguese gate. The *istana* belongs to the descendants of Syarif

Neighbouring Sarawak was the base of the "White Raja", James Brooke.

BELOW: Siam crocodiles

Camp Leakey was established by Birute Galdikas in 1971 for her research into orang-utan behaviour. A disciple of Louis Leakey, whose life's work was to establish a link between humans and apes, Galdikas was the only scientist among his protégés, who included Jane Goodall and Dian Fossey. For 20 years Galdikas continued her research here, and although she no longer works in the camp, her presence brought it international renown.

BELOW: tarsiers are nocturnal primates found in the depths of the Borneo jungle.

Abdul Rahman, an Arab rover who founded the city in the late 18th century with Dutch backing.

Located bang on the equator, the coastal road heading north 3km (2 miles) from Pontianak towards the Pinyuh river passes a strange-looking monument called **Tugu Khatulistiwa** (Equator Monument). Having become somewhat symbolic of Pontianak, miniatures of the monument are available in local shops. About 120km (75 miles) northwest of Pontianak on the road to Singkawang is **Kampung Saham**, a Kendayan longhouse settlement with a beauty all its own. At **Mempawah** is the **Amantubillah Palace**, built in 1780, and the **Juang Mandor Cemetery** commemorating the 21,000 people killed in Japanese skirmishes and buried in mass graves.

Just outside **Singkawang** ⑭ are a couple of huge ceramic kilns turning out vases and jars. The large Chinese population in this area descended from the miners who arrived here to work during the gold rush at the beginning of the 19th century. There are several striking Buddhist temples in the area.

Near Singkawang, **Pasir Panjang** beach is ideal for swimming. Also in the vicinity, the **Gunung Poteng** hill resort is a great place for nature-lovers with its cool, fresh air. Raya Pasi is home to a variety of flora and fauna, including the parasitic Rafflesia, the largest flower in the world. Singkawang is also near the Lo Fat Fun, Niyut and Prinsen nature reserves.

North of Pontianak (5 hours by car) is **Sambas**, a former sultanate and pirate's lair. There is not a lot to see in Sambas, and the town is a centre for the production of *kaim sambas*, a fine textile interwoven with gold and silver threads. Similar to the Malay *songket* and those from Palembang (Sumatra), the cloth is sold at a much lower price by the weavers in their homes than in Pontianak shops.

The **Istana Sambas**, a palace remnant of the former kingdom, is still in good condition and houses many antiques. Adjacent to the palace is a mosque. Both are similar to the ones in Pontianak, though not as grand.

Deep into Dayak land

For trips inland to Dayak country, riverboats are the generally accepted mode of transport, but facilities are geared for local travellers, and it takes 2–3 days to reach Sintang and five to six days to Putussibau. Riverboats depart from downtown Pontianak. There are now regional flights into both towns.

East of Pontianak, on the way to Sintang is the forested area around **Sanggau**, good for trekking. There are basic overnight facilities in Sanggau.

Sintang ⑮, the home of some of West Kalimantan's most traditional Dayak groups, is situated in the middle portion of the Kapuas Basin. It can be reached by road (12 hours by bus), small plane (about 45 minutes via a small Trigana aircraft) or boat (2 days by houseboat) up the Sungai Kapuas from Pontianak. There is a small museum in Sintang that is worth a visit, and it is possible to visit some of the area's longhouses.

Nearby, **Gunung Kelam** (Dark Mountain) looms over the countryside. This superb, sheer-walled rock is a challenge to even the best of climbers. For traditional Dayak country, head up the Sungai Melawi, which flows into the Kapuas at Sintang. Take either the Sungai Kayan, a tributary of the Melawi close to Sintang, or else go up the main stream of the Melawi, past **Nanga Pinoh** and to Gunung Schwaner. In the far upriver villages, there are carved funerary structures.

Putussibau ⓰, the last town in West Kalimantan on the Sungai Kapuas, can be reached by plane, boat, or via bus from Sintang (about 6 hours) on a good road. From here, visit traditional Kayan villages on the Sungai Mendalam or the Maloh longhouses a short way upstream on the Kapuas. Further inland, in Gunung Muller, most Dayak have been proselytised by American fundamentalist missionaries who frown on just about all aspects of traditional life. For the adventurous, it is possible to make the week-long trek from upper Kapuas across Kalimantan to upper Mahakam.

Putussibau near the Sarawak border, in addition to mammals and birds, the park protects at least 120 fish species, including Asian bony tongue and clown loach, as well as estuarine and Siamese crocodiles and false gharials.

Betung Kerihun National Park, north of Putussibau, is also near the Malaysian border and contains both lowland and montane rainforests harbouring orang-utans, Muller's Bornean gibbons, slow lorises and tarsiers. Smelly Rafflesia also grow here. Many outdoor experiences await the adventurous in this park: climbing Gunungs Lawit and Kerihun, exploring ancient caves and shooting class IV and V rapids.

South of Pontianak is **Sukadana**, gateway to **Gunung Palung National Park ⓱**. There are homestays at Buntok and Lubak Baji. The park is a vital conservation area because of its diversity of habitats, from mangroves and swamp forests to montane forest. Thought to be the world's largest population, orang-utans are the flagship species here, but there are also sun bears, red-leaf monkeys, crocodiles and cobras.

A Kenyah Dayak ceremony, Pampang

Little-visited national parks

There are several obscure conservation areas in West Kalimantan. Travel to these regions on a budget via public transport is arduous and time-consuming, and the alternative – chartered vehicles and boats – is expensive. For determined adventurers, though, the rewards are considerable.

On the border of East and Central Kalimantan, **Bukit Baka-Bukit Raya** contains a section of the Schwaner Mountains. Bukit Raya (2,278 metres/7,474ft) is its highest point and also the habitat of sun bears, clouded leopards, gibbons, slow lorises and proboscis monkeys.

From Putussibau it is possible to visit two other parks. A Ramsar protected wetlands site, **Danau Sentarum National Park**'s importance is its seasonal lakes, freshwater swamp forest and peat swamp forest. Lying west of

The Dayaks of Kalimantan

The term "Dayak" is an amorphous one. Although its origin is unclear, "Dayak" distinguishes the 200 or more ethnic groups living in the interior of Kalimantan from the coastal-dwelling Malays. While Malays make their living through trade, sea fishing and farming settled areas, the Dayak prefer to fish the rivers, hunt and gather forest produce.

The Dayak were romanticised in the past – and with good reason. They were noted head-hunting jungle warriors, lived in massive longhouses and practised strange rituals. One of the more novel practices of Dayak men was the *palung*, the practice of inserting objects into the foreskin of the penis as sexual enhancers. One British explorer wrote of this practice in the 19th century: "One lively range of objects can be so employed – from pigs' bristles and bamboo shavings to pieces of metal, seeds and beads . . ."

While the *palung* – mostly used by the Kenyah and Kayan – never hurt a man's chances with women, there was, however, the bride price to come up with. Back in the old days, no suitor needed to apply to marry the chief's daughter unless he could produce several freshly severed heads. These heads were believed to be essential for the spiritual and material welfare of the village. Thankfully, for most, head-hunting is now outlawed.

SULAWESI

This strangely shaped island with unusual jagged contours contains an astonishing variety of life within its jungles and offshore reefs, as well as fascinating indigenous cultures

t is little wonder that nature-lovers regard Sulawesi as paradise on earth, as its terrestrial fauna is a mosaic of Asian and Australian animals that has evolved into new species found nowhere else on the planet. The mountainous regions of the central highlands are separated by deep gorges and fast-flowing rivers, and are dotted with highland lakes. In the lush rainforests – such as in Lore Lindu National Park – live an astonishing array of mostly endemic fauna, including babirusa pig-deer, anoa dwarf buffalo, eccentric maleo birds, saucer-eyed tarsiers and scores of fabulous butterflies. A Neolithic settlement, cave stencils, megaliths, sarcophagi and other artefacts have also been found here.

The waters surrounding the island are equally compelling. Teeming with an incredible abundance of marine life, rich coral reefs, underwater valleys and vertical drop-offs, coupled with crystal-clear waters and white-sand beaches, they really are a paradise for divers and snorkellers. Long known to the international diving community is Bunaken Marine National Park on the far northeastern tip of the island. Further northeast, more islands are being developed for marine tourism. Together with Wakatobi Marine National Park – located in the Coral Triangle in the southeastern quadrant – they may soon replace Bunaken in popularity. The Togian Islands Marine National Park between the northern "arms" of the islands is also attracting increasing attention, as is the Taka Bone Rate National Park off the southwest coast.

The population of nearly 17.5 million is also diverse, made up of peoples who speak more than 40 languages. Sulawesi, meaning Island (sula) of Iron (wesi), is aptly named for its rich deposits of nickel-iron, copper and gold. Its best-known tribes are the coastal Bugis, Indonesia's primary shipbuilders and seafarers, and the Torajans whose arc-roofed houses and effigy-guarded burial caves decorate breathtakingly scenic valleys in the southwestern part of the island. But there are also the outspoken Makassarese of the area surrounding the capital city and the Minahasan in the northeast, whose favourite foods include rats and bats.

PRECEDING PAGES: evening light in a South Sulawesi village. **LEFT:** effigies at a Torajan grave. **ABOVE LEFT:** rubber plantation. **ABOVE RIGHT:** Torajan festival.

WEIRD WILDLIFE

Thanks to its diverse ecological zones, Indonesia has a range of fauna and marine life that is quite unlike anything else seen on the planet

The Indonesian islands have intrigued naturalists for hundreds of years because of their enormous number of endemic species and incredible range of animals of both Asian and Australian origin. To the west of the Wallace Line biological divide *(see page 267)* is Sundaland – Sumatra, Java, Bali and Kalimantan – where tapirs and sun bears dwell among Asian rhinos, tigers, elephants and orang-utans. To the east is Papua, home to Australasian species such as tree kangaroos, wallabies, echidnas and large, flightless cassowaries. Sulawesi and the islands of Maluku and Nusa Tenggara have a unique mixture of both Asian and Australasian species.

Jewels of land and sea

Due to the islands' separation from any mainland for 200 million years, an unusually large number of endemics have evolved here. More than 125 of Wallacea's 220-plus mammal species are found nowhere else in the world. Sulawesi is home to the anoa (dwarf buffalo), babirusa (pig-deer), at least five species of tiny nocturnal tarsiers, and the odd mound-building maleo bird. The most famous species is the Komodo dragon *(see page 281)* of Nusa Tenggara, but the Indonesian islands also house nearly 50 frog species of which 30 are native to this region.

The marine life is equally diverse. Warm, clean, plankton-rich seas are an ideal environment for some of the most biologically diverse coral reefs in the world, where a kaleidoscope of fish species thrive and new discoveries are not unusual.

ABOVE: Alfred Russel Wallace originally came to the Indonesian archipelago in search of magnificent birds of paradise, which were first seen in Europe adorning ladies' hats. Many of the 26 species found in Papua, such as the male lesser bird of paradise *(Paradisa minor)* pictured here, perform spectacular displays to attract mates

BELOW: the dwarf cuscus is the smaller of the two Sulawesi species. Its relative, the bear cuscus, is twice its size. In Papua, the spotted cuscus is prevalent and ranges to northern Australia. All are marsupials and are the largest of the world's possums.

LEFT: the babirusa is a unique species. Endemic to Sulawesi, its name translates as "pig-deer", although there is no genetic link to deer and the animal is only distantly related to pigs.

THE OLDEST FISH IN THE WORLD

In 1998, shark net fishermen from Manado Tua, North Sulawesi, shocked the scientific world with their catch of a living coelacanth *(pictured above)*. This extremely rare and endangered fish was assumed extinct for 70 million years until a fishing trawler accidentally dragged one up in South Africa in 1938. Since then, a small population of the prehistoric fish, dating back 400 million years, was thought to exist only as an isolated group off eastern Africa.

Coelacanths inhabit underwater lava caves at a depth of between 20 and 600 metres (70–2,000ft) during the day, emerging to drift-hunt during the night. Their fleshy, lobed fins resemble legs, which places them at the base of four-legged animal evolution.

The Manado Tua coelacanth, hailed as a new species, *Latimeria menadoensis*, was found an amazing 10,000km (6,200 miles) from its African counterparts. The specimen is preserved in the Museum Zoologicum Bogoriense in Cibinong, Java.

LOW: in prehistoric times, orang-utans ranged throughout Asia n China to Java. Nowadays, however the are found only in parts 3orneo and Sumatra.

RIGHT: the warty frogfish is one of nine frogfish species found in the Lembah Strait north of Sulawesi. Although frogfish have been recorded throughout the Indo-Pacific region, Indonesia has the highest concentration. Pictured here are an orange adult and juvenile.

SOUTH SULAWESI AND TANA TORAJA

Two groups with rich cultural traditions co-exist in this beautiful corner of Indonesia: the once-powerful seafaring Buginese with their proud history, and the highland Torajans with their elaborate death rituals

Ujung Pandang

Striking landscapes and remarkable people are the hallmarks of **Sulawesi Selatan** (South Sulawesi). Makassar, its capital, is the largest city in eastern Indonesia and is a vibrant conglomerate of government offices, businesses and trade.

The coastal and lowland regions of South Sulawesi are inhabited mainly by the proud and outspoken Buginese. These Mongolian descendants are believed to have settled along these shores well over 1,000 years ago and have since had one of the more colourful histories of any Indonesian people. Also on the coasts are the Mandarese, renowned throughout the archipelago for their shipbuilding and expert sailing skills.

It is Tana Toraja, however, that visitors come here to see. In the highlands at the northern end of the peninsula is a mountainous, landlocked region whose people retain ancient ways and take pride in their crescent-roofed homes. Toraja, as it's fondly called, is certainly the Shangri-La of South Sulawesi.

Bugis glory days

The Bugis have always been great seafarers and shipbuilders. During the Hindu period they returned from sojourns abroad – as far away as Madagascar and Australia – with foreign goods and treasures from the sea, and with new beliefs and practices as well. These influences

lasted for many centuries, elevating Bugis kingdoms to power between the 12th and 15th centuries. After 1500, trade relations with sultanates on Java's north coast were strong, eventually converting the Bugis to Islam.

Though later subdued and dominated by the Dutch, even in the 18th and 19th centuries Bugis groups continued to found new sultanates on the Malay peninsula and in the Riau archipelago. Today, there is hardly a bay or estuary without a Bugis settlement on it.

Main attractions

BENTENG ROTTERDAM, MAKASSAR
PELABUHAN PAOTERE, MAKASSAR
MUSEUM BALLALOMPOA, MAKASSAR
TANA BERU – PINISI-BUILDING
TANA TORAJA HIGHLANDS
RANTEPAO
TAKA BONE RATE NATIONAL PARK

LEFT: traditional Bugis house on stilts. **RIGHT:** boat-building at Bira.

Fishing at sunrise.

The Bugis courtly heritage is not well preserved. Cultural performances seem to be limited to displays of fire-breathing and *takraw* ball manoeuvres. Most tourists are wont to bypass the Bugis homelands en route to Toraja in the north, although there is much history and natural beauty in the south.

Makassar

Makassar ❶ is a big modern city of about 1.7 million people – the business centre for eastern Indonesia and the capital of South Sulawesi province. Following independence, the city was renamed Ujung Pandang (meaning Lookout Point). In 1999,

however, it reverted to its colonial name, Makassar, which had been coined by the Dutch after they conquered the medieval Gowa kingdom and established a fortified trading post there in 1667.

The city flourished as the port and trading centre for Gowa. The old fort (*benteng*) was one of the 11 Gowanese strongholds when it was first erected in 1545. The Dutch conquered and reconstructed it in 1667, renaming it **Benteng Rotterdam**. With its interior church and trading offices, it stands as an excellent example of 17th-century Dutch fortress architecture. The fort now houses

the **Museum Provincial Makassar** (Tue–Sun 8am–2pm; charge), with displays of old ceramics, manuscripts, coins, musical instruments and ethnic costumes. In the southwest corner of the fort is a dungeon where one of Indonesia's national heroes, Prince Diponegoro of Yogyakarta (1785–1855), was imprisoned for 27 years after defying both the Dutch and his own family by leading a series of popular uprisings in Central Java between 1825 and 1830. The **Tomb of Diponegoro** is located in the middle of town on a street which carries his name.

In the late afternoon, **Pelabuhan Paotere** in the northern part of Makassar makes a pleasant place to stroll and watch the activity aboard the many *pinisi* schooners. **Pantai Losari**, a sand-free seafront promenade and cruising strip, is a popular sunset gathering place. Also on Pantai Losari is Trans Studio Theme Park, a 3-hectare (7½-acre) indoor recreational centre with entertainment, safaris and rides inspired by children's programming on the owners' two television stations. A nearby getaway, **Samalona** island, offers good snorkelling and sandy beaches.

Just south of Makassar lies **Sungguminasa**, the former capital of the Tallo sultanate. Today, the wooden palace houses the **Museum Ballalompoa** and contains many weapons, royal costumes and a gem-studded gold crown weighing 15.4kg (34lbs) that may be viewed on request. Near Sungguminassa are tombs of the Gowa kings, of whom Sultan Hasanuddin (1629–70) is the most famous for his brave leadership in the struggle against the Dutch. Just outside the cemetery, a small fenced-off plot holds **Batu Tomanurung**, the stone upon which the kings of Gowa were once crowned. On a side road nearby lies the tomb of Arung Palakka, the king of Bone and arch-enemy of Sultan Hasanuddin.

Southern round-trip

To escape the lowland heat of Makassar, travel 70km (45 miles) to **Malino ❷**, lying on the slopes of Gunung Bawakaraeng, about 760 metres (2,500ft) above sea level. This cool, quiet pine-forest resort area is noted for its *markisa* (passion fruit) orchards. The seedy fruit produces a refreshing drink. The lovely **Takapala Waterfall** is an easy 6km (4-mile) walk south of the town.

A road from Malino leads east to **Sinjai** on the southern coast of the peninsula. From there, a coastal road – breathtaking for its steep precipices and spectacular views – leads east to **Tana Beru ❸**, heart of the Bugis shipbuilding industry. Round-bellied *pinisi* (schooners) are still fashioned here with simple hand tools and without the use of metal or nails. Teak cords are hewn into planks, then fastened with wooden pegs according to an ancient design retained in the communal memory. Sails were once made of plaited banana and pineapple fibres, then later of woven cotton and silk. Rituals are employed in all phases of

Pare Pare is the hometown of Indonesia's third president, Bacharuddin Jusuf Habibie, who took over the reins after Suharto's ousting. Habibie served a disastrous short term from 1998–9.

BELOW: the 17th-century Dutch fortress at Benteng Rotterdam.

The tympanum-like triangles over the doorways of Bugis homes are composed of three, five, seven or nine parts, indicating the social rank of the inhabitants. Nine parts are reserved for royalty.

BELOW: playing on Pantai Bira beach.

construction, from the selection of the tree to the final launching, to ensure that the craft will be seaworthy. The finished 200-tonne *pinisi* or a lighter vessel called *bago* appear to be unstable until fully loaded with copra or timber – then they are among the best cargo ships afloat today.

Further down the southeast tip of the peninsula lies **Bira**, a relaxed white-sand beach resort area featuring caves, reefs for snorkelling and diving, boat-building and traditional weaving crafts. Turning westwards along the southern **Bulukumba Coast**, the road returns to Makassar through small towns like Bantaeng, Jeneponto and Takalar, names found in a Chinese text six centuries ago.

Ancient caves

A mountainous 180km (110-mile) road heads northeast from Makassar towards Watampone, the former capital and port city of the Bugis kingdom Bone. En route, it passes a series of gushing waterfalls at **Bantimurung**. **Bantimurung-Bulusaraung National Park** encompasses the second-largest

karst mountain range in the world. Out of the 250 butterfly species Alfred Russel Wallace discovered in the valleys near waterfalls here, only about 100 remain. Nearby are **Gua Leang-Leang** caves, which contain 5,000-year-old red-henna hand stencils. To the east is the brisk mountain resort **Camba**, where the views are superb and there are many mysterious caves.

The once-bustling port town of **Watampone ➍** (or Bone) is quiet now, but retains its former dignity. The **Museum Lapawawoi** houses the regalia of the kings of Bone, as well as a copy of the 1667 Treaty of Bonggaya that ended the Dutch economic dominance over the area; both may be seen on request. Watampone's harbour is still a centre for inter-island shipping, and a ferry leaves here for Kolaka in Southeast Sulawesi. Boat-building and fishing are the principal industries, although beautiful cotton and silk *sarong*s are still woven here, as well as unusual orchid-fibre plaiting. South Sulawesi's largest cave system, **Gua Mampu**, is about 30km (20 miles) away. Stalactites and stalagmites here

Taka Bone Rate National Park

Another of Sulawesi's difficult-to-reach locations, Taka Bone Rate National Park appears to be in the middle of nowhere in the Flores Sea, some 30km (20 miles) offshore from the southwest coast. The third-largest atoll in the world, Takabonerate (a Bugis name meaning "coral piled up on sand") is a proposed Unesco World Heritage Site. The islands are surrounded by table reefs, making the marine park a paradise for snorkellers and divers, who can spot four species of endangered sea turtles, jackfish, wrasse, eels, groupers and giant clams. Underwater visibility is usually excellent, while above water the bird life is also of interest. The problem is getting there. The journey takes at least 14 hours from Makassar on a series of bus and boat rides, and the only accommodation on the islands is in villagers' homes.

resemble animals and humans, and give rise to local legends.

On the mountain plateau northwest of Watampone, nestled on the shores of Danau Tempe, lies **Sengkang**, seat of another feudal kingdom of old. It is best known today for its hand-loomed silk weavings. South of Sengkang in the hill country is the town's twin-court centre, **Watangsoppeng**.

From Watangsoppeng, a road leads northwest to **Pare Pare** on the coast. This was once the site of the powerful Supa trading kingdom that connected Makassar to the highlands and the ports of the Mandar kingdom. In the days of *pinisi* and Portuguese galleons, Pare Pare's deep natural harbour was favoured over Makassar's. Further to the north and west, the Mandar kingdom once stretched all along the coast of what is now Mandar Bay. The Mandarese are distinct from the Bugis, yet, as great sailors, are often confused with them. Their shipbuilding tradition still rivals that of their southern neighbours and is centred on **Balangnipa**, between Polewali and Majene. On the eastern coast lies the Bugis Luwu kingdom, its harbour, **Palopo**, deemed the oldest of all Bugis kingdoms, and today, an important gateway to South Sulawesi.

Highland Toraja tribes

Tucked amid the rugged peaks and fertile plateaus of inland South Sulawesi live many isolated tribes known collectively as the Torajan. According to traditional accounts, the Torajan left Pongko island, located to the southwest, some 25 generations ago and crossed the ocean in canoes *(lembang)*. Arriving in Sulawesi, they made their way up the Sungai Sa'dan, which now cuts diagonally across **Tana Toraja ⑤**, and settled on its banks.

The Torajan remained here growing rice and vegetables. Today, the region is particularly known for its fine coffee. Traders and missionaries exerted a certain degree of influence,

but for the most part Torajan animistic customs and social structures endure as before.

The Torajan traditionally live in small settlements perched on hilltops surrounded by stone walls. Several extended families inhabit a series of *tongkonan* houses in each village, which are arranged in a circle around an open field. In the middle stands a sacred stone or banyan tree used for ritual offerings. Granaries *(lumbung)* face the dwellings. The roofs of *tongkonan* rise at both ends like the bow and stern of a boat; ritual chants compare these dwellings to the vessels that carried their ancestors here. House panels are exquisitely carved with symbolic geometric and animal motifs executed in the sacred colours of white, red, yellow and black. The roof represents the heavens, and the house – representing the universe – is always oriented northeast to southwest, the directions of the two ancestral realms according to Torajan cosmology.

In the early 20th century, Dutch missionaries penetrated the Tana Toraja highlands, and in 1905, many

TIP

International cruise liners frequently call at Makassar's Sukarno-Hatta harbour en route to Komodo and Bali.

BELOW: traditional houses in Lemo.

The Sulawesi coastline is longer than that of the entire continental United States, and any given location on the island is no more than 100km (60 miles) from the sea.

Torajan villages were brought under direct Dutch control. To facilitate their administration, they were ordered to move from their hilltop perches and settle in more accessible valleys and plateaus. Instead of stone walls, hedges now ring these villages.

The winding mountain road from Makassar to Tana Toraja, which even at local drivers' breakneck speeds takes a minimum of 7 hours, passes Pare Pare and inland Enrekang. From here, the road enters a land of steep terraced slopes, tall bamboo forests and high mountain peaks. Across the Sungai Sa'dan from Salubarani, there is a large boat-shaped arch, marking the entrance to Tana Toraja. The road continues through Bambapuang Valley and past the shapely Buntu Kabobong (Erotic Hills).

Some 18km (11 miles) past Makale lies **Rantepao ❻**, the centre of the Toraja tourist trade. In nearby *tongkonan* villages, Torajans practise weaving and woodcarving. Interspersing rice paddies are several cave tombs (*liang*) where rows of wooden effigies (*tau tau*) stare eerily from suspended balconies like sentries of their stony graves. The best-known gravesite is at **Londa**, about 2km (1.2 miles) off the main road connecting Makale with Rantepao. Here, the effigies are those of noblemen and other high-ranking community leaders. Similar tombs can be seen at **Lemo**, where the burial chambers are carved out of a sheer rock face. On a hillside behind **Ke'te**, coffins are guarded by life-sized statues.

Especially beautiful *tongkonan* grace **Palawa**, a village on a small hill about 9km (5.5 miles) from Rantepao. Other traditional villages are located north and east of Rantepao. A journey from Makale northeast to Sangalla is worth the effort, as older *tongkonan* houses here provide a more traditional atmosphere.

West Toraja

If time is abundant and legs are strong, the 120km (75-mile) hike north from Rantepao to Rongkong or the 80km (50-mile) trek west through the mountains to **Mamasa** introduces other facets of Toraja life.

Very few travellers visit Mamasa, also known as West Toraja. From Makassar it is a hard 10–12 hours, and the road up from the Mandar coast west of Pare Pare is mountainous and not well maintained. However, as it winds its way between and up river valleys, it is one of the most scenic, if rough, drives in all Sulawesi. Mamasa's spectacular villages rest on rugged tracks, but several are accessible with a jeep and a guide. From Polewali at Mandar Bay, it is a 98km (61-mile) journey, taking 4–5 hours via an equally bad road.

The best way to see Mamasa is on foot in order to capture the fabulous views en route of traditional houses, tombs and villages. Guided treks taking 3–4 days can be arranged with prior notice. If time is short, it is possible to trek to Bituang and go by jeep to Mamasa. This is the only place in Sulawesi where copper is worked and a dazzling array of jewellery with unique designs produced.

BELOW: distinctive Torajan *tongkonan* dwellings are a feature of the region.

Feasts for the Dead

In Torajan culture a death merits an enormous banquet, after which the body is laid to rest under the watchful eyes of life-sized effigies

The Torajan are perhaps best known for their elaborate funerary feasts, offered to ensure that souls of the dead will pass to the afterworld *(puya)* in a manner appropriate to their living status. Only when the rites have been performed, it is believed, will the ancestors bestow their blessings upon the living, thus maintaining the fragile balance between the various realms of the cosmos.

The week-long feasts require an enormous outlay of material wealth – kin groups save and work for many years to ensure a suitably elaborate funeral is held between July and September, following harvest. A person is considered dead only when his or her funeral feast has been held. Before that, the deceased is regarded as merely "sick", and the body is embalmed and kept in the southwest end of the *tongkonan*, where it is fed and visited as if still alive, for weeks, sometimes months.

When enough money has been saved, under the guidance of a *tomebalun* (death specialist), the ceremonies begin. Family members and friends return to the village from cities where they have gone to work bringing gifts of buffaloes, pigs, betel nut, fruit, cigarettes and *tuak* (palm wine). The body is placed in a tongkonan-shaped coffin, then placed on an open platform in the village ceremonial field *(rante)*.

Feasting, chanting and dancing continue all night, with buffalo fights and boxing matches during the day. The rites culminate in the slaughter of as many as 100 buffalo and pigs, depending on the wealth and status of the deceased. The blood is collected, cooked with the meat, and distributed among the guests. On the last day of the feast, the coffin is lowered from the platform and carried to the village gravesite. From here, the soul of the deceased ascends to the realm of the deified ancestors *(deata)*.

Terrifying tau tau

Each village has its own burial site, some in cliff faces, others carved out of large rocks scattered in verdant rice fields. Only the very wealthy in certain villages are buried in caves carved into the cliff face where they are guarded by *tau tau* – life-sized wooden effigies of the dead. The coffins of lesser members of the community are placed on overhanging rocks close to the burial caves; bones and skulls from decayed caskets litter the ground below.

As the *tau tau* are exposed to the elements, they become weatherbeaten and faded over time. Statues are repaired once every 25 years, and in a ceremony known as *ma'nene*, the clothing of the *tau tau* is replaced. Over the years, many burial sites have been plundered by grave robbers, as genuine *tau tau* effigies are highly prized by collectors in the West.

ABOVE & RIGHT: cliff burials and Tau Tau puppets, Londa, Tana Toraja.

SOUTHEAST AND CENTRAL SULAWESI

Travel is challenging in this land of remote tribes and great mountain ranges, but the rewards are unequalled: ancient megaliths, wild natural beauty, rare animals and outstanding diving

Sulawesi's out-of-the-way Central and Southeastern provinces have some of the lowest densities of people in all of Indonesia. They also have some very sizeable tracts of wilderness in their national parks and nature reserves, as well as some superb diving and snorkelling in their marine national parks. In addition to nature opportunities, Central Sulawesi also has some cultural and historical points of interest, such as the megaliths in the valleys of Lore Lindu National Park.

In the past, both provinces were largely ignored by travellers due to transport challenges. However, with the growing popularity of diving and snorkelling in the Togian islands and at Wakatobi, access to these remote areas is improving.

CENTRAL SULAWESI

Central Sulawesi is the largest province in Sulawesi, with about 60 percent of its terrain swathed in rainforest. The majority of the province's 2.6 million people live along the coastlines, while the remainder inhabit rifts and valleys of the mountainous landscape. Extensive mountain ranges have proved formidable barriers to migration and many of the inland dwellers are still relatively isolated. Twelve ethnic groups and 24 languages are officially recognised.

Palu ❼, its capital, is a pleasant port town surrounded by grassy hills and located at a bottleneck of land between Tomini Bay and the Makassar Strait. A visit to the Museum Negeri Propinsi Sulawesi Tengah gives a preview of Indian-inspired silk *(kain Donggala)* woven by the indigenous Kaili people, as well as displays of arts and crafts, traditional bark cloth and megalith replicas from the valleys around Lore Lindu.

Main attractions

LORE LINDU NATIONAL PARK
NAPU, BESOA AND BADA VALLEY MEGALITHS
TOGIAN ISLANDS MARINE NATIONAL PARK
WAKATOBI MARINE NATIONAL PARK

LEFT: hornbill. **RIGHT:** Tonkean macaques at Lore Lindu National Park.

Tomini Bay offers superb diving, with great visibility and a rich variety of marine life.

Lore Lindu and Morawali

Arguably one of the country's most important biological refuges, **Lore Lindu National Park ❽**, a Unesco Biosphere Reserve, hosts incredibly diverse plant and animal life within its rugged geography. Seventy-seven bird species endemic to Sulawesi and eye-catching butterflies abound, and three of the island's strangest and most elusive mammals, *anoa* (dwarf buffalo), *babirusa* (pig-deer) and nocturnal Sulawesi palm civets, reside in the park. Patience and a bit of luck will reveal tarsiers, the Tonkean macaque, maleo fowls and cuscus.

More than 400 megalithic statues, estimated between 700 and 5,000 years old, dot Napu, Besoa and Bada valleys in Lore Lindu. The origin of these carvings is unknown, although they almost certainly related to ancestor worship. While the smaller stones are just 50cm (20ins) high, the decidedly phallic-inspired stone images of humans are up to 4 metres (13ft) high.

Further along the eastern peninsula, the land becomes increasingly infertile and isolated, but no less captivating. The administrative centre, Poso, is the usual hub to **Morawali Nature Reserve ❾** and Kepulauan Togian, two infrequently visited but remarkable areas. Kolonodale, a tiny town on spectacular Teluk Towori, is the most convenient starting point into Morawali. Transport and guides can be arranged in Kolonodale to visit the Wana people, who still hunt wild boar and other Sulawesi fauna with poisoned-dart rattan pipes.

BELOW: tropical forest at Lore Lindu National Park.

Kepulauan Togian Marine National Park

Towards the north, the remote forest-capped **Togian Islands Marine National Park ❿** consists of 56 islands clustered in the huge, calm, azure Tomini Bay. Sheer limestone cliffs, secluded white-sand beaches, and wonderful snorkelling and diving can be found here. Species to spot are hawksbill and green turtles, coconut crabs and dugongs. The beautiful setting and relaxed pace often lull travellers into extending their stay to include trekking in the forests for many of Sulawesi's unique birds and mammals. Here, the once-nomadic sea gypsies, or Bajo people, live in stilt houses over the water. Una-una, a volcano island with spectacular coral reefs, violently erupted and blew off its cone in 1983, causing extensive damage but, fortunately, no human lives were lost.

SOUTHEAST SULAWESI

Southeast Sulawesi is a rugged province with impassable mountains to the north, savannah to the east and a chain of fragmented islands to the south. Although isolated from the rest of the island by land, air and sea links are quite good. The majority of the 2.2-million population lives in the south. The settlers include the Tolaki and Tomekongga people, the Buginese and Makassarese from

South Sulawesi, and government-sponsored transmigrants from Java and Bali.

The capital of Southeast Sulawesi is **Kendari** ⓫, a port town whose craftsmen are renowned for their intricate silver filigree work. Outside the town, fine beaches and snorkelling are located at Hari island. In nearby Morame, spectacular seven-tiered waterfalls canopied under lush foliage are wonderful to visit for a day of soaking and swimming. **Rawa Aopa National Park** ⓬, about 70km (44 miles) west of Kendari, has a number of ecological habitats to explore with the assistance of guides arranged by the Kendari tourist office. *Babirusa* and both species of *anoa* live in the park's sub-montane and coastal forests, and a paddle in a dugout along mangrove forests and peat swamps is a good way to catch sight of many of the 155 bird species, of which 37 are endemic.

Muna and Buton islands

On the larger islands south of the mainland, the area around Raha on Muna island attracts tourists who come to see the red-ochre cave depictions at Goa Mabolu, but the highlight is the incredible scenic beauty of **Napabale Lagoon**.

Although Muna is largely deforested, neighbouring **Buton** – Sulawesi's largest island and former seat of the powerful Wolio sultanate – is still cloaked in impenetrable virgin rainforest. The more accessible secondary rainforest in **Lambusango Nature Reserve** ⓭, about a 2-hour drive from Bau-Bau, offers a good chance to see macaques, tarsiers and hornbills. Operation Wallacea (www.opwall.com) has a research site here. Benteng Keraton in **Bau-Bau**, Buton's main settlement, was a fortress and palace protected by a 3km (2-mile) stone wall overlooking the Buton Strait. During the 17th-century Dutch era, Bau-Bau was an important stop between Makassar and

the Maluku Spice Islands to the east. There is good snorkelling and diving at Pantai Nirwana, 9km (5.5 miles) outside Bau-Bau.

Southeast Sulawesi's biggest attraction is **Wakatobi Marine National Park** ⓮, its name derived from the first two letters of its four biggest islands: Wangi-Wangi, Kaledupa, Tomia and Binongka. The park is significant for its position in the Coral Triangle containing a high biodiversity of corals and marine life, thus offering spectacular diving.

In addition to sea explorations, nearby there are Bajo villages where sea gypsies live in stilted houses. There is a Marine Biology Research Base on Hoga island near Kaledupa that is visited by top European and North American marine biologists and students every July and August, where Operation Wallacea also runs research and training expeditions.

Until recently the area was difficult to reach, but now Bau-Bau has an airport with regular flights from Makassar.

TIP

Sulawesi's distilled *tuak* liquor – stored in bamboo containers – can leave you with a nasty hangover, so go easy on it.

BELOW: coconut crab at Wakatobi.

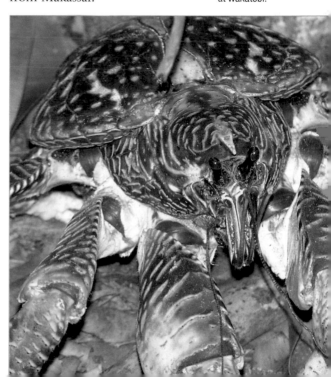

NORTH SULAWESI

Fabulous underwater scenery, the Minahasan highlands' primeval beauty and some of the planet's oddest creatures make their homes in volcanic North Sulawesi

BELOW: coconuts are a significant part of the local economy.

Something of an anomaly, Sulawesi Utara (North Sulawesi) is a fertile, snake-like volcanic peninsula outstretched in the middle of the vast Maluku Sea. World-class diving surrounds the province, and a menagerie of exotic wildlife resides in its national parks and reserves.

The full spectrum of diving activities ranges from magnificent coral gardens at Bunaken National Park and Bangka Strait to the underwater volcanoes at the Sangihe-Talaud islands and the unusual and rarely seen critters of Lembeh Strait. Land-based activities focus on rainforest hiking in Tangkoko-Dua Saudara Nature Reserve and Bogani Nani Wartabone National Park, along with volcano-climbing, river-rafting, treks to powerful waterfalls and even golf. Exploring the scenic Tomohon-Tondano highlands area rounds out the choices. The people are genuinely friendly and open.

Seaside Manado

Nearly 2.5 million people make their homes in North Sulawesi, about 10 percent of whom reside in **Manado** ⓯, the pleasant provincial capital. The city lies at the foot of the lovely mountainous Minahasa region, which is dotted with active volcanoes, highland lakes and hot-water springs. Coconut plantations stretch for miles along the coasts (18,000 tonnes of copra are produced in North Sulawesi every month) that teem with fish and coral. Inland there are bountiful clove and coffee plantations, terraced rice fields and vegetable and flower gardens.

Alfred Russel Wallace called Manado "one of the prettiest towns in the East", but the city has since lost its initial lustre and offers little in the way of urban attractions apart from the 19th-century **Ban Hin Kiong** Buddhist temple, the **Museum Negeri Propinsi Sulawesi Utara**, which displays ethnographic artefacts from Minahasa, and a 30-metre (98ft) statue of **Jesus Christ**, the world's fourth-largest of its kind. The real attractions, however, are the nearby mountains, coral reefs and rainforests.

Bunaken Marine National Park

Manado is an excellent staging point for diving and snorkelling trips to **Bunaken Marine National Park** ⑯, 15km (10 miles) offshore. The coral reefs teem with thousands of species of colourful tropical fish along steep drop-offs that plunge thousands of metres into the abyss. Sea turtles, sharks and pods of dolphins make their way around the park, and there is also a World War II-era wreck to explore.

Further to the north, the 70-odd islands in the **Sangihe-Talaud** chain offer white-sand beaches and equally spectacular diving. Dotted with volcanoes and unusual rock formations, some of the islands are over 1,500 metres (4,920ft) high and are densely covered by coconut palms.

Like most unspoiled areas, the islands are not easy to get to. Divers who are not deterred by the long journey and want to discover the unknown are rewarded with 60-metre (200ft) visibility and 100-year old gigantic sponges. Some of the other highlights include an underwater lava flow and Mahangetang, a submarine volcano that releases silver bubbles into the sea – an unforgettable sight.

A very good road network radiates from Manado. One interesting route runs 55km (35 miles) east to **Bitung** ⑰ on the eastern coast of the peninsula. Bitung is situated along **Lembeh Strait**, which is a divers' Mecca for unusual muck-dwelling creatures such as hairy frogfish and mimic octopus. Along the way, the road passes through Airmadidi (Boiling Water), and the main road continues east to the coastal Kema, populated by *burghers* (Minahasan-Dutch settlers), who all have Dutch surnames. South of Kema there is a stretch of coastline ideal for water sports, with coral gardens, around Nona island.

Tangkoko-Dua Sudara Nature Reserve

From Bitung, a fairly bumpy northern road winds through to the **Tangkoko-Dua Sudara Nature Reserve** ⑱, one of the most important places for terrestrial nature conservation in Minahasa. There are few places in the world where such a wide variety of habitats, plants and animals are crammed into one small forest (8,890 hectares/21,990 acres). To date, scientists have documented 26 mammal, 18 bird, 15 reptile and over 200 plant species here, including spectral tarsiers – one of the world's smallest primates – troops of endangered crested black macaques, marsupial cuscus, endemic red-knobbed hornbills and eight species of kingfishers. Local guides are available at Batu Putih village at the entrance of the reserve.

Minahasan hills

A road south from Airmadidi winds up through the **Minahasa highlands**

Preparing for a dive at Manado's Bunaken National Park.

BELOW: sunset at Bunaken.

TIP

At Pinawetengan, about a 30-minute drive from Tomohon, there is a small but well-endowed mini-museum as well as a weaving handicraft area. Visitors can watch the weavers at work and purchase their lovely woven handicrafts, which are named after the village.

to the lovely lake district at **Tondano** ⑲, an attractive town surrounded by rice fields and forested hills. On the way to Tondano there is an open-air museum in **Sawangan** displaying *waruga* – stone sarcophagi hewn from boulders – with engraved depictions of the deceased's prior occupation. Dating from the 12th century, Minahasans once encased their dead in *warugas* in a crouching foetal position to facilitate rebirth, together with their most valued possessions.

On a hill outside Tondano at Kampung Java, a Muslim enclave in a Christian region, lies the mausoleum of Kyai Maja, a Javanese leader who fought with Diponegoro during the Java Wars (1825–30) and was exiled here by the Dutch. There are a number of interesting towns around **Danau Tondano**, including Ranopaso and Pulutan, noted for hot springs and ceramics. At the southern end of the lake is the **Kolongan Kawangkoan**, site of *kolintang* performances, bullock cart races and Japanese caves. Bukit Temboan Rurukan offers a panoramic vantage point.

West from Tondano, the road cuts through more hills on the way to **Tomohon**, a busy centre for market, education and missionary activities. There are hot springs nearby at Lahendong amid a clove tree plantation, and several at Langowan. A short walk from Tincep brings you to an impressive waterfall, and construction of made-to-order Minahasan houses can be seen at **Woloan**. An easy hour's hike up a wide path on **Gunung Mahawu** volcano is rewarded by a 360-degree view of Minahasa and the surrounding islands.

Tomohon

When Alfred Russel Wallace travelled through this region, he wrote of "fine volcanic peaks 6,000 or 7,000 feet high, forming grand and picturesque backgrounds to the landscape" in the Minahasa highlands. North Sulawesi is the only part of a strangely sprawling island that has volcanoes. Nestled between two of them, **Tomohon** means "people who pray".

For energetic travellers a trek to the top of either of Tomohon's adjacent

BELOW: fishing boat at Gorontalo.

All the way from Mongolia

The fair-skinned Minahasans of North Sulawesi are thought to be descended from Asians who arrived several thousand years ago, probably from Mongolia, and over the centuries intermarried with Chinese and European settlers. The remaining islanders – accomplished fishermen and farmers – share ethnic roots with the Filipinos to the north. There are a large number of Catholics and Protestants, the result of 16th-century conversions by Spanish missionaries from Manila, followed by the efforts of Dutch Calvinist missionaries.

Minahasans have a vigorous culture, their dances warrior-like and their music oddly European, using bamboo instruments. They are also known for their unusual taste in food: spicy dog, cat, forest rat and bat dishes are all popular.

peaks, Lokon or Mahawu, is both challenging and worthwhile for spectacular views. Lokon erupts from time to time; its last episode was in May 2001, showering Manado and surrounding areas with ash. On a clear morning from the rim of Mahawu's crater there is a bird's-eye view of the whole region, including Manado and Bunaken island to the north, and as far as Bitung and Gunung Duasudara to the east.

Surrounded by neat rows of vegetable crops are highland lakes; the largest and best known is **Lake Tondano**. This makes a pleasant lunch stop, as colourful stilted restaurants serving fresh seafood decorate the water's edge. Lake Linow is fed by a steaming volcanic spring, and on a hot day its colour changes from deep blue to turquoise, green and sulphur-yellow. A short drive from Tomohon is Kali waterfall, within a moderately energetic walk from the car park through luxuriant rainforest. Kali has a charming fairytale quality, with surrounding rock walls covered with beard moss that blows in the breeze and spray. Take a raincoat and something to cover your camera to avoid getting wet.

Amurang, a small harbour town located 80km (50 miles) southwest of Manado, has a thriving trade with East Kalimantan across the Sulawesi Sea. Surrounded by lovely hills, this is the gateway to southern Minahasa and the colonial town Gorontalo, a day's drive west via the Trans-Sulawesi highway.

Gorontalo

Diving has been available for several years in **Gorontalo** ⑳, with the season being November to April. Twenty dive sites include dramatic coral walls, multiple pinnacles, caverns, muck, shallow coral gardens and two wrecks. A particularly important feature is Sulawesi's continental wall, which comes within a few metres of the coastline bringing deep blue water to the shore. Gorontalo has a growing list of new, undescribed and endemic species, as well as some of the most dense and diverse hard coral growth in the Indo-Pacific region. The huge, surreal Salvador Dali sponge can only be found in Gorontalo.

A scenic inland road heads east to the Kotamobagu coffee plantation region. Nearby is **Gunung Ambang Nature Reserve** ㉑, an active nesting site for the unusual mound-building maleo bird. Further west lies **Bogani Nani Wartabone National Park** ㉒ (formerly called Dumoga Bone National Park), a vast mountainous rainforest rich in fruit-bearing trees such as durian, nutmeg and figs, and home to a collection of endemic Sulawesi animals including babirusa (the Sulawesi "pig-deer") and the shy anoa. The New York-based Wildlife Conservation Society, established in 1895, partners with a local conservation group to manage three of the largest communal nesting grounds for the maleo birds in the park. Its southern coast is the last known site of beach nests for the endangered land-bird.

Coral at Bunaken National Park.

BELOW: *waruga* stone sarcophagi.

MALUKU AND PAPUA

The mysterious Papua, Indonesia's last frontier, remains largely unexplored. To the west, Maluku has slipped into obscurity from its former fame as the centre of the spice trade

The little-known islands of Maluku province quietly conceal the influence they had in the shaping of the world as it is today. These far-flung outposts were once among the most valuable real estate on earth; many battles were fought over the rights to control the trade of the exotic Spice Islands' produce. Nutmeg, mace and cloves were once worth their weight in gold, and many artefacts from this golden age of the Spice Race can be uncovered when exploring Maluku. The adventurous traveller will be well rewarded with rich experiences here.

Ambon, in central Maluku, is the provincial capital and logistical hub of the region, with Halmahera to the north and Tanimbar to the south. Southeast of Ambon is the Banda archipelago, nine small islands that remain under a sleepy spice-laden spell.

Today the islands are a destination for international dive tourism and a Mecca for underwater photographers. There is an array of sites ranging from the pristine coral-encrusted walls of the Banda islands to the more accessible reefs of Ambon Bay.

Papua

Head-hunters and cannibals, penis sheaths and grass skirts, poisonous birds and water-spitting fish – Papua is captivating, diverse and remote. This region occupies the western half of New Guinea, formerly called Irian Jaya, the third-largest island in the world (after Australia and Greenland). The Indonesian half of the island has a population of more than 3.6 million on a landmass almost twice the size of Great Britain, representing 22 percent of Indonesia's total area.

Until recently, the relatively few intrepid travellers who visited Papua went to see its indigenous tribespeople – the Dani, Lani and Yali of Baliem Valley and the south coast's Asmat, Amungme and Kamoro who still live very primitive lifestyles, and the stunning vistas of their homeland. These days it is the pristine waters and the incredible biodiversity of the Raja Ampat islands that lure the greatest number of travellers, who come for the outstanding diving. Even non-divers will find many reasons to visit Raja Ampat, with newly-developed kayaking and birdwatching programmes and a range of other activities.

PRECEDING PAGES: crocodile festival in the Papuan interior. **LEFT:** a Dani mummy.
ABOVE LEFT: bird of paradise. **ABOVE RIGHT:** Tenate Harbour, Maluku.

Maluku

The fabled Spice Islands, once a prize coveted by European powers, are a sleepy backwater today. Aside from shipwrecks and crumbing forts, there are some immaculate beaches and outstanding dive sites

Once famed as the Spice Islands, the Moluccas, now known as Maluku, were zealously sought for many years before Portuguese mariners finally located them in the 1500s. Explorers like Christopher Columbus, Vasco da Gama, Ferdinand Magellan and Sir Francis Drake all dreamed of finding their wealth there. In fact, one of the main incentives for Europe's Age of Discovery was the avid search for spices, easily worth their weight in gold at that time. Cloves, nutmeg and mace were used to camouflage the taste of spoiled meat in the days before refrigeration, and for medicine. While its current production of nutmeg and mace is negligible, for centuries the tiny Banda islands supplied every last ounce of both, their origin a well-kept secret by Arab traders in Venetian markets prior to the arrival of the Portuguese. Control of the spice-producing islands assured vast fortunes, and countless lives were lost in the quest for them. But the introduction of refrigeration and British success in propagating nutmegs and cloves in Sri Lanka was to end the spice wars for ever.

Scattered across the sea north of Timor and east of Sulawesi, part of Maluku extends to the Arafura Sea south of Papua. Due to remoteness, Maluku's two national parks bring in few visitors, but its spice trade-era and World War II historic sites are of interest to history buffs. It is the sensational diving, however, that lures most visitors. With so much sea, virtually every type of marine topography waits to be explored and enjoyed.

Flora and fauna

With eastern Maluku in the Wallacea transition zone, there are only a dozen or so species of land mammals. Indigenous marsupials include the squirrel-like flying opossum; three kinds of wide-eyed, prehensile-tailed

Main attractions
BENTENG VICTORIA, AMBON
AUSTRALIAN WAR CEMETERY, AMBON
MANUSELA NATIONAL PARK, SERAM
BANDANEIRA FORTS AND MUSEUMS
GUNUNG API
TERNATE
AKETAJAWA-LOLOBATA NATIONAL
    PARK, HALMAHERA

LEFT: Naulu man on the island of Seram.
RIGHT: marbled cat

Dried salted fish is a food staple in many remote islands.

furry cuscus; a tree-climbing kangaroo; and the wallaby. There are also over 25 species of bats.

Birdlife, however, is prolific. The 300-odd species of birds include over 40 different kinds of birds of paradise, which are concentrated in the Aru archipelago; a couple of dozen species of parrot, headed by the large, handsome red-crested palm cockatoo; beautiful crimson lories; and strange mound-building megapods. These can be seen in Maluku's two national parks.

Ambon

Ambon ❶ is the metropolitan focus of Maluku. By the 19th century, due to Dutch influence, about half of Ambon's population had converted to Christianity. The newly baptised Ambonese availed themselves of educational opportunities, forming the backbone of the Dutch colonial army. Not even World War II could shake their loyalty to Holland. Maluku was overrun by superior Japanese forces in spite of heroic Australian resistance in Ambon, and the area became a central Japanese base. After the war, the Dutch returned to a rousing welcome in Ambon. When Indonesia became independent later, Ambon resisted; thousands fled to Holland while others fought a guerrilla war against the Indonesian military.

Map opposite

Ambon city's architecture, functional but nondescript due to bombing in 1944, was almost entirely destroyed during the 1999–2000 upheaval. Fortunately, the entrance to the 18th-century **Benteng Victoria**, Ambon's most worthwhile colonial relic, remains. However, it is difficult to find, and it is forbidden to take photographs unless one has a permit from military security in Jakarta. At the end of Ambon's main street, Jalan Patty, is **Mesjid Al Fatah**, the main mosque next to the handsome old **Mesjid Jame**.

The **Museum Siwalima** is located on a hill just beyond the urban area. Off the paved road on the way up, see the impressive Japanese shore battery, still protected by its concrete bunker. The museum displays aspects of Maluku's natural history and geology, but the emphasis is on ethnography, with many fine objects, including ancestral carvings from the southern islands. Unlike many museums in Indonesia, most of the interesting showcases have an English description. The summit of **Gunung Nona** has the best view of the bay and Ambon town.

Ambon Bay hosts some intriguing dive sites in **The Twilight Zone**, with strange-looking creatures inhabiting slopes beneath the traditional fishing fleet; there's also a Dutch shipwreck.

On the outskirts of town, in the opposite direction from the museum, the large, well-trimmed **Australian War Cemetery** holds the remains of Australian and other Allied troops who died during World War II. Lovingly maintained by the Australian government, many of those buried here were prisoners of war who perished in spite of the heroic aid given to them by the Ambonese.

Beyond the city

Soya Atas village is less than halfway up the slopes of 950-metre (3,100ft) high **Gunung Sirimau ❷**. There is a fine church there, but be sure also to check out the *baileo* – a ritual meeting place with sacred megaliths. From Soya Atas, a path leads up to a sacred

Ambon.

BELOW: nutmeg was once worth a fortune.

Banda and the nutmeg saga

At the heart of wars between European nations and Indonesia from the 14th to the 17th century was a small egg-shaped seed from the nutmeg tree *(Myristica sp.)* and the colourful orange-red membrane surrounding it called mace. For many centuries these treasures only grew on Run island in the Banda archipelago and were sold by Arab traders in Venice for a profit of as much as 2,500 percent.

By the time the first Europeans – the Portuguese – arrived in the 16th century, unlike its neighbouring Islamic sultanates, Banda was organised into several democratic republics. Not only did the Bandanese take great pride in their active role in the shipping of their own goods between Maluku and Java, they had a thriving entrepôt trade in equally precious cloves.

Whereas the sultans of Tidor and Ternate made deals with Portuguese (and later the Dutch and the English) in return for increased power over all of Maluku, the Bandanese remained independent until the VOC arrived. With the consent of the Tidor and Ternate sultans, the VOC drove the Bandanese into slavery, destroyed their plantations and massacred as many as 15,000 inhabitants in 1621 for refusing Dutch control. The VOC eventually resettled the Banda islands with imported labourers.

hilltop site with more megaliths and a water container that never dries out. Drinking this water is said to bring health, love and prosperity. Footpaths from Soya Atas descend to some of Ambon's most traditional villages. A guide is recommended. Beware of the local Luhu ghost in the area, the beautiful daughter of a former *raja* with a predilection for handsome foreign men.

A couple of popular beaches lie to the west of town. **Amahusu** is 7km (4 miles) away on the bay side, while , 16km (10 miles) out, faces the island's southwestern shore. In the other direction, east of Ambon, the beach at **Natsepa** offers protected, shallow water. Beyond Natsepa, the road leads to Tulehu village and on to **Waai ❸**, which has sacred eels living in a spring-fed cave whose waters flow into a crystal-clear pool. Their keeper entices the eels to slither out of the cave by flicking his fingers on the water's surface, then cracking open raw eggs. Near **Honimua** village at Liang, there is a long, deserted beach and a pier from which dolphins and skipjacks can be spotted. The

best swimming and snorkelling is off **Pombo island**, accessible by boat from either Tulehu or Honimua.

Rounding the bay out of Ambon city, a paved road cuts across Hitu to the island's north coast. On this road are clove plantations, occasional stands of mace and nutmeg and – with luck – you can see villagers processing sago tree trunks into a starchy paste, the staple diet for many people. On the north coast, the road swings to the west. At **Hila** village is Immanuel Church and the Mesjid Wapauwe, whose foundations were laid in 1414. A short stroll away are the seaside ruins of the majestic but neglected Benteng Amsterdam.

Diving near Ambon

Ambon's diving is diverse and exciting. In 2008 Maluku Divers discovered a new species of frogfish, *Histiophryne psychedelica*, found only on the slopes of The Twilight Zone. This discovery has generated huge international interest in the destination, which is now extremely popular for underwater photographers. Regular trips set

BELOW: pitcher plant.
BELOW RIGHT: Australasian species, such as this cockatoo, are a feature of Maluku.

off in search of vibrant fish life and explorations of dramatic underwater topography on the southern and eastern coasts as well. There are several sites off Seram island, too, and the fish-smothered slopes around nearby **Pulau Tiga**.

Among the islands near Ambon, **Saparua ❹**, a 2-hour ferry ride from Tulehu, offers several interesting attractions. **Ouw** village produces pottery – simple, elegant and functional – for practical use and for sale in Ambon. Dominating a turquoise bay, **Benteng Duurstede** has been restored and bristles with cannons.

Manusela National Park

Seram, the largest and among the least-known islands in Maluku, hovers over Ambon, Saparua and Molana. Seram lies within the Wallacea Transitional Zone and is a key area for global studies on species evolution. The central **Manusela National Park ❺**, which is home to 2,000 species of butterflies and moths and 120 species of birds, covers an area of 189,000 hectares (467,103 acres). **Wahai** village is the northern entrance to the park, and **Sanulo** village, overlooking the Bay of Teluti, is the southern gateway.

Many of Ambon's traditions are said to have originated in Seram, including the division into two sets of customs, the *patasiwa* and the *patalima*, as well as the *pela* alliances between two villages, often located far apart. Seram is also steeped in magic, for the Ambonese anyway, with many anecdotes of men who can fly and change their shape at will. While the western part of the island has lost its mystery, thanks to a thriving lumber industry, the remote eastern mountains are where the magic is concentrated. **Gesser**, on the eastern tip of Seram, has the exotic Bati hill tribe, known to have exceptional supernatural powers. They remain secluded from civilisation by choice.

Another group of mountain people, the Naulu, live close to **Masohi ❻**. Of the few remaining tribes in Maluku who closely adhere to ancient traditions without the veneer of a foreign religion, the Naulu are the easiest to reach. The men's distinctive red headbands, worn after initiation

National hero Thomas Matulessy, known as Pattimura, was a native of Saparua island. He fought Dutch oppression but was defeated in Saparua, and subsequently hanged in Ambon in 1817.

BELOW: Banda's underwater life.

The clove is not a seed or fruit, but the unopened flower bud of the clove tree. A single tree will yield about 2kg (4lbs) of cloves, best picked between the months of August and September.

rituals, distinguish the Naulu from their Malukan neighbours. The initiation requires a 5-day trek in the mountains of their ancestral homeland, where they must kill a deer and a boar with a spear and a tree-dwelling cuscus with a single arrow. Explorations further into Naulu lands require hiking (with a guide) inland to the mountainous Manusela National Park.

Banda

South of Seram and Ambon is **Kepulauan Banda** ❼, or the Banda archipelago. "Founded" by the Portuguese in 1512, it was the Dutch who arrived a century later to set up a spice monopoly. The English, who came later, undercut the Dutch efforts of price control by shipping nutmeg and mace to Europe from Run island, in the Bandas. The Dutch monopoly was restored when Manhattan was traded for Run, but as spices were increasingly produced elsewhere, the nine Banda islands faded into obscurity.

The Bandas' importance in the English–Dutch struggle to control the spice trade is evidenced in its remaining forts. A military headquarters until 1860, **Benteng Belgica** was restored in the early 20th century and dominates **Bandaneira** ❽, the major island of the archipelago. Closer to the sea, **Benteng Nassau**, important during VOC governor-general Jan Pieterszoon Coen's efforts to control Banda in 1621, crumbles in neglect. The string of forts continues on neighbouring **Banda Besar** ❾ island with Benteng Concordia and Benteng Hollandia, built by Coen high on a ridge to command the surrounding seas, and destroyed by earthquake in 1743. Benteng Revingil (Revenge) rises from the ocean on **Ai** island. On both islands, old nutmeg smokehouses line trails through fragrant nutmeg groves, dotted with huge mango and *kanari* (tropical almond) trees, coffee and other exotic plants as tropical birds fly overhead.

Energetic souls may want to climb **Gunung Api** ❿, an active volcano directly opposite Bandaneira. It last erupted in 1988, but fortunately almost all of the lava and ash fell on the side away from the town. The view from the summit is spectacular. Attempt this with a guide and get an early start to beat the heat of the day. In Bandaneira, the **Museum Rumah Budaya** holds many historical artefacts. Other sites include a church dating from 1852, its interior stone slab graves inscribed with the names of Dutch colonialists, and the **Mesjid Hatta-Syahrir**. The **Istana Mini**, the old governor's mansion, has the former resident's suicide note carved on one of the window panes. Next door is the former **VOC headquarters**, which has a statue of King William III, the great-grandfather of the present Dutch queen. The **Museum Muhammad Hatta** and the **Museum Sjahrir** contain memorabilia of Indonesia's top nationalist leaders who were exiled in Bandaneira in the mid-1930s. The **Museum Captain Cole** was named after the British leader who captured Banda from the Dutch in 1811.

BELOW: active Gunung Api is an ever-present threat.

Banda's islands, like the majority of Maluku's fertile waters, offer excellent diving opportunities. Snorkelling is also possible on sites within Banda's huge natural harbour. One special site, **Lava Flow**, situated upon the lava from Gunung Api's 1988 eruption, has been identified as having the world's fastest-growing table corals, with layer upon layer reaching a span of 3 or 4 metres (10–13ft). Sharks and pelagic species patrol deeper waters, while a myriad of colourful fish swarm coral-encrusted walls. Banda has a unique mandarin fish; every evening divers can observe and photograph its mating ritual. In April and October, the seas are calm and visibility excellent. The Bandas also have seasonal fishing, primarily for tuna, marlin and snapper.

Beyond Banda

East and southeast from the Banda islands, travel becomes more difficult. Yet both Tual in the Kepulauan Kai archipelago as well as Saumlaki in the Kepulauan Tanimbar offer attractions. The airstrip near Tual was built by the Japanese during World War II. Nearby, in the grounds of the Roman Catholic mission, a relief sculpture depicts the history of Catholicism in the area, starting with the arrival of Jesuits in the late 19th century. During the war, the Japanese invaded the Kai islands, murdering the bishop and 13 foreign priests.

Tual ⓫ on **Dullah** island is the capital of the Maluku Tenggara (Southeast Maluku) district and the transportation hub for an extensive network of roads and sea lanes. A half-hour ride away is Dullah village, where the **Museum Belawang** displays a splendid ceremonial canoe, complete with carved decorations. Close to Tual is **Pasir Panjang**, a powder-white beach that stretches for 3km (2 miles). From Tual, motorised canoes depart for the mountainous **Kai Besar** island. Occasional boats from Tual also head for **Dobo ⓬**, Maluku's pearl capital and the largest town of the Kepulauan Aru

archipelago. Comprising 25 islands, the coastlines of the Aru islands are mangrove swamps, housing an abundance of pearl oysters, shrimp, lobsters and other fish. Its low-lying palm forest holds unusual butterflies, flocks of several species of birds of paradise and wallabies. Aru is also significant as a turtle nesting ground. Rare dugongs are still easily spotted in the seagrass beds found throughout Aru.

Nicobar pigeon

Kepulauan Tanimbar

South of the Kai islands is the **Kepulauan Tanimbar** group of islands. The area only went under Dutch control in the first years of the 19th century, during the final phase of Holland's colonial expansion in Indonesia. **Saumlaki** on **Yamdena** island was a Japanese air base during World War II. Tanimbar artists carve strange statues of humans with big heads.

At **Sangliat Dol ⓭**, on northeast Yamdena, there is a megalithic staircase that leads to the village ceremonial ground featuring a huge stone boat with a carved prow. The local people believe that their ancestors arrived

BELOW: exploring a coral reef off Banda.

in this sacred craft. Near Saumlaki is an island known for its rare species of orchids.

Ternate and Tidore

North of Ambon, the administrative and geographical district of the northern third of Maluku is dominated on maps by Halmahera, but tiny **Ternate** island is the real centre of power and communications as it is the capital of North Maluku province. Two-thirds of the island's people live in Ternate town, the business and market centre of the region.

One of the major clove-producing islands of Maluku, Ternate had been trading with Chinese, Arab and Javanese merchants hundreds of years before the first European arrival. The Portuguese were there in the early 1500s, followed by the Dutch at the start of the 17th century. **Benteng Oranje** was built by the Dutch in 1667 and is currently used by the Indonesian police and military. There are many ancient cannons in the large complex. On the outskirts of town, towards the airport, there is a mosque

BELOW: Benteng (Fort) Toloko.

whose foundations date back to the 15th century. Its multi-tiered roof covers an airy space, beautifully designed for prayer and meditation.

A bit further out on the road to the airport, the **Kedaton**, or Sultan's Palace, built in 1796, houses a museum. Prior arrangements can be made through the local tourism office to see the museum's jewel, the magical crown reputed to be a personal gift from Allah to the first sultan who submitted to Islam. Some hair attached to the crown is said to be growing, requiring periodic trimming. A few years ago, when Gunung Gamalama threatened to erupt, the son of the last officially recognised sultan took the crown on a boat ride around Ternate to calm the impending eruption. It worked. Three times a week the crown and the resident spirits receive offerings of flowers, holy water and betel nuts.

A 45km (30-mile) paved road encircles Ternate, never wandering far from the coastline and the volcanic slopes of the 1,720-metre (5,640ft) Gunung Gamalama. At **Dufa-Dufa** village, the Portuguese **Benteng Toloko** fort stands on a seaside cliff, in surprisingly good shape and with a still-legible seal on its main entrance. **Batu Angus** (Burnt Rock) is a former lava flow, now jagged rock, which continues underwater for quite a distance. On the northeast coast, the steep slopes of **Hiri** island pop into view. Nearby, there are two crater lakes, both called **Danau Tolire**.

After rounding the north of Ternate, the crumbling Portuguese **Benteng Kastella** fort comes into view. From here, there is a path to the sacred Akerica royal springs and to the huge old Afo clove tree. Past Kastella and just before Ngade village is **Danau Laguna**. This lake, partially covered with lotus plants, is home to sacred crocodiles who, it is believed, trace their ancestry to a princess. Seeing one of them is said to lead to a lifetime of good luck. A path along one side of the lake rises to give a splendid view of Danau Laguna, with Maitara and Tidore islands in the background. The last stop, **Benteng Kayu Merah** fort, offers a sea-level view of the same islands.

Tidore 🅖 island, a bit larger than Ternate, is for the less energetic, belying its history as a former rival of Ternate's clove production in the 17th century. Frequent boats leave Bastion for **Run**, where there is a weekly market. Tidore is dominated by the volcano Gunung Kiematubu. A paved road encompasses most of the island, but beyond the main town of **Soa Siu**, the surface degenerates considerably.

Halmahera and Morotai

At one time governed by the sultanates of Tidore and Ternate, **Halmahera's** 🅖 main town is **Tobelo**, which lies on the eastern shore of the island's northern peninsula. **Daru** village is south of Tobelo, while further south near the bottom of the bay is **Kao**, which hosted some 80,000 Japanese troops during World War II, earning itself the name of Little Tokyo. Prior to landing on Morotai further north, Allied planes bombed the installations here. A few anti-aircraft guns still guard the

landing strip, which was built by the Japanese. There are several bunkers near the runway. Offshore, superstructures of Japanese shipwrecks protrude above the surface of the water.

On the northeastern peninsula of Halmahera is **Aketajawa-Lolobata National Park** 🅖, a small (1,673-sq km/646-sq mile) conservation area by Indonesian standards. Out of 51 mammal species found in North Maluku, seven are endemic to Halmahera.

Morotai island 🅗 was the site of a major battle during World War II. The task force led by General Douglas MacArthur swept ashore after destroying the light Japanese defence there, as well as the concentration of power at Kao Bay. Morotai was vital to MacArthur's island-hopping strategy towards the Philippines and onwards to Japan. Although many of the relics from the war were carted off to a steel mill in Java, there are still remnants of war machinery. In 1973, a Japanese soldier came out of the jungle, nearly three decades after Japan surrendered. It is rumoured that there may still be Japanese survivors on the island.

Abandoned cannon at Benteng Oranje.

BELOW: dried cloves from Ternate

PAPUA

As one of the world's last great wildernesses, Indonesia's easternmost land offers great promise to explorers, but advance planning is essential. Allow lots of time for any expedition to the region

Papua, the western half of the large island of New Guinea, is Indonesia's final frontier and one of the most extraordinary places on earth. Yet its sheer isolation (and therefore the expense of getting here), along with past news reports of social unrest, have kept all but the hardiest adventurers away: the few who have made the journey return home with rave reviews.

The "Stone Age" Dani, Lani and Yali tribes of the breathtakingly beautiful Baliem Valley render accounts of men wearing *koteka* (penis gourds) and bare-breasted women in grass skirts carrying piglets and babies in fibre bags hanging from their heads. The former head-hunting, cannibalistic Asmat have long been known throughout the artistic world for their primitive woodcarvings. A very few nature purists venture to the southeast, to Wasur National Park, where aboriginal tribes, and wildlife such as wallabies and cassowaries, make it appear more like Australia than Indonesia.

Papua also has a reputation for superb diving at Raja Ampat. A secret from the world until recently, news of the region's amazing diversity of fish and coral species has captured the attention of divers globally,

who have placed it top of their must-see lists.

Jayapura and around

Jayapura ❶, the capital of Papua province, lies on Yos Sudarso Bay. Its constricted site along several indented, steep-walled coves is gorgeous. Highly recommended is the splendid view of the city from the base of a communications tower, on a steep hill just at the back of the harbour.

Jayapura and Sentani were unknown to the outside world until General

Main attractions
DANAU SENTANI
BALIEM VALLEY TRIBES
ASMAT ART AND TRIBAL VILLAGES
WASUR NATIONAL PARK
RAJA AMPAT DIVING

LEFT: a Lani man at a festival wearing traditional wig made of human hair.
RIGHT: fishermen and desert island.

Papuan school children.

MacArthur and the Allies arrived in 1944, turning the area into a giant military base. **Hamadi**, about 4km (3 miles) south of Jayapura, is the spot where the Americans landed in their quest to drive the Japanese out of New Guinea. Jayapura saw the biggest amphibious operation of World War II in the southwestern Pacific, involving 80,000 Allied troops. Rusting tanks and aeroplanes still rest half-buried in the sand. **Tanjung Ria** beach, known as Base G during the war, lies to the west.

While waiting for travel documents to be processed, many elect to go to **Abepura**, between Jayapura and Sentani, to visit the excellent **Museum Loka Budaya** (Mon–Fri 7.30am–4pm; charge), on the Cendrawashih University grounds. It has a good collection of ethnographic pieces, as well as an impressive collection of Asmat art donated by the Rockefeller Foundation. On the same road, the **Museum Negeri** houses an interesting collection of both natural history exhibits and ethnographic pieces. Nearby, a crocodile farm displays several thousand crocodiles in

varying stages of development waiting to become purses and shoes – give it a miss.

Danau Sentani is the third-largest lake in Papua and has a very good restaurant for a lunch stop. Boats can be hired here to **Apayo** island, where the residents still produce Sentani bark paintings. A visit can also be made to the island village of **Doyo Lama**, famous for its large woodcarvings and unexplained rock paintings.

At **Gunung Ifar**, 6km (4 miles) outside of Sentani, the remains of General MacArthur's World War II headquarters can be seen. As the hill is on a military base, visitors have to report to the local military office to deposit their passports.

Inland to Baliem Valley

The fertile **Baliem Valley** lies in Papua's highlands, a 45-minute flight southwest from Jayapura. At 1,500 metres (4,900ft), the valley is cool, especially at night, but the midday sun can still burn. The area is surrounded by the steep Sudirman Mountain Range that kept it hidden

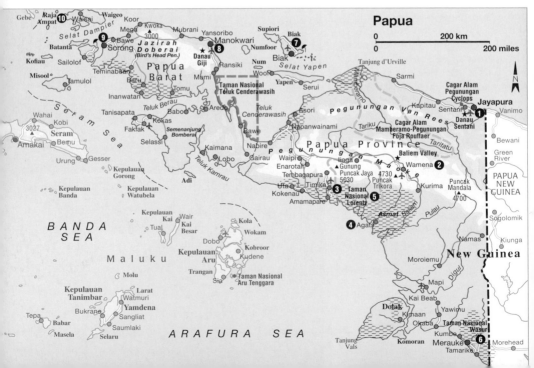

from Western eyes until 1938 when American explorer Richard Archbold flew his seaplane over the mountains and sighted a lush valley dotted with the thatched roofs of Dani huts. The *National Geographic* reported the discovery in its March issue of 1941, but it was not until 1945, when the first missionaries made contact with the estimated 95,000 tribespeople, that the world was made fully aware of the valley and its inhabitants. The creamy-brown Sungai Baliem, 55km (34 miles) long and 15km (9 miles) wide, snakes through the valley before pouring out through a southern gorge to the Arafura Sea.

The Dutch established **Wamena ❷**, the only urban centre in the Baliem Valley, in 1958. It has a bustling, colourful traditional market – Pasar G.B. Wenas where all the local tribes gather to sell forest and farm products and handicrafts: stone axes, baskets, fibre bags, bows and arrows.

The indigenous people of the Baliem Valley – Dani, Lani and Yali – are a Neolithic race with unknown origins. Until the 1960s, when steel was introduced to them, they were using wood, flint and stone for weapons and tools. Although foreign influence continues to chip away at their beliefs and traditions, in villages people live as they have done for centuries, following tribal laws and time-honoured customs. Older men still wear *koteka* (penis gourds), while some women wear grass skirts and carry babies, piglets or sweet potatoes in their fibre bags, known as *noken*, while younger folk often don Western wear. Disputes, which occur over land, pigs or women, are settled by fines and payment in pigs.

In the early 1990s, the government opened **Balai Latihan Kerja**, a cooperative to teach the Dani and Lani skills in pottery making, rattan weaving and leather working. This facility is located near the police station and visitors are welcome. There is no admission charge.

To visit the small **Museum Wamena** (free, but a donation is welcome), you have to ask for it to be opened for you. It showcases the daily life, traditions and ceremonial items of

Papuan man, Wamena.

BELOW: tribesman in the Wamena region sporting a penis sheath.

Mamberamo-Foja Mountain Nature Reserve

The **Mamberamo-Foja Mountain Nature Reserve**, west of Jayapura, comprises 8 million hectares (nearly 20 million acres), much of which is untouched forest. With little human impact, scientists are discovering numerous previously unknown species each time they conduct research there. Exploration began in the late 1890s when women's hats adorned with a bird that ornithologists had never seen before arrived in Europe in a shipment from the East. Subsequent British expeditions to find the origins of the bird failed. Fast-forward one century, when a team led by anthropologist Jared Diamond discovered the golden-fronted bowerbird in the Foja Mountains in 1979.

The region is so remote and bureaucracy, together with local opposition to admitting strangers, so intense that saying that arranging further expeditions has been "difficult" is an understatement. However, after years of negotiations and confidence-gaining, a team from the Indonesian Institute of Sciences, Cenderawasih University, the Smithsonian Institution, Conservation International and others was finally allowed to enter in 2005. Results of subsequent explorations are now beginning to be published, the delay caused by the arduous task of determining what species the new discoveries belong to.

the Dani, Lani and Yali tribes. Behind the building is a suspension bridge over the Sungai Baliem, leading to a small Dani compound which welcomes visitors. You will be expected to pay to take photographs; 5,000 rupiah per shot should suffice.

Trekking in the Baliem Valley

In addition to unique ethnic groups, the main reason to visit Wamena is for the trekking – suitable for varying levels of capability – through breathtaking landscapes not seen elsewhere in Indonesia. In the highlands south of town, one- or two-day jaunts take hikers into the Baliem Gorge through sweet-potato fields and over stone fences surrounding Dani villages. Walk along the powerful **Baliem River** and cross a suspension bridge to Sogogmo village, surrounded by terraced fields and groves of wild sugar cane, ending at **Kurima**.

On another outing, hike to the top of **Gunang Sekan** for outstanding views of the southern Baliem and the Siepkosi valleys, passing fields of flowers, including orchids, mosses and carnivorous plants. It's an easy walk into the fertile **Pugima Valley** from Siepkosi, the only area where beautiful pottery is made using primitive methods.

Travellers with only a few days usually arrange for a Dani village to perform a mock war and pig feast. **Amomoge** village, a 45-minute drive northwest of Wamena, is the most popular choice. Elderly village warriors will gladly show their arrowhead scars, attesting to wartime bravery.

A 15-minute walk from here is **Jiwika**, famous for its blackened, mummified warrior. In the past, important Dani were preserved with the use of herbs and a process of smoking in a secret ritual known only to a select few. Although the secret is still handed down to one couple in every village each generation, it has not been used for over 250 years. There is also a mummy at **Akima**, a 10-minute drive from Jiwika.

Behind Jiwika in the northern part of the valley is the **Kotilola Cave**, with lush vegetation, and further on is the vibrant market at **Uwosilomo**. From here, drive through a mountain pass surrounded by forest, taking time to study the fauna in the highland woodlands. Heading back to Wamena, there is another mummy at **Meagaima**.

A drive along the western side of Baliem Valley through grassy savannahs and acacia forests reveals a landscape totally different from the fertile, terraced fields elsewhere. Follow the route through **Elagaima** and **Kimbim** (where there are local markets), and on to **Gunung Magi** in the Pyramid region for a view overlooking a western segment of the Baliem River. The white clapboard houses with chimneys here were built by American missionaries, perhaps lonely for home, in the early 1950s.

A five-day trek will take those in good shape to **Yali country**, where it is easy to negotiate a night's stay in a traditional hut or a local schoolteacher's house. Or, weather permitting,

BELOW: Dani tribal chief

drive to **Habema Lake** (about 3 hours; 90km/60 miles), a lake within a swamp surrounded by orchid-producing high mountain forest. On a clear day, you can see **Gunung Trikora** (4,730 metres/15,520ft) from here.

Into Asmat territory

Timika ❸ is dominated by the Freeport-McMoRan mine, the richest copper and gold mine in the world. Officially opened in March 1973 by then-President Suharto, Freeport is Indonesia's fourth-largest taxpayer, and the mine is continuously surrounded by controversy.

Timika is also the jumping-off point for travel to **Agats ❹**, the only town in **Asmat** (the land as well as the people share this name). The Asmat, once feared head-hunters and cannibals and now fishermen and carvers, live in the harsh environment of an alluvial swamp on the south coast of Papua, bordered on the north by towering central highlands, making travel and exploration in this area extremely difficult. In 1770, English explorer James Cook stopped in Asmat territory near the Casuarina coast in search of fresh water. As Cook and his men approached the jungle, Asmat warriors appeared. Cook, fearing danger, fired at the group and returned to his ship. In 1913, this place was named **Cook's Bay**.

The first Asmat carvings were taken to Holland in the early 20th century, thus beginning the art world's interest in these "primitive" carvers. Although primitive art experts recognised the carvings of the Asmat as unique, the objects had no value to the Indonesian government. The Dutch gave up control of Papua in 1962, and when Indonesian officials arrived in Asmat in 1963, they ordered the destruction of the statues and put an indefinite ban on carving and on feast ceremonies, which were part of the rituals surrounding head-hunting, cannibalism and warfare. The ban proved effective and did indeed bring head-hunting and cannibalism under control.

Five years later the ban was lifted when the Indonesian government, in consultation with the United Nations, decided to open up the Asmat area to outside visitors. Around that time,

Danau Sentani is home to one of Papua's largest freshwater fish – the sawfish. It can reach some 5 metres (16ft) long and weigh half a tonne. The Sentani believe their ancestral spirits live in the sawfish and refuse to consume it.

BELOW LEFT: Dani mask. **BELOW:** in the interior many waterways are traversed by precarious-looking bridges.

TIP

Those wishing to visit Papua's interior must have their *surat jalan* (travel permit) processed at the police headquarters in either Jayapura, Biak or Sorong *(see Travel Tips, Transport, page 374)*. If you arrive at the airport at Sentani, a 45-minute drive from Jayapura, you will need to hire a car to get into the city and allow a day for your *surat jalan* to be processed.

BELOW: Dani warriors.

the mysterious death of Michael Rockefeller, son of American billionaire Nelson Rockefeller, who came to Agats to buy Asmat carvings for museums in the United States, brought the art to world attention.

As the Indonesian government went about systematically destroying the art of the Asmat, Catholic missionaries Bishop Alphonse Sowada and Father F. Trenkenschug bought as many pieces as their funds would allow. Their collection now resides in the **Asmat Museum of Culture and Progress** (Mon–Sat 9am–noon, afternoons by appointment; charge), the finest collection of Asmat art in the world. It is rare to find an old, high-quality piece of Asmat art today. In the past, the tools used by the Asmat were suitable for use only on soft woods. Many of these carvings were intended for a specific ceremony and then discarded. The recent introduction of metal tools now allows the Asmat to use hard woods such as ironwood.

The best way to proceed upon arrival in Agats is to go to one of the two hotels in town and ask around for an Asmat guide who speaks English. There are two villages near Agats – **Syuru Kecil** (small) and **Syuru Besar** (large). Syuru Kecil can be reached by elevated boardwalk, Syuru Besar by longboat. Either of these villages can be "hired" for several hours to don their traditional dress and perform dances and perhaps even a ceremony. A motorised longboat can provide transport to either upriver or downriver villages more removed from Agats. However, the villages within only a one-day longboat journey are very similar to those near Agats.

On a longer trip, it is often possible to negotiate to spend a night in the *jeu* or men's house. The Asmat speak their own language, but there is usually at least one person in each village who speaks Bahasa Indonesia, so the guide can act as translator. An introduction to the chief is the first order of business. The Asmat are usually quite happy to assemble their members in the men's house and answer questions. It is not considered impolite to ask if there are any former head-hunters who wish to be interviewed. Having visitors

is an exciting time for the Asmat, and they enjoy talking about the past. Often they will conclude such a session with drum-playing and chanting.

Lorentz National Park

Between Timika and Agats is **Lorentz National Park 5**, a Unesco World Heritage Site (permits to visit are required from the police headquarters in Jayapura, the Forestry Ministry in Jakarta and the Freeport mining company). At 2.5 million hectares (6.2 million acres), it is the largest protected area in Southeast Asia, with the rare feature of incorporating a tropical marine environment, lowland wetlands and a snow-capped mountain, **Gunung Puncak Jaya** (formerly called Gunung Cartenz Pyramid). At 5,030 metres (16,503ft), Puncak Jaya is the tallest peak between the Himalayas and the Andes, and one of only three equatorial glaciers on the planet.

Wasur National Park

Merauke, the easternmost town in Indonesia, is the entry point to southern Papua. It was founded in 1904 by the Dutch in answer to complaints from British citizens concerning Asmat head-hunting raids on their side of the border to the east. Today, it is virtually one long street – Jalan Raya Mandala. There is a bank and a police station, where permits to enter Wasur National Park, southeast of Merauke, may be processed.

Wasur National Park 6 is a 400,000-hectare (990,000-acre) natural treasure trove. A Ramsar wetlands protected site, the park contains several diverse habitats: extensive open-water swamplands (Rawa Biru), vast tidal mudflats, dry savannah grasslands, luxuriant mangroves, lowland forest and eucalyptus woodlands. In the rainy season Rawu Birus overflows its banks and the only access is by canoe. In the dry season, a jeep is required. An English-speaking guide can be found in Merauke if you enquire at your accommodation. The wildlife is more Australian than Indonesian; look for wallabies, bandicoots, cuscus and echnidas. Fabulous birdlife includes cassowaries, lapwings, spoonbills, crowned pigeons and eclectus parrots. The

Amat Art

BELOW: an Asmat armada in the Agats area.

Kanum, Marori, Marind and Yei people who inhabit the park's 14 villages are hunter-gatherers, and they actively participate in discouraging poachers.

North coast explorations

Boot-shaped **Biak** ❼ island, lying one degree off the equator on Papua's north coast, is the site of an Indonesian naval base, but during World War II it was the location of some of the worst battles fought between the Allies and the Japanese over control of New Guinea. Divers can explore shipwrecks sunk from these battles. The **Japanese Caves** are also of interest. Near the entrance to the caves, on Jalan Sisingamangarja, the **Museum Cenderawasih** contains a collection of war relics – one half for the Allied memorabilia and the other for the Japanese.

Southwest of Biak lies **Teluk Cenerawasih National Park**, encompassing the waters around Mioswaar, Nusrowi, Roon, Rumberpon and Yoop islands. The reef ecosystem here is part of the Coral Triangle region and is rich in many coral varieties, more than 200 fish species, four types of sea turtles, dugongs, blue whales and dolphins.

Bird's Head peninsula

The **Bird's Head peninsula** (Jazirah Doberai), located on the western tip of Papua, is so called because, on the map, it resembles the head of a huge westward-flying bird. **Manokwari** ❽, the capital of West Papua province, and Sorong are the principal towns on the peninsula. Manokwari was the site of the first European settlement and the first permanent Christian mission. Today, it remains a strong missionary centre. **Gereja Koawi**, a monument to the first missionaries, is located just past the hospital and behind the church. A **Japanese War Memorial** is also sited in the town.

Manokwari is host to over 30 separate language groups. The three main ethnic groups in the area are the Wamesa in the south, the Arfak in the Arfak Mountains and the Doreri along the coast. While here, take a side trip to **Danau Unggi** in the Arfak Mountains either by air or hike the distance in four days. The panorama is truly spectacular. The area is home to the endemic Arfak butterfly, famous for its shimmering wings.

The Sougb people make their home in the Unggi region. Although Christian, The Sougb still believe in black magic. The men wear red, the women black, and they have retained their traditional huts and customs.

Sorong ❾, the other large town in this area, has good beaches and reefs and attracts dive charters. The town has two World War II memorials to the Japanese who died here. As the hub of Indonesia's lucrative eastern oil and gas fields and a timber export centre, it has an airport serviced by international flights incoming from Biak. It is also the gateway to Raja Ampat, the mention of which sends divers into a swoon.

Diving at Raja Ampat

Although there are more than 1,500 small atolls in the **Raja Ampat** ❿

BELOW: Southern crowned pigeon at Wasur National Park.

group, there are four main islands: Waigeo, Batanta, Salawati and Misool. Raja Ampat ("Four Kings") gained notoriety when scientific data seeped out that the area may very well be the epicentre of oceanic biodiversity. Its position in the Coral Triangle– comprising Indonesia, Malaysia, the Philippines, the Solomon islands and New Guinea – is significant. According to research conducted by The Nature Conservancy, 1,320 fish species, 553 varieties of coral and 699 molluscs have already been recorded, and the discovery of new species – such as the walking shark – are common. Couple this with crystal-clear waters, rainforests and mangroves, and no amount of difficulty getting here seems to be too much trouble. Alfred Russel Wallace visited Raja Ampat in 1860 in search of birds of paradise, and this amazing area lies just east of the line named in his honour.

Infrastructure here is rather basic, but is already changing quickly, with two airports under construction. In the meantime, flights land at Sorong and from here the islands are accessible by boat. At Wasai, the capital of Raja Ampat regency, there are new roads and a small health clinic, and budget cottages near Wasai beach as well as a few homestays. Several cruises and liveaboards have jumped on the band-wagon, and there are a few resorts.

Diving, of course, is the main event; frequently encountered are manta rays, giant groupers and large schools of barra-cudas and jacks, as well as sharks, whales and dolphins. In the shallows are pygmy shrimp and octopus and nudibranchs. Most explorations are drift dives due to strong currents. But there are also other activities. Kayak4conservation is a com-munity development project and offers homestay-to-homestay programmes for experienced kayakers and with a guide and support boats for the less adventur-ous. The homestays are owned by villag-ers, trained by Westerners. Snorkelling is included in the adventure. Birdwatching is as exciting as the undersea world. While the fabulous bird of paradise is at the top of most avian enthusiasts' must-see lists, there are lowland forest, moun-tain and riverine species to search for, as well as waders.

BELOW: extraordinary festival costumes are a feature of Papuan highland tribes.

Karowai tree people

Papua's Karowai people are often referred to as "tree people" because their homes can be as high as 45 metres (150ft) above the ground. They live in the dense jungles of eastern Papua, a three-day journey by boat, charter plane and foot from Asmat on the south coast. They may also be reached from the highlands of the Baliem Valley. An extended family or two small families might share a tree-house consisting of one large room with no room dividers, but with separate male and female areas. (Intimate relations are never allowed inside.) Hunting dogs and baby pigs live alongside.

The Karowai women spend their days caring for the children, cooking and sometimes making a foray into the jungle to collect their staple food, sago, and sago worms, the larvae of the scarab beetle. The men make bows and arrows, discuss the next hunt and clear land for growing sago palms. They also organise ceremonies, such as the yearly sago worm ceremony.

The Karowai have encountered people from the outside world, primarily missionaries but also a few tourists; however, a related group, the Karowai Batu, rejects any contact with outsiders. They are one of the few peoples left in the world today who choose to remain totally isolated.

INSIGHT GUIDE TRAVEL TIPS
INDONESIA

TRANSPORT

ACCOMMODATION

EATING OUT

ACTIVITIES

A – Z

LANGUAGE

Transport

Getting There
and Getting Around

GETTING THERE

By Air

The vast majority of international flights arrive either at **Sukarno-Hatta International Airport** (also spelled Soekarno-Hatta), 20km (13 miles) west of **Jakarta** on Java, or **Ngurah Rai Airport**, near **Denpasar**, Bali. In addition, there are international arrivals using smaller aircraft at major cities throughout the country. For example, **Yogyakarta** (Jogja) has direct flights to Singapore and Kuala Lumpur.

Garuda Indonesia is the national carrier, covering both international and domestic routes. In addition to the government-owned Merpati Nusantara, which primarily focuses on domestic routes, there are privately owned regional airlines, making travelling to and from as well as within Indonesia easier than ever before. For domestic flights, it is advisable to check with a reliable travel agent in Indonesia (often found in hotels) as schedules change frequently.

Singapore is a major hub in the region, with a number of flights to various Indonesian destinations. Singapore-based SilkAir (a sister company of Singapore Airlines), AirAsia (Malaysia-based) and Lion Air (Indonesia-based), offer direct flights from Singapore, Kuala Lumpur, Bangkok and Hong Kong to several of Indonesia's larger cities.

Departing Indonesia: reconfirm international reservations prior to departure as instructed by the airline (not all require you to do this). Arrive at the airport 2 hours prior to departure. International departure tax varies from one airport to another and

must be paid in rupiah. The average is about Rp 150,000.

By Sea

If you're one of the lucky ones with plenty of time (and money), an **ocean cruise** to Indonesia should not be missed. Luxury cruise lines offer fly/cruise arrangements that allow you to fly to Bali and other ports, then catch a ship on the way home, or vice versa. Contact a travel agent in your home country to see which cruise operator is offering Indonesia as part of its itinerary.

Batam and Bintan islands (Sumatra) are served by **high-speed ferries** which connect to Singapore. There are also ferry connections from Penang and Malacca in Malaysia to Medan and Dumai in Sumatra respectively.

By Land

The only access by road is at Entikong, between Kalimantan and Sarawak, Malaysia. Entry point is at the Pontianak–Kuching expressway. You may need a visa to cross into Malaysia.

GETTING AROUND

By Road

Every Indonesian city, town and village has inexpensive public transport: buses, minivans (*bemo*), horse-drawn carts (*andong, cidomo, dokar*), *becak* (pedicabs) or *ojek* (motorcycles). All except Jakarta's Transjakarta buses can be flagged down anywhere on the street. Enquire what the fare is before getting in. Between towns on all islands, **public buses** run frequently.

A few are safer than others, but all except the air-con express varieties (most with reclining seats, videos and toilets) are noisy and crowded.

The alternative is to hire a **taxi**, car or minivan, which would allow stops along the way. The hire of a **car and driver** can be arranged at even the smallest *losmen* (homestay) at rates by the day. Negotiate better rates if you are booking a vehicle for a week or longer, but note that you are responsible for the driver's food and lodging, and for the petrol.

The quality of the roads varies greatly, and distances in kilometres are irrelevant when calculating time over mountainous routes. Don't bother driving, as the experience is not worth the effort of having to deal with near-manic drivers.

By Air

Note that in remote areas, flights may not be connected to a central reservations system, so it's best to purchase tickets in the town itself rather than pre-book them from a larger city. Seats are not always assigned in advance. Be sure to get a computer printout with a confirmation number on it, and reconfirm all domestic flights to be sure they are on schedule. Domestic departure tax is set locally, so varies from airport to airport. The average is about Rp 40,000.

By Sea

PELNI (Pelayaran Nasional Indonesia; www.pelni.co.id), the state-owned shipping company, serves about 30 ports, with each ferry accommodating 1,000–1,500 passengers in four classes. They are basic and often dangerously overloaded. PELNI tickets can be purchased at their local offices or at travel agencies. There are also privately owned ferry services to many small port towns. Check with a ticketing agency locally for schedules and prices.

In bad weather, especially during the rainy season (Oct–Apr), the seas can be quite rough, particularly between Sumatra and Java, Bali and Lombok, and around Komodo, and all ferry runs may be cancelled. Enquire at the local ticketing office if the weather looks ominous.

By Train

There is a reasonable railway network in Java, and a more limited one in Sumatra, but train services are virtually non-existent elsewhere. *(See Java and Sumatra below for more details.)*

JAVA

By Air

Jakarta is served by most of the world's airlines, and there are numerous flights to other Indonesian cities from here. *(See listings of international and regional airlines above.)* Elsewhere in Java, domestic airports with some international flights are found in **Yogyakarta** (Jogja), **Surakarta** (Solo) and **Surabaya**.

As routes and schedules of regional airlines change frequently, check with Indonesian ticketing offices or travel agencies for the latest details.

By Sea

The national ferry passenger line, PELNI, has fixed schedules for services from Java to destinations throughout Indonesia. There are four ports in Java: Jakarta, Cirebon, Semarang and Surabaya.

By Train

Java's train network, running from east to west, offers services to all its major cities. In the east, it connects with ferries to Bali, and in the west, with ferries to Sumatra. The trains may be slow, but they are inexpensive and a nice way to see the countryside.

There are two basic routes: (north) Jakarta–Cirebon– Semarang– Surabaya; and (south) Jakarta–Bandung–Yogyakarta– Surakarta–Surabaya.

Executive Class reservations are recommended for comfort; all have air-conditioning and a dining car.

Key International Carriers

AirAsia (www.airasia.com)
British Airways (www.ba.com)
Cathay Pacific (www.cathaypacific.com)
China Airlines (www.china-airlines.com)
EVA Air (www.evaair.com)
Garuda Indonesia (www.garuda-indonesia.com)
Japan Airlines (www.jal.com)
KLM Royal Dutch Airways (www.klm.com)
Korean Air (www.koreanair.com)

Lion Air (www.lionair.co.id)
Lufthansa (www.lufthansa.com)
Malaysia Airlines (www.malaysiaairlines.com)
Qantas Airways (www.qantas.com.au)
Royal Brunei Airlines (www.royalbruneiairlines.com)
SilkAir (www.silkair.com)
Singapore Airlines (www.singaporeair.com)
Thai Airways International (www.thaiair.com)

Economy Class can be hot, crowded, noisy and dirty. Trains are often late, sometimes by many hours. For night travel, it is best to purchase tickets the day before; for day travel, buy tickets 1–2 hours ahead or through a travel agent. Train tickets can be purchased on the day of your departure at the station (allow 1 hour or more before departure), or 2 days beforehand from local travel agencies. There are four main stations in Jakarta: **Gambir Station**: Jl. Medan Merdeka, tel: 021-386 2362 or 384 2777, serves south- and eastbound train routes, including Bogor and Bandung. **Kota Station**: Jl. Stasiun Kota, tel: 021-692 8515, serves south- and eastbound trains. **Senen Station**: Jl. Stasiun Senen, tel: 021-421 0164, serves eastbound and Cirebon trains. **Tanan Abang Station**: Jl. Jatibaru, tel: 021-384 0048, serves westbound trains, including the Sumatra ferry connection.

By Road

In the large cities, the road systems are good, with modern inner-city highways in or around Jakarta, Surabaya, Bandung and Yogyakarta. Once in the countryside, potholes and poor road conditions are common.

By Bus

Most Indonesians travel by long-distance buses – the least expensive way to travel. Many operate at night, leaving major cities at one end of Java and arriving at the other end in the early morning. Note that local bus drivers are often reckless and accidents are quite common. Beware of pickpockets.

On **regular public buses**, seats are narrow – six across. Some have air-con and screen noisy videos. **Long-distance buses** operate from three terminals in Jakarta. All can be

reached by taxi and are connected by local city buses. The other alternative is "**Express**" or **First Class buses** that are roomier, air-conditioned and quieter. Check with a local travel agent for timetables and prices.

Jakarta has three main terminals: **Kalideres Terminal** (west Jakarta) operates services to Sumatra and West Java; **Kampung Rambutan Terminal** (in northeast Jakarta, near the old Halim Airport) is the hub for services to Bandung, Bogor and southwards; while **Pulo Gadung Terminal** (Jl. Bekasi Timur Raya) has services heading to Central and East Java.

By Car/Minivan Hire

The most comfortable way to travel is by chartered vehicle. With a group of four or five people, you can go from Jakarta all the way to Yogyakarta for about the same cost as flying, with the added bonus of being able to stop along the way. Work out the details in advance, including the amount you will give the driver every day for food and lodgings (tips are not mandatory, but will be appreciated). You may have to pay extra for a driver who speaks English. Count on an extra day's hire and a full tank of petrol for the driver to get home.

Jakarta

By Car

Chauffeur-driven cars are highly recommended as a way to get around. Offered by many companies, the use of such cars can be arranged through your hotel.

Hourly or daily rates are charged within the city; trips out of town are charged on a round-trip basis. The most reputable companies are: **Avis**, tel: 021-314 2900; **Hertz**, tel: 021-830 7460; **White Horse**, tel: 021-6385 5005; and **Bluebird**, tel: 021-798 9000. Self-drive car hire is available, but is not recommended.

You must have an international licence to drive in Indonesia.

By Taxi

Taxi fares are reasonable. Check that the meter is working and that your driver knows the location of your destination before getting in; alternatively, book a taxi from **Bluebird** (tel: 021-7917 1234) or **Pusaka** (which is owned by the Bluebird Group) or its sister company, **Silverbird** (tel: 021-798 1234). Also recommended are **Express** (tel: 021-2650 9000) and **TransCab** (tel: 021-5835 5500), which is equipped with cable TV.

Taxis are easily found at large hotels and shopping malls, or by flagging one down on major streets. Note that it is advisable to be selective when taking a taxi on the street, as not all are safe and reliable. Look for the driver's ID card on the dashboard to make sure he is an authorised driver.

By Bus

Regular city buses are cheap but are hot and crowded – an adventure for the intrepid traveller. They can be dangerous, as they tend not to stop completely when picking up or discharging passengers. Beware of pickpockets, especially during peak hours; the orange "Metro Mini" buses have a particularly bad reputation.

The **Transjakarta** bus (also known as the "busway") operates 10 corridors linking five Jakarta areas. More than 400 air-conditioned buses ply special car-free lanes for US30 cents one-way. Convenient stops along the way are: Kebayoran, Thamrin, Majapahit, Gajahmada and Pintu Besar Selatan and vice versa. The busway is the fastest way to get from one end of town to the other. Visitors can alight at the Kota bus terminal and begin their

walking tours of Old Batavia (Kota) from there.

By Boat to Kepulauan Seribu

Motorboat launches can be hired to all the Kepulauan Seribu islands from Ancol marina, located within the vast Ancol amusement park on Jakarta's north shore. The islands closest to the mainland are only 20–30 minutes away, making them an easy beach escape from the city. The furthest islands are about 2 hours away. The resorts will arrange the boat transfer when you make your booking with them.

West Java

West Coast

Most of West Java is easily accessible from Jakarta, connected by modern express toll roads or by high-speed trains. Take note, however, that the highways in and out of Jakarta at weekends and during holidays are extremely crowded.

Bandung

The Argo Parahyangan train travels from Jakarta to Bandung in 2 hours and has comfortable reclining seats, videos and offers a seat-side meal service. The fastest alternative is the regularly scheduled (less waiting time) minivan shuttle service (6–9 passengers) via Cipularang toll road, which takes around 2½ hours. Call Day Trans (tel: 021-7063 6868; www.daytrans.co.id), X-trans (tel: 021-315 0555; www.xtrans.co.id) or Cipaganti (tel: 022-731 9498; www.cipaganti.co.id) for stopping-off places. Prices start from US$6 per person one-way.

Central Java

By Air

Central Java's airports are at Yogyakarta (Jogja), Surakarta (Solo) and Semarang.

AirAsia has daily flights to **Jogja** from Singapore and Malaysia Airlines operates direct flights from Kuala Lumpur (Malaysia) to Jogja. From Jakarta, Bali and other points in Indonesia, options include Batavia Air, Citilink, Garuda, Lion Air, Merpati and Sriwijaya. SilkAir has direct flights from Singapore to **Solo**. From Solo to Jogja it is 65km (40 miles) or an hour by car on a good highway. **Semarang** is served by Garuda and Merpati, connecting it with Jakarta and other points in Indonesia.

By Train and Bus

Jogja can be reached by train from Bandung, Jakarta and Surabaya and is connected to Jakarta and Denpasar and points in between by several classes of **bus**. Non-stop Executive Class buses are recommended. For an excellent **car hire** company for day trips around or outside Jogja contact JogjaRentCar (www.jogjarentcar.com). Service is efficient and rates are reasonable. A bonus is English-speaking drivers who do not accept commissions at tourist shops.

Magelang does not have an airport, so the only way to get there is by bus, car or taxi. It is less than 1 hour north of Jogja or 2 hours south of Semarang. Local travel agents can help you arrange your trip. **Semarang** is connected with Jakarta and Surabaya and other points in Indonesia by train and bus.

Solo can be reached by express minibus from Jogja; book a seat at any local travel agency (check with your accommodation for the closest one). There are services running throughout the day, departing every 30 minutes, which will drop you anywhere in Solo. You can also flag down a bus or minibus heading east, from Jogja's Jl. Jend. Sudirman or Jl. Solo; they will take you to Solo for about half the price, but the ride will take a good bit longer and the vehicle is usually packed. Another option is to charter your own taxi or minivan from Jogja and share the cost with other passengers. It is also possible to reach Solo by **train**. The Prambanan Express runs from Jogja to Solo five times daily.

East Java

Surabaya

Convenient domestic **air services** connect Surabaya with many cities in Indonesia, with regular shuttles to and from Jakarta among others. Many flights heading for the northern and eastern islands stop over

BELOW: Java-Bali ferry.

at Surabaya. As Surabaya is an important commercial hub, there are also direct services from Singapore and Kuala Lumpur.

In addition to many of the key domestic carriers listed above, Sky Aviation flies small aircraft from Surabaya to other regions in Java and Sumatra and is also available for charter flights.

A large number of trans-Java express **trains** (www.kereta-api.com) and **buses** terminate or originate in Surabaya, with many immediate onward connections.

PELNI **ferries** connect Surabaya, an important port of call, with other major ports. There are frequent ferries from Ketapang, East Java, to Gilimanuk, Bali. *Bemos* (minivans) shuttle travellers between the bus terminal, 4km (2½ miles) north of Ketapang, and the ferry terminal.

Malang

Sri Wijaya Air has daily flights to Malang from Jakarta and other cities. From Surabaya, express buses leave regularly from the Purabaya

Key Domestic Carriers

Batavia Air (www.batavia-air.com) flies from Jakarta to most provincial capitals and other cities.
Citilink (www.citilink.co.id), a Garuda subsidiary, serves Jakarta and several major cities.
Express Air (www.expressair.biz) serves destinations in Sulawesi and Papua.
Indonesia Air Transport (http://indonesia-air.com) serves Lombok.
Kalstar (www.kalstaronline.com) serves destinations in Kalimantan.
Merpati Nusantara Airlines (www.merpati.co.id) connects remote cities to major hubs.
Sendawar Air (www.sendawar.com) serves destinations in Kalimantan.
Sky Aviation (www.sky-aviation.co.id) serves destinations in Sumatra and Java not covered by other airlines.
Sriwijaya Air (www.sriwijayaair.co.id) is one of the best airlines for regional routes.
Susi Air (www.susiair.com) runs a scheduled commuter service to remote destinations in Java, Sumatra, Kalimantan, Timor and Papua.
TransNusa Air Services (www.transnusa.co.id) links Bali to Nusa Tenggara.
Trigana Air (www.trigana-air.com) connects Denpasar and Lombok, and serves destinations in Kalimantan.

ABOVE: horse-drawn carts in Denpasar

bus terminal for the 2-hour ride to Malang's Arjosari station, 5km (3 miles) north of the town. The morning Jatayu train leaves Surabaya's Gubeng station for the 90-minute journey to Malang. Ask your hotel to book train or bus seats.

SUMATRA

Medan is Sumatra's largest city, with **international flights** arriving from Singapore and Kuala Lumpur, as well as from other points in Sumatra and elsewhere in Indonesia. A few international carriers also serve Padang, Palembang, Pekanbaru and Batam. Indonesian air carriers connect the major cities – Banda Aceh, Bandar Lampung, Benkulu, Kota Jambi, Medan, Padang, Palembang, Pekanbaru and Batam – and other points in Indonesia.

Numerous **ferry services** connect Sumatra to Malaysia and other Indonesian islands, and there are frequent crossings between Singapore and Bintan and Batam resort islands.

On mainland Sumatra, there are good highway systems in the north, west and south, but in the east, travel is more difficult. There are frequent **buses**, and shorter-distance **minibuses**, locally called "Travel".

There are three unlinked **rail systems** in Sumatra. The North line runs from Medan north to Banda Aceh and south to Rantauprapat; West, from Padang north to Bukittinggi and Payakumbuh and south to Solok and Sawah Lunto. In South Sumatra, the line begins at Tanjung Karang and runs north to Prabumulih, east to Palembang and west to Lubuklinggau.

North Sumatra

Medan

Medan's **Polonia International**

airport has daily flights from Jakarta, Singapore (SilkAir) and Kuala Lumpur (Malaysia Airlines). In terms of distance, Singapore, Kuala Lumpur and Penang (Malaysia) are closer to Medan than Jakarta. Garuda flies from Medan to Jakarta 10 times a day. Merpati, Batavia Air and Lion Air also serve Medan.

It is also possible to travel by **ferry** from Singapore to Batam island in the Riau archipelago and then fly direct to Medan. Between Medan and Penang there are fast hydrofoil boats that make the twice-weekly crossing in 5 hours. Contact Langkawi Ferry Service in Medan (tel: 061-452 1666 or 452 7555; www.langkawi-ferry.com).

Banda Aceh

Banda Aceh can be reached by an 11-hour express bus ride from Medan, and there are direct flights on Garuda from Jakarta and Medan. Lion Air and AirAsia operate flights from Kuala Lumpur. In addition, a railway line runs from north Medan to Banda Aceh.

Prapat/Samosir island

Scheduled bus services from Medan make the trip to Prapat within 4 hours. Alternatively, rent a minivan and hire a driver.

West Sumatra

Padang

Padang's international airport is 23km (14 miles) north of town. AirAsia flies from Jakarta three-times daily. Garuda flies from Jakarta twice daily and from Medan four times a day. Garuda and Singapore's Tiger Airways fly direct from Singapore to Padang. AirAsia, Garuda, Tiger Airways, Batavia Air and Lion Air serve Padang.

Bukittinggi

Bukittinggi is a 2-hour bus, taxi or "Travel" (minivan) ride from Padang

Airport. Taxis are booked for a flat fee at the airport; buses stop in Padang; minivans will wait until most seats are filled before departing. From Medan, the journey may take more than 18 hours.

Nias

There are daily **flights** on Lion Air (operated by Wings Air) and Merpati to Nias island from Medan. Sibolga can be reached **by** road from either Medan (in 9 hours) or Padang (10 hours). You can also take a boat from there; daily **ferries** make the 4–10-hour crossing to the Nias capital, Gunung Sitoli. Note: Storms are frequent and the waves can be quite dangerous. ASDP ferries depart nightly from Sibolga for the 10-hour journey to Gunung Sitoli.

Siberut

The 150km (90-mile) boat trip from Padang to Siberut island takes 12 hours. From Padang's Teluk Bayur Harbour, small passenger **ferries** depart twice a week for Muara Padang on Siberut. The boats can be very crowded, so book in advance (tel: 0759-21064; Siberut office, Jl. B.T. Arua No. 31, Teluk Bayur; tel: 0725-21941) or contact Regina Adventures (Jl. Pampangan No. 54, Padang; tel: 0751-64884; www. reginaadventures.com).

South Sumatra

Palembang

AirAsia connects Palembang with Kuala Lumpur; Garuda and SilkAir with Singapore. AirAsia, Garuda, Sriwijaya and Merpati fly from Jakarta, with additional services originating from other Sumatran cities such as Medan, Pekanbaru and Batam island.

BELOW: Jakarta backstreet.

ABOVE: becak pedicabs awaiting customers, Makassar.

Pekanbaru

Garuda flies direct from Singapore three times weekly. AirAsia flies three times a week from Kuala Lumpur. Garuda, Lion Air, Batavia Air and AirAsia fly from Jakarta to Pekanbaru. Note that during the dry season (July–Oct) Sumatra's forest fires can disrupt air travel in the region. Check timetables.

Batam island

AirAsia, Garuda, Batavia Air, Lion Air and Merpati have **flights** from Jakarta to Batam. **Ferries** frequently zip back and forth between Singapore and the Riau islands. Crossings from Singapore's Harbourfront Centre (the main terminal) take 30–60 minutes, depending on type of boat and destination on Batam. Ferry operators from Harbourfront Centre include Penguin (www. penguin.com.sg) and Dino/Batam Fast (www.batamfast.com). Note that you will have to go through Immigration upon arrival at Batam.

Bintan island

Tanjung Pinang, the capital of Riau on the southwest coast, is served by **high-speed ferries** from Singapore's Tanah Merah Ferry Terminal (45 minutes away), Johor Bahru (Malaysia), Batam and other Riau islands. In Bintan, you can obtain a visa on arrival (if appropriate) at Bandar Bentan Telani terminal on the western tip of the Bintan Resort area (Lagoi). Schedules and online booking for Bintan Resort Ferries are available at www.brf.com.sg.

Transport from the ferry terminal to the resort is generally included in hotel packages, which may also include ferry fares. Car hire companies are also located at the ferry terminal for trips to other parts of Bintan island.

BALI

Getting There

By Air

Bali's **Ngurah Rai International Airport** (information, tel: 0361-751 011) is served by direct flights from cities in Europe, the US, Australia and Asia, as well as key Indonesian cities. The airport is very compact, with the domestic and international terminals within a few minutes' walking distance of each other. Domestic departure tax in Bali to other Indonesian cities is currently Rp 30,000.

Some international airlines fly only to Jakarta's Soekarno-Hatta International Airport, from where domestic flights to Bali are frequent. *(See pages 365 and 367 for listings of international and domestic airlines and for departure information.)*

By Bus

With improved roads, the *bis malam* (night bus) from Java to Bali now travels faster than the train, but drivers can be reckless. Unless you particularly want the overland experience, check air fares, as promotional rates can be cheaper. There are numerous bus companies that make the journey; ask a travel agent locally. All connect with the ferries on the east coast, arriving in Denpasar within 24 hours, after stopping at three or four cities, depending on the bus company. To break the journey, stop over at Yogyakarta; from there it's 15–16 hours to Bali, or from Surabaya, 11 hours.

Perama (www.peramatour.com) buses are safe, clean and efficient, and travel daily from major cities in Java to several destinations in South and North Bali and also within Lombok and Flores.

By Sea

For all ferry crossings, be prepared for delays, particularly in bad weather and in peak season, and for long waits while cargo and passengers are offloaded. From Java: Ferries ply the 30-minute trip between Ketapang in East Java and Gilimanuk in West Bali. From Lombok: From Lembar Harbour in Lombok, ferries take 4 hours to reach Padangbai in East Bali. Contact Perama *(see By bus, above)* for transport packages that include land transfers and ferry tickets.

Getting Around

Balinese roads double as parade grounds for festival processions. They are becoming increasingly crowded, and traffic jams are frequent. Keep in mind that patience is a virtue.

By Public Transport

Minivans *(bemo)* operate on fixed routes from terminals or marketplaces in cities and major towns. Some transfer points are at important crossroads. There are no marked places to get off and on; just flag one down, and call out "stop" when you want to get out. Fares are based on distance travelled (ask a local what the fare is while waiting). As passengers and products of all sorts are loaded off and on, things can get hot and crowded. This mode of transport does take time, but allows you to meet the local people; beware of pickpockets, though.

Major **bus terminals**, with *bemo* stations alongside, are at Tegal in Denpasar (services to Kuta), Kereneng in Denpasar (services to places in the city, Batubulan and Sanur), Ubung (services to Tabanan, Singaraja and Jembrana), Batubulan (services to Gianyar, Singaraja, Bangli, Klungkung and Karangasem), and in Singaraja (services to Jembrana, Tabanan, Denpasar and Karangasem).

By Private Transport

Taxis
Airport taxis have fixed rates, which are posted at the taxi counters outside the domestic and international terminals, where you pay. Taxis are air-conditioned and metered; however, outside the airport, many drivers will offer to charge a flat rate instead of using the meter. If you do not know the going rate (ask at your hotel), tell the driver to use the meter. Few taxis, outside the Kuta-Legian-Seminyak area, cruise the

streets for passengers, so call **Bali Taxi** (tel: 0361-701 111) – owned by Jakarta's reputable Bluebird Group, it has the highest percentage of English-speaking drivers. If you can't get a Bali Taxi, **Praja Taxi** (tel: 0361-389 090) is also good.

In Ubud, the only taxis are the ones that have brought passengers from other areas and are hoping for a fare back. Your hotel can arrange private transport, or negotiate a fare with one of the men offering transport on the street. *(See Vehicle with driver, below, for more details.)*

Motorcycle Taxis
Motorcycle taxis *(ojek)* wait at designated places and take you wherever you want to go, which is very convenient for locations not served by public transport. Agree on the price beforehand, and make sure you wear the extra helmet that the driver provides, as it's required by law. The drivers do weave in and out of heavy traffic but are very experienced. Fares are negotiable, usually just a few thousand rupiah for a short journey.

Vehicle with Driver
Hiring a car or minivan with driver can be done by the half-day or full day. Tip: rates are cheaper if negotiated on the street rather than from your hotel; look out for young men who call out "transpor" and move their hands as if driving a car. Check the condition of the vehicle and get a feel for the driver before agreeing to anything.

Rates vary according to the kind of vehicle, its condition, actual travel time and total number of hours. This amount should include fuel. Full-day rates generally range from Rp 400,000 during peak season. Half-day will cost Rp 200,000–300,000.

It is courteous to give your driver money for a meal if you pause for lunch or dinner. If you are pleased with his service, a tip of Rp 30,000–50,000 is

appropriate and Rp 50,000–100,000 for English-speaking guides. You will usually get a better rate if you arrange to use the same driver for all the trips during your stay.

It is easy to charter a vehicle with a driver (and a guide, if needed) for an hour, day or month. Check with **Golden Bird Limousine & Car Rental** (24-hour reservations): tel: 701 111; www.bluebirdgroup.com. **Autobagus Rent a Car**: Jl. Tukud Balian Renon, Denpasar; tel: 7222 222; www.autobagus.com.

Self-drive Car Hire
Driving in Bali can be dangerous. Generally, drivers do not drive defensively, the roads are narrow and poorly maintained, and stray dogs and chickens frequently dart out. If you collide with anything, you are responsible for all costs. It's safer to hire a driver while you relax and enjoy the sights.

Self-drive cars are available throughout South Bali, for which you must have a valid international driving licence. It's also advisable to pay the extra costs to ensure you have full insurance coverage. Petrol is not included in the price. You can book a car through your hotel or from the companies listed above – they will deliver the car to you and pick it up at the end of the rental period. Always test-drive the car before paying. Note: drive on the left side of the road.

Prices (per day) range from US$20–35 for a Suzuki Jeep to US$30–45 for a larger Toyota Kijang. These rates should include collision insurance, unlimited mileage and pick-up and delivery service.

Motorcycle Hire
Motorcycles are a convenient and inexpensive way to get around the island, but there are risks due to heavy traffic and poor roads. Helmets are required by law, but the cheap

BELOW: the national airline.

ones provided by rental agencies offer little protection, so bring your own or buy a good one from a local shop, especially one with a face shield for protection from sun, rain, bugs and dust. Drive slowly and defensively, as locals and tourists are injured or killed every year in accidents.

The cost of motorbike hire varies according to the model, condition of the machine, length of rental and time of year. Expect to pay Rp 60,000 per day in high season. Petrol is not included. Buy full insurance so that you are not responsible for any damage. Be sure to test-drive it to check that everything is in working order, especially brakes and lights.

You must have an international driving permit valid for motorcycles, or else go to the Denpasar Police Office to obtain a temporary permit, valid for three months on Bali only. Normally the person who rents you the motorbike will accompany you to the police office. Take your passport, driving licence from your home country and three passport-sized photos.

Bicycle

Bikes are available for rent everywhere, and many hotels have them. Before you pay for one, make sure the wheels are properly aligned and that the brakes and light work well. Then be selective about where you ride. The main roads of Bali are congested and full of potholes, and motor vehicles spew exhaust fumes into your face, so stick to the quieter country roads. Wear a helmet for extra safety, and try not to ride at night, because roads are very poorly lit, or not lit at all. Prices vary from Rp 20,000–30,000 per day.

BELOW: on the road in central Bali.

NUSA TENGGARA

Lombok

Getting There

By Air
At the time of writing, Lombok flights are served by Selaparang Airport near the capital, Mataram. Scheduled to open in late 2011 is the new **Lombok International Airport** 40km (25 miles) south of Mataram, which will replace Selaparang. Most visitors head straight for one-of the beaches upon arrival. If you need a visa on arrival (and qualify for one), you can get it at the airport *(see page 413 for more information about visas)*.

Currently, SilkAir is the only international airline arriving in Lombok (direct flights from Singapore to Mataram); however, more are scheduled once the new airport opens. At present, Lion Air, Merpati and Citilink fly from Surabaya. Batavia Air, Garuda, Lion Air and Merpati have flights from Jakarta; Indonesia Air Transport, Merpati and Trigana Air have flights from Denpasar. TransNusa connects Lombok with islands to the east.

By Sea
Public (slow, overcrowded) **ferries** depart every 2 hours for the picturesque sea crossing between Padangbai Harbour (Bali) and Lembar Harbour (Lombok), about 20km (12 miles) south of Mataram; the crossing takes 4 to 5 hours. Note that on a windy day with high waves, the crossing will be choppy and uncomfortable. Seasickness medication is advised. Several companies offer **speedboat service** from Bali directly to the Gilis and

mainland Lombok. Check out Gili Cat (http://gilicat.com).

From Senggigi, Lembar Harbour is about 1 hour away. Buy tickets direct from the desk there, or get a complete transfer package from a reputable tour company such as **Perama Tours** (www.peramatour.com), which includes pick-up from destinations throughout Bali and Lombok, bus transfer to the local harbour, ferry ticket and transfer from the harbour to your destination on either island. Contact Perama in Lombok, tel: 0370-693 007/693 008; Bali, tel: 0361-751 551/751 875.

Getting Around
By Motorcycle and Bicycle
Motorbike rental is available in Senggigi. Enquire at your hotel or any motorcycle shop on the main streets. A motorcycle licence is required – obtainable at the police station – as is a helmet. You can bring a motorcycle from Bali on the public ferry. Many hotels have bicycles for hire.

By Taxi
Lombok Taxi (tel: 0370-627 000), owned by Jakarta's reliable Bluebird Group, operates light-blue taxis that are metered and have courteous drivers. Flag one down on the street, or phone ahead to book one. Hourly or day-rate hire also available.

By Bemo and Bus
Minivans *(bemos)* and buses serve all the towns on the island, but they are slow and uncomfortable. The central terminal is at the crossroads at Sweta, just to the east of Cakranegara; there is a signboard displaying the fares to all destinations. **Perama** (tel: 0370-693 007; www.peramatour.com) operates shuttle buses that connect to key places on the island.

Car Hire
It is worth paying a bit more for a taxi or rented car with an English-speaking driver. Most hotels have a travel disc that can arrange cars for you with or without driver and guide. Self-driving is not advised, but if you decide to try it, you must have an international drivers' licence. To see what types of vehicles are available, check www.lombokcarrentals.com or http://lombokrentcar.com.

Sumbawa

Merpati and TransNusa **airlines** serve both Sumbawa Besar (West Sumbawa) and Bima (East Sumbawa). **Ferries** from Lombok to West Sumbawa are regularly scheduled. Check with a Lombok travel agent for current scheduling and prices. Minivans *(bemos)* meet the ferries to take passengers to either Sumbawa Besar (another 3 hours) or to Bima (9 hours).

Komodo and Rinca

Komodo National Park can be reached only by sea. There are two entry points to the park. TransNusa flies from Denpasar to Bima, on Sumbawa, and to Labuhanbajo, western Flores. From Bima, travel overland to Sape Harbour by public bus or hired vehicle (1½ hours over curving mountain road). At both Sape and Labuhanbajo harbours there are local boats (bargain for reasonable fares) and a scheduled ferry service (buy a ticket at the ferry terminal).

Departure times depend entirely upon the tides and currents, and service is frequently halted because of high seas, particularly in January and February. The crossing from Sape to Komodo takes 8 hours in calm seas, longer if the waves are strong. From Labuhanbajo, it's about 3 hours to Komodo and is a far more scenic crossing. From either direction, ferries will stop near Komodo island, where small local boats will take you to land for a nominal fee. Be sure to inspect the vessel for seaworthiness before getting in. The currents are strong in these seas, and although boatmen don't take unnecessary risks, boats do sink with alarming regularity.

Alternatively, chartered boats from either Sape or Labuhanbajo may be prearranged through travel agents throughout Indonesia or chartered through tour operators in Bima, Sape or Labuhanbajo. Or you may choose to cruise and dive with one of several dive operators.

Foreigners visiting Komodo National Park must pay an entrance fee of Rp 50,000 plus Rp 50,000 per camera and Rp 150,000 per video camera. Permits are valid for 3 days and easily extendable. Entrance fees may be paid at the ranger station at either Loh Liang, Komodo or Loah Buaya on Rinca. The 3-day pass is good for both islands.

Flores

TransNusa operates **flights** to Labuhanbajo from Denpasar (Bali), Kupang (Timor), Mataram (Lombok) and Ruteng (Flores). TransNusa also flies to Bajawa, Ende, Larantuka and Maumere from Kupang and between Ende and Maumere.

ABOVE: Sanur beach.

TransNusa's flights into Ruteng originate in Denpasar, Ende, Kupang, Labuhanbajo and Mataram. Merpati flies to Maumere, Labuhanbajo and Ende from Denpasar. PELNI **ships** have several routes to Labuhanbajo.

Travelling overland across Flores should not be attempted with limited time. The Trans-Flores highway reaches from Labuhanbajo in the west to Larantuka in the east – which can be done by public transport – but be aware that the 670km (400-mile) road is often shut down for hours or days due to landslides during the rainy season (Oct–Apr). It takes a good 4 to 5 days to complete, as public transport seldom runs at night, but for those with plenty of time, by breaking up the journey into 5-hour segments, overnighting and touring for a day or two, then beginning the next leg of the trip, you can see practically all of one of Indonesia's most geographically and culturally diverse islands.

Elsewhere in Nusa Tenggara

There are daily return **flights** to Kupang from Jakarta, Surabaya and Denpasar. Be forewarned that small-aircraft flights in this area – although scheduled – are frequently delayed or cancelled altogether. Flexibility and patience are essential to travelling here. TransNusa and Merpati serve the Solor and Alor archipelagos and Sumba from Kupang. Susi Air flies from Kupang to Rote and Savu. As small planes are used, tickets must be booked well in advance at the Susi Air office at the respective airports. via Garuda, Lion Air, Batavia Air, Sriwijaya Air and Merpati.

PELNI sails between the islands and there are also local **ferries**. The bigger the port town, the more frequent the stops. Note that the seas are rough in Jan and Feb, and ferries often do not run. Travellers should

avoid visiting East Nusa Tenggara islands by sea during these months.

KALIMANTAN

Many travellers enter Kalimantan via **Balikpapan**, which has daily flights from Singapore, Jakarta, Manado and other Indonesian cities, as well as ferries from Java *(see below)*. The West Kalimantan gateway is **Pontianak**, connected by air with Kuching in East Malaysia, as well as major Indonesian cities. Visitors seeking orang-utans in Central Kalimantan can fly to Palangkaraya or Pangkalanbun. *For more details on getting to Kalimantan, see below.*

Kalimantan is a huge island with relatively poor infrastructure. The major cities are far apart and public buses are erratic, making it sensible to travel by air. For short distances, there are several varieties of boats, ranging from large passenger ferries to water taxis.

East Kalimantan

Balikpapan

A busy oil and timber town, Balikpapan holds little interest for travellers and sees mostly business visitors. Independent travellers head straight for Samarinda – the gateway to Dayak country – by air, or drive up the 115km (70-mile) paved road to begin their journey up the great Sungai Mahakam into the interior.

Silk Air has daily flights from Singapore. Domestic flights between Jakarta, Manado and Balikpapan and other points in Indonesia are served by Batavia Air, Garuda, Lion Air, Merpati and Sriwijaya Air. Passengers flying to the more remote parts of Kalimantan may experience frequent delays, cancellations or overbooking.

There are three PELNI ferry

services to Balikpapan. One connects to Surabaya in Java, the other to Makassar in Sulawesi, and the third goes to Tarakan in northern East Kalimantan, near the Sabah border.

The Trans-Kalimantan highway extends from Batakan, south of Banjarmasin, to Balikpapan and then to Samarinda. It eventually connects to Bontang and Tarakan. Buses run on a regular schedule from Banjarmasin to Balikpapan and Samarinda. Because of the thick forest, water transport is the key means of getting around in Kalimantan. Riverboats and ferries – *taksi sungai* (river taxi) or *bis air* (water bus) – are popular forms of transport.

Samarinda

Buses from Balikpapan make the journey to Samarinda in about 2 hours. Chartered **taxis** are much faster but more expensive. **Speedboats** depart Samarinda daily and arrive in Bontang about 5 hours later. **Water taxis** take about twice as long. Try to catch a ride with MAF (Missionary Aviation Fellowship, www. maf.org) in small Cessna planes to reach the inaccessible places. MAF has no fixed schedules and operates strictly on a seat-available basis.

South Kalimantan

Banjarmasin

In addition to the commercial **airlines**, Batavia, Garuda, Lion Air, Merpati, Sriwijaya Air and Kalstar Aviation fly to Banjarmasin. Check with an Indonesian travel agent for schedules.

PELNI **ferries** call at Banjarmasin on the run between Surabaya and Semarang in Java. Marina Nusantara sails to Banjarmasin from Surabaya in 16 hours. Contact a Banjarmasin travel agent to make a booking. From Balikpapan and Samarinda, overnight **buses** make the journey to Banjarmasin

BELOW: scooters are ubiquitous.

in 12 and 14 hours, respectively.

Riverboats are the main mode of travel in much of Kalimantan. From Banjarmasin, you can go northwards on Sungai Barito to its headwater. If you have a couple of weeks, you can explore the whole river. Boats can be chartered upriver as far as Mauratewe. From there, switch to a canoe as you approach the headwater.

A long trek northeast (you can shorten the journey by road) over swamps leads to Intu and finally to Long Iram on Sungai Mahakam. Samarinda is 36 hours away down the Mahakam River. But if you are game for more river travel, on arrival in Long Iram go by boat up the Mahakam to the Dayak villages at Longbangun, through the rapids to Long Pahangai, Tiong Ohang and further.

Central Kalimantan

Palangkaraya

Garuda, Batavia Air and Sriwijaya Air fly to Palangkaraya from Jakarta. Garuda also files in from Surabaya. By bus or car from Banjarmasin across a new road takes about 8 hours, or travel the way the local people do, by *bis air* (water bus) or speedboat. Or fly to Pangkalanbun and travel by road to Palangkaraya.

Pangkalanbun

There are daily flights between Pangkalanbun and Semarang, Ketapang and Pontianak on Kalstar Aviation.

Tanjung Puting National Park

Visitors must register with the PHPA (Forestry Department) office in Pangkalanbun to obtain a permit to go into the park. You will need a photocopy of your passport (including the white embarkation card you received when you entered Indonesia). Current registration fee is about US$5.

From Pangkalanbun, it is 20 minutes by taxi to Kumai, the riverside village that is the entry point into Tanjung Puting National Park. At Kumai Harbour, rent a *klotok* (motorised local boat) for about US$35 per day for one to four people. If you plan to eat and sleep on the boat, you will pay extra for a cook. Be sure to buy food and water in Kumai before heading upriver.

West Kalimantan

Pontianak

Malaysia Airlines **flies** to Pontianak from Kuching (Sarawak, Malaysia), where there are international

Getting to the Gilis

Perama (tel: 0370-693 007; www. peramatour.com) has daily shuttles to the Gilis from Mataram, Senggigi and Kuta (Lombok). Also check the dive shops for shuttle service. Public boats leave from Bengsal beach. To get to the official ticket office from the main road requires passing through a horde of greedy touts who are out to rip you off. Ignore them and go to the ticket office on the left. Note that boats to the Gilis do not depart until they are full.

connections from Singapore and Kuala Lumpur. Domestic airlines serving Pontianak are Batavia Air, Garuda, Merpati and Sriwijaya Air. Trigana Air flies small aircraft from Pontianak to Ketapang, Pangkalanbun, Banjarmasin, Sintang and Putussibau. The trip from the airport into town takes about 20 minutes, depending on traffic conditions. Taxis are available.

Three PELNI **ferries** stop at Pontianak, and connect to Surabaya, Semarang and Jakarta. Prima Vista (Jl. Pak Kasih 90B; tel: 0561-761 145) sells ferry tickets and has schedules.

The **road trip** from Pontianak to Sambas takes 5 hours. To go to Sintang, you can fly there in 45 minutes on a small Trigana plane. You can also ride 12 hours by bus or go by houseboat (2 days) up the Sungai Kapuas. From Pontianak, a serviceable road runs north and forks at Seipenyu village. The road on the left heads northwards towards the border with East Malaysia (you need a visa to cross). The road on the right heads east to Sintang. Logging roads provide a crude path for sturdy vehicles in a few areas. Bridges are often made with rotting logs, and erosion and mud slides create common obstacles. In dry weather, it is possible to travel by jeep.

SULAWESI

Makassar is the provincial capital of Sulawesi and has the largest number of **flights**. However, there are good connections in Manado, serving the north and gateway to Bunaken, and in Palu. Kendari is the entry point for Southeast Sulawesi, including Wakatobi. By **sea**, PELNI is the main connection with other Indonesian islands.

In Sulawesi, the major cities are far apart, the **roads** are poorly maintained and are either hilly or winding, or both. Travel by air is advised whenever possible. PELNI ferries schedule routes to the Wakatobi area but are unreliable, making it best to use one of the fast boat services there.

South Sulawesi

Makassar

Confusingly, Makassar city was formerly called Ujung Pandang, and although it officially changed its name to Makassar over a decade ago, the airport is still called Ujung Pandang. Several **airlines** originating in Jakarta and Surabaya serve Makassar. See an Indonesian travel agent for flight timetables for Batavia Air, Garuda, Lion Air, Merpati and Express Air. AirAsia arrives several times a week on direct flights from Kuala Lumpur, and Garuda has daily direct flights from Singapore. From the airport, it is about 40 minutes to town. To ride in an authorised taxi, purchase a coupon at the taxi counter outside the arrivals hall.

PELNI **ferries** operate routes to Makassar from Balikpapan, Bau-Bau and various points in Java and Flores.

For **short trips** in the city, *becak* (pedicabs) are an environmentally-friendly way to get around. To travel by air-con metered taxis, either hail one on the street or call one by phone (Bosowa Taxi; tel: 0411-454 545).

Boats to Samalona island or other places can be chartered from Pantai Benteng (across from Benteng Rotterdam) for about US$35 for a round-trip. The price to Kayangan island is US$3.50 by shuttle boat. Tickets can be purchased at kiosks across from Benteng Rotterdam.

Rantepao

SMAC Air (Sabang Merauke Raya Air; no website) operates **flights** from Makassar to Tana Toraja twice a week. Several attempts over the years to establish regular flights to and from Toraja – helping travellers to avoid the excruciating road trip there – have failed. With luck, this one will endure.

From the airport in Makassar it takes 20 minutes to get to Daya Bus Station. **Air-con buses** leave for Toraja four times daily. Purchase tickets at the bus station, or book a seat on an express bus 1 day in advance. The most comfortable buses are found at **Litha & Co.** (tel: 0411-324 847), **Alam Indah** (tel: 0411-458 405) and

ABOVE: the livestock market at Rentepau, Sulawesi.

Bintang Prima (tel: 0411-477 2888).

Travel agents can arrange **chartered vehicles** for the 7–8-hour trip from Makassar to Rantepao via Pare Pare, a good place to stop for a seafood lunch overlooking the ocean. From there the road is winding and hilly and drivers are aggressive. Motion sickness medication is advised if you are susceptible.

Rantepao is small enough to explore on foot. You can also hop into a *becak* (pedicab) or ride around on a rented bicycle. Minivans *(pete-pete)* make the 20-minute run between Rantepao and Makale several times throughout the day, starting their trip from Terminal Bolu, and can be flagged down anywhere along Jalan A. Yani for travel to nearby destinations.

Hiking is the best way to explore Tana Toraja. One-day walks can be made around the area, but several days are needed to see remote areas such as Mamasa Valley. May–Oct is the best time, otherwise your hike may well end up being just a long slog in the mud.

Central Sulawesi

Palu

Merpati **flies** from Makassar to Palu four times a week. Batavia and Lion Air fly daily from Makassar. The Batavia flight continues on to Balikpapan. PELNI passenger **ships**

travel overnight from Balikpapan, Bitung, Makassar and Pare Pare. Daily public **buses** leave for Palu from Daya Bus Station in Makassar and from Rantepao.

To get to most of Central Sulawesi, a combination of trekking, taxis, four-wheel-drive vehicles, buses and boats is required. For a hassle-free holiday, ask a tour operator to make all the arrangements for you.

Poso/Tentena

Buses make the journey from Palu to Poso in about 6 hours, but as the roads are rough, the journey is a tedious one. From Poso, there are regular minibuses to Tentena (a 2-hour trip). A chartered taxi is a more comfortable option and can take you direct to Tentena.

Togian islands

Getting to the Togian islands is rough, especially during the wet season. For further information ask the staff at your hotel in Gorontalo or Ampana, or visit www.blackmarlindive.com.

Kendari

Kendari, the capital of Southeast Sulawesi, is a good place to break your journey because of its decent range of lodgings. Spend a day soaking and swimming at the spectacular seven-tiered waterfall at Morame.

Getting to Melak and Derawan island

Melak, the starting point for Dayak expeditions, can be reached by ferry (20 hours) or bus (7–8 hours) from Samarinda. Sendawar Air flies from Balikpapan and Samarinda to Melak three times weekly. The roads around Melak are good, but there is no public transport. Hire a car or motorcycle to reach Kersik Luwai, Eheng and Tering.

There are two main ways to get to Derawan island. You can take Kalstar from Balikpapan to Berau (1 hour), from where it's 30 minutes by speedboat to Derawan. Alternatively, from Balikpapan, Sriwijaya Air flies to Tarakan (1 hour). From there, take a 3–4-hour speedboat to Derawan. A new international airport is opening on Berau in 2012.

Merpati, Lion Air, Garuda, Batavia and Sriwijaya Air fly to Kendari daily from Makassar, and there are also some **direct flights** from Jakarta. PELNI **ferries** sail once every couple of weeks from Makassar to Kendari.

As Kendari has only one main road, you can't get lost. *Pete-pete* (minivans) run frequently, stopping anywhere along the way for a low fixed fare; they can also be chartered to any destination in the city. There are also metered taxis and *becaks* (pedicabs) for shorter distances.

Bau-Bau

Lion Air and Express Air **flights** to Bau-Bau operate daily from Makassar. Merpati also flies from Makassar to Bau-Bau several days a week. PELNI **ferries** sail between Makassar and Bau-Bau (12 hours) a few times a week. Times vary radically.

Superjet and Sagori Express operate twice-daily **express boat services** to and from Kendari and Bau-Bau, taking 5 hours. Ticket prices are the same, but the Sagori boats are newer and more comfortable. Purchase your tickets at booths near the harbour.

Wakatobi

Getting There
Wangi-Wangi is the first island in the Wakatobi archipelago, and it is the main port of entry by air and sea. Express Air **flies** to Wangi-Wangi daily from Makassar and Bau-Bau, and to and from Kendari each week.

There are **overnight ferries** between Bau-Bau and Wangi-Wangi, departing each destination daily at 9pm and arriving around 6am. These are wooden boats, equipped with mattresses to sleep on in large comunal areas. A few cabins are available for those wishing to pay extra, but the communal area is more spacious than the cramped cabins. Purchase tickets on the boat.

Passenger boats run between Kendari and Wangi-Wangi four times a week (10 hours), departing each destination at 9am and arriving around 7pm. The boats are similar to the Bau-Bau to Wangi-Wangi boats, only bigger. Tickets can be bought in the harbour or directly on the boat.

There are also some direct boats from Bau-Bau to Kaledupa and Bau-Bau to Tomia, but the times are variable and unpredictable. Get information on timetables at Bau-Bau Harbour.

Getting Around
There are four main islands in Wakatobi, and daily public **speedboat**

ferries operate between three of them: Wangi-Wangi and Kaledupa, and Wangi-Wangi and Tomia.

The **Kaledupa boats** depart Kaledupa at 5am and arrive in Wanci (Wangi-Wangi's main town) at 7.30am, then head back from Wanci to Kaledupa at 9 or 10am, and arrive there at about noon. Tickets can be bought on the boat, and the boats depart from Jembatan Mola.

Once on Kaledupa it is easy to charter a small boat across to Hoga island. The **Tomia boats** also depart from Jembatan Mola at 9 or 10am, and the journey to Tomia takes 2–3 hours. The boats from Tomia to Wanci depart Tomia at 10am and arrive in Wanci around noon. Tickets can be bought on the boat.

North Sulawesi

Manado

SilkAir **flies** from Singapore four times a week. Garuda and Lion Air arrive daily from Bali via Makassar, and Garuda, Batavia, and Lion Air service Manado several times daily from Jakarta. Merpati flies daily from Surabaya, Ternate and Papua.

Ships from Ambon, Sangihe, Talaud, Sorong, Ternate, Bau Bau and Banggai islands sail overnight to arrive in Bitung Harbour, 1 hour east of Manado city.

MALUKU AND PAPUA

The main entry points to **Maluku** are Ambon and Ternate. Daily return flights from Jakarta, Bali and Manado serve Ambon, the logistical hub of Maluku; intermittent flights serve other islands in the Maluku province.

Lion Air has direct **flights** from Jakarta, and also from Bali via Surabaya and Makassar to Ambon. Garuda, Batavia and Sriwijaya depart daily out of Jakarta via Makassar or Surabaya. Be prepared to show your passport at the airport upon arrival. PELNI **sails** throughout the Maluku islands from many ports. Check with the local office for schedules, which are subject to changes, delays and cancellations.

Nearly all visitors arrive in **Papua** by air via Biak or directly into Jayapura. Before booking a flight into Jayapura, compare timetables, as most make many stops en route. Garuda is the only airline that has direct flights to Jayapura from Jakarta. PELNI is the major carrier by sea. The

only land crossing open to tourists is into Jayapura via Vanimo, Papua New Guinea, and is not advised.

Travel into **Papua's interior** past the main coastal towns (ie Jayapura and Biak) requires a travel permit *(surat jalan)*, so that if you get lost the authorities will know where to start looking for you. You must list on the permit every area you plan to visit – no exceptions. You can get the permit at police headquarters in Jayapura, Biak or Sorong, usually in one day, with two passport-sized photos, a copy of your passport and a small administration fee. While you are in the city, make plenty of passport and *surat jalan* photocopies to take with you, as hotels and tour operators may ask for them.

Jayapura/Sentani

Flights to Jayapura actually land at Sentani, a 45-minute drive from Jayapura. Batavia, Garuda and Merpati have daily services. Flights transit through Makassar (also called Ujung Pandang) and other Indonesian cities. Check with the airlines for details. Express Air serves Jayapura to Tanah Merah, Wamena, Nabire, Manokwari and Sorong. Garuda has a route from Jayapura to Timika before continuing on to Jakarta. From Timika, Agats is 20 minutes by public bus.

It's worth trying to hitch free rides on one of the **coastal steamers**, as the oil industry in Papua is served by a number of sea-going vessels. On the south coast, Merauke is the major port. Other boats carry passengers, but for a fee. If you are in no hurry, the PELNI **ferry** sails from Jakarta to Jayapura and other points in Papua.

Manokwari

As the capital of West Papua province, Manokwari is linked by Merpati, Batavia and Sriwijaya Air. Susi Air connects Manokwari with other destinations on the Bird's Head peninsula and Biak.

Raja Ampat

Sorong, on the northwest tip of Bird's Head peninsula, is the entry point to Raja Ampat and is accessible on some international **flights** via Biak. Merpati, Batavia Air, Lion Air and Express Air are among the airlines that fly to Sorong from Jakarta.

Regularly scheduled **ferries** or chartered boats ply the waters between Sorong and Raja Ampat. Check with your Raja Ampat accommodation to determine if they provide transfers from the harbour.

ACCOMMODATION

HOTELS, VILLAS AND GUESTHOUSES

ACCOMMODATION

In Bali and the major business centres in Java, hotels range from five- to one-star and below, catering to every budget and taste. Jakarta and Bali's luxury hotels are among the best in the world and feature first-class service and facilities. Apart from the international five-star chains such as Hyatt, Four Seasons and Ritz-Carlton, there are also high-quality local chains and numerous boutique properties. In Banding, Surabaya, Jogja and other cities there are also heritage properties, whereas in Kalimantan overnights in Dayak longhouses can be arranged.

In provincial and regency capitals there are always two- and three-star hotels where government workers and business travellers stay, but in more remote regions anticipate only the basics, and take heart that you can delight in Indonesian hospitality.

Every area of this vast country has something special to offer, and so the biggest choice you need to make about where to stay (other than price) is what you came to experience. For example, surfers and divers will want to be near the sea and nature-lovers near forests, but there are many beaches and jungles here. We suggest reading the Places chapters first to get a feel for what each region has to offer, and then look at the listings below as a step forward in making your decision.

Prices and Bookings

Throughout Indonesia, advance reservations are recommended during the peak June–Aug and Christmas–

ABOVE: Grand Hyatt, Jakarta

New Year periods. Also be aware that prices are usually higher at these times or surcharges are added. In addition, during Indonesian public holidays and school breaks (June–July) all recreation areas plus Bali and Jogja are crowded with domestic travellers.

Look for better rates during "low" (non-peak) season. In small establishments, it is perfectly acceptable to ask for a discount when they are not fully booked. Many larger hotels have special internet rates. When travelling from island to island within Indonesia, local travel agents can often get the best rates on two- and three-star hotels by booking with hotels they frequently do business with.

There is a government tax of 11 percent, which is charged by all but small establishments, and the larger ones also usually include a 10

percent service tax (in lieu of tipping).

Many of the hotels in the following listings offer a broad choice. Inexpensive and moderately priced hotels may have rooms without air-conditioning and hot water for budget travellers as well as rooms with all amenities, termed "VIP". Moderately priced and expensive hotels may also have "presidential suites" or private villas.

The price guidelines shown are just that – guidelines – using the highest possible rate in high season. Note that the "under US$30" category includes budget *losmen* (small, family-run guesthouses) for $4–5 per night, while the "above US$150" category can also mean US$800-per-night luxury villas. Check with individual hotels for current rates during the time of your visit.

JAKARTA

If you arrive at Jakarta International Airport, you can book a hotel room at a discount at the **Indotel** and KAHA counters (located next to the baggage claim). Jakarta has a wide selection of first-class luxury hotels – most are found along the city centre of Jl. Sudirman-Thamrin.

Moderately priced hotels are a taxi ride away, while backpackers' guesthouses and *losmen* are found in the Jl. Jaksa and Jl. Kebon Sirih Dalam area near Monas/Medan Merdeka (Freedom Square).

The Dharmawangsa
Jl. Brawijaya Raya, No. 26
Tel: 021-725 8181
www.the-dharmawangsa.com
Intimate boutique-style hotel with only 100 rooms, a third of which are suites. A haven of understated luxury, with expensive artworks throughout. The dramatic Sriwijaya restaurant combines Western flair and presentation with local ingredients and traditional Indonesian flavours. **$$$$$**

Grand Hyatt Jakarta
Jl. Jend M.H. Thamrin, Kav. 28–30
Tel: 021-2992 1234
www.jakarta.grand.hyatt.com
Considered to be the best in Jakarta, this sophisticated hotel sits above the Plaza Indonesia mall. Excellent

BELOW: Surabaya Shangri-La.

service and fabulous restaurants. **$$$$$**
Gran Meliá Jakarta
Jl. H.R. Rasuna Said, Kav. X-0
Tel: 021-526 8080
www.granmeliajakarta.com
A five-star hotel, part of the Spanish-run Meliá Sol chain. An elegant 428-room hotel with beautiful landscaped gardens. Known for its good Sunday brunch. **$$$$$**
J.W. Marriott
Jl. Lingkar Mega Kuningan, Kav. E 1–2, No. 122
Tel: 021-5798 8888
www.marriott.com
Located in the Golden Triangle business district, its restaurant is popular with businessmen at lunchtime. Rooms are comfortable and spacious. **$$$$$**
Mid Plaza
InterContinental
Jl. Jend. Sudirman, Kav. 10–11
Tel: 021-251 0888
www.ichhotelsgroup.com
Jakarta's five-star InterContinental hotel features lots of wood and black marble and has easy access to the central business district. **$$$$$**
Mulia Senayan
Jl. Asia Afrika Senayan
Tel: 021-574 7777
www.hotelmulia.com
Located in the shopping district near Blok M, this hotel features spacious and luxurious rooms and all the amenities you expect from a five-star hotel. **$$$$$**
Ritz-Carlton Jakarta
Jl. Lingkar Mega Kuningan, Kav. E-1.1, No. 1
Tel: 021-2551 8888
www.ritzcarlton.com
This five-star de luxe hotel is located between Jl. Jend. Sudirman and Jl. H.R. Rasuna Said (Kuningan), Jakarta's business districts. **$$$$$**
Ritz-Carlton Pacific Place Jakarta
Sudirman Central Business District
Jl. Jend. Sudirman, Kav. 52–53
Tel: 021-2550 1888
www.ritzcarlton.com
Adjacent to Pacific Place Mall and Residence, this

Ritz-Carlton has only 60 boutique rooms. **$$$$$**
Shangri-La
Kota BNI
Jl. Jend. Sudirman, Kav. 1
Tel: 021-570 7440
www.shangri-la.com
One of the more popular luxury hotels, this 32-storey establishment is centrally located and offers free morning shuttle services to major office addresses. An excellent Chinese restaurant serves dim sum on Sundays, while the popular B.A.T.S. bar is on the first level. **$$$$$**
Sultan
Jl. Gatot Subroto
Tel: 021-570 3600
www.sultanjakarta.com
The largest five-star hotel in the city sits adjacent to the Jakarta Convention Centre. More than 200 apartments in separate wings cater to long-term guests. The hotel serves a great Sunday brunch, and offers monthly cooking classes. **$$$$$**
Hotel Nikko
Jl. M.H. Thamrin, No. 59
Tel: 021-230 1122
www.nikkojakarta.com
This comparatively older but well-run hotel is located in the heart of the city and has a spa, business and wellness centres and swimming pool. **$$$$**
Alila Jakarta
Jl. Pecenongan, Kav. 7–17
Tel: 021-231 6008
www.alilahotels.com
Trendy four-star boutique hotel with cutting-edge minimalist-abstract design and large rooms that attracts young executives and urbanites. Excellent fitness centre on-site. **$$$**
Ibis Arcadia
Jl. K.H. Wahid Hasyim, No. 114
Tel: 021-230 0050
www.ibishotel.com
This small hotel is well located and has a good range of services. Offers discounts at weekends, when businessmen check out. **$$$**
MaxOneHotels.com@
Sabang
Jl. Agus Salim, No. 24

Tel: 021-316 6888
www.maxonehotels.com
A new eight-storey hotel 50 metres/yds from Jl. Thamrin in downtown Jakarta. The 87 rooms are small but clean, with flat-screen TV – a fresh option for budget travellers. **$$**
Paragon
Jl. K.H. Wahid Hasyim, No. 29
Tel: 021-391 7070
www.paragon.co.id
Centrally located between Menteng and Jalan Thamrin. Small gallery hotel displays local and international fine art in rooms, lobby and corridors. **$$**
Pulau Bidadari
Bidadari island
Reservations: Terminal Pulau Bidadari, Marina Jaya Ancol
Tel: 021-6417 0048
www.bidadariisland.com
Offers comfortable bungalows, both air-conditioned and fan-cooled. Restaurant, bar and a range of water sports. Ask for packages which include meals and transfers. Ruins of a historical Dutch fortress are on this island. **$$**

Kepulauan Seribu

Pulau Ayer
Ayer island
Reservations: Jl. K.H. Samanhudi, No. 47–49
Tel: 021-385 2004
www.pulauayer.com
The closest resort to

PRICE CATEGORIES

Price categories for standard rooms, usually without breakfast:
$$$$$ = above US$150
$$$$ = US$101–150
$$$ = US$51–100
$$ = US$30–50
$ = under US$30

Jakarta, 30 minutes from Marina Pier. Day trips, including boat transfer, lunch and water antivities, are offered. **$$$**
Pulau Pelangi
Pelangi island
Reservations: PT Pulau Seribu Paradise

Jl. Pantai Mutiara R/1
Tel: 0878-8874 1833, 0818-0676 0968
www.pelangiisland.com
Reachable in 1½ hours from Jakarta's Marina Pier. All bungalows face the sea. Water-sports centre, floating

restaurant, dive shop, tennis court and clinic are among the facilities. **$$$**
Pulau Putri
Putri island
Reservations: PT Buana Bintang Samudra, Jl. Sultan Agung, No. 21

Tel: 021-828 1093, 830 5877
www.putriisland.com
In addition to the usual facilities, it also has an aquarium housing a collection of tropical fish and corals. Reachable in 1½ hours from Marina Pier. **$$$**

WEST JAVA

Bandung

Grand Hotel Preanger
Jl. Asia Afrika, No. 81
Tel: 022-423-1631
www.aerowisatahotels.com
Bandung's best, this charming colonial-style five-star hotel is located in the centre of town. The traditional dance performances at the weekend are a treat. **$$$$**
Hyatt Regency Bandung
Jl. Sumatera, No. 51
Tel: 022-421 1234
www.bandung.regency.hyatt.com
De luxe hotel within walking distance of Bandung Indah Plaza and food stalls on crowded Jl. Merdeka. Also has a café, restaurants (Chinese and Indonesian) and a pub. **$$$$**
Sheraton Bandung Hotel and Tower
Jl. Ir. H. Juanda, No. 390
Tel: 022-250 0303
www.starwoodhotels.com
Located 6km (4 miles) from the city centre on the slopes of the Dago area. The hotel is surrounded by mountains, conveniently situated just a few minutes from the main business district. 157 spacious guest rooms. **$$$$**
Jayakarta Bandung

Jl. Ir. H. Juanda, No. 381A
Tel: 022-250 5888
www.jayakartahotelsresorts.com
Comfortable and reasonably priced hotel with a good location. Restaurant serves Western and Sundanese food. Large free-form pool. **$$$**
Savoy Homann Bidakara
Jl. Asia Afrika, No. 112
Tel: 022-423 2244
www.savoyhomann-hotel.com
This four-star 1939 hotel was refurbished in the early 1990s with stylish Art Deco detailing. Live music pulsates nightly, while dinner is served in an interesting garden atrium restaurant. **$$$**

West Coast

Banten Beach Resort
Jl. Raya Sirih, Km 15, Anyer
Tel: 0254-600 982
Villa-style beach hotel set in landscaped gardens and with views of the ocean. Swimming pool, restaurant and bar. **$$$$$**
Marbella
Jl. Raya Karang Bolong, Km 135, Anyer
Tel: 254-602 345
www.marbellaanyer.com
This hotel is located right

on the beach. It has swimming pools, shops and restaurants and organises a full range of activities. **$$$$**
Tanjung Lesung Beach Resort
Jakarta Reservations Office
Tel: 021-572 7220
www.tanjunglesung.com
Comprises 61 cottages (114 rooms), with a beachfront restaurant, bar, children's playground, kids' club, ocean-view swimming pool, and a beach club for jet-skiing, snorkelling and yachting. Rental bicycles are available for going around the resort or to Bodur beach for stunning sunsets. **$$$$**
Hotel Mambruk Anyer
Jl. Raya Karang Bolong, Anyer
Tel: 0254-601 602
www.mambruk.co.id
A de luxe beachfront resort with a water-sports centre, children's playground, pool and a view of Krakatau. **$$$**
Pulau Umang Resort
Marketing office:
Barcelona Square E-9/RK 53, Nusa Loka sector 14, BSD city Tangerang
Tel: 021-5315 3008

www.pulau-umang.com
Pulau Umang is an island east of Sumur and the nearest gateway to Ujung Kulon National Park. Reached by speedboat in 15 minutes, the resort offers cottages, all facing the sea. **$$$**
Sunda Jaya Home Stay
Desa Taman Jaya
Ujung Kulon National Park
Kec. Sumur, Pandeglang
Tel: 0818-0618 1209
www.sundajaya.blogspot.com
Built in cooperation with the WWF, on the border of Ujung Kulon National Park, accommodation comprises 4 rooms with 2 single beds each including mosquito nets. Bathroom outside. Offers surfing and sailing in addition to trekking in the park. **$**

CENTRAL JAVA

Borobudur

Amanjiwo Resort
Borobudur, Magelang
Tel: 0293-788 333
www.amanresorts.com
One hour from Jogja Airport, the Amanjiwo is the ultimate in opulence, surrounded by four volcanoes and

overlooking Borobudur in the distance. **$$$$$**

Cirebon

Hotel Prima
Jl. Siliwangi, No. 107
Tel: 0231-205 411
A good-value three-star

business hotel that has some style in its Islamic architecture. There is also an in-house restaurant. **$$$**
Patra Jasa Cirebon
Jl. Tuparev, No. 11
Tel: 0231-209 400
www.patra-jasa.com
A three-star hotel and the

TRANSPORT

ACCOMMODATION

EATING OUT

ACTIVITIES

A – Z

LANGUAGE

only one in town with bungalow-style accommodation. It also has a restaurant, swimming pool and jogging track. **$$–$$$**

Hotel Santika Cirebon
Jl. Dr Wahidin, No. 32
Tel: 0231-200 662
www.santika.com
Part of the Santika group, the hotel has 87 luxurious rooms, restaurant, bar, fitness centre and tennis cour and pool. **$$–$$$**

Magelang

Losari Coffee Plantation Resort & Spa
Desa Losari Grabag, Magelang
Tel: 0298-596 333
www.losaricoffeeplantation.com
A lovely boutique resort situated on 22 hectares (54 acres) of working coffee plantation nestled in the highlands 900 metres (2,953ft) above sea level. Approximately 1-hour drive from Jogja, Solo and Semarang, it has 26 restored *joglo* villas, a spa, infinity-edge swimming pool, delicious food and, of course, great coffee. **$$$$$**

Semarang

Hotel Ciputra
Jl. Simpang Lima
Tel: 024-844 9888
www.hotelciputra.com
In the heart of Semarang, adjacent to the city's largest mall with restaurants and shops. Five-star hotel with 200 rooms, including executive club rooms. **$$$–$$$$**

Novotel Semarang
Jl. Pemuda, No. 123

BELOW: elephant ride Amanjiwo resort

Tel: 0243-563 000
www.accorhotels-asia.com
Located in the town centre, a four-star hotel with 174 rooms in a range of types; restaurants, aerobics studio and fitness centre. **$$$**

Hotel Santika Premier
Jl. Pandanaran, No. 116–120
Tel: 024-841 3115
www.santika.com
A four-star hotel with 128 rooms in the heart of the city; restaurant, bar, fitness centre and sauna. **$$$**

Solo

Lor-In Solo
Jl. Adisucipto, No. 47
Tel: 0271-724 500
http://lorinhotel.com
An oasis surrounded by sparkling lagoons, garden sanctuaries and pools, the Lor-In has 114 luxury rooms, swimming pool, health club, restaurants and bar. **$$$$**

Novotel Solo
Jl. Slamet Riyadi, No. 272
Tel: 0271-724 555
www.accorhotels-asia.com
A four-star hotel in the heart of business and shopping districts. 141 rooms, swimming pool, fitness centre, snooker/billiards. **$$–$$$**

Solo Paragon Hotel & Residences
Jl. Dr Soetomo
Tel: 0271-765 5888
http://soloparagonhotel.com
Comprising 237 newly refurbished rooms and suites on 25 floors near Jl. Slamet Riyadi, this four-star hotel also has a restaurant, lounge, pool, fitness centre, basketball court, jogging track, spa and kids' club. **$$–$$$**

Ibis Solo
Jl. Gajah Mada, No. 23
Tel: 0271-724 555
www.accorhotels.com
Alongside the Novotel Solo and offering excellent value. 152 rooms. **$–$$**

Wonosobo

Gallery Hotel Kresna
Jl. Pasukan Ronggolawe, No. 30
Tel: 0286-324 111
www.kresnahotel.com
In the cool highlands near Dieng plateau, historic hotel

---

of mixed Dutch colonial and Javanese style. Famous guests included Charlie Chaplin. 115 rooms and suites with modern amenities, restaurant, tearoom, bar and gallery featuring contemporary Indonesian artists. **$$$**

Yogyakarta (Jogja)

As Indonesia's second-largest tourist destination (after Bali), Jogja has a wide range of accommodation – from luxurious presidential suites to simple *losmen* in the Pasar Kembang area near the train station and along Jl. Prawirotaman, Jl. Dagen and Jl. Sosrowiajyan. There is currently a building boom, with more hotels to be completed 2012–13.

Rumah Sleman
Jl. Purboyo, No. 111
Warak Kidul, Sumberadi, Mlati, Sleman
Tel: 0274-866 611, 866 622
www.rumahsleman.com
A private villa located in a village outside the busy city centre, this is a fine example of traditional *joglo* architecture. Rental of one of two wings, one furnished in classical Javanese style and the other Western, entitles guests to use of the entire villa, staff and gardens. **$$$$$**

Meliá Purosani
Jl. Suryotomo, No. 31
Tel: 0274-589 521
www.solmelia.com
This five-star hotel in the centre of the city is just a short walk from Jl. Malioboro and the Keraton. Set amid beautiful landscaped gardens, it has a resort-style swimming pool. **$$$$–$$$$$**

Dusun Jogja Village Inn
Jl. Menukan, No. 5
Tel: 0274-373 031
www.jvidusun.co.id
This small, tranquil boutique hotel offers a unique and artistic atmosphere where intimacy, comfort and style come together. Rooms have terraces or balconies with views of the gardens. Saltwater swimming pool. **$$$–$$$$**

---

d'Omah Yogya
Jl. Parangtritis, Km 8.5,
Sewon Bantul
Tel: 0274-368 050
www.d'omah.com
Located 20 minutes south of Jogja; rooms are in restored traditional Javanese houses. There is also a Javanese Culture Museum nearby. Swimming pool. **$$$**

Hyatt Regency Yogyakarta
Jl. Palagan Tentara Pelajar
Tel: 0274-869 123
www.hyatt.com
An idyllic resort designed to symbolise Borobudur. Offers spa, golf course, Camp Hyatt for kids, excellent restaurants, tiered swimming pool and five-star pampering. **$$$–$$$$**

Ibis Malioboro Yogyakarta
Jl. Malioboro, No. 52–58
Tel: 0274-516 974
www.accorhotels-asia.com
Located in the heart of the well-known shopping district, Jl. Malioboro, the Ibis also connects to a modern shopping mall. **$$$**

Novotel Yogyakarta
Jl. Jend. Sudirman, No. 89
Tel: 0274-580 930
www.accorhotels-asia.com
Only 30 minutes from the airport and 15 minutes from the train station, the Novotel is modern and clean. Restaurants, swimming pool and excellent bakery. **$$$**

Phoenix Hotel
Jl. Jendral Sudirman, No. 9
Tel: 0274-56617
www.accorhotels.com
Located near the city centre of the city in a Dutch heritage building, this is an MGallery Accor hotel. Swimming pool, restaurant, bar. **$$$**

Rumah Mertua
Jl. Tentara Pelajar, Gang Padma, No. 5
Tel: 0274-866 680
http://rumahmertua.com
A lovely little boutique hotel where guests are well looked after. Located 10 minutes from the city centre behind the Hyatt. Swimming pool, restaurant and spa treatments. Highly recommended. **$$**

Indraloka Family Homestay
Jl. Cikditiro, No. 18
Tel: 0274-544 428
www.jogjapages.com

A home-away-from-home in a small and friendly hotel, constructed in 1930 of mixed Javanese-European style. Situated near Gadjah Mada University, this homestay is popular with foreign students. **$–$$**

EAST JAVA

Baluran National Park

Rosa's Ecolodge
Dusun Sidomulyo
Sumberwaru, Banyuputih,
Situbondo
Tel: 0338-453 005
www.rosasecolodge.com
Situated near Baluran National Park; five air-conditioned cottages with Western toilets, and a Madurese-style main lodge and restaurant. Mountain, savannah and birdwatching treks; excursions to Baluran beaches with Dutch- or English-speaking guides. Guest fees help finance environmental education for villagers. **$$$**

Gunung Bromo

Java Banana Bromo Lodge, Gallery & Café
Jl. Raya Bromo
Wonotoro, Sukapura
Tel: 0335-541 193
http://java.banana.com
With a view of Gunung Bromo from every room, this new lodge is a welcome addition to replace the older, musty accommodation. Features include fireplace, cable TV, café and photo

gallery. Can arrange tours. **$$**
Yoschi's Guesthouse
Jl. Wonokerto, No. 1
Wonokerto (2km/1¼ miles downhill from Ngadisari)
Tel: 0335-541 018
An excellent choice: options include clean, basic rooms or comfortable cottages, with hot water. Garden and a good restaurant. You can buy bus tickets, arrange for guides and buy trekking maps here. **$**

Gunung Ijen

Ijen Resort and Villas
Randu Agung, Licin
Banyuwangi
Tel: 0333-773 3338
www.ijendiscovery.com
Surprising, luxurious accommodation in the middle of nowhere, offering a choice of rooms, bungalows and suites, with vistas of volcanoes, rainforest, rice fields and the Bali Strait. Restaurant, bar and massages. **$$$$**

Malang

Kartika Graha

Jl. Jaksa Agung Suprapto, No. 17
Tel: 0341-361 900
This good-value hotel is bright and cheerful, with rooms that are very comfortable. Facilities include a 24-hour café and two pools. **$$$**
Regent's Park
Jl. Jaksa Agung Suprapto, No. 12
Tel: 0341-363 388
www.hotelregentspark.com
A pleasant hotel with nice rooms. It's comfortable, has good views and hot tubs, a spa, three restaurants and a karaoke bar. **$$$**
Hotel Tugu Malang
Jl. Tugu No. 3
Tel: 0341-363 891
www.tuguhotels.com
This award-winning boutique hotel has splendidly appointed rooms. The luxuriously cosy ambience of the museum hotel is punctuated by superb Javanese and Chinese antiques. **$$$**

Surabaya

Hotel Bumi Surabaya
Jl. Jend. Basuki Rachmat, No. 106–128
Tel: 031-531 1234
Formerly Hyatt Regency, this

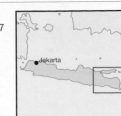

luxury hotel is conveniently located, and has four restaurants and a bar with live entertainment. **$$$$**
Hotel Majapahit Surabaya
Jl. Tunjungan, No. 65
Tel: 031-545 4333
www.hotel-majapahit.com
Built in 1910 by one of the Sarkies brothers (architects of Singapore's famous Raffles Hotel), this landmark hotel exudes colonial charm and elegance. A quiet haven in the city's centre. **$$$$**
Surabaya Plaza Hotel
Jl. Pemuda, No. 31
Tel: 031-531 6833
www.surabayaplazahotel.com
This non-smoking and all-suites hotel is centrally located downtown, near heritage buildings. A bonus is its Semanggi Corner, a great place to try inexpensive local fare. **$$$**

NORTH SUMATRA

Banda Aceh

Hermes Palace Hotel
Jl. Panglima Nyak Makam
Tel: 0651-755 5888
www.hermespalacehotel.com
Banda Aceh's first four-star hotel; six storeys with a

good range of facilities, including café, bar, spa, swimming pool and internet access. Rooms are contemporary and spacious. Located in the centre of town near the governor's office and 10 minutes from the Mesjid Raya Baiturrahman. **$$$$**
The Pade Hotel
Jl. Soekarno Hatta, No. 1
Desa Daroy Kameu
Kacamatan Darul Imray
Aceh Besar
Tel: 0651-49999
http://thepade.com
Located in the "new town"

on higher ground away from the city centre, this hotel's 65 clean rooms each have private balconies. Pool is small and is closed to guests when meetings are held. Beer and wine served to foreigners. **$$$**

Gunung Leuser National Park

Ecolodge Bukit Lawang
Bukit Lawang, Langkat
Tel: 081-2607 9983
www.ecolodge.yelweb.org
Run by a foundation for sustainable ecosystems;

rooms are decorated with bamboo and rattan supplied by villagers. Revenue goes to community development and nature conservation. Offers rafting and caving

TRANSPORT

ACCOMMODATION

EATING OUT

ACTIVITIES

A – Z

LANGUAGE

tours; has traditional medicine garden and grows organic food served in restaurant. **$**

Tangkahan Ecotourism
Desa Namo Sialang
Kecamatan Batang Serangean
Langkat
Tel: 0813-6142 3256
http://tangkahanecotourism.com
Eight lodges, each with rooms and a restaurant, run by a conservation and community-empowerment group. Also offers caving, elephant safari, jungle trekking and river-cruising trips. **$**

J.W. Marriot
Jl. Putri Hijau, No. 10
Tel: 061-455 3333
www.marriot.com
The first five-star luxury hotel in Medan. Located in the downtown, facilities include swimming pool, fitness centre, spa and restaurants serving Western and Indonesian food. **$$$$**

Soechi International Hotel
Jl. Cirebon, No. 76A
Tel: 061-456 1234
www.soechi-hotel.com
This four-star hotel, managed by Novotel, is situated 15 minutes from the airport, near shopping malls and places of interest. Facilities include swimming pool, fitness centre, tennis court, spa and sauna. **$$$$**

My Dream Hotel
Jl. Surabaya, No. 88
Tel: 061-4107 7777
www.myhotel.com

The best value in Medan: a new, clean hotel in minimalist style at an excellent location. Restaurant and bar and 183 rooms in an eight-storey building. **$–$$**

Samosir Cottages
Tuk-Tuk, Lake Toba
Tel: 0625-451 311
www.samosircottages.com
Clean rooms and friendly staff and situated right on Lake Toba. Provides several computers for internet access and a TV/DVD room. Traditional Batak dance and music performed on Saturday nights. **$$**

Carolina Cottages and Hotel
Tuk-Tuk Sindong

Tel: 0625-451 210
www.carolina-cottages.com
A Tuk-Tuk favourite located on the lakefront with a private swimming beach and superb views. Rooms range from basic to Batak-style bungalows. The open-air restaurant serves freshly baked bread. Dance performances featured every Saturday night. This place is popular, so be sure to book ahead. **$**

Toledo Inn
Tuk-Tuk Sindong
Tel: 0625-41181
The oldest hotel on the island, it has the best swimming beach and is still the top choice with international groups. The rooms are comfortable, and there is a large open restaurant that serves local and Western cuisine. **$**

WEST SUMATRA

The Hills
Jl. Laras Datuk Bandaro
Tel: 0752-35000
www.thehillsbukittinggi.com
The only luxury hotel in the area, it is also the most elegant. Aside from the swanky decor, a big plus is the heated pool. **$$$$**

Pusako
Jl. Sukarno-Hatta, No. 7
Tel: 0752-32111
www.pusakohotel.com

A 15-minute walk to the city centre, though a shuttle service is provided. The rooms are large with full facilities, the staff are friendly and helpful and, best of all, it has nice views. **$$$**

For birdwatching and Gunung Kerinci climbs (2 days) most visitors stay at

BELOW: Rumah Sleman Hotel.

Losmen Subandi, tel: 0812-7411 4273, in Kersiktuo, at the foot of the mountain, 60km (37 miles) from Sungaipenuh. The National Park Bird List is kept here. This *losmen* is also makes an excellent base camp for climbs to the beautiful crater lake on Gunung Tujuh (1 day) or treks to the highland peat swamp in Ladeh Panjang (allow 3 days return).

Most of the tourist attractions are in the south, a 2–3-hour journey on decent roads from Gunung Sitoli. There are a handful of *losmen* at **Sorake beach** in Lagundri Bay, ranging from simple to fairly good. For a listing, see http://sorake-beach.org.

Hotel Batang Arau
Jl. Batang Arau, No. 33
Tel: 0751-24700
www.batangarau.itgo.com

In a Dutch colonial building, a cosy place to relax and refresh. Pizzas are good, white wine is chilled and there are almost always interesting people passing through. **$$**

Bougenville Hotel
Jl. Bagindo Aziz Chan, No. 2
Tel: 0751-32423
www.bougenvillehotel.com
Located a 20-minute drive from Minangkabau International Airport. Easy access to places of interest in Padang; near restaurants and shopping complex. **$$**

Mariani International Hotel
Jl. Bundo Kandung, No. 35
Tel: 0751-25466
This four-storey hotel is centrally located in downtown Padang. Restaurants and beach are walking distance from the hotel. **$$**

Siberut Island

There are a handful of very basic *losmen* In Muara Siberut. The best options are **Christine Losmen** or **Bu Tio Homestay** (tel: 0759-21030). Elsewhere, you will need to stay with local families or Christian missionaries. Malaria is endemic, so take precautions *(see Health and Medical Care, page 414).*

Mentawai Surf Camp
Siberut island
Tel: 0852-7477 5975
www.mentawai-surfcamp.
com
A private, three-bedroom *Uma* traditional house that can accommodate up to six people. This is by some distance the best accommodation in Siberut among the world-renowned "Playgrounds", popular among the surfers. **$$$$**

SOUTH SUMATRA

Bandar Lampung

Marcopolo
Jl. Dr Susilo, No. 4
Tel: 0721-262 511
www.marcopololampung.
com
The hotel sits on a hillside and has a wonderful view of the bay. The rooms are clean and comfortable, with a pool on the grounds. There is also a restaurant. **$$**

Batam Island

Harris Resort Batam
Waterfront City
Tel: 0778-381 888
www.waterfront-batam.
harrishotels.com
Located outside the city centre, with 188 rooms, suites, residences and beachfront cabanas. Cafés and restaurants, grill and bar, music lounge, swim-up pool bar, kids' club and water sports. **$$$**
Holiday Inn Resort Batam
Waterfront City
Tel: 0778-381 333
www.holidayinn.com

Offers all-suites accommodation and award-winning Tea Tree Spa. Outdoor and indoor swimming pool, gymnasium, tennis court, kids' programme, mini-golf putting, paintball and low-element team-building. **$$$**
Planet Holiday Hotel & Residence
Jl. Raja Haji, Sei Jodoh
Tel: 0778-433 555
www.planetholidayhotel.com
Avant-garde concepts blended with modern functionality, guaranteeing an unforgettable stay. Fitness club, spa, lounge and restaurant, exceptional pool facilities with extensive choice of beverages. **$$$**

Bengkulu

Nala Seaside Cottages
Jl. Pariwisata, No. 2
Tel: 0736-344 855
The resort, which rests on the beach just 5 minutes from town, has air-conditioned cottages but with cold showers.

BELOW: Yoga at Melia Purosani.

The restaurant overlooks the Indian Ocean. **$**

Bintan Island

Banyan Tree Bintan
Jl. Teluk Berembang
Laguna Bintan, Lagoi
Tel: 0770-693 100
www.banyantree.com
This quietly luxurious and ecologically minded resort has 74 secluded villas hugging a rainforest-clad cliff which looks out over the sea. A few villas have their own private pools and Jacuzzi. Extensive spa facilities. **$$$$$**
Club Med Bintan
Site A 11, Lagoi
Bintan resort
Tel: 0770-692 801
www.clubmed.com
In addition to the usual Club Med features of parties, courses and lavish meals, there is an in-house circus school. This four-star resort offers 302 superior and de luxe rooms, plus suites, and an 18-hole Greg Norman golf course, spa, restaurants, nightclub, bar. **$$$$**
Nirwana Beach Club
Bintan resort
Tel: 0770-692 505
www.nirwanagardens.com
A two-star group of 50 cabana rooms that are a favourite with water-sports enthusiasts: pick from banana boating, snorkelling, diving, windsurfing, kitesurfing, jet-ski, kayaking, boogieboard, sailing and fishing. Surf shop, restaurant. **$$$**

Palembang

Aston Palembang Hotel & Convention Center
Jl. Basuki Rahmat, No. 189
Tel: 0711-388 999
www.aston-international.com

Comprising 174 rooms in the heart of the business district, with bars, restaurants, spa, fitness centre and swimming pool. **$$$**
Novotel Palembang
Jl. R. Sukamto, No. 8A
Tel: 0711-369 777
www.novotel.com
Located in the city centre, it has 194 rooms, fitness centre, sauna, jogging track, swimming pool, two restaurants and four bars. **$$$**
Swarna Dwipa
Jl. Tasik, No. 2
Tel: 0711-313 322
www.hotelswarnadwipa.com
This old colonial building in a quiet residential area 2km (1¼ miles) west of the city centre overlooks a park. You can choose between a room in the new modern wing, or a restored de luxe one in the old wing. The service is friendly and there is a fitness centre. **$$–$$$**

Pekanbaru

Grand Jatra
Jl. Tengku Zainal Abidin, No.

1, Komplek Mal Pekanbaru
Tel: 0761-850 888
www.jatrahotelpekanbaru.com
A five-star hotel located
near Pekanbaru Mall, banks
and entertainment spots.
Restaurants, spa, sauna,
health club. **$$$**
Amaris Hotel Pekanbaru
Jl. Wahid Hasylm

Reservations Tel: 021-270 0027
www.amarishotel.com
A new branch of the
Indonesian-owned Santika
Hotels Group; all Amaris
properties are contempo-
rary and starkly furnished,
but new and clean and
priced for the budget
crowd. **$–$$**

Way Kambas National Park

Satwa Elephant Eco Lodge
Way Kambas
Tel: 0725-764 5290
www.ecolodgesindonesia.
com
Located only 500 metres/
yds from the park

entrance, the four cot-
tages, in a walled garden,
each sleep up to four people and come with fans
and hot-water showers.
The lodge contributes to
conservation projects in
the park and follows
Australian green hotel
regulations. **$$**

SOUTH BALI

Denpasar

There is no real reason to
stay in Denpasar unless you
have urgent business that
can't wait for the short
(15-minute) commute from
Kuta. There are scores of
hotels for under US$20,
most of them catering to
domestic tourists.
INNA Bali
Jl. Veteran, No. 3
Tel: 0361-225 681
www.innabali.com
Dutch colonial atmosphere
on a busy but centrally
located street. Rooms in the
main section are basic, but
have air-conditioning, hot
water, TV and telephone.
More comfortable executive
suites across the road.
Restaurant, bar, swimming
pool. 74 rooms. **$$**

Jimbaran and Bukit Badung

The calibre of Jimbaran's
and Bukit Badung's hotels
attract jet-setters who come
for hideaway holidays. In
Jimbaran, international-

BELOW: water lilies in an
Ubud hotel courtyard.

chain hotels are situated
around a tranquil white-
sand bay with beachside
seafood restaurants provide
dining alternatives to hotel
food. Resorts in Bukit
Badung are perched atop a
large limestone plateau.
Bali InterContinental
Jl. Uluwatu
Jimbaran
Tel: 0361-701 888
www.bali.intercontinental.com
418 luxury rooms set on 14
hectares (35 acres) of landscaped gardens and pools
on a beautiful beach. An
ideal viewing spot for Bali's
sunsets. **$$$$$**
The Bvlgari Resort Bali
Jl. Goa Lempeh
Uluwatu, Bukit Badung
Tel: 0361-847 1000
www.bulgarihotels.com
Ultra-de luxe villas set high
above the sea, with priceless works of art scattered
about public areas. Private
beach is accessible far
below by the hotel's inclined
elevator. **$$$$$**
**Four Seasons Resort at
Jimbaran Bay**
Jl. Bukit Permai
Jimbaran
Tel: 0361-701 010
www.fourseasons.com
Built on a terraced hillside
amid landscaped gardens,
this award-winning resort
has a spectacular view of
the bay and Gunung Agung.
An all-villa resort, each with
its own plunge pool. **$$$$$**

Kuta and Tuban

Kuta has the best seafront
on the island, although it is
rather frenetic, catering for
budget travellers who like
to be in the thick of things.

The Legian-Seminyak end
of the beach is quieter and
better for a prolonged stay.
South of Kuta, Tuban is
peaceful and good for families, as the surf here is
safer.
Hard Rock Hotel
Jl. Pantai Kuta
Kuta
Tel: 0361-761 869
www.balihardrockhotels.net
418 rooms and suites
stretch along the beach,
along with Bali's largest
free-form pool, a children's
club, spa and retail outlets.
Dining options include Hard
Rock Café, of course. A
great place for families.
$$$$$
**Kupu-Kupu Barong
Beach Hotel**
Jl. Wana Segara
Tuban
Tel: 0361-753 780
www.kupubarongbeach.com
A five-star resort with 10
suites, four with private
plunge pools. Sunset Bar on
the beach is a popular spot
for sundowners. **$$$$$**
Poppies Cottages I
Gang Poppies I
Kuta
Tel: 0361-751 059
www.poppiesbali.com
A selection of well-designed
cottages in a beautiful gar-
den that is only 300
metres/yds from the beach.
Very popular, so reserva-
tions are essential. 20
rooms. **$$$**

Legian, Seminyak, Petitenget and Canggu

Legian and Seminyak are
north of the Kuta beach strip.
Further north are Petitenget
and Canggu. Located just

15–20 minutes from the
centre of Kuta, yet free of the
hype, these villages are per-
fect for extended holidays.
Find what suits you best by
shopping around.
The Legian
Jl. Kayu Aya
Seminyak
Tel: 0361-730 622
www.ghmhotels.com
An upmarket resort with 67
luxury suites set on a wide
beach. Excellent fine-dining
restaurant and a spa. Even
more exclusive is **The Club
at The Legian**, 11 luxury vil-
las across the street. **$$$$$**
Oberoi Bali
Jl. Katu Aya
Seminyak
Tel: 0361-730 361
www.oberoihotels.com
Located on the beach, luxu-
rious rooms and villas with
sea or garden views, some
with private pool, all
equipped with satellite TV
and CD systems. The
resort's coral-rock veran-
dahs and villas are adapta-
tions of classic Balinese
palace designs. **$$$$$**
Hotel Tugu Bali
Jl. Pantai Batu Bolong
Canggu beach
Tel: 0361-731 701
www.tuguhotels.com
A living museum of priceless
antiques, including two
suites replicating the stu-
dios of 1930s painters. This

stunning boutique hotel and spa is set between the rice fields and the quiet rugged beach. 21 suites and pavilions. $$$$$

Nusa Dua

If you want isolation from the rest of Bali, this is it. This exclusive resort area with its white-sand beaches (a rarity in Bali) is quite sterile, but the hotels have tried to make up for it by providing everything on the premises. Don't be alarmed that there are few street addresses here. Most resorts are aligned on one main road running parallel to the beach.

Amanusa
Jl. Amanusa
Nusa Dua
Tel: 0361-772 333
www.amanresorts.com
One of the wildly extravagant Aman Resorts, this one certainly measures up with 35 suites, fabulous architecture and view of the golf course and ocean. Completely self-contained with spa, Reiki, reflexology and sports facilities. $$$$$

The Bale
Jl. Raya Nusa Dua Selatan
Tel: 0361-775 111
www.thebale.com
This exclusive boutique property has only 20 oversized pavilions, all with individual lap pools. Combines

ethnic Balinese materials with chic minimalist architecture. In-house Faces gourmet restaurant serves excellent fare. $$$$$

Grand Hyatt Bali
Nusa Dua
Tel: 0361-771 234
www.bali.grand.hyatt.com
648 rooms, suites and villas replicating a Balinese king's water palace, with a huge range of facilities, including five swimming pools, restaurants, bars, kids' club, water sports. $$$$$

The Laguna Resort & Spa
Nusa Dua
Tel: 0361-771 327
www.starwoodhotels.com
271 newly redecorated rooms and suites come with butler service and are set amid cascading waterfalls and swimming lagoons. While still pricey, it is not as exorbitant as some of the other Nusa Dua resorts. $$$$$

Sanur

Sanur is peaceful and quiet. The main choice is between the convenience and luxury of the large five-star establishments or the quietude of a private bungalow by the sea. There is a nice shallow beach with a minimal number of beach hawkers, and lots of space for everyone.

Villa Mahapala
Jl. Pantai Sindhu

Tel: 0361-286 222
www.villamahapala-bali.com
A new option to supplement some of the old standby resorts. There are 20 villas, each with private pool, plus restaurant, bar, spa, fitness centre. $$$$$

Segara Village
Jl. Segara Ayu
Tel: 0361-288 407
www.segaravillage.com
Here, 120 renovated guest rooms are arranged in "villages" bordering the sea. Three swimming pools, water-sports facilities, spa and massage. The hotel holds classes in traditional Balinese dance, music and painting. $$$$

La Taverna Bali
Jl. Danau Tamblingan, No. 29
Tel: 0361-288 497
www.latavernahotel.com
Old hotel with a good reputation. Rooms are delightful thatched bungalows with Italian stucco walls and elegantly styled decor set in a garden with private beach. 36 rooms and suites. $$$

Sativa Sanur Cottages
Jl. Danau Tamblingan
Tel: 0361-287 881
http://sativahotels.com
Well managed, peaceful and cosy, this congenial hotel represents very good value. Only 5 minutes away from the beach; all rooms are just steps away from a

swimming pool with swim-up bar. 10 two-storey cottages. $$

Tanjung Benoa

Tanjung Benoa, at the northern end of Nusa Dua, is a long, finger-shaped peninsula with a white-sand beach that is lined with upmarket hotels and water-sports operations. At low tide its waters can be as still as a mill pond because of the protective coral reef offshore.

Conrad Bali Resort & Spa
Jl. Pratama, No. 168
Tanjung Benoa
Tel: 0361-778 788
www.conradhotels.com
A magnificent five-star property set amid tropical gardens and waterfalls. Most of its 360 tastefully appointed rooms and suites have sea views. There is a complete range of five-star facilities including a spa and five restaurants. $$$$$

The Royal Santrian
Jl. Pratama
Tanjung Benoa
Tel: 0361-778 181
www.theroyalsantrian.com
The ultimate in seclusion and privacy, with 20 villas set amid lush gardens sloping to the sea. Private pools, living areas, dining pavilions and a Martini bar and cigar lounge. $$$$$

CENTRAL BALI

Ubud

Amandari
Kedewatan
Tel: 0361-975 333
www.amanresorts.com

BELOW: batik scarves.

Luxurious isolation within the resort's 30 villas that overlook the Ayung River. The main swimming pool (**filtered** with salt, not chlorine) is modelled after a Balinese rice paddy. Out of this world. $$$$$

Four Seasons Sayan
Sayan
Tel: 0361-977 577
www.fourseasons.com
Spectacular resort overlooking the Ayung River and occupying 7 hectares (17 acres) of terraced rice slopes. The luxuriously appointed suites and villas

(many with private plunge pools and outdoor showers) and the decadent spa facilities promise a sublime experience. $$$$$

Komaneka Resort
Jl. Monkey Forest
Tel: 0361-976 090
www.komaneka.com
Central location but set back from main road so very quiet. Charming bungalows, gardens, pool, restaurant, spa, art gallery and boutique. $$$$$

Ubud Hanging Gardens
Buahan, Payangan
Tel: 0361-982 700

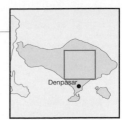

Denpasar

PRICE CATEGORIES

Price categories for standard rooms, usually without breakfast:
$$$$$ = above US$150
$$$$ = US$101–150
$$$ = US$51–100
$$ = US$30–50
$ = under US$30

www.ubudhanginggardens.com
An Orient-Express hotel, offering 38 luxurious Balinese-style villas perched on a hillside enveloped in nature, and ultimate privacy. In the gardens are flamboyant cacao and coffee trees intermingled with bamboo. Two restaurants and a bar. **$$$$$**
Uma Ubud
Jl. Raya Sanggingan
Tel: 0361-972 448

http://theumaubud.com
Overlooks Campuhan Valley. Conceived by Japanese interior designer Koichiro Ikebuchi, the architecture is minimalist but the rooms are outfitted with every luxury. Excellent restaurant. Shambalala retreat centre offers yoga, meditation classes and spa treatments.-24 rooms and suites. **$$$$$**

Alam Indah
Nyuhkuning village (opposite side of the Monkey Forest)
Tel: 0361-974 629
www.alamindahbali.com
Owned by the Café Wayan family, it has 10 rooms ranging from double to family suite. The bonus is excellent, friendly service and delicious food. Swimming pool. **$$$**
Okawati Hotel
Near Jl. Monkey Forest

Tel: 0361-975 063
www.okawatihotel.com
Located down a quiet lane in the midst of a verdant area of rice fields; 19 cosy rooms, some with hot-water showers. The owner, Ibu Oka, is one of Ubud's legends and still runs her hotel hands-on. Restaurant's speciality is *bebek betutu*. Swimming pool. **$$**

WEST AND NORTH BALI

Balian Beach

There are already a few bungalows and villas here, with more under construction.
Pondok Pitaya Surfer Hotel & Restaurant
Balian River
Tel: 081-9998 4054
www.baliansurf.com
Four rooms and one riverside villa located just steps from the beach, feauring all-wood, classical Indonesian architecture. Restaurant serves fresh food, pizza, sangria, guacamole. Board rentals. **$**

Bedugul Highlands

Clean mountain air-lovers happily ensconce themselves in the Bedugul highlands and don't want to leave. Homestays start at about US$10; for a little more comfort, try **Pacung Indah Hotel** (wwwlpacung-bali.com; **$**), a cosy cabin with wood-burning fireplace at **Strawberry Hill Hotel** (www.strawberryhill-bali.com; **$$–$$$**), or go for the full treatment at **De'Kahyangan Spa, Restaurant & Villa** (www.dekahyangan.baliklik.com; **$$$–$$$$**), overlooking

PRICE CATEGORIES

Price categories for standard rooms, usually without breakfast:
$$$$$ = above US$150
$$$$ = US$101–150
$$$ = US$51–100
$$ = US$30–50
$ = under US$30

strawberry farms and vegetable plantations.

Medewi Beach

Construction for new resorts and villas abounds, but currently the best full-service, but cosy and friendly, resort right on the beach is:
Puri Dajuma Cottages, Beach Eco-Resort & Spa
Medewi beach
Tel: 0365-43955, 470 018
www.dajuma.com
Designed to reduce the impact on the environment, it has cottages and two suites with garden and ocean views, air-conditioning and hot water. Villas with private pools opening 2012. Spa, pool, innovative cultural tours. **$$$**

Pemuteran

Many visitors stay at Pemuteran, a haven for all-season diving and snorkelling in its own right, and take a 30-minute boat ride to Menjangan island. There is a wide range of accommodation here; especially recommended are:
Puri Ganesha Villas
Pemuteran
Tel: 0362-94766
www.puriganeshabali.com
Four two-bedroom villas with antique furnishings, garden bathrooms, kitchens and private saltwater swimming pools. The ultimate for people who are seeking privacy, quality and personal service. Gourmet restaurant. **$$$$$**

Matahari Beach Resort
Pemuteran
Tel: 0362-92312
www.matahari-beach-resort.com
Environmental award-winning beach resort. Five-star villas with full spa and gourmet restaurant. Dive excursions to Pulau Menjangan can be arranged. **$$$$**
Pondok Sari Beach Resort & Spa
Pemuteran
Tel: 0362-92337
www.pondoksari.com
Standard air-conditioned rooms and bungalows are decorated with wood and bamboo and have hot-water showers in semi-open-air bathrooms. Spa; dive centre. Guests are invited to join resort's social programmes. **$$–$$$$**

Pemuteran to Lovina

En route from Pemuteran to Lovina on the north coast beaches are some unexpected getaway spots. One is **Munduk Moding Coffee Plantation Nature Resort & Spa** (www.mundakmoding-plantation.com; **$$$$**) near Seririt, a luxury boutique hotel offering horse riding and plantation tours. Between Seririt and Ume Anyar is an entire complex of villas for rent (search the web for Ume Anyar villas), as well as wellbeing resorts, such as **Ganesha Bali Retreat & Villas** (www.ganesha-bali.

com), **Shanti Loka Resort for Body & Soul** (http://shanti-loka.com) and **Zen Resort Bali** (www.zenresortbali.com).
Lovina has evolved beyond being merely an alternative to the beaches of the south to a base for exploring North Bali and the Bedugul highlands. The snorkelling is superb, with the reef close enough even for beginner swimmers, and there is a wide range of accommodation, much of which has been renovated. Highly recommended is **Puri Bagus Villa Resort Lovina** (www.puribagus.net; **$$$$$**), or try **Bali Taman Lovina Resort & Spa** (www.balitamanlovina.com; **$$$–$$$$**) or family-run **Rambutan Beach Cottages, Boutique Hotel & Spa** (www.rambutan.org; **$**).

West Bali National Park

There are four resorts near or inside the park; all are in the luxury category, and all are dedicated to preserving and restoring the environment. Check out:
Manjangan Resort
Jl. Raya Gilimanuk-Singaraja, Km 17
Desa Pajarakan

Tel: 0362-94700
www.themanjangan.com
Situated inside the national park, the villas and rooms in the lodge have LCD TV, DVD player and iPod dock. Built following environmentally-friendly guidelines, the resort is surrounded by forest, wildlife and nesting birds. Snorkelling and diving on-site and to Manjangan island. **$$$$$**
Novus Gawana Resort & Spa
West Bali National Park

Banyuwedang
Tel: 0362-94500
www.novushotels.com
Located on tranquil Manjangan Bay with views of the sea and North Bali Mountains. All suites are decorated in natural colours, fabrics and textures with natural hot-spring water tubs. Spa, games room, restaurant and bar; diving on premises or to Menjangan island.

$$$$$
Waka Shorea
West Bali National Park
Reservations Tel: 0361-723 629
www.wakaexperience.com
The 14 terraced bungalows and two villas are designed to exist in harmony with the landscape. Restaurant at water's edge, spa, freshwater swimming pool. Sea-kayaking, sailing, diving, snorkelling and nature treks among activities offered. **$$$$$**

Mimpi Resort
Mejangan
Banyuwedang
Tel. 0362-94497
www.mimpi.com
Simulating a Balinese village, 30 terraced patio rooms and 24 walled courtyard villas are located at the park boundary. Each of the villas are equipped with private hot-spring tubs. Diving, snorkelling, canoeing and sea-biking offered. **$$$$-$$$$$**

EAST BALI

Amed and environs

Many travellers now base themselves at one of the many bungalows or resorts that line seven beaches, collectively known as Amed, and make day trips into East Bali at low tide, when the snorkelling is not good. However, there are several homestays around Tirtagangga favoured by trekkers and one very nice hotel at the top of the hill overlooking the royal water gardens: **Tirta Ayu Hotel & Restaurant** (www.hoteltirtagangga.com; **$$$$**).

Candidasa and environs

At Candidasa, there is everything from bungalows to villas, many with dive shops, and most along the main road fronting the beach. Try **Kelapa Mas Homestay** (www.welcome-tokelapamas.com; **$**), **Bali Sangrila Beach Club** (www.balishangrila.com; **$$$**) or **Puri Bagus Candidasa**

(www.puribagus.net; **$$$$$**). There are two luxury resorts on Balina beach at Manggis, "next door" to Candidasa: **Amankila** (www.amankila.com; **$$$$$**) and **Alila Manggis** (www.alilahotels.com; **$$$$$**). Good choices at Amed include: **Kembali Beach Bungalows** (www.kembali-beachbungalows.com; **$**), **Aiona Garden of Health** (www.aionabali.com; **$–$$**), **Life in Amed Bali** (www.life-bali.com; **$$$**) and **Jepun Bali Villas** (www.jepunbaliv-illas.com; **$$$$**).

Gunung Batur (Kintamani)

The *losmen* that trekkers use are primarily in the Toya Bungkah area, near Lake Batur. **Under the Volcano ($)**, with three locations, is particularly popular. For a major splurge, check out exclusive **The Ayu** (www.theayu.com; **$$$$$**). Next door is **Toya Devasya Resort & Spa**, a natural hot-spring

swimming pool, restaurant and campsite complex.

Nusa Penida and Nusa Lembongan

There are only basic homestays on Nusa Penida, but **Friends of the National Parks** (www.fnpf.org) has a few rooms used by researchers and volunteers at its field station, which are rented when not in use. On Nusa Lembongan, accommodation now lines the west coast beaches, with a few lodgings on the southern coast, ranging from budget to luxury. The best known is **Waka Nusa Resort** (www.wakanusa.com; **$$$$**), offering a full range of water sports, tours and spa.

Padangbai

The road that hugs the shore here has side-by-side budget and moderately priced accommodation, cafés and dive shops, with more along small

perpendicular streets. **Bloo Lagoon Sustainable Village** (www.bloolagoon.com; **$$$$**) is a villa compound on the cliff overlooking the sea.

Sidemen

Isolated in agricultural heartland with gorgeous views, there are a few getaway places and one wellbeing centre here, three with excellent prices. Have a look at **Nirarta Centre for Living Awareness** (www.aware-ness-bali.com; **$$**), **Lihat Sawah Guest House** (www.lihatsawah.com; **$$**), **Surya Shanti Villa** (www.suryashantivilla.com; **$$$$**) and **Pondok Soria Moria** (www.balisoriamoria.com; **$$**).

LOMBOK

Gili Islands

Gili Air

This island has the largest local population and is a great place for families. There are a few bars.
Coconut Cottages

Tel: 0370-635 365
www.coconuts-giliair.com
Possibly the best place to stay on laid-back Gili Air, the cottages here are set back slightly from the beach in a shady coconut grove set

within lovely gardens. All have hot water, air-conditioning or fan, and one bedroom. **$$–$$$**
Hotel Gili Air
Tel: 0370-662 1448
www.hotelgiliair.com

Located on the north of the island, 31 chalets with air-conditioning, satellite TV and private terrace. Bar and restaurant. **$$$–$$$$**

Gili Meno

The smallest and least developed of the Gili islands, it gives the illusion of a real island escape.
Villa Nautilus
Tel: 0370-642 143
www.villanautilus.com
Small resort with a better standard than most on the island. Five bungalows in a peaceful location, with a restaurant on-site. Spacious rooms have air-conditioning and hot water, sun lounges and large terraces with lovely views of the ocean. **$$$**

Gili Trawangan

There are two entirely different atmospheres on "Gili T". To the southeast is the party area, and the many *losmen* and better hotels are generally fully booked in July and August. Beachfront restaurants, bars, money-changers, internet cafés – the works – are in this area, which turns into a disco scene after dinner. On the northern and northeastern coasts, guests enjoy quiet solitude.

Alam Gili
Reservations: Tel: 0361-974 629
www.alamindahbali.com
On the quiet northern shore of Gili T, six bungalows, two suites and a swimming pool are combined with the family hospitality popular among fans of Ibu Wayan (Café Wayan; Alam Indah), in Ubud (Bali). This resort is run by Ibu's daughter and her husband. **$$–$$$**
Vila Ombak
Tel: 0370-642 336
www.hotelombak.com
Traditional, air-conditioned Sasak-inspired huts and bungalows. One of the best hotels on the island. An interesting feature is the three-level swimming pool with whirlpool. It has a seaside pizzeria, beach and pool bars, a spa and a diving school. **$$$–$$$$$**

Puri Mas Boutique Resorts & Spa
Jl. Raya Senggigi
Tel: 0370-693 023
www.purimas-lombok.com
Private cottages, suites and villas on the beach with great restaurant, pool, yoga garden, fitness, spa, dance lessons and art gallery. **$$$–$$$$$**
Quinci Villas

Jl. Raya Mangsit
Tel: 0370-693 800
www.quincivillas.com
A gorgeous boutique hotel on the beachfront with ocean and garden view rooms and villas in minimalist style, set in lovely gardens. Cosy restaurant, spa and pool. **$$$–$$$$$**

Sheraton Senggigi Beach Resort
Jl. Raya Senggigi, Km 8
Tel: 0370-693 333
www.starwoodhotels.com
Suites and villas, some with disability access, and all the amenities: pools, spa and wellness, tennis courts, health club, water sports, bike rental. Turtle hatchery on-site. **$$$$–$$$$$**
The Santosa Villas & Resort
Jl. Raya Senggigi, Km 8
Tel: 0370-693 090
www.santosavillasresort.com
Recently refurbished de luxe rooms, suites and villas with restaurants, sunken bar, pool spa. Cultural activities, water sports and land and seaside adventures. **$$$–$$$$$**

Novotel Lombok Mandalika Resort

Pantai Putri Nyale, Kuta
Tel: 0370-653 333
www.novotel-lombok.com
A delightfully unusual resort that is a re-creation of an ancient Sasak village. Thatched bungalows on the beachfront surround water-garden pools and statuary. There are three pools, a spa and two restaurants. **$$$$$**
The Oberoi Lombok
Medana beach, Tanjung
Tel: 0370-613 8444
www.oberoihotels.com
This luxurious resort has 20 villas and 30 terrace rooms along a remote beach; they feature sunken baths, satellite TV and CD sound systems. Most villas have a garden shower and private pool. The resort has restaurants, a health club and a spa. **$$$$$**
The Tugu Lombok
Sire Beach, Tanjung
Tel: 0370-612 0111
www.tuguhotels.com
One of the fabulous family-owned Tugu Hotels, each full to the brim with antiques and objets d'art. The lobby is a 100-year-old building that was moved here. Suites, bungalows and villas, pool. Yoga and meditation, wine cellar, bike rental, private boat for water activities. **$$$$$**

ELSEWHERE IN NUSA TENGGARA

Pelangi Indah
Jl. Diponegoro, No. 34
Tel: 0397-21251
Good standard rooms and facilities. There is no restaurant, but meals can be provided with advance notice. **$**

Bajawa

Bintang Wisata Hotel
Tel: 0384-21744
A small hotel in the heart of Bajawa next to the market, shopping areas and restaurants. Caters for travellers who are visiting the megalithic villages and climbing

the volcanoes of the Bajawa area. **$**
Villa Silverin
Tel. 0384-222 3865
Rooms have king-size bed or twin, en suite bathroom and hot-water shower, TV with international channels, towels and blankets. Choice of either Gunung Inarie or town views. **$**

Ende

Dwi Putra Hotel
Jl. Yos Soedarso, No. 27
Tel: 0381-21685
The most upmarket hotel in Bajawa, this is also one of the few that has hot water. Some of the rooms are equpped

with air-conditioning. **$**
Hotel Ikhlas
Jl. Ahmad Yani, No. 69
Tel: 0381-21695
Owner Djamal Alhadad speaks English and German and has many years' experience assisting travellers. Can arrange tours with English-speaking guides. Go for one of the newer rooms with a small terrace. The restaurant serves good, simple fare. **$**

Labuhanbajo

Aman Emerald Resort
Batu Gosok, Labuhanbajo
Tel: 0385-41319

Bali office: I Gusti Ngurah Rai By-Pass, No. 178
Tel: 0361-778-666
www.purikomodoresort.com
Six rooms with shared terraces and 12 bungalows, all with ceiling fans. Water sports and dive centre on-site, restaurant and bar. **$$$**

Bajo Komodo Eco Lodge
Jl. Pantai Pede
Tel: 0385-41391
www.ecolodgesindonesia.com
Located on the beach, the
lodge offers a range of
accommodation, including
fan and air-conditioned
rooms and cottages. Pool,
restaurant, bar. Adheres to
Australian green hotel
standards. Part of the
grounds are breeding areas
for coucals, a pheasant-like
bird. **$–$$$**

Chez Felix
Jl. Prof. W.Z. Johanes
Tel: 0385-41032
Located up on a hill over-
looking the harbour. A clean
place with a nice view from
the restaurant. **$**

Maumere

Sea World Club Hotel Waiara
Jl. Sawista
Tel: 0382-21570
www.sea-world-club.com
A seaside hotel on calm Waiara
beach, next to the beautiful div-
ing at Maumere Bay. Has its
own dive centre. **$$–$$$**

Moni

**Kelimutu Crater Lakes Eco
Lodge**
3 Gorontalo, Labuhanbajo
Tel: 0385-41391, 0813-3977
6232
www.ecolodgesindonesia.com
Opened in 2010, five bed-
rooms and five chalets with
solar-powered hot water
and traditional grass thatch
roofing and local stone.
Restaurant, bar, terraces
near river. Can arrange
tours. Same owners as Bajo
Komodo Eco Lodge in
Labuhanbajo. **$$$**

Ruteng

MBC Susteran
Jl. A Yani
Tel 0385-22835
12 rooms with cold and hot
water. Only 10 minutes by
foot from the hotel to the
centre of Ruteng town. **$**

Komodo and Rinca

Basic accommodation and
cheap meals are available
at the ranger stations at
both Loh Liang on Komodo
and Loh Buaya on Rinca.
Charges are minimal.

Upon arrival at either
island, register and pay
the fee at the ranger station. Visitors leaving the
compound for trekking
must be accompanied by
a ranger, who charges a
nominal daily fee.

Lembata

Lamalera

There are two places to stay
in Lamalera, one in the village square beyond the
beach and the other at Guru
Ben's house on the hillside
looking down on the beach.
Guru Ben was a great
source of information to visitors of Lamalera. He died in
2003 of malaria, and his
wife, Yudis, continues to run
the small homestay.

Guru Ben Homestay
Located on the hillside
overlooking Lamalera Bay.
Two private rooms and
one communal room,
shared family bath. Meals
are meagre, so you might
want to bring your own
snacks. **$**

Lewoleba

Lile Ile
Jl. Trans Lembata
Tel: 0383-41250
About 400 metres/yds
east of the harbour, a
clean, friendly homestay
with four rooms and a
common bath. Owners Jim
and Kalis are helpful
guides. Delicious local
dishes are served with lots
of vegetables and fish,
tempe or tofu. **$**

Rote

Nemberala Beach Resort
Nemberala beach, Rote
www.nemberalabeachresort.
com
New, fully renovated
bungalow-style resort on
Nemberala beach, the
heart of Rote's interna-
tional surf scene. A very
nice place to stay, but a bit
expensive for the average
surfer. **$$$**

Tiberias Hotel
Batu Termanu, Rote
Tel: 0380-805 8555
New hotel on the beach with
spacious rooms, 5km (3

ABOVE: Villa Ombak.

miles) north of Ba'a, with
white sandy beaches and
great sunsets. Same owner
as Hotel Ricky (Jl. Palapa,
No. 1; tel: 0380-871 025) in
Ba'a. **$$**

Savu

Savu has no accommoda-
tion of international standard yet. In Seba, there are
two homestays and one
losmen. All offer basic
accommodation.
Scheduled to open in late
2011 is Rai Hawu Hotel
(Desa Eilode, Sabu Tengah;
email: raihawuhotel@
gmail.com): 25 bungalow-
style rooms, restaurant and
swimming pool perched
atop a hill with pleasant
views of the Savu Sea and
cool afternoon breezes. **$$**

Yacob Rajapona Homestay
Jl. Simpang Tiga
Tenihawu, Seba, Savu
Tel: 0821-4526 6407
New homestay with clean
rooms. Friendly owner and
nice setting. Price includes
three meals. **$**

Sumba

East Sumba

Elvin
Jl. A. Yani, No. 73
Waingapu, Sumba
Tel: 0387-61443
Formerly the Elim Hotel, the
rooms here have private
showers. Meals are
available. **$**

West Sumba

Nihiwatu Resort
Bali office: Jl. Raya

Seminyak, No. 12
Seminyak
Tel: 0361-752 374
www.nihiwatu.com
Set on a secluded bay on
Sumba's southwestern
coast, seven bungalows
and three villas with sea
views. Pool and a restau
rant. Deep-sea fishing,
surfing, diving and horse
riding. Guests can do vol-
unteer work through the
resort's Sumba
Foundation. **$$$$**

Newa Sumba Resort
Newa, Sumba
Jakarta office: Tel: 021-
522 9117/8
www.newasumbaresort.com
On the northwestern coast
near Waikelo, 10 minutes
from Tambolaka Airport.
Simple bungalows have liv-
ing rooms and private balco-
nies hidden in a coastal
wilderness, 100 hectares
(247 acres) fringed by a
white-sand beach. The
grounds also encompass a
nature reserve. **$$**

Manandang
Jl. Pemuda, No. 4
Waikabubak, Sumba
Tel: 0387-21197, 21292
The nicest place in town, with
an excellent restaurant.
Vehicle hire available. **$**

PRICE CATEGORIES

Price categories for
standard rooms, usually
without breakfast:
$$$$$ = above US$150
$$$$ = US$101–150
$$$ = US$51–100
$$ = US$30–50
$ = under US$30

Sumbawa

Bima

Bima has several *losmen*, a few cleaner and more popular than others, to accommodate backpackers en route to Komodo.

Lambitu Hotel
Jl. Sumbawa, No. 14
Tel: 0374-42222, 43333
The best hotel downtown, it has standard rooms with a fan and shower, as well as air-conditioned suites with hot water. **$**

Hu'u (Lakey beach)

Aman Gati
Jl. Raya Hu'u, Nangadoro, Dompu
Booking office:
Gang Merak, No. 5X, Kuta, Bali
Tel: 0361-743 8073
www.amangati.com
Located directly in front of the renowned Lakey Peak and a short walk from Periscope, a clean, safe and friendly environment. Surfing, kayaking, fishing, kite-surfing, diving and snorkelling are offered, and surfing tours to Mentawi, G-Land,

Lombok and Bali can be arranged. **$$**

Moyo Island

Amanwana
Moyo island
Tel: 0371-22233
www.amanresorts.com
Accessible only by the resort's private yacht. The almost undeveloped Moyo island, 15km (9 miles) off the Sumbawa coast, also has a wildlife sanctuary. Accommodation at the resort is in the form of 20 ultra-luxurious "tents". There is open-air dining and a bar and lounge area. It's all supremely stylish **$$$$$**

Sumbawa Besar

Kencana Beach Cottages
Jl. Raya Tano, Km 11, Badas
Tel: 0371-270 8855
Just outside Sumbawa Besar town, these bungalows occupy a private beach with clear waters for swimming, snorkelling, diving or just relaxing on the beach. Owner also has a

travel agency.

West Coast Beaches

There are many budget hotels on the west coast beaches and one a bit ritzier. Tropical Beach Resort (tel: 08133-7670 1532; www.tropical-beachresort.com), minutes away from Yo-Yo's, Scar Reef and Super Suck, has a gym, massage and beauty centre, 9-hole golf course and deep-sea fishing boat. Rooms are let for a minimum of seven nights. **$$$$$**

Timor

Kupang

There are many decent hotels in Kupang, as it is the regional capital of East Nusa Tenggara, regularly hosting government and business conventions and conferences. Scheduled to open in 2012 is Aston International Hotels' Aston Kupang, a four-star, 300-room hotel near the beach.

Hotel Kristal
Jl. Timor Raya, No. 59
Tel: 0380-825 100
www.kupangklubhouse.com/kristalhotel.htm
A large, 140-room beachfront hotel with its own restaurant, swimming pool and conference facilities. **$$$**

Sasando International
Jl. Kartini, No. 1
Tel: 0380-833 334
This recently renovated hilltop hotel is a 15-minute taxi ride from town. It has good views over Kupang Bay, a swimming pool and a handy in-house travel agency which can book airline tickets and arrange other transport. **$$$**

Hotel Pantai Timor
Jl. Sumatra, No. 44
Tel: 0380-83165
www.kupangklubhouse.com/pantaitimor.htm
This good mid-range hotel in central Kupang, on the seafron has its own restaurant serving Indonesian, Chinese and European meals. One of the best options in Kupang **$**

KALIMANTAN

East Kalimantan

Balikpapan

Le Grandeur Balikpapan
Jl. Jenderal Sudirman
Tel: 0542-420 155
www.legrandeurhotels.com
This hotel combines an attractive setting with first-class facilities. It sits amid extensive gardens adjoining a beautiful sandy beach overlooking the Makassar Strait. **$$$–$$$$**

Adika Hotel Bahtera
Jl. Jend. Sudirman, No. 2
Tel: 0542-738-000
www.bahterahotel.com
162 rooms with spa, swimming pool, tennis court, fitness centre and restaurants in the city centre, with sea views of the Bahtera Menara Tower. **$$$**

Samarinda

Hotel Grand Victoria
Jl. Letjen S. Parman, No. 11

Tel: 0541-203 001
http://hotelvictoriagroup.com
Primarily used by businessmen, situsted in front of Lembuswana Mall. Internet, spa and fitness centre, international and Chinese restaurants. Live music in lobby lounge nightly except Thursday and Sunday. 80 rooms. **$$$**

Swiss-Belhotel Samarinda
Jl. Mulawarman, No. 6
Tel: 0541-200 888
www.swiss-belhotel.com
140 rooms in the city centre overlooking the Mahakam River. Spa, swimming pool, restaurant and bar. **$$$**

South Kalimantan

Banjarmasin

Hotel Arum Kalimantan
Jl. Lambung Mangkurat
Tel: 0511-436 6818
Well-equipped hotel, 30 minutes from the airport,

with facilities that include a business centre, massage and fitness centre and a pool. **$$$**

Swiss-Belhotel Borneo
Jl. Pangeran Antasari, No. 86A
Tel: 0511-327 1111, 326 1369
www.swiss-belhotel.com
Located in centre of Banjarmasin overlooking the Martapura River and opposite Mitra Plaza, Banjarmasin's largest shopping complex. A variety of restaurants are within walking distance. **$$$**

Amaris Banjarmasin
Jl. A. Yani, Km 7
www.amarishotel.com
Designed for budget-conscious young professionals and offering all the amenities without the big price. Stark, minimalist design, but clean and new. 93 rooms next to Food Square. Rate includes breakfast. **$$**

Banjarmasin

Central Kalimantan

Palangkaraya

Aquarius Boutique Hotel
Jl. Iman Bonjol, No. 5
Frequented by businessmen, a new multi-storey hotel that has all the necessary facilities, including health club and restaurant. Live music and disco club and karaoke bar. **$$$**

Hotel Dandang Tingang
Jl. Yos Sudarso, No. 13
Tel: 0536-322 1805
The high-end rooms have air-conditioning, TV and hot water, and a private dining

room. The restaurant serves Indonesian, Chinese and European food, and turns into a disco in the evening, fuelled by a live band. **$$**

Pangkalanbun

Blue Kecubung Hotel
Jl. Domba
Tel: 0532-322 1211
www.bluekecubunghotel.com
The poshest hotel in town, though it's seen better days, and the only one to offer a bar with live music on most nights. Good Chinese restaurant. Large, airy single rooms, most with nice views. Breakfast and snacks included in the price. **$$**

Abadi Hotel
Jl. P. Antasari, No. 150
Tel: 0532-322 1021
Clean and comfortable, well located near shopping, food, banks and transport. Three floors, each with a common lounge area. All have private bathrooms. **$**

Hotel Bone
Jl. Domba, No. 21
Tel: 0532-322 1213
Budget hotel with basic

rooms. Shared bathrooms are basic but clean. **$**

Purnama Indah Hotel
Jl. A. Yani, Km 2
Tel: 0532-322 4990
Large hotel built around 1998, unfortunately located away from shopping and transport and next to bad roads. Standard rooms have fan, some with shower, air-conditioning, TV and small fridge. **$**

Tanjung Puting National Park

Rimba Orangutan Ecolodge
www.ecolodgesindonesia.com
32 rooms, some with air-conditioning and hot water, all with mosquito nets, Western showers and toilets. This lodge follows Australian green hotel standards. **$$–$$$**

Sekonyer River Ecolodge
Jakarta reservations office: Kalpataru Adventures Jl. Kenaga II/2, Jaka Permai Kompleks Bekasi, Jakarta
Tel: 021-889 1183
Kalpataru travel agency owns the lodge and also

ABOVE: Kenyah Dayak ceremony.

organises tours to Tanjung Puting and Dayak country. Basic accommodation in the village directly behind the lodge. **$$**

West Kalimantan

Pontianak

Grand Mahkota Hotel Pontianak
Jl. Sidas, No. 8
Tel: 0561-736 022/3
Aside from easy access in the centre of town, this high-rise hotel has

140 rooms and an excellent restaurant. A buffet breakfast is included in the room price. **$$$**

Hotel Santika Pontianak
Jl. Diponogoro, No. 46
Reservations: Tel: 021-270 0027
www.santika.com
A three-star hotel located within the central business district and only 20 minutes from the airport. Caters for both business and leisure travellers. **$$$**

SULAWESI

South Sulawesi

Bira

Amatoa Resort Bira
Jl. Pasir Putih, No. 6
Bulukumba Bira
Tel: 0813-5337 6865
www.amatoaresort.com
Seven air-conditioned bungalows built into a cliff, some with private sea access. Restaurant serves European and Indonesian food. Swimming pool, good snorkelling and diving, white-sand beach. **$$$$$**

Makassar

Hotel Pantai Gapura
Jl. Pasar Ikan, No. 10
Tel: 0411-362 5791
www.pantaigapura.com
The resort has lovely de luxe cottages over the water, and a plus is the remarkable swimming pool. **$$$**

Pondok Suada Indah
Jl. Hasanuddin, No. 12
Tel: 0411-361-7179

15 budget rooms in the city centre next to KFC and near Losari beach. Very friendly staff. **$**

Rantepao

Toraja Heritage Hotel
Jl. Kete Kesu
Tel: 0423-21192
http://torajaheritage.com
160 rooms and suites in Torajan-style clan houses, all with balconies facing rice fields. Swimming pool, two restaurants, spa. Mountain bikes available; can arrange trekking and rafting tours. **$$$$**

Luta Resort Toraja
Jl. Dr Ratulangi, No. 26
Phone: 0423-21060
www.torajalutaresort.com
36 modern rooms and suites ranging from standard to presidential suite with rice field and mountain views. Health-and-beauty spa, restaurant; Riverside

Bar plays live music some nights. **$$$**

Hotel Pondok Torsina
Jl. Paorura, No. 37
Tel: 0423-21293
A simple but clean two-star hotel set in a rice field about 1.5km (1 mile) from Rantepao. Rooms have hot water and nice views. Two-storey Torajan architecture, swimming pool. **$**

Central Sulawesi

Palu

Swiss-Belhotel Silae Palu
Jl. Malonda, No. 12
Tel: 0451-461 888
www.swiss-belhotel.com
Situated in the central business district of Palu, 54 rooms and 27 villas overlook the breathtaking Palu Bay, a popular venue for windsurfing. Eight food and beverage options. **$$$**

Poso/Tentena

Hotel Victory
Jl. Diponegoro, No. 18
Tentena
Tel: 0458-21392
Airy rooms, helpful

PRICE CATEGORIES

Price categories for standard rooms, usually without breakfast:
$$$$$ = above US$150
$$$$ = US$101–150
$$$ = US$51–100
$$ = US$30–50
$ = under US$30

management in a hotel with the cleanest kitchen in town. Tour information available on Morowali, Togian islands and Lore Lindu. **$**

Togian islands

Black Marlin Dive Resort
Kadadiri island
www.blackmarlindiving.com
15 stylish bungalows just a few steps from the ocean. All rooms have double spring-beds with full mosquito nets, ceiling fans, Western-style bathrooms and filtered running water. Dive shop. Electricity 10am–12pm, eco-friendly. See website for dive site map. **$$**
Kadadiri Paradise
Bungalows
Kadadiri island, Togian
Tel: 0464-21058
www.kadidiriparadise.com
Located on the beach, very near snorkelling and dive sites. Simple bamboo bungalows, some recently renovated. Can arrange jungle trekking on the island. Stargazers welcome. **$$**

Bau-Bau
Hill House Villa
Tel: 0402-270 0456
Stunning hilltop location 7km (4 miles) from town, with beautiful 360-degree views of the bay and mountains. Recently renovated; air-conditioning and hot-water en suite bathrooms. Family atmosphere; small restaurant serves good local food. **$$**

Kendari

The Cendrawasi Hotel is very cheap, basic and clean. It is not too far from the harbour, in front of Kendari beach strip of night warungs. **$**. Otherwise, try:

Wakatobi

Patuno Resort Wakatobi
Wangi-Wangi island
Tel: 081-1400 2221
www.patunoresortwakatobi.com
Beautiful beachside bungalows, tastefully designed and very clean. Air-conditioning, hot-water en suite bathrooms. Other facilities include

Dive Center, Jetty Restaurant serving local and Western dishes, bar. Tours and day trips. **$$$**
Hoga Island Resort
Hoga island
Tel: 0852-4162 8287
www.tukangbesidiving.com
Basic beach bungalows with shared bathrooms on a remote uninhabited island with no roads. Tasty food and three meals per day included in prices. Small, friendly homestay atmosphere. **$$**

Bunaken island

Bastianos Cottages
Liang beach, Bunaken island
Tel: 0431-864 025
www.bastianos.com
Simple wooden cottages featuring terraces and waterfront views. Mosquito nets and cooling fan. Meals are included in the price. **$**

Manado

Kima Bajo Resort and Spa
Desa Kima Bajo

Tel: 0431-860 999
www.kimabajo.com
Luxury hotel on Wori Bay, overlooking Manado Tua island. Stylish villas in a former coconut plantation with swimming pool, spa, bar and restaurant. Range of tours offered, including diving and snorkelling expeditions. **$$$$**
Sintesa Peninsula
Hotel Manado
Jl. Jend. Sudirman,
Gunung Wenang
Tel: 62-431-855 008
www.sintesapeninsulahotel.com
Located in the very heart of Manado city, this five-star hotel provides luxurious standards and easy access to central business district. Dining, lounges, spa, health club, pool. 147 rooms. **$$$**
Minahasa Hotel
Jl. Sam Ratulangi, No. 199
Tel: 0431-862-559
www.hotelminahasa.com
This colonial-design hotel is conveniently located and offers rooms with air-conditioning and hot water. **$**

MALUKU

Maluku Divers Resort
Jl. Raya Air Manis
Desa Laha, Ambon
Tel: 0911-336 5307

www.divingmaluku.com
This new dive resort has individual bungalows set beneath mature mango trees in a tranquil

waterfront plot. Great food and spacious air-conditioned rooms with en suite bath. Packages include accommodation and meals. **$$$$**
Aston Natsepa
Jl. Raya Natsepa
Ambon
www.aston-international.com
Constructed in 2009, a large-occupancy hotel with rooms set in three multi-storey blocks. Large open-air swimming pool. Central reservations through website. **$$$**
Swiss-Belhotel
Jl. Pasifik Permai
Ambon City
Tel: 0911-322-888
www.swiss-belhotel.com
Constructed in 2010, the hotel is located in Ambon city, convenient for city exploration. Comfortable rooms and more amenities than most Ambon hotels. **$$$**

Colin Beach Resort
Jalan Raya
Latuhalat village
Formerly a dive resort, now locally owned. Three blocks of terraced accommodation. All rooms have en suite bath and air-conditioning. **$$**
Michael's Homestay
Michael Puturuhu works as head of tourism relations in Ambon Airport. Minutes from the airport and offers three fan-only rooms, shared bathroom and shower, cared for by his warm and welcoming family. **$**

BELOW: on the beach near Ambon.

Banda

Maulana Hotel
Banda Neira
Tel: 0910-21022
The largest hotel in Banda Neira by some distance. At the time of writing, the hotel

is a little tired and in need of some repair. The Maulana benefits from a great waterfront location, with views across to the spectacular to Gunung Api volcano. **$$**

Ternate

Archie Hotel
Jl. Nuku, No. 6
Tel: 0921-311 0821
Clean rooms and modern facilities set this hotel apart from others in Ternate. **$$**

Bukit Pelangi Hotel
Jl. Jati Sit, No. 338
Tel: 0921-22180
Not particularly well-decorated rooms, but comfortable and clean enough, in the Bastiong area. **$$**

PAPUA

Agats

Asmat Inn
Very basic rooms, no restaurant. Meals have to be pre-ordered. Water is rationed during the dry season. **$**

Losmen Pada Elo
A two-storey place offering very basic rooms. The second floor is cooler and a little nicer. Standing fans are available on request. A simple breakfast is served; other meals may be ordered in advance. Water is rationed during the dry season. **$**

Biak

Hotel Arumbai
Jl. Selat Makassar, No. 3
Tel: 0981-21835, 22159
Located in the centre of Biak town, Arumbai has clean, air-conditioned rooms but no view. The restaurant is small, but the food is good. **$$**

Irian Hotel
Jl. Professor Moch Yamin
Tel: 0981-21139, 21939
Decent, basic, air-conditioned rooms and food. Good value. **$**

Jayapura

Swiss-Belhotel
Jl. Pasifik Permai
Tel: 0967-551 888
www.swiss-belhotel.com
Located in the town centre on the waterfront. Clean, air-conditioned rooms. The restaurant overlooks Jotefa Bay. **$$$**

Yasmin Hotel
Jl. Percetakan Negara, No. 8
Tel: 0967-533 222
Located in downtown Jayapura, the rooms here are clean, but small. There is a good restaurant with the best iced coffee in town. The Garuda office is next door. **$$**

Manokwari

Swiss-Belhotel
Jl. Yos Sudarso, No. 8
Tel: 0986-21299
www.swiss-belhotel.com
Located on the water looking out over Dore Bay, 10 minutes from the Manokwari town centre. Clean, air-conditioned rooms. **$$$**

Merauke

Megaria Hotel
Jl. Raya Mandala, No. 166
Tel: 0971-321 932
Rooms include a few with Western-style bathrooms and hot water. Breakfast is included; other meals have to be pre-ordered. The reception desk stocks cold beer. **$**

Nirmala Hotel
Jl. Raya Mandala, No. 66
Tel: 0971-321 849
A very basic hotel with a huge restaurant that serves good food. The economy rooms come with a fan and use of a common bathroom, the mid-priced rooms have air conditioning but no hot water, while the de luxe rooms have both air-conditioning and hot water. **$**

Raja Ampat

Sorido Bay Resort
Mansoear archipelago,
Raja Ampat
Tel: 0815-2700-0610,
081-1480 4610
www.rajaampatdiving.com
Pioneers in the region, the resort is located in the centre of Raja Ampat overlooking the bay and surrounding islands. The restaurant is one of the best in the area. **$$$$$**

Kri Eco Resort
Mansoear archipelago, Raja Ampat
Tel: 0815-2700 0610,
081-1480 4610

www.papua-diving.com
Traditional Papuan bungalows on stilts over the water. Back to nature. Fresh and healthy food with freshly caught fish dishes daily. **$$$$**

Sentani

Sentani Indah
Jl. Raya Hawai
Tel: 0967-592 828
Located 10 minutes from Sentani Airport, this standard hotel has a nice pool and a good restaurant specialising in grilled fish. There is disco dancing at weekends. The rooms at the back offer a good view of the Cyclops Mountains. **$$$**

Sorong

Je Meridian Hotel
Jl. Basuki Rahmat, Km 7
Tel: 0951-327 999
Clean, air-conditioned rooms and good food. Very good value. **$$**

Royal Mamberamo Hotel
Jl. Dr Sam Ratulangi, No. 35
Tel: 0951-325 666
Situated in the centre of Sorong town, the Royal Mamberamo has clean, air-conditioned rooms but no view. The restaurant is one of the best in town. **$$**

Timika

Sheraton Timika
P.O. Box 3
Tel: 0901-394 949
www.sheraton.com
Beautiful and expensive, but well worth the price. Located 10 minutes from the airport, the resort has the full range of de luxe facilities, including an attractive pool, and a nature walk. Another plus is the excellent restaurant

right on the premises. **$$$$**

Hotel Serayu
Jl. Ahmad Yani, No. 10
Tel: 0901-321 777
Located in downtown Timika, the rooms are basic but they do come equipped with air-conditioning. There is also a restaurant serving passable food. **$$$**

Wamena

Baliem Pilamo
Jl. Trikora
Tel: 0969-31043
Located on the main street, offering a range of rooms from basic to standard. The water supply is always a problem. The restaurant offers simple but good food. **$$**

Nayak Hotel
Jl. Gatot Subroto
Tel: 0969-31067
A favourite with budget travellers, the Nayak is a 2-minute walk from the airport. Standard rooms and a small restaurant with simple fare. **$**

PRICE CATEGORIES

Price categories for standard rooms, usually without breakfast:
$$$$$ = above US$150
$$$$ = US$101–150
$$$ = US$51–100
$$ = US$30–50
$ = under US$30

Eating Out

Recommended Restaurants, Cafes & Bars

Eating Out in Indonesia

The staple for the majority of Indonesians is rice, although in the eastern islands corn, sago, cassava or sweet potatoes dominate, and in smaller towns and villages that's what you'll be served. Coconut milk and hot chilli peppers are popular cooking ingredients nationwide. Dishes range from very spicy meat, fish and vegetables, such as the Padang food found everywhere in restaurants called Rumah Makan Padang or Rumah Makan Minang, to those which are quite sweet, for instance Jogja's speciality, *gudeg*. Almost all come with steamed white rice *(nasi puti)*. The most popular dishes among visitors are *nasi goreng* (fried rice), *mie goreng* (fried noodles), *sate* or *satay* (grilled meat or chicken on skewers) and

gado-gado (cold, steamed vegetables served with a peanut sauce). *Nasi campur* is a good choice for travellers because it is a complete meal, including rice, a vegetable and a piece of meat, usually chicken.

Chinese restaurants are found in almost every town and offer less spicy food and vegetarian dishes. In the main tourist centres and resorts, many restaurants cater for visitors and serve a wide variety of cuisines, including Western. All cities have American fast-food outlets such as KFC (Kentucky Fried Chicken), and larger ones have McDonald's and Pizza Hut.

Drinks

While the local beer, Bintang, is reasonably priced, imported beers,

cocktails and wine (only available in larger cities) are expensive and can equal the price of a meal. Bottled drinking water can be purchased everywhere. The *Aqua* brand is preferred, and in fact the name is synonymous with mineral water. In tourist-centre restaurants, free room-temperature or cold water may be poured from a pitcher at the table *(air putih)*, which has been filled from a large mineral water container in the kitchen, saving you the cost (and environmental waste) of buying bottled water. If in doubt, just ask. In cheaper establishments, *air putih* may be served hot in a glass or in a thermos, indicating that it has been boiled and is safe to drink.

Hygiene and Etiquette

It is recommended to avoid ice served in *warungs* (roadside food stalls), since the origin of the water used to make it is unknown; however, in resorts catering to tourists purified water is used in ice-making, so is acceptable. Also be aware that the hygienic standards of *warungs* and street vendors are usually not what Westerners are accustomed to. Plates and cutlery are not washed with hot water and food may not be refrigerated until cooked. Proceed with caution.

If visiting someone's home, for example in a village, you will almost always be offered a drink and a snack. It is impolite to refuse, so if unsure of cleanliness, stick with coffee or tea (which have been boiled), cooked food or fresh fruit. *(For more about food and drink, see Spice Islands Cuisine, page 77).*

Left: *rijsttaeffel* (rice table).

JAKARTA

Jakarta eateries offer something for everyone: from fine dining to Western-style fast-food joints and very simple local fare at *warungs* (roadside food stalls). These days, some of the best food and the widest diversity of choices are in the shopping malls. Just wander around and see what tickles your fancy; quality can be judged by the size of the crowd. Or go shopping at the boutiques along Jl. Kemang Raya in the suburbs and stop for lunch at one of the popular cafés and delis.

Café Batavia
Jl. Pintu Besar Utara, No. 14
Tel: 021-691 5531
A stylish restaurant housed in a 19th-century Dutch heritage building. Good Indonesian and international dishes served in a charming, eclectic decor. **$$$**

Oasis
Jl. Raden Saleh, No. 47
Tel: 021-315 0646
A landmark restaurant reminiscent of old-world colonial elegance. The speciality is *rijsttaefel*, served by waitresses in traditional dress, each carrying a separate dish. **$$$**

Shang Palace
Shangri-La Hotel
Kota BNI, Jl. Jend.
Sudirman, Kav. 1
Tel: 021-570 7440
A Chinese restaurant with wide selections of Cantonese and vegetarian dishes. Serves dim sum at lunchtime; also live seafood selections. **$$$**

Bistro Baron
Plaza Indonesia Extension, Level 1, No. E20–21 (below Hyatt)
An amazingly good, but small, restaurant decorated in French bistro style with a limited menu that includes pasta, sandwiches, grills and desserts. Also open for breakfast. **$$**

Canteen
Adjacent to Aksara bookstore, Plaza Indonesia and Pacific Place malls.
Spacious, great light for reading, internet hotspot and good food; what more could a diner want? Check out the Sunday brunch. Other goodies include smoothies, breakfast pizza, sandwiches and soups. **$$**

The Duck King
Senayan City, Pondok Indah and Kelapa Gading Malls, Tangerang (western Jakarta), Bandung and Surabaya
Main dishes are roasted and Peking duck; also serves dim sum and seafood prepared by chefs from Malaysia, Singapore and Hong Kong. **$$**

Hazara
Jl. Dr Kusuma Atmaja, No. 85, Menteng
Tel: 021-3192 5037
Good North Indian food amid curios and antiques in an interesting setting. **$$**

Jun Njan Seafood Restaurant
Grand Indonesia, West Mall,

ABOVE: satay is a popular street food.

Level 5, No. 11 A-BMH
Jl. M.H. Thamrin, No.1
Tel: 021-2358 0647
A seafood restaurant with seven outlets throughout Jakarta. Try the delicious fresh boiled shrimp and crabs in oyster sauce. **$$**

Koi Gallery
Jl. Mahakam 1, No. 2
Tel: 021-722-2864 and Jl. Kemang Raya
The European and Asian menu changes regularly to complement the exhibits in this gallery-cum-eatery. **$$**

Payon
Jl. Kemang Raya, No. 17
Tel: 021-719 4826
Exquisite cuisine from West, Central and East Java served in a typical Yogyakarta-style house. Gamelan music tinkles in the background while you partake of your food. **$$**

Sushi Tei
Plaza Indonesia, No. 1–102 A & C
Jl. M.H. Thamrin, Kav. 28–30
Tel: 021-3983 5103
A group of Japanese restaurants that has 11 outlets throughout Jakarta, mostly in shopping malls. It prepares the best sushi and Japanese curried rice in town. **$$**

VOC Galangan Café & Restaurant
Jl. Kakap, No. 1
Tel: 021-667 0981
A Jakarta institution set in an old Dutch warehouse located just opposite the Pasar Ikan and Bahari Museum. Serves Indonesian and Dutch fusion food. **$$**

Bumbu Desa
Jl. Cikini Raya, No. 72
Tel: 021-390 4747
A franchised traditional Sundanese restaurant with an elegant modern ambience. Specialities are chicken or fish wrapped in a banana leaf and roasted. **$**

D'Cost Seafood
Jl. Kemang Raya, No. 84
Tel: 021-7179 2661
A group of seafood restaurants in Java, Sumatra, Kalimantan, Sulawesi and Bali. Its motto, "five-star quality with street hawker prices", means business: hot tea costs only US$0.01. **$**

WEST JAVA

Anyer

Blue Moon Bar & Restaurant
Jl. Raya Bojong, No. 10
Tel: 0254-600 251
Frequented by holidaying Jakarta expatriates, who are expert at finding good food. Indonesian dishes and cold Bintang beer. **$**

Makassar
Jl. Raya Bojong
Tel: 0254-601 450

Specialises in South Sulawesi grilled fish and ribs. **$**

Mbok Sarikah
Jl. Raya Sirih
Tel: 0254-600 041
Speciality is grilled fish fresh from the catch of the day. **$**

Midori
Jl. Raya Cikoneng
Tel: 0254-601 974
The only Japanese restaurant in the Anyer-Carita beach area. Popular among Japanese expatriates working in the industrial complex at nearby Cilegon. **$**

Bandung

BMC
Jl. Aceh, No. 30
Tel: 022-420 4595
In a historic building, BMC

TRANSPORT

ACCOMMODATION

EATING OUT

ACTIVITIES

A – Z

(Bandoengsche Melk Centrale) was a milk factory in 1928 and is now a restaurant. The main attraction is fresh milk and yoghurt, but it also serves Western and Indonesian dishes. **$$**

Kampung Daun
Jl. Sersan Bajuri, No. 88
Tel: 022-278 7915
An outdoor Sundanese restaurant set on a cliff with dining huts arranged between lush trees. Offers authentic Sundanese dishes such as ikan *gurame goring* (fried carp), *karedok* (raw salad in peanut sauce) and oxtail soup. **$$**

Queen
Jl. Dalem Kaum, No. 79

Tel: 022-420 4561, 423 1659
Around since 1954, the best Chinese (Cantonese) dishes in Bandung. Within walking distance of Grand Preanger and Savoy Bidakara hotels. **$**

Sindang Reret
Jl. Surapati, No. 53
Tel: 022-250 1474
The best authentic Sundanese food in town, with branches at Jl. Raya Lembang (near Tangkuban Perahu volcano) and Jl. Raya Ciwidey (south of Bandung). Spacious restaurant and ample parking. **$**

Bogor to Puncak

Bogor and Cianjur are linked

by a highway known locally as Jl. Raya Puncak, even though the name changes many times from one end to the other.

Cimory
Jl. Raya Puncak, No. 435
Tel: 0251-825 7888
A restaurant within a creamery that makes fresh milk and yoghurt. Serves Western food, such as grilled ribs and sausages, and Indonesian fare, such as oxtail soup. **$$**

Grand Hill Bistro Café
Jl. Raya Puncak, Km 84
Tel: 0251-825 0516
The newest area restaurant, set on a pine tree-covered hill with a great

panorama. It offers European and Asian cuisines. **$$**

Puncak Pass Resort
Jl. Raya Puncak, Km 90
Tel: 0263-512 503
The oldest restaurant in Puncak, established in 1928. Speciality is Dutch fare, including *pannekoek* (apple pancakes), *Hollandsche poffertjes* (buckwheat pancakes), beef croquette (small beef roll), *bitter ballen* (meat-based snack) and beef steak. An ideal place for having good food in a historic atmosphere overlooking Puncak landscape. **$$**

CENTRAL JAVA

Cirebon

Jumbo
Jl. Siliwangi, No. 191
The seafood here is cooked according to Sundanese and Chinese recipes. Good grilled dishes. **$$**

Maxim's
Jl. Bahagia No. 45–47
The best Chinese seafood place in town, just a short walk from Thay Kak Sie Buddhist temple. Try the steamed giant crabs and prawns. **$**

Semarang

Toko Oen
Jl. Pemuda, No. 52

BELOW: Bintang beer.

In a wonderful old colonial building, serves Dutch-Indonesian food in a nostalgic atmosphere. Delicious sweets, favoured by Indonesians and foreigners. **$$**

Solo

Every evening at 6pm, Solo's Jalan Mayor Sunaryo off the main street, Jl. Slamet Riyadi, is closed to traffic and becomes a pedestrian-way where local food vendors gather.

O-Solo-Mio Galleria & Ristorante
Jl. Slamet Riyadi, No. 253

Tel: 0271-706 0842
Open for breakfast, lunch and dinner; very interesting menu of mostly Western food, with great pizza, pasta and salads. **$$**

Sari
Jl. Slamet Riyadi, No. 351
Tel: 0271-719 317
The overall best Javanese restaurant in Solo. Specialities here are *nasi liwet* (a Solo speciality consisting of rice cooked in coconut cream with garnishes), fried chicken and various types of *pepes* (steamed or grilled seafood or mushrooms wrapped in banana leaf). **$$**

Segar Ayam
Jl. Secoyudan (opposite Pasar Klewer, the central batik market, and within walking distance of the Keraton)
The iced fruit drinks are excellent, meant to accompany the simple Javanese dishes like *gado-gado*, *pecel* (boiled vegetables with peanut sauce) and *nasi rames* (sampler dishes). **$**

Tojoyo
Jl. Kepunton Kulon, No. 77
Here, you get the best Javanese fried chicken in town, but only at dinner (6–9pm). Arrive early or you will be disappointed. **$**

Warung Buru

Jl. Ahmad Dahlan, No. 23
High-quality Indonesian and Western food, good value and friendly, helpful staff. Also organises transport bookings, bicycle tours and batik courses. Highly recommended. **$**

Yogyakarta (Jogja)

The Jogja speciality is *gudeg* – a combination plate consisting of rice with boiled *nangka muda* (young jackfruit), chicken, egg, coconut gravy and spicy sauce with boiled *sambal kulit* (spicy buffalo hide). Having a large student population, here cheap food is aplenty, particularly at sundown when little eateries pop up along the sidewalks. Foreigners accustomed to more hygienic food and cutlery handling, however, should exercise caution. Some restaurants with good standards follow.

Gadjah Wong
Jl. Gejayan
Tel: 0274-588 294
Three different dining areas offer guests a choice of ambience, accompanied by Javanese, jazz or other Western music. Remarkably good food in a friendly, upmarket setting

surrounded by tropical gardens. **$$**

Sasanti Restaurant
Jl. Pelagan Tentara Pelajar
Tel: 0274-650 9860, 866 789
Authentic Indonesian and delicious Western food, excellent service and ambience. Garden or indoor seating; serenity pool. **$$**

The House of Raminten
Jl. FM Noto, No. 7, Kota Baru
Serves Indonesian food in a restaurant with Javanese architecture and ambience. Try one of the Javanese *jamu* (herbal) drinks. **$**

Ministry of Coffee
Jl. Prawirotaman, No. 15A
Tel: 0274-747 3828

www.ministryofcoffee.com
An interesting menu of primarily Western dishes in the heart of the budget accommodation district. A wide selection of coffees and teas and excellent desserts. **$**

Via Via Café
Jl. Prawirotaman, No. 30
Tel: 0274-386 557

www.viaviajogja.com
Serves Indonesian and Western food, both vegetarian and non-vegetarian, and is popular with budget travellers. Offers excellent travel information and alternative tours, such as bicycle trips and caving, and courses such as batik and Indonesian language. **$**

EAST JAVA

Malang

Inggil Restaurant and Museum
Jl. Gajah Mada, No. 4
Tel: 0341-332 110
Serves Indonesian dishes in a restored Dutch colonial house-cum-museum displaying the collections of its art-lover and historian owner. Speciality is *ayam goreng* (Indonesian fried chicken). **$$**

Melati Pavilion
Hotel Tugu Malang
Jl. Tugu, No. 3
Tel: 0341-363 891

This beautiful garden restaurant offers delicious Indonesian home-cooking, Chinese Peranakan and Dutch colonial cuisine. Freshly baked bread served at breakfast. **$$**

Toko Oen
Jl. Basuki Rachmat
Tel: 0341-364 052
In an old Dutch building, this restaurant serves Indonesian and Dutch food, delicious desserts and bakery items. Also has an outlet in Semarang. **$$**

Surabaya

The Café, House of Sampoerna
Jl. Taman Sampoerna, No. 6
Tel: 031-353 9000
Art Deco interior with a dash of history, The Café offers a special sensory and culinary experience. In the Dutch colonial House of Sampoerna compound. **$$**

La Rucola
Jl. Dr Soetomo, No. 51
Tel: 031-567 8557
Authentic Mediterranean food in a European setting

unique to Surabaya. Excellent steaks and pizzas and an extensive wine list. **$$**

Dream of Kahyangan Restaurant Art Resto
Jl. Puri Widya Kencana, LL5
Citraland-Surabaya
Tel: 031-741 1999, 742 1999, 7122 1999
Authentic Indonesian cuisine showcased by lavish Javanese-Chinese architecture and interior design reflecting the owner's love of art and culture. Live traditional music. **$**

SUMATRA

North Sumatra

Medan

Lyn's Café and Restaurant
Jl. Jend. Ayani, No. 98
A good place for Western food, not least because of its lively bar. A favourite place with the expat community. **$$**

Omlandia Restaurant
Deli River Resort
Jl. Raya Namorambe
Pasar 4, No. 129
Tel: 061-703 2964
A special restaurant with beautiful architecture in the middle of unspoiled Sumatran nature on the banks of the Deli River. Serves traditional Indonesian and European cuisines. **$$**

Restaurant Garuda
Jl. Pemuda, No. 20 (next to the luxury market)
Tel: 061-451 3893
www.restorangaruda.com
Everything on the menu in

this 24-hour eatery is good. Try its freshly squeezed fruit juices. **$**

Night market
Jl. Selat Panjang
The roadside stalls are a must-try, providing a fun (and delicious) way to soak up the local culture. There is a range of low-priced local fare and fresh seafood, including finger-licking chilli crabs.

Samosir

Carolina Restaurant
Carolina Cottages and Hotel
Tel: 0645-451 210
By far the best place on the island to eat: good food, good prices and a wonderful lakeside setting. Batak dances add excitement on Saturday evenings. **$**

Juwita Café
Tuk-Tuk
Tel: 0625-451 217
www.juwitacafe.com

Next to Samosir Villa Resort, this café offers good food and cooking classes. **$**

Rumba's Pizzeria
Southern end of Tuk-Tuk
The food here is very decent, and the pizzas are good. **$**

West Sumatra

Bukittinggi

The Coffee Shop
Jl. Jend. A Yani, No. 105
A Bukittinggi institution and a favourite meeting point for travellers, the eatery serves a wide range of Western food, including delicious pancakes. Very crowded in the evenings. **$**

Family Benteng
Jl. Yos Sudarso
Tel: 0752-21102
Serves good Padang and Western fare. **$**

Padang

This is the home of *nasi*

Padang, which consists of 20–25 small dishes of spicy vegetables or meat pre-prepared and laid out on the table. It is the ultimate fast food – there is no waiting at all – and is nutritious too. Each diner pays for the portion he or she eats. The popularity of *nasi Padang* has spread throughout Indonesia, and to Southeast Asia as well. Most of the dishes are hot, and a few favourites are *rendang* (curried

PRICE CATEGORIES

The price guidelines shown are per person for an Asian meal that includes a meat dish and two vegetables or a Western three-course meal, without drinks.

$ = under US$10
$$ = US$11–25
$$$ = US$26–50

beef), *dendeng balado* (crispy beef with red chillies) and boiled egg in curry.

Simpang Raya
Jl. Bagindo Aziz Chan
This is the best place to sample *nasi Padang*. The

eatery has a branch on Jl. Bundo Kandung. **$**
Taman Sari
Jl. Yani

Good Javanese and Chinese food is served here. Try the *kway teow goreng* (fried flat noodles). **$**

SOUTH BALI

Every hotel will have at least one restaurant. Listed below are some culinary experiences beyond hotel confines.

Bukit Badung

Bali Buddha
Jl. Raya Uluwatu, Pecatu
Tel: 0361-701 980
www.balibuddah.com
Serves vegan, raw food and vegetarian to eat in or take away. Small shop sells organic and baked goodies. Delivers to area hotels and villas. **$$**

Denpasar

The capital city sees mostly locals and domestic tourists. There are many small Indonesian and Chinese restaurants, particularly along Jl. Teuku Umar. Don't expect much in terms of Western fare.
OZIGO Country
Jl. Moh. Yamin, No. 59
Tel: 0361-241 570
Continental and local food. Upstairs is an air-conditioned restaurant. Downstairs has live country music three nights a week. Highlights are the outdoor barbecue of pork ribs, steaks and lobster. **$**

Jimbaran

Beachside dining under the stars is a favourite indulgence. Scores of *warung*-style restaurants offer grilled seafood. **$$**

BELOW: gado gado.

Kuta and Legian

Poppies Restaurant
Gang Poppies I
Tel: 0361-751 059
A long-time favourite with consistently good food and service. Steaks, seafood, salads, shish kebabs and Indonesian food plus a nicely stocked wine cellar. Reservations necessary during high season. **$$$**
TJ's Mexican Restaurant
Gang Poppies I
Tel: 0361-751 093
Serves large portions of the best Tex-Mex dishes in Bali, plus margaritas, ice-cold beer and desserts. Nice indoor garden setting. **$$**
Yut'z Place
Jl. Werkudara, No. 521
Tel: 0361-765 047
An eclectic menu features an array of interesting Continental dishes, appetisers, cold plates and Indonesian food. **$$**

Sanur

This was the first area to attract Western tourists and is still Bali's largest expatriate area today. The variety is expanding rapidly, and new restaurants open regularly.
Café Batujimbar
Jl. Danau Tamblingan, No. 152
Tel: 0361-287 374
www.cafebatujimbar.com
An expat favourite, has a varied menu featuring healthy foods, salads, fruit drinks. Daily specials. **$$**
Kayu Manis
Jl. Danau Tamblingan
Tel: 0361-289 410
Popular with expats who know good food; expect

delicious international dishes at moderate prices. No credit cards. **$$**
Massimo Il Ristorante
Jl. Danau Tamblingan, No. 206
Tel: 0361-288 942
www.balimassimo.com
Excellent Italian cuisine; pizza, pastas and risotto all very tasty. Both indoor and outdoor seating available. Set lunches are good value. **$$**
Sanur Deli
Jl. Danau Poso, No. 67
Tel: 0361-270 544
The best sandwich shop in Bali. Select rye, wheat or wholemeal bread, then choose your fillings from a large selection. Also Australian-style pies, English pasties and quiches. After 6pm turns into a small restaurant offering good pork, beef and chicken dishes. **$**

Seminyak and Petitenget

Gado Gado
Jl. Dhayna Pura, No. 99
Tel: 0361-736 966
www.gadogadorestaurant.com
Trendy, relaxing beachfront restaurant. Sit under the trees and watch Bali's famous sunset and the surf rolling in. The lunchtime crisp-skinned *wasabi* chicken breast on a bed of spiced Thai noodles is fusion food at its best. Dinner options are more varied (and more expensive). **$$$**
Ku dé Ta
Jl. Kayu Aya, No. 9
Tel: 0361-736 969
www.kudeta.net
A hip, upmarket restaurant with a beautiful beachside location. Serves trendy modern Australian cuisine. Recommended are the impressive breakfasts and 4–6pm tapas served in time for the sunset. **$$$**
La Lucciola

Jl. Kayu Aya, No. 9
Tel: 0361-730 838
Excellent Mediterranean food served in a big, two-level thatched structure on the beach. Great for sunset cocktails and Sunday brunch. Reservations are essential. **$$**
The Living Room Fine Dining Restaurant & Lounge
Jl. Petitenget, No. 2000X
Tel: 0361-735 735
www.thelivingroom.com
Lovely, romantic, garden-oriented and indoor setting presenting Pan-Asian fusion food in very relaxed yet posh surroundings. Popular DJ music in the lounge after dinner. **$$**
Mykonos Taverna
Jl. Laksmana, No. 52
Tel: 0361-733 253
www.mykonos-bali.com
A simple little Greek taverna with wonderful and hardy Greek food and a thoroughly fun atmosphere. **$$**
Trattoria Cucina Italiana
Jl. Laksmana
Tel: 0361-737 082
Packed almost every night of the week, which says a lot about the food (and the reasonable prices) here. Fantastic pastas, pizzas and salads, as well as beef and seafood dishes, but be prepared to wait if you haven't made a reservation. Located about 100 metres/yds from its smaller branch of the same name. Food is equally good at both places. **$$**

Nusa Dua, Tanjung and Benoa

The restaurant pickings are slim in Nusa Dua and mainly confined to the luxury hotels. The restaurant section of the Bali Connection shopping mall offers a variety of eateries with a good range of eating options, but all are quite expensive compared with

other areas of Bali.

Tanjung Benoa

Bumbu Bali
Tanjung Benoa
Tel: 0361-774 502
www.balifoods.com

Beautifully presented
authentic Balinese dishes.
Try the multi-course *rijstaeffel*. Cooking classes
offered. Free transport provided from/to area hotels.
$$$

CENTRAL BALI

Ubud

Ubud's eateries are almost
as varied as Kuta's. There is
egg *lawar* and yoghurt
shakes, feta salads and
brown bread, and some of
the best *nasi campur* on
the island.
Ary's Warung
Jl. Raya Ubud
Tel: 0361-975 053
www.dekco.com
Contemporary Asian Cuisine
blending Western food and
techniques with Asian
spices and ingredients. The
tasting menu is a good way
of sampling food you might
not have otherwise ordered.
$$$
Lamak
Jl. Monkey Forest
Tel: 0361-974 668
www.lamakbali.com
Serves excellent fusion food
like duck breast in Asian
spices and lamb rack cutlets
coated with a tangy Hunan
sauce. Also has one of the
most stylish cocktail bars in
Bali. **$$$**
Mozaic
Jl. Raya Sanggingan
Tel: 0361-975 768
www.moziac-bali.com
Highly recommended for

those who appreciate fine
cuisine and top-class pres-
entation and service, rare
elsewhere on the island.
Reasonably priced for such
a high standard.
Established by chef and
owner Chris Salans in 2001,
you must reserve in
advance. **$$$**
Bebek Bengil (Dirty Duck)
Jl. Raya Hanoman, Padang Tegal
Tel: 0361-975 489
An old favourite, Balinese
bales (pavilions) scattered
among ponds and gardens
overlooking rice paddies.
The menu caters for many
tastes: Western, traditional
Indonesian and Balinese,
including local specialities
like the *bebek betutu* (fried
crispy duck), which sells out
quickly. **$$**
Café Lotus
Jl. Raya Ubud
Tel: 0361-975 660
Set in an open-air court-
yard with a lotus pond,
the menu includes a good
mix of Western staples,
home-made pastas,
Indonesian-style dishes
and tempting cheese-
cakes. Balinese dance
performances and music

ABOVE: coffee plant in the Sumatran highlands.

evenings. **$$**
Café Wayan
Jl. Wanara Wana (Monkey
Forest Road)
Tel: 0361-975 447
www.alamindahbali.com
One of Ubud's legends,
run by Ibu Wayan and her
ever-smiling family. The
Wayan Special Salad is
delicious with a bowl of
soup and garlic toast. The
seafood and pizza are
scrumptious. Ask for a
table at the back where
you can gaze at rice fields.
$$
Casa Luna
Jl. Raya Ubud
Tel: 0361-973 282
www.casalunabali.com
Tasty Balinese and
Indonesian food; interna-
tional offerings are not as
consistently good. Bakery at
the front of the restaurant
serves good breads, cakes
and pastries. The café also
conducts Balinese cooking
classes. **$$**
Naughty Nuri's
Jl. Raya Lunsgsiakan (across

from Neka Museum)
Tel: 0361-977 547
Excellent steaks, ribs and
other grilled fare and arguably the best Martinis on the
island, all in a roadside
shack. **$$**
Warung TutMak
Jl. Dewi Sita, No. 97
Tel: 0361-975754
One of the most interesting
menus in Ubud. Surprises
include enchiladas, rarely
found on Bali. Excellent cof-
fee roasted on-premises.
Located next to the Jl.
Monkey Forest football field.
$$
Ibu Oka
Jl. Suweta
Tel: 0361-975 345
Most famous outlet in Bali
for *babi guling* (roast suckling pig), the island's most
revered dish. From opening
until about 2.30pm there is
a constant queue. When the
street is closed for royal ceremonies the *warung* is
operated from the owner's
house at Jl. Tegal Sari, No.
2, nearby. **$**

NORTH AND WEST BALI

Balian Beach

**Pondok Pitaya
Surfer Hotel &
Restaurant**
Balian beach
Tel: 0819-9984 9054
www.baliansurf.com
Right on the beach, an
open-air restaurant so
near the ocean you can
feel the spray on your
face on a windy day.
Can become rather

rambunctious with beer
and surfer talk at night.
$$

Lovina

Jasmine Kitchen
Jl. Binaria, Kalibukbuk
Tel: 0362-41565
Authentic Thai food upstairs
in a two-storey building dec-
orated simply and pleasantly.
Good service is a plus. **$$**

Lovina Bakery
Jl. Raya Lovina
Tel: 0362-42225
An excellent choice for
those times when you're
craving something
besides rice. Fragrant
freshly baked breads and
also a café with a wine
menu. **$$**
Spunkey's Bar-Restaurant
Banyualit beach, Kalibukbuk
Tel: 0813-3736 5094

As the name suggests,

PRICE CATEGORIES

The price guidelines shown
are per person for an Asian
meal that includes a meat
dish and two vegetables or
a Western three-course
meal, without drinks.
$ = under US$10
$$ = US$11–25
$$$ = US$26–50

this is a great hang-out place in a quieter location than the main Binaria beach, away from the more crowded locations nearby. It's the perfect place to wash down good Australian, international or Indonesian food with a cold beer, juice or coffee, or drop round for cock-tails. **$$**

Pemuteran

Matahari Beach Resort & Spa
Jl. Raya Seririt-Gilimanuk
Tel: 0362-92312
A first-class restaurant in a luxury resort that is highly recommended by expatri-ates who come here from South Bali to relax. Balinese dances performed twice weekly. **$$$**
Puri Genesha Villas
Pantai Pemuteran

Tel: 0362-94766
Specialises in healthy meals, including vegan and organic; also offers "healing through food" packages. Small seaside restaurant has a different menu every night. **$$$**

West Bali National Park

Manjangan Resort
Jl. Raya Gilimanuk-

Singaraja, Km 17
Desa Pejarakan
Tel: 0362-94700
An eco-resort set in the forest; its outdoor restau-rant has fabulous views. There is a watchtower above the canopy for birdwatching, or take a short trek around the property to burn off extra calories. **$$–$$$**

EAST BALI

Amed

Sails Restaurant
Lean village, Bunutan
Tel: 0363-33006
The only real restaurant in Amed, with a wide-scope menu to please vegetarians as well as those hungry for chicken curry, steak, sau-sages or fish. Try the des-sert crêpes. Free pick-up and drop-off in Amed area.

Reservations essential dur-ing high season.

Candidasa

Garpu
Rama Candidasa Resort & Spa
Jl. Raya Sengkidu
Tel: 0363-41974
www.ramacandidasahotel.com

Air-conditioned restaurant with ocean views; serves international, Mediterranean, Italian and Balinese cuisine. Recently renovated and upgraded. **$$**
TJ's Café
Hotel Taman Air
Tel: 0363-41540
A breezy garden restaurant serving Indonesian and European dishes, including

salads and yummy des-serts. Bar serves cocktails. **$$**
Vincent's
Jl. Raya Candidasa
Tel: 0363-41368
Serves mix of local and European cuisines in a cosy atmosphere with friendly service. Pleasant garden; jazz played softly on the second floor. **$$**

NUSA TENGGARA

Flores

Ende

Pangan Lokal Restaurant
Jl. Melati
Contact: Sister Martini, Tel: 0852-390 2274
Operated by the Catholic Vocational School Muktayasa, managed by the Business Studies Foundation, and overseen by the Congregation of

BELOW: drying spices.

Sisters of the Followers of Jesus (CIJ). Speciality is *Rumpu Rample Set:* locally grown red rice, grilled fish, chilli *sambal* and *moke* (home-made *arak* wine) served in natural coconut shells and *lontar* plaited dishes. **$$**

Labuhanbajo

Laveria Restaurant

Jl. Gorontalo, next to Bajo Komodo Eco Lodge
Quiet place serving Indonesian, Chinese and Western dishes. **$$**
Treetop Restaurant
Jl. Sukarno-Hatta
Serves Indonesian, European and Chinese food in a setting overlooking the sea. **$$**

Maumere

Loka Ria Restaurant
Jl. Nai Roa (Paris beach), in front of Lokaria Chapel
Tel: 0813-3942 9690
Authentic Flores dishes served on the beach under large, shady trees. The sea is safe for swimming here, and the restaurant has changing rooms. **$**

Lombok

Senggigi

The main road to Senggigi is lined with a good number of restaurants, and most offer free pick-up and drop-off to

area hotels. In Mangsit, the innovative fare at Quinci Restaurant, at Quinci Villas, Jl. Raya Mangsit (tel: 0370-693 800) is highly recom-mended, as is anything on the menu at any of The Tugu Lombok restaurants on Sire beach, Tanjung (tel: 0370-612 0111). Lunch or dinner at The Tugu is worth what-ever it costs for the chance to see this special property.
Asmara Restaurant
Jl. Raya Senggigi
Tel: 0370-693 619
www.asmara-group.com
German-owned, with fresh, tasty and innovative food, including a good range of international dishes, fresh seafood, steaks and pastas. The menu also includes local Sasak-style food and a good selection of vegetarian dishes. **$$**
Café Alberto
Jl. Raya Senggigi
Tel: 0370-693 039
www.cafealbertolombok.com

Authentic wood-fired pizzas and pasta on the beach, thanks to an Italian owner and his Indonesian wife. Who could ask for more? Daily 9am–midnight. **$$**

Square Restaurant & Lounge
Jl. Raya Senggigi
Tel: 0370-693 688
http://squarelombok.com
The first – and only – fine-dining restaurant in Senggiggi outside the resorts, Square presents mouth-watering cuisine including *foie gras*, Australian tenderloin, rack of lamb and fish dishes. Try the Caesar salad and cheesecake. **$$**

Timor

Kupang

Pantai Laut Bar and Resto
Jl. Ikan Tongkol, No.3
Tel: 0380-802 0999
www.kupangklubhouse.com/pantailaut.htm
Great outdoor seaside bar and restaurant. Steaks (local), seafood, Chinese and Indonesian food served alfresco. Free Wi-fi and pool table keep Pantai Laut one of the busiest establishments in town for Westerners. Guest DJs and live bands nightly. **$$**

Restoran Nelayan
Jl. Timor Raya, No. 14
Tel: 0380-823 000
www.kupangklubhouse.com/nelayanrestaurant.htm
Specialising in fresh seafood, good Chinese and Indonesian food in an outdoor setting by the sea. Also regularly hosts parties and weddings. **$$**

Rotterdam Steak House
Jl. Timor Raya, No. 19
Tel: 0380-832302
www.kupangklubhouse.com/rotterdamsteakhouse.htm
Great steaks (local), Chinese and Indonesian and an even better atmosphere by the sea. For a relaxing night of dining, look no further. Live music (tasteful and unobtrusive) most nights. **$$**

KALIMANTAN

Balikpapan

Bondy
Jl. Pulau Antarsari, No. 137A (near Adika Hotel Bahtera)
Tel: 0542-424 438
Fronted by an ice-cream and pastry parlour is an open-air restaurant specialising in grilled fish. Local and imported steaks are also on the menu. **$$**

Jack's Place
Jl. Mulawarman, No. 56
Tel: 0542-760 120
This beachside restaurant has a profusion of plants, so you could be forgiven for thinking you were eating in a forest. Home-cooked Western fare: steaks, gumbo, beef brisket, stews and meatloaf. Top off a satisfying meal with apple pie and coffee. **$$**

New Shangrila
Jl. Jend. Ahmad Yani, No. 250 (about 15 minutes' walk from Adika Hotel Bahtera)
Tel: 0542-423 124
The house special is a hot dish (either chicken, prawns or beef) with vegetables and pigeon eggs. **$**

Banjarmasin

Jorong Steak House
Jl. S. Parman
An extensive, out-of-the-ordinary menu with everything from grilled lobster at the high end to burgers, hot dogs and fries. Also serves ox tongue, lamb chops and venison. **$$**

Shinta Restaurant
Jl. Lambung Mangkurat, No. 62
Housed in the Arjuna Plaza complex, this Chinese restaurant is the city's nicest eatery. On offer are shark's-fin or bird's-nest soup. Quiet in the day and very busy at

ABOVE: Seminyak restaurant.

dinner. **$$**

Pontianak

The hotels have the best restaurants, or take your pick of the local delicacies and simple rice meals at the many *warung*s at the night market on Jl. Diponegoro.

Bakso PSP
Jl. A.R. Hakim
Specialises in beef-ball soup. **$**

Kabar Gembria
Jl. Siam, No. 206
A vegetarian restaurant with a primarily Chinese menu. **$$**

Rumah Makan Borneo
Jl Setia Budi
A Chinese restaurant specialising in seafood. **$$**

Samarinda

Lezat
Jl. Mulawarman, No. 56
Tel: 0541-743 031
Excellent Chinese dishes such as squid, oysters, prawns, frog and crab, as well as pork and chicken. **$$**

Sari Pacific
Jl. Panglima Batur, No. 5–7
Tel: 0541-743 289
A good place to come for Javanese cuisine and European steaks. **$$**

Sari Rasa
Jl. Agus Salim, No. 26
Tel: 0541-732 569
Specialises in Chinese and Western dishes; large menu. Imported beef and Japanese dishes. A little pricey, but recommended. **$$**

SULAWESI

Bau-Bau

There is a string of street vendors around Pantai Kamali (near the harbour). The stalls open every evening and set up tables and chairs along the seafront; there is always a festive buzz in the air, with market stalls and kids' fairground rides. Highly recommended is the Ambon Manise stall with a blue neon sign out the front. They serve *nasi kuning* (yellow rice). Lots of fresh and traditional vegetable dishes, and a range of grilled seafood, fish and chicken with tasty sauces and *sambal*s. **$**

Lakeba Restaurant
This place is approx. 7km (4 miles) out of town. The dining tables are set in little

TRANSPORT | ACCOMMODATION | EATING OUT | ACTIVITIES | A – Z | LANGUAGE

pagodas in the garden and along the seafront, and it has a nice ambience. Serves mainly Indonesian food with a few Western dishes, juices and ice cream. **$$**

Rumah Makan Boga
Between the harbour and Pantai Kamali, this simple eatery serves good *gado-gado*. **$**

Warung Pangkep
Near the harbour, this is the largest and busiest of the many eating houses serving grilled fish. **$**

Makassar

Surya Super Crab
Jl. Nusa Kambangan, No. 16
The extensive seafood menu includes giant tiger prawns and spicy crab in the shell. **$$$**

Lae-Lae and Kayangan
Both located on Jl. Datumuseng, offer excellent fish, baked or fried, served with spicy or sweet and sour sauce. **$$**

Kios Semarang
Jl. Penghibur, No. 73
The third floor of the multi-storey restaurant is a long-time favourite of expats, who go for the cheap beer, decent Chinese-Indonesian food and the view over Losari beach. **$**

Manado

For the adventurous palate, Minahasan restaurants serve a spread of fruit bat on the spit, chopped forest rat and spicy wild pig with gener-

ous chunks of fat.

Bumi Beringin Restaurant
Jl. Sam Ratulangi
Superb atmosphere, air-conditioned; great mix of Indonesian and Manadonese cuisine. **$$**

Green Garden
Jl. Sam Ratulangi, No. 52
Tel: 0431-870 089
Serves Chinese and Indonesian dishes, with consistently good food and efficient service. **$**

Raja Sate
Jl. Piere Tendean, No. 39
Tel 0431-852 398, 846 679
Great sate (beef, chicken, goat, squid and more). Vegetables are fresh, beer is cold, service is fast. Better-than-average atmosphere; owner speaks English. **$**

Rantepao

Torajan specialities such as *papiong* (meat cooked in a bamboo tube) and Bale Tollopamarasan (cooked with special Torajan spices) can be ordered in advance from restaurants catering for tourists along Jl. A. Yani and Jl. Andi Mappanyukki. Restaurant Mambo and Riman, both on Mappanyukki (**$**), and Mart's Café (**$**) at 44a Jl. Ratulangi, are good examples.

Wakatobi

Rumah Makan Wisata
Wanci
A small restaurant on stilts on the seafront with nice views. Serves seafood and general Indonesian fare. **$**

MALUKU AND PAPUA

Maluku

Ambon

Local warung food abounds, but there aren't many Western-

style restaurants as yet

Café Panorama Restaurant
Jl. CM Tiahahu

BELOW: sushi.

Northern Ambon city
Tel: 0911-351 884
For a varied menu, including a few Western dishes. **$$**

CAF Restaurant
Jl. Raya Pattimura, Southern Kota Ambon. The best place for seafood. **$$**

Ternate

In addition to warung food, there are a few places that can be recommended. Try Pondok Katu for Chinese and seafood, Rumah Makan Jailolo for Indonesian food, and Kafe Citra Rasa, popular at night.

Papua

Biak

Arumbai Restoran
Jl. Selat Makassar, No. 03
Tel: 0981-22159, 21835
Very good Chinese and Western food at reasonable prices. **$**

Restoran 99
Jl. Imam Bonjol, No. 32
Tel: 0981-21450
A simple restaurant with good Chinese food. **$**

Jayapura/Sentani

Pondok Wisata Yougwa
Lake Sentani
This pleasant, open-air

restaurant has great grilled fish, especially gabus, a local lake fish. The kang-kung (water spinach) is also good. Great sunset views. **$**

Restoran Mickey
Main street, Sentani
One of the old standbys in Sentani, it serves good Chinese and Indonesian food. **$**

Wamena

Mentari Restaurant
Jl. Yos Sudarso, No. 47
Tel: 0969-31771
A 10-minute walk from Wamena's main street, Mentari has a pleasant atmosphere and good food at reasonable prices. Try the udang sungai (crayfish) from the Sungai Baliem. The Chinese dishes are also good. **$**

ACTIVITIES

FESTIVALS, THE ARTS, NIGHTLIFE, SHOPPING AND SPECTATOR SPORTS

THE ARTS

Every village in Indonesia has its own traditional dances and music that are performed for celebrations. Enquire at your accommodation if there are any events being held in the area during your stay.

Java

Jakarta

Visual Arts

Art galleries are scattered throughout Jakarta. **Edwin's Gallery** in Kemang (www.edwinsgallery.com) is among the most active venues for photography, sculpture and painting exhibitions.

Performing Arts

For culture in any form, the first place to check is **Taman Ismail Marzuki** (TIM; tel: 021-3193 7325) at Jl. Cikini Raya. TIM hosts a variety of Indonesian modern and traditional theatre productions, as well as visiting performances and international film festivals.

   Gedung Kesenian, Jl. Gedung Kesenian (tel: 021-380 8283; charge) is a restored Dutch *Schouwburg* playhouse, and offers dance and musical performances. **Wayang Orang Bharata Purwa**, Jl. Kalilio, No. 15, Pasar Senen (tel: 817-007 9177; Sat 8pm; charge) hosts *wayang orang* (dance-drama) and *ketoprak* (folk drama) performances.

   Dome of Sarbini (Balai Sarbini; Plaza Semanggi, South Jakarta; tel: 021-739 2919) is home to the **Nusantara Symphony Orchestra** and is also a venue for art and cultural performances.

   Aula Simfonia Jakarta stages performances by the **Jakarta**

ABOVE: Sundanese *wayang golek* wooden puppets, Bogor.

Simfonia Orchestra (tel: 021-6586 7808; www.aulasimfoniajakarta. com), a collaboration of local and international musicians. **Twilite Orchestra** (tel: 021-7581 8957; www.twiliteirchestra.org) plays pop music at both venues.

Bandung

Angklung performances are held regularly in the afternoons at **Pak Ujo's Saung Angklung** (Jl. Padasuka, No. 118; daily 3.30–5.30pm; charge), an *angklung* school and a workshop. *Wayang golek* and dance performances are held on request.

   The open-air theatre **Taman Budaya** (Jl. Bukit Dago Selatan, No. 53; tel: 022-250 5365; charge) has dance, music and drama every weekend, as well as art exhibitions.

Bogor

At Pak Dase's *wayang golek* (wooden puppet) **workshop** (Lebak Kantin RT 02/VI; tel: 0251-838 3758), visitors can see the puppets being made and watch performances.

Surabaya

From June to Nov there are fortnightly (first and third Sat of each month) *sendratari* classical Javanese dance-drama performances at the open-air **Candra Wilwatikta** amphitheatre in Pandaan, 45km (30 miles) south of Surabaya.

   East Javan traditional *reog* **performances,** often called the "lion peacock dance", are held every Sun 9–11am at Balai Pemuda. The heavy headdress weighs in at 55kg (121lbs) and is held in place by the dancer's teeth.

Yogyakarta (Jogja)

Visual and Performing Arts

While **Affandi Museum and Gallery** (Jl. Laksda Adisucipto, No. 167; tel: 0274-562 593) attracts the most visitors, there is another outstanding gallery near Borobudur: **H. Widayat Museum, Gallery & Art Shop** (Jl. Letnan Tukiyat, Sawitan, Kota Mungkid, Magalang; tel: 0274-788 251). Several venues offer rotating visual and performing arts exhibitions. **Bentara Budaya**: Jl. Suroto, No. 2, Kota Baru, tel: 0274-560 404; www. bentarabudaya.com.

Cemeti Art House: Jl. D.I. Panjaitan, No. 41; tel: 0274-371 105; www.cemetiarthouse.com.

Kedai Kebun Forum & Restaurant: Jl. Tirtodipuran, No. 3; tel: 0274-376 114.

Taman Budaya: Jl. Sriwedari, No. 1 (east of Benteng Vredeburg); tel: 0274-523 512.

Cultural Performances

The **Keraton** hosts a different performance every morning (usually 9.30am–noon), including gamelan, *wayang kulit* (leather shadow puppets), *wayan golek* (wooden puppets), *wayan orang* (human dance-drama) and Javanese poetry.

The most magical place to experience the beauty of traditional Javanese dance is the **Prambanan Temple Open Air Theatre's** *Ramayana*, with 250 dancers accompanied by 50 gamelan players (May–Oct). In the rainy season the *Ramayana* is performed at Prambanan's indoor theatre, **Trimurti Theatre Prambanan.**

Sumatra

Bukittinggi

Dance performances are held every evening at **Saayun Salangkah** on Jalan Yamin. Local entertainment favourites are *pencak silat*, a dance that incorporates martial arts movements, and the plate dance, in which plates are tossed onto the ground to form a carpet of broken shards over which the dancers perform.

Parapat/Samosir Island

The Batak dramatic *gondang sabangunan* (drums and reed instruments) is performed at Simanindo (23km/14¼ miles north of Tuktuk), daily 10.30am–12.30pm, and includes dance and wooden puppet performances. More informal *gondang hasapi* ensembles with flutes, guitars and percussion can be heard Saturday nights at Carolina Cottages.

Bali

Denpasar

Bali Arts Festival (www.baliartsfestival.com) is held from mid-June to mid-July at the Taman Werdi Budaya (Art Centre) on Jl. Nusa Indah in Denpasar. A full month of dance, drama, and art and handicrafts exhibitions. The opening ceremony is a parade beginning in downtown Denpasar worthy of international attention.

Ubud

Visual Arts

Ubud's selection of art museums

and galleries is astonishing, but the not-to-be-missed ones are: **Museum Puri Lukisan** on Jl. Raya Ubud, **Neka Art Museum** (www.museumneka.com) and its sales outlet **Neka Art Gallery** on Jl. Raya Ubud, **Seniwati Gallery of Art by Women** (www.seniwatigallery.com), **Agung Rai Museum of Art** (www.armamuseum.com) and **Museum Rudana** (www.museumrudana.com).

Performing Arts

Nightly performances of *legong*, *kecak*, *barong* and other dances are held at the Pura Dalem Ubud and other locations in central Ubud, as well as in nearby villages. Check at the Tourist Information Centre on Jl. Raya Ubud for schedules and ticketing.

Kecak Srikandhi is the only all-female *kecak* dance troupe on the island. Performances are held at 7.30pm on Weds at Pura Batu Karu.

FESTIVALS

Indonesians love to gather with family and friends to celebrate practically any occasion, and these events promise entertainment for everyone. Many festivals and ceremonies are based on religious or cultural calendars, meaning the dates change every year. Enquire upon arrival if there are any events being held in your area, and you might get lucky.

Cultural Festivals

Chinese New Year: Many cities host elaborate festivals to celebrate Chinese New Year (Feb/Mar). In Manado (Sulawesi) the **Toa Peh Kong Festival,** a large procession including horses, decorated floats and children in Chinese costumes, begins at a Confucian temple if the gods grant permission through a ritual.

Dayak Erau Festival (Kalimantan): Held throughout the region, the best known is in Kutai Kartanegara, a showcase for Dayak cultural arts, dances and handicrafts. Scheduling is based on auspicious dates chosen by traditional leaders.

Pasola (Sumba): A mock-battle, usually held Feb/Mar, at a date determined by the annual migration of *nyale* sea worms. "Warriors" on horseback try to unseat their opponents, and any blood spilled is believed to fertilise the soil and benefit the next harvest. Held in three areas: West Sumba's Wanakola and Kodi districts, and Waingapu in East

Sumba. On Mandalika beach, Lombok and in Savu similar rituals are held.

Lake Sentani Festival (Papua): Usually in June, local dancers perform on floating dugout canoes; there are drum competitions, lake tours, fireworks, and bark-painting and hair-weaving contests.

Lake Toba Festival (Sumatra): June or July on Samosir island, this festival features Batak art, cultural performances, boat and horse races, and handicrafts exhibitions.

Labuhan (Java): In Jogja, every 25 Aug there is a procession to Parangkusumo beach where offerings are made to Nyi Roro Kidul, Queen of the Southern Sea. Similar ceremonies are held at Gunung Merapi, Gunung Bromo and Gunung Lawu, and throughout the country to give thanks for successful harvests or catches and to ask blessings for the coming season.

Madura Bull Races (Java): Races are held from Sep to Nov in East Java and in Madura showcasing the strength and speed of prized bulls. In Oct in Pamekasan, the **Sapi Sono Festival** is held to name the most "beautiful" buffalo in the region.

Religious Festivals

Waisak Day (Java): Thousands of Buddhists from throughout Asia join a procession from Mendut temple to Borobudur to meditate in honour of the Day of Enlightenment (June/July), the biggest day on the Buddhist calendar.

Easter (Flores): Laruntuka's Easter celebrations draw devotees by the hundreds from nearby islands. On Good Friday, the ceremony begins with a procession through town led by shrouded bearers of Christ's coffin and the bathing of a Virgin Mary statue in a tradition dating back to Portuguese ancestors.

Sports Festivals

Many sporting events are held during school holidays (June/July), at the height of the tourist season.

Raja Ampat Marine Festival (Papua): Promotes the beauty of culture, adventure and nature, held in Waisai in May. Activities include underwater orientation and photo competitions, parades, dragon-boat races and beach sports.

Indonesian Surfing Championship (Seminyak, Bali): June events include Pro, Junior, Women's, Master and Longboard competitions. Local and international surfers participate in a one-week championship competition and surfing film festival (www.isctour.com).

Bali International Triathlon: Held every June, Olympic and sprint-distance events, team relays and fun runs. Balinese bicycle blessing ceremony; post-race live music and beach party (www.balitriathlon.com).

Tour de Singkrak (Sumatra): An annual bicycle race that draws participants from throughout Asia and Europe begins in Padang and traverses 743.5km (462 miles), ending at Lake Singakaral. Held in June or July (http://tourdesingkrak.com).

International Kite Festival (Bali): Part of the **Sanur Village Festival** (June/July). Teams from Indonesia and abroad fly enormous kites up to 10 metres (33ft) long – taking as many as five men to launch – and compete in various divisions, including traditional Balinese and contemporary kite designs.

Darwin–Ambon Yacht Race: Held annually since 2007 (July–Aug) and attracting over 100 boats, the Darwin–Ambon Yacht Race (www.darwinambonrace.com.au) also inspires other marine festivals en route, such as **Sail Banda** and **Sail Wakatobi**, with game-fishing competitions, beach sports, diving tournaments and conferences.

August Celebrations

Beginning the first week in Aug in every village, town and city, competitions and games are held in celebration of Indonesia's **Independence Day** on 17 Aug, and visitors are always welcome. Two spectacular ones are:

Sanur Village Festival (Bali): An annual celebration held in July–Aug, drawing hundreds of locals and tourists to its many events. A four-day feast of contests includes water sports and an international kite-flying competition, music, dance and food, food, food. A great opportunity to mingle with the local people, hear some great music and eat some really good food (www.gotosanur.com).

Baliem Valley Festival (Papua): Fabulous mock battles held in August between tribes accompanied by traditional dance, music and art exhibitions and a pig feast.

NIGHTLIFE

Jakarta

Nightlife in Jakarta pulsates. As the sun sets and temperatures drop, the

ABOVE: Batak ceremony, Sumatra.

skyline lights up, as does the energy of crowds unwinding in the city's myriad pubs, bars, nightclubs and karaoke dens. The range is endless, with something on the menu for everyone.

Most of the major hotels have comfortable upmarket bars. Local favourites are **O'Reiley's** in the Grand Hyatt Hotel, **Kudus** in the Sultan Hotel and Shangri-La's **B.A.T.S** bar. Techno music can be found at **M Club** at Blok M Plaza. **Parkit DejaVu** on Jl. Wahid Hasyim hosts a young crowd, while long-time favourite **Jamz Jazz Club** at Lippo Sudirman Grand Suite Hotel has the best live jazz. **JJ** at Jl. Tanah Abang Timur is always crowded.

Blowfish Kitchen and Bar at Wisma Mulia, Jl. Jend. Gatot Subroto, No. 42, is known for its R&B and hip hop music. **Dragonfly** at Graha BIP, Jl. Jend. Gatot Subroto, No. 23, is another great club. **IndoChine** at fX Lifestyle Center Senayan and **Immigrant** in Plaza Indonesia share the spotlight as the best upmarket nightlife and have regular overseas DJ performances. **Red Square**, Senayan Plaza Arcade Unit X210-211, Jl. New Delhi, No. 9, Pintu I, is another popular spot.

Bali

Kuta's nightlife attracts young party animals, and most of it is centred on Jl. Legian. The fun begins with late-afternoon happy hour and lasts until 2am. Current hotspots include **Apache, Macaroni Club** and **Bounty**. **Seminyak**'s lounges are frequented by a more sophisticated crowd and start getting busy around 11pm. At popular **Double Six** (tel: 0361-756

666; www.doublesixclub.com) crowds start gathering around 10pm but really start swinging around 2am. Especially favoured are **De ja vu** (tel: 0361-732 777) and **Benny's Bistro** (tel: 0361-732 917). **Hu'u Bali** on Jl. Petitenget (tel: 0361-736 443; www.huubali.com) draws tourists and expats.

Lombok

Nightlife in **Senggigi** begins with sundowners anywhere with good sunset views. After hours, **The Office Bar & Restaurant** (Jl. Raya Senggigi; tel: 0370-693 162), **Papaya Café** (Jl. Raya Senggigi; tel: 0370-693 136) and **Tropicana** (Jl. Raya Senggigi; tel: 0370-693 432) are popular with locals and tourists.

SHOPPING

Java

Jakarta

Handicrafts

Pasaraya at Blok M is the best one-stop shop for the full gamut of Indonesian products; also good are **Sarinah** on Jl. Thamrin and **Keris Gallery** in Menteng. All three stock everything from baskets to placemats, paintings, carvings and batik.

Bandung

Bandung is known for its hand-woven baskets and mats from nearby Tasikmalaya, bamboo *angklung* instruments and *wayang golek* puppets. **Batik Semar** (Istana Plaza, Jl. Pasir Kaliki, No. 121–123)

Conservation and Marine Expeditions

Operation Wallacea (www.opwall. com) runs 2–10-week research conservation expeditions, July–Aug, for students and volunteers. Participants stay in villages and/or forest base camps, and do jungle training and data collecting – a great way to see a lot of wildlife and

experience local community living. The company also conducts 2–10-week marine biology research expeditions, July–Aug, from Hoga island. Volunteers stay in rustic beach bungalows and dive/snorkel every day to help marine biologists collect data.

---

has a selection of paintings, batik, embroidered textiles, *angklung* instruments and ceramics.

Bandung is the jeans-producing capital of Indonesia. Head to the **Cihampelas Jeans Shop** along Jl. Cihampelas for good bargains. Shoes are a good buy at the **Cibaduyut Shoe Industry** at Jl. Cibaduyut. Factory outlet shops along Jl. Cihampelas, Jl. Juanda (Dago area) and Jl. Riau (**R.E. Martadinata**) are popular.

Yogyakarta (Jogja)

For many, shopping for batik or locally made handicrafts is a major mission on their trip to Jogja. For one-stop shopping, try:
Titon Handicraft, Jl. Minggiran MJI/1627, Dukuh, Jogja 55142 (Ring Road Selatan, on the road to Bantul); tel: 0274-378 476, 371 105. Daily 8.30am–4.30pm. A wide array of handmade home accessories and rattan furniture in one location.
Pasar Seni Gabusan Bantul, Jl. Parangtritiskm, No. 9.5, Bantul; tel: 0274-367 959, 788 2049, 749 0553. A large marketplace displaying the work of

Ubud Walking Tours

There are three Ubud-based walking tour groups, and all are recommended.
Bali Bird Walks: http://balibirdwalk.com.
Keep Walking Tours: www.balispirit.com/tours.
Ubud Herb Walks: www.baliherbalwalk.com.

area craftsmen: pottery, natural products, stone-carvings and much more.

Keris
For the real thing (not the souvenir version found locally), visit Empu Sungkowo (*keris*-maker) Harum Brodjo, Gatak, Sumberagung, Moyudan, Sleman; tel: 81-2273 1372; donation) welcomes visitors by appointment only. Be aware that it takes more than two months to finish one *keris* and prices start at US$700.
Pottery
Best known is **Kasongan**, Bantul, 10km (6 miles) south of Jogja. About 1km (mile) of shops lining both sides of Jl. Raya Kasongan. Pottery is also made in **Pundong**, Bantul (8km/5 miles south of Jogja off Jl. Parangtritis) and in **Pagerjurang hamlet, Klaten** (43km/27 miles east of Jogja on the way to Solo). Expect to find vases, tableware, pots.
Silver
Kota Gede, south of Jogja, is renowned for its silver jewellery. Recommended are the small shops along both sides of Jl. Monodorakan, the main street, but at larger establishments you can see silversmiths at work.

Surakarta (Solo)
Batik
The three largest batik mass-producers in Solo are: **Batik Danar Hadi** (Jl. Slamet Riyadi; tel: 0271-713 140) for good-quality cloths and ready-made batik clothing (also has a museum); **Batik Semar** caters to the mass market with its printed

batik dresses and shirts; and **Batik Keris** (also found in major airports) is somewhere in between.

Bapak Gunawan (Jl. Cakra, No. 21, Kauman; tel: 0271-632 214) is an important traditional batik master. **Hardjonagoro** (Jl. Yos Sudarso, No. 176, and Jl. Kratonan, No. 101; tel: 0271-643 289) is one of Indonesia's national treasures. Make an appointment before visiting.

"Antiques" and Traditional Crafts
Pasar Triwindu on Jl. Diponegoro is a marketplace filled with "antiques" of all kinds. To buy an antique *keris* dagger, visit **Pak Suranto Atmosaputro** at his home at Jl. Kestalan, No. III/21. Pak Suranto is a *keris* aficionado and always has pieces for sale.

For *wayang kulit* puppets, visit **Manyaran** village, about 35km (22 miles) southwest of Solo. Wares by its craftsmen are organised by the village head and sold for reasonable, fixed prices.

To buy a gamelan instrument or a whole ensemble, or just to observe them being forged, visit **Pak Tentrem Sarwanto** (Jl. Ngepung RT 2/RK I, Semanggi), whose family has made gamelan instruments for generations.

Sumatra
Bukittinggi

West Sumatra is renowned for its beautiful hand-loomed *songket* cloth, fine embroidery, silverwork and woodcarvings.

The best-known *songket* weaving centre is **Silungkang**, a small town on the Agam plateau. Another popular village is **Pandai Sikat**, on the main road from Padang to Bukittinggi, which is also renowned for its embroidery and woodcarvings. Silversmiths in hilltop **Koto Gadang** produce fine filigree.

Bali

The entire island is given over to thousands of artisans of all kinds. The southern beaches are filled with vendors selling everything from fake Rolex watches to pineapples. Try to keep a sense of humour in crowds of sellers.

Ceramics
Jenggala Ceramic: Jl. Uluwatu II, Jimbaran; tel: 0361-703 310; www.jenggala-bali.com. Internationally acclaimed (and pricey) range of ceramics and household accessories, café and classes.

BELOW: bull racing on Madura.

Fashions and Home Accessories

Stroll down Jl. Raya Seminyak or Jl. Laksmana and shop 'til you drop for fashions and home furnishings made for export. Top clothing shops such as **Animale**, **By The Sea**, **Mama and Leon**, **Paul Ropp** and **Uluwatu** have several outlets elsewhere.

Handicrafts

Practically everyone in Batubulan is involved in **stone-carving**, and Mas village artisans specialise in **woodcarvings** and masks. Shops line the main road in both villages. Highly recommended for exquisite **masks** is I Wayan Muka (Br. Batan Ancak, Mas; tel: 0361-974 530). The best one-stop-shopping spot for handicrafts is **Pasar Seni** in Sukawati, which is packed to the rafters with everything sold in South Bali, but for half the price.

Jewellery

Silver showrooms and workshops line the main road at Celuk. In Ubud, there are many jewellery shops. Especially respected are **Jean Francois** (Jl. Raya, No. 7, and Jl. Suweta, No. 6; www.if-fcom), **Runa House of Design and Museum** (Lod Tunduh) and **Treasures** (Jl. Raya Ubud, next to Ary's).

Textiles

For ikat weavings from throughout Indonesia, visit **Threads of Life** (Jl. Kajeng, No. 24, Ubud; tel: 0361-972 187; www.threadsoflife.com). A non-profit organisation which supports weavers of traditional cloths in remote village, it also offers demonstrations and workshops.

Nusa Tenggara

Flores

Hand-woven textile aficionados cannot go to East Flores without stopping in at one or more of its ikat-weaving villages. This is one of the few places in Indonesia where these cloths are still used for daily wear, and each village has its own distinctive motifs and colours. Ikat cloths can be bought in the local *pasars* (markets), but for a look at how they are made and a deeper appreciation of the time and skill involved, visit Watublapi, Sikka and Nita villages, near Maumere.

Lombok

Lombok is known for its hand-woven textiles, pottery and basketry. Traditional textiles are woven by hand in: **Sukarare** *(tenun Lombok)*, **Pujung** *(kain lambung)*, **Purbasari** *(kain Purbasari)*, **Balimurti** (sacred

ABOVE: Legong dance, Bali.

beberut cloth) and **Pringgasela**. The **Lombok Pottery Centre** (Jl. Sriwijaya, No. IIIA, Banyumulek; tel: 0370-640 350) offers high-grade earthenware. For contemporary ceramic tableware try **Citra Lombok Ceramics**, at Jl. Brawijaya, No. 26, in Cakranegara (tel: 0370-634 502). **Banyumulek**, **Masbagik** and **Penujak** villages all produce distinctive and elegant pottery.

Baskets

Lombok's rattan and grass baskets are extremely fine and sturdy, and many of these are produced in the eastern villages **Kotaraja** and **Loyok**. Baskets, pots and handicrafts are cheap and plentiful at the **Mandalika** Market by the bus terminal in Sweta, or at the **Cakranegara Market** to the west of the Pura Meru temple.

Kalimantan

Dayak Arts and Crafts

Dayak arts and crafts display extraordinary and vibrant design. The characteristic flowing geometrical patterns used in portraying scenes of jungle life come from Chinese and Vietnamese Dong Son influences. More than any other ethnic group in Indonesia, the Dayaks are famed for their beadwork. They use thousands of tiny glass beads to decorate purses, tobacco pouches, scabbards, prams,

Batik Hotpots in Jogja

Renowned for its batik, Jogja is heaven for textile enthusiasts. There are several shops on **Jl. Tirtodipuran**. Recommended is **Winotosastro Batik** (Ibu Hani), with some of the highest-quality batiks in town. Other hot batik spots are:
Afif Syakur Batik: Jl. Pendega Marta, No. 37A; tel: 0274-589 914, 580 665. Highly acclaimed for sophisticated designs using traditional motifs. Also many silk pieces.
Batik & Embroidery Museum: Jl. Sutomo, No. 13; tel: 0274-562 338; Mon–Sat 8am–noon; charge. A small museum with two sections: one with batik dating from the 1880s, the other *sulaman* embroidery fancied by Javanese ladies for formal wear.
Bima Sakti Batik Collective: Located in Giriloyo, Imogiri (near Kota Gede), this is a whole village of traditional batik-makers, with shops at the base of the

Royal Cemetery. Nearby is **Joglo Ciptowening Batik Museum**: Wukirsari, Imogiri; tel: 083-2876 2759; Tue–Sun 10am–4pm. Exhibits Imogiri-style and other regional batik *tulis*.
Bixa Batik Studio: Pengok PJKA, GK 1/7/43F; tel: 0274-546 545. Well known for its natural dyed batiks.
Brahma Tirta Sari: Desa Tegal Cerme Kd. V, RT 08/ RW14, Banguntapan, south Jogja; tel: 0274-377 881; www.brahmatirtasari.com; daily 8am–4pm. The studio focuses on its unique batik style using traditional motifs in contemporary designs, and holds workshops, courses and demonstrations by appointment. Call for directions.
Gallery Batik Jawa: Mustakaweni Hotel, Jl. AM Sanghaji, No. 72; tel: 0274-515 268. Beautiful Javanese batik in indigo and mahogany natural dyes.

TRANSPORT
ACCOMMODATION
EATING OUT
ACTIVITIES
A – Z

basket lids, dress hems, caps and headbands.

Another Dayak craft is basketry in a wide variety of types in characteristic two-tone patterns. Weaving had almost died out until it was revived for the tourist trade in Tanjung Isuy village in East Kalimantan.

Ikat is the common technique in weaving, originally using bark fibre and natural dyes. Now, commercial yarn and dyes are common.

Gender roles differentiate most of the Dayak crafts. Men are more at home carving wood and working metal, while the women tend towards plaiting, weaving and beadwork.

Sulawesi

Bau-Bau and Wakatobi

Traditional handicrafts available in this area include hand-woven sarongs in a range of bright colours, usually stripes for women and chequered patterns for men. The local Butonese and Wakatobi people still regularly wear this traditional cloth for religious and festive occasions. It can be found at **Pasar Wameo**, Bau-Bau and **Pasar Central**, Wangi-Wangi. It's best to go in the morning to both markets.

Rantepao

Todi Shop on Jalan Pembangunan (www.todi.co.id) sells Torajan ikats and silk weavings and supports women weavers in isolated areas.

Look for Torajan handicrafts in shops along **Jalan Andi Mapanyukki**; they stock a wide range of quality merchandise. Torajan woven cloths are not plentiful (and are expensive) but may be purchased in **Sa'dan Sangkombong** and **Sa'dan Tobarana** villages.

Papua

Agats

Agats has four shops offering a wide variety of Asmat pieces, but it is easy to purchase pieces directly from the villages nearby. The quality varies considerably, and it is becoming

Local Sensibilities

Over the years, predominately Muslim Lombok has become more tolerant of the strange behaviour of foreigners. Nevertheless, be aware that public intoxication, immodest dress and public displays of affection are frowned upon.

difficult to find older pieces. Two of the shops – **Kios Asmat** and **Toko Anda** – are owned by immigrants from other islands. Better still, enquire at one of the two small hotels how you can buy art pieces. In a matter of hours, you will find Asmat villagers turning up with a few pieces for sale.

Jayapura/Sentani

The increased demand for Asmat carvings has produced many low-quality pieces. Shop carefully. Simple colours – red, black and white – are an Asmat trademark. There are several shops in Hamadi, a suburb of Jayapura, which have good selections of pieces from Asmat and Sentani.

Wamena

Don't miss the local market in Wamena for stone axes, penis gourds, orchid-fibre skirts, shell necklaces, slate "bride stones", and bows and arrows.

OUTDOOR ACTIVITIES

Indonesia is one of the best places on earth for trekking, diving and surfing, as well as some more unusual adventure sports and activities.

Java

Biking

West Java has excellent mountain-biking sites between Bogor and Garut. Bicycle trekking is good around the national parks, Bogor, Puncak and Sukabumi. Contact **Bogor Mountain Biking** (www.bogormountainbiking.com).

Birdwatching

Pulau Dua and **Pamojan Besar** are havens for migratory birds. Pamojan Besar is north of Pulau Dua, Banten Bay, and is accessible in 1 hour by boat. Between Apr and Aug each year, migratory birds flock to both islands by the hundreds. Contact **Burung Indonesia;** www.burung.org; tel: 0251-835 7222 ext 113 for further information.

Deep-sea Fishing

The waters off **Ujung Kulon National Park** and **Krakatau** in the Sunda Strait are top fishing sites year-round for blue marlin, yellow-fin tuna, dogtooth tuna, wahoo, dorado and sailfish. Contact **Badak Club Ujung Kulon Krakatau Ecotourism**

Organizer at ofatbadak@yahoo.com.

Diving

The **Kura-Kura Resort** (www.kurakuraresort.com) at Kerimunjawa Marine National Park in Central Java operates various activities including dive courses, snorkelling and sea-kayaking.

Golf Courses

Jakarta

Jakarta's golf courses are located in and around the city. Visit their websites or contact them for further information. **Cengkareng Golf Club**: www.cengkarenggolfclub.com. **Jakarta Golf Club**: http://jakartagolfclub.org. **Klub Golf Senayan**: tel: 021-5711 0181, 573 2508. The only golf course located in the heart of the capital. **Damai Indah Golf, Pantai Indah Kapuk Course**: http://damaiindahgolf.com.

Bandung

Bandung's four golf and country clubs attract cool mountain air duffers. However, there are also other countryside activities that can be done in a day trip. **Cipanas Hot Springs**: East of Bandung, 5–6km (3–4 miles) north of Garut. Experience healing sulphurous waters at the hot spring-fed swimming pool Kampung Sumber Alam Resort (http://resort-kampungsumberalam.com). **Lembang Hill Resort**: Spend the day having spa and massage therapies and lunch in the hills at Jadul Village Villas and Spa (http://jadulvillage.com), 30 minutes from Bandung.

Paragliding

Gunung Mas tea plantation at Puncak Pass is the ideal place for tandem paragliding. Fly with a licensed pilot to view mountainous Puncak from above. Contact **Gendon Subandono** (www.gendonsubandono.blogspot.com).

Rafting

Sukabumi's rivers flow to Pelabuhan Ratu beach. To try white-water rafting on the Cicatih River, contact **Riam Jeram** (www.riamjeram.com), and on the Citarik River, contact **Arus Liar** (www.arusliar.co.id) or **Caldera** (www.calderaindonesia.com) .

Trekking

West Java's three national parks are ideal for day- or overnight-trekking. Contact **Badak Club Ujung Kulon Krakatau Ecotourism Organizer** at ofatbadak@yahoo.com for Ujung Kulon and Krakatau national parks and **Base Camp Adventure Shop** (www.basecampindonesia.com) for Halimun-Salak and Gede-Pangrango national parks.

Outdoor adventure opportunities abound near **Jogja** but are rarely promoted. Contact **Agus Setiawan** (tel: 086-256 2392; email: agusvenuz@yahoo.com) for climbing Gunung Merbabu, hiking Gunung Sindoro and Gunung Sumbing, as well as birdwatching and caving trips.

Jakar (tel: 0293-788 845; email: jackpriyana@yahoo.com.sg) specialises in the Borobudur area, with sunrise treks to Mahitan hill for spectacular views overlooking Borobudur and village visits to see glass noodles, tofu and pottery being made.

Equator Sinergi Indonesia: www.equator-indonesia.com. An experienced climber, owner Jarody Hestu offers caving, climbing, trekking and rafting expeditions.

Citra Elo Rafting (www.yogyes.com) takes novices and experts on thrilling white-water rafting trips on the Elo and Progo rivers.

East Java's national parks offer superb trekking, wildlife-spotting and birdwatching opportunities.

Alas Purwo National Park First collect a permit at the PHKA office in Tegaldelima, drive 4km (2½ miles) to Sadengan, park your vehicle, then begin an easy walk to a watchtower for views of grazing cattle, peacocks, wild hens and boars.

The waves at **G-Land** (www.g-land.com), in the park's southeasternmost tip, are said to be second only to the famous Pipeline in Hawaii.

Baluran National Park After obtaining a permit at the park entrance, take guided walks to see dry-terrain fauna not appearing in other areas of Java. For tour information and guided walks contact **Rose's Ecolodge** (www.rosaecolodge.com).

Meru Betiri National Park
The main attractions here are turtle conservation, hornbills, Java warty pigs and giant owls. Accommodation is basic and the journey rugged, but worth it for the chance to see endangered sea turtles climbing up on the beach to lay their eggs. In a sturdy vehicle, take the main road from Banyuwangi to Genteng and turn south to Sukamade. The 35km (21-mile) trip to the park centre can take from 1 to 3 hours. The dry season is the best time to visit.

Volcano Adventures
Ndeso Adventure Consultant (www.exploredesa.com) is a volcano- and eco-adventure specialist committed to responsible travel principles and excellent customer service.

Tasikoki Wildlife Reserve

About 1 hour from Manado on the way to Tangkoko-Dua Sudara Nature Reserve, the **Tasikoki Wildlife Reserve** (www.tasikoki.org) harbours animals rescued from the illegal wildlife trade. Visitors are welcome for day tours and overnight stays at the on-site lodge. All proceeds support conservation and education efforts in North Sulawesi. Volunteers are always needed and appreciated.

Experienced guides lead volcano-climbing and walking expeditions and adventure trips throughout Java and can organise tailored trips to active **Gunung Bromo** and **Gunung Semeru** in the magnificent Bromo-Tengger-Semeru National Park, as well as to **Gunung Kerinci** and **Gunung Ijen**, where sulphur miners carry heavy loads from the odiferous crater surrounded by rainforests, coffee plantations and breathtaking scenery. Their itineraries also include 12- and 21-day volcano explorations in Java and active volcanoes from Central to East Java.

Sumatra

Diving
Cubadak island off the west coast near Padang offers Indian Ocean dives to see rich underwater biodiversity and ecosystems. Contact **Cubadak Paradiso Village**, www.cubadak-paradisovillage.com.

Paragliding
West Sumatra's paragliding sites range from the Bukittinggi hills to the west coast off Padang. Tandem paragliding by highly skilled pilot **Joe Mairi** (www.sumatra-paragliding.id.or.id).

Surfing
Siberut and Sipora islands in the Mentawai archipelago have excellent waves all year. Contact **Mentawai Surf Camp** (www.mentawai-surfcamp.com) for further information.

Krui beach in West Lampung is the second-best Sumatra surfing after Mentawai. Less crowded and cheaper, it has year-round great waves at lower prices. Contact **Krui Surf**; www.kruisurf.com.

Trekking and Rafting
Two-day trekking to the Gunung Kerinci summit can be booked at **Homestay Subandi** (tel: 0812-7411 4273). Trekking to Gunung Merapi or Gunung Singgalang in Bukittinggi is available through **Regina Adventure** (www.reginaadventures.com).

Bukit Lawang Ecolodge (www.ecolodge.yelweb.org) offers wildlife-spotting treks into Gunung Leuseur National Park in search of some of the park's 700 animal species. All proceeds go to community development and nature conservation.

Friendship Guesthouse and Restaurant in Ketambe (www.ketambe.com) guides 1–7-day Gunung Leuser National Park trekking trips and 1–5-day rafting expeditions on the Alas River.

Tangkahan Ecotourism (http://

ABOVE: carving on coconut shells.

tangkahanecotourism.com) is a conservation and community-empowerment project at Gunung Leuser National Park. Arranges tubing adventures, caving, elephant safaris and jungle trekking.
Trijaya Tour (www.trijaya-travel.com) offers rafting on the Wampu River at Bukit Lawang, near the Bohorok Orang-utan Centre.

Bali

Cycling Tours

A range of interesting outdoor activities are available, allowing visitors to enjoy the "real Bali" via cycling through villages or walking through rice fields. For guided bicycling geared to suit capabilities, contact I Wayan Kertayasa at **Bali Sport** (www.balicycling.com), member of both the Bali and the Indonesia Cycling federations.

Diving

Bali's top dive destination is Pulau Menjangan in West Bali National Park, with nearby Pemuteran on the north coast running a close second. The USS Liberty shipwreck at Tulamben also draws many divers. There is good diving at Nusa Penida as well, where the waters are in a marine reserve. There are dozens of dive shops in South Bali, and most arrange dive trips to other areas, sell gear and offer PADI dive courses. Recommended are **Scuba Duba Doo Dive Center** in Kuta (www.divecentrebali.com), **Eco-Dive Bali** in Amed (www.ecodivebali.com) and **Reef Seen Aquatics** in Pemuteran

(www.reefseenbali.com).

Golf

There are three golf courses in South Bali, each of them special:
Bali Golf & Country Club: www.baligolfandcountryclub.com.
Bali Beach Golf Course: www.innagrandbalibeach.com.
New Kuta Golf Club: http://newkutagolf.com.
In North Bali, the **Bali Handara Kosaido Country Club** (www.balihandarakosaido.com) is an 18-hole Peter Thompson championship course in the Bedugal highlands. The only course in the world set inside a volcano, it has been voted one of the world's top 50 most beautiful courses.

Horse Riding

Umalas Equestrian Resort (www.balionhorse.com) offers everything from sunset beach rides and lessons to dressage tuition. Thirty horses, including thoroughbreds and ponies, to suit adults and children.

Rafting

White-water rafting takes place on either the Ayung or Telaga Waja rivers. Contact **Bali Adventure Tours** (www.baliadventuretours.com) and **Sobek** (www.sobek.com): they also specialise in mountain biking and jungle trekking.

Sailing and Cruises

Benoa Harbour berths many boats that operate day trips to Nusa Lembongan, dinner cruises, and sailing adventures throughout Indonesia. Visit the following for

further details: **Bali Hai Cruises** (www.balihaicruises.com), **Bounty Cruises** (www.balibountygroup.com), **Seatrek Sailing Adventures** (www.seatrekbali.com) and **Waka Experience** (www.wakaexperience.com).

Surfing

Reasonably good throughout the year, the best surfing period is June–Aug. Beginners should start at Kuta, Legian and Seminyak. Bingin south of the airport or Canggu north of Seminyak are good for intermediate surfers. Much further west are Balian and Medewi and to the southeast, Nusa Lembongan. The breaks at Dreamland, below Pura Uluwatu, and Lebih, on the east coast, attract international champions. See www.wannasurf.com for more information.

Many of the surf shops in South Bali give lessons as well as selling gear. **Quiksilver** (Jl. Legian 318, Kuta; tel: 0361-752 693) and **Ripcurl** (Jl. Legian, Kuta; tel: 0361-765 889) are both well established and reputable.

Nusa Tenggara

Lombok

Diving and Snorkelling
Good snorkelling and great diving draw visitors to the Gili islands. The snorkelling at Senggigi is not world-class, but good; many hotels hire out snorkel gear. Certified foreign and Indonesian dive instructors offer courses in several languages, and most dive operators have outlets at Senggigi and on the Gilis. Recommended are:
Big Bubble: www.bigbubblediving.com.
Blue Marlin Dive: www.bluemarlindive.com.
Manta Dive: www.manta-dive.com.
The southwest peninsula is just beginning to develop, and **Secret Island Resort** (www.secretislandresort.com) is just one of the establishments offering snorkelling and diving, as well as kayaking and trekking trips.

Golf
Two golf courses grace Lombok: **Rinjani Country Club** (http://lombok-golf.com) and **Lombok Golf Kosaido Country Club** (www.lombok-network.com).

Trekking
Rinjani Trek Center (Senaru: tel: 0868-1710 4132; Mataram office: Hotel Lombok Raya, Jl. Usaha, No. 11, Mataram; tel: 0370-641 124) and **Rinjani Trekking Club** (www.rinjanitrekking.com) offer guides,

Hand-woven Textiles

East Nusa Tenggara has won acclaim from textile aficionados throughout the world for its ikat cloths, all still hand-woven on backstrap looms, and some using hand-spun cotton threads and natural dyes. Motifs and colours vary from one district to another, making them particularly distinctive. The best place to shop for ikats is at traditional markets (pasar), where the local women shop, but some villages welcome shoppers with demonstrations as well as sales. Ask for suggestions at your accommodation. Shop carefully, as much inferior work appears on the market. Bargain hard, as the final price could well be one-third of the first asking price. Below are a few other tips.
Solor: Traditional cloths have red

backgrounds rather than the dark indigo found in other regions.
Lembata: Excellent-quality indigo cloths here fetch a high price as they are treasured as "bride's wealth", but lesser cloths will satisfy most amateur shoppers.
Alor: Alor ikats are generally indigo cloths with ikat motifs on the borders.
Sumba: The only ikats bearing bold, often garish, but always symbolic animistic designs. Prailiu and Mangili villages, outside Waingapu, are the centres of the weaving industry. Note that sellers here are particularly aggressive. Bargain hard, while smiling, of course.
Rote: Look for bright red, white and black designs.
Savu: Perhaps the most finely woven of the ikats in the area, with intricate motifs.

maps, tourist information and Gunung Rinjani climbing and walking tours.

Sumbawa

Climbing Gunung Tamboro
Summiting Gunung Tamboro (2,820 metres/9,250ft) should only be attempted by the physically fit, accompanied by an experienced guide, as it entails passing through dense forest, overgrown trails, slippery rocks, deep gulleys and overnighting on the mountain.

At **Calabai**, a logging town, ask permission to stay in the timber company's guesthouse and register with the local police, which is essential. Pancasila village, 15km (9 miles) away, is the starting point, and you can arrange a guide here, who will also act as porter and cook.

The ascent passes through thick woodland and further up through pine forest. From here the track rises steeply to the crater. From the summit, on a clear morning, the crater is visible, as are Pulau Moyo and Gunung Rinjani on Lombok. Take warm clothes, as it can get very windy and cold on the peak.

Diving and Snorkelling
The strait south of **Pulau Moyo** has clear waters and untouched reefs, providing excellent snorkelling. There is a guesthouse at **Tanjung Pasir**, on the mainland. There are small boats for hire at Ai Bari, which will take you to Pulau Moyo for trekking, Tanjung Pasir beach or **Tanjung Manis**, where there is a nice white-sand beach and a few homestays accommodating snorkellers, divers and fishing expeditions.

Flores

Trekking, Caving and Diving
Flores has such a varied terrain that there are many options for outdoor adventures. Tourism outside the island's major attractions is just beginning to blossom and travel is rough, but to see unspoiled areas before the world focuses on them

ABOVE: weaving, Flores.

makes the difficulty worthwhile.

Mountains to climb on Flores include **Gunungs Inerie** and **Ebulobo**, near Bena, and **Golo Curu** (Welcome Mountain) and **Ranaka**, near Ruteng. (See www.gunungbagging.com for more information.) There is an extensive cave system, **Batu Cermin** (Mirror Rock) near Labuhanbajo.

There is good diving and snorkelling from either end of the island, and dive charters to Komodo National Park can be arranged in Labuhanbajo. There is also a marine reserve at Riung.

"Cultural trekking" goes to traditional villages around Ruteng and Bena and two community-run ecotourism villages. One is in the Mbeliling Forest Nature Reserve, 3 hours southeast of Labuhanbajo, and the other is at Waerebo mountain village, accessible from Ruteng. For information, contact **Flores Exotic Tours** (http://floresexotictours.blogspot.com). To make your own Mbeliling arrangements independently, contact Mr Zhakarias at the Roe Ecotourism Association (tel: 0813-5378 1200), or Mr Ketrin (tel: 0852-3906 1205).

Komodo

Wildlifespotting, Trekking and Diving
Trekking through Komodo National Park requires the accompaniment of a park ranger for a nominal fee and can range from 2-hour hikes on Komodo or Rinca to 2 days on Komodo island. As part of the Wallacea transitional zone, birdwatching is excellent on Komodo.

Diving and snorkelling in national park waters is superb. See http://floresexotictours.blogspot.com for a complete list of dive sites and descriptions and tours to the park. There are also many live-aboard dive charters that can be arranged in advance, such as those found at http://komododiving.com, www.indocruises.

com and www.divekomodo.com.

Elsewhere in Nusa Tenggara

Diving
Many travellers who visit East Nusa Tenggara come for the superb diving and snorkelling at Alor, where there are sunfish, schooling orcas and muck diving. Contact **Dive Alor Dive** (www.divealordive.com) for courses in several languages, day trips, backpacker prices or fully guided diving tours, land-based, resorts and live-aboards.

Special features in Kupang (Timor) are freshwater cave diving, muck diving and a 1942 Japanese wreck. Beginning in 2012, Dive Kupang Dive will offer dive trips to Savu island. Contact **Kupang Dive** (www.divekupangdive.com) for further information.

Trekking
East Nusa Tenggara's forests, volcanoes, mountains – **Gunung Ili Api** on Lembata and **Gunung Sirung** on Pantar island – and hills provide ample climbing and trekking opportunities, but as infrastructure is not well developed, be prepared to ask at your accommodation for a local guide.

There are two little-known national parks on Sumba island protecting dozens of bird and butterfly species: **Laiwangi Wanggameti National Park** in the southeast and **Manupeu Tanah Daru National Park** in West Sumba.

Kalimantan

Diving
Diving in the Sangalaki archipelago off Kalimantan's east coast is in the early stages of development and looks set to become a big phenomenon. A few dive resorts have already been established, including **Derawan Dive Resort** (www.divederawan.com).

Bargain Sensibly

There are many good buys to be found in Indonesia. In the tourist places, prices are always inflated, so it's worth your while to bargain down to around half of the asking price. In the villages, however, the difference of a few rupiah may mean a day's meals, so exercise common sense. Don't start haggling if you have no intention of buying, and remember to smile.

TRANSPORT

ACCOMMODATION

EATING OUT

ACTIVITIES

A – Z

LANGUAGE

Trekking

Visiting Dayak villages and orang-utan-spotting are Kalimantan's two major attractions. For trekking, mountain climbing, birdwatching, caving, river rafting and other expeditions in less developed areas, **De'Gigant Tours** (www.borneotourgigant.com) is recommended, and its website has excellent information.

Samboja Lodge (www.sambojaloge.com) is operated by the Borneo Orang-utan Survival (BOS) Foundation and offers treks to virgin rainforests or island sanctuaries to see wild orang-utans as well as volunteer opportunities with animals and tree-planting. The property includes a Sun Bear Sanctuary and a lodge. All proceeds go to conservation projects.

An ecotourism project at **Wehea**, near Derawan island in East Kalimantan, is unique because it was instigated by the villagers themselves. They began their ecotourism project with settlement money from a dispute with a logging company, and conduct canoe tours to longhouses and guide rainforest treks. To visit the area, first obtain a permit from The Nature Conservancy (TNC) office at Samarinda (Jl. Kuranji, No. 1, Voorvo) or Berau (Jl. Pemuda, No. 92, Tanjung Redap).

Yayasan RASI (www.ykrasi.110mb.com) is an NGO focusing on protecting marine flora and fauna and their ecosystems, particularly freshwater dolphins. Its Tourist Information Centre in Muara Pahu focuses on non-intrusive wildlife observations, and its website has good information about their research.

Sulawesi

Diving

South Sulawesi

Makassar-based **Wira Tours** (www.sulawesi-celebes.com) operates trips to **Togian Islands National Park**, where there is outstanding diving and snorkelling. Trekking through the forests for wildlife-spotting and Gorontalo tours can also be arranged. **Wasage Divers** (www.wasagedivers.com) offers day trips for certified divers and also hires out snorkel gear. Some great new dive sites have been discovered around Bau-Bau and Buton islands in Southeast Sulawesi, and Pantai Nirwana, Pasarwajo and Siompu islands offer exciting diving suitable for the adventurous looking for something new.

Southeast Sulawesi
Wakatobi Marine National Park is known for its spectacular underwater

world of fantastic colourful corals and high species diversity. Expect stunning coral topography, sculpted overhangs, steep walls plunging to unimaginable depths, gently sloping coral gardens, pinnacles rising out of the deep, and a dense coverage of highly diverse hard and soft corals, giant sponges, whips and sea fans. Dive companies include:
Patuno Resort Wakatobi: Wangi-Wangi island, www.patunoresortwakatobi.com.
Tukangbesi Diving: Hoga island, www.tukangbesidiving.com.
Tomia Dive Center: Tomia island, www.tomiadivecenter.com.
Wakatobi Dive Resort: Tomia island, www.wakatobi.com.
Wasage Divers: Hoga and Tomia islands, www.wasagedivers.com.
For non-divers wishing to experience the delights of **Wakatobi**, snorkelling is the perfect option. Pantai Nirwana (9km/6 miles outside Bau-Bau) and Hoga island are ideal for snorkelling straight from white-sand beaches. Wangi-Wangi island also has some of the best snorkelling sites around.

North Sulawesi
The reason most visitors go to North Sulawesi is the splendid diving in **Bunaken National Park**, where there are many dive operators. To narrow down the choice, visit www.divenorthsulawesi.com, the website of **North Sulawesi Watersports Association (NSWA)**. All its members are also Green Fins supporters, dedicated to protecting and conserving coral reefs by promoting sustainable diving.

Rafting

Scenic 1- or 3-day rafting trips in the **Toraja highlands** are particularly exciting during the rainy season from Nov to Mar. Tour operators provide pick-up from the hotel, and excursions include guides, equipment and meals. **Torango Buaya** (Jl. Poros Makale Rantepao, Eran Batu; tel: 0423-25717/ 21336) is a recommended white-water-rafting outfitter.

Indo Sella (Jl. Restorant Riman Mappanyukki, No. 113; tel: 0423-25210, 0813-4250 5301; www.sellatours.com) excursions include rafting on the Ma'ting, Sa'dan and Rongkong rivers, kayaking, mountain biking and trekking.

Safari Tours & Travel (www.manadosafaris.com) in Manado offers a thrilling ride down a Minahasan highlands river (1½ hours) in rafts holding up to six people, including an experienced guide.

City Centre Recreation

Car-free day is held in Jakarta twice a month on the second and fourth Sun 6am–noon. Thousands of cyclists enjoy worry-free pedalling between the Welcome Statue and Monas along Jl. Sudirman and Jl. Thamrin and share the road with joggers and skateboarders. The Trans-Jakarta busway remains open.

Trekking

South and Central Sulawesi
Wira Tours (www.sulawesi-celebes.com) in Makassar offers tours in South and Central Sulawesi that are difficult to arrange alone. Highlights include **Lore Lindu National Park** treks to see some of Sulawesi's rarest animals and the megalithic stones in Napu, Besoa and Bada valleys. Also offers treks to **Bantimurung-Bulusaraung National Park**, including a 3-hour trek to the Gunung Bulusaraung peak through rainforest for birdwatching, caving and wildlife-spotting. There are magnificent views from the summit. Meet the people at Tompobulu ecotourism village and see their daily lives.

Southeast Sulawesi
There are many short jungle and waterfall treks which can be reached from Bau-Bau. Places to visit include Bungi and Bau-Bau waterfalls and the rice fields at Ngkari-Ngkari. Most people hire a bicycle and guide and go exploring. **Hill House Villa** (tel: 0402-270 0456) can help arrange bike rental, and often a member of staff is happy to come along as a guide for short walks around the Bau-Bau area.

About 2 hours away from Bau-Bau by car, Lambusango Nature Reserve protects tarsiers, macaques, cous-cous and hornbills. These creatures are out and about at dusk, making it a good idea to stay overnight in Labundo-Bundo village. **Wasage Divers** (www.wasagedivers.com) can arrange guides for 1–2-day jungle trips.

Cultural Tours
Wakatobi culture can be experienced by getting out and about in the local villages. The locals are very friendly and welcoming to tourists, and throngs of children will happily follow you around. You will notice a distinct difference between the island dwellers and the Bajo sea-gypsies who are now settled in houses on stilts in the sea.

Hoga Island Diving Resort (http://wakatobi-hoga-diving.com) can arrange a Bajo guide to Samepla Bajo village. Walk around this stilted village on little bridges or hire a canoe to take you around by sea.

The locals will be happy to show you around and have their picture taken with you.

Patuno Resort Wakatobi (www. patunoresortwakatobi.com) offers guided cultural tours, taking in a Bajo sea-nomad village, seaweed farming, traditional weaving, an old fort and mosque which were outposts of the Buton sultanate, local markets and caves which are still used by locals for washing and bathing. This resort also hires out bicycles for seeing some of the local nature and culture. Wangi-Wangi island has a number of tarmac roads through quiet villages and farms, with many small dirt tracks to explore.

North Sulawesi Highly recommended **Safari Tours & Travel** (www.manadosafaris.com) in Manado offers several outdoor adventures that would be very difficult to arrange on your own. Among them are: **Mahawu Volcano Trek**: A 1-hour trek up Gunung Mahawu, near Tomohon. Stunning vistas, a steaming crater lake and the smell of sulphur from the pools. **Lokon Volcano Trek**: A 2-hour trek to Gunung Lokon's crater, near Tomohon, about halfway to the summit, with outstanding views overlooking the village. **Tangkoko-Dua Sudara Nature Reserve**: Hike through the forest, 2 hours from Manado, in search of endemic wildlife. **Tasikoki Wildlife Rescue and Education Centre**: Visit the home of animals rescued from the illegal wildlife trade, learn more about their plight, and have lunch with volunteers from around the world.

Whale and Dolphin Watching

Wakatobi in the southeast is home to a few resident dolphin and pilot whale pods that can be easily spotted all year round. Passing sperm whales, grey whales and other larger whale species can also be seen Aug–Oct. Contact **Patuno Resort Wakatobi** for full- and half-day snorkelling trips and half-day Whale & Dolphin Watching Tours on a comfortable traditional fishing boat.

ABOVE: a blue marlin.

Maluku

Diving

Diving is good throughout Maluku, but infrastructure is not yet well developed. For a well-established dive operator, contact **Maluku Divers** (www.divingmaluku.com), which recommends Ambon and Banda dives for beginners or experienced divers with PADI certified dive masters. Internationally managed, it also owns two resorts and can assist with day tours. Visit its website for great information and photos.

Trekking

Maluku's two national parks – **Aketajawa-Lolobata** on Halmahera and **Manusela** on Seram – are excellent for birdwatching. Do not expect well-developed tourism facilities just yet. BirdLife International is very active here; a list of Maluku species can be found at www.birdlife. org. Manusela also has 2,000 species of butterflies and moths.

Climbing **Gunung Gamalama** on Ternate island is strenuous and dangerous. Do not attempt to summit without an experienced local guide. For more information on climbing this and other Indonesian mountains, visit www. gunungbagging.com.

Papua

Birdwatching

Sorong-based and owned by a local family, **Papua Expeditions** (www.bird-watching-papua-adventure-travel. com) at Raja Ampat is dedicated to the true meaning of ecotourism, including community participation and development. Extensive list of birding tour choices and a large Papua bird list are available on the website.

Diving

Highly recommended is **Papua Diving** (www.papua-diving.com), with two resorts: an eco-establishment on Kri island and the other at Sorido Bay. The Dutch owner and long-time Papua resident is heavily involved in several community-empowerment programmes.

Kayaking

An exciting new sport opportunity has been instigated by The Raja Ampat Research and Conservation Centre (tel: 081-5270 00605), through which local tribes own either kayaks or homestays along the main route, thus enjoying some of the benefits of tourism. Trips can be solo or with a guide and can include snorkelling, diving, hiking and birdwatching. Contact **Kayak4Conservation** at www. kayak4conservation.com.

Trekking

Trekking adventures in the fabulously scenic Baliem Valley range from easy walks across Dani sweet-potato fields on the valley floor to extreme hikes to Lake Habema or to meet the mountain Yali people. **Jefalgi Tours** (Jl. Kamp Walker, Griya Lestari D-06, Jayapura; http://jefalgitours.com) is a locally owned, low-impact travel company, and also runs tours to the Korowai treehouse people.

Surabaya Activities

Get away from the city centre to learn more about Surabaya's people. Below are some suggested venues: **Kenjeran recreational beach** is surrounded by fishing villages. Give the fish and chips sold by the local people a try. **Kalimas Harbour**: See traditional wooden boats and watch animated trading activity, daily 8am–5pm. Hire a fishing boat and explore the **mangrove forest** at Wonorejo, home to a variety of birds, monkeys and other wildlife. Afterwards, discover the treasures made by the local people, such as mangrove-patterned batik and delicious mangrove syrup.

TRANSPORT

ACCOMMODATION

EATING OUT

ACTIVITIES

A – Z

LANGUAGE

A – Z

A HANDY SUMMARY OF PRACTICAL INFORMATION, ARRANGED ALPHABETICALLY

A

Addresses

It can be difficult for visitors to find addresses in Indonesia, as villages often flow into one another with no apparent boundary demarcations in sight, particularly in Bali. To add to the confusion, many of the street names have changed, but some establishments continue to use the old forms while others have switched to the new.

B

Budgeting for Your Trip

How much you'll spend depends largely on whether you are staying in a large city or a tourist destination – where options are greater and prices are higher – or a remote area; how many islands you plan to visit – air fare being a rather large expense – and how ardently you shop.

Accommodation can cost per night from US$15 in budget establishments to US$40 for a standard room and all the way up to thousands of dollars for villas and fancy resorts.

Anything imported is expensive, and this is most noticeable in terms of food and drinks. A canned local beer (Bintang) costs about US$1.50, with large bottles containing two servings around US$2.50, but imported beers are roughly double that. Likewise, local wines (such as Bali-produced Hatten) sell for about US$20 per bottle, and the price

of imported wines can be at least double, and often much more. Simple Indonesian food can be had for as little as US$2.50 almost anywhere, a moderately priced meal for around US$6 (without drinks), and the sky is the limit for fine dining, averaging US$30–40. Of course, prices in luxury resorts will be much higher.

Taxis are relatively cheap, for example the journey from Jakarta's airport to town costs about US$15, but local transport is cheaper. The Damri Airport shuttle bus costs around US$3 for the same journey. A Transjakarta bus ticket is US$3.50 one-way.

Admission charges are another consideration and range from a small donation at Balinese temples to US$3 for most museums and up to US$15 for theme parks.

Business Hours

In most places, government offices are generally open from Monday to Thursday, 8am–3pm, and close at 11.30am on Friday. On Saturday, they close at around 2pm. Business offices are open from Monday to Friday, 8 or 9am until 4 or 5pm. A few companies work on Saturday mornings as well. Banks are open 8am–3pm on weekdays, but in Jakarta some have branches in shopping malls that are open at weekends.

Business Travellers

Big hotels in cities and towns have conference rooms and business centres that are internet- and email-friendly, can send and receive faxes, make appointments and handle typing, photocopying and other administrative chores. In larger cities,

internet and email are available. Wi-fi "hotspots" are easily found in hotels, cafés and malls.

Business etiquette: The correct protocol is of the utmost importance when doing business in Indonesia. Apprise yourself of the rules by reading books on the subject. Here are a few pointers.

The terms *Bapak* or *Pak* ("Sir") and *Ibu* ("Madam"), are universally applicable in Indonesia and used to address business counterparts. Both men and women shake hands on introduction. If drinks are served, don't reach for yours until your host has gestured for you to do so. Observe the formalities until your Indonesian counterpart takes the lead to be more relaxed. At first meetings, business may not be discussed at all, paving the way for subsequent consultations.

Meetings usually begin with the conversation centring on social or predictable topics. Specific or personal enquiries are avoided. The best way to air a grievance is to talk politely around the subject until your business partner sees your point of view. Do not be too direct; rather than saying "no" directly, most Indonesians would say "*belum*", meaning "not yet". Consensus is fundamental to all relationships.

Business with Indonesians requires endurance, and most negotiations on deals will take far longer than hoped or planned.

C

Children

All Indonesians love children. Reliable

babysitters are available at all major hotels, and even small inn owners are happy to look after youngsters. Many hotels have kids' clubs and children's programmes, and shopping malls in large cities often provide pushchairs. Disposable nappies and baby food are scarce outside major cities.

Climate

Indonesia's climate is fairly even all year round, roughly divided into two seasons, wet and dry. The northeast monsoon brings drenching rain to the western islands roughly between November and April, and the tropical sun and the oceans combine to produce continuously high humidity (75–100 percent) everywhere. The dry season kicks in from May to October when high humidity levels are lessened by the cool dry air blowing in from the Australian land mass in the west. The further east you move, the shorter the rainy season is, making the dry season longer.

The transitional period between the two seasons alternates between sun-filled days and occasional thunderstorms. Even amid the wet season, temperatures range from 21–33°C (70–90°F), except at higher altitudes, which can be much cooler, and warm clothes are required. The heaviest rainfalls are usually in December, January and February. The seas surrounding the eastern islands can be very rough during these months.

Crime and Safety

Indonesia is certainly safer, on the whole, than most Western cities. As with everywhere, watch out for pickpockets in crowded areas, thieves in cheap hotels, and the occasional scam artist. Take the usual precautions. Don't leave valuables unattended, and be careful of your purse, wallet and backpacks in crowded areas. Don't lend money if you expect it to be returned. Report any theft immediately to police or security officers. (Without a police report, new passports and travel documents are difficult to obtain.) In some tourist areas, such as Jakarta, Jogja and Bali, there are English-speaking "tourist police" in specially marked uniforms and cars who are trained to handle foreigners' questions and lend assistance.

Exercise caution by carrying photocopies of your passport, tickets and travel documents, and keep the originals in hotel safes.

All narcotics are illegal in Indonesia and prosecution means a long prison term – perhaps even death – and/or huge fines.

Disabled Travellers

There is little awareness in Indonesia for the special needs of the disabled, and anyone looking other than "normal" will certainly draw stares, maybe even laughter, which camouflages embarrassment. Wheelchair ramps and van lifts are not the norm, though large international chains may have facilities. Ask your tour operator in advance for extra assistance.

Electricity

Electricity is usually 220V to 240V AC in Indonesia. Power failures are common and voltage fluctuates considerably, so using a stabiliser is advised. Wall plugs are the standard Western European variety: two round pins. International hotels may have adaptors for guests to use.

Embassies and Consulates

Embassies are found only in Jakarta. In Bali, Medan (Sumatra), Jogja (Java) and Surabaya (Java), a few countries maintain small consular offices. Only addresses in Jakarta and Bali are given here.

Jakarta

(Telephone area code 021)
Australia: Jl. H.R. Rasuna Said, Kav. 15–16; tel: 2550 5555; www. indonesia.embassy.gov.au.
Britain: Jl. M.H. Thamrin, No. 75, Menteng; tel: 2356 5200; www. ukinindonesia.fco.gov.uk.
Canada: Jl. Jend. Sudirman, Kav. 29, World Trade Center 6th floor; tel: 2550 7800; www. canadainternational.gc.ca.
New Zealand: Sentral Senayan 2, Floor 10, Jl. Asia Afrika, No. 8; tel: 2995 5800; www.nzembassy.com/indonesia.
Singapore: Jl. H.R. Rasuna Said, Kav. X-4, No. 2, Kuningan; tel: 2995 0400; www.mfa.gov.sg/jkt.
United States: Jl. Medan Merdeka Selatan, No. 5, Jakarta Pusat; tel: 3435

9000; www.jakarta.usembassy.gov.

Bali

(Telephone area code 0361)
Australia, Canada, New Zealand, Ireland and Papua New Guinea: Jl. Tantular, No. 32, Renon; tel: 241 118; www.dfat.gov.au.
Uk: Jl. Tirta Nadi, No. 20, Sanur; tel: 270-601,
Denmark and Norway: Mimpi Resort, Kawasan Bukit Permai, Jimbaran; tel: 701 070.
France: Jl. Mertasari, Gang II, No. 8, Sanur; tel: 285 485.
Germany: Jl. Pantai Karang, No. 17, Sanur; tel: 288 535.
Holland: Jl. Raya Kuta, No. 127, Kuta; tel: 761 506.
Spain: Jl. Raya Sanggingan, Br. Lungsiakan, Kedewatan, Ubud; tel: 975 736.
Sweden and Finland: Jl. Segara Ayu Sanur; tel: 288 407.
Switzerland and Austria: Jl. Patih Jelantik, Komplek Istana Kuta Galeri, Blok Valet 2, No. 12, Kuta; tel: 751 735.
United States (Consular): Jl. Hayam Wuruk, No. 310, Denpasar; tel: 233 605; http://surabaya.usconsulate. gov/bali2.html.

Entry Regulations

Each adult is permitted to bring a maximum of 1 litre of alcoholic beverages, 200 cigarettes, 50 cigars, or 100 grammes of tobacco, and a reasonable quantity of perfume. Prohibited from entry are the following: narcotics, arms and ammunition, pornography and fresh fruit. There is no restriction on import and export of foreign currencies and travellers' cheques; however, import or export of Indonesian currency exceeding Rp 5 million is prohibited. It is also prohibited to import or export products made from endangered species.

Visas and Passports

All travellers to Indonesia must be in possession of a passport valid for at least six months after arrival and tickets proving onward passage. Some immigration officials will require six blank passport pages, so it's better to be safe than sorry.

Visitors from countries not approved as either visa-free or eligible for visa-on-arrival must obtain a 30-day tourist visa from their local Indonesian embassy or consulate before entering Indonesia.
Visa-free: Visitors from the following 12 countries automatically receive a 30-day visa permit free upon arrival in Indonesia: Brunei, Chile,

TRANSPORT
ACCOMMODATION
EATING OUT
ACTIVITIES
A – Z
LANGUAGE

Ecuador, Hong Kong SAR, Macau SAR, Malaysia, Morocco, Peru, Philippines, Singapore, Thailand and Vietnam. **Visa-on-arrival**: Regulations are constantly changing. At press time, 65 countries have been approved for visa-on-arrival (VOA). Currently the fees are US$10 for 7 days or US$25 for 30 days. It is recommended that you check with your local Indonesian embassy or consulate in advance of travelling for current regulations.

The visa-on-arrival can be extended one time for a maximum 30 days and cannot be converted into a different visa. The only way to stay longer in Indonesia than your visa allows is to leave the country and come back in again, the nearest place being Singapore. Alternatively, apply for a 60-day visa at an Indonesian embassy or consulate before arriving in Indonesia. For further information, check the Indonesian Foreign Affairs Department website: www.deplu. go.id.

Travel Permits

A *surat jalan* (travel permit) is required for visits to the interior of Papua. After landing in Sentani, hire a car at the airport and go directly to the police station in Jayapura (a 45-minute drive), where travel permits are processed. Have on hand 2–4 passport-sized photos (depending on the number of places you plan to visit), photocopies of your passport, and your embarkation card. (Expatriate residents need a copy of their KITAS instead of the embarkation card.)

When applying for the *surat jalan*, be certain to list all of the places you plan to visit in the interior – Baliem Valley, Asmat, Wasur, for example – and make photocopies of it. You will have to leave one copy at each area visited, as police checkpoints often ask for it, even in non-restricted areas.

Permits are also required to enter all national parks. In some parks there is an officer on the premises, but in others permits must be obtained prior to arrival. Check locally for regulations before visiting any national park.

Etiquette

Indonesians are remarkably friendly and courteous, but they are also staunchly conservative. Travellers who observe a few basic rules of etiquette will be assured of a warm welcome.
• Using the left hand to give or to receive

anything is taboo (the left hand is reserved for hygiene acts), as is pointing or crooking a finger to call someone.
• Don't make any offers to purchase unless you intend to buy. When bargaining, start at half the asking price and then work out a compromise. Rp 1,000 can mean the difference of a day's meal, so avoid quibbling over small sums. Many Indonesians are still very poor, so be prudent and don't display large sums of money.
• Begging is not a tradition. However, a small contribution at a temple, a village or a cultural conservation centre is appropriate and will be appreciated.
• Hands on the hips indicates defiance or arrogance, especially when also standing with legs apart.
• When sitting, feet should be tucked away, not propped up with the soles facing another person.
• When visiting mosques and other places of worship, dress modestly and remove shoes.

Gay and Lesbian Travellers

Although homosexuals are broadly accepted in Indonesia, note that overt displays of affection are not. Such behaviour is considered distasteful – whether exhibited by homosexuals or heterosexuals. Indonesians, however, are wont to show open affection among one's own sex rather than between the sexes. It is common, for instance, to see two men hugging or holding hands, or girls walking with hands intertwined.

In Java and Bali there are gay communities and establishments that cater for them. Utopia, the Asian Gay & Lesbian Resources Centre (www.utopia-asia.com), has excellent information on gay travel in Indonesia as well as other Asian countries.

Health and Medical Care

The health risks when travelling in a tropical country such as Indonesia depend greatly on how you choose to travel and where you are going to go. Nonetheless, you should not travel to Indonesia without comprehensive medical insurance.

Yellow fever vaccinations are required if arriving within six days of leaving or passing through an infected

area. Check with your home physician regarding vaccinations for other ailments like typhoid, cholera and hepatitis A and B.

Diarrhoea and stomach upsets may be a problem, often a reaction to a change in food and environment. Tablets such as Lomotil and Imodium are invaluable, but offer only a temporary solution, best taken only when toilet facilities are lacking. A fever accompanying cramps and diarrhoea may require doctor-prescribed antibiotics.

Probably more stomach upsets are due to **dehydration** than anything else, as most people simply don't drink enough water. Drink more than you think you need, particularly if taking part in outdoor activities. Take precautions against the sun and the heat. Wear a hat as protection. Tanning oils and creams are expensive in Indonesia and difficult to find outside the big cities. Bring them from home.

Malaria is carried by night-biting mosquitoes. Prophylactics are increasingly questionable; strains are developing in Southeast Asia that are resistant to most medications; some, like Larium, can cause dizziness, stomach upset, even hallucinations. Before consulting a physician, first determine if you will be travelling in a malaria-infected area (not all of Indonesia is). Upon arrival, minimise contact with mosquitoes by using repellent; and as mosquitoes are most active around dawn and dusk, wear long-sleeved shirts and long trousers during those times. Sleep under a mosquito net in infected areas. All bites, cuts and abrasions can easily become infected in the tropics; treat them immediately.

Dengue fever, carried by daytime mosquitoes, is far more prevalent in Indonesia than malaria. There is no prophylactic; take the precautions described above if travelling in an infected area.

All **water** must be made safe before consumption. Bottled purified water is readily available in even the smallest villages, but if caught in a bind, bringing water to a rolling boil for 20 minutes is an effective method of sterilisation. All fruit should be peeled before eaten; avoid raw vegetables.

AIDS and other sexually transmitted diseases are increasing in Indonesia. Local sex workers have multiple partners from around the world. Act responsibly and use condoms, available over the counter at city *apotik* (pharmacies), supermarkets and mini-marts.

Most drugs are available at pharmacies *(apotik)* in major cities without prescription, but if you need special medication, bring adequate supplies with you. International-standard medical treatment and specialist care is available in Jakarta and Bali at hospitals and clinics.

Jakarta

The following clinics are of international standard and are popular with expatriates living in Indonesia. Both have staff who can handle problems in English.
SOS Medika (AEA International Clinic): Jl. Puri Sakti, No. 10, Cipete, Jakarta; tel: 021-750 6001 (24-hour emergency); www.sosindonesia.com.
MMC (Metropolitan Medical Center): Jl. H.R. Rasuna Said, Kav. C 20–21; tel: 021-527 3473; www.rsmmc.co.id.

Bali

Bali International Medical Centre (BIMC): Jl. By-Pass Ngurah Rai, No. 100X, Kuta; tel: 0361-761 263; www.bimcbali.com. Provides 24-hour general medical treatment and emergency evacuation, under supervision by Australian, English, American, New Zealand, Japanese and Indonesian medical personnel.
International SOS Medika, Bali Clinic: Jl. By-Pass Ngurah Rai, No. 505X, Kuta, tel: 0361-710 544; www.internationalsos.com. Provides international-standard medical care, including specialist and ambulance services. Routine care, including dental and psychological, and emergency care 24 hours a day.

Internet

Most internet cafés have now become Wi-fi-friendly "hotspots", handy if you have a laptop or smartphone. Wi-fi is also available in most hotels. For those with no laptop, large hotels usually have business centres where guests can log on; if not, ask at the front desk for directions to the nearest internet café.

Media

The Jakarta Post is the major

ABOVE: drinks stalls outside the mosque at Banten, Java.

English-language newspaper. In addition, a few international newspapers – English-language and others – are available at the newsstands of large hotels and major airports. *Tempo* magazine is published in Indonesian and in English and is a good source of political and business news.

Television is available everywhere, even in the most remote locations. Larger hotels have cable TV, so in addition to Indonesian channels, they receive CNN, MTV, at least one sports and one movie channel.

Money

Rupiah (Rp) come in banknote denominations of 100,000; 50,000; 20,000; 10,000; 5,000; 2,000; and 1,000. Coins come in 1,000, 500, 200, 100 and 50 rupiah.

Change is often not available in smaller shops. Carry a variety of coins and small notes, especially when travelling outside cities.

Changing Money

Bring only new notes (no coins), as practically no one will change dirty or marred bank notes. The best exchange rate is usually obtained at money-changers, found at the airports of all major cities. Hotels usually offer a lower rate, and banks often offer even worse rates.

Particularly in Bali, where illegal money-changers know every scam in the book, stick to those advertising themselves as "Authorised". Count your money before leaving the counter and get a receipt. It is advisable to convert most of your money in the cities before moving towards the interior. Leftover rupiah notes are easily changed back into foreign currency at departure. At time of press, US$1 was roughly equivalent to Rp 9,000; £1 equalled Rp 14,250.

Credit Cards

MasterCard and Visa are accepted in most large hotels and shops, but don't count on using them in the hinterland. Diner's Club and American Express are less prevalent. Don't be surprised if an additional 3–5 percent "handling charge" is added to the bill; this is an accepted practice.

ATMs

ATMs are found everywhere in the larger cities. Look for those affiliated with your international ATM network.

Tipping

Major hotels add a 10 percent service charge to bills. If it is not included in upmarket restaurants, a tip of 5–10 percent is appropriate if the service has been satisfactory.

In small-town eateries, tipping is not expected. Airport and hotel porterage is Rp 5,000 per piece. Tipping taxi and hired-car drivers is not mandatory, but rounding up the fare to the nearest Rp 1,000 is standard. However, if you are travelling with a hired-car driver and/ or a guide, a tip is a good idea.

Photography

Most Indonesians love to be photographed, especially if they have children, but it's still nice to ask before shooting. Practically everyone understands *"Foto?"*. Just point at the camera and, if you get a nod or a smile, click away. Older people may be shy; if they indicate "no", politely move on. It isn't polite to photograph people praying.

Digital-photo shops are abundant in cities; convenient for downloading photos from camera to USB devices.

Postal Services

There are post offices in every major town and village. Hours are generally as follows: from Monday to Thursday 8am–2pm; Friday 8am–noon; and Saturday 8am–1pm.

Smoking

Large cities are making an effort to ban smoking in public places. Look for smoking rooms in airports, and enquire if smoking is permitted in special sections of restaurants and hotels.

Telecommunications

The telephone service is rapidly being modernised and overhauled throughout the country, meaning telephone numbers and area codes change frequently. If a number listed in this guide doesn't work, it has probably been upgraded.

Establishments such as hotels may have several telephone numbers, which may come in five to eight digits. Thus, listings never seem to match. Major hotels offer International Direct Dial (IDD). Dial 001, 007, 008 and 017 for an international line. Indonesia's cellular phone system is GSM. Prepaid SIM cards that can be inserted into your phone allow you to make local and international calls at lower prices than landline calls. These can be purchased in varying amounts

BELOW: odalan festival, Bali.

at many kiosks and supermarkets in Indonesia's towns and cities.

Time Zone

Indonesia is divided into three time zones following provincial boundaries:
Waktu Indonesia Barat (WIB, Western Indonesia Standard Time): Sumatra, Java, western half of Kalimantan. UTC +7 of Greenwich Mean Time (GMT).
Waktu Indonesia Tengah (WITA, Central Indonesia Standard Time): Eastern half of Kalimantan, Sulawesi, Bali, Nusa Tenggara. UTC +8.
Waktu Indonesia Timur (WIT, Eastern Indonesia Standard Time): Papua, Maluku. UTC +9.
Daylight saving time is never observed in Indonesia.
During non-daylight saving time in other countries:
At noon in Western Indonesia (WIB), it's 0.00 (midnight) the previous day in New York (ie New York is 12 hours behind Jakarta) and 5am on the same day in London (ie London is 7 hours behind Jakarta).
At noon in Central Indonesia (WITA), it's 11pm the previous day in New York (ie New York is 13 hours behind Denpasar) and 4am the same day in London (ie London is 8 hours behind Denpasar).
At noon in Eastern Indonesia (WIT), it's 10pm on the previous day in New York (ie New York is 14 hours behind Jayapura) and 3am on the same day in London (ie London is 9 hours behind Jayapura).

Toilets

Most places catering to tourists have at least one Western toilet. In shopping malls, there is often an attendant who collects a small fee (Rp 1,000) to pay for keeping toilets clean. Otherwise, and in remote areas, "squat" toilets are the norm. Toilet tissue is often not available, as most Indonesians clean themselves with the water that's provided. If you prefer not to go native, bring your own tissue and dispose of it in the bin next to the toilet, if there is one.

Tourist Information

While there is plenty of information about Indonesia on the web, much of it is conflicting and a lot of it is just plain wrong. Unfortunately, most of the provincial government tourist information websites are

either in Bahasa Indonesia only or have not been updated in several years. Also shown below are current websites in English for reliable tourist information, usually posted by local tourism promotion boards comprising tourist-related businesses or travel agencies. Some of them also display languages other than English. *(For more websites, see "Tour Operators", below, and Outdoor Activities starting on page 406).*

Note that the provincial tourist information offices are difficult to reach by telephone and they close at odd hours, ie for lunch, at weekends and during public holidays. The best bet is to drop by their offices before noon on a weekday.

Java

Jakarta
Ministry of Culture and Tourism: Gedung Sapta Pesona, Jl. Medan Merdeka Barat, No. 17; tel: 021-383 8167; www.indonesia.travel.
Jakarta City Government Tourism and Culture Office: Jl. Kuningan Barat, No. 2; tel: 021-520 5455, 520 5454.
PHKA (Forest Protection & Nature Conservation): Manggala Wanabakti Building Blok I, 8th Floor, Jl. Jend. Gatot Subroto; tel: 021-573- 4818. Information about permits for Indonesia's national parks.
Visitor Information Centre: Jakarta Theatre Bldg (across from Sarinah), Jl. M.H. Thamrin; tel: 021-315 4094.
Bandung
For useful tourist information about Bandung, visit www.visitbandung.net.
Banten Tourism Office: Jl. Raya Serang–Pandeglang, Km 4, Komplek Tembong Indah, No. 1, Serang; tel: 0254-219 836.
West Java Provincial Tourist Office: Jl. R.E. Martadinata, No. 209, Bandung; tel: 022-727 1385, 727 3209.
Cirebon
Provincial Tourist Services: Jl. Brigien Darsono, No. 5; tel: 0231-208 856.
Solo
Provincial Tourist Services: Jl. Slamet Riyadi; tel: 0271-711 435.
Surabaya
Provincial Tourist Services: Jl. Wisata Menanggal; tel: 031-853 1814/1817/1820/1821.
Tourist Information Centre: Balai Pemuda, Jl. Gubernur Suryo, No. 15; tel: 031-5340 4444.
Tourist Information Centre: House of Sampoerna, Taman Sampoerna, No. 6; tel: 031-353 9000; www.houseofsampoerna.museum; Tue–Sun 9am–4pm.

For useful information about East Java, visit www.eastjava.com, www.sparklingsurabaya.com, www.eastjavatourism.com, www.jogjapages.com, www.tourismsleman.com, and www.visitbandung.net

Yogyakarta
Yogyakarta Tourism Board: Jl Malioboro, No. 56; tel: 0274-587 486. For Jogja tourism information, visit www.jogjapages.com and www.yogyes.com.

Sumatra

Bandar Lampung
Lampung Tourism Office: Jl. Jend. Sudirman, No. 2, Bandar Lampung; tel: 0721-261 430.
Bengkulu
Bengkulu Tourism Office: Jl. P. Tendean, No. 17, Bengkulu; tel: 0736-21272.

Medan
North Sumatra Tourism Office: Jl. Jend. A. Yani, No. 107, Medan; tel: 061-453 8101.

Padang
West Sumatra Tourism Office: Jl. Khatib Sulaiman, No. 7, Padang; tel: 0751-705 5711.

Palembang
South Sumatra Tourism Office: Jl. Demang Lebar Daun, Kav. IX, Palembang; tel: 0711-356 661, 311 345, 357 348.

Riau
Riau Tourism Office: Jl. Jend. Sudirman No. 200, Pekanbaru; tel: 0761-31452, 40356. For useful Sumatra tourist information, also visit: www.acehhotels.com, www.medanku.com, www.west-sumatra.com.

Bali

Denpasar
Denpasar Government Tourist Office: Jl. Surapati, No. 7, Denpasar; tel: 0361-234 569.

Legian
Bali Tourist Information: Century Plaza, Jl. Bensari, No. 7, Legian; tel: 0361-754 090.
Legian Tourist Information: Jl. Legian, No. 37; tel: 0361-755 424.
Provincial Tourist Services: Jl. S. Parman Niti Mandala, Renon; tel: 0361-222 387; www.balitourismauthority.net.

Singaraja
Singaraja Tourist Information Office: Jl. Gajah Mada, No. 117; tel: 0362 25141.

Ubud
Ubud Tourist Information Service: Jl. Raya Ubud, Ubud; tel: 0361-973 285. Helpful tourist information can also be found at www.balicalendar.com,

Above: use mosquito repellent.

www.bali-tourism-board.com, www.karangasemtourism.com, www.godivingbali.com.

Nusa Tenggara

Flores
West Manggarai Regency Tourist Office: Labuhanbajo; tel: 0385-41107. Useful tourist information websites: http://floresexotictours.blogspot.com, www.florestourism.com, www.floreskomodo.com, www.komodonationalpark.org.

Sumbawa
Tourist Information Office: Jl. Sukarno-Hatta, Raba, Bima; tel: 0374-44331.
Tourist Information Office: Jl. Akasia, No. 2, Dompu; tel: 0373-21177.
Tourist Information Office: Jl. Bungur, No. 1, Sumbawa Besar; tel: 0371-261-658.

Timor
Provincial Tourist Services: Jl. Jend. Basuki Rahmat, No. 1, Kupang; tel: 0380-21540, 21824; www.goseentt.com.
Kupang Klub House: Jl. Hati Mulia, No. 2/6, Kupang; tel: 0380-840 244; www.kupangklubhouse.com, online information directory for Kupang and East Nusa Tenggara.
Other useful websites for East Nusa Tenggara tourist information: www.alordiver.com, www.lavalontouristinfo.com.

Kalimantan

Useful tourist information websites, Kalimantan: www.kalimantantours.com, www.extremeborneo.com.

Banjarmasin
Provincial Tourist Services: Jl. Pramuka, No. 4, Banjarmasin; tel: 0511-274 252.

Palangkaraya
Provincial Tourist Services: Jl. Tjilik Riwut, Km 5, Palangkaraya 73112; tel: 0536-323 1110.

Pontianak
Provincial Tourist Services: Jl. Letjen. Sutoyo, Km 17, Pontianak; tel: 0561-736 172.

Samarinda

Provincial Tourist Services: Jl. Sudirman, No. 22, Samarinda; tel: 0541-736 850, 747 241.

Sulawesi

Bau-Bau
Buton Tourist Office: tel: 0402-23588.
Kendari
Provincial Tourist Services: Jl. Lakidende, No. 9; tel: 0401-21764.

Makassar
Provincial Tourist Office: Jl. Jend. Sudirman, No. 23, Makassar; tel: 0411-872 366, 878 912; Mon–Fri 8am–4pm.
There is also a **Tourist Information Centre** inside Benteng Rotterdam organised by the Indonesia Tour Guide Association.

Manado
Provincial Tourism Office: Jl. Sam Ratulangi; tel: 0431-837 674.
Manado City Tourism Office: Jl. Wolter Monginsidi (Bahu); tel: 0431-851 723, 852 730.
Useful tourist information websites for North Sulawesi: www.north-sulawesi.com, www.north-sulawesi.org, www.divenorthsulawesi.com.

Palu
Provincial Tourist Services: Jl. Dewi Sartika, No. 91; tel: 0451-455 260.

Rantepao
Government Tourist Office: Jl. A. Yani, No. 62; tel: 0423-21297.
Tourist Information: Toraja Decouverte, Jl. Pahlawan, No. 7 (behind Modern Foto); email: mailto:toraja-decouverte-splendeurs@gmail.com, torajainfo@gmail.com. Organises tours, hiking, rafting, and car/motorbike rental.

Maluku

Tourism Information Centre: Jl. Bhayangkara, Tobelo, Ambon; www.halmaherautara.com.

Papua

Provincial Tourist Services: Jl. Soa Siu Dok II, Jayapura; tel: 0967-33381, 35923,

Tour Operators and Travel Agents

See Travel Tips – Activities, page 406 for recommended tour operators and their specialities. A few others are listed below.

Java

Jakarta

Sahabat Museum (Friends of the Museum): contact Mr Ade Purnama; tel: 021-769 6283; mobile tel: 081-949 682; email: adep@cbn.net.id, sahabatmuseum@yahoogroups.com. An expert historian, Mr Ade conducts tours of museums and other historical sites in Jakarta as well as elsewhere in Java. A popular walking tour is in Old Batavia, stopping to eat in restaurants with traditional menus. **Karash Adventure & Training**: Jl. Gabus Raya, No. 37, Pasar Minggu, Jakarta; tel: 021-7884 3830; www. karashteambuilding.com. Specialises in introducing Indonesia's nature and culture to travellers who want to go off the beaten path. Organises trekking, mountain climbing and team-building for businesses and families.

Panorama Tours: Head Office, Panorama Building, 3rd Floor, Jl. Tomang Raya, No. 63; tel: 021-2556 5555; www.panorama-tours.com. Incoming tour operator in Jakarta with several branches in Java and Bali. Specialises in Java-overland-to-Bali tours with multilingual guides. Also does ticketing and hotel reservations.

West Java

Visits to Ujung Kulon National Park and Krakatau can be arranged with these Jakarta-based tour companies specialising in these areas.

Ujung Kulon Tours & Travel: Jl. Sultan Agung Tirtayasa, No. 49, Simpang Tiga, Cilegon; tel: 0254-384 159; www.ujungkulon-tour.com.

Ujung Kulon Ecotourism Information Centre: Jl. Raya Labuan, Km 10, Carita, Pandeglang; tel: 0253-880 609; www.ujungkulonecotourism.com.

East Java

East Java Overland Tours

For 1–7-night East Java Discovery excursions contact: **Aneka Kartika Tours & Travel Services**: Jl. Manyar Kertoarjo V-50, Surabaya; tel: 031-592 9000; www.aneka-tours.co.id.

Baluran National Park

For tourist information, mountain and savannah hiking, birdwatching treks and excursions to Baluran beaches, contact **Rosa's Ecolodge** (www.rosasecolodge.com). Guides speak Dutch and English. Proceeds help to finance environmental education for villagers.

Gunung Ijen

For information on Gunung Ijen, its 54-hectare (133-acre) sulphuric crater lake, and clove, cocoa and coffee plantations (which helped the Dutch to corner the world's coffee market in the 19th and 20th centuries), contact the **Banyuwangi Tourism Office** (tel: 0333-422 128) or call the very helpful Pak Hanyono in that office directly (mobile: 081-5590 5197). **Ijen Villa and Resort** (tel: 0333-773 3338, www.ijendiscovery.com).

Bali

By letting travel agents arrange logistics for you, you get more time for having fun. They can organise car hire, guides, tours, airline tickets and hotel reservations. Most hotels have a travel desk or can suggest an agency nearby. Some of the large full-service agencies are:

Asian Trails: Jl. By-Pass Ngurah Rai, No. 260, Sanur; tel: 0361-285 771; www.asiantrails.com.

Bagus Discovery: Jl. By-Pass I Gusti Ngurah Rai, No. 300B, Denpasar, tel: 0361-751 223, www.bagus-discovery.com.

Golden Kris Tours: Jl. By-Pass Ngurah Rai, No. 7, Sanur, tel: 0361-289 225; www.goldenkrisbali.com.

KCBJ Tours & Travel Services: Jl. Raya Kuta, No. 127, Kuta; tel: 0361-751 517; www.kcbtours.com.

Pacto: Jl. Bypass, Sanur; tel: 0361-288 247; www.pactoltd.com.

Sutra Tours: Jl. Sekarangi, No. 14, By-Pass Prof. Dr IB Mantra, Kesambi, Denpasar, tel: 0361-741-6665; http://sutatour.com.

Vayatour: Jl. By-Pass Ngurah Rai, No. 143, Sanur; tel: 0361-285 555; www.vayatour.com/bali.

Nusa Tenggara

Flores, Solor and Lembata

Area Codes

Location	Code		Location	Code
Indonesia	62		**Lombok**	0370
Java			**Sumbawa**	
Bandung	022		Sumbawa Besar	0371
Jakarta	021		Bima	0374
Yogyakarta (Jogja)	0274		**Flores**	
Surakarta (Solo)	0271		Labuhanbajo	0385
Semarang	024		Maumere	0382
Surabaya	031		Ende	0381
Malang	0341		Sumba	0387
Sumatra			Timor	0380
Medan	061		**Kalimantan**	
Banda Aceh	0651		Balikpapan	0542
Prapat, Samosir	0625		Samarinda	0541
Padang	0751		Banjarmasin	0511
Bukittinggi	0752		Palangkaraya	0536
Palembang	0711		Pontianak	0561
Bengkulu	0736		**Sulawesi**	
Bandar Lampung	0721		Makassar (Ujung Padang)	
Batam	0778			0411
Bintan	0770		Rantepao	0423
Bali			Palu	0451
Denpasar, Badung, Tabanan			Manado	0431
	0361		**Maluku**	
Gianyar, Ubud			Ambon	0911
	0361		Bandaneira	0910
Kuta, Sanur, Nusa Dua			Ternate, Tidore	0921
	0361		**Papua**	
Buleleng, Singaraja, Lovina			Jayapura	0967
	0362		Wamena	0969
Amlapura (Karangasem)			Biak	0981
	0363			
Candidasa	0363			
Jembrana				
	0365			
Semarapura (Klungkung)	0366			
Bangli, Kintamani				
	0366			
Bedugul	0368			

Note: The telecommunications system in Jakarta has reached its limit for 6- and 7-digit numbers. All new telephone numbers have 8 digits. Therefore, it's not unusual for some businesses to have 6-, 7- and 8-digit numbers if they have added new telephone lines over the years.

Above: surf shop, Kuta, Bali.

CV Latour: Jl. Podor Lewolere, Larantuka, Flores; tel: 0383-21388. Arranges tours to Solor and Lembata, including the Lamalera whaling village, as well as traditional villages in eastern Flores.

Lombok

Perama Travel Club: Jl. Pejanggik, No. 66, Mataram; tel: 0370-635 928; www.peramatour.com. Organises tours, sightseeing trips, ferry tickets, surfing, snorkelling and diving trips. It has branches in Senggigi, Gili Terawangan and Labuan Lombok, six offices in Bali, and one each in Jakarta, Surabaya and Balikpapan (East Kalimantan), the Netherlands and Germany.

Kalimantan

Ateng Tour: Jl. Gajah Mada, No. 201, Pontianak; tel: 0561-732-683. Offers tours to West Kalimantan Dayak country near Singkawang and Sambas, and a Serimbu rapids adventure with local boats. Other itineraries include expeditions to Mount Kelam and to Gunung Palung National Park, as well as to Mulu Caves in Sarawak.

Ragus Travel: Jl. Sulawesi, No. 17, Banjarmasin 70115; tel: 0511-59979. Well-thought-out South Kalimantan itineraries ranging from city tours and three-day diamond-mining, bamboo-rafting or trekking trips, to 10-day Dayak expeditions. There is also an itinerary for Tanjung Puting National Park.

De'Gigant Tours: Jl. Martadinata Rauda 1, No. 21 RT 11, Samarinda; tel: +62 (0)81-2485 6578; www.borneotourgigant.com. A full-service tour operator specialising in adventure tours throughout Kalimantan. Its website has the most complete information on the island available.

Sulawesi

Wira Tours & Travel: Jl. Gunung Lokon, No. 25, Makassar; tel: 0411-312-298; www.sulawesi-celebes.com. With 20 years' experience in cultural and adventure travel in Sulawesi, this is an excellent resource for customised group or individual tours. Safari Tours & Travel: Jl. Sam Ratulangi, No. 178, Manado; tel: 0431-857-637; Error! Hyperlink reference not valid.A complete service tour operator and travel agency focusing on North Sulawesi, offers diving, trekking, horse riding, rafting and cultural tours.

Papua

Raja Ampat
For further information about Raja Ampat's diverse species, visit the websites of **World Wildlife Fund** (www.worldwildlife.org), which also occasionally conducts tours, **Conservation International** (www.conservation.org) and **The Nature Conservancy** (TNC) (www.nature.org) or visit the TNC field office at Jl. Gunung Merapi, No. 38, Sorong; tel: 0951-323 437.

Weights and Measures

Indonesia follows the metric system.

What to Bring

Travel as lightly as possible, as there are many good buys to be found in Indonesia and never enough luggage space for them. Essentials are insect repellent, sunscreen, prescription medicines and perhaps an extra set of spectacles. Always hand-carry medicines, as checked-in luggage can get delayed or lost. Make sure all luggage is locked.

What to Wear

Indonesians are concerned with how they present themselves, and are particularly mindful of modesty. As most Indonesians are Muslim, it is polite for women to keep their knees, midriffs and armpits covered. Singlets, halter tops, shorts and miniskirts are frowned upon, as are swimsuits anywhere other than on the beach or at the pool.

As the weather is hot and humid year-round, bring all-cotton clothing or the synthetic quick-dry variety for sale in camping stores throughout the world. Sandals or footwear that can be slipped off easily are a good idea, especially if planning to visit mosques or homes, as shoes are always removed before entering. Hiking boots may be required for trekking.

For formal occasions, men wear batik shirts and tailored trousers; women, modest dresses or ethnic outfits.

Women Travellers

It is highly unusual for a young woman to travel alone in Indonesia, and solo females may have to put up with being pestered by gregarious Indonesian men; young local women almost always move around in company. However, you will be quite safe as long as you dress and behave modestly; women with bare legs and minimal tops are considered disrespectful.

Take the usual precautions: don't walk down dark alleys or beaches alone at night. In Bali and Jakarta, be wary of gigolos and "cowboys" offering free rides.

TRANSPORT

ACCOMMODATION

EATING OUT

ACTIVITIES

A - Z

LANGUAGE

Language

Understanding the Language

Indonesia's motto, *Bhinneka Tunggal Ika* (Unity in Diversity), is seen in its most potent form in language. Although there are over 700 distinct languages and countless dialects spoken in the archipelago, the one national tongue, Bahasa I ndonesia, will carry you from the northernmost tip of Sumatra to Java and across the string of islands to Papua.

Bahasa Indonesia is both an old and a new language, and is based on Malay, which has been the lingua franca throughout much of Southeast Asia for centuries. The construction of basic sentences is relatively easy. Indonesian is written in the Roman alphabet and, unlike some other Asian languages, is not tonal.

To show respect, an older man is addressed as *bapak* or *pak* (father or Sir) and an elder woman as *ibu* (mother or Madam). *Bung* (in West Java) and *mas* (in Central and East Java) roughly translate as "brother" and are used to address your equals, people of your own age whom you

don't know all that well. You can also use it to address strangers, even service personnel such as hotel clerks, taxi drivers, tour guides and waiters.

Pronunciation

a short as in "father"
(*apa* = what, *ada* = there is)
ai rather like the "i" in "mine"
(*kain* = material, *sampai* = to arrive)
k hard at the beginning of a word as in "king", but hardly audible at the end of a word
(*kamus* = dictionary, *cantik* = beautiful)
kh (ch) slightly aspirated, as in "khan" or the Scottish "ch" in "loch"
(*khusus* = special, *khabar* = news)
ng as in "singer"
(*bunga* = flower, *penginapan* = cheap hotel)
ngg like the "ng" in "Ringo"
(*minggu* = week or Sunday, *tinggi* = high, tall)
r always rolled
(*rokok* = cigarette, *pertama* = first)
u (oe) as in "flute"
(*umum* = public, *belum* = not yet)
y (*j*) as in "you"
(*saya* = I or me, *kaya* = rich)
c (*tj*) like the "ch" in "church"
(*candi* = temple, *kacang* = nut)
e 1. often unstressed as in "open"
(*berapa* sounds like *b'rapa* = how much?)
2. sometimes stressed, somewhere between the "e" in "bed" and "a" in "bad"
(*boleh* = may, *lebar* = wide)
g hard as in "golf"
(*guntur* = thunder, *bagus* = good)
h generally lightly aspirated
(*hitam* = black, *lihat* = to see)
i either short as in "pin", or longer, like "ee" in "meet"
(*minta* = to ask for, *ibu* = mother)
j (*dj*) as in "John"
(*jalan* = road or street, *jahit* = to sew)

Spelling

Two minor points about spelling. Despite ever-changing rules, there are many instances where the names of people continue to be spelled with the old "**oe**" rather than the current "**u**". Some may change, but most stick to their birthright. For example, the former president, whose name is Suharto, is spelt by the local press as Soeharto.

Greetings and Civilities

Thank you	*Terima kasih*
Good morning	*Selamat pagi*
Good day	*Selamat siang*
Good afternoon/good evening	
Selamat sore (pronounced *soray*)	
Goodnight	*Selamat malam*
Goodbye	*Selamat jalan (to*
person going)	
Goodbye	*Selamat tinggal*
(to person staying)	
I'm sorry	*Ma'af*
Welcome	*Selamat datang*
Please come in	*Silakan masuk*
Please sit down	*Silakan duduk*
What is your name?	*Siapa nama Anda*
My name is . . .	*Nama saya . . .*
Where do you come from?	*Saudara berasal dari mana?*
I come from . . .	*Saya berasal dari . . .*

Pronouns/Forms of Address

·I	*Saya*
You (singular)	*Anda*
He, she	*Dia*
We (excluding the listener)	*Kami*
We (including the listener)	*Kita*
You (plural)	*Anda semua*
Mr	*Pak/bapak*
Mrs	*Ibu/bu*
Miss	*Nona*

Directions/Transport

left	*kiri*
right	*kanan*
straight	*terus*
near	*dekat*
far	*jauh*
from	*dari*
to	*ke*
inside	*di dalam*
outside	*di luar*
here	*di sini*
there	*di sana*
in front of	*di depan/muka*
at the back	*di belakang*
next to	*di sebelah*
pedicab	*becak*
car	*mobil*
bus	*bis*
train	*kereta api*
bicycle	*sepeda*
motorcycle	*sepeda motor*
Where do you want to go?	*Mau kemana?*
I want to go to . . .	*Saya mau ke...*
Stop here	*Berhenti di sini*
bank	*bank*
post office	*kantor pos*
tourist office	*kantor pariwisata*
embassy	*kedutaan*

Eating Out

restaurant	*restoran/rumah makan/resto*
food	*makanan*
drink	*minuman*
breakfast	*makan pagi*
lunch	*makan siang*
dinner	*makan malam*
boiled water	*air putih/air matang*
iced water	*air es*
tea	*teh*
coffee	*kopi*
milk	*susu*
rice	*nasi*
noodles	*mie/bihun*
fish	*ikan*
prawns	*udang*
vegetables	*sayur*
fruit	*buah*
egg	*telur*
sugar	*gula*
salt	*garam*
pepper	*merica, lada*
cup	*cangkir*
plate	*piring*
glass	*gelas*
spoon	*sendok*
knife	*pisau*
fork	*garpu*

Shopping

shop	*toko*
money	*uang*
change (from a bill)	*uang kembali*
to buy	*beli*

price	*harga*
expensive	*mahal*
cheap	*murah*
fixed price	*harga pas*
How much is it?	*Berapa?/Berapa harganya?*

Signs

open	*buka, dibuka*
cashier	*kasir, kassa*
closed	*tutup, ditutup*
entrance	*masuk*
exit	*keluar*
don't touch	*jangan pegang/ sentuh*
no smoking	*dilarang merokok*
gate	*pintu*
ticket window	*loket*
ticket	*karcis*
information	*informasi*
city	*kota*

GLOSSARY OF TERMS

A

adat customary law
arak strong spirit from sugar palm

B

bale (also *balai*) open-air pavilion with roof
banjar neighbourhood association; the basic social and political unit
banten religious offerings (Bali)
barat west
Barong mythical beast portrayed in dance by two costumed men (Bali)
bemo public minibus
bukit a hill or hilly area

C

candi bentar split entrance gateway to a Balinese temple

D

dalang puppet master
danau lake
desa village
dewa generic name for god
dewi generic name for goddess
Dewi Sri Goddess of Rice

G

Galungan Balinese New Year
gamelan percussion orchestra
gang small lane or alley
garuda mythological bird
geringsing double *ikat* cloth
gunung mountain

I

ikat traditional handwoven textile

J

jalan street, road; to walk

K

kain cloth; also sarong
kantor office
kepulauan archipelago
keris ceremonial dagger with a wavy blade

L

legong Balinese dance; also the name given to the dancer
lingga a Hindu phallic symbol
lombok chilli
lontar a palm-leaf manuscript
losmen small family-run guesthouse
lumbung a traditional rice barn

N

naga dragon, water serpent
nusa island (also called *pulau*)

O

odalan Balinese temple festival
ojek motorcycle taxi

P

pantai beach
pasar market
pura temple
puri palace

S

sawah rice field
selatan south
sungai river

T

taman garden
teluk bay
tenggara southeast
timur east
topeng mask
tuak palm wine

U

utara north

W

wartel telecoms office
warung simple café where food and drinks are served
wayang Javanese puppet

TRANSPORT
ACCOMMODATION
EATING OUT
ACTIVITIES
A – Z
LANGUAGE

FURTHER READING

Fiction

A Tale from Bali by Vicki Baum (Periplus, 1999). First published in 1937, this classic tale of love and death in Bali is set against the backdrop of turmoil faced by the Balinese in their struggle against the Dutch colonialists.

Bali Behind The Seen: Recent Fiction from Bali translated by Vern Cork (Darma Printing, 1996). A wonderful collection of fiction from contemporary Balinese writers, these works provide a fascinating insight into the complex relationships and quirks of living on this tourist paradise.

The Buru Quartet by Pramoedya Ananta Toer (Penguin, 1990–7, English translations). A four-part series (*This Earth of Mankind*, *Child of All Nations*, *Footsteps*, *House of Glass*), the first volume was originally recited orally by Toer while a political prisoner, and all four were banned in Indonesia for many years. The series tells the multifaceted story of Indonesia's birth as a nation through the eyes of Javanese citizens in what has been called "one of the twentieth century's great artistic creations . . ."

Midnight Shadows by Garrett Kam (Trafford, 2003). Historical novel with the communist coup of 1965 as the setting, it looks at the reasons behind the terrible violence that engulfed Bali by interweaving actual events and history with mythology, dreams and rituals.

The Year of Living Dangerously by C.J. Koch (St Martin's Press, 1978). Also banned in Indonesia for many years and later made into a film, this is the tale of a nation in crisis with the *wayang kulit* as a backdrop. Masterfully told.

General

Bali Today: Real Balinese Stories by Jean Couteau (Spektra Communications, 1998). Couteau is well known for his humorous stories in the Indonesian press about Bali and the Balinese way of life. His observations are witty, ingenious and hilariously funny.

Fragrant Rice – A Tale of Love, Marriage and Cooking in Bali by Janet De Neefe (HarperCollins, 2003). What started as Neefe's desire to put together a collection of Balinese recipes developed into a life story with food as the main ingredient. Geography and Natural History

A Dark Place in the Jungle: Science, Orangutans and Human Nature by Linda Spalding (Algonquin Books of Chapel Hill, 1999). Spalding went to Kalimantan to follow the trail of orang-utan researcher Biruté Galdikas and discovered an unholy mix of foreign scientists, government workers, tourists, loggers, Dayaks and half-tame orang-utans vying for control of the jungle.

Krakatoa: The Day the World Exploded August 27, 1883 by Simon Winchester (HarperCollins, 2003). Geologist Winchester puts an entirely new perspective on the iconic 1883 eruption of Krakatoa that was followed by an immense tsunami that killed nearly 40,000 people, and he does it in language that laymen can comprehend.

The Malay Archipelago: The Land of the Orang-utan and the Bird of Paradise by Alfred Russel Wallace (Graham Brash, 1983, reprint). Tales from the 19th-century naturalist's eight-year journey through one of the most biologically diverse areas of the world are written with great gusto. His theories of evolution and genetic discoveries provided the foundation for the scientific study of botany and zoology in many parts of the world.

Nature's Treasurehouse: The Wildlife of Indonesia by Kathy MacKinnon (Gramedia Press, 1992). Although a bit out of date, this volume remains the most comprehensive description of Indonesia's national parks and the animals who live there, complete with English, Latin and Indonesian names.

Reflections of Eden: My Years with the Orangutans of Borneo by Biruté M.F. Galdikas (Little, Brown and Company, 1995). Louis Leakey's "third angel", Galdikas reveals the story of her life with the orang-utans of Kalimantan for more than 20 years.

Soul of the Tiger: Searching for Nature's Answers in Exotic Southeast Asia by Jeffrey A. McNeely, et al (Doubleday, 1988). The results of two decades of living and learning in Southeast Asia, the authors' fascinating, bizarre and sometimes humorous accounts reveal the vital connection between these people and their animals.

Tropical Herbs and Spices of Indonesia by Wendy Hutton (Periplus Editions, 1997). This handy pocket-sized book with photos is ideal for identifying the exotic spices used in Indonesian cooking and their scientific classifications.

Zoo Quest for a Dragon by David Attenborough (Lutterworth Press, 1957). A classic travel tale of Attenborough's journey to Indonesia in the 1950s to capture Komodo dragons for London Zoo, the people he met and the animals he saw.

History and Culture

Bali: A Paradise Created by Adrian Vickers (Periplus, 1989). Bali, the "last paradise", seen through Western eyes. Fresh insights on the history and culture of a traditional island faced with a massive invasion of paradise-seekers.

Bali Sacred and Secret by Gill Marais (Saritaksu Editions, 2006). A remarkable revelation of a rarely witnessed, mystical world of Balinese ritual and magic.

Bali: Sekala & Niskala Volumes I and II by Fred B. Eiseman, Jr (Periplus, 1990). Essays by a long-time Bali resident: Volume I is an exploration of Balinese religion, rituals and performing arts; Volume II covers the geography, social organisation, language, folklore, as well as Bali's material culture.

The Batak: Peoples of the Island of Sumatra by Achim Sibeth (Thames and Hudson, 1991). A wonderfully photographed, large-format edition exploring Batak art objects found in private collections and museums in Indonesia and abroad.

Indonesia: Land Under the Rainbow, by Mochtar Lubis (Oxford University Press, 1990). This is

a most interesting book and the first popular history of Indonesia through the eyes of a distinguished native author to appear in English. It covers the maritime trade that put the archipelago on the world map from the beginning of time to the 20th century. *The Island of Bali* by Miguel Covarrubias (Periplus, 1999). First published in 1937, this book is still regarded by many as the most authoritative text on Bali and its intriguing culture and people.
Jamu: The Ancient Indonesian Art of Herbal Healing by Susan-Jane Beers (Periplus, 2001). The culmination of 10 years' research, Beers provides a comprehensive look at the background, materials and applications of the holistic *jamu*, herbal tonics, massage oils and creams used by Indonesians for hundreds of years.
Java: The Garden of the East by E.R. Scidmore (Oxford University Press, 1989, reprint). This travel book written by an American visitor to Java in 1899 literally opened the eyes of the Western world to a little-known island in the East. Her journey during the heyday of colonial rule is both astonishing and amusing and brings to life a world of yesteryear.
Jogja: Sites out of Site by M. Rizky Sasono, et al (Enrique Indonesia, 2002). A treasure trove of information about the obscure temple remains near Prambanan, Borobudur and the Gunung Merapi plains compiled by archaeologists and anthropologists. In English, French and Indonesian, with maps.
A Little Bit One o'Clock: Living with a Balinese Family by William Ingram (Periplus, 2002). A beautifully written mini-memoir explores the web of relationships between a foreigner and a Balinese family.
Nusantara: A History of Indonesia by Bernard H.M. Vlekke (Quadrangle Books, 1959). A rare English-language account of Indonesian history from the dawn of time through the revolution from the Dutch. Out of print for decades; history buffs will want to take the trouble to locate a copy.
Our Hotel in Bali by Louise G. Koke (Pepper Publications, 2001). A reissue of the 1987 publication that documents how a young American couple, Bob Koke and Louise Garret, came to build Bali's first hotel, the Kuta Beach Hotel, in 1936.
A Short History of Bali by Robert Pringle (Allen & Unwin, 2004). The history of Bali from before the Bronze Age to the presidency of Megawati

Sukarnoputri and the tragedy of the Kuta bombings in 2002.

Textiles

Batik Belanda 1840–1940 by Harmen C. Veldhuisen (Gaya Favorit Press, 1993). A detailed, illustrated account of Dutch influence on Javanese batik, complete with history and stories.
Contemporary Tie and Dye Textiles of Indonesia by Kim Jane Saunders (Oxford University Press, 1997). A comprehensive look at hand-woven and hand-spun textiles as a dynamic art form, this is an introduction to the diversity of the textiles of each of Indonesia's main weaving islands as they exist in modern times.
Indonesian Textiles by Michael Hitchcock (Periplus, 1991). Hitchcock examines the survival of traditional designs, significant colours, techniques and types of decorative applications in Indonesian textiles, with illustrations.
Lurik: The Magic Stripes by Nian S. Djoemena (Penerbit Djambatan, 2000). One of the few compilations in existence of *lurik* motifs and colours and their symbolism, this book is Djoemena's attempt to keep alive this traditional Yogyakarta hand-woven cloth, perhaps older than batik.
Story Cloths of Bali, by Joseph Fischer (Ten Speed Press, 2004). Story cloths are used as ritual decorations and offerings in Balinese temples. Indonesian art expert Fischer describes how to appreciate Balinese culture via its array of textiles.

The Arts

Balinese Paintings by A.A.M. Djetantik (Oxford in Asia, 1990, second edition). A concise but well-documented guide to traditional Balinese painting, including the work of Ubud's Pitamaha painters and Batuan and Penestanan's Young Artists.
Dance and Drama in Bali by Beryl de Zoete and Walter Spies (Oxford, 1973). Spies lived in Bali for 12 years from 1927 and was an accomplished painter, musician and dance expert; De Zoete was trained in European dance. This important ethnographical book documents the history of Balinese dance and drama.
A House in Bali by Colin McPhee (Periplus, 2000). First published in 1947 and one of the most enchanting books ever written about Bali, this is the story of how, in 1929, a young Canadian-born musician

chanced upon rare gramophone recordings of Balinese gamelan music that were to change his life for ever.
Offerings, the Ritual Art of Bali by Francine Brinkgreve and David Stuart-Fox (Image Network Indonesia, 1992). This beautifully illustrated book provides a rare glimpse into the pageantry, ritual and devotion that accompany the creation of offerings in Bali.

Other Insight Guides

Insight Guides covering the Southeast Asia region include titles on Bali and Lombok; Malaysia; Singapore, Southeast Asia; Thailand; Thailand's Beaches and Islands.
Insight Step by Step Guides advise on the best and most rewarding things to see, including up to 20 tailor-made itineraries exploring the main attractions. Southeast Asian titles include Bali and Singapore.
Titles in the *Insight Smart Guides* series, compact practical guides in an A–Z format, include Bangkok, Kuala Lumpur and Singapore.
The laminated *Insight FlexiMaps* have an informative easy-to-read approach. *FlexiMaps* to Bali, Bangkok; Phuket and Kuala Lumpur are available.

Send Us Your Thoughts

We do our best to ensure the information in our books is as accurate and up-to-date as possible. The books are updated on a regular basis using local contacts, who painstakingly add, amend and correct as required. However, some details (such as telephone numbers and opening times) are liable to change, and we are ultimately reliant on our readers to put us in the picture.
We welcome your feedback, especially your experience of using the book "on the road". Maybe we recommended a hotel that you liked (or another that you didn't), or you came across a great bar or new attraction we missed. We will acknowledge all contributions, and we'll offer an Insight Guide to the best letters received.

Please write to us at:
**Insight Guides
PO Box 7910
London SE1 1WE**
Or email us at:
insight@apaguide.co.uk

Art and Photo Credits

Agência Brasil 53
AidEnvironment 332
akg–images **34, 36, 40, 46**
Alamy 148, 155B, 158, 173, 162B,
163, 169B, 237, 268BL, 312B, 343,
347
APA Archives 359
Asiaimages 192B
asiapulppaper 213
Athendra 345T
Atid Kiattisaksiri 266B
AWL Images 169T, 338/339, 342
Drew Avery 333
Steve Bickell I 290
Bình Giang 31.
BirdPhotos.com 118
Ole Johan Brett 250T
Emmett Brown 313
Tom Casadevall 206T
Christoph Chauvin 331
Christian Goupi 277B
Corbis 188, 289
D Dunlop 300T
David Fleetham 321TR
DavidDennisPhotos.com 303BL
Dimas Ardian 121
Dimitry Dudin 151, 193R
Fotolia 246T, 254T, 269, 277, 278,
298T, 303T, 332T
Garuda Airlines 369
Getty Images 23, 27B, 52, 140B,
150, 208, 211
Government of Republic of
Indonesia 49
Gunawan Kartapranata 37
Gunkarta Gunawan Kartapranata
161
JJ Harrison 417
Guy Harvey 411
H Hart 139
Hans Hofer 66, 151T, 182T, 183T,
195, 213, 306, 308, 322,
Hotel Bumi Surabaya 382
Paul Hessels 157
APA/Jack Hollingsworth 74R, 104,
105, 106, 179, 196, 202T, 223,
230, 248T, 268, 268T, 272, 285,
309,
Hyatt Hotels 375
Indonesian Tourist Board 6MR, 8B,
32, 117, 184/185, 193L, 194, 279,
281, 297, 298, 299B, 310, 325,
338, 358, 368T,
iStockphoto 7B, 21, 75, 174T,
182B, 190B, 198, 200T, 204L, 275,
280, 281T, 282, 286, 287, 288,

291T, 304, 330, 337T, 341T, 341B,
349B, 352, 354, 355B, 355T, 356,
357R, 359T, 422
Jakarta Tourism 142
Kenrick95192T
Leon Schadeberg / Rex Features
51
Leung Cho Pan 346L
Luca Tettoni 160T, 164T
Luc-Henri Fage 30
Masgatotkaca 139T
Mentawi Surf Camp 205
Meursault2004 165
Sakurai Midori 366
John Mose 346R
Only the Best 361
Hotel Ombi 387
Paul C. Pet 180B
Jordon R. Beesley 190T
Photobank 350
Melia Purosani 381
Reef Seen Aquatics Dive Center 247T
Relic38 349T
Rimba Restaurant 391
Robert Francis 236B
Robert Harding 171, 351
roberto adrian 357L
Rumah Sleman Hotel 380
Ryan Somma 29
APA/Sylvaine Poitau 345B
Shangri-La 376
Specialist Stock 119, 274, 300B
Snuff Puppets 90
Neil Straw 303BR
Willem Strien 11, 209
Tirto 41
Topfoto 50
Luc Viator 360
Verstandort 267
APA Martin Westlake 18, 76, 87,
99, 108, 138T, 173T, 204L, 206,
207, 216, 247, 284, 285T, 291,
334, 335T, 344, 348, 351,
APA/Corrie Wingate 1, 2, 2B, 3, 4B,
4T, 5, 6ML, 6BR, 6BL, 7TR, 7ML,
7BL, 6/7T, 7MR, 8T, 9TL, 9BR, 10B,
10T, 12/13, 14/15, 16/17, 19T,
19B, 20, 22, 24/25, 26, 28, 33, 35,
44, 54/55, 56/57, 58, 59, 60, 61,
62, 63, 64L, 65, 67, 68, 69, 70, 71,
72, 73, 74L, 77, 78, 79, 80, 81, 82L,
82R, 83, 84, 85, 86, 88, 89, 91, 92,
93, 94, 95, 96, 97, 98, 100, 101,
107, 109, 110, 111, 112, 113, 114,
115, 116, 124/125, 126/127,
128/129, 130, 131, 132, 133T,

133B, 134, 135, 137T, 137B, 138B,
140T, 141, 143, 144, 145, 146,
149, 152, 153, 156, 157T, 159,
160B, 162T, 164B, 166B, 166T,
167B, 167T, 168, 170, 171T, 172B,
172T, 174B, 175, 176, 177, 178,
180T, 181, 183B, 186, 187T, 187B,
189, 195B, 196T, 197, 199, 200B,
201, 202B, 217T, 217B, 218, 219,
220BL, 220BR, 220TL, 221T, 221B,
222L, 222R, 223T, 224TL, 224BL,
224BR, 225B, 225T, 226, 227, 228,
229, 230T, 231R, 231L, 232, 233B,
233T, 234L, 234R, 235, 236T,
238B, 238T, 239B, 239T, 241TR,
241ML, 241BR, 241BR, 242, 243,
244, 245, 246B, 248BL, 248BR,
250BL, 250BR, 251B, 251T, 252,
253, 254B, 255T, 255B, 256, 257T,
257B, 258, 259T, 259B, 262, 263T,
263B, 264, 265, 266T, 270B, 270T,
271, 272L, 273, 292/293, 294,
295T, 305BR, 305BL, 305TR, 307B,
307T, 310T, 311, 312T, 315,
316/317, 318, 319T, 319B, 321BL,
323, 324, 326, 327, 328, 329B,
329T, 362, 364, 367, 368B, 370,
371L, 372, 373L, 389L, 390, 392T,
392B, 393L, 394, 397, 398, 399L,
400, 400/401T, 400/401M, 403L,
405L, 407L, 409L, 412, 415L, 416,
419L, 420T, 420B
Frank Wouters 302
Lip Kee Yap 120

Photo Features

102–103: Corrie Wingate
102/103T, 102BR, 103BL, 103BR,
103TR, J Marshall – Tribaleye
Images / Alamy 102BL
122–123: Carsten Peter 123BL,
Corrie Wingate 122BL, Danita
Delimont / Alamy 123TR, DEA / A.
DAGLI ORTI 123BR, simon gurney
122BR, © Biosphoto / Alain
Compost 122/123T
240/242: All images APA/Corrie
Wingate except Andrea Pistolesi
240BR
320–321: Istockphoto 320/321,
320BL, 321BR, Getty 320 BR, APA
Corrie Wingate 321BL, Nature
Picture Library 321TR

Main attractions are in bold type